Lecture Notes in Computer Science 2784

Edited by G. Goos, J. Hartmanis, and J. van Leeuwen

T0297981

Springer

Berlin
Heidelberg
New York
Hong Kong
London
Milan
Paris
Tokyo

Marcela Genero   Fabio Grandi
Willem-Jan van den Heuvel   John Krogstie
Kalle Lyytinen   Heinrich C. Mayr
Jim Nelson   Antoni Olivé   Mario Piattini
Geert Poels   John Roddick   Keng Siau
Masatoshi Yoshikawa   Eric S.K. Yu (Eds.)

Advanced Conceptual Modeling Techniques

ER 2002 Workshops
ECDM, MobIMod, IWCMQ, and eCOMO
Tampere, Finland, October 7-11, 2002
Revised Papers

Springer

Series Editors

Gerhard Goos, Karlsruhe University, Germany
Juris Hartmanis, Cornell University, NY, USA
Jan van Leeuwen, Utrecht University, The Netherlands

Volume Editors

Antoni Olivé
Universitat Politecnica de Catalunya, Campus Nord, C5-D207
Jordi Girona 1-3, 08034 Barcelona, Spain
E-mail: olive@lsi.upc.es

Masatoshi Yoshikawa
Nagoya University, Information Technology Center
Furo-cho, Chikusa-ku, Nagoya 464-8601, Japan
E-mail: yosikawa@itc.nagoya-u.ac.jp

Eric S.K. Yu
University of Toronto, Faculty of Information Studies
140 St. George St., Toronto M5S 3G6, Canada
E-mail: yu@fis.utoronto.ca

Cataloging-in-Publication Data applied for

A catalog record for this book is available from the Library of Congress

Bibliographic information published by Die Deutsche Bibliothek
Die Deutsche Bibliothek lists this publication in the Deutsche Nationalbibliographie;
detailed bibliographic data is available in the Internet at <http://dnb.ddb.de>.

CR Subject Classification (1998): H.2, H.3-5, C.2.4-5, J.1

ISSN 0302-9743
ISBN 3-540-20255-2 Springer-Verlag Berlin Heidelberg New York

Springer-Verlag Berlin Heidelberg New York
a member of BertelsmannSpringer Science+Business Media GmbH

http://www.springer.de

© Springer-Verlag Berlin Heidelberg 2003
Printed in Germany

Typesetting: Camera-ready by author, data conversion by Christian Grosche, Hamburg
Printed on acid-free paper   SPIN: 10931554   06/3142   5 4 3 2 1 0

Preface

The objective of the workshops held in conjunction with ER 2002, the 21st International Conference on Conceptual Modeling, was to give participants the opportunity to present and discuss emerging hot topics, thus adding new perspectives to conceptual modeling. To meet this objective, we selected the following four workshops:

- 2nd International Workshop on Evolution and Change in Data Management (ECDM 2002)
- ER/IFIP8.1 Workshop on Conceptual Modelling Approaches to Mobile Information Systems Development (MobIMod 2002)
- International Workshop on Conceptual Modeling Quality (IWCMQ 2002)
- 3rd International Joint Workshop on Conceptual Modeling Approaches for E-business: a Web Service Perspective (eCOMO 2002)

ER 2002 was organized so that there would be no overlap between the conference sessions and the workshops. This proceedings contains workshop papers that were revised by the authors following discussions during the conference. We are deeply indebted to the members of the organizing committees and program committees of these workshops for their hard work.

July 2003   Antoni Olivé, Masatoshi Yoshikawa, and Eric S.K. Yu
Workshop Co-chairs
ER 2002

ECDM 2002

Change is a fundamental but sometimes neglected aspect of information and database systems. The management of evolution and change and the ability of database, information and knowledge-based systems to deal with change is an essential component in developing and maintaining truly useful systems. Many approaches to handling evolution and change have been proposed in various areas of data management, and this forum seeks to bring together researchers and practitioners from both more established areas and from emerging areas to look at this issue. The second ECDM workshop (the first ECDM workshop was held with ER 1999 in Paris and its report can be found in SIGMOD Record 29(1):21–25, March 2000) dealt with the manner in which change can be handled, and the semantics of evolving data and data structure in computer-based systems. The workshop topics included:

- Semantics of Change in Time and Space
- Modelling and Management of Time-Varying Data, Temporal Databases
- Handling Changes and Versioning of Semi-structured Data
- Handling Changes of Metadata, Schema Evolution and Versioning

- Change Detection, Monitoring and Mining
- Evolution and Change in Internet-Based Information Systems
- Evolution and Change in E-services and E-world Systems
- Induction of Cause and Effect, Logics for Evolution
- Maintenance of Views, Summaries, Dictionaries and Warehouses
- Managing Evolution of Sources in Information Integration

With respect to the main ER conference, the ECDM workshop aims at stressing the evolutionary aspects involved in conceptual modelling and in the development and implementation of systems, ranging from the modelling of information dynamics to the dynamics of the modelling process itself. Another explicit aim of ECDM 2002 (as it was also for ECDM 1999) was to bring together scientists and praticitioners interested in evolution and change aspects in different research fields and, thus, people who often belong to completely separate communities. It is our opinion that such interactions can be tighter and cross-fertilization can be more useful in the context of a collaborative workshop like ECDM than in the context of the main conference sessions. Moreover, since the emphasis is on the evolutionary dimension, a special insight is sought upon this specific aspect, one that could hardly find an appropriately broad coverage in the scope of the main ER conference.

Following the acceptance of the workshop proposal by the ER 2002 organizing committee, an international and highly qualified program committee was assembled from research centers worldwide. As a result of the call for papers, the program committee received 19 submissions from 15 countries, and after rigorous refereeing 10 high-quality papers were eventually chosen for presentation at the workshop, and these appear in these proceedings.

We would like to thank both the program committee members and the additional external referees for their timely expertise in reviewing the papers. We would also like to thank all authors for submitting their papers to this workshop. Last, but not least, we would like to thank the ER 2002 organizers for their support, and in particular the workshop co-chairs, Antoni Olivé, Eric Yu, and Masatoshi Yoshikawa.

September 2002   Fabio Grandi and John Roddick
                                                 Program Co-chairs
                                                      ECDM 2002
                  http://kdm.first.flinders.edu.au/events/ECDM02.html

MobIMod 2002

Mobility is perhaps the most important market and technological trend in information and communication technology. With the advent of new mobile infrastructures providing higher bandwidths and constant connections to the network from virtually everywhere, the way people use information resources is predicted to be radically transformed. The rapid developments in information technology (IT) are substantially changing the landscape of organizational computing. Workers in many business areas are becoming increasingly mobile. Workers in more and more areas will be required to act more flexibly within the constraints of the business processes they are currently engaged in. At the same time they will often want to use the same information technology to support their private tasks. During the last few years, a new breed of information system has emerged to address this situation, referred to as m-commerce systems or mobile information systems. The objective of the workshop was to provide a forum for researchers and practitioners interested in modeling methods for mobile information systems to meet, and exchange research ideas and results.

The relevant topics for the workshop included the following aspects of m-commerce and mobile information systems:

- Mobile commerce models and architecture
- Service modeling
- Mobile access to enterprise systems (ERP, CRM, SCM, etc.)
- Enterprise modeling and business process re-engineering
- Workflow modeling
- Meta-modeling and method engineering
- Evaluation of modeling languages and experience
- Modeling of access control to provide security and privacy
- Content personalization and user modeling
- Context modeling
- Requirement modeling
- Information and database modeling
- Component engineering and integration
- Geographical information systems and location-based services
- Cross-platform conceptual interface modeling
- Mobile modeling tools
- Modeling of embedded systems
- (Mobile) Agent modeling and design
- Agile modeling, extreme modeling, and extreme programming

October 2002

John Krogstie
Program Chair
MobIMod 2002

IWCMQ 2002

Conceptual modeling has been recognized as a key task that lays the foundation of all later design and implementation work. The early focus on conceptual modeling may help in building better systems, without unnecessary rework at later stages of the development when changes are more expensive and more difficult to perform. Quality in conceptual modeling has been a topic of research since the early 1990s but recently a stronger emphasis has been given to the assessment, evaluation, and improvement of the models produced in the early phases of the system development life-cycle. The theme of the 1st International Workshop on Conceptual Modeling Quality was methodologies and instruments for the quality assurance of conceptual modeling processes and products. The workshop intended to provide a forum for researchers and practitioners working on approaches, frameworks, methods, techniques, guidelines, and tools for measuring, predicting, evaluating, controlling, and improving the quality of conceptual modeling processes and artifacts.

February 2003

Geert Poels
Workshop Co-chair
IWCMQ 2002

eCOMO 2002

The Internet is changing the way businesses operate. Organizations are increasingly relying on the Web to deliver their goods and services, to find trading partners, and to link their existing legacy applications to other applications. Web services are rapidly becoming the de facto enabling technology of today's e-business systems, and will soon transform the Web as it is now into a new distributed application-to-application computation network. This will be the basis for the future network economy which comes with the need for new and adapted business models, business technologies and, as a consequence, new challenges for the developers and users of e-business systems. They will have to supply and to adopt Web-based services over the complete supply chain as well, in the context of new digital products. In particular, services that allow enterprises to combine or integrate their business processes will have to be developed, respectively their models, with those of the partners when forming a dynamic network or a virtual enterprise.

Web service technology is generally perceived as an ideal candidate to fulfil the requirements of modern networked enterprises because they allow both loose-coupling and dynamic composition at both the enterprise and the business application level. Progress has been made in the area of Web service description and discovery, and there are some important standards emerging. Nevertheless, there is still a list of issues that need to be addressed and researched in connection with conceptual modeling methodologies that are tailored to deal with the specifics of Web-services and their alignment with e-business requirements before Web services becomes the prominent paradigm for distributed computing and electronic business. Industry is delivering new exciting solutions at a fast rate, but most of them lack a firm scientifically validated foundation.

The eCOMO workshop series was started in 2000. It aims to bring together experts from practice and academia who are working from different, but related perspectives on the same research questions, such as from the perspectives of business modeling, enterprise application integration, the semantic Web, business metadata and ontologies, process management, business re-engineering, business models, and business communication languages.

The contributions to eCOMO 2002 that are collected in these proceedings passed a careful review process in which each of the submitted papers was assessed by three experienced reviewers. They deal with modeling aspects of e-business processes, the model-based composition of processes and Web services, specific approaches to managing unstructured e-business information and to extracting relevant data from Web forms, and with the question of designing successful e-business Web applications.

Many persons deserve appreciation and recognition for their contribution to making eCOMO 2002 a success. First of all we have to thank the authors for their valuable contributions. Similarly, we thank the members of the program committee, who spent a lot of time in assessing submitted papers and participating in the iterated discussions on acceptance or rejection. Special appreciation is due to Christian Kop, who organized and co-ordinated the whole preparation process including the composition of these proceedings. We also express our thanks to Jian Yang and Klothilde Pack for the organizational support they provided. Last, but not least, we thank the ER organizers and the ER workshop co-chairs (Antoni Olivé, Masatoshi Yoshikawa, and Eric Yu) for their support in integrating eCOMO 2002 into ER 2002.

February 2003   Willem-Jan van den Heuvel
                                                    Heinrich C. Mayr
                                                    Program Co-chairs
                                                    eCOMO 2002

Organization

ER 2002 Workshops Chairs

Antoni Olivé   Universitat Polytecnica de Catalunya, Spain
Masatoshi Yoshikawa   Nagoya University, Japan
Eric S.K. Yu   Univeristy of Toronto, Canada

ECDM 2002 Program Committee Co-chairs

Fabio Grandi   University of Bologna, Italy
John Roddick   Flinders University, South Australia

ECDM 2002 Program Committee

Michael Böhlen   Aalborg University, Denmark
Curtis Dyreson   Washington State University, USA
Ramez Elmasri   University of Texas, USA
Enrico Franconi   University of Manchester, UK
Kathleen Hornsby   University of Maine, USA
Richard McClatchey   University of the West of England, UK
Erik Proper   University of Nijmegen, The Netherlands
Chris Rainsford   DSTO, Australia
Sudha Ram   University of Arizona, USA
Elke Rundensteiner   Worcester Polytechnic Institute, USA
Maria Rita Scalas   University of Bologna, Italy
Myra Spiliopoulou   Leipzig Graduate School of Management,
                               Germany
Babis Theodoulidis   UMIST, UK
Carlo Zaniolo   UCLA, USA

MobIMod 2002 Workshop Co-chairs

John Krogstie
Kalle Lyytinen
Keng Siau

MobIMod 2002 Program Committee

R. Baskerville   J. Dietz   R. Kalakota
S. Brinkkemper   G. Grosz   S. Kelly
J. Dhaliwal   H. Kangassalo   J. Krogstie

K. Lyytinen	M. Rossi	K. Smolander
S. March	K. Siau	J. Veijalainen
A.L. Opdahl	G. Sindre	G. Wijers
B. Pernici	M.B. Skov	

IWCQM 2002 Organization Committee – Workshop Co-chairs

Marcela Genero	University of Castilla-La Mancha, Spain
Jim Nelson	The Ohio State University, USA
Geert Poels	Ghent University, Belgium

IWCQM 2002 Program Committee Chair – Workshop General Chair

Mario Piattini	University of Castilla-La Mancha, Spain

IWCQM 2002 Program Committee Members – Referees

Sjaak Brinkkemper	Baan, The Netherlands
Giovanni Cantone	University of Rome, Italy
Guido Dedene	Katholieke Universiteit Leuven, Belgium
Reiner Dumke	University of Magdeburg, Germany
Donal Flynn	UMIST, UK
Marcela Genero	University of Castilla-La Mancha, Spain
Bill Hardgrave	University of Arkansas, USA
Brian Henderson-Sellers	University of Technology, Sydney, Australia
Paul Johannesson	Stockholm University, Sweden
Barbara Kitchenham	Keele University, UK
John Krogstie	Sintef, Norway
Ronald Maier	University of Regensburg, Germany
Heinrich Mayr	University of Klagenfurt, Austria
Roberto Meli	GUFPI, Italy
David Monarchi	University of Colorado, USA
Daniel Moody	Norwegian University of Science and Technology, Norway
Jim Nelson	Ohio State University, USA
Risto Nevalainen	FiSMA, Finland
Oscar Pastor	Valencia University of Technology, Spain
Jeff Pearsons	Memorial University of Newfoundland, Canada
Geert Poels	Ghent University, Belgium
Gustavo Rossi	National University of La Plata, Argentine
Houari Sahraoui	Université de Montréal, Canada

Reinhard Schuette   University of Essen, Germany
Martin Shepperd   Bournemouth University, UK
Keng Siau   University of Nebraska-Lincoln, USA
Guttorm Sindre   Norwegian University of Science
                           and Technology, Norway
Monique Snoeck   Katholieke Universiteit Leuven, Belgium
Eva Söderström   Stockholm University, Sweden
Bernhard Thalheim   Brandenburg University of Technology
                           at Cottbus, Germany
Yuhong Tian   University of Nebraska-Lincoln, USA
Benkt Wangler   Stockholm University, Sweden

eCOMO 2002 Chairs

Heinrich C. Mayr   University of Klagenfurt, Austria
Willem-Jan van den Heuvel Tilburg University, The Netherlands

eCOMO 2002 Workshop Organization

Christian Kop   University of Klagenfurt, Austria
Jian Yang   Tilburg University, The Netherlands

eCOMO 2002 Program Committee Members

Boldur Barbat   Roland Kaschek   Daniel Schwabe
Boualem Benatallah   Stephen Liddle   Il-Yeol Song
Anthony Bloesch   Zakaria Maamar   Rudi Studer
Antonio di Leva   Norbert Mikula   Hiroyuki Tarumi
Vadim A. Ermolayev   Oscar Pastor   Bernhard Thalhiem
Marcela Genero   Barbara Pernici   Jos van Hillegersberg
Martin Glinz   Matti Rossi   Carson Woo
Jozsef Györkös   Klaus-Dieter Schewe   Jian Yang
Bill Karakostas   Michael Schrefl

Table of Contents

ER/IFIP8.1 Workshop on Conceptual Modelling Approaches to Mobile Information Systems Development (MobIMod 2002)

International Workshop on Conceptual Modeling Quality (IWCMQ 2002)

Research in Quality of Conceptual Models

Requirements and Entity Relationship Models

Class Models and Architectures

Web and Interactive Models

Third International Joint Workshop on Conceptual Modeling Approaches for E-business: A Web Service Perspective (eCOMO 2002)

Process, Models, and Web Services

E-business Methods and Technologies

Success Factors for Conceptual Modeling in E-business

Change Management for a Temporal Versioned Object-Oriented Database*

Renata de Matos Galante, Nina Edelweiss, and Clesio Saraiva dos Santos

Instituto de Informática - Universidade Federal do Rio Grande do Sul
{galante,nina,clesio}@inf.ufrgs.br

Abstract. In this paper, we propose a schema versioning mechanism to manage the schema evolution in temporal object-oriented databases. The schema evolution management uses an object-oriented data model that supports temporal features and versions definition - the Temporal Versions Model - TVM. One interesting feature of our proposal is that TVM is used to control not only the schema versioning, but also the storage of extensional database and propagation of the changes performed on the objects. The extensional data level supports integration with the existing database, allowing the maintenance of conventional and temporal versioned objects. The instance propagation approach is proposed through the specification of propagation and conversion functions. These functions assure the correct instance propagation and allow the user to handle all instances consistently in both backward and forward schema versions. Finally, the initial requirements concerning data management in the temporal versioning environment, during schema evolution, are presented.

1 Introduction

Object-oriented databases offer powerful modeling concepts as those required by advanced application domains as CAD and Case tools. Typical applications handle large and complex structured objects, which frequently change their value and structure. As the structure is described in the database schema, support to schema evolution is a highly required feature. In this context, the version concept has been applied to maintain all the history of the database evolution.

Schema evolution and schema versioning are two techniques that allow schema modifications while consistency is maintained between a schema and its data. According to accepted terminology [1], a database supports schema evolution if it allows schema changes without losing extentional data. In addition, the schema versioning support allows not only the maintenance of data, but also the access to all data through schema versions.

However, the representation of the temporal dimension is essential to keep the whole evolution history. This feature is necessary in many computer applications, as medical control, geographical information systems and flight reservation. Schema versioning with temporal features has been studied extensively

---

* This work has been partially supported by Capes and CNPq.

A. Olivé et al. (Eds.): ER 2002 Ws, LNCS 2784, pp. 1–12, 2003.

in relational environments [2,3,4]. Bitemporal schema versioning [2,5] enabling retro and pro-active schema changes to produce past, present and future schema versions has been specially analyzed.

Most proposals found in the literature approach schema versioning through temporal features [2,3,5,6,7] or version control mechanisms [8,9,10]. The main contribution of this paper is to present a schema evolution mechanism that integrates features of both versions and time.

The main attempt of this paper is to present a schema versioning mechanism to manage the schema evolution in a temporal object-oriented database. The schema evolution management uses an object-oriented data model that supports temporal features and versions definition - the Temporal Versions Model - TVM [11]. In order to fulfill the schema evolution requirements, the instance propagation approach is also presented. Concerning physical implementation, propagation and conversion functions are specified to assure the correct instance propagation and allow the user to handle all instances consistently in both backward and forward schema versions. The initial requirements concerning data management in a temporal versioned environment, during schema evolution, are also exposed.

The rest of this paper is structured as follows. Section 2 briefly presents the Temporal Version Model. Section 3 shows an overview of the schema evolution architecture proposal. In section 4, the schema versioning approach is presented. The instance propagation approach is presented in Section 5 . The main requirements concerning data management during schema evolution are exposed in section 6. Section 7 cites some related work. Section 8 summarizes the main ideas of this paper and proposes some topics for future work.

2   Temporal Versions Model - TVM

The *Temporal Versions Model* (TVM) is proposed as an object-oriented (OO) data model that extends a version model by adding the temporal dimension to the instance versioning level [11]. Indeed, the user may model the database considering the design alternatives as well as the data evolution. It is important to notice that TVM does not require all classes to be temporal and versionable, allowing the integration with existing applications. Only the main features of TVM are presented here, which are necessary to understand the schema evolution process proposed in this paper.

Time is associated with objects, versions, attributes and relationships, allowing better and more flexible modeling of reality. An object has a time line for each of its versions. TVM supports two different temporal orders: *branched* time for a versioned object, and *linear* time within a version. Time varies in a discrete way, and temporality is represented in the model through temporal intervals and bitemporal timestamp (transaction and valid time).

During its lifetime, a version changes its status, which can be: *working, stable, consolidated*, and *deactivated*. Figure 1 shows the state diagram of a version, showing the possible status, as well as its transitions, and the events that cause these transitions.

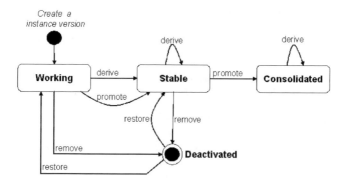

Fig. 1. State diagram of a version

3   An Overview of the Schema Evolution Architecture

This section presents an outline of the *Temporal and Versioning Approach to Schema Evolution*. The general architecture of the approach reported here is depicted in figure 2, which is split into four main parts:

- *Schema Versioning Manager* - implements the schema versioning through TVM features, the basis on which our proposal is founded.
- *Schema evolution manager*- controls the schema evolution management (*change manager*) and accomplishes instance change update (*propagation manager*) according to schema transformation in order to assure consistency between the schema versions and heir corresponding data.
- *Data Manager* - controls the schema changes, change propagation and data manipulation through transaction processing.
- *Storage Manager* - controls the storage of schema versions and their corresponding data. This module is divided into two parts: *Metadata Structure* and *Intention and Extension Storage*.

The schema evolution management uses TVM to control not only the schema versioning, but also the storage of extensional data and the propagation of the changes in the objects. Concerning the extensional data level, it supports integration with the existing database, allowing the maintenance of conventional and temporal versioned objects.

The next sections present our proposal and how the requirements explained here can be achieved.

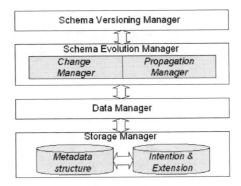

Fig. 2. Schema Evolution Architecture

4   The Schema Versioning Approach

This section explains the schema versioning approach using TVM. A metadata structure is defined to store information concerning the evolving schema, as well as their classes, attributes and relationships. Also, two alternatives are defined for the intentional and extensional data management.

4.1   Schema Versioning Using the Temporal Version Model

In order to complete the requirements for the temporal management of applications, the occurrence of schema versions besides data evolution shall also be supported. TVM already presents versions and temporal features on the data level, as presented in section 2. This section adds to TVM the support to schema versioning.

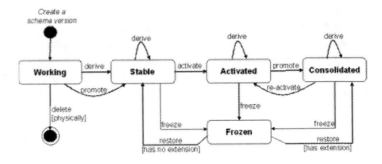

Fig. 3. Schema Version Status

Similar to instance versions, the schema versions also have a status, reflecting its robustness. The available status are: *working, stable, activated, consolidated,* and *frozen*. Figure 3 illustrates the status that a schema version can assume during its lifetime, and the actions that can cause such transitions.

New versions are created in the *working* status. When a version is derived from another one, its predecessors are automatically promoted to *stable*, thus avoiding modifications on versions that were important from a historical point of view. Only in the *working* status the version can be physically modified, otherwise a new version is created as successor from that changed. Finally, while the *frozen* versions represent a logical exclusion (only used to solve queries), the *consolidated* versions cannot be populated, but can be used as base for a new derivation besides solving queries.

4.2 Metadata Structure

A *metadata structure*[1] is defined to store information concerning the evolving schema status, as well as their classes, attributes and relationships. Figure 4 illustrates the specification of a metadata structure using a UML class diagram notation.

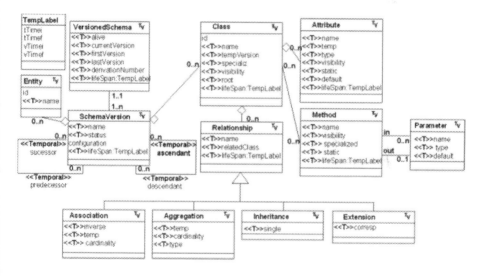

Fig. 4. Metadata specification to a schema temporal versioning

The metadata is modeled through the following main classes: *versioned schema, schema, class, attribute, relationship* and *method*. The *VersionedSchema* class keeps control of information about the schema versioning storage, and *Schema* class stores data concerning the schema versions. Each schema version can have classes that maintain temporal information about their corresponding classes, methods, attributes and relationships.

---

[1] The metadata structure is completely specified in [12].

4.3   Intention and Extension Data Management

Currently there are two main approaches [2] to convert the database structure
after applying schema changes in temporal database: *single* and *multiple* repositories. In the former, the data corresponding to all schema versions are maintained into a single repository, with a completed schema. In the latter, distinct
repositories are maintained for each schema version.

The approach proposed in this paper uses two strategies to store extensional
data during schema evolution, according to the kind of modification made in the
schema structure, integrating both single and multiple repositories. The multiple
repositories solution is adopted for extensional database in case a schema change
modifies the schema structure as schema and relationship. Otherwise, when a
schema change modifies the class structure as class and method changes, the
single repository solution is adopted for the storage of extensional data. Concerning the physical representation, both approaches can be used in the same
application.

Multiple Repository Storage   The management of temporal schema evolution is performed through *schema versioning* and *multiple repositories*. Any
schema change leads to a derivation of the new schema version and a new data
repository is created. In addition, data of the previous repository is copied to
the new repository, updated according to the new schema.

Figure 5 illustrates the inclusion of a new class, named *Subject*, in the first
schema version (*Schema,1*). A new schema version is derived (*Schema,2*), whose
data are stored in the intention database. A new data repository containing the
changes performed is created (*Repository,2*).

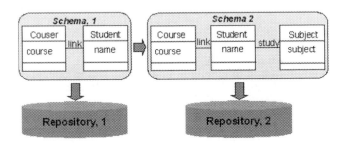

Fig. 5. Schema Versioning using multiple repositories

Single Repository Storage.   The schema versioning approach always handles versions of the complete schema, which can cause a high number of version
derivations. In this case, the quantity of data repositories can be greatly increased. Another implementation proposal is defined here in order to improve

the performance of the system, avoid frequent interruption during data propagation and assure the integrity of stored data.

In this context, in which the class description is changed, the propagation of changes is performed in the same data repository, in order to decrease data duplication, and all the history of the schema evolution is kept (in other words, schema versions are conceptually created for each change).

For instance, in figure 6, the *address* attribute is included in the *Student* class. In this case, the first schema version (*Schema,1*) is modified, causing the derivation of a new schema version (*Schema,2*), and the instance propagation is stored in the already existing data repository.

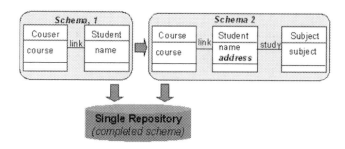

Fig. 6. Schema Versioning using single repository

5   The Instance Propagation Approach

The database schema cannot be changed without considering what should happen to the data whose structure is described in the schema. Once the schema is changed, the data and schema shall be consistent one with the other. Besides, new data may be created under the new schema that has a different structure of data created under the old schema. For fulfilling this requirement, the following steps must be accomplished: (*i*) identify the objects which should be updated; and (*ii*) propagate the changes to the database instances.

There are two important approaches for implementing the instance propagation mechanism [13]: *immediate* and *deferred* propagation. This proposal presents a hybrid method, which allows the use of both approaches, depending on the application necessities. A schema change causes an immediate update in those objects that are being used by applications. That means that only objects that have active valid time must be immediately updated. Therefore, an object can be required by an application, and then updated through the deferred mechanism, following the same rules of immediate propagation.

Figure 7 shows the access scope of the schema versions and their corresponding database instances. Immediate propagation is accomplished considering current data and should be performed in the repository that has the same temporal pertinence of its schema version. Otherwise, deferred propagation will be performed when an instance is requested, considering a schema version that has different temporal pertinence from its schema version.

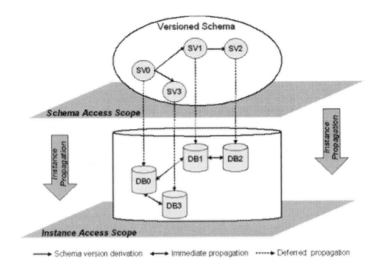

Fig. 7. Instance propagation scope

Concerning physical implementation, two kinds of functions have been defined in order to convert the database instances: *propagation* and *conversion*. These functions have been specified to assure the correct database conversion and to allow the user to handle all instances consistently in both backward and forward schema versions.

5.1   Propagation Functions

Propagation functions must be specified in order to update the instance values required by schema versions (specifically when multiple repository strategy is adopted). Two kinds of functions must be defined for each schema structure modification: *forward* and *backward*. The former describes the value of the instances when they are required by the new schema version and must be associated with the previous one. In an opposite direction, the latter describes the values of the instances required by the previous schema version, but being associated with the new schema version. The propagation functions are reversible, which means the instances can be freely converted among several schema versions. Besides, if it is needed, the user can manually specify propagation functions in order to specify semantic relationships among schema versions.

Figure 8 shows the algorithms [2] which specify both propagation functions, forward and backward, applied to a schema modification (add class *Subject*)

---

[2] A specific algorithm is defined for each schema modification operation.

represented previously in figure 5. The former defines the operations involved in this change: (*i*) create the object with its values, and (*ii*) specify the relationship *study* with *Student* class. The latter excludes object and relationship.

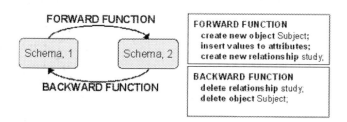

Fig. 8. Examples of the propagation functions

5.2   Conversion Functions

Conceptually, when the class structure is modified, a new schema version is derived. This change is performed physically in the same data repository. Thus, conversion functions must be specified in order to update the instance values required when changes are applied to the class structure. Two kinds of functions are defined for each class structure modification: *forward* and *backward*. The former describes the instance values when they are required by the new schema version and the latter describes the values of the instances required by the previous schema version. However, both functions are associated with the class changed; the backward function is associated with the class of the new schema version, and the forward function is associated with the class of the previous one.

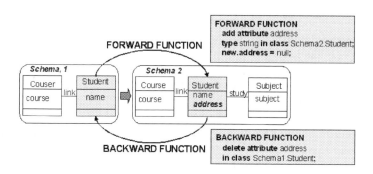

Fig. 9. Examples of the conversion functions

Figure 9 illustrates both conversion functions, forward and backward, applied to class modification (add attribute *address* in class *Student*), represented previously in figure 6. Through the former function, the attribute *address* is excluded. Through the later, the attribute *address* is included and it receives a value *null.*

6 Data Management during Schema Evolution

The schema evolution management involves not only the schema change and data propagation but also data manipulation operations. For instance, object handle through *insert, update* and *delete* operations could be made while a schema change operation is performed. Many of the conventional techniques employ lock mechanisms to manage schema evolution, restricting the concurrence. Thus, there is a direct relationship between schema evolution and transaction processing.

Since transactions are constructs that change the database state, we are analyzing their effects during the schema evolution and the instance propagation approaches. The result will be a mechanism to control schema changes, instance propagation and data manipulation, operations which can be specified inside the same transaction. Then, the first requirements are the following[3]:

- *Transaction specification* - Specification of how operations must be handled inside transactions and definition the effects caused in the TVM environment, considering schema, instances and version derivation.
- *Data manipulation rules* - Specification of rules to assure consistency of data manipulation during schema evolution.
- *Integrity rules* - Specification of rules to assure that the database outcome is always correct and consistent. Otherwise, the transaction must be aborted.
- *Concurrence mechanisms* - Specification of techniques for the performance of transactions processing with interleave operations, including schema change, data propagation and data manipulation.

7 Related Work

The appropriate treatment of changes performed in a database schema during its lifetime has been the objective of many research works. Consequently, a great number of proposals which aim at dealing properly with this subject have emerged.

Historically, three fundamental techniques have been employed for modifying the conceptual structure of an object-oriented database. First, schema evolution [14], in which the database has one logical schema and change operations are applied to the class definition and the class hierarchy. Second, schema versioning [8], in which several versions of one logical schema can be created and manipulated independently. Third, class versioning [9] is the creation of a new version for the class definition, in which the previous class definition is retained, allowing multiple versions of a class definition to co-exist. The Sades Evolution

---

[3] Since our work in this area is quite recent, more concrete results will be reported in future papers.

System [10] proposes the use of schema evolution for class versioning and views for conceptual database evolution.

In the temporal database context, [5] defines a formal model for the support of temporal schema versions in object-oriented database. The model is provided with a complete set of schema change primitives, for which an operational semantics and formal analysis of their correct behavior are also specified. Another formal model for schema version management is defined in [7]. This research formally defines a model that uses concepts of time and version in an object-oriented environment. In this model only transaction time is adopted. Axioms are predefined in order to ensure the schema consistency, but it does not define rules that guarantee the validity of the changed objects. Also TIGUKAT proposes the use of a temporal object model [6] for management of schema changes and adaptation of instances.

Temporal concepts and versions modeling are mostly treated individually in literature. In contrast to the approaches above our proposal presents a schema evolution management approach, which is based on TVM, thus adding time and version features to the class, schema and instance levels. Finally, the main achievement of this paper in relation to [12] is that TVM is used as the basis for intentional and extensional database, allowing the management of the instance propagation process. Furthermore, we have adopted branched time, which provides more than one active schema version at the same instant of time.

8   Summary and Concluding Remarks

This paper proposes a schema evolution management approach, which is based on the Temporal Versions Model, adding time and version features to the schema, class and instance levels. The union of version and time concepts keeps different schema versions as well as stores the schema changes performed. It also allows both retroactive and proactive updates and queries in the schema and database. The use of bitemporal schema versioning increases the flexibility of our proposal, allowing access to past, present and future schema versions.

The instance propagation approach is also proposed through the specification of propagation and conversion functions. These functions assure the correct instance propagation and allow the user to handle all instances consistently in both backward and forward schema versions. One interesting feature is that the extensional data level supports integration with existing database, maintaining conventional and temporal versioned objects. Thus, it represents the main achievement of this paper in relation to [12], since the management of the instance propagation process is made through TVM.

Currently we are working on an extension of the present approach in two directions. First, we are specifying a mechanism to control concurrently schema changes, instance change propagation and data manipulation through the transaction processing. Second, a TVM object definition language is being specified as extension of the TVQL [15] in order to fulfill the schema evolution management and data manipulation.TVQL (*Temporal Versioned Query Language*) is a query language proposed to TVM. As a final result, we intend to propose a complete schema evolution model with temporal and version features. In addition, this schema evolution model will be implemented on top of a commercial database, whose main attempt is to simulate the feasibility of the proposed model.

References

1. C.S. Jensen, et al., The consensus glossary of temporal database concepts - february 1998 version, in: Temporal Databases: Research and Practice, Vol. 1399 of LNCS, Springer-Verlag, 1998, pp. 367–405.
2. C. de Castro, F. Grandi, M.R. Scalas, Schema versioning for multitemporal relational databases, Information Systems 22 (5) (1997) 249–290.
3. V. P. Moreira, N. Edelweiss, Schema versioning: Queries to the generalized temporal database system, in: Spatio-Temporal Data Models and Languages, in conjuntion with Int'l. Conf. on Database and Expert Systems Applications, IEEE Computer Society, Florence, Italy, 1999, pp. 458–459.
4. J. F. Roddick, F. Grandi, F. Mandreoli, M. R. Scalas, Beyond schema versioning: A flexible model for spatio-temporal schema selection, GeoInformatica 5 (1) (2001) 33–50.
5. F. Grandi, F. Mandreoli, A formal model for temporal schema versioning in object-oriented databases, Tech. Rep. TR-68, Time Center (jan 2002).
6. I.A. Goralwalla, D. Szafron, M.T. Özsu, R.J. Peters, A temporal approach to managing schema evolution in object database systems, Data & Knowledge Engineering 28 (1) (1998) 73–105.
7. L. RodrÂŋguez, H. Ogata, Y. Yano, TVOO: A temporal versioned object-oriented data model, Information Sciences 114 (1-4) (1999) 281–300.
8. S.-E. Lautemann, A propagation mechanism for populated schema versions, in: Int'l. Conf. on Data Engineering, IEEE Computer Society, Birmingham U.K, 1997, pp. 67–78.
9. S.R. Monk, I. Sommerville, Schema evolution in oodbs using class versioning, SIGMOD Record 22 (3) (1993) 16–22.
10. A. Rashid, P. Sawyer, E. Pulvermueller, A flexible approach for instance adaptation during class versioning, in: Int'l. Symposium Objects and Databases, Vol. 1944 of LNCS, Springer, Sophia Antipolis, France, 2000, pp. 101–113.
11. M.M. Moro, S.M. Saggiorato, N. Edelweiss, C. S. dos Santos, Adding time to an object-oriented versions model, in: Int'l. Conf. on Database and Expert Systems Applications, Vol. 2113 of LNCS, Springer, Munich, Germany, 2001, pp. 805–814.
12. R.M. Galante, A.B. da Silva Roma, A. Jantsch, N. Edelweiss, C. S. dos Santos, Dynamic schema evolution management using version in temporal object-oriented databases, in: Int'l. Conf. on Database and Expert Systems Applications, Vol. 2453 of LNCS, Springer, Aix-en-Provence, France, 2002, pp. 524–533.
13. F. Ferrandina, T. Meyer, R. Zicari, Implementing lazy database updates for an object database system, in: Int'l. Conf. on Very Large Data Bases, Morgan Kaufmann, Santiago, Chile, 1994, pp. 261–272.
14. J. Banerjee, W. Kim, H.F. Korth, Semantics and implementation of schema evolution in object-oriented databases, in: ACM Sigmod Int'l. Conf. on Management of Data, San Francisco, CA, 1987, pp. 311–322.
15. M.M. Moro, N. Edelweiss, A.P. Zaupa, C.S. dos Santos, TVQL - temporal versioned query language, in: Int'l. Conf. on Database and Expert Systems Applications, Vol. 2453 of LNCS, Springer, Aix-en-Provence, France, 2002, pp. 618–627.

Towards Temporal Information in Workflow Systems

Carlo Combi[1] and Giuseppe Pozzi[2]

[1] Università di Verona, strada le Grazie 15 I-37134 Verona - Italy
combi@sci.univr.it
[2] Politecnico di Milano, P.za L. da Vinci 32 I-20133 Milano - Italy
giuseppe.pozzi@polimi.it

Abstract. A workflow management system (WfMS) is a software system that supports the coordinated execution of different simple activities, assigning them to human or automatic executors, to achieve a common goal defined for a business process. Temporal aspects of stored information cannot be neglected and the adoption of a temporal database management system (TDBMS) could benefit.

By this paper we scratch the surface of the topic related to the use of a TDBMS in a WfMS, identifying some advantages in managing temporal aspects by a TDBMS inside some of the components of a WfMS. E.g., queries to reconstruct the schema of the business process or to assign activities to executors balancing their workload over time, or the definition of constraints among tasks can benefit from the use of a TDBMS.

1 Introduction

Workflows are activities involving the coordinated execution of multiple tasks performed by different processing entities. A worktask (or task) defines some work to be done by a person, by a software system or by both of them. Specifying a workflow involves describing those aspects of its component tasks (and the processing entities that execute them) that are relevant to control and coordinate their execution, as well as the relationships between the tasks themselves.

Information needed to run a workflow are stored by a database management system (DBMS). In most cases, the adopted DBMS is a traditional, off-the-shelf, relational DBMS which does not provide any facility to manage temporal aspects of stored information, forcing the designer to explicitly define and manage those aspects. Temporal information to be managed in a workflow involves several aspects, such as the starting and ending timestamps of a task, the deadline for completing an activity, the validity time of a data item, the time interval between the execution of two different activities, to mention few of them.

With regards to these temporal aspects, the adoption of a temporal DBMS (TDBMS), which is based on a data model where time and time dimensions are suitably represented and managed [12], could easily improve the development of a system devoted to the automatic management of workflows (workflow management system: WfMS). Indeed, the adoption of a temporal data model and of a related temporal query language, could help to:

A. Olivé et al. (Eds.): ER 2002 Ws, LNCS 2784, pp. 13–25, 2003.
© Springer-Verlag Berlin Heidelberg 2003

- manage in a homogeneous way information related to different aspects of a workflow system, providing a uniform data model to all the software components of a workflow system;
- express in a general way those temporal aspects that are not application-dependent, thus allowing the focus on specific issues of the application when designing a workflow;
- allow a powerful specification of workflows, where application-dependent temporal aspects of real world situations can be simply expressed.

This paper provides a first analysis of specific temporal issues of workflow systems which could be suitably faced by the adoption of a TDBMS; more specifically, we first consider temporalities of information modeled in workflow systems and then examine the temporal issues related to the management of this information during the automatic execution of workflows. In this paper we shall adopt a generic temporal relational data model and the widely known temporal query language TSQL2 [13], to show how to model and manage different temporalities in WfMSs. Throughout the paper, we shall mainly consider the two basic temporal dimensions, namely valid and transaction times, which have been extensively considered in the temporal database literature [12]; more recent topics in the temporal database area will be mentioned for specific needs of WfMSs.

In the following, Section 2 provides some basic concepts on workflow systems, a motivating example, and a description of used models. Section 3 discusses the workflow models which require temporal dimensions, and describes the components of a workflow system that could greatly benefit from the adoption of a TDBMS, mentioning also relevant related work. Finally, Section 4 sketches out some conclusions and general remarks.

2   Workflow Management Systems - WfMSs

Workflow Management Systems (WfMSs) are software systems that support the specification of business processes (described by their *process model* or *schema*), the execution of process instances (*cases*) described in terms of activities (*tasks*) and of dependencies among tasks. A business process may refer to the management of a car rental company, of a travel agency, of an assurance company or even a bank loan. WfMSs control process executions by scheduling activities and by assigning them to executing agents. WfMSs are very complex systems and include many different components, such as: the interpreter of the process definition language (PDL) used to formally model the business process; the process model designer, which helps the user to suitably define a process model according to the supported PDL; the resource management unit, to assign tasks to executing agents; the database connectivity unit, to access data stored into a DBMS; the transaction manager; and the e-mail feeder.

2.1   A Motivating Example

Throughout the paper, as motivating example of a business process that can be managed by a WfMS, we shall refer to a car rental company: Figure 1 depicts the car rental example. Although the semantics of the graphical representation is very intuitive, we refer to the conceptual model described in [5].

A new case is started as the car rental company receives a reservation request. The task GetRentalData collects customer's data and pick-up and return date and place. Next, ChooseCar specifies the type of car the customer prefers (Ferrari, Cadillac, ...). The task CheckCarAvailability queries the database and verifies whether the specified car is available by defining a value for the variable Available. According to the value of Available observed by routing task R1, the outgoing left arch may be followed, leading to the task RejectReservation which informs the customer about failure in reserving the car: otherwise, if the car is available, the task MakeReservation performs the reservation and informs the customer, while SendConfirmation sends the customer a mail with reservation details.

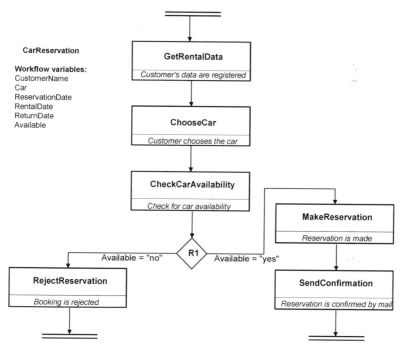

Fig. 1. Schema for the CarReservation process

2.2 Workflow Models

A WfMS stores all the information it needs inside a database managed by a DBMS. Several models can be defined for a WfMS considering the organization where the process is enacted and managed, the formal description of the process model, the data used by the process, the exception model to manage expected events which may force a deviation from the main flow [6], the transaction model to manage aspects of concurrent access to shared data [5]. In the following, we categorize some of the models we shall refer to, as defined in [5].

The Organizational Model The organizational model formally depicts the organization of the company where the process is being enacted. Information mainly relates to agents, owned skills and hierarchy inside the company: all this information is stored by suitable database tables, whose structure is independent both from the organization and from the application domain. Every agent belongs to a group: a group collects agents either involved in the same project or working in the same geographical area. Every agent has a function (or role) specifying the skills the agents owns and the tasks he/she can be assigned, and a supervisor. A generic description of the organizational model includes several tables: however, for clarity reasons, we shall assume that all the information are stored into one unique table, namely Agent, storing the name and the Id of the agent, the e-mail address, the role owned, the group the agent belongs to, and the Id of the manager for that agent. The structure of the table, with some tuples for the CarRental process, is the following:

Agent	AgentName	AgentId	E-mail	Role	Group	ManagedBy
	Hernest	H03	hernest@mailer	PhoneOperator	Boston	B08
	Rudy	R01	rudy@mailer	PhoneOperator	Boston	B08
	Laura	L05	laura@mailer	PhoneOperator	Harvard	B08
	Ken	K13	ken@mailer	PhoneOperator	Harvard	B08
	Doug	D10	douglas@mailer	CarExpert	Syracuse	B08
	Bob	B08	mass_dealer@mailer	LocalDealer	Boston	B01
	Luke	B01	boss@mailer	CEO	Arlington	B01

The Process Model The process model describes the schema of the process; all the information is stored inside suitable database tables whose structure is statically determined and independent from the application domain. At process model design time, the process engineer specifies which is the first task to be executed, the subsequent tasks, the conditions to be evaluated to select different outgoing arcs, the criteria used to assign tasks to agents.

Namely, the tables of the process model are: Workflow, storing the names of the process models registered into the WfMS with their respective first task to be activated; Worktask, storing the names of the tasks of all the process models and the required role for the executing agent; RoutingTask, describing the type of all the routing tasks of any process model; Next, storing the successor task for any task of any process model; AfterFork, storing the criteria adopted to activate arcs outgoing from a routing task of any process model. Their structures with some tuples related to the process model CarReservation are the following:

Workflow	SchemaName	StartTask
	CarReservation	GetRentalData

WorkTask	SchemaName	TaskName	Role
	CarReservation	GetRentalData	PhoneOperator
	CarReservation	ChooseCar	CarExpert
	CarReservation	CheckCarAvailability	InformationSystem
	CarReservation	RejectReservation	PhoneOperator
	CarReservation	MakeReservation	PhoneOperator
	CarReservation	SendConfirmation	InformationSystem

RoutingTask	SchemaName	RTName	Type
	CarReservation	R1	mutualex_fork

Next	SchemaName	TaskName	NextTask
	CarReservation	GetRentalData	ChooseCar
	CarReservation	ChooseCar	CheckCarAvailability
	CarReservation	CheckCarAvailability	R1
	CarReservation	MakeReservation	SendConfirmation
	CarReservation	SendConfirmation	end_flow
	CarReservation	RejectReservation	end_flow

AfterFork	SchemaName	ForkTask	NextTask	Cond
	CarReservation	R1	RejectReservation	Available = "no"
	CarReservation	R1	MakeReservation	Available = "yes"

The Information Model. The information model describes the application domain data the process has to manage and the history of different cases.

Process Specific Data. The structure of process-specific tables is defined at schema design time and tables are automatically derived. Even though in most cases several tables are used, for clarity reasons in the following we assume that all the data about the cases of the process model CarReservation is stored within one single table: tables can eventually be reconstructed as a view. The table Rental-Data stores the process variables defined at process design time: case identifier, customer's name, date when the reservation was made, date of picking up the car, date for returning the car, and availability of the car as a result of the reservation. This latter variable is used by routing task R1 to activate the successor task (RejectReservation or MakeReservation). Table RentalData, with 2 runs of the CarReservation process, is depicted as:

RentalData	CaseId	CName	Car	ReservationDate	RentalDate	ReturnDate	Available
	50	Marple J.	Cadillac	01-03-09	01-12-01	02-01-06	"yes"
	51	Wallace E.	Lamborghini	01-07-11	02-02-01	02-02-02	"no"

Historical Data. Historical data contains information related to the execution of tasks and cases and is independent from the application domain. A generic description of historical data is obtained by the tables CaseHistory (storing the identifier of all the executed cases, the name of their respective process model, the responsible agent, which in most cases is the starting agent, and temporal information about the start time and the duration of the entire case) and TaskHistory (storing the name of the task, the identifier of the case the task belonged to, the name of the executing agent, the final status of the task and the time of start and end of the task itself). Their structures with some tuples from the process model CarReservation are the following:

CaseHistory	CaseId	SchemaName	Responsible	StartTime	Duration
	47	CarReservation	H03	01-03-09 10:03:10	8 min 40 sec
	48	CarReservation	L05	01-07-11 9:00:10	3 min 49 sec

TaskHistory	CaseId	TaskName	StartTime	EndTime	FinalState	AgentId
	47	GetRentalData	01-03-09 10:03:10	01-03-09 10:05:50	Completed	H03
	47	ChooseCar	01-03-09 10:06:00	01-03-09 10:08:50	Completed	D10
	47	CheckCarAvailability	01-03-09 10:08:51	01-03-09 10:08:52	Completed	auto
	47	MakeReservation	01-03-09 10:08:53	01-03-09 10:08:55	Completed	R01
	47	SendConfirmation	01-03-09 10:09:10	01-03-09 10:11:50	Completed	auto
	48	GetRentalData	01-07-11 9:00:10	01-07-11 9:01:43	Completed	L05
	48	ChooseCar	01-07-11 9:01:45	01-07-11 9:02:01	Completed	D10
	48	CheckCarAvailability	01-07-11 9:02:03	01-07-11 9:02:07	Completed	auto
	48	RejectReservation	01-07-11 9:02:10	01-07-11 9:03:59	Completed	K13

3   Temporal Aspects in WfMS

In this section, we show that several aspects managed by a WfMS have relevant temporal dimensions. We first introduce some examples of temporalities we need to consider when representing and storing information related to the different models of Section 2.2; then, we show how this information should be managed by the WfMS through a TDBMS.

3.1   Temporalities of the Models

Several temporal aspects of data could be managed by a TDBMS, providing a unified support for all the models the WfMS needs. In the following we shall focus on the application to workflow models of those temporal dimensions which are widely recognized as the fundamental temporal dimensions of any fact relevant to a database [12]: valid and transaction times. The *valid time* (VT) of a fact is the time when the fact is true in the considered domain, while the *transaction time* of a fact is the time when the fact is current in the database.

Temporality in the Organizational Model. In defining the organizational model, temporal aspects have to be considered: indeed, we need to represent when agents are available to perform any task suitable for their roles. Let us consider the case of human agents in the CarReservation process: each agent is working only during certain hours of the day and only during some days of the week; furthermore, each agent spends some holidays out of work during the year. All these aspects have to be managed in any case by the WfMS. The adoption of an organizational model which explicitly considers these temporal features can improve the usability of the system by the workflow designer, which can suitably represent the temporal constraints of the organization under consideration. As an example, in the following table we describe when a given agent is available.

AgentAvailability	AgentId	VT
	H03	working days in $[00\text{-}08\text{-}09 \div +\infty]$
	R01	mondays, tuesdays in $[00\text{-}01\text{-}05 \div +\infty]$
	L05	working mornings in $[00\text{-}05\text{-}07 \div +\infty]$
	K13	working days in $[01\text{-}01\text{-}23 \div +\infty]$
	D10	working days in $[01\text{-}01\text{-}09 \div +\infty]$
	B08	working days in $[01\text{-}11\text{-}11 \div +\infty]$
	B01	all days in $[00\text{-}01\text{-}03 \div +\infty]$

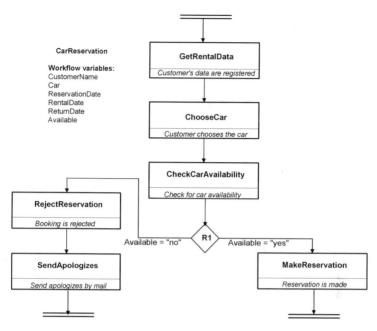

Fig. 2. Schema for the CarReservation process after a change to schema has been applied

In the previous example we assume we are able to express valid time according to different granularities, suitably defined and managed by the TDBMS. Several works on time granularity have been done within the temporal database community, which should be deeply considered in modelling this kind of temporal data for a WfMS [1,8,13,10].

Temporality in the Process Model. In the process model we mainly distinguish two different temporal aspects: versioning and temporal constraints.

Versioning. A process can have different versions, which result from the modification of the process schema due to the evolution of the application needs: for example, we can imagine that the schema of the process CarReservation, defined on January 5th, 2000, is that one depicted in Figure 1 until October 12th 2001, when it is modified as depicted in Figure 2. As a difference from the previous version of the schema, if the reservation succeeds, the customer is no longer sent a confirmation: if the reservation fails, the customer is informed and an apologizing mail is sent along with some advertising flyers (task SendApologizes). Each version of the process model has, thus, a valid time, which identifies the temporal interval during which the given version was used. Tables WorkTask and Next, which are now valid time relations, are suitably updated according to the changes to the schema as follows:

WorkTask	SchemaName	TaskName	Role	VT
	CarReservation	GetRentalData	PhoneOperator	[00-01-05 ÷ +∞]
	CarReservation	ChooseCar	CarExpert	[00-01-05 ÷ +∞]
	CarReservation	CheckCarAvailability	InformationSystem	[00-01-05 ÷ +∞]
	CarReservation	RejectReservation	PhoneOperator	[00-01-05 ÷ +∞]
	CarReservation	MakeReservation	PhoneOperator	[00-01-05 ÷ +∞]
	CarReservation	ConfirmReservation	InformationSystem	[00-01-05 ÷ 01-10-12]
	CarReservation	SendApologizes	InformationSystem	[01-10-13 ÷ +∞]

Next	SchemaName	TaskName	NextTask	Tcons	VT
	CarReservation	GetRentalData	ChooseCar	[0 m ÷ 2 m]	[00-01-05 ÷ +∞]
	CarReservation	ChooseCar	CheckCarAvailability	[0 m ÷ 10 m]	[00-01-05 ÷ +∞]
	CarReservation	CheckCarAvailability	R1	[0 m ÷ 1 m]	[00-01-05 ÷ +∞]
	CarReservation	MakeReservation	ConfirmReservation	[0 m ÷ 1 m]	[00-01-05 ÷ 01-10-12]
	CarReservation	ConfirmReservation	end_flow	[0 m ÷ 0 m]	[00-01-05 ÷ 01-10-12]
	CarReservation	RejectReservation	end_flow	[0 m ÷ 0 m]	[00-01-05 ÷ 01-10-12]
	CarReservation	MakeReservation	end_flow	[0 m ÷ 0 m]	[01-10-13 ÷ +∞]
	CarReservation	RejectReservation	SendApologizes	[0 m ÷ 2 m]	[01-10-13 ÷ +∞]
	CarReservation	SendApologizes	end_flow	[0 m ÷ 0 m]	[01-10-13 ÷ +∞]

Temporal Constraints. A process model includes the definition of temporal constraints among the different tasks and their durations [1]. For instance, the column labelled Tcons in table Next defines a constraint for the scheduler of the WfMS, specifying that the successor task is to be scheduled, after the current task finished, within the minimum and maximum time stated by Tcons. Similarly, also time constraints for the maximum allowable task duration can be defined for every task, serving as temporal constraints on the execution time. TDBMS should be able to represent temporal constraints even with different temporal granularities, as discussed in [1,2].

Temporality in the Information Model. Several different temporal dimensions can be considered for data inside the information model; in this context, valid and transaction times are very important, managing both the history of workflow data and of possible changes on entered data. As an example, the table RentalData, managed by a bitemporal database system [12], allows the WfMS to discover changes both in the customer preferences and in entered data.

The table RentalData presents two situations. In the first one, customer Smith for case 47 modified his reservation. In fact, the customer named Smith on November 12th 2001 made the reservation for a car to be returned on January 6th 2002 (see the first tuple with CaseId=47). The valid time for the case started on November 12th 2001. On November 21st 2001 he changed the return date to January 7th 2002 - thus forcing the same case to be still opened and closing the first transaction for case 47 - and asked for a new car type FIAT.

In the second situation, data originally entered were wrong. Customer Jones did not change anything about his reservation; there has been only an error in data insertion (collection). Indeed, in this case, there is only one tuple about Jones in the current database state (i.e., the state consisting of tuples having the transaction time with +∞ as upper bound): valid time of this tuple confirms that the reservation of Jones was valid from its definition up to now.

The table RentalData is the following:

CaseId	Cname	Car	RentDate	RetDate	Avlb	VT	TT
47	Smith J.	Ferrari	01-12-01	02-01-06	yes	[01-11-12 ÷ +∞]	[01-11-12 ÷ 01-11-21]
48	Jones J.	Lotus	02-02-01	02-02-02	no	[01-08-02÷ +∞]	[01-08-02 ÷ 01-08-03]
47	Smith J.	Ferrari	01-12-01	02-01-06	yes	[01-11-12 ÷ 01-11-21]	[01-11-21 ÷ +∞]
47	Smith J.	Fiat	01-12-01	02-01-07	yes	[01-11-21 ÷ +∞]	[01-11-21 ÷ +∞]
48	Jones J.	Lotus	02-02-01	02-02-03	no	[01-08-02÷ +∞]	[01-08-03÷ +∞]

As for historical data of the information model, by a TDBMS we are able to manage in a homogeneous way temporal data already present into the database and explicitly managed by the WfMS as user-defined times. Indeed, tables Case-History and TaskHistory depicted in Section 2.2 represent the valid time of stored information by attributes StartTime, Duration and StartTime, EndTime, respectively; being these attributes user-defined times [12], the WfMS has to deal with them explicitly. Using a TDBMS, instead, these two tables would be simply valid time relations, directly and homogeneously managed be the temporal database system. Instances of tables CaseHistory and TaskHistory, when represented in a temporal database system as valid time relations, are depicted in the following:

CaseHistory	CaseId	SchemaName	Responsible	VT
	47	CarReservation	H03	[01-11-12 10:03:10 ÷ 01-11-12 10:11:50]
	48	CarReservation	L05	[01-08-02 9:00:10 ÷ 01-08-02 9:03:59]

TaskHistory	CaseId	TaskName	FinalState	Agent	VT
	47	GetRentalData	Completed	H03	[01-11-12 10:03:10 ÷ 01-11-12 10:05:50]
	47	ChooseCar	Completed	D10	[01-11-12 10:06:00 ÷ 01-11-12 10:08:50]
	47	CheckCarAvailability	Completed	auto	[01-11-12 10:08:51 ÷ 01-11-12 10:08:52]
	47	MakeReservation	Completed	R01	[01-11-12 10:08:53 ÷ 01-11-12 10:08:55]
	48	GetRentalData	Completed	L05	[01-08-02 9:00:10 ÷ 01-08-02 9:01:43]
	48	ChooseCar	Completed	D10	[01-08-02 9:01:45 ÷ 01-08-02 9:02:01]
	48	CheckCarAvailability	Completed	auto	[01-08-02 9:02:03 ÷ 01-08-02 9:02:07]
	48	RejectReservation	Completed	K13	[01-08-02 9:02:10 ÷ 01-08-02 9:03:59]

Observation. *To reconstruct the complete history of a case, it could be useful to distinguish at the modelling level both the time during which the task has been executed, i.e., the valid time of the task, and the time at which the task has been assigned to the agent. This latter temporal dimension could be suitably modeled by the concept of event time, which is the occurrence time of a real-world event that either initiates or terminates the validity interval of the modeled fact [7].*

3.2   Managing Temporal Aspects

All the components of a WfMS heavily interact with the DBMS to store and reference all the data from the different models (organizational, process and information models). If the adopted DBMS does not feature the management of temporal information, all the components of the WfMS have to explicitly manage those temporal aspects of data: on the other hand, if a TDBMS is adopted, temporal aspects of data are directly managed by the DBMS itself. Without loss of generality, in the following we shall use the widely known temporal query language TSQL2 [13], to show how the interaction of the WfMS with a TDBMS could be powerfully performed by a temporal query language. In the following, we briefly outline some of the components of a WfMS that could take the greatest advantages from the adoption of a TDBMS.

Process Instancer: This component defines the proper process model to be adopted for all the running cases and also for completed ones. Obviously, if no change has never been applied to the model of a given process, there is no need to manage temporal aspects related to schema migration of the process model itself: however, a very very small percentage of process models (a good reasonable estimation is less than 1%) does not need for a change during their life, not even for adaptive, perfective or corrective maintenance [4]. On the other hand, if the process model has been changed, one may want to reconstruct the exact process model defined for all the cases, no matter if completed or not. For completed cases, the table CaseHistory defines only the executed tasks, while the table does not allow one to completely reconstruct the schema: in fact, if in front of a routing operator with three or more outgoing arcs one of them only was followed, the table CaseHistory does not specify which outgoing arcs were available but only the followed outgoing arcs. The complete reconstruction of the process model is thus not feasible by the workflow history only.

Assuming that a case evolves according to the process model valid at the time of its initiation [4], the temporal query in TSQL2 [13] to reconstruct the process model for any case should sound like:

SELECT CaseId, TaskName, NextTask
FROM Next N, CaseHistory C
WHERE C.SchemaName = N.SchemaName AND
      VALID(N) OVERLAPS BEGIN(VALID(C))

On the other hand, whenever a new case is started, the process instancer has to define which is the current process model to be followed for the starting case. The TSQL2 query to reconstruct the *current* process model for CarReservation, if many different versions are defined, should sound like:

SELECT TaskName, NextTask
FROM Next N
WHERE N.SchemaName = "CarReservation" AND
      VALID(N) OVERLAPS CURRENT_DATE

In both the described situations, the reconstruction of the correct process model would be completed by considering the information about routing tasks stored in the table AfterFork, with the same approach previously described.

Scheduler of the Workflow Engine: This component assigns tasks to agents for execution based on their skills. The component has to mainly consider working time and work load of agents, which are very critical and may vary continuously.

Working time: the scheduler should not assign to an agent a task whose expected completion, computed as the maximum task duration started from the initiation of that task, will fall into or will include an holiday period for that agent. Additionally, holiday time for agents is in most situations made of a set of intervals, e.g., agent Bob will be on holiday on 02-04-04÷02-04-11 and on

02-05-01÷02-05-06. If the task is expected to start on 02-04-02 and the expected duration is 3 days, the agent will suspend the execution of the task on 02-04-03 (beginning of holiday) and will resume its execution at the end of the holiday on 02-04-11, resulting in a duration of the execution of that task of approximatively 10 days, much beyond the expectancy of 3 days. The scheduler, thus, has to compare intervals of holidays of agents and expected execution time of tasks by suitable techniques, to be able to manage comparisons between intervals at different levels of granularities and/or with indeterminacy [1,8]. In this direction, Bettini and colleagues in [1] study the problem of specifying, even with different granularities, time constraints for tasks and for delays between tasks; they also propose a general algorithm for finding *free schedules*, i.e. schedules which do not impose further constraints on the task durations, for a workflow.

Work Load: The scheduler has to assign tasks to agents balancing the load of work among them. When evaluating the history of tasks executed by agents, the scheduler could consider, for example, whether there is some agent which is not working when some other agent (with the same role) is working. Let us consider the following TSQL2 query:

```
SELECT A.AgentId, TaskName
FROM AgentAvailability A, TaskHistory T, Agent G1, Agent G2
WHERE A.AgentId <> T.Agent AND A.AgentId = G1.AgentId AND
    T.AgentId = G2.AgentId AND G1.Role = G2.Role AND
    NOT EXISTS (SELECT *
        FROM TaskHistory T1
        WHERE T1.Agent=A.AgentId AND VALID(T1) OVERLAPS VALID(T))
```

Through this query, by using the default semantics of TSQL2 in the FROM clause, tuples of tables AgentAvailability, TaskHistory, and Agent are associated only if their valid times intersect (in this case, tuples of atemporal tables are considered as always valid); the condition expressed in the WHERE clause is then evaluated on these tuples. Valid times of tuples in the result are the intersection of the tuples considered in the evaluation of the query.

Process Model Designer Tool: The process model engineer uses a tool, namely workflow designer, to formally define the schema inside the WfMS. The process engineer has to define for every task an expected task duration (i.e., the average duration for a task) and the maximum allowable duration (i.e., a deadline for the completion of the task): if the execution of a task exceeds the maximum duration, the agent has to be urged to complete the task and if the delay persists, a compensation action could possibly be executed. The tool also has to enable the engineer in defining temporal constraint (e.g., through suitable values of the attribute Tcons in table Next of Section 3.1) over dependencies among tasks, identifying the maximum allowable interval between the completion of a predecessor task and the activation of its successor(s): these constraints must be observed by the workflow scheduler.

Exception Designer Tool: The process model engineer, after having defined the process model, has to define *expected exceptions* [6,11], i.e., those anomalous situations that are part of the semantics of the process and that are known in advance at workflow design time. Exceptions are an important component of workflow models and permit the representation of behaviors that, although abnormal, occur with high frequency (sometimes even more than 10% of the times). Examples of expected exceptions are the violation of either constraints over data or temporal conditions, a car accident in a car rental process, as well as a change in the RentalDate or in the ReturnDate: if the customer postponed the ReturnDate, some compensation actions must be performed, e.g., re-arranging the subsequent rentals of the same car to other customers. Exception management modules in a WfMS are periodically invoked, sometimes with a frequency ranging from tens of minutes to several hours: such a frequency considers that business processes are long-running activities [9] and in most cases there is no need for an immediate management of exceptions. These modules manage exceptional situations that may have occurred during the process enactment since the previous activation of the modules themselves [6] and consider for execution the several exceptions occurred to different cases, grouping them by exception type: e.g., all the task instances that for any reason exceeded their maximum allowable task durations are processed altogether. In order to select all the exceptions to be processed, a temporal query must be performed to select all the exceptions that actually occurred since the last execution of the exception manager: the use of a TDBMS could easily help.

Additionally, a TDBMS can help in retrieving values of process specific data at given instants. Let us assume that we need an exception detecting whether the customer switched from a car to another car. The exception mechanism has to compare the currently booked car with the previously booked one. The event of the exception is a modify of an attribute, namely Car: the condition part has to monitor the value of Car with its previous value. By a TDBMS the query to reconstruct the changes to the Car attribute sounds like the following:

```
SELECT SNAPSHOT R1.Car, R2.Car
FROM RentalData R1, RentalData R2
WHERE R1.CaseId = R2.CaseId AND R1.Car <> R2.Car AND
    VALID(R1) BEFORE VALID(R2) AND
    NOT EXISTS (SELECT *
        FROM RentalData R
        WHERE R.CaseId = R1.CaseId AND VALID(R) AFTER VALID(R1)
            AND VALID(R) BEFORE VALID(R2))
```

It can be easily observed that if the adopted DBMS is not a temporal one, the query would result in a more specific expression: indeed, the attributes representing the valid time would be treated as application-dependent ones. Furthermore, the query would be executed without any special support by the DBMS.

4   Conclusions

In this paper, we showed how temporal database systems applied to WfMS could greatly improve performances, e.g. by allowing one to define different versions of the same process model, picking the last one for new cases to be started and using the original one valid at the time the already running case was started, and ease-of-usage of WfMSs, e.g. by storing the subsequent changes to process-specific data. We also showed how to model and query in a homogeneous way temporal information concerning different models needed by WfMSs.

The management of temporal information in WfMSs is an underestimated research topic, where research results from the temporal database area could be extensively applied and suitably extended. To this regard, we are going to consider the following possible future research directions:

Design of visual tools for process model design: the process engineer can define real world temporal constraints among tasks and on task/case durations, possibly by a powerful and easy-to-use tool;

Exception modelling: the process engineer can define suitable compensation actions if deadlines and/or temporal constraints are violated. Compensation actions, on the other hand, can be immediately executed, delayed, or temporally grouped, depending on the violated constraints and on the specific process.

References

1. Bettini C., Sean Wang X., Jajodia S. Free Schedules for Free Agents in Workflow Systems. Seventh International Workshop on Temporal Representation and Reasoning, TIME 2000, IEEE Computer Society, 31–38
2. Brusoni V., Console L., Terenziani P., Pernici B. Qualitative and Quantitative Temporal Constraints and Relational Databases: Theory, Architecture, and Applications. *IEEE TKDE* 1999, 11(6): 948–968
3. Casati F., Ceri S., Pernici B., Pozzi G. Deriving Production Rules for Workflow Enactment. In: Proceedings of the 7th Database and Expert Systems Applications International Conference, Springer-Verlag, LNCS, 1996, 94–115
4. Casati F., Ceri S., Pernici B., Pozzi G. Workflow Evolution. *Int. Journal Data and Knowledge Engineering* 1998, 24(1): 211–239
5. Casati F., Pernici B., Pozzi G., Sánchez G., Vonk J. Conceptual Workflow Model. In: *Database Support for Workflow Management*, Dordrecht, Kluwer Ac., 1999, 23–45
6. Casati F., Ceri S., Paraboschi S., Pozzi G. Specification and Implementation of Exceptions in Workflow Management Systems. *ACM TODS* 1999, 24(3): 405–451
7. Combi C., Montanari A. Data Models with Multiple Temporal Dimensions: Completing the Picture. In: Advanced Information Systems Engineering, 13th International Conference, CAiSE 2001, Berlin, Springer, LNCS, 2001, 187–202
8. Combi C., Pozzi G. HMAP - A temporal data model managing intervals with different granularities and indeterminacy from natural language sentences. *VLDB Journal* 2001, 9(4): 294–311
9. Dayal U., Hsu M., Ladin R. Organizing long-running activities with triggers and transactions. SIGMOD Record, 1990, 19(2): 204–214.
10. Dyreson C. E., Evans W. S., Lin H, Snodgrass R. T.: Efficiently Supported Temporal Granularities. *IEEE TKDE* 2000, 12(4): 568-587 (2000)
11. Eder J., Liebhart W. The Workflow Activity Model WAMO. Proceedings of the 3rd International Conference on Cooperative Information Systems, 1995, 87–98.
12. Jensen C., Snodgrass R.T. Temporal Data Management. *IEEE TKDE* 1999, 11(1): 36–44
13. Snodgrass R.T. (ed.) The TSQL2 Temporal Query Language. Boston, Kluwer Ac., 1995.

Preserving and Querying Histories of XML-Published Relational Databases

Fusheng Wang and Carlo Zaniolo

Department of Computer Science, University of California, Los Angeles
Los Angeles, CA 90095, USA
{wangfsh, zaniolo}@cs.ucla.edu

Abstract. There is much current interest in publishing and viewing database-resident data as XML documents. In fact, such XML views of the database can be easily visualized on web browsers and processed by web languages, including powerful query languages such as XQuery. As the database is updated, its external XML view also evolves. In this paper, we investigate the problem of representing the evolution history of such a view as yet another XML document, whereby the complete history of the database can also be visualized on web browsers, processed by web languages, and queried using powerful query languages such as XQuery. We investigate various approaches used for publishing relational data, and identify and select those which are best for representing and querying database histories. We show that the selected representations make it easy to formulate in XQuery temporal queries that are difficult to express using SQL on database relations. Finally, we discuss briefly the storage organization that can be used to support these queries efficiently.

1 Introduction

There is a much current interest in publishing database-resident data as (concrete or dynamic) XML documents, which can then be viewed on web browsers, and processed by various web-based applications, including queries written in languages such as XPath and XQuery [4]. As the underlying database is updated, its external XML view also changes (continuously for dynamic documents and at refresh time for concrete ones). Most users who are interested in viewing and querying the current database are also interested in viewing and querying its past snapshots and evolving history—preferably, using the same browsers and query languages. In fact, in many applications, (such as inventory control, supply chain management, surveillance, etc.) changes in the database being monitored are of critical interest. To address this need, web data warehouses have been proposed recently [25]; these detect changes in web sites of interest, preserve their past contents, and answer continuous queries for subscribing users [25]. As in the case of more traditional warehouses, changes can be monitored in two ways:

1. The site publishing the database sends to the web warehouse the log of its recent updates (either continuously or at regular intervals), or

A. Olivé et al. (Eds.): ER 2002 Ws, LNCS 2784, pp. 26–38, 2003.

2. The web warehouse downloads from the site frequent snapshots of the XML-published data, and then computes the delta between the new version and the previous one.

The second problem can be reduced to the first one, by computing the delta between the two versions and then deriving an edit script that shows how one version can be transformed into the other; algorithms to support this computation were proposed in [25,17]. Since we are dealing with XML-published <u>relational</u> data, the order of the tuples is immaterial and we can also use the change detection algorithm for semistructured information proposed in [9]. All these algorithms represent the deltas between the documents as edit scripts and return minimum deltas that will transform the old version into the new one. As discussed in [6], for elements that are logically identified by keys, it is semantically preferable to detect changes between elements denoted by the same key. The X-Diff algorithm proposed in [33] applies in this situation; this algorithm was in fact designed for detecting changes in unordered XML documents with keys, as in the case of our XML-published relational data. By utilizing node signatures and node XHash values, the algorithm tries to find the minimum-cost matching. The algorithm can reach a high matching accuracy, and has complexity $O(n^2)$ [33].

The additional step of computing the edit script is avoided when the publishing site communicates the changes directly to the web warehouse. Thus in the rest of the paper, we assume that the update log is given. Moreover, we will not go into details about the particular form in which the corresponding updates to the XML document are represented. While somewhat different representations have been used in the past, these differences are not significant in our study, and they are bound to disappear once a standard XML update language will emerge [30]. Moreover, the use of the database update log avoids the temporal indeterminacy problems that instead occur when the remote database is sampled at regular intervals and the edit script is reconstructed using various diff algorithms.

All the approaches previously discussed focus on the preservation and retrieval of past versions of web documents; in this paper, we instead focus on relational tables and discuss how to preserve their content and support complex historical queries via XML and XQuery. Thus, we examine alternative ways to represent the history of XML-published relational tables as XML documents, and show that some of these representations allow the expression of powerful historical queries in a natural fashion. The conceptual and practical interest of this conclusion is underscored by the fact that expressing temporal queries directly on relational databases had instead proven to be a difficult problem that required major extensions to SQL [16,35,36,26]. Thus viewing the history of relational tables as XML documents could provide an appealing venue for supporting historical queries on databases. Observe that the publication of the current database as an XML document is actually not required for representing the *database history* as an XML document, since this can be constructed directly from the update log of the database.

2   Preserving the History of Documents

Traditional schemes for version management, such as RCS [32] and SCCS [28], are widely used in applications such as software configuration control and support for cooperative work; version-control techniques have also been proposed for databases, often in the context of O-O systems and CAD applications [24]. The emergence of web information systems and many new web-based applications has generated a flurry of interest and research activities, at first focusing on semistructured information [9], and now on XML [13,25,14,6]. This interest is due to the fact that (i) traditional version management applications are now migrating to a web-based environment [3], (ii) there is an increasing realization that e-permanence must be achieved and the broken link problem must be fixed [23], and (iii) very interesting queries can now be answered (using XQuery or XPath) on the preserved history of multiversion documents.

The e-permanence problem has motivated a significant amount of previous work. In particular the Wayback machine crawls the whole web [23], preserving the past content, but without much support for queries (temporal or otherwise). Transaction-time web servers were instead proposed in [18] to archive previous versions of web resources to support transaction timeslice requests by remote browsers. As further enhancement was proposed in [19], where it was shown that the XPath data model and query language can be naturally extended to support transaction time semantics.

The problem of efficiently storing and querying the history of versioned XML documents was discussed in [12,13,25,14]. The reference-based model proposed in [13] unifies the logical representation and the physical one, but can only handle simple queries; in fact, different storage representations are needed for more complex queries[14]. An extension of the SCCS scheme [28] was recently used for representing versions of hierarchically structured documents [6]. Here, we will use a similar version scheme to represent and query the history of XML-published databases at the logical level. Since many different XML-based representations can be used for publishing [29,30] the same database tables we will also study alternative representations and determines which are most suitable for supporting temporal queries. We will also show that still different representations are needed at the physical level.

3   Publishing Relational Data History as XML Documents

Table 1 and 2 describe the history of employees and departments. These transaction-time tables are shown here for illustration and *they are not stored in the actual database*. Instead, our database only contains the evolving snapshots of these relations—e.g., a single tuple for the employee in the example.

Therefore, we propose to represent and preserve the evolving history of these database relations by means of the XML documents shown in Figure 1 and Figure 2. We will call these *H-documents*. Each element in a H-document is assigned two attributes *tstart* and *tend*, which represent the inclusive time-interval of the

element. The value of *tend* can be set to *now*, to denote the ever-increasing
current time.

Our H-documents use a temporally grouped data model [16]. Clifford, et al.
[16] show that temporally-grouped models are more natural and powerful than
temporarily-ungrouped ones. Temporal groups are however difficult to support in
the framework of flat relations and SQL. Thus, many approaches proposed in the
past instead timestamp the tuples of relational tables. These approaches incur
into several problems, including the coalescing problem [35]. TSQL2's approach
[35] attempts to achieve a compromise between these two [16], and is based on
an implicit temporal model, which is not without its own problems [10].

Our model supports temporal grouping by taking advantage of the richer
structure of XML documents, and the expressive power of XQuery. An advantage of our approach is that powerful temporal queries can be expressed in
XQuery without requiring the introduction of new constructs in the language.
We next show how to express temporal projections, snapshot queries, joins and
historical queries on *employees* and *departments*. These queries were tested with
Quip [2] (SoftwarAG's implementation of XQuery) and can be downloaded from
http://wis.cs.ucla.edu/~wangfsh/ecdm02/.

Table 1. The snapshot history of employees

Name	Salary	Title	Dept	DOB	Start	Stop
Bob	60000	Engineer	QA	1945-04-09	1995-01-01	1995-05-31
Bob	70000	Engineer	QA	1945-04-09	1995-06-01	1995-09-30
Bob	70000	Sr Engineer	RD	1945-04-09	1995-10-01	1996-01-31
Bob	70000	Tech Leader	RD	1945-04-09	1996-02-01	1996-12-31

Table 2. The snapshot history of departments

Name	Manager	Start	End
QA	Johnson	1994-01-01	1998-12-31
RD	Joe	1992-01-01	1996-12-31
RD	Peter	1997-01-01	1998-12-31
Sales	Frank	1993-01-01	1997-12-31

3.1   Each Table as an XML Document: Columns as Elements

A natural way of publishing relational data is to publish each table as an XML
document by converting relational columns into XML elements [29]. Figure 1
shows the history of the table `employee` and Figure 2 shows the history of
the `dept` table. Thus the history of each relation is published as a separate
H-document.

Based on the published documents, we can specify a variety of queries in
XQuery:

```
<employees tstart="1995-01-01" tend="1996-12-31">
  <employee tstart="1995-01-01" tend="1996-12-31">
    <name tstart="1995-01-01" tend="1996-12-31">Bob</name>
    <salary tstart="1995-01-01" tend="1995-05-31">60000</salary>
    <salary tstart="1995-06-01" tend="1996-12-31">70000</salary>
    <title tstart="1995-01-01" tend="1995-09-30">Engineer</title>
    <title tstart="1995-10-01" tend="1996-01-31">Sr Engineer</title>
    <title tstart="1996-02-01" tend="1996-12-31">Tech Leader</title>
    <dept tstart="1995-01-01" tend="1995-09-30">QA</dept>
    <dept tstart="1995-10-01" tend="1996-12-31">RD</dept>
    <DOB tstart="1995-01-01" tend="1996-12-31">1945-04-09</DOB>
  </employee>
</employees>
```

Fig. 1. The history of the `employee` table is published as `employees.xml`

```
<depts tstart="1992-01-01" tend="1998-12-31">
  <dept   tstart="1994-01-01" tend="1998-12-31">
      <name   tstart="1994-01-01" tend="1998-12-31">QA</name>
      <manager tstart="1994-01-01" tend="1998-12-31">Johnson</manager>
  </dept>
  <dept tstart="1991-01-01" tend="1998-12-31">
      <name tstart="1991-01-01" tend="1998-12-31">RD</name>
      <manager tstart="1991-01-01" tend="1996-12-31">Joe</manager>
      <manager tstart="1997-01-01" tend="1998-12-31">Peter</manager>
  </dept>
  <dept tstart="1993-01-01" tend="1997-12-31">
      <name tstart="1993-01-01" tend="1997-12-31">Sales</name>
      <manager tstart="1993-01-01" tend="1997-12-31">Frank</manager>
  </dept>
</depts>
```

Fig. 2. The history of the `dept` table is published as `dept.xml`

QUERY 1: Temporal projection: retrieve the salary history of employee "Bob":

```
element salary_history{
  for $s in document("employees.xml")/employees/employee
      [name="Bob"]/salary
  return $s }
```

QUERY 2: Snapshot queries: retrieve the departments on 1996-01-31:

```
for $d in document("depts.xml")/depts/dept
    [@tstart <= "1996-01-31" and @tend >= "1996-01-31"]
let $n := $d/name[@tstart<="1996-01-31" and @tend>="1996-01-31"]
let $m := $d/manager[@tstart<="1996-01-31" and @tend>="1996-01-31"]
return( element dept{$n,$m } )
```

QUERY 3: Find employees history from 1995-05-01 to 1996-04-30:
```
for $e in document("employees.xml")/employees/employee
let $ol:= overlap($e/@tstart, $e/@tend, "1995-05-01","1996-4-30")
where not (empty($ol))
return ( $e/name, $ol )
```

Here *overlap($v1s, $v1e, $v2s, $v2e)* is a user-defined function that returns an element `overlap` with overlapped interval as attributes (tstart, tend). If there is no overlap, then no element is returned which satisfies the XQuery built-in function `empty()`. The next query is a containment query:

QUERY 4: Find employee(s) who worked in the "QA" department through the history of that department:

```
for $d in document("depts.xml")/depts/dept[name="QA"]
for $e in document("employees.xml")/employees/employee[dept="QA"]
where $e/@tstart = $d/name/@tstart and $e/@tend = $d/name/@tend
return $e/name
```

QUERY 5: Find the manager of each employee:

```
for $e in document("employees.xml")/employees/employee
for $d in document("depts.xml")/depts/dept[name=$e/dept]
for $m in $d/manager
let $ol :=overlap($m/@tstart,$m/@tend,$e/@tstart,$e/@tend)
where not (empty($ol))
return ( $e/name, $m, $ol )
```

This query will join employees.xml and depts.xml by *dept*, and the *overlap()* function will return only managers that overlap with the employee with the overlapped version timestamp intervals.

QUERY 6: Find the history of employees in each dept:

```
element depts{
  for $d in document("depts.xml")/depts/dept
  return
    element dept { $d/@*, $d/*,
     element employees {
       for $e in document("employees.xml")/employees/employee
       where  $e/dept = $d/name and
           not(empty(overlap($e/@tstart, $e/@tend, $d/@tstart,$d/@tend)))
       return ($e/name, $e/dept,
           overlap($e/@tstart, $e/@tend, $d/@tstart,$d/@tend) )
     }
   }
}
```

This query will join depts and employees document and generate a hierarchical XML document grouped by dept(Figure 5).

3.2   Multiple Tables as a Single XML Document: Flat Structure

Another way to publish relational data is to publish multiple relational tables into a single XML document(Figure 3), but still with the flat structure as shown in Figure 2. Essentially there is not much difference between this approach and the previous one.

Queries on this representation are similar to those described in the last section.

```
<company tstart="1995-01-01" tend="1996-12-31">
 <employees tstart="1995-01-01" tend="1996-12-31">
    <!-- <employee>... see Fig. 1 ...</employee> ...    -->
 </employees>
 <depts tstart="1992-01-01" tend="1998-12-31">
    <!-- <dept>... see Fig. 2 ... </dept> ...   -->
 </depts>
</company>
```

Fig. 3. The history of the `employee` and `dept` tables is published as `company.xml`

3.3   Multiple Tables as an XML Document: Flat Structure with IDs

To facilitate query processing, when multiple relational tables are published as XML document, tuples can be assigned IDs, which can be referred by IDREF from other elements. For example, in Figure 4, the IDs assigned to dept element, are referred to from employee.

```
<company tstart="1995-01-01" tend="1996-12-31">
 <employees tstart="1995-01-01" tend="1996-12-31">
   <employee ID="emp1" tstart="1995-01-01" tend="1996-12-31">
    <!-- name,salary,title,DOB ... -->
    <dept IDREF="dept1" tstart="1995-01-01" tend="1995-09-30">QA</dept>
    <dept IDREF="dept2" tstart="1995-10-01" tend="1996-12-31">RD</dept>
    <DOB tstart="1995-01-01" tend="1996-12-31">1945-04-09</DOB>
   </employee>
 </employees>
 <depts tstart="1992-01-01" tend="1998-12-31">
   <dept ID="dept1"  tstart="1994-01-01" tend="1998-12-31">
    <name  tstart="1994-01-01" tend="1998-12-31">QA</name>
    <manager tstart="1994-01-01" tend="1998-12-31">Johnson</manager>
   </dept>
   <!-- more dept... -->
 </depts>
</company>
```

Fig. 4. The history of the `employee` and `dept` tables is published as `company2.xml`

This representation supports queries similar to those discussed in the previous sections, but simplifies joins:

QUERY 7: Retrieve the dept Bob worked on 1995-10-15:

```
return document("company2.xml")/company/employees/
            employee[name='Bob'])/dept/@ID=>dept/name
            [@tstart<= "1995-10-15" and @tend >="1995-10-15"]
```

3.4 Multiple Tables as a Single XML Document: Hierarchical Structure

Another approach is to generate a hierarchical XML document from multiple relational tables(Figure 5). This approach is also taken by XPERANTO [8] through grouping in XML views and SQLX [21] through extended aggregate functions.

```
<depts tstart="1991-01-01" tend="1998-12-31">
  <dept  tstart="1994-01-01" tend="1998-12-31">
     <name  tstart="1994-01-01" tend="1998-12-31">QA</name>
     <manager tstart="1994-01-01" tend="1998-12-31">Johnson</manager>
     <employees tstart="1994-01-01" tend="1998-12-31">
      <employee tstart="1995-01-01" tend="1995-09-30">
       <name tstart="1995-01-01" tend="1995-09-30">Bob</name>
       <salary tstart="1995-01-01" tend="1995-05-31">60000</salary>
       <salary tstart="1995-06-01" tend="1995-09-30">70000</salary>
       <title tstart="1995-01-01" tend="1995-09-30">Engineer</title>
       <DOB tstart="1995-01-01" tend="1995-09-30">1945-04-09</DOB>
      </employee>
    </employees>
  </dept>
  <dept tstart="1991-01-01" tend="1998-12-31">
    <name tstart="1991-01-01" tend="1998-12-31">RD</name>
    <manager tstart="1991-01-01" tend="1996-12-31">Joe</manager>
    <manager tstart="1997-01-01" tend="1998-12-31">Peter</manager>
    <employees tstart="1991-01-01" tend="1998-12-31">
       <employee tstart="1995-10-01" tend="1996-12-31">
        <name tstart="1995-01-01" tend="1996-12-31">Bob</name>
        <salary tstart="1995-10-01" tend="1996-12-31">70000</salary>
        <title tstart="1995-10-01" tend="1996-01-31">Sr Engineer</title>
        <title tstart="1996-02-01" tend="1996-12-31">Tech Leader</title>
        <DOB tstart="1995-10-01" tend="1996-12-31">1945-04-09</DOB>
       </employee>
    </employees>
  </dept>
  <!-- ... -->
</depts>
```

Fig. 5. The history of `employee` and `dept` is published as `depts3.xml`

This approach simplifies some queries but complicates others. For example, if we want to retrieve employees in each department (containment query), we can simply write:

QUERY 8: Find employee(s) who worked in the QA department through the dept's history:

```
for $d in document("depts3.xml")/depts/dept[name='QA']
let $e := $d/employees/employee
```

```
let $e_all := document("depts3.xml")/depts/dept
              /employees/employee[name=$e/name]
where  count ($e_all) = 1
       and $e/@tstart = $d/name/@tstart and $e/@tend = $d/name/@tend
return $e/name
```

However, coalescing is needed for other queries in the hierarchical representation.

QUERY 9: Find the salary history of employee "Bob" in the company:

```
for $s in document("depts3.xml")/depts/dept/
          employees/employee[name='Bob']/salary
return coalesce($s)
```

Here we rely on a user-defined function *coalesce()* (Figure 6) to coalesce the employees. This function can also be defined in standard XQuery, as follows:

```
define function coalesce(xs:AnyType $e)  returns xs:AnyType {
if (count($e) =1) then $e
else
   if( $e[1]/text() != coalesce(subsequence($e,2)) [1]/text() )
   then ($e[1], coalesce(subsequence($e,2)) )
   else
     if( string($e[1]/@tend) <
         string(coalesce( subsequence($e,2) )[1]/@tstart)   )
     then $e
     else ( element {name($e[1]) }
            {$e[1]/@tstart, coalesce( subsequence($e,2)[1]/@tend ),
             $e[1]/text()},
             subsequence( coalesce( subsequence($e,2) ), 2) ) }
```

Fig. 6. A coalescing function defined in XQuery

3.5   Relational Tables as XML Document: Columns as Attributes

A relational table can also be published as XML document as attributes (Figure 7), e.g., the *FOR XML* statement in Microsoft SQL Server 2000 [7]. The published XML document is essentially a flat structure that corresponds to the tuple snapshots.

This approach is similar to that of timestamping the whole tuple in the relation. Temporal queries tend to be more complex and most queries require coalescing. Thus, in general, we recommend against this approach when publishing the history of relational tables.

In summary, XML representations that map columns as elements are preferable, and hierarchical representation can only be justified for special cases.

```
<employees>
<employee name="Bob" salary="60000" title="Engineer" dept="QA"
     DOB="1945-04-09" tstart="1995-01-01" tend="1995-05-31"/>
 <employee name="Bob" salary="70000" title="Engineer" dept="QA"
     DOB="1945-04-09" tstart="1995-06-01" tend="1995-09-30"/>
 <employee name="Bob" salary="70000" title=" Sr Engineer" dept="RD"
     DOB="1945-04-09" tstart="1995-10-01" tend="1996-01-31"/>
 <employee name="Bob" salary="70000" title="Tech Leader" dept="RD"
     DOB="1945-04-09" tstart="1996-02-01" tend="1996-12-31"/>
</employees>
```

Fig. 7. History of `employee` published as `employees2.xml` by mapping the table columns into attributes

4   Efficient Implementation

In the previous sections, we have shown how it is possible to preserve the history of XML-published data as XML documents, and to express complex queries on such documents using XQuery. However, the design of an efficient archival and querying system for such documents present many difficult challenges, due to the need to satisfy multiple competing performance requirements. In fact the design must achieve good performance on

- storage utilization,
- maintaining the archive (i.e. storing the latest changes),
- querying the archive (e.g., to reconstruct past snapshots of a database table, or the salary history of an employee).

For instance, the approach based on the SCSS [28] and recently used in [6] incurs in excessive costs when retrieving a snapshot of a database table—as needed to, e.g., support a query such as 'find the count of employees in each department on 1999-01-01'. In fact, in the SCCS storage scheme, the successive elements of the snapshot table tend to be scattered uniformly throughout the document history. Thus retrieval of a snapshot normally requires reading the whole document history. When the number of pages in the snapshot grows larger than the number of elements in the document, a temporal index can be used to identify which pages contain elements for a given snapshot. Even so, the number of page reads can be equal to the number of document elements, whereas page reads can be significantly reduced using temporal clustering schemes such as those proposed in [13,14].

In the archival scheme used in RCS [32], the changes to the document are appended at the end of the current history. Thus the cost of maintaining the archive is minimal with this scheme; the reconstruction of a snapshot, however, can require the traversal of the whole document history. This situation can be greatly improved (at the cost of some additional storage) with the usefulness based clustering approach discussed in [11,14], which is briefly discussed next.

Usefulness-Based Clustering. The usefulness-based clustering scheme (UBCC) [11,14] clusters the objects of a version into a new page if the percentage of valid objects in a page(i.e., its usefulness) falls below a threshold. When a page's usefulness falls below a minimum, all the valid records in that page are copied to a new page. Since the records for a given version are clustered, reconstructing the document at a version only requires to retrieve the pages that were useful at that version [15]. The usefulness-based clustering techniques can also play an important role in managing XML-published database histories.

Document Shredding. This technique is often used to manage efficiently XML documents stored in relational databases. Basically, the original XML document is decomposed into pieces that because of their more regular and simpler structure can be efficiently supported with current database engines. Each document piece is identified by an unique ID that then facilitates the reconstruction of the original document through various joins and outer-joins queries [31,14]. A natural way to shred XML published documents, is to decompose them along the attribute of the original relation—thus, e.g. the history of the employee relation might be shredded into a salary table, a position table, and a department table. No special new ID is here needed, since the relation key or the tuple ID can be used in this role.

Support for Complex Queries. Efficient indexing schemes [15] and query processing algorithms [14] can be used to support complex queries on multiversion documents. For instance, multiversion B-Trees (MVBT) [5] indexing is used to support complex queries. The MVBT is a directed graph with multiple roots, and each root is associated with a consecutive version interval.

Finally, while complex operators such as coalesce can be expressed directly in XQuery, much faster execution can be achieved by their direct implementation as built-in primitives.

5   Conclusions

In this paper, we have shown that XML-based representations and query languages provide effective ways for representing and querying the database history. In particular, we have concentrated on a situation where relational data is published using XML: we have shown that the history of the database can be represented as an XML document and queried using XQuery. The resulting XML representation is quite natural, and similar to the temporally grouped data models that were proposed in the past as the most natural approach to dealing with historical data [16]—but one that is difficult to realize in the context of the flat relational data model. In this paper, we studied alternative XML representations and identify those that best support temporal queries. We have shown that XQuery without any modification can express complex temporal queries on such representations. We have briefly discussed the physical representations and indices that are needed to ensure a more efficient execution of these queries.

The historical representations and queries discussed here find applications in data warehouses that archive and collect data from sites of interest to assure the e-permanence [1] of critical information and support complex queries on changes [25]. Efficient support for archiving warehouse data is already supported in some commercial systems, and various techniques have been proposed for supporting complex queries on such historical data warehouses [34,27]. Many of the problems that considered in this paper are similar to those that occur in the context of transaction-time web servers and XPath extensions along the transaction time axis [18,19]. An integration of the web-server and web-warehouse functions on the historical axis is possible and desirable and represents an interesting topic for future investigations.

In this paper, we have focused on how to preserve through XML the change history of the database. But similar representations and queries could, respectively, be used to capture valid-time information in XML documents, and to support temporal queries on such documents. This is a very interesting problem [22] that can be expected to become the focus of much future research. Various techniques developed in the valid-time context [20] can also be effective for dealing with the temporal indeterminacy problems that occurs in warehouses that periodically crawl remote web sites.

References

1. National Archives of Australias policy statement Archiving Web Resources: A Policy for Keeping Records of Web-based Activity in the Commonwealth Government. http://www.naa.gov.au/recordkeeping.
2. Software AG's XQuery prototype Quip. http://www.softwareag.com/tamino.
3. WebDAV, WWW Distributed Authoring and Versioning. http://www.ietf.org/html.charters/webdav-charter.html.
4. XQuery 1.0: An XML Query Language. http://www.w3.org/TR/xquery/.
5. Becker, B., Gschwind, S., Ohler, T., Seeger, B., Widmayer, P.: On Optimal Multiversion Access Structures. Proc. of Symposium on Large Spatial Databases, Vol 692 (1993) 123–141.
6. Buneman, P., Khanna, S., Ajima, K., Tan, W.: Archiving Scientific Data. Proc. ACM SIGMOD (2002).
7. Burke, P.J., et. al.: Professional Microsoft SQL Server 2000 XML. Wrox Press (2001).
8. Carey, M., Kiernan, J., Shanmugasundaram, J., et al.: XPERANTO: A Middleware for Publishing Object-Relational Data as XML Documents. VLDB (2000).
9. Chawathe, S., Rajaraman, A., Garcia-Molina, H., Widom, J.: Change Detection in Hierarchically Structured Information. Proc. ACM SIGMOD (1996).
10. Chen, C.X., Zaniolo, C.: Universal Temporal Extensions for Database Languages. ICDE (1999) 428-437.
11. Chien, S.Y., Tsotras, V.J., and Zaniolo, C.: Version Management of XML Documents. WebDB 2000 Workshop, Dallas, TX (2000) 75-80.
12. Chien, S.Y., Tsotras, V.J., and Zaniolo,C.: Copy-Based versus Edit-Base Version Management Schemes for Structured Documents. 11th RIDE Workshop (2001)
13. Chien, S.Y., Tsotras, V.J., and Zaniolo,C.: Efficient Management of Multiversion Documents by Object Referencing. Proc. VLDB (2001).
14. Chien, S.Y., Tsotras, V.J., Zaniolo, C., and Zhang, D.: Efficient Complex Query Support for Multiversion XML Documents. EDBT (2002).

15. Chien, S.Y., Tsotras, V.J., Zaniolo, C., and Zhang, D.: Storing and Querying Multiversion XML Documents using Durable Node Numbers. WISE (2001).
16. Clifford, J., Croker, A., Grandi, F., and Tuzhilin, A.: On Temporal Grouping. Proc. of the Intl. Workshop on Temporal Databases (1995).
17. Cobena, G., Abiteboul, S., Marian, A.: Detecting Changes in XML Documents. Proc. ICDE (2002).
18. Dyreson, C.: Towards a Temporal World-Wide Web: A Transaction Time Web Server Proc. of the Australian Database Conf. (2001).
19. Dyreson, C.: Observing Transaction-time Semantics with TTXPath. WISE (2001).
20. Dyreson, C.E., Snodgrass, R.T.: Supporting Valid-Time Indeterminacy. TODS 23(1) (1998) 1–57
21. Eisenberg, A., Melton, J.: SQL/XML and the SQLX Informal Group of Companies. http://www.sqlx.org.
22. Grandi, F., Mandreoli, F.: The Valid Web: an XML/XSL Infrastructure for Temporal Management of Web Documents. Proc. of ADVIS (2000).
23. Kahle, B., Alexa et al.:The Internet Archive–The Wayback Machine–Surf the Web as it was. http://www.archive.org/index.html.
24. Katz, R.H., Chang, E.: Managing Change in Computer-Aided Design Databases. Proc. of VLDB (1987).
25. Marian, A., et al.: Change-centric management of versions in an XML warehouse. Proc. of VLDB (2001).
26. Ozsoyoglu, G., and Snodgrass, R.T.: Temporal and Real-Time Databases: A Survey. IEEE Trans. on Knowledge and Data Engineering, 7(4) (1995) 513–532.
27. Papadias, D., Tao, Y., Kalnis, P., Zhang, J.: Indexing Spatio-Temporal Data Warehouses. ICDE (2002).
28. Rochkind, M.J.: The Source Code Control System. IEEE Trans. on Software Engineering, SE-1, 4 (1975) 364–370.
29. Shanmugasundaram, J., et al.: Efficiently Publishing Relational Data as XML Documents. Proc. of VLDB (2000) 65–76.
30. Tatarinov, I., Ives, Z.G., Halevy, A.Y., Weld, D.S.: Updating XML. Proc. of SIGMOD (2001).
31. Tian, F., DeWitt, D. J., Chen, J., and Zhang, C.: The Design and Performance Evaluation of Various XML Storage Strategies. http://www.cs.wisc.edu/niagara/Publications.html.
32. Tichy, W.F: RCS–A System for Version Control. Software–Practice&Experience 15, 7 (1985) 637–654.
33. Wang, Y., DeWitt, D.J., and Cai, J.: X-Diff: A Fast Change Detection Algorithm for XML Documents. ICDE (2003).
34. Yang, J.: Temporal Data Warehousing. Ph.D. Dissertation, Stanford University (2001)
35. Zaniolo, C., Ceri, S., Faloutsos, C., Snodgrass, R.T., Subrahmanian, V.S., and Zicari, R.: Advanced Database Systems. Morgan Kaufmann Publishers, (1997) 97–160.
36. The TSQL2 Language Design Committee: TSQL2 Language Specification, ACM SIGMOD Record, 23(1), (1994) 65–86.

A Lightweight XML Constraint Check and Update Framework

Hong Su, Bintou Kane, Victor Chen, Cuong Diep, De Ming Guan, Jennifer Look, and Elke A. Rundensteiner

Department of Computer Science
Worcester Polytechnic Institute
100 Institute Road, Worcester, MA 01609-2280
{suhong,bkane,vchen,cdiep,deguan,jlook,rundenst}@cs.wpi.edu

Abstract. Support for updating XML documents has recently attracted interest. When an XML document is to conform to a given schema, the problem of *structural consistency* arises during updating, i.e., how to incrementally guarantee that the modified XML document continues to conform to the given XML Schema. To achieve this following the traditional database approach, the XML Schema would first have to be analyzed to construct a structured repository and the XML documents would have to be loaded into this repository before any update could be checked for possible schema constraint violation. Due to the very nature of XML being lightweight and freely shared over the Web, we instead propose a novel approach towards incremental constraint checking that follows the loosely-coupled web paradigm. Namely, we propose to rewrite an XML update query into a safe XML update query by extending the original query with appropriate constraint checking subqueries. This enhanced XML update query can then safely be executed using any existing XQuery engine that supports updates. In order to verify the feasibility of our approach, we have implemented a prototype, *SAXE*, that implements the above techniques by extending the Kweelt XML query engine by University of Pennsylvania with both XML update support as well as incremental constraint support.

Keywords: XML Update, XQuery, XML Schema, Structural Consistency.

1 Introduction

1.1 Motivation

Change is a fundamental aspect of persistent information and data-centric systems. Information over a period of time often needs to be modified to reflect perhaps a change in the real world, a change in the user's requirements, mistakes in the initial design or to allow for incremental maintenance.

However, change support for XML in current XML data management systems is only in its infancy. First of all, practically all change support is tightly tied to the underlying storage system of the XML data. For example, both in IBM DB2 XML Extender [IBM00b] and Oracle 9i XSU [Ora02] who support

A. Olivé et al. (Eds.): ER 2002 Ws, LNCS 2784, pp. 39–50, 2003.
© Springer-Verlag Berlin Heidelberg 2003

decomposition of XML data into relational storage or object-relational storage respectively, the user would then need to work with the relational data representing the original XML document as with any other relational data. In particular, any update on the XML data has to be specified using SQL and then will be executed on the underlying relational data. This requires users to be aware of not only the underlying storage system but also the particular mapping chosen between the XML model and the storage model. In other words, there is a lack of abstraction for specifying native updates to XML data independent of the different underlying storage models.

As the first step for native XML update support, a native language for updating XML must be proposed. In this paper, since no World Wide Web Consortium proposal on XML updating has emerged to date, we utilize an extension of XQuery [W3C01b] to support powerful XML updates [TIHW01]. We will further discuss choice of XML update language in Section 2.

An indispensable next step towards supporting updates is to provide a mechanism for maintaining the *structural consistency* of the XML documents with all associated XML schemata (if any) during the course of the update. Structural consistency is a desired property in database systems since they require that the data must always conform to its schema. An update is considered to be *safe* only if it will not result in any data violating the associated schema. For example, in a relational database, if an attribute is defined as NOT NULL in the schema, an insertion of a tuple with a NULL value for this attribute will be regarded as an unsafe operation and thus would be refused by the system. Though it is not required that XML documents must always have associated schemata due to their "self-describing" nature, many application domains tend to use some schema specification in either DTD [W3C98] or XML Schema [W3C01a] format to enforce the structure of the XML documents. Whenever XML schemata are associated with the XML data, then structural consistency should also be taken care of during update processing. No work has been done to date to address this issue for native XML.

1.2   Illustrating Example

For example, Figures 1 and 2 show an XML schema *juicers.xsd* and an XML document *juicers.xml* conforming to the schema respectively. Suppose the user specifies to remove the cost of the juicer with name "Champion Juicer" (the first juicer in *juicers.xml*). This operation will render the Champion juicer to no longer have a *cost* subelement. Such an updated XML document is inconsistent with the schema *juicers.xsd* since a *juicer* element is required to have at least one *cost* subelement, indicated as <xsd: element ref = *cost* minOccurs = 1 maxOccurs = unbounded/> in *juicer.xsd*. This update would however have been allowed for the second juicer (i.e., Omega Juicer). Some mechanisms must be developed to prevent such violation of structural consistency.

```
<xsd: schema xmlns: xsd =                                    >        <juicers>
  <xsd: element name = "juciers">                                       <juicer>
   <xsd: complexType>                                                     <name> Champion Juicer </name>
    <xsd: sequence>                                                       <image> images\champion.gif </image>
     <xsd: element ref = "juicer" minOccurs = "0" maxOccus = "unbounded"/>  <cost> 239.00 </cost>
    </xsd: sequence>                                                     </juicer>
   </xsd: element>                                                       <juicer>
   <xsd: element name = "juicer">                                         <name> Omega Juicer </name>
    <xsd: complexType>                                                    <image> images\omega.jpg </image>
     <xsd: sequence>                                                      <cost> 234.00 </cost>
      <xsd: element ref = "name"/>                                        <cost> 359.50 </cost>
      <xsd: element ref = "image" minOccurs = "unbounded">              </juicer>
      <xsd: element ref = "cost" minOccurs = "0" maxOccurs = "unbounded" />  </juicers>
     </xsd: sequence>
     <xsd: attribute ref = "quality" use = "optional"/>
    </xsd: complexType>
   </xsd: element>
   <xsd: element name = "name" type = "xsd: string"/>
   <xsd: element name = "cost" type  = "xsd: string"/>
   <xsd: element name = "image" type = "xsd: string"/>
   <xsd: attribute name = "quality" type = "xsd:string"/>
 </xsd: schema>
```

Fig. 1. Sample XML Schema: *juicers.xsd*   **Fig. 2.** Sample XML Document: *juicers.xml*

1.3   Desiderata of Preserving Structural Consistency

In our current work, we assume the schema is the first-class citizen. In this sense, an update to an XML document is only allowed when the update is *safe*, i.e., the updated data would still conform to the given XML schemata. In this section, we discuss the desiderata of the mechanism for checking the safety of XML data updates.

Native XML Support. There have been some techniques proposed for translating constraints in XML to constraints in other data models, say the relational model [KKRSR00] or the object model [BGH00]. Once the mapping is set up, XML constraint checking would be achieved by the constraint enforcement mechanism supported in the other underlying models. However we prefer a native XML support for several reasons. Primarily, we want to avoid the overhead of a load into a database management system (DBMS) as well as the dependency of XML updates on some specific alternate representation.

Loosely-Coupled Constraint Checking Support. Following the traditional database approach shown in Figure 3, the XML Schema would first be analyzed to construct a fixed structure and XML documents could then be loaded into a repository in order to allow updates on the document to be checked. It is preferable to have the validity checking a lightweight standing-alone module rather than being tightly coupled to an XML DBMS. Ideally the constraint checking tool should be a middleware service so that it is general and portable over all XML data management systems.

Incremental Constraint Checking. A naive approach to ensuring the safety of data updates is to do a validation from scratch (shown in Figure 4), namely, to first execute the updates, then run a validating parser[1] on the updated XML document, and lastly decide whether to roll back to the original XML document based on the validation result. Such an approach is inefficient since it involves redundant checking on those unchanged XML fragments. It is preferable to have an incremental checking mechanism where only the modified XML fragments rather than the complete XML document are checked. Moreover when the validating parser is run on an XML document modified by a batch of updates and any inconsistency is detected, the parser is unable to tell which updates have caused the inconsistency. Hence, this would make a roll back of only the unsafe updates (but not the changes made by safe updates) impossible.

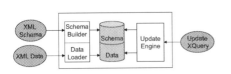

Fig. 3. Tightly-Coupled Approach

Fig. 4. From Scratch Validation Approach

1.4   Our Approach and Contributions

In this paper we introduce a native, incremental and lightweight framework for checking the validity of data updates specified in an XQuery update language *Update-XQuery* [TIHW01]. The key concept we exploit is the capacity of the XQuery query language to not only query XML data but also XML Schema. This allows us to rewrite Update-XQuery statements by extending them with appropriate XML constraint checking sub-queries.

In summary, we make the following contributions in this work:

1. We identify the issue of preserving structural consistency during the update of XML documents in a loosely-coupled native XML context.
2. We propose a general constraint checking framework that provides native, incremental and lightweight XML constraint checking support.
3. We describe the prototype system *SAXE* we have implemented. We verified the feasibility of this proposed approach by comparing its performance against that of current state-of-the-art solutions.

2   Related Work

Several XML update languages have been proposed [IBM00b] [Obj99] [SKC+00] [TIHW01]. The expressive power of the language concerns two capabilities: i.e.,

---

[1] Most XML document parsers [IBM00a] support validating the XML document against the given DTD or XML Schema.

the power to specify (1) what nodes to update (i.e., querying over the data to select target nodes) and (2) what actions to take on the selected nodes.

[IBM00b] provide their own language for native XML update support in DB2 XML Extender. The expressive power of the update language is limited. XML Extender allows to specify target nodes in the XML document using XPath expressions [W3C99]. XPath is a subset of XQuery, e.g., in particular, XPath does not support variable bindings. Moreover Extender only allows in-place content update on the selected nodes without other basic support such as inserting new nodes or removing existing nodes. Excelon [Obj99] offers an update language. The disadvantage of this language is that it uses its own proprietary query specification which detracts from its compatibility with the standard XML query language. An XML working group XML:DB [XML02] proposes XUpdate [XUp02] which also has the expressive power limitation in that it uses XPath as the query specification. [TIHW01] stands out among the XML update languages in terms of its expressive power and compatibility with XQuery. It is a natural extension of XQuery that supports the application of a set of update operations including insertion of new data, removal or in-place modification of existing data on bound variables.

None of the above work deals with the problem of incremental validation after the updates. To the best of our knowledge, our earlier work on XEM [SKC⁺00] is one of the first efforts addressing this problem. XEM proposes a set of update primitives each of which is associated with semantics ensuring the safety of the operation. In XEM, a data update primitive on the other hand is only executed when it passes the validity check. The main limitations of XEM are: (1) the data update primitives in XEM can be only performed on one single element selected by an XPath expressions; (2) XEM is a tightly-couple approach, namely, we implemented an engine on top of PSE (a lightweight object database), mapped the DTD to a fixed schema and loaded the data into object instances. Such a paradigm requires schema evolution support from PSE and specialized constraint enforcement has to be hardcoded into the PSE system.

3   XML Query and Update Language

3.1   XML Query Language: XQuery

XQuery [W3C01b] is an XML query language proposed by W3C. An XQuery statement is composed of several expressions. An important expression in XQuery is the FLWR expression constructed from FOR, LET, WHERE and RETURN clauses.

1. FOR and LET clauses bind values or expressions to one or more variables.
2. WHERE clause (optional) filters the bindings generated by FOR and LET clauses by any specified predicates.
3. RETURN clause constructs an output XML document.

We give an example XQuery over the XML document in Figure 2:

```
For $p in document(''juicers.xml'')/juicer, $c in $p/cost[1]
Return $c.
```

The variable $p is bound to iterate over each element node satisfying the expression document(''juicers.xml'')/juicer. For each identified binding of $p, $c is bound to the first *cost* child node of $p and returned.

3.2   XML Update Language: Update-XQuery

[TIHW01] proposes a set of update operations and embeds them into the XQuery language syntax. Each update operation is performed on a target object indicated as *target*. Table 1 gives the set of update operations and their semantics.

Table 1. Taxonomy of Update Operations

Update Operation	Description
Delete *child*	Remove *child* from children list of *target*
Rename *child* To n	Rename *child* to name n
Insert new_attr(n, v)	Insert new attribute with name n and value v to *target*
Insert c Before/After *child*	Insert XML fragment with content of c directly before/after *child*
Replace *child* With new_attr(n, v)	Replace *child* with attribute with name n and value v
Replace *child* With c	Replace *child* with XML fragment with content c

[TIHW01] extends XQuery's original FLWR expressions to accommodate the update operations by introducing FOR... LET... WHERE... UPDATE..., i.e., FLWU expressions. We will refer to this extension of XQuery now as *Update-XQuery*. The BNF of FLWU expression syntax is shown in Figure 3.2 while the BNF for the UPDATE clause (subOp in Figure 3.2) in particular is shown in Figure 6.

```
FOR $binding_1 IN XPath-expr, ...
LET $binding := XPath-expr, ...
WHERE predicate1, ...
UPDATE $binding {subOp{, subOp}*}
```

```
DELETE $child |
RENAME $child TO name |
INSERT (new_attr(name, value) |
        content [BEFORE | AFTER $child] |
        $copyTarget [BEFORE | AFTER $child]) |
REPLACE $child WITH (new_attr(name, value) |
                     content |
                     $copyTarget) |
FOR $binding IN XPath-expr, ...
WHERE predicate1, ...
UPDATE $binding {subOp {, subOp}*}
```

Fig. 5. Syntax of Update-XQuery

Fig. 6. BNF of subOp

The semantics of FOR, LET and WHERE clauses are exactly the same as that in a FLWR expression as briefly described in Section 3.1. The UPDATE clause specifies the target node to be updated and a sequence of update operations or FLWU expressions to be applied on the target node.

Figure 2 shows a sample Update-XQuery on the XML document in Figure 2. The variable $p is bound to iterate over each element node satisfying the expression document(''juicers.xml'')/juicer (line 1). For each identified binding of $p, $c is bound to the first *cost* child nodes of $p (line 2) and $p is updated by deleting its child node, i.e., the binding of $c (line 4).

4   XML Framework For Safe Updates

Our Overall Approach. In order to allow only consistent updates to be processed on XML documents, we aim to develop a loosely-coupled update strategy that supports incremental schema constraint checking that accesses only updated parts of the XML document. The key idea is to first generate a safe Update-XQuery statement from a given input Update-XQuery statement. This generated safe Update-XQuery statement, still conforming to the standard Update-XQuery BNF, can then be safely executed on any XQuery update engine. This way we succeed in separating the concern of constraint check verification from that of developing the XML query and update engine.

For this safe query generation, we design appropriate *constraint checking subqueries*. The constraint checking subqueries take input parameters from the update operation and determine whether the update operation is valid or not. For this, we exploit the capacity of the XQuery query language to not only be able to query XML data but also XML Schema. This allows us to rewrite Update-XQuery statements by extending them with appropriate XML constraint check sub-queries for each update operation as in Table 1. The execution of an update operation is conditional on passing the constraint checking.

Illustrating Example. For example, Figure 2 shows the rewritten Update-XQuery from the Update-XQuery in Figure 2. There is one update operation in the query, i.e., DELETE $c in line 4. We can see that lines 3, 5 and 6[2] in Figure 2 have been inserted into this update operation so that this update is only executed when delElePassed(...) (line 5) returns true. delElePassed(...) is a constraint check function which determines the validity of the update DELETE $c. The subquery schemaChkDelEle(...) in line 3 is a function that provides information that is needed by delElePassed(...) to make the determination. We will further discuss the details of these two functions in Section 5.3.

```
1 FOR $p in document("juicers.xml")/juicer,
2      $c in $p/cost[1]
3 UPDATE $p {
4      DELETE $c
5 }
```

```
1 FOR $p in document("juicers.xml")/juicer,
2      $c in $p/cost[1]
3 LET $constraint =
   schemaChkDelEle("juicers.xsd","juicer","cost")
4 UPDATE $p {
5 WHERE delElePassed($c,$p/cost,$constraint)
6      UPDATE $p {
7           DELETE $c
8      }
9 }
```

Fig. 7. Sample Update-XQuery   **Fig. 8.** Sample Safe Update-XQuery

SAXE Architecture. Figure 9 shows the architecture of $SAXE^3$, the framework for generating a safe Update-XQuery statement given an input Update-

---

[2] Line 6 is added only to meet the syntax requirement.

[3] SAfe Xml Evolution.

XQuery. The *safe Update-XQuery generator SAXE* is composed of the five components described below:

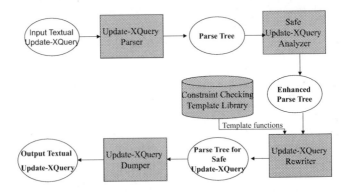

Fig. 9. An Incremental Yet Loosely-Coupled Update Processing Framework Supporting XML Updates with Schema Constraint Validation

1. *Update-XQuery Parser.* The parser takes an Update-XQuery statement and constructs a parse tree representation [ASU86] from it.
2. *Update-XQuery Analyzer.* Given a parse tree, the analyzer identifies more detailed information about types of update operations in the parse tree and derives an enhanced parse tree (refer to Section 5.2).
3. *Constraint Checking Template Library.* We generalize the constraint checking procedures by defining named parameterized XQuery functions called *constraint checking templates.* Each constraint checking template is in charge of checking constraints for one update type.
4. *Update-XQuery Rewriter.* The rewriter handles the actual generation of a safe Update-XQuery. It determines how to rewrite the original Update-XQuery statement by plugging in the appropriate constraint checking functions from the template library and correspondingly modifying the enhanced parse tree.
5. *Update-XQuery Dumper.* The dumper constructs a textual format of the modified Update-XQuery statement from the enhanced parse tree, which now is in the standard Update-XQuery syntax.

5 Components of Constraint Checking Framework

We now describe the main components of the framework shown in Figure 9.

5.1 Update-XQuery Parser

Given an Update-XQuery statement, the Update-XQuery parser constructs a parse tree which is composed of objects of classes that were designed to store the parsed query. For example, a class *Update* is defined to store update clauses. Subclasses of class *Update* are defined for four types of update operations, i.e., *Delete, Rename, Insert* and *Replace*, respectively.

5.2 Safe Update-XQuery Analyzer

Given an internal representation of an Update-XQuery, the analyzer will determine a more specific sub-type of an update operation. For example, the analyzer
would examine the content of an object of class *Delete* to classify the update as
either deleting an element or deleting an attribute. The detailed information of
update types would then be embedded into the original parse tree. We call the
new parse tree an *enhanced parse tree.*

5.3 Constraint Checking Template Library

The library stores templates that account for every type of update possible
using our Update-XQuery language (See BNF in Figure 3.2). A constraint check
is composed of three steps which are:

1. Query the XML schema to identify any constraints that may be violated by
   the specified update.
2. Query the XML document to gather information pertaining to the target
   elements or attributes.
3. Compare the information retrieved from the two previous steps and thus
   identify whether the constraints would be violated by the update.

We illustrate how this constraint check is done for a delete-element operation.
The constraint checking functions `schemaChkDelEle` and `delElePassed` shown
in Figures 5.3 and 5.3 jointly achieve the three steps mentioned above.

```
Function integer schemaChkDelEle($xsdName, $parentEleName, $childEleName) Return Integer
1 {
2  For $pDef In document($xsdName)/xsd:element[@name = $parentEleName],
3      $cRef In $pDef//xsd:element[@ref = $childEleName]
4  Let $cRefMinOccurs:= $cRef/minOccurs
5  Return $childRefMinOccurs }
```

Fig. 10. Constraint Checking Function *schemaChkDelEle*

```
Function delElePassed($childBinding, $childBindingPath, $childMinOccurs) Return Boolean
1 {
2    LET $childInstCount := count($childBindingPath)
3    Return
4    If ($childMinOccurs <= $childInstCount - 1
5      Then TRUE
6      Else FALSE
7 }
```

Fig. 11. Constraint Checking Function*delElePassed*

The Constraint Checking Function. `schemaChkDelEle` queries over the schema (i.e., step 1) for the information related to the constraints that may be violated when deleting an element. Deleting an element e of element type t can only violate the constraint of a required minimum occurrence of the elements of type t in the content model of e's parent. `schemaChkDelEle` is to retrieve the minimum occurrence of elements of type $childEleName$ in the parent type $parentEleName$. In particular, line 2 queries the XML schema file, specified by the file name $xsdName$, to find the element definition $pDef$ for type $parentEleName$. The element definition of *parentEleName*'s subelement referring to type *childEleName* is stored in $childRef$ in line 3. Line 4 then retrieves the minimum occurrence of element type *childEleName* in *parentEleName*.

Constraint Checking Function. `delElePassed` checks whether the data update is safe based on the schema constraint information collected by `schemaChkDelEle`. `delElePassed` is composed of two parts:

1. **Query over Data** (i.e., step 2). Line 2 begins querying over the XML document to find the actual count of instances of type *childEleName* that are subelements of the target object. These instances can be retrieved by the XPath expression $childBinding$. Function *count* on the retrieved instances returns the count of these instances. Thus there would be only *childInstCount* - 1 instances of type *childEleName* if the update is allowed to occur.

2. **Integration of Query Result over Schema and Data** (i.e., step 3). Line 4 compares the information from the XML schema and data. It compares the minimum occurrence requirement (i.e., *childRefMin*) and the actual occurrence if the update were indeed to proceed. In this example, this would be *childInstCount* - 1. If actual occurrence after the update had occurred were larger than the minimum occurrence requirement, this check is passed and the update operation is regarded as valid.

5.4   Safe Update-XQuery Rewriter

The Safe XQuery Rewriter traverses the enhanced parse tree. For each update operation, based on the update type, the Rewriter determines which template function should be used for checking the constraints of the update. Since the template is parameterized, the Rewriter also instantiates the parameters. Values for these parameters can be identified through the analysis of different parts of the parsed XQuery.

This can be seen in Figure 2. The `delElePassed` template function takes in three parameters to execute its query. For this particular example, *"juicer.xsd"* (the file name of the XML Schema), *"juicer"* (the type name of the parent element of the to-be-deleted element) and *"cost"* (the type name of the to-be-deleted element) are the three instantiated parameters respectively.

Once all parameters have been assigned values, the Rewriter needs to insert the instantiated template function into the original query. The Rewriter modifies the parse tree by inserting the constraint checking function for example via a where clause after the associated update clause (line 5 in Figure 2). After all modifications have been done to the original update XQuery, the safe Update-XQuery generation is complete. Finally, a resulting safe Update-XQuery statement is produced by the query rewriter module.

6   The *SAXE* System

We have designed and implemented the above proposed query rewriting techniques as a prototype system, called *SAXE*. Our system is based on Kweelt [SD02], a query engine for the Quilt XML query language [CRF02], a precursor of the XQuery standard, developed by the University of Pennsylvania. Kweelt is composed of two parts, i.e., the language parser and language evaluator. The parser takes a Quilt statement and constructs a parse tree. The evaluator then executes the query against the data. First, we extended the Java Compiler Compiler file (JavaCC) which is a Java parser generator in Kweelt so that the Update clauses are accepted by the language parser. Second, we have extended the evaluator so that an Update-XQuery statement can be executed.

We compare *SAXE* against the from-scratch validation solution, which means we first perform the given update using the extended Kweelt update engine and then we run the modified XML document through an XML-Schema Validator [Tom02] to check for conformance with the given XML schemata. We added the time for regular XQuery execution to the time needed to run the update document through the validator. Generating a typical safe Update-XQuery takes about 400 - 500 milliseconds. For some cases, the safe Update-XQuery execution takes slightly longer than the from-scratch validation solution. However, this does not mean that a safe Update-XQuery is less efficient than using validators after updates are executed. The argument is that the safe Update-XQuery is a one step process where updates are only performed once the updates are deemed safe so that all the attempts for invalid updates will be prevented. On the other hand for the execution of non-safe Update-XQuery, as mentioned in Section 1.3, the system may need to iterate several times between attempting updates and then verifying if the updates leave the XML document in a consistent state.

7   Conclusion

In this paper, we propose a lightweight approach to ensure the structural consistency of XML documents after updates. More precisely, we propose that an Update-XQuery statement can be rewritten into a safe Update-XQuery statement by embedding constraint checking operations into the query. This approach is lightweight in the sense that it can be implemented as a middleware independent of any underlying system for XML data management. To ensure the structural consistency, any Update-XQuery statement is first fed to our safe Update-XQuery generator, *SAXE*, while the returned safe Update-XQuery statement can then be executed by any system supporting Update-XQuery.

Currently, our safety checking semantics is at the atomic level, i.e., each atomic update on a single object is allowed if this update leads to a valid XML document. As a next step, we want to explore the concept of transactional update, i.e., a batch of updates are only allowed to be executed if the overall effect of executing them leads to a valid document.

References

ASU86.   V. Aho, R. Sethi, and J.D. Ullman. *Compilers: Principles, Techniques and Tools* . Addison-Wesley, 1986.

BGH00.   L. Bird, A. Goodchild, and T. A. Halpin. Object role modelling and xml-schema. In *International Conference on Conceptual Modeling / the Entity Relationship Approach*, pages 309–322, 2000.

CRF02.   Don Chamberlin, Jonathan Robie, and Daniela Florescu. Quilt, 2002.

IBM00a.   IBM. XML Parser for Java, 2000. http://www.alphaworks.ibm.com/tech/xml4j.

IBM00b.   IBM Software: Database and Data Management. DB2 XML Extender. http://www-4.ibm.com, 2000.

KKRSR00. G. Kappel, E. Kapsammer, S. Rausch-Schott, and W. Retschitzegger. X-ray - Towards integrating XML and relational database systems. In *International Conference on Conceptual Modeling / the Entity Relationship Approach*, pages 339–353, 2000.

Obj99.   Object Design. Excelon Data Integration Server. http://www.odi.com/excelon, 1999.

Ora02.   Oracle. Oracle9i application developer's guilde - xml release 1 (9.0.1): Database support for xml. http://download-east.oracle.com/otndoc/oracle9i/901_doc/appdev.901/a88894/adx05xml.htm, 2002.

SD02.   A. Sahuguet and L. Dupont. Querying xml in the new millennium, 2002.

SKC+00.   H. Su, D. Kramer, K. Claypool, L. Chen, and E.A. Rundensteiner. XEM: Managing the Evolution of XML Documents. In *International Workshop on Research Issues in Data Engineering*, pages 103 – 110, 2000.

TIHW01.   I. Tatarinov, Z. Ives, A.Y. Halevy, and D.S. Weld. Updating XML. In *SIGMOD*, pages 413 – 424, 2001.

Tom02.   Henry Tompson. xsv: schema validator, 2002.

W3C98.   W3C. *Guide to the W3C XML Specification ("XMLspec") DTD, Version 2.1.* http://www.w3.org/XML/1998/06/xmlspec-report-v21.htm, 1998.

W3C99.   W3C. XML Path Language (XPath) Version 1.0. http://www.w3.org/TR/xpath, 1999.

W3C01a.   W3C. *XML Schema* . http://www.w3.org/XML/Schema, 2001.

W3C01b.   W3C. *XQuery 1.0: An XML Query Language.* http://www.w3.org/TR/xquery/, 2001.

XML02.   XML:DB. http://www.xmldb.org/, 2002.

XUp02.   XUpdate. XML:DB. http://www.xmldb.org/xupdate/xupdate-wd.html, 2002.

Change Discovery in Ontology-Based Knowledge Management Systems

Ljiljana Stojanovic[1], Nenad Stojanovic[2], and Alexander Maedche[1]

[1]FZI - Research Center for Information Technology at the University of Karlsruhe
Haid-und-Neu-Str. 10-14, 76131 Karlsruhe, Germany
{Ljiljana.Stojanovic,maedche}@fzi.de

[2]Institute AIFB, University of Karlsruhe
76128 Karlsruhe, Germany
nst@aifb.uni-karlsruhe.de

Abstract: In this paper, we present a novel approach for the change discovery in ontology-based knowledge management systems. It extends our previous work in the ontology evolution by taking into account the usage of an ontology in the knowledge management system. The approach is mainly based on the analysis of the user's interaction with the system in providing annotations for knowledge resources, as well as in the process of accessing the knowledge by querying the knowledge repository. We defined several assessment criteria to estimate the quality of annotations and the user's needs from the point of view of the knowledge management. These criteria result in the recommendations for the continual system improvement. Two evaluation studies illustrate the benefits of our approach.

1   Introduction

Knowledge management systems in general are not developed to remain stable, but are subjects to continual change, which is caused by several factors:
- The environment in which KM systems operate can change unpredictably, thereby invalidating the assumptions that were made when the system was built. For example, acquiring a new subsidiary in an enterprise adds new business areas as well as functionalities to the existing system.
- Users' requirements often change after the system is already built, warranting system's adaptation. For example, hiring new employees may lead to new competencies and greater diversity within the enterprise, which need to be reflected in the system.
- Some changes in the domain are implicit and can be discovered only through the analysis of user's interaction with the system. For example, if many users are interested in two topics in conjunction (e.g. debug and java), and there is no knowledge resource matching this criterion, then an efficient knowledge management system should signal that a knowledge resource about the combination of these topics is needed (e.g. a document on how to perform debugging of java code).

A. Olivé (Eds.): ER 2003 Ws, LNCS 2784, pp. 51-62, 2003.
© Springer-Verlag Berlin Heidelberg 2003

Ad hoc management of the changes in knowledge management systems may work in the short-term, but to avoid unnecessary complexity and failures in the long run, the management has to be interpreted at the conceptual level. In ontology-based knowledge management systems ontologies are used as a conceptual backbone for providing information about knowledge resources and for accessing to the knowledge resources [1]. Therefore, in ontology-based knowledge management systems the changes caused by above-mentioned factors should be applied to the ontology.

The changes can be defined explicitly by the knowledge officer or by the end user. These changes cover business strategy evolution, modification in the application domain, additional functionality, etc. and they are captured in a variety of ways: direct discussion or interviews, customer specifications, surveys, observations. However, some changes may be discovered by analysing log-files tracking user's interaction with the system. The application of these changes enables the continual improvement of the knowledge management systems according to the changes in the users' needs. Although this facility enhances the efficiency of the system, as known to the authors there are no methods and tools that take into account change discovery.

In this paper we present an approach that supports discovery of the changes in ontology-based knowledge management systems. Change discovery is the first phase in the ontology evolution process [2] that enables the timely adaptation of an ontology, as well as the consistent management/propagation of the ontology changes to dependent elements. More details about ontology evolution can be found in [3].

Our primary goal is to suggest the knowledge engineer how to adapt the underlying ontology or annotation in order to enhance the whole system. In that sense we do not only discover the changes, but also estimate their effects on the functionality of the system and choose the most useful one.

The paper is organized as follows: In the second section we discuss the methods to discover changes in ontology-based knowledge management system. Moreover we introduce several assessment criteria to estimate the quality of annotations and the user's needs from the point of view of knowledge management. Section 3 contains two evaluation studies. After a discussion of related work in the section 4, concluding remarks summarize the importance of the presented approach.

2   Change Discovery in Ontology-Based KM Systems

Change discovery can be defined as a process of inducing the changes from existing data. In the ontology-based knowledge management system it should consider (i) the ontology as a domain model that underpins that system, (ii) the annotations[1] that are results of the knowledge providing phase and (iii) the user's activities in the knowledge management system. Consequently, we have identified the following ways of discovering changes [2]:

- *Structure-driven change discovery* identifies the set of heuristics to improve an ontology based on the analysis of the ontology structure. Based on our experience in the ontology development [1], the most frequently used heuristics are:

---

[1] An annotation consists of a set of ontology instances. We use term metadata as a synonym for an ontology instance.

- A concept with a single subconcept should be merged with its subconcept;
- If all subconcepts have the same property, it may be moved to the parent;
- If there are more than a dozen subconcepts for a concept, then an additional layer in the concept hierarchy may be necessary;
- The concept without properties is a candidate for deletion;
- If a direct parent of a concept can be achieved through a non-direct path, then the direct link should be deleted.

- *Data-driven change discovery* detects the changes that are induced through analysis of existing instances. For example, if no instance of a concept C uses any of the properties defined for C, but only properties inherited from the parent concept, we can make an assumption that C is not necessary;
- *Usage-driven change discovery* takes into account the usage of the ontology in the knowledge management system. For example, by tracking when the concept was last retrieved by a query, it may be possible to discover that some concepts are out of date and should be deleted or updated.

2.1   Changes Discovered from the Annotations

The experience from information retrieval research shows that the "quality" of annotations is crucial for the retrieval of relevant knowledge resources. Our primary objective was not only to monitor the quality of annotations over time, but also to suggest how to adapt them or the underlying ontology, in order to enhance the whole system. Indeed, this type of change discovery is based on the analysis of the quality of the annotations. We define the quality of annotations according to two criteria:

- Validity – if metadata in annotation is inconsistent with the domain ontology, then it is not treated in the knowledge sharing;
- Optimality - if metadata in the annotation is redundant, inaccurate or incomplete, then it can seriously damage the users' confidence in the system;

To note that assessment is performed on the annotation level, and the ontology structure is the basis for all measures. From the point of view of the information retrieval, the analysis of the first criterion enables increasing of the recall of the system, whereas the second ensures enhancing of the precision.

2.1.1 Validity

One annotation is valid only if all its metadata are valid. One piece of metadata is valid if it satisfies all constraints implied by ontology itself. We identified several types of inconsistency: the presence of errors in format, the usage of undefined entities, the usage of unexpected values etc.

Independently of the sources of the inconsistency of the annotation and whether annotations are embedded in the knowledge resources or they are in the knowledge repository [4], they have to keep the consistency with the ontology. The role of the change discovery is not only to find all invalid annotations, but also to make recommendation for changes in the annotations, in order to achieve the syntactic and semantics consistency.

From the knowledge management point of view, the validity of annotations is a pre-request for the successful knowledge retrieval in the highly changeable business environment, since only the annotations that conform to the ontology can be taken into consideration in the knowledge searching process. By considering the knowledge repository in which the content of some resources is annotated with invalid annotations, the knowledge searching process can result not only in the low precision – missing some relevant answers, but also in the incorrectness – the delivery of wrong answers.

2.1.2 Optimality

In order to emphasise the real need of the optimal annotation, we use examples from the MEDLINE database, which represents the state-of-the-art in human indexing. However, our experiments with MEDLINE show that there are many possibilities to optimise the annotations, which may trigger discovery of changes.

To estimate the optimality of an annotation, we introduce the following three criteria that are important from the knowledge management point of view:

Compactness – A semantic annotation is incompact or redundant if it contains more metadata than is needed and desired to express the same "idea". In order to achieve compactness (and thus to avoid redundancy), the annotation has to comprise the minimal set[2] of the metadata without exceeding what is necessary or useful. The repetition of the metadata or the usage of several metadata with the same meaning only complicate maintenance and decrease the system performance.

Concept hierarchy and property hierarchy from the domain ontology are used to check this criterion. For example, if the knowledge resource is annotated, after all, with the concept **Person** and its subconcept **Female**, then this annotation is incompact. When someone searches for all knowledge resources about **Person**, she searches for the resources about all its subconcepts (including **Female**) as well. Consequently, she gets this resource (minimum) twice. Moreover, such annotation introduces an ambiguity in the understanding of the content of a knowledge resource, which implies problems in knowledge sharing. Let us examine the meaning of the annotation of a medical document using the set of metadata **Person**, **Female**, **Aspirin**, **Complications**. Does it mean that the document is about complications in using aspirin only in females, or in all persons? When the second answer is the right one, then this document is also relevant for the treatment of male persons with aspirin. This implies new questions: is the annotation using metadata **Female** an error, or the metadata **Male** is missing? Anyway, there is an ambiguity in annotations, which can be detected and resolved by using our approach.

In order to prevent this, a knowledge resource should be annotated using as special metadata as possible (i.e. more specialised sub-concepts). In this way, the mentioned ambiguities are avoided. Moreover, the maintenance of the annotations is also alleviated, because the annotation is more concise and only changes linked to the concept **Female** can provoke changes in the annotation.

Completeness – An annotation is incomplete if it is possible to extend the annotation only by analysing existing metadata in the annotation, in order to clarify its semantic. It means that the annotation is not finished yet, and requires that some additional metadata have to be filled up.

---

[2] An annotation is not minimal if excluding metadata results in the same retrieval for the same query i.e. precision and recall remain the same.

This criterion is computed based on the structure of the domain ontology. For example, one criterion is the existence of a dependency in the domain ontology between the domain entities, which are already used in the annotation. If an annotation contains concepts with many relationships between them (e.g. properties *"cures"* and *"causes"* exist between concepts **Therapy** and **Disease**), then its interpretation is ambiguous, e.g. are the knowledge resources about how a disease (i) can be cured by a therapy, or (ii) caused by a therapy. In order to constrain the set of possible interpretations, the annotation has to be extended with one of these properties.

This problem is especially important when the knowledge repository contains a lot of resources annotated with the same concepts, because the search for knowledge retrieves irrelevant resources that use certain concepts in a different context. Consequently, the precision of the system is decreased.

Aggregation – An annotation is aggregative if it contains a set of metadata that can be replaced with semantically related metadata in order to achieve a shorten annotation, but without producing any retrieval other than the original annotation. For example, this pattern for the annotation refinement occurs when a resource is described with all subconcepts of one concept (e.g. concepts **Female** and **Male** are subconcepts of the concept **Person**). From the searching for knowledge point of view, it is the same whether a resource is annotated using the combination of concepts (e.g. **Female** and **Male**) or using only the parent concept (e.g. **Person**). It is obvious that the second case of annotation makes the management much easier. Moreover, since the standard approaches for the ranking results of querying [5] exploit conceptual hierarchies, for example in a querying for persons a resource annotated using **Female** and **Male** will be placed at the same level as a resource annotated using only one of these concepts. It has to be ranked on the top level (level of concept **Person**), because it covers all subtypes of concept **Person**.

2.2   Changes Discovered from the End-Users' Activities

The task of a knowledge management system is to deliver the right knowledge in the right moment (at the right place). Interpreted on the level of the searching for knowledge, it means that a user has the opportunity to easily find relevant knowledge resources for the topics, which are important for the problem she solves. In other words, the list of retrieved knowledge resources for a user query should not be empty, and should also contain only highly relevant sources.

It implies that the management component of a knowledge management system should track the interests of users, as well as the list of answers for the posted queries. In order to support this task, the user's interactions with the knowledge management system have to be recorded. The prerequisite for the meaningful analysis is that this log information is properly organized and interpreted. In order to use as much as possible of the existing mechanism for storage and query, we use the log ontology that is defined in [4]. The role of the log ontology is to model what happens, and why, when, by whom, how it is performed. Each user's activity is captured in a log file in the form instances of the log ontology.

In order to analyse users' preferences, we define the rate of interest IRate(E) of users for an ontology entity E as:

$$IRate(E) = IFrequency(E) \cdot Clarity(E) \qquad (0 \leq IRate(E) \leq 1) \quad (1)$$

IFrequency(E) represents the users' interest in ontology entity E, and it is calculated as a ratio between the numbers of the users' interactions with the system related to the ontology entity E and the total number of the interactions. Indeed, we use the formula:

$$IFrequency(E) = \frac{Q(E)}{Q} \qquad (Q \neq 0,\ 0 \leq IFrequency(E) \leq 1)$$

whereas Q(E) is the number of queries that contains entity E, and Q is the total number of queries, i.e. Q(E)<= Q. In the case that there is no query related to the entity E, the users' interest in ontology entity E (IFrequency(E)) is 0, whereas when all queries are about entity E, then IFrequency(E) is equal to 1.

The clarity factor represents the uncertainty to determine the user's interest in a posted query. For example, when a user makes a query using a concept **Person**, which contains two subconcepts **Female** and **Male**, it could be matter of discussion: whether she is interested in the concept **Person** or in its subconcepts, but she failed to express it in a clear manner. Our experiences show that users who are not familiar with the given ontology used to use a more general concept in searching for knowledge resources, instead of using more specific concepts. In other words, the clarity factor makes the calculation of the users' interest more sensitive to the structure of the ontology by accounting possible "errors" in the query formulation.

The formula for the clarity factor depends on the entity type:

$$Clarity(E) = \begin{cases} k(E) \cdot \dfrac{1}{numSubConcepts(E)+1} & E \text{ is a concept} \\[3mm] k(E) \cdot \dfrac{1}{numSub\,Propeties(E)+1} \cdot \dfrac{1}{numDomains(E)} & E \text{ is a propetry} \end{cases}$$

0<Clarity(E)≤1,

whereas numSubConcepts(E) is the number of subconcepts of a concept E, numSubProperties(E) is the number of subproperties of a property E and numDomains(E) is the number of domains defined for the property E.

The coefficient k is introduced in order to favour the frequency of the usage. It is calculated using the following formula:

$$k(E) = \frac{1}{numLevel(E)+1} \qquad (0<k\leq 1)$$

where numLevel(E) is the depth of the hierarchy of the entity E.

Our primary goal is to decrease the impact of the non-leaf concepts, since they represent the common view to the set of their subconcepts, as described above. The similar strategy is applied to the properties and their hierarchy. However, the unclearness of reasons for a property usage can also arise when multiple domains for a property are defined. Thus, in order to clarify the context of a property usage, we require the explicit specification of the domain of that property, or otherwise we decrease its clarity factor.

The IRate value is calculated for all entities, and two extreme cases are analysed: the frequently used and unused entities. The first extreme corresponds to the entities with the highest rates that should be considered for changes. The formula (1) expresses our experience that the frequent usage of an entity in queries can be a consequence of the bad modelling of the hierarchy of that entity, i.e. in modelling that entity the hierarchy is not explored in details. For example, in a medical domain the concept **Person** is not split into concepts **Male** and **Female**, although there are a lot of differences between medical treatment of male and female patients. In end effect, any time the user wants to find knowledge resources related to either the male or female patients, she has to make a query with the concept **Person** and consequently the number of retrieved queries is huge. Therefore, our analysis can suggest that the concept **Person** should be divided into several subconcepts. The knowledge engineer decides whether and how to do that. If the considered concept already has a hierarchy, then its suitability (probability) for change is decreased by the clarity factor. The similar strategy is applied to the properties, too.

In the case that nobody is interested in an entity, i.e. the rate of interest for that entity is equal 0, then the entity should be considered for deleting from the ontology and consequently from annotations. However, the problem arises when the knowledge repository contains a lot of resources annotated with that entity. It can be interpreted in various ways. One interpretation might be that the topic is interesting for the community, but it is a new one and it is not used in previous projects. Other interpretation might state that employees are very familiar to this topic and therefore do not search for it.

The previous analysis takes into consideration only one entity. For the simultaneous analysis of the set of entities, the modifications of the frequency of interest IFrequency($E1,...,En$) is straightforward. However, the calculation of the clarity factor requires further analysis. Due to the lack of space, we mention the most frequently occurring cases:

$$Clarity(C1,C2) = \begin{cases} \dfrac{Clarity(C1) \cdot Clarity(C2)}{num\,\mathrm{Pr}operties(C1,C2)+1} & num\,\mathrm{Pr}operties(C1,C2) \geq 1 \\[2ex] 1 & else \end{cases}$$

$$Clarity(C1,C2,...,Cn) = \prod_{\substack{i=1,n \\ j=1,n}} Clarity(Ci,Cj)$$

$$Clarity(C,P) = \begin{cases} Clarity(C) \cdot Clarity(P) \cdot numDomains(P) & C \text{ is domain of } P \\[2ex] 1 & else \end{cases}$$

whereas C, $C1$, ..., Cn are concepts and P is a property. Note that the values of all clarity factors are between 0 and 1.

The high value of the rate of interest for the set of entities indicates the following changes:

If two concepts frequently occur in the same queries, it means that the users are very interested in the relationship between them. If such ontology property doesn't exist, then the system makes the highly ranked recommendation to create it since the clarity factor is set to 1. In case that such property already exists, it is possible that it is too general, i.e. defined for the concepts on the higher level in the concept hierarchy. This is a frequently occurring example of a bad ontology modelling. The recommendation is to specialise this property by creating subproperty whose domain is one of subconcept in the considered concept hierarchy.

Similar to the previous discussion, the frequent occurrence of the n ontology entities simultaneously indicates that these concepts are related. However, since the ontology properties are binary, the set of recommendation is delivered. First, a new concept should be created. Second, this concept should be related to each of the n frequently occurring concepts through the newly created property. At the end, the annotations should be extended in order to satisfy the optimality criteria mentioned in the section 2.1.

The high number of queries related to a concept and a property indicates the importance of the concept for that property. Consequently, if the concept is neither a domain nor a range of that property, it should be defined as is recommended by our system. Otherwise, we consider the possibility to specialise the property.

3   Evaluation

In order to prove the validity of our approach, we conducted two case studies, one for each of the proposed strategies for changes discovery: (i) changes discovered from the annotations and (ii) changes discovered from the end-users' activities.

3.1   Analysis of Annotations in MEDLINE

MEDLINE is one of the largest index and abstract databases of medical journal articles, which contains over 11 million references to articles from 4,600 worldwide journals in life sciences. It is maintained by the U.S. National Library of Medicine, which has developed a sophisticated controlled vocabulary called the Medical Subject Headings[3], used in the indexing of articles. The assignment of MeSH topics to articles, from the MEDLINE database, represents the state-of-the-art in human indexing; the professional indexers who perform this task train for at least 1 year. Ten to twelve topics in the form MainHeading/Qualifier are associated to the each article, which can be interpreted as the concept-relation relationship. Although such annotations help in searching for articles, MEDLINE suffers from the overload of information. For example, searching the MEDLINE using the MeSH topic "common cold"[4] yields over 1,400 articles written in the last 30 years. Finding a relevant article might take 20-30 minutes.

In order to prove whether our approach can discover some inconsistencies in MEDLINE annotations, which lead to the decreasing of the precision of the system, we analysed a corpus of MEDLINE articles and corresponding annotations regarding criteria we mentioned in the section 3.2.1. About 200 articles are randomly selected from the MEDLINE database and the results are presented in Table 1.

---

[3] MeSH (http://www.nlm.nih.gov/pubs/factsheets/mesh.html) is so-called medical ontology.
[4] The example is taken from http://www.ovid.com.

Discussion:

Validity is perfect - Since the management of MEDLINE annotations is performed very systematically, such inconsistency does not exist in the repository. Indeed, each year in November and December MEDLINE is in irregular operation as it makes the transition to a new year of MeSH.

The rate of compactness is small - High-frequent occurrence of this inconsistence can be explained by the format of the annotations itself. Since all metadata in an annotation are assigned separately to the corresponding knowledge resource and are not grouped according to the context, the concept-subconcept pairs occur very often in the annotations (e.g. **Human** and **Female**).

Completeness is medium - A part of the problem lies in the format of annotations itself: articles are annotated using topics and not relation metadata [6]. Consequently, it is not possible to express any relationship between medical concepts. Therefore, in lots of annotations the meaning of used topics has to be specified by adding a property, or the range of the property.

Aggregation is high - The small number of cases we found are related to the explanation given for the Compactness.

Table 1. The result of the analysis of the MEDLINE annotations (to note that in some articles two or more inconsistencies were found)

Criteria	Validity	Optimality		
		Compactness	Completeness	Aggregation
% of documents where the criterion failed	0	80	43	10

3.2   Analysis of Users' Queries in a Semantic Portal

The Semantic Portal (SEAL) [5] is an ontology-based application, which provides a "single-click" access to the almost all information related to the organisation, people, researches and projects of our Institute. It is widely used by our research and administrative staff as well as by our students. One of the most usable features is the possibility to search for people, research areas and projects on the semantic basis, i.e. using corresponding Institute Ontology. The portal provides a very user-friendly interface, which enables formation of arbitrary queries using entities from the underlying ontology. The search is performed as an inference through metadata, which is crawled from Portal pages.

Since the installation of the new version of the portal three months ago, the information about users' activities, regarding querying the portal, are logged in a file. The primary goal was to test the stability of the used version of inference engine. However, we reused the log file in order to evaluate our methods for discovering changes in the ontology. We set up a "what-if" experiment concerning this log file as follows:

1. We rewrote 1000 randomly selected queries under following hypothetical conditions:

a) The hierarchy of the concept **Person** that originally had five levels is shorten to only one level including the sub-concepts **Researcher** and **Student**;
b) The hierarchy of the concept **Project** that originally had two levels is deleted;
c) The hierarchy of the concept **ResearchArea** is shorten to the first level only. Consequently, we use 20 subconcepts instead of 80 subconcepts in the original hierarchy.

The hypothetical conditions given above are used for query rewriting. For example, from the original query in the form of (**Professor, pastProject, Knowledge_Acquisition**), meaning that a user is interested in information about professors whose past project was related to the knowledge acquisition, one gets the rewritten query in the form (**Researcher, Project, Knowledge_Based_Systems**).

2. We started searching (inferencing) using these queries.

3. We calculated interesting rate IRate (formula 1 in the section 3.2.2) for concepts **Person, Researcher, Project** and research areas **Knowledge_Based_System** and **E-Commerce**. In order to simplify the analysis, for the coefficient k we used the value 1. Table 2 shows the result of our analysis.

Table 2. The result of the interesting rate analysis

Concept	Researcher	Project	Knowledge_Based_System	E-Commerce	Person
IRate Value	(202/1000) *(1) = 0,202	(100/1000) *(1) = 0,1	(10/1000)*(1) = 0,01	(2/1000)*(1) = 0,002	(4/1000)* (1/2) = 0,002

Discussion:

We made a hypothetical situation in which the ontology is badly modelled and some hierarchies are not explored at all. A user can select only some restricted, higher-level concepts and for each specialisation he or she has to use one of higher-level concepts (e.g. for the query about professors she has to use the concept **Researcher**). In such a way we modelled the situation in which **the underlying ontology did not correspond to the users' needs**. The task of our method was to recognize which of badly modelled hierarchies do not reflect users' needs. We discuss several results:

• *The concept Researcher has the highest IRate* - it should be considered firstly - This is the right decision while a lot of queries contain concept **Researcher** and it has no hierarchy in the hypothetical situation. It means that we could conclude that concept **Researcher** is used as a replacement for the users' need to search for some specializations of researchers.

• *The concept Knowledge_Based_Systems should be considered before the concept E-Commerce* - In our experiment the both hierarchies are shorten. However, in the original ontology the first one was larger and therefore should be firstly considered for a change. The number of queries, which contain topic "knowledge-based system", reflects users' needs for more specialized areas of the knowledge-based system.

• *The concept Person has the lowest IRate* - This is the right estimation, since the concept **Person** has one level of the hierarchy, which satisfies users' needs regarding this concept.

4   Related Work

This section gives an overview of the researches related to our approach.

In [7] authors discuss the possibilities to combine the two research areas Semantic Web and Web Mining. The idea is to improve, on the one hand, the results of Web Mining by exploiting the new semantic structures in the Web, and to make the use of the Web Mining to , on the other hand, for building up the Semantic Web. Our paper shows the benefits of the both of methods. We define semantics for the log information in the form of the log ontology and we use the log information to enhance ontologies that are the underlying model for the Semantic Web.

Change mining in the context of decision tree classification for real-life application is studied in [8]. Their primary goal is to know what is changing and how it has changed in order to provide the right products and services to suit the changing market needs. In contrast to this approach, our system discovers changes for the users' interactions with the systems with the goal not only to predict changes but to improve the efficiency of the system.

[9] sets up a framework for stability of conceptual schemas and proceeds to develop a set of metrics from it. The metrics are based on straightforward measurements of conceptual features. A set of measures we defined takes into account the conceptual structure of the ontology, quality of the annotations as well as the users' needs.

In [10] the author presents the guiding principles for building consistent and principled ontologies in order to alleviate their creation, the usage and the maintenance in the distributed environments. They define set of the operational guidelines based on the structure of the ontology. In our approach it corresponds to the set of heuristics for the structure-driven change discovery. Moreover, we go a step further by incorporating the data-driven and the usage-driven change discovery.

The area of maintaining knowledge management systems is rather seldom explored in the research community, although the practical importance is elsewhere announced [11]. Our approach enables a systematic analysis of changes in the user's needs and dynamic adaptation of the system to these changes.

5   Conclusion

In this paper, we present a novel approach for the change discovery in ontology-based knowledge management systems. The approach is based on the analysis of the user's interaction with the system in providing annotations for knowledge resources, as well as in the process of accessing the knowledge by querying the knowledge repository. Our previous work in ontology evolution is used as a basis for this research. We defined several assessment criteria to estimate the quality of annotations and the user's needs from the point of view of knowledge management. These criteria result in the recommendations for the continual system improvement. The benefits of the proposed approach are manifold: dynamic adaptation of the system to the changes in the business environment, dynamic analysis of the user's needs and the usefulness of particular knowledge resources and the organisation of the knowledge repository to fulfil these needs, to name but a few.

The evaluation experiments show that our approach can be applied in the real-world applications successfully. We find that it represents a very important step in the achievement of a self-adaptive knowledge management system, which can discover some changes from the user's interactions with the system automatically and evolves its structure correspondingly.

References

[1]   Staab, S., Schnurr, H.-P., Studer, R., and Sure, Y.: Knowledge Processes and Ontologies, IEEE Intelligent Systems, 16(1) , 2001.

[2]   Maedche, A., Motik, B., Stojanovic, L., Studer, R. and Volz, R.: Ontologies for Enterprise Knowledge Management. IEEE Intelligent Systems, November/December 2002.

[3]   Stojanovic, L., Maedche, A., Motik, B., and Stojanovic, N.: User-Driven Ontology Evolution Management. Proceedings of the 13th European Conference on Knowledge Engineering and Management, EKAW-2002, Springer, LNAI, Madrid, Spain, 2002.

[4]   Stojanovic, N., and Stojanovic, L.: Usage-oriented Evolution in the Ontology-based Knowledge Management Systems. Proceedings of the First International Conference on Ontologies, Databases and Application of Semantics (ODBASE), Springer, 2002.

[5]   Stojanovic, N., Maedche, A., Staab, S., Studer, R., and Sure, Y.: SEAL - A Framework for Developing SEmantic PortALs, ACM K-CAP 2001, Vancouver, October, 2001.

[6]   Handschuh, S., and Staab, S.: Authoring and Annotation of Web Pages in CREAM, Proceedings of the 11th Int. World Wide Web Conference WWW-2002, 2002.

[7]   Berendt, B., Hotho, A., and Stumme, G.: Towards Semantic Web Mining. Proceeding of the ISWC 2002 - First International Semantic Web Conference, Sardinia, Italy, June 9-12, pp. 264-278, 2002.

[8]   Liu, B., Hsu, W., Han, H.S., and Xia, Y.: Mining Changes for Real-Life Applications. Proceedings of the 2nd International Conference on Data Warehousing and Knowledge Discovery (DaWaK-2000), Sept 4-6, London, UK, pp. 54-63, 2000.

[9]   Wedemeijer, L.: Defining Metrics for Conceptual Schema Evolution. In: Balsters, H., Brock, B., Conrad, S. (Eds.): Database Schema Evolution and Meta-Modeling,. Lecture Notes in Computer Science, Vol. 2065, Springer, 2001.

[10] McGuinness, D.: Conceptual Modeling for Distributed Ontology Environments. Proceedings of the ICCS 2000, August 14-18, Darmstadt, Germany , 2000.

[11] Lindgren, R., Hardless, C., Pessi, K. and Nulden, U.: The Evolution of Knowledge Management Systems Needs to be Managed. Journal of Knowledge Management Practice, Volume 3, 2002.

An Architecture for Managing Database Evolution*

Eladio Domínguez, Jorge Lloret, and María Antonia Zapata

Dpt. de Informática e Ingeniería de Sistemas, Facultad de Ciencias
Universidad de Zaragoza. E-50009 – Zaragoza, Spain
{noesis,jlloret,mazapata}@posta.unizar.es

Abstract. This paper presents an architecture for managing database evolution when all the components of the database (conceptual schema, logical schema and extension) are available. The strategy of evolution in which our architecture is based is that of 'forward database maintenance', that is, changes are applied to the conceptual schema and propagated automatically down to the logical schema and to the extension. In order to put into practice this strategy, each component of a database is seen under this architecture as the information base of an information system. Furthermore, a translation information system is considered in order to manage the translation of conceptual elements into logical schema elements. A current Oracle implementation of this architecture is also presented.

Keywords: Information Systems, Database Evolution, Forward Database Maintenance, Meta-modelling.

1 Introduction

The requirements of a database do not remain constant during its life time and therefore the database has to evolve in order to fulfil the new requirements. In general, database evolution activities are considered of great practical importance since they normally consume a large amount of resources [10]. As a consequence, much research has been focused on analysing ways of facilitating this type of activity [1,16].

Several problems related with databases evolution have been outlined in [6]. In particular, we are interested in the forward database maintenance problem ('redesign problem' according to [16]), that is, how to reflect in the logical schema and in the extension changes that have occurred in the conceptual schema of a database. Although a lot of research papers have been written in relation with this problem (see, for example, [16] and [10]) no completely satisfactory solution has been proposed.

---

* This work has been partially supported by DGES, projects TIC2000-1368-C03-01 and PB-96-0098-C04-01, and by University of Zaragoza, project UZ-00-TEC-04.

A. Olivé et al. (Eds.): ER 2002 Ws, LNCS 2784, pp. 63–74, 2003.

As a contribution towards achieving a more satisfactory solution, in this paper we propose an architecture for managing database evolution within the context of forward engineering. The main difference with respect to other proposals is that we consider a translation component besides the conceptual, logical and extension components. The translation component stores information about the way in which a concrete conceptual database schema is translated into a logical schema. This component plays an important role in enabling the automatic propagation of the conceptual database schema evolution down to the logical database schema making it possible to reflect in the extension of the database the changes performed in its conceptual schema.

Another important difference with respect to other authors [16,8] is that a meta-modelling approach [3,11] has been followed for the definition of the architecture. We have chosen this approach because it allows modelling knowledge to be represented and because it has been proven that it facilitates the definition of data model translations [11]. Within the architecture, three meta-models are considered which capture, respectively, the conceptual, logical and translation modelling knowledge. At the same time, the notion of information system, such as is defined in [5], is brought into play not only at the model level (which is the way in which it is normally used) but also at the meta-model level (like in [10]).

So as to show a concrete application of our architecture, we present a current Oracle implementation, which follows the common approach [16,15] of modelling the conceptual (logical) schema of the database by using the ER (relational) model. It should be noted that we have chosen these concrete models only with the aim of illustrating our architecture. However, the architecture is of general applicability and therefore can also be applied to other approaches such as, for example, within the context of object oriented databases [1,2]. Like other authors [10], we have chosen to represent the meta–schemas by means of UML class diagrams [13] in the belief that they will be easily understood thanks to the fact that UML is an increasingly widely accepted standard modelling language.

The remainder of the paper is organised as follows. Section 2 explains our view of dealing with database evolution, presenting in Section 3 the architecture we propose. Section 4 is devoted to showing a current Oracle implementation of our architecture. In Section 5 we discuss related work and finally conclusions and future work are outlined in Section 6.

2   The Database Evolution Issue

In order to design a database, users' information requirements are represented by means of a conceptual database schema S_C (for example, an ER model or a UML diagram). This schema is translated into a logical database schema S_L (see Figure 1) which will be implemented by means of a DBMS. The database is then populated to create a consistent database state σ.

Within this framework, the database evolution issue can be stated in a general way rephrasing the ideas explained in [16] as follows. Due to varied reasons (changes in the real world [16], optimisation procedures for improving the performance of the system [7]...), the conceptual schema S_C is modified generating

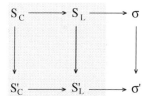

Fig. 1. Database Evolution

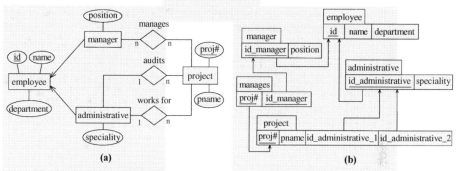

Fig. 2. Examples of Conceptual and Logical Database Schemas

a new conceptual schema S'_C. Ideally this modification at the conceptual level should be managed following the strategy of 'forward database maintenance' [6] according to which changes at the conceptual level should be automatically propagated down to the logical schema and its population. That is, the logical schema S_L has to be modified in order to generate a new logical representation S'_L and the database state σ has to be mapped into a new database state σ' consistent with S'_L.

The changes to be performed in the conceptual database schema in order to carry out the desired evolution can be expressed by means of schema transformations [7]. A schema transformation accomplishes modifications in the structure of the database and maps the population of the source schema into an allowable population of the resultant schema [2,7].

In order to illustrate an example of database evolution, we will use the schema of Figure 2(a) as the conceptual schema S_C, which has been obtained combining different examples included in [9]. In this example the E/R model has been used as the conceptual modelling technique and, as usual, entity types, relationship types and attributes are represented, respectively, by rectangles, diamonds and ovals. This schema represents a company where it is perceived that there are employees and projects. The employees can be managers (managing projects) or administrative staff (working for projects or auditing projects).

Traditionally the relational model has been used as the logical modelling technique when the E/R model is used at the conceptual level. Following this criteria, the proposed example of E/R schema has been translated into a relational model (see Figure 2(b)) using the algorithm proposed in [4]. In Figure 2(b) the foreign key constraints have been represented by means of arrows. With regard to this example we only want to emphasise that the n–n relationship type manages has been translated into a relational table which is not the case with the 1–n relationship types works_for and audits.

In the course of this paper we are going to consider two examples of evolution of the conceptual schema of Figure 2(a). One is the case in which the audits relationship type, together with its instances, must be deleted. This example seems to be very simple but we will see later on that it is more complex than it appears. Moreover, it will serve to illustrate the suitability of the translation component we include in our proposed architecture. As for the other example, we are going to suppose that the attribute department of the entity type employee must be transformed into an entity type. This transformation (1) adds to the conceptual schema an entity type department described by means of two attributes (id_department and department), id_department being its primary key, (2) adds a relationship type employee has department and, (3) deletes the attribute department. With respect to the extension, this transformation maps each distinct non–null value of the attribute department in the old schema into a distinct 'department' entity in the new schema. Furthermore, the corresponding 'employee has department' relationships are added.

3   Database Evolution Architecture

The architecture we propose aims at providing a general framework which makes it feasible to manage database evolution following a forward maintenance strategy. Therefore, the architecture has to be defined in such a way that the changes performed in the conceptual database schema can be reflected in the logical schema and its extension. It is more or less obvious that some component has to allow conceptual, logical and extensional information to be stored. Let us go on to illustrate, by means of an example, the necessity of also storing knowledge with regard to the translation process from the conceptual into the logical schema.

Let us suppose that the audits relationship type must be deleted from the conceptual schema of Figure 2(a). This modification must be automatically reflected in the logical schema of Figure 2(b) deleting some element. According to the translation algorithm applied to the conceptual schema, it is known that the audits relationship type has been translated into an attribute of the project table, this attribute being a foreign key referencing the administrative table. The problem is that this table contains two columns (id_administrative_1 and id_administrative_2) verifying these conditions. If there is no information about the specific process followed for obtaining the logical schema of Figure 2(b), it is not known which attribute should be deleted. Our proposal is to store knowledge about the translation process explicitly in a component of our architecture, in the same way that the conceptual, logical and extensional information is stored. This component will include, for example, information about the column which the relationship type audits has been translated into.

A meta-modelling approach has been followed for the definition of the components storing conceptual, translation and logical information (a modelling ap-

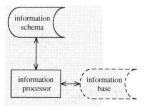

Fig. 3. Components of an Information System

proach is used with regard to the extensional information). The meta-modelling approach consists of representing modelling knowledge by means of a meta-model, where a *meta-model* is a conceptual schema of the elements constituting a data model or technique [3]. Following this approach the elements of a conceptual database schema, logical database schema or translation process are seen as instances of the corresponding meta-model. In order to capture this fact, [10] inspired us with the idea of bringing into play the notion of information system, such as is defined in [5], not only at the model level (which is the way in which it is normally used) but also at the meta-model level.

According to [5] an *information system* (see Figure 3) consists of three components: an information schema, an information base and an information processor. The information schema[1] defines all the knowledge relevant to the system, the information base describes the specific objects perceived in the Universe of Discourse, and the information processor receives messages reporting the occurrence of events in the environment. In order to respond to the events received, the information processor can send structural events towards the information base and/or towards the information schema and can generate internal events that inform other information systems of the changes performed in it.

The notion of information system is used within our architecture giving rise to four information systems which are used to store, respectively, the conceptual modelling knowledge, the translation process, the logical modelling knowledge and the extension. The corresponding components of each one of these information systems as well as the way in which they are related appear in Figure 4. The name of each one of these components has been modified in an attempt to capture the type of knowledge that they store (in any case the graphical symbol that surrounds each component stands for the type of component it represents).

It must be noted that three different abstraction levels are involved in the architecture. On the one hand, the information schemas of the three former information systems are situated at the most abstract level (meta-model layer according to [13]) and, on the other hand, the information base which stores the population of the database is situated at the least abstract level (user data layer [13]). All the other elements are situated at the model layer [13]. Let us now explain each one of the four information systems of the architecture.

---

[1] In fact, in [5] this component is called 'conceptual schema'. However, with the aim of avoiding misunderstandings, we have considered it inappropriate to use the term 'conceptual' since we are going to use this component not only at the conceptual level of the database but also at the logical and physical levels.

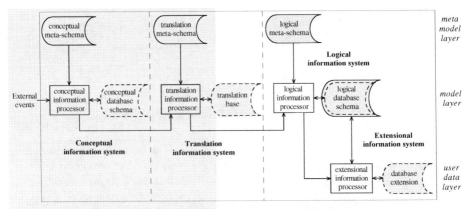

Fig. 4. Architecture for Database Evolution

3.1   Conceptual Information System

The population of this information system (that is, its information base) represents the constituent elements of a given conceptual database schema. For example, with respect to the E/R schema of Figure 2(a), facts such as that employee is an entity type and that department is an attribute have to be stored. These facts will be stored following the structure established in the conceptual meta–schema.

The conceptual information system has to react to external events received from the environment. The type of events in which we are interested are those related with database evolution. Each event issued from the environment is handled by the information processor which checks its validity according to the restrictions imposed by the conceptual meta–schema. If it is valid, the information processor induces a collection of structural events necessary to change the conceptual database schema (that is, the information base) according to the semantics of the received event. The conceptual information processor also generates a collection of internal events that inform the translation information system of the changes performed in the conceptual database schema.

3.2   Translation Information System

The goal of this information system is to store all the information necessary to enable any change performed in the conceptual database schema to be automatically reflected in the logical schema. This goal is achieved by storing the way in which conceptual schema elements are translated into logical schema elements. In order to do this, the translation accomplished by the chosen translation algorithm is specified as a set of elementary translations each of which represents the translation of only one conceptual element into a logical element. For example, the translation of the E/R schema of Figure 2(a) following the algorithm proposed in [4] performs, among others, the elementary translations of transforming the entity type employee into a table with the name employee, and transforming the attribute department into a column with the same name. The elementary translations are stored in the translation base (that is, the information base) specifying the type of translation, the element of the conceptual schema it is applied to and the element of the logical schema it gives place to.

The translation information system has to react to the internal events generated by the conceptual processor which inform it about the changes performed in the conceptual database schema. In accordance with these events, the information processor determines the elementary translations that must be added, deleted or updated from the translation base. After these changes, the translation base contains the set of elementary translations that translates the new conceptual schema (resulting from the evolution process) into a logical one. The information processor also generates a collection of internal events that inform the logical information system of the changes performed in the translation base.

It must be noted that the new set of elementary translations is determined without it being necessary to apply once again the translation algorithm from scratch. The knowledge stored in the translation information system avoids having to recalculate the logical elements that result from the conceptual elements that have not been modified. The idea of using an information system to store the elements related with the translation process and the way in which this knowledge is used during the database evolution process are, from our point of view, a significant contribution of our work.

3.3   Logical and Extensional Information Systems

The logical information base stores the elements of the logical schema obtained as a translation of a given conceptual database schema. For example, with respect to the relational schema of Figure 2(b), facts such as that employee is a table and that department is a column of it have to be stored. These facts will be stored following the structure established in the logical meta–schema.

The logical information processor receives a collection of internal events from the translation information processor, according to which it generates the structural events necessary to change the logical database schema in order to reflect the evolution performed at the conceptual level.

In Figure 4, the information base of the logical information system is surrounded with both the information base and information schema symbols. This is because the logical database schema can be seen as the information base of the logical information system (as we have explained) or as the information schema of the extensional information system. For this reason two different components of our architecture store the same information. This fact obliges us to define some rules, called *correspondence rules* (in the same sense as in [10]). These rules govern the correspondence between the elements of each one of the two components. In order to hold these rules, the logical information processor sends the internal events reporting the changes made in the logical database schema, and the extensional information processor, according to the received events, changes the database extension and the database schema (that is, the information schema). This is the only case in which the information processor changes the information schema of its information system.

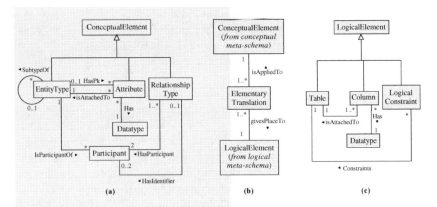

Fig. 5. Meta-models of the Information Systems

4   An Implementation of Our Architecture

In this section, we describe a concrete implementation of our architecture. This implementation is based on the RDBMS Oracle 8i Release 8.1.7 and the programming language PL/SQL Release 8.1.7 [17]. Within this implementation, the E/R technique has been chosen as the conceptual modelling technique and the relational as the logical modelling technique. We will use UML meta–schemas in order to conceptually describe the structure of the three information schemas that belong to the meta-model level. The graphical representation of these meta–schemas appears in Figure 5 in which only the name is included for each class (its attribute compartment does not appear).

The meta–schema of the **conceptual information system** (see Figure 5(a)) conceptualises the different modelling elements of the E/R model (the version we use is based on the E/R model proposed in [9]). For example, it is represented that a relationship type is related with exactly two participants and that an entity type is related with the attributes that conform to its primary key (PK). This meta–schema also has several meta–constraints associated to it. For example, two constraints (expressed by means of OCL [13]) with context EntityType are the following:

1. If an entity type is not a subtype of any entity type, then it must have one primary key.
   SubtypeOf → size $= 0$ **implies** HasPK → size ≥ 1

2. An entity type cannot be a subtype of itself.
   SubtypeOf → forAll(e | e <> self)

   In order to carry out database evolution tasks the external event types that we have implemented appear in Table 1 (their arguments have been omitted). Six of these external events are basic operations of addition or deletion of modelling elements (entity type, attribute or relationship type), two of them allow the modification of a primary key, one adds an entity type as a specialisation of another entity type and, finally, one transforms an attribute into an entity type.

Table 1. External Event Types

For entity types	For attributes	For relationship types	For primary keys
NewEntityType	NewAttribute	NewRelType	AddAttrToPk
DropEntityType	DropAttribute	DropRelType	DropAttrFromPk
NewEntitySubtype	AttributeToEntityType		

We are aware that this is a relatively small number of external events, and that more are needed for facilitating the database evolution.

As an illustration of database evolution, the example of schema evolution described at the end of Section 2, according to which the attribute department is transformed into an entity type, will be performed using the external event:

AttributeToEntityType('employee.department')

This event has only one parameter which expresses the attribute that has to be transformed into an entity type. As a consequence of this event the following tasks have to be performed: (1) create a new entity type called department with two attributes (id_department and department) and primary key id_department, (2) create a new relationship type, called has, between employee and department, and (3) delete the attribute department of the entity type employee.

The information processor of the conceptual information system has been implemented as a set of PL/SQL procedures, one for each of the established external event types. For example, there exists a procedure that is executed when the event AttributeToEntityType occurs and this procedure accomplishes the tasks associated with the event.

The meta–schema of Figure 5(b) represents that the **translation information system** stores the elementary translations that have to be applied to the given conceptual database schema in order to be translated into a logical schema (the elementary translations are determined following the translation algorithm proposed in [4]). Each translation is related with the conceptual element to which it is applied and with the logical element to which it gives rise.

The information processor of this information system is implemented as a collection of PL/SQL triggers which are fired by the insert, delete or update operations performed in the conceptual database. For example, the addition of the entity type department fires a trigger which adds to the translation base an elementary translation that translates the entity type department into a table. The deletion of the attribute department fires a trigger which deletes the elementary translation that translates the attribute department into a column.

The meta–schema of the **logical information system** (see Figure 5(c)) conceptualises the different elements that conform to a relational model. The information processor of this information system is also implemented as a collection of PL/SQL triggers which are fired by the insert, delete or update operations performed in the translation base. For example, the addition of the elementary translation that translates the entity type department into a table fires a trigger which adds the table department. In the same way, the deletion of the elementary

Table 2. SQL sentences automatically generated and executed

```
1   CREATE TABLE department(department varchar2(30), id_department
    integer);
2   INSERT INTO department (department) SELECT DISTINCT department
    FROM employee WHERE department IS NOT NULL;
3   execute giveidvalues('department','id_department','department');
4   ALTER TABLE department ADD (PRIMARY KEY (id_department));
5   ALTER TABLE employee ADD id_department integer;
6   ALTER TABLE employee ADD (CONSTRAINT restr22 FOREIGN KEY
    (id_department) REFERENCES department(id_department));
7   execute matchvalues('employee','id_department','department',
    'department','id_department','department');
8   ALTER TABLE employee DROP COLUMN department;
```

translation that translates the attribute department into a column fires a trigger which deletes the column department.

The **extensional information system** stores the Oracle 8i database schema and its data. The information processor of this information system is also implemented as a collection of PL/SQL triggers which are fired by the insert, delete or update operations performed in the logical database. These triggers automatically generate and execute the SQL sentences that perform the changes that have to be made in the Oracle 8i database in order to accomplish the correspondence rules and to reach a consistent database state. For example, the SQL sentences generated in order to transform the attribute department into an entity type appear in Table 2. These sentences perform the following tasks:

1. Create the new table department with the values of attribute id_department created by means of the procedure giveidvalues (lines 1–4).
2. Create the relational structures corresponding to the new relationship type between entity types employee and department (lines 5–6).
3. Assign values to attribute employee.id_department using the procedure matchvalues (line 7).
4. Drop attribute employee.department (line 8).

5   Related Work

Database evolution has been widely discussed in the literature and therefore very varied approaches have been proposed. The evolution of object-oriented databases and relational databases, including the propagation of changes automatically down to the extension of the database, has received great attention and the research results have been included in prototypes or in commercial DBMS (see, for example [1]). However they lack the consideration of a conceptual level which allows the designer to work at a higher level of abstraction [10].

In [6] an abstract framework which takes into account both conceptual and logical levels is presented and the necessity of automatically propagating down (forward strategy) the changes performed at the conceptual level is stated. The different papers dealing with forward engineering mainly differ in the way they address the propagation of the conceptual changes down to the logical schema and to the extension. For example, a taxonomical approach is followed in [15], which proposes a taxonomy of changes for ER structures and the impact of these changes on relational schemes is analysed. However this paper does not study how to reflect the schema evolution in the extension of the database.

Other approaches, more similar to ours, propose various ways to capture knowledge about the mappings performed to obtain the logical schema of a conceptual schema. This information is used subsequently in order to obtain the new logical schema associated to the changed conceptual schema. In [8], for example, the sequence (called history) of mappings performed in order to obtain the logical schema is stored. In this way the mappings affected by the changes can be detected and modified, whereas the rest can be reexecuted without any modification. Our approach has the same aim as this one but differs in that we follow a meta-modelling approach.

A meta-modelling approach is also proposed in [10], [14] and [12]. In the case of [10] only a conceptual meta-model is considered whereas we also make use of a logical and a translation meta-model. With respect to [14], the authors make use of a meta-modelling approach with a different goal since the paper deals with the definition of a query language for evolving information systems. In [12] a generalisation of the traditional information system notion similar to ours has been proposed. However, some differences with respect to our proposal are worth noting. Firstly, in [12] not only data modelling is taken into account (as we do) but also process and behaviour specification. Secondly, in [12] only the conceptual level is under consideration so that the proposed architecture includes only one information system. Finally, the information processor of an information system is concerned with the modification of the structure and also of the population, instead of using different information processors for each one of these processes as we propose.

6   Conclusions

In this paper we have presented an architecture for managing database evolution with a forward strategy. The architecture consists of four information systems whose information schema capture the relevant modelling elements. As the main contribution, a translation information system is considered, which reflects the translations performed between the conceptual and logical schemas of the database. Evolution changes performed in the conceptual database schema are reflected in the logical schema and the extension of the database making use of structural and internal events. An implementation of our architecture using Oracle has also been presented.

As a direction of future work, the problems related with the evolution of integrity constraints have to be analysed. Furthermore, a comprehensive support within our architecture for relationship evolution, following the ideas of [2], is a goal for further development.

References

1. L. Al-Jadir, M. Léonard, Multiobjects to Ease Schema Evolution in an OODBMS, in T. W. Ling, S. Ram, M. L. Lee (eds.), *Conceptual modeling, ER-98*, LNCS 1507, Springer, 1998, 316–333.
2. K. T. Claypool, E. A. Rundensteiner, and G. T. Heineman, ROVER: A Framework for the Evolution of Relationships, in A. H. F. Laender, S. W. Liddle, V. C. Storey (eds), *Conceptual modeling, ER-2000*, LNCS 1920, Springer, 2000, 409–422.
3. E. Domínguez, M. A. Zapata, J. J. Rubio, A Conceptual Approach to Meta-modelling, in A. Olivé, J. A. Pastor (Eds.), *Advanced Information Systems Engineering, CAISE'97*, LNCS 1250, Springer, 1997, 319–332.
4. R.A. Elmasri, S.B. Navathe, *Fundamentals of Database Systems (3rd ed.)*, Addison-Wesley, 2000.
5. J.J. van Griethuysen (ed.), *Concepts and Terminology for the Conceptual Schema and the Information Base*, Publ. ISO/TC97/SV5-N695, Mars 1982.
6. J.L. Hainaut, V. Englebert, J. Henrard, J.M. Hick, D. Roland, Database Evolution: The DB-MAIN approach, in P. Loucopoulos (ed.), *Entity-Relationship approach-ER'94*, Springer Verlag, LNCS 881, 1994, 112–131.
7. T.A. Halpin, H.A. Proper, Database Schema Transformation and Optimization, in M. P. Papazoglou (ed.), *Object–Oriented Entity-Relationship Modelling Conference- ER'95*, Springer Verlag, LNCS 1021, 1995, 191–203.
8. J.M. Hick , J.L. Hainaut, V. Englebert, D. Roland et al., Strategies pour l'evolution des applications de bases de donnes relationelles: L'approche DB-MAIN, *Proceedings XVIII Congres Inforsid*, La Garde, France, 1999.
9. A.H.F. Laender, M.A. Casanova, A.P. de Carvalho, L. F.G.G.M. Ridolfi, An Analysis of SQL Integrity Constraints from an Entity-Relationship Perspective, *Information Systems*, 10, 4, 1994, 331–358.
10. J.R. López, A. Olivé, A Framework for the Evolution of Temporal Conceptual Schemas of Information Systems, in B. Wangler, L. Bergman (eds.), *Advanced Information Systems Eng., CAiSE 2000*, Springer, LNCS 1789, 2000, 369–386.
11. C. Nicolle, D. Benslimane, K. Yetongnon, Multi–Data Models Translations in Interoperable Information Systems, in J. Mylopoulos, Y. Vassiliou (Eds.), *Advanced Information Systems Eng., CAISE'96*, LNCS 1080, Springer, 1996, 1–21.
12. J.L.H. Oei, H.A. Proper, E.D. Falkenberg, Evolving Information Systems: Meeting the ever–changing environment, *Information Systems Journal*, 4, 3, 1994, 213–233.
13. OMG, *UML specification version 1.4*, formal/01–09–67, 2001, http://www.omg.org
14. H.A. Proper, Th. P. van der Weide, Information Disclosure in Evolving Information Systems: Taking a Shot at a Moving Target, *Data & Knowledge Engineering*, 15, 1995, 135–168.
15. J.F. Roddick, N.G. Craske, T.J. Richards, A Taxonomy for Schema Versioning Based on the Relational and Entity Relationship Models, in R. A. Elmasri, V. Kouramajian, B. Thalheim (eds.), *Proc. of the 12th Int. Conf. on the Entity-Relationship Approach*, Elsevier, LNCS 823, 1994, 137–148.
16. A.S. da Silva, A.H.F. Laender, M.A. Casanova, An Approach to Maintaining Optimized Relational Representations of Entity-Relationship Schemas, in B. Thalheim (ed.), *Conceptual Modeling- ER'96*, Springer Verlag, LNCS 1157, 1996, 292–308.
17. S. Urman, *Oracle 9i PL/SQL Programming*, Osborne, 2002.

Reifying Design Patterns to Facilitate Systems Evolution

Florida Estrella[1,2], Zsolt Kovacs[2], Jean-Marie Le Goff[2],
Richard McClatchey[1], and Norbert Toth[1, 2]

[1]Centre for Complex Cooperative Systems, UWE
Frenchay, Bristol BS16 1QY UK
Tel: +44 1179 656261, FAX: +41 22 767 8930
{Florida.Estrella,Richard.McClatchey,Norbert.Toth}@cern.ch
[2]ETT Division, CERN, Geneva, Switzerland
Tel +41 22 767 6559, FAX: +41 22 767 8930
{Zsolt.Kovacs,Jean-Marie.Le.Goff}@cern.ch

Abstract. In the Web age systems must be increasingly flexible, reconfigurable and adaptable in addition to being developed rapidly. As a consequence, designing systems to cater for change is becoming critical to their success. Allowing systems to be self-describing or *description-driven* is one way to enable this. To address the issue of evolvability in information systems, this paper proposes a pattern-based description-driven architecture. The proposed architecture embodies four pillars - firstly, the adoption of a multi-layered and reflective meta-level architecture, secondly, the identification of four modeling relationships that must be made explicit to be examined and modified dynamically, thirdly the identification of five patterns which have emerged from practice and have proved essential in providing reusable building blocks, and finally the encoding of the structural properties of these design patterns by means of one pattern, the Graph pattern. A practical example of this is cited to demonstrate the use of description-driven data objects in handling system evolution.

1   Background

A crucial factor in the creation of flexible web-based information systems dealing with changing requirements is the suitability of the underlying technology in allowing the evolution of the system. Exposing the internal system architecture opens up the architecture, consequently allowing application programs to inspect and alter implicit system aspects. These implicit system elements can serve as the basis for changes and extensions to the system. Making these internal structures explicit allows them to be subject to scrutiny and interrogation.

A reflective system utilizes an open architecture where implicit system aspects are reified to become explicit first-class *meta-objects* [1]. The advantage of reifying system descriptions as objects is that operations can be carried out on them, like composing and editing, storing and retrieving, organizing and reading. Since these meta-objects can represent system descriptions, their manipulation can result in change in system behaviour. As such, reified system descriptions are mechanisms that can lead to dynamically modifiable and evolvable systems. Meta-objects, as used here, are the self-representations of the system describing how its internal elements can be accessed and manipulated. These self-representations are causally connected to the internal structures they represent; changes to these self-representations immediately affect the underlying system. The ability to dynamically augment, extend

A. Olivé (Eds.): ER 2003 Ws, LNCS 2784, pp. 75-87, 2003.
© Springer-Verlag Berlin Heidelberg 2003

and re-define system specifications can result in a considerable improvement in flexibility. This leads to dynamically modifiable systems that can adapt and cope with evolving requirements, essential in a web-oriented system.

There are a number of OO design techniques that encourage the design and development of reusable objects. In particular design patterns are useful for creating reusable OO designs [2]. Design patterns for structural, behavioural and architectural modeling have been documented and have provided software engineers rules and guidelines that they can immediately (re-)use in software development. Reflective architectures that can dynamically adapt to new user requirements by storing descriptive information that can be interpreted at runtime have led to so-called Adaptive Object Models [3]. These are models that provide meta-information about domains that can be changed on the fly. Such an approach, proposed by Yoder, is very similar to the approach adopted in this paper.

A Description-Driven System (DDS), as defined by the work reported in this paper, is an example of a reflective multi-level architecture [4]. It makes use of meta-objects to store domain-specific system descriptions, which control and manage the life cycles of meta-object instances, i.e. domain objects. The separation of descriptions from their instances allows them to be specified and managed and to evolve independently and asynchronously. This separation is essential in handling the complexity issues facing many computing applications and allows the realization of interoperability, reusability and system evolution since it gives a clear boundary between the application's basic functionalities from its representations and controls. As objects, reified system descriptions of DDSs can be organized into libraries or frameworks dedicated to the modeling of languages in general, and to customizing its use for specific domains in particular.

This paper shows, for the first time, how the approach of reifying a set of design patterns can be used as the basis of a description-driven architecture and can provide the capability of system evolution. (The host project, CRISTAL, is not described in detail here. Readers should consult [4] & [5] for further detail). The next section establishes how semantic relationships in description-driven systems can be reified using a complete and sufficient set of meta-objects that cater for Aggregation, Generalization, Description, Dependency and Relationships. In section 3 of this paper the reification of the Graph Pattern is discussed and section 4 investigates the use of this pattern in a three-layer reflective architecture.

2   Reifying Semantic Relationships

In response to the demand to treat associations on an equal footing with classes, a number of published papers have suggested the promotion of the relationship construct as a first-class object (reification) [6]. A first-class object is an object that can be created at run-time, can be passed as an actual parameter to methods, can be returned as a result of a function and can be stored in a variable. Reification is used in this paper to promote associations to the same level as classes, thus giving them the same status and features as classes. Consequently, associations become fully-fledged objects in their own right with their own attributes representing their states, and their own methods to alter their behavior. This is achieved by viewing the relationships themselves as patterns.

Different types of relationships, representing the many ways interdependent objects are related, can be reified. The proper specification of the types of relationships that exist among objects is essential in managing the relationships and the propagation of operations to the objects they associate. This greatly improves system design and implementation as the burden for handling dependency behavior emerging from relationships is localized to the relationship object. Instead of providing domain-specific solutions to handling domain-related dependencies, the relationship objects handle inter-object communication and domain consistency implicitly.

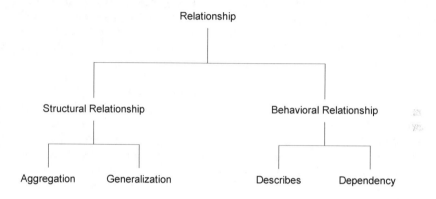

Fig. 1. Relationship classification

Reifying relationships as meta-objects is a fundamental step in the reification of design patterns. The next sections discuss four types of relationships, as shown in Figure 1. The relationship classification is divided into two types - structural relationship and behavioral relationship. A structural relationship is one that deals with the structural or static aspects of a domain. The Aggregation and the Generalization relationships are examples of this type. A behavioral relationship, as the name implies, deals with the behavioral or dynamic aspects of a domain. Two types of behavioral relationships are explored in this paper - the Describes and Dependency relationships.

It is not the object of this paper to give an exhaustive discussion of each of these relationships. Those which are covered are the links which have proved essential in developing the concepts of description-driven systems and these have emerged from a set of five design patterns: the Type Object Pattern [7], the Tree Pattern, the Graph Pattern, the Publisher-Subscriber Pattern and the Mediator Pattern [8]. Interested readers should refer to [9] for a more complete discussion about the taxonomy of semantic relationships.

2.1   The Aggregation Meta-object

Aggregation is a structural relationship between an object whole using other objects as its parts. The most common example of this type of relationship is the bill-of-materials or parts explosion tree, representing part-whole hierarchies of objects. The familiar Tree Pattern [10] models the Aggregation relationship and the objects it relates. Aggregated objects are very common, and application developers often re-implement the tree semantics to manage part-whole hierarchies. Reifying the Tree pattern provides developers with the Tree pattern meta-object, providing applications with a reusable construct. An essential requirement in the reification of the Tree pattern is the reification of the Aggregation relationship linking the nodes of the tree. For this, aggregation semantics must first be defined.

Typically, operations applied to whole objects are by default propagated to their aggregates. This is a powerful mechanism as it allows the implicit handling of the management of interrelated objects by the objects themselves through the manner in which they are linked together. By reifying the Aggregation relationship, the three aggregation properties of transitivity, anti-symmetry and propagation of operations can be made part of the Aggregation meta-object attributes and can be enforced by the Aggregation meta-object methods. Thus, the state of the Aggregation relationship and the operations related to maintaining the links among the objects it aggregates are localized to the link itself. Operations like copy, delete and move can now be handled implicitly and generically by the domain objects irrespective of domain structure.

Figure 2 illustrates the inclusion of the reified Aggregation relationship in the Tree pattern. In the diagram, the reified Aggregation relationship is called Aggregation, and is the link between the nodes of the tree. The Aggregation meta-object manages and controls the link between the tree nodes, and enforces the propagation of operations from parent nodes to their children. Consequently, operations applied to branch nodes are by default automatically propagated to their compositions.

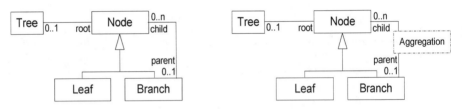

Fig. 2. The Tree Pattern with Reified Aggregation Relationship

2.2   The Generalization Meta-object

Generalization is a structural relationship between a superclass and its subclasses. The semantics of generalization revolve around inheritance, type checking and reuse, where subclasses inherit the attributes and methods defined by their superclass. The subclasses can alter the inherited features and add their own. This results in a class hierarchy organized according to similarities and differences. Unlike the Aggregation relationship, the generalization semantics are known and implemented by most programming languages, as built-in constructs integrated into the language semantics. This paper advocates extending the programming language semantics by reifying the Generalization relationship as a meta-object. Consequently, programmers can access the generalization relation as an object, giving them the capability of manipulating superclass-subclass pairs at run-time. As a result, application programs can utilize mechanisms for dynamically creating and altering the class hierarchy, which commonly require re-compilation for many languages.

As with the Aggregation relationship, generalization exhibits the transitivity property in the implicit propagation of attributes and methods from a superclass to its subclasses. The transitivity property can also be applied to the propagation of versioning between objects related by the Generalization relationship. Normally, a change in the version of the superclass automatically changes the versions of its subclasses. This behavior can be specified as the default behavior of the Generalization meta-object. Figure 3 illustrates the Tree pattern with the Generalization and Aggregation relationships between the tree nodes reified.

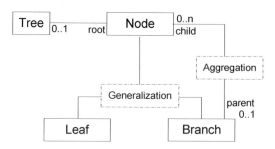

Fig. 3. Reification of the Generalization and Aggregation Relationships

2.3   The Describes Meta-object

In essence the Type Object pattern [7] has three elements, the object, its type and the Describes relationship, which relates the object to its type. The Type Object pattern illustrates the link between meta-data and data and the Describes relationship that relates the two. Consequently, this pattern links levels of multi-level systems. The upper meta-level meta-objects manage the next lower layer's objects. The meta-data that these meta-objects hold describe the data the lower level objects contain. Consequently, the Type Object pattern is a very useful and powerful tool for run-time specification of domain types.

The reification of the Describes relationship as a meta-object provides a mechanism for explicitly linking object types to objects. This strategy is similar to the approach taken for the Aggregation and Generalization relationships. The Describes meta-object provides developers with an explicit tool to dynamically create and alter domain types, and to modify domain behavior through run-time type-object alteration.

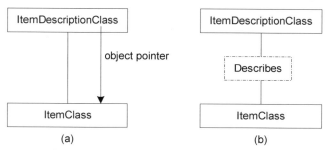

Fig. 4. The Type Object Pattern with Reified Describes Relationship

The Describes relationship does not exhibit the transitivity property. This implies that the propagation of some operations is not the default behavior since it cannot be inferred for the objects and their types. For example, versioning a type does not necessarily mean that objects of that type need to be versioned as well. In this particular case, it is the domain that dictates whether the versioning should be propagated or not. Thus, the Describes meta-object should include a mechanism for specifying propagation behavior.

Consequently, programmers can either accept the default relationship behavior or override it to implement domain-specific requirements. Figure 4 illustrates the transformation of the Type Object pattern with the use of a reified Describes relationship. The object pointer (in Figure 4a) is dropped, as it is insufficient to represent the semantics of the link relating objects and their types. Instead, the Describes meta-object (in Figure 4b) is used to manage and control the Type Object pattern relationship.

2.4   The Dependency Meta-object

The Publisher-Subscriber pattern models the dependency among related objects. To summarize the Publisher-Subscriber pattern, subscribers are automatically informed of any change in the state of its publishers. Thus, the association between the publisher and the subscriber manages and controls the communication and transfer of information between the two. Reifying the Publisher-Subscriber dependency association (hereafter referred to as the Dependency association), these mechanisms can be generically implemented and automatically enforced by the Dependency meta-object itself and taken out of the application code. This represents a significant breakthrough in the simplification of application codes and in the promotion of code reuse.

The reification of the Dependency relationship is significant in that it provides an explicit mechanism for handling change management and consistency control of data. The Dependency meta-object can be applied to base objects, to classes and types, to components of distributed systems and even to meta-objects and meta-classes. This leads to an homogeneous mechanism for handling inter-object dependencies within and between layers of multi-layered architectures.

The Event Channel of the Publisher-Subscriber pattern [11] and the Mediator of the Mediator pattern are realizations of the Dependency relationship. The Event Channel is an intervening object, which captures the implicit invocation protocol between publishers and subscribers. The Mediator encapsulates how a set of objects interacts by defining a common communication interface. By utilizing the Describes relationship, an explicit mechanism can be used to store and manage inter-object communication protocols. Figure 5 illustrates the use of reified Dependency meta-object in the Publisher-Subscriber pattern (a) and the Mediator pattern (b).

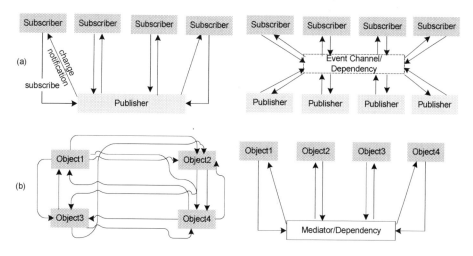

Fig. 5. The Event Channel and the Mediator as Reified Dependency

Reifying relationships as meta-objects is a fundamental step in the reification of design patterns. The four relationship meta-objects discussed above manifest the links that exist among the objects participating in the five design patterns listed in the introduction to this section. With the use of reified relationships, these five patterns can be modeled as a single graph, using the Graph pattern. Consequently, the five design patterns can be structurally reified as a Graph pattern, as shown in the next section, with the appropriate relationship meta-object to represent the semantics relating the individual pattern objects.

3   The Reified Graph Pattern

The graph and tree data structures are natural models to represent relationships among objects and classes. As the graph model is a generalization of the tree model, the graph model subsumes the tree semantics. Consequently, the graph specification is applicable to tree representations. The compositional organization of objects using the Aggregation relationship also forms a graph. Similarly, the class hierarchy using the Generalization relationship creates a graph. These two types of relationships are pervasive in computing, and the use of the Graph pattern to model both semantics provides a reusable solution for managing and controlling data compositions and class hierarchies and a valuable approach to enabling system evolution.

The way dependent objects are organized using the Dependency association also forms a graph. Dependency graphs are commonly maintained by application programs, and their implementations are often buried in them. The reification of the Dependency meta-object 'objectifies' the dependency graph and creates an explicit Publisher-Subscriber pattern. Consequently, the dependency graph is treated as an object, and can be accessed and manipulated like an object. The same argument applies to the Describes relationship found in the Type Object pattern. The link between objects and their types creates a graph. Reifying the Describes relationship results in the reification of the Type Object pattern. With the reification of the Type Object pattern, the resulting graph object allows the dynamic management of object-type pairs. This capability is essential for environments that dynamically change.

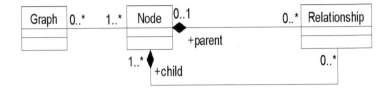

Fig. 6. An UML diagram of the Graph Meta-object

A UML diagram of the Graph meta-object is shown in Figure 6. The Node class represents the entities of the domain objects, classes, data, meta-data or components. The Relationship is the reification of the link between the Nodes. The aggregated links between the Node and the Relationship are bi-directional. Two roles are defined for the two aggregated associations - that of the parent, and that of the child. The parent aggregation, symbolized by the shaded diamond, implies that the lifecycle of the relationship is dependent on the lifecycle of the parent node. The child aggregation behaves similarly.

The use of reflection in making the Graph pattern explicit brings a number of advantages. First of all, it provides a *reusable* solution to data management. The reified Graph meta-object manages static data using Aggregation and Generalization meta-object relationships, and it makes persistent data dependencies using the Describes and Dependency relationships. As graph structures are pervasive in many domains, the capture of the graph semantics in a pattern and objectifying them results in a reusable mechanism for system designers and developers. Another benefit of having a single mechanism to represent compositions and dependencies is its provision for interoperability. With a single framework sitting on top of the persistent data, clients and components can communicate with a single known interface. This greatly simplifies the overall system design and architecture, thus improving system maintainability. Moreover, clients and components can be easily added as long as they comply with the graph interface.

Complexity is likewise catered for since related objects are treated singly and uniformly. The semantic grouping of related objects brings transparency to clients' code and the data structures provided by the Graph meta-object organize data into atomic units, which can be manipulated as single objects. Objectifying graph relationships allows the implicit and automatic propagation of operations throughout a single grouping. Another benefit in the use of the reified graph model is its reification of the link between meta-data and data. As a consequence, the Graph meta-object not only provides a reusable solution for managing domain-semantic groupings, but can also be reused to manage the links between layers of meta-level architectures.

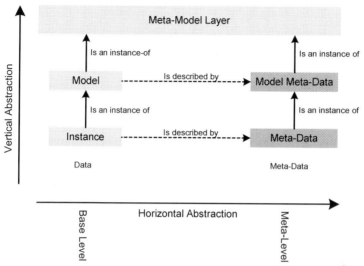

Fig. 7. Three-layer reflective Description-driven system architecture

4   Putting It All Together – Reified Patterns as the Basis of DDSs

This paper proposes that the reified Graph pattern provides the necessary building block in managing data in any DDS architecture. Figure 7 illustrates a proposed description-driven architecture. The architecture on the left-hand side is typical of layered systems such as the multi-layered architecture specification of the OMG [12]. The relationship between the layers is *an Instance-of*. The instance layer contains data that are instances of the domain model in the model layer. Similarly, the model layer is an instance of the meta-model layer. On the right hand side of the diagram is another instance of model abstraction. It shows the increasing abstraction of information from meta-data to model meta-data, where the relationship between the two is also *an Instance-of*. These two architectures provide layering and hierarchy based on abstraction of data and information models.

This paper proposes an alternative view by associating data and meta-data through description (the *is Described by* relationship). The Type Object pattern makes this possible. The Type Object pattern is a mechanism for relating data to information describing data. The link between meta-data and data using the Describes relationship promotes the dynamic creation and specification of object types. The same argument applies to the model meta-data and its description of the domain model through the Describes relationship. These two horizontal dependencies result in an horizontal meta-level architecture where the upper meta-level describes the lower base-level (see figure 8). The combination of a multi-layered architecture based on the Instance-of relationship and that of a meta-level architecture based on the Describes relationship results in a description-driven architecture (DDS). The reified Graph pattern provides a reusable mechanism for managing and controlling data compositions and dependencies. The graph model defines how domain models are created. Similarly, the graph model defines how meta-data are instantiated. By reifying the semantic grouping of objects, the Graph meta-object can be reused to hold and manage compositions and dependencies within and between layers of a DDS (see figure 9). The meta-level meta- data are organized as a meta-level graph. The base-level data are organized as a base-level graph. Relating these two graphs forms a further graph whose nodes are related by the Describes relationship. These graphs indicate the reuse of the Graph pattern in modeling relationships in a DDS architecture.

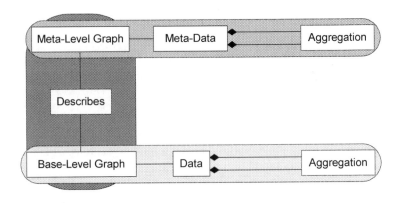

Fig. 8. The reuse of the Reified Graph Pattern in a description-driven system

5   CRISTAL as an Example of a Description-Driven System

The research which generated this paper has been carried out at the European Centre for Nuclear Research (CERN) based in Geneva, Switzerland. CERN is a scientific research laboratory studying the fundamental laws of matter, exploring what matter is made of, and what forces hold it together. Scientists at CERN build and operate complex accelerators and detectors whose construction processes are very data-intensive, highly distributed and ultimately require a computer-based system to manage the production and assembly of components. In constructing detectors like CMS, scientists require data management systems that can cope with complexity, with system evolution over time (primarily as a consequence of changing user requirements and extended development timescales) and with system scalability, distribution and interoperation.

A research project, entitled CRISTAL (Cooperating Repositories and an Information System for Tracking Assembly Lifecycles [4],[5]) has been initiated to facilitate the management of the engineering data collected at each stage of production of CMS. CRISTAL is a distributed product data and workflow management system that makes use of an OO database for its repository, a multi-layered architecture for its component abstraction and dynamic object modeling for the design of the objects and components of the system. CRISTAL is based on a DDS architecture using meta-objects.

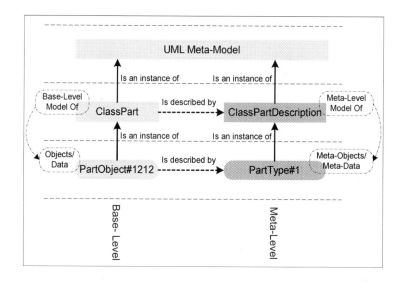

Fig. 9. The CRISTAL description-driven system architecture

The design of the CRISTAL prototype was dictated by the requirements for adaptability over extended timescales, for system evolution, for interoperability, for complexity handling and for reusability. In adopting a description-driven design approach to address these requirements, the separation of object instances from object description instances was needed. This abstraction resulted in the delivery of a three-layer description-driven architecture. The model abstraction (of instance layer, model layer, meta-model layer) has been adopted from the OMG MOF specification [13], and the need to provide descriptive information, i.e. meta-data, has been identified to address the issues of adaptability, complexity handling and evolvability.

Figure 9 illustrates the CRISTAL architecture. The CRISTAL model layer is comprised of class specifications for type descriptions (e.g. PartDescription) and class specifications for classes (e.g. Part). The instance layer is comprised of object instances of these classes (e.g. PartType#1 for PartDescription and Part#1212 for Part). The model and instance layer abstraction is based on model abstraction and *Is an instance of* relationships. The abstraction based on meta-data abstraction and *Is described by* relationships leads to two levels - the meta-level and the base-level. The meta-level is comprised of meta-objects and the meta-level model that defines them (e.g. PartDescription is the meta-level model of PartType#1 meta-object). The base-level is comprised of base objects and the base-level model which defines them.

Separating details of model types from the details of single parts allows the model type versions to be specified and managed independently, asynchronously and explicitly from single parts. Moreover, in capturing descriptions separate from their instantiations, system evolution can be catered for while production is underway and therefore provide continuity in the production process and for design changes to be reflected quickly into production. The approach of reifying a set of simple design patterns as the basis of the description-driven architecture for CRISTAL has provided the capability of catering for the evolution of a rapidly changing research data model.

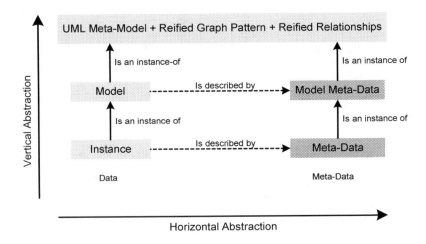

Fig. 10. Extending the UML Meta-model using a Reified Graph Pattern

In the two years of operation of CRISTAL it has gathered over 26 Gbytes of data and been able to cope with more than 20 evolutions of the underlying data schema without code or schema recompilations.

6   Conclusions

As shown in figure 10, the reified Graph pattern and the reified relationships enrich the meta-model layer by giving it the capability of creating and managing groups of related objects. The extension of the meta-model layer to include constructs for specifying domain-semantic groupings is the proposition of this paper. The meta-model layer defines concepts used in describing information in lower layers. The core OMG/UML meta-model constructs include Class, Attribute, Association, Operation and Component meta-objects. The inclusion of the Graph meta-object in the meta-model improves and enhances its modeling capability by providing an explicit mechanism for managing compositions and dependencies throughout the architecture. As a result, the reified Graph pattern provides an explicit homogeneous mechanism for specifying and managing data compositions and dependencies in a DDS architecture.

This paper has shown how reflection can be utilized in reifying design patterns. It shows, for the first time, how reified design patterns provide explicit reusable constructs for managing domain-semantic groupings. These pattern meta-objects are then used as building blocks for describing compositions and dependencies in a three layer reflective architecture - the description-driven systems architecture. The judicious use and application of the concepts of reflection, design patterns and layered models create a dynamically modifiable system which promotes reuse of code and design, which is adaptable to evolving requirements, and which can cope with system complexity. In conclusion, it is interesting to note that the OMG has recently announced the so-called Model Driven Architecture as the basis of future systems integration [14]. Such a philosophy is directly equivalent to that expounded in this and earlier papers on the CRISTAL description-driven architecture.

Acknowledgments

The authors take this opportunity to acknowledge the support of their home institutes.

References

1. G. Kiczales, "Meta-object Protocols: Why We Want Them and What Else Can They Do?",Chapter in OO Programming: The CLOS Perspective, pp 101-118, MIT Press, 1993.
2. E. Gamma, R. Helm, R. Johnson and J. Vlissides, "Design Patterns: Elements of Reusable Object-Oriented Software", Addison-Wesley, 1995.
3. J. Yoder, F. Balaguer, and R. Johnson., "Architecture and Design of Adaptive Object-Models". Proc of OOPSLA 2001, Intriguing Technology Talk, Florida. October 2001.
4. F. Estrella et al., "Handling Evolving Data Through the Use of a Description Driven Systems Architecture". LNCS Vol 1727, pp 1-11 Springer-Verlag, 1999
5. F. Estrella et al., "Meta-objects as the Basis for System Evolution". Proc of the Web Age Information Management (WAIM'2001) conference. Beijing China, June 2001.
6. F. Demers and J. Malenfant, "Reflection in Logic, Functional and Object-Oriented Programming: A Short Comparative Study", Proceedings of the International Joint Conferences on Artificial Intelligence (IJCAI), Workshop on Reflection and Meta-level Architectures and their Applications in AI, Montreal, August 1995.
7. B. Woolf and R. Johnson, "The Type Object Pattern" in Pattern Languages of Program Design 3, Addison-Wesley, 1997. Originally presented at the Third Conference on Pattern Languages of Programs (PLoP), 1996.
8. F. Estrella, "Objects, Patterns and Descriptions in Data Management", PhD Thesis, University of the West of England, Bristol, England, December 2000.
9. M. Blaha, "Aggregation of Parts of Parts of Parts", Journal of Object-Oriented Programming (JOOP), September 1993.
10. M. Blaha and W. Premerlani, "Object-Oriented Modeling and Design for Database Applications", Prentice Hall, 1998.
11. F. Bushmann, et.al., "Pattern-Oriented Software Architecture: A System of Patterns", John Wiley & Sons, 1996.
12. The Object Management Group (OMG), URL http://www.omg.org
13. The Meta- Object Facility (MOF) Specification, URL: http://www.dstc.edu.au/Products/CORBA/MOF/.
14. OMG Publications., "Model Driven Architectures - The Architecture of Choice for a Changing World". See http://www.omg.org/mda/index.htm

Managing Configuration
with Evolving Constraints in Design Databases

Tom W. Carnduff [1] and Jeevani S. Goonetillake [2]

[1]School of Computing, University of Glamorgan, Pontypridd CF37 1DL UK
tcarnduf@glam.ac.uk
[2]Computing Division, UWIC Business School, UK

Abstract. Artifacts in engineering design are structurally complex and may be represented in software as recursively composite objects. Due to the evolutionary nature of the design process each artifact and its components may evolve through several versions. This paper describes enhanced database system facilities that are used to group mutually consistent component versions together into useful configurations. The versioning system includes integrity management facilities that allow evolving design constraints to be captured flexibly at individual component/object level. In order to permit evolution, integrity constraints are represented within versionable objects, so-called constraint version objects (CVOs). Inter-dependency constraints can be modelled to express the consistency semantics necessary to combine component artifact versions into useful configurations. The evolution of these configurations can be captured in the database, as configurations are also represented as versioned objects.

1   Introduction

Design objects are either primitive (fine-grained objects) or composite (coarse-grained). Generally a composite object is composed of its own attributes and other objects. These constituent objects may themselves be composite or primitive. A composite design artefact can be logically decomposed into its component parts which in turn may be decomposed recursively in such a way to allow the individual/group of designers to address them separately [1]. Subsequently during the design process, this decomposed complex artifact is recomposed by combining its constituent component objects. In a versioning environment each composite and component design object may have number of versions making this composition task cumbersome. For example, if a composite object/artifact is composed of m objects, each one in n versions, there can be up to n^m different combinations to be used for the construction of configurations out of which only a few may be actually consistent or relevant. A configuration is defined as a structurally composite object formed by combining other configurations (known as sub configurations) and versions of different objects. Useful configurations are formed from versions of constituent objects that are consistent together [2]. Even though several version models have been proposed in the literature only a few address configuration management. Since different configurations may exist due to differing constituent version combinations, it would be useful if the designer had the facility to store meaningful configurations and to keep track of configuration evolution. This can be achieved if configurations can be managed as

A. Olivé (Eds.): ER 2003 Ws, LNCS 2784, pp. 88–99, 2003.

versions. Another benefit in this situation is that versions and configurations may be freely combined to construct higher-level configurations [3].

To produce a consistent configuration all of the component versions participating in that configuration should satisfy the inter-dependency constraints imposed on them. Inter-dependency constraints are known as global constraints since their validity spans multiple objects. Successful validation of inter-dependency constraints ensures that a configuration is consistent with its constituent component versions. Consequently, it is important to augment configuration management with an integrity mechanism that checks each configuration for data correctness and consistency. A common problem encountered during the design process is that of frequent constraint changes. Different versions of the same configuration object may have to satisfy different sets of inter-dependency constraints at different times. In [4] an integrity validation model for object versions was presented, which considered the means of representing and managing evolving integrity constraints in a collaborative engineering design environment. We have not located in the literature, a version model that deals with the consistency of design configurations, through constraint management. The objective of this paper is to show how this may be achieved.

2   Related Work

Even though version management and configuration management are strongly related areas, little attention has been paid in existing version models to configuration management. Most proposed configuration management systems are either superficial or otherwise unsatisfactory. Versions of different objects are bound together either statically or dynamically to form a configuration [5, 6, 7, 8, 9]. Dynamic references are resolved later by placing the versions that go together in the same *layer* [10], *environment* [11], database version [2] or assigning these versions to the same configuration identifier [12]. The selection of these versions is based on either the most recent or the default version. Significantly, these models do not provide any integrity mechanism to capture possible inconsistencies between the versions forming a configuration. This makes the formation of inconsistent configurations very likely. It is a designer's responsibility to check whether the constructed configuration is consistent. Furthermore, some configuration management mechanisms are inherently unsatisfactory due to:

- version proliferation (cause by static binding) [5, 6, 7, 8, 9], or
- problems in sharing component versions between configurations (e.g. an object version cannot be part of more than one configuration) [13], or
- explicit copying of versions every time they are used in a configuration [12], or
- lack of facilities for the designer to save and track important configurations for his/her reference, as these systems can deal with only one configuration at a time, e.g. at the released time [14].

Versions and configurations are treated as different concepts in most of the existing version models. This distinction provides some drawbacks, such as difficulty in freely combining versions and configurations to form higher-level configurations [3]. Some research has focused on reducing this distinction between versions and configurations by treating and managing configurations as versions [3, 15]. Nevertheless, none of these version models addresses support for the consistency of configurations using evolving constraints.

The model proposed by Doucet and Monties [16] addresses both versions and evolving integrity constraints using a Database Version (DBV) approach [2]. Each database version contains a configuration composed of one version of each constituent object. Constraint evolution also involves the production of multiple DBVs. Consistency is confined to each database version and consequent configuration level. The checking of some constraints spans multi-database versions, which adds to the complexity. It is not clear whether this model can be applied to a cooperative and distributed design environment. We believe that in a cooperative design environment, the system may end up with a large number of database versions, which will impose a considerable storage and organisational overhead.

3   Version Binding

There are two object-binding mechanisms used in forming configurations namely, static and dynamic (or generic). With static binding each composite version refers directly to specific sub component versions. The creation of a new sub component version may lead to the creation of a new composite object version with consequent version proliferation. To illustrate version proliferation (or version percolation) we consider a bicycle tyre system (figure 1(a)), which consists of the two components wheel and tyre. A wheel is in turn composite, with the two components hub and rim. The first version of the composite tyre system is depicted in figure 1(b). Suppose a new version of rim (R2) is created then figure 1(c) shows how this leads to the creation of new versions of the other components in the composition hierarchy.

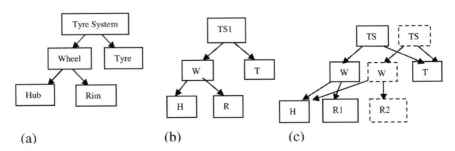

(a)   (b)   (c)

Fig. 1. Static Binding

With dynamic binding on the other hand a composite version refers to the generic version of its components and not to a specific version. In this paper, a configuration which uses dynamic binding is referred to as a generic configuration. Generic references are often more appropriate than static references for to two reasons [14]. Firstly, versioning a component object does not lead to the creation of a new version of the composite artifact (and vice versa). Secondly, it is possible to bind the generic reference to any required version of the component object so long as the inter-dependency constraints are satisfied. The replacement of a dynamic reference with a reference to a specific version is called *dynamic reference resolution*. The disadvantages associated with dynamic referencing relate to the extra levels of indirection. On balance, however, dynamic references are preferable to static references and we have adopted this technique in our configuration management model. The generic configuration concept is used initially to identify the constituent component objects of the composite artifact. To this end, we recognise two possible ways of using dynamic references. We illustrate these points using a bicycle wheel consisting of the two components, rim and hub.

i) Version-Generic: In this method each version of a composite object refers to the generic versions of its component objects as depicted in figure 2 (a). The shaded nodes denote a generic configuration. With this method the composite object is modelled (in this case wheel) as shown in figure 2(b) with references to generic versions of the component objects. Each instance of this class represents a generic configuration.

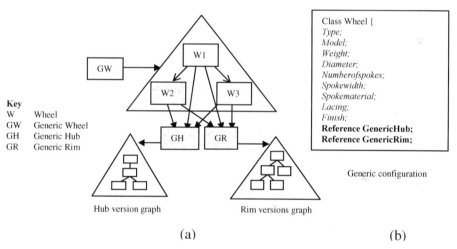

Fig. 2. Dynamic Binding – (Version-Generic)

ii) Generic-Generic: In this method the generic version of the composite object refers to the generic versions of its components (figure 3 (a)). The versions of the composite object can be handled independently from its components, while an indication of its components can still be provided through the generic version. This mechanism enables the composite object to be modelled as a separate object independent from generic references as shown figure 3(b). The shaded nodes in figure 3(a) indicate the generic configuration. There is only one generic configuration unlike the version-generic approach. This is a deviation from the widely used generic configuration representation, however, it still achieves its main purpose of identifying component objects in a generic configuration.

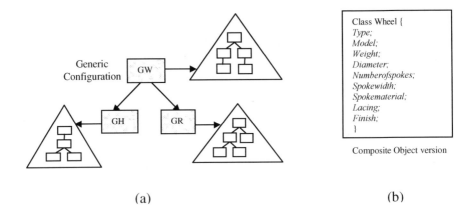

(a)   (b)

Fig. 3. Dynamic Binding – (Generic-Generic)

Most existing configuration management systems that employ dynamic binding use the *Version-Generic* approach. Dynamic reference resolution takes place only when the configuration is to be released or accessed. In general, one configuration is constructed when required, based on a version selection procedure (for example by combining all of the default versions, or the most recent versions in the composition hierarchy). This method leads to the creation of different configurations at different times as new versions are introduced. Consequently information on previously created configurations is lost. We submit that this is inappropriate since the designer should be able to save important configurations for later reference. Furthermore, there is no guarantee that the selected versions are consistent together. For example it would be incorrect to assume that the latest version of one component would always be consistent with the latest version of another component, without checking their inter-dependency constraints.

4   Configuration Management Requirements

In practical terms, the designer should be able to construct configurations by selecting and combining component versions. The environment should be flexible enough to allow experimentation with different version combinations. For example the designer may experiment with a bicycle structure version (a sub configuration of bicycle) made of titanium with both hybrid and mountain bicycle versions (figure 4(a)). Alternatively the designer may experiment with a mountain bicycle version with structure versions made of different materials (figure 4(b)). The designer should be provided with a facility to store important configurations and to keep track of configuration evolution. The sub configurations should be able to be combined freely with other versions and sub configurations to construct higher-level configurations. These objectives can be achieved by managing configurations as versions. From the system point of view maintaining a number of configuration versions should not lead to the data redundancy that would arise due to the unnecessary copying of object versions for each configuration.

Fig. 4. Combining versions for configurations

Consistency between the version objects participating in a configuration is achieved by satisfying the inter-dependent constraints imposed on them. In terms of the designer's role in managing the data validation aspects of configuration consistency, he/she should be freed from the need for:

- typing selection criteria to produce views every time a configuration is constructed, or
- changing and compiling application programs when constraints change, or
- any manual checking of the inter-dependency constraints to ensure the consistency of configurations.

Checking the consistency of the selected versions of the configuration should be handled automatically by the configuration management system based on the pre-defined inter-dependency constraints.

5   Proposed Configuration Management Model

In meeting the configuration management requirements set out in the previous section, we have utilised the version model described by Goonetillake et al. [4]. We begin by looking at how composite artifacts are represented within versioned configurations using dynamic referencing. If a composite artifact is modelled using dynamic referencing (figure 2(a)), it is not possible to replace the generic version reference with a specific version reference unless the generic and specific versions are both instances of the same class. Since they contain different information they are instances of different classes. A class must be declared which incorporates references to the specific version types, so that specific configurations can be constructed.

5.1   The Configuration Object and Version Sharing

It is evident that both of the methods of moving from generic to specific configurations are problematic. Attribute values must be copied every time a specific configuration is created. Consequently, there will be considerable data duplication as different component versions are selected for configuring with a single composite version during tentative experimentation. Figure 5(a) shows the data redundancy involved in tentatively combining a wheel version with a number of rim and hub versions. As a solution to these issues we have used the *generic-generic* approach (option (ii) in section 3) to represent the generic configuration. This allows us to define a composite object with a separate class which is independent of references to generic versions - see figure 3(b). A separate configuration object is used to combine the corresponding object versions to form a configuration - see figure 5 (b). This provides the flexibility required to combine object versions whilst avoiding redundancy through version sharing. Modelling the configuration object in this way allows the selection of specific versions of a particular object (irrespective of whether it is physically composite) and versions of a configuration object. For example a wheel object and wheel configuration are two different entities. A wheel object version is part of a wheel configuration version. This may not represent the aggregation (is part of) relationship that should exist between a composite object version and its component versions (as in figure 5 (a)). However, the advantage of this approach is that it enables the same composite object version to be shared by many configurations without data duplication (figure 5(b)). The version of the main/composite object (in this case the wheel object version) is the key object in the configuration version. The component versions should be selected in combination with this key object version. The key object version should reflect the main characteristics of the whole configuration version (for example the wheel object version should represent the main features of the wheel configuration version, for example a small wheel with 32 spokes, coloured blue weighing less than 900g). This is important in the validation of inter-dependency constraints when constructing higher-level configurations.

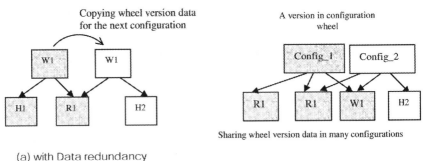

Fig. 5. Constructing Specific Configuration versions

5.2   Configurations as Versions

We now go on to illustrate how configurations are managed as versions. For illustrative purposes we return to the composite tyre system artifact (figure 1(a)). From the configuration management point of view, the composite object wheel with its hub and rim form a sub configuration version. Unless otherwise stated sub configurations are referred to as configurations since there is no semantic difference in the way they are both managed. The generic version of a wheel refers to the generic versions of both hub and rim, to form a generic configuration (figure 6 (a)). Each generic version in turn refers to its corresponding version set. The designer explicitly creates specific configuration versions by selecting specific versions from each version set. A specific configuration version is an instance of the corresponding configuration object class, which is modelled to combine the object versions that go together – see figure 6(b). To this end, references are made from the configuration object to the corresponding constituent objects (e.g. figure 6(b)). As shown in figure 6(c) it is possible to share object versions between configuration versions without duplicating data.

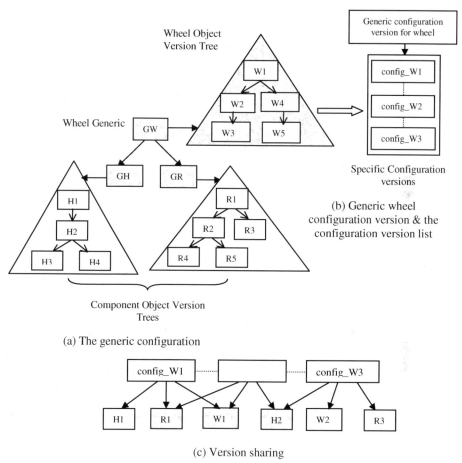

(a) The generic configuration

(b) Generic wheel configuration version & the configuration version list

(c) Version sharing

Fig. 6. Construction of wheel sub configuration

A configuration version can have at most one version from each component. Each configuration version is associated with its version information including configuration number, time of creation and status details (e.g. default, active, last, deleted). The configuration number is generated and assigned by the system so that each configuration is identified uniquely within the system. The designer has freedom to set any configuration as the default configuration so long as it adheres to the currently applicable set of constraints (see section 6). The new configuration versions are not derived from preceding configurations, but are created from scratch by selecting corresponding object versions. Consequently a configuration version set is represented as a list and it is not therefore possible to logically cluster revisions of alternative configurations. However, an alternative configuration version and its revisions are identifiable through the use of configuration number. As with version management, this list is referenced by a generic configuration *version* (not the generic configuration referred to earlier), which contains meta information relating to the configuration version set (e.g. the default configuration, total number of configurations, the last configuration, owner of the configuration). In this way, higher-level configurations can be constructed by freely combining configuration object versions.

A version may or may not belong to a configuration. Moreover, an object version which is consistent in one configuration, may not be consistent in another configuration. A configuration version can be constructed in either a top down or bottom up manner. Our approach allows partial configurations to be defined where one or more constituent object versions have not yet been selected.

6   Integrity Validation Model

6.1   Constraint Evolution

It is necessary to check whether the selected versions constitute a consistent configuration through satisfying a given set of constraints. The constraints that are used to validate configurations are known as inter-dependent or global constraints. The scope of these constraints spans multiple objects. At the configuration level, validation is mainly concerned with selecting valid sub components. However, a set of design constraints will evolve over time with modifications [17, 18, 19, 20], the addition of new constraints and the omission of existing constraints. A constraint management framework for engineering design was described by Goonetillake et al. [4]. In essence this framework is based around an object version model in which the constraint categories are value based (e.g. range, enumeration, relationship). The constraints are represented and stored in Constraint Version Objects (CVOs). A CVO aggregates a set of currently active constraints applicable to a particular artifact. Constraint evolution is effected by producing new CVOs, that is new versions of the set of constraints contained in a CVO. This model takes cognisance that a designer/user is not a computer programmer. The designer is provided with a graphical user interface to create new CVOs in a form-filling manner in the event of constraint changes. The creation of an executable CVO is transparent to the designer and handled by the system.

In summary a child CVO contains only modified and new constraints and inherits unchanged constraints from its parent CVO. This avoids the unnecessary redefinition of constraints. Usually, the last CVO created in the system for a particular artifact will become the default CVO for that artifact. The default CVO for each artifact determines the validity of its versions. The new versions are automatically associated with the default CVO at the creation time. In a collaborative and distributed design environment the default CVO enables designers to identify consistently the current active CVO for a particular artifact. The default object version of an artifact should generally be linked to the default CVO. This work on CVOs is related to object versioning, and as the configuration management model presented here deals with configuration versions, CVO concepts can be applied to configuration management. In constructing a configuration version it is important that each constituent version is individually consistent with the set of constraints in the corresponding default CVO.

In a CAD environment some (global) constraints on complex objects may be decomposed into a set of local constraints on sub components or leaf objects [21]. For example a weight constraint on an artifact may be decomposed into local weight constraints on its sub components as shown in figure 7. A change in such a global constraint will require a change to the corresponding local constraints. However, this change propagation is not automatic and should be carried out by collaborating designers through a process of discussion. Because constraints are created and refined by human specialists through analysis and engineering judgement, no design framework/model should change the design information (constraints) arbitrarily without the necessary human involvement.

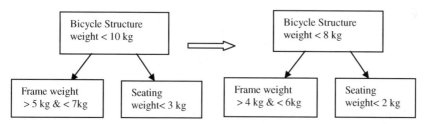

Fig. 7. Breaking down of global constraints to local constraints

The terms local and global are relative in relation to CVOs and depend on the number of levels in the design database hierarchy. A global object at one level may be a local object at the next level up in the hierarchy.

6.2   Configuration Versions and CVOs

In this section we give a detailed explanation of the means by which the integrity validation system validates configuration versions. The explanation is framed around the wheel structure example. Versions of the wheel object are first validated against their local constraints (e.g. diameter < 55 cm, {blue, red} $\supseteq$ finish) . These local constraints are imposed on the attribute values of the wheel object. Each CVO contains the active set of local constraints for the wheel object at some point in time.

Since the sub components are first validated against their local constraints, the constituent component versions of a configuration are assumed to be individually consistent with their local constraints. Consequently, a configuration version will only have to be validated against its global constraints (or inter-dependency constraints) as imposed on the constituent versions of that configuration. These global constraints specify the dependencies between attribute values in each selected component object version. For example for the wheel configuration, the inter-dependencies could be (number of spoke holes in hub = number of holes in rim) and (wheel finish = blue) $\rightarrow$ (rim finish = black and hub finish = blue). Each configuration version is automatically associated with the default CVO to be validated against the constraints in that CVO at its creation time

Tyre system object versions are managed in the same way as wheel object versions and are validated independently against their local constraints. The construction of a tyre system configuration version requires the combination of a tyre system object version, a wheel configuration version and a tyre object version. The resulting configuration version will have to be validated against its corresponding global constraints. These global constraints specify the dependencies between attribute values in the selected tyre system, wheel configuration and tyre object version (for example wheel weight + tyre weight < 1.5 kg). Each global CVO contains the active set of global constraints for the tyre system configuration at some point in time.

7   Conclusion

In this paper we have presented a configuration management model in which configurations are managed as versions. This enables the designer to store useful configurations and to keep track of configuration evolution. Moreover, it reduces the distinction between the version and configuration concepts and thus provides the facility to freely combine configurations and versions together to form higher-level configurations. The way in which the configuration object is modelled provides the means to be able to flexibly combine any composite artifact version with any number of constituent versions in the construction of different configurations, without data duplication. The uniform treatment of versions and configurations provides the means to combine them freely in the construction of higher-level configurations. The integrity validation system checks the consistency of versions selected for a configuration. The configuration model manages the consistency of object versions (including configuration versions) through the management of constraint evolution. The system described has been implemented in prototype form using the Java programming language, the Objectivity object database system, and for constraint management aspects of the work, the Prolog declarative programming language. For reasons of space no further consideration is given to implementation here, but will be described in a future paper.

References

1. Sauce, R., Martini, K., and Powell, G. (1992). Object Oriented Approaches for Integrated Engineering Design Systems, *ASCE Journal of Computing in Civil Engineering*, 6(3), 248-265.
2. Cellary, W., Jomier, G. (1990). Consistency of Versions in Object Oriented Databases, *Proc. 16th Int. Conf. on Very Large Databases (VLDB 16)*, 432-441, Australia.

3. Golendziner, L.G., Santos, C.S. (1995). Versions and Configurations in Object-Oriented Database Systems : A Uniform Treatment, *Proc. 7th Int. Conf. on Management of Data*, Pune, India, 18-37.
4. Goonetillake, J.S., Carnduff, T.W., and Gray, W.A (2001). Integrity Validation for Object Versions in a Co-operative Design Environment, *Proc. 6th Int. Conf. on Computer Supported Cooperative Work in Design (CSCWD'01)*, eds. Shen, W., Lin, Z., Barthes, J. and Kamel, M., Ontario, IEEE, pg:89-94.
5. Krishnamurthy, K., and Law, K. (1995). A Data Management Model for Design Change Control, *Concurrent Engineering: Research and Applications*, 3(4): 329-343.
6. Andonoff, E., Hubert, G., Parc, A., and Zurfluh, G. (1996). Integrating Versions in the OMT Models, *Proc. 15th Intl. Conf. on Conceptual Modeling*, Cottbus, Germany, 472-487.
7. Ahmed, R. & Navathe, S. (1991). Version Management of Composite objects in CAD databases, *Proc. ACM SIGMOD Int. Conf. on Management of Data*, eds. Clifford, J. and King, R., 218-227, Denver, USA.
8. Kafer, W., and Schoning, H. (1992). Mapping a Version Model to a Complex-Object Data Model, Proc. *8th Int. Conf. on Data Engineering*, Tempe, Arizona, 348-357.
9. Santoyridis, I., Carnduff, T.W., Gray, W.A ,and Miles, C.J. (1997). An Object Versioning System to Support Collaborative Design within a Concurrent Engineering Context. *Proc. 15th British National Conf. on Databases (BNCOD 15)*, Advances in Databases, 184-199. London, UK, Springer.
10. Katz, R.H. (1990). Towards a Unifying Framework for Version Modeling in Engineering Databases, *ACM Computing Surveys*, 22(4), 376-408.
11. Dittrich, K.R., and Lorie, R. (1988). Version Support for Engineering Database Systems, *IEEE Transactions on Software Engineering*, 14 (4), 429-437.
12. Carnduff, T.W. (1993). *Supporting Engineering Design with Object-Oriented Databases*, PhD thesis, Department of Computer Science, University of Wales Cardiff, UK.
13. Kim, W., Banerjee, J., Chou, H.T., Garza, J.F., and Woelk, D. (1987). Composite Object Support in an Object-Oriented Database systems, *Proc. 2nd Int. Conf. on Object-Oriented Programming Systems, Languages and Applications (OOPSLA'87)*, Florida, 118-125.
14. Sciore, E. (1994). Versioning and Configuration Management in an Object-Oriented Data Model, *VLDB Journal*, 3(1), 77-106.
15. Al-Khudair, A., Gray, W.A., and Miles, J.C. (2001). Object-Oriented Versioning in a Concurrent Engineering Design Environment, *Proc. British National Conf. on Database (BNCOD 18)*, Lecture Notes in Computer Science 2097, Springer, 105-125.
16. Doucet, A., and Monties, S. (1997). Versions of Integrity Constraints in Multiversion Databases. *Proc. 8th Int. Conf. on Database and Expert System Applications (DEXA'97)*, pg. 252-261, Toulouse, France, Springer.
17. Dieter, E.G. (1991). *Engineering Design, A Materials and Processing Approach*, Second Edition, McGraw-Hill, Inc.
18. Thompson, D.R., Tomski, T., Ellacott, S.W., and Kuczora, P. (1993). An Expert System for Preliminary Design of Timber Roofs, *Information Technology for Civil and Structural Engineers*, eds. B.H.Topping and I.Khan, Civil-Comp Press, 187-196.
19. Ramachandran,B. (1989). A Framework for Design Problem Solving, *Research in Engineering Design*, 1(2), 75-86.
20. Ram,D.J., Vivekananda, N., Rao, C.S.. and Mohan.,N.K. (1997). Constraint Meta-Object: A New Object Model for Distributed Collaborative Designing, *IEEE Transactions on Systems, Man and Cybernetics*, 27(2), 208-220.
21. Lin, J., Fox, M.S., and Bilgic, T. (1996). A Requirement Ontology for Engineering Design, *Proc. Advances in Concurrent Engineering (CE'96)*, eds. Sobolewski, M, Fox, M., Toronto, 343-351.

Intentions of Operations –
Characterization and Preservation

Mira Balaban[*] and Steffen Jurk[**]

[1] Ben-Gurion University
Beer-Sheva, Israel
mira@cs.bgu.ac.il
[2] Brandenburg Technical University
Cottbus, Germany
sj@informatik.tu-cottbus.de

Abstract. Frequent changes of software requirements imply changes of the underlying database, like database schema, integrity constraints, as well as database transactions and programs. Tools like ERWin, DBMain and Silverrun help developers in applying these changes. Yet, the automatic derivation might pose a problem: Since the developer is not aware of the details of the derivation applications, the resulting programs might include contradictory actions. That is, intentions of programs might be reversed by the automatic derivation, resulting a different behavior than expected by the developer.

In this paper, a compile-time algorithm that achieves preservation of intentions is suggested. The algorithm revises a composite program into a program without contradictory actions. It is based on a fine analysis of effects, that is sensitive to computation paths. The output program is expressive and efficient since it interleaves run-time sensitive analysis of already reduced effects within the input program. The compile-time reduction of effects accounts for the efficiency; the run-time sensitivity of effects accounts for the expressiveness. The novelty of the proposed approach is in combining static and dynamic analysis in a way that run-time overhead is minimized without sacrificing the expressivity of the resulting program.

1   Introduction

Frequent changes of software requirements imply changes of the underlying database, like database schema, integrity constraints, as well as database transactions and programs. Methods supporting the design of database programs [9,10,8,13] and tools like ERWin, DBMain and Silverrun help developers in applying these changes. Yet, the automatic derivation might pose a problem:

[*] This work was supported in part by the Paul Ivanir Center for Robotics and Production Management at Ben-Gurion University of the Negev.
[**] This research was supported by the DFG, Berlin-Brandenburg Graduate School in Distributed Information Systems (DFG grant no. GRK 316).

A. Olivé et al. (Eds.): ER 2002 Ws, LNCS 2784, pp. 100–111, 2003.
© Springer-Verlag Berlin Heidelberg 2003

Since the developer is not aware of the details of the derivation applications, the resulting programs might include contradictory actions. That is, intentions of programs might be reversed by the automatic derivation, resulting a different behavior than expected by the developer. The work described in this paper deals with the characterization and preservation of program intentions.

Example 1. Assume a developer is designing (changing) a database where inclusion and exclusion dependencies have to be inserted or removed, due to some changing requirements. The design tool repairs insertions or deletions by adding necessary insertions or deletions, so that the current dependencies are satisfied. The problem is that certain dependency combinations can lead to intention contradiction, of which neither the developer nor the users, are aware.

For example, assume a unary relation A and a binary relation B, with an inclusion relation between $\pi_1(B)$ (the first column of B) and A, and an exclusion relation between $\pi_2(B)$ and A. The design tool repairs an insertion of (x, y) into B by inserting x into A and deleting y from A. Analogously, an insertion of x into A is repaired by deleting from B all tuples with x as a first element. For the action $insert(B, (x, y))$ the following consistent program S is derived:

$$S(x, y) = insert(B, (x, y));$$
$$\text{if } x \notin A \text{ then}$$
$$insert(A, x);$$
$$\text{while } \sigma_{2=x}(B) \neq \emptyset \text{ do: } delete(B, \bar{t}) \text{ where } \bar{t} \in \sigma_{2=x}(B);$$
$$\text{if } y \in A \text{ then}$$
$$delete(A, y);$$
$$\text{while } \sigma_{1=y}(B) \neq \emptyset \text{ do: } delete(B, \bar{t}) \text{ where } \bar{t} \in \sigma_{1=y}(B);$$

Now consider the action $insert(B, (x, x))$, whose natural intention is $(x, x) \in B$. A careful examination of $S(x, x)$ reveals that while the dependency requirements are indeed being enforced, the original intention of an action insert $(B, (x, x))$ might get lost. That is, the tuple (x, x) is not inserted, although A might be changed. An intention preservation policy requires that if the original intention is lost than the repair program is rejected and not completed successfully. In this example it means that $S(x, x)$ should be rejected if the tuple (x, x) can not be inserted properly.

Problems of intention contradiction arise frequently in Rule Triggering Systems (RTSs) ([13,7,14]), and have also been studied within the context of integrity enforcement in databases, where repairing updates can undo each other ([2,11]). However, the problem is not handled in regular database maintenance systems like RTSs.

In this paper we introduce an intention (effect) preserving mechanism, that combines static analysis of an action with run-time tests. The mechanism is based on characterization of contradictory actions. Actions are assumed to have *intentions* (*effects*), which are logic constraints. Actions contradict if their intentions do so ([5]). The intentions of actions (atomic operations) are set by the user (action initiator). The intentions of programs (composite operations like transactions) are computed by the program management system.

The effect preserving mechanism that we introduce in this paper is a program transformation. The main idea is to augment computation paths that might lead to an unsatisfiable intention, with necessary intention preserving tests. The delicate problem here is to avoid unnecessary tests that might lead to unnecessary rejections, and still achieve performance that improves run-time testing for intention violation. Therefore, there is a need to characterize intentions (effects) in a way that distinguishes between actions that lie on different computation paths, and reduce the amount of intention testing that is required at run-time. The mechanism suggested here combines static transformation with run-time tests. At compile-time, a computation tree that analyzes all computation paths of the program is constructed, and the program is augmented with tree navigation and intention tests. The nodes of the tree are associated with maximally reduced constraints that capture the intention preservation requirements.

The mechanism achieves a better performance than run-time methods for intention preservation since the time consuming operation of tree construction and constraint reduction is applied at compile-time. Only statically unresolved intentions are left for run-time evaluation. The run-time overhead is linear in the size of the program since the size of the reduced conditions is independent of the program size, and is expected to be rather small and easy to evaluate. The novelty of our approach is in combining compile-time and run-time processing in a way that run-time overhead is minimized, without sacrificing the expressivity of the revised program.

In Section 2 the language of programs is defined, and Section 3 introduces the path sensitive characterization of effects (intentions of actions and programs). Section 4 presents the combined static-dynamic revision of programs, that enforces the effect preservation property. Section 5 concludes the paper.

2   A Restricted Language of Database Programs

The language of database programs studied in this paper is restricted to an imperative language with a sequence and a conditional combinator. Programs are built over a finite set of typed *state variables* X (a state space). A *state* is a well typed value assignment to the variables in X. For example, in a relational database with relations $R_1, \ldots, R_n$, the state space is $\{R_1, \ldots, R_n\}$, and any assignment of concrete relations to the relation variables results a database state. A language over X is denoted $\mathcal{L}(X)$.

The language symbols include, besides the state variables, input and local variables, and self-evaluating symbols (language constants). Input variables are not assignable. The primitive actions are *skip* (a no-op operation), *fail* (rollback, the impossible action), and *assignment action* – well typed assignments to state variables. Assignments include, besides the assigned state variable, only input variables and constants, i.e., non-assignable symbols. The *fail* action leads to the *undefined state*, which in transactional databases correspond to a *rollback*, which undoes undefined states by restoring the old state.

The two constructors that are studied in this paper are sequential composition, denoted $(S_1; S_2)$ and guarded deterministic choice (conditional), denoted (if P then S_1 else S_2) where S_1 and S_2 are programs and P a condition. We use if P then S for abbreviating if P then S else *skip*. The formal semantics of the language is defined as in Dijkstra's guarded commands language ([1,6,2].

3   Path Sensitive Characterization of Effects

In this section we define the effects of composite programs, on the basis of effects of primitive actions. First we define effects of sequences of primitive actions. We distinguish between *desired effects*, denoted $effects_D(S)$, to *executed effects*, denoted $effects_E(S)$: The first, expresses the aggregated desired effects of all primitive actions in a program and it might not hold after the program is completed. The second, expresses the historical effects of all primitive actions in a program, as they were when executed, and it always holds after a program is executed. Then, we introduce the notion of a *computation tree* associated with a program. Finally, we define the desired/executed effects of a program as the conjunction of the guarded desired/executed effects of the leaves in its computation tree, respectively. The section ends with a formal definition of the *effect preservation* property of programs.

3.1   Effects of Primitive Actions

Primitive actions are atomic elements of the language $\mathcal{L}(X)$. Their intentions, denoted $effects(S)$ express postconditions that should hold following the action. The desired/executed distinction does not apply to primitive actions, since their effects are both desired and executed. For the two primitives *skip* and *fail*, their effects derive from their intended semantics[1]: $effects(skip) = true$, $effects(fail) = false$. For assignments, the effects are domain specific and developer provided. Clearly, we expect that developer provided effects are non-trivial, e.g. $effects(S) = true$.

Example 2 (Possible effects of primitive assignments in different domains).

- **Sets** – insert or delete an element e from a list x: $effects(x := insert(x, e)) = (e \in x)$, and $effects(x := delete(x, e)) = (e \notin x)$.
- **Lists** – insert an nth element e to a list x: $effects(x := insert(x, n, e)) = (e = element(x, n))$.
- **Trees** – insert an element e to a tree x: $effects(x := insert(x, path, e)) = (e = element(x, path))$.

---

[1] Recall that *fail* is the impossible action, i.e., rejection. Its semantics in Dijkstra's guarded commands language [1,6] states that "everything holds following a *fail*".

The effects in the last example involve conditions that can be expressed in terms of the final values of the state variables, i.e., static conditions. In this paper we deal only with static effects, and most of the examples are taken from the domain of sets.

3.2   Effects of Sequences of Primitive Actions

Primitive actions modify the values of state variables. These modifications have to be considered in the account of the desired and executed (historical) effects, because repetitive modifications of a state variable might interfere. Therefore, the computation of effects requires repeated application of the modifications to the state variables. The following examples demonstrate these notions in the set domain. They use the actions $x := insert(x, e)$ and $x := delete(x, e)$, for a set variable x and an element variable e, with the effect formulae $e \in x$ and $e \notin x$, respectively.

Example 3 (Desired Effects). Consider the program:

$$S(e_1, e_2, e_3) = \big(x := insert(x, e_1); x := insert(x, e_2); x := delete(x, e_3)\big)$$

The desired effects are: $effects_D(S(e_1, e_2, e_3)) = e_1 \in x \wedge e_2 \in x \wedge e_3 \notin x$. Clearly, $effects_D(S(e_1, e_2, e_3))$ does not hold in case that $e_1 = e_3$ or $e_2 = e_3$.

Example 4 (Executed (Historical) Effects). Consider the program S above. The executed effects of S certainly include $e_3 \notin x$. The insertion of e_2 occurs before the last deletion. Therefore, in terms of the final value of x, its effect is $e_2 \in insert(x, e_3)$, i.e., the last *delete* action must be reversed. The insertion of e_1 occurs before the insertion of e_2. Therefore, in terms of the final value of x, its effect is $e_1 \in delete(insert(x, e_3), e_2)$. Altogether we have: $(e_1 \in delete(insert(x, e_3), e_2)) \wedge (e_2 \in insert(x, e_3)) \wedge (e_3 \notin x)$. Yet, these executed effects fall short of handling the case where $e_1 = e_2$. The problem has to do with idempotent actions (like set insertion and deletion), where repetitions are redundant since $((x\ op\ a)\ op\ a) = (x\ op\ a)$. If $e_1 = e_2$, the second insertion is a *skip* action, but in the executed effects account it is reversed by a non-*skip* action.

We handle sequences of redundant primitive actions by factoring out repetitions. In this example, the second action $x := insert(x, e_2)$ is transformed into $x := insert(x, e_2 - e_1)$, where the element subtraction stands for singleton set subtraction. Therefore, the executed effects are: $effects_E(S(e_1, e_2, e_3)) = (e_1 \in delete(insert(x, e_3), e_2 - e_1)) \wedge (e_2 \in insert(x, e_3)) \wedge (e_3 \notin x)$

Definition 1 (Desired Effects). *For simple actions that involve a single state variable, the desired effects of a sequence are simply the conjunction of the effects of the primitive actions (as in the above example).*

Definition 2 (Executed Effects). *Let S be a sequence of primitive actions $x_1 := A_1, \ldots, x_n := A_n$. The executed effects of S are obtained in two steps:*

1. **Factorization**: *Each action $x_i := A_i$ is factored with respect to all previous actions $x_j := A_j$ where $x_i = x_j$ and $j < i$. The exact factorization procedure is type dependent.*
2. **Inductive definition**:
   (a) *For a primitive action U, $effects_E(U) = effects(U)$.*
   (b) – *$effects_E(S;\ skip) = effects_E(S)$.*
       – *$effects_E(S;\ fail) = false$.*
       – *$effects_E(S;\ x := A) = effects(x := A) \wedge (effects_E(S)_{\{x/A^{-1}\}})$,*
       with A^{-1} as inverse action of A.

It can be shown that $effects_E(S)$ of sequences of primitive actions are valid postconditions of any execution of S. A formal proof requires introduction of a calculus for reasoning about imperative operations, such as Dijkstra's guarded commands. The proof appears in the full paper [4].

3.3 Computation Paths and Effects

Compile-time effect preservation requires fine analysis of the computation paths of a program and their effects. The following examples demonstrate the weakness of effects that are assigned to a program as a whole, and the advantage of an effect preservation theory that relies on path sensitive effects.

Example 5 (Path Sensitive Effects).

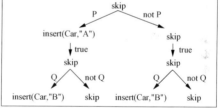

The program

$S(\text{``A''}, \text{``B''}) =$
if P then $Car := insert(Car, \text{``A''})$;
if Q then $Car := insert(Car, \text{``B''})$

has four computation paths,
with the desired effects: "A" $\in Car \wedge$ "B" $\in Car$, "A" $\in Car$, "B" $\in Car$, or *true* (the latter effect means that only *skip* is performed). Each formula corresponds to the effects of a possible sequence of primitive actions.

In order to define effects on paths of a computation, we use an auxiliary data structure termed the *computation tree* of a program. Each program is associated with a single finite computation tree, whose paths span all the possible evaluations of the conditions in the program. The nodes of the computation tree are labeled with primitive actions, and the arcs are labeled by conditions.

Definition 3 (Computation Tree). Let $Node(U)$ be a constructor for a node tree labeled with a primitive action U, and $addLeft(node, P, T)$ and $addRight(node, P, T)$ methods that add a left or right child T to a node, with P as the arc condition. The computation tree $Tree(S)$ of a program S is inductively defined:

1. For a primitive action U, $Tree(U) = Node(U)$.
2. $-$ $Tree(S_1; S_2) =$ for all leaves l of $Tree(S_1)$ do: $addLeft(l, true, Tree(S_2))$.
   $-$ $Tree(\text{if } P \text{ then } S_1 \text{ else } S_2) =$
   $\quad root = Node(skip)$, $addLeft(root, P, S_1)$, $addRight(root, \neg P, S_2)$.

Each node in a computation tree stands for a sequence of primitive actions given by the labels on the path that leads to the node. Further, each node is associated with a *guard* constraint that characterizes the initial condition for following the path (a *pre-condition*).

Example 6 (Guards and Sequences of a Computation Tree Nodes). Consider example 5. The four leaves are associated with the following sequences and guards:

sequence	guard
$insert(Car, \text{“A”}); insert(Car, \text{“B”})$	$P \wedge Q_{\{Car/insert(Car,\text{“A”})\}}$
$insert(Car, \text{“A”}); skip(\equiv insert(Car, \text{“A”}))$	$P \wedge \neg Q_{\{Car/insert(Car,\text{“A”})\}}$
$skip; insert(Car, \text{“B”})(\equiv insert(Car, \text{“B”}))$	$\neg P \wedge Q$
$skip; skip(\equiv skip)$	$\neg P \wedge \neg Q$

Guards of nodes can be defined inductively, similarly to the definition of executed effects ([4]). Computation trees can be optimized by pruning branches that include internal $fail$ nodes, and removing nodes whose guards are equivalent to $false$.

Each node in a computation tree is associated with the desired effects of its sequences. For example, the left most leaf in the computation tree in example 5 is associated with the desired effects "A" $\in Car \wedge$ "B" $\in Car$. The *guarded desired/executed effects* of a node n are the implication conditions $guard(n) \Rightarrow effects_D(n)$ and $guard(n) \Rightarrow effects_E(n)$, respectively.

3.4   The Effect Preservation Property

The effects of a general composite program should take into account its different computation paths. For example, the program of example 5 cannot have as its effects simply the conjunction of the contradictory effects of its primitive actions.

Definition 4 (The Desired/Executed Effects). *The* desired/executed effects *of a program S are given by the conjunction of the guarded desired/executed effects of the leaf nodes in the computation tree of S.*

Following the intuitive discussion of effect preservation above, we define a program as effect preserving if its desired effects follow from its executed effects. That is, the history that followed a modification did not affect its effect:

Definition 5 (The Effect Preservation Property). *A program S is effect preserving if $effects_E(S) \Rightarrow effects_D(S)$.*

Proposition 1. *A program is effect preserving if and only if for each leaf node* n *of its computation tree,* $effects_E(n) \Rightarrow effects_D(S)$ *is valid.*

Example 7. The program from example 5 is effect preserving, since it can be easily verified that for each leaf node the last proposition holds. For example, for the left most leaf, ["A" $\in delete(Car,$ "B") $\wedge$ "B" $\in Car$] $\Rightarrow$ "A" $\in Car \wedge$ "B" $\in Car$ is valid.

4 The Effect Preservation Transformation

An effect preserving transformation turns an input program into an effect preserving one, by inserting tests that act as guards against violation of previous intentions. The two criteria for a good transformation are: (1) Minimize rejections caused by effect preservation and (2) Minimize the run-time overhead. The task of effect preservation can be carried out at run-time, or at compile-time, or in a combined mode. A run-time only transformation achieves the first criterion, since rejections are triggered only in case of past effect violation. However, the run-time overhead is maximal, since at every modification all past effects must be checked. A compile-time only transformation achieves the second criterion since all effect violations are pre-computed and interleaved within the program, but the first criterion is not achieved since evaluation of effects requires run-time information.

In a combined compile-time run-time approach both criteria can be achieved using static analysis and partial evaluation of effects. The path sensitive effects characterized in the previous section guarantee that tested effects reflect the intentions of actions that are actually executed, and do not enforce effects of computation paths that are not followed. The static analysis in the presented transformation includes the construction of the computation tree with its path sensitive effects. Furthermore, in each tree node, the relevance between the aggregated path effects and the immediate primitive modification is pre-computed. This relevance singles out *delta-conditions* that must be checked, following the previous tests. This way, repeated time consuming evaluations of full path effects before or after modifications are saved. The delta-conditions provide a form of partial static evaluation of effects. The final evaluation of the delta-conditions is left to run-time. Run-time overhead is minimized by interleaving the tree navigation within the resulting program, and computation of delta-conditions in compile-time.

4.1 Delta-Conditions

Intuitively, executing an assignment, corresponding to some node n of the tree, the effects can be preserved, if the condition $effects_D(n)$ is tested after n has been executed. However, this is still costly, since the size of $effects_D(n)$ is proportional to the size of the program. Therefore, the run-time overhead is in the worst case $\mathcal{O}(size(S)^2)$, for a program S, assuming that primitive effect tests take constant time, and that primitive actions have atomic effects. Unfortunately, this is the run-time overhead of run-time only effect preservation. The run-time overhead can be improved by minimizing the formula $effects_D(n)$ which is the idea behind delta-conditions.

Delta-conditions extract the possible interaction between aggregated path effects and an immediate primitive action. Consider, for example, the program $S(u, v) = (x := insert(x, u); x := delete(x, v))$. The desired effects of the 2nd assignment are: $u \in x \land v \notin x$. Again, static analysis of these effects leaves the delta-condition $u \neq v$ to be tested prior to the application of the second assignment.

Definition 6 (Delta Conditions). *Let n be an assignment node in a computation tree of a program, with an action label $x := f(\bar{e})$. If n is the root node, then $delta\_condition(n) = true$. Otherwise, $delta\_condition(n)$ is any condition satisfying: $effects_D(parent(n)) \land delta\_condition(n) \Rightarrow effects_D(parent(n))_{\{x/f(\bar{e})\}}$*

Thus, delta-conditions guarantee that the desired past effects of the parent node hold after the assignment. Clearly, $effects_D(parent(n))_{\{x/f(\bar{e})\}}$ is a legal $delta\_condition(n)$, but the worst. The best $delta\_condition(n)$ is simply $true$, which indeed is the case, if the action of n does not interfere with $effects_D(parent(n))$.

Delta-conditions can be computed by a rough syntactic method that is based on a "no common state variables" consideration, as in the above example with a delta-condition $u \neq v$. Or by a fine, domain dependent method, that exploits knowledge about the domain primitives, i.e., actions and predicates. Since delta-condition specifies a test for possible interference between an action and a constraint, its static evaluation can be performed with methods developed in the field of *Integrity Constraint Checking* [12,5], where static analysis results minimal conditions that are left to be tested at run-time.

4.2   Effect Preservation Transformation

A given, possibly non effect preserving, program is transformed into a effect preserving one by interleaving the program code with commands for navigating the computation tree. Thus, precomputed delta-conditions are taken from the tree in a path sensitive manner and checked at run-time.

Algorithm 1 (Effect-Preservation with Delta-Conditions). *The ref variable refers to the current position in the computation tree.*
```
reviseProgram( S , T ) =
  replace each [if P then S1 else S2] in S by:
    (if P then ref:=left(ref);S1 else ref:=right(ref);S2)
  for each primitive U in S
    if U = skip or U = fail then replace U by: (U;ref:=left(ref))
    else
       if for all n ∈ nodes(U) delta−condition(n) = true then
```

```
    replace U by: (U; ref:=left(ref))
else
    replace U by:
    (if delta-condition(ref) then U else fail; ref:=left(ref))
```

Algorithm 1 includes an additional static optimization step aimed at saving redundant tests of delta-conditions. Clearly, such tests at run-time are needed only if there exists at least one execution path in $nodes(A)$ with a delta-condition different from $true$. This optimization is especially important since we expect that effect violations would be rather rare, and the more common situation is that delta-conditions reduce to $true$ at compile-time.

Finally, we present the main result showing that effect preservation is indeed achieved by the above algorithm, with run-time overhead that depends only on the delta-conditions. Since we believe that delta-conditions tend to be small and do not depend of the overall program size, then the run-time overhead is linear in the size of the program, instead of a quadratic overhead, in run-time only effect preservation.

Proposition 2 (Correctness and Efficiency of the Algorithm). *For a program S in $\mathcal{L}(X)$, $\texttt{reviseProgram}(S)$ is an effect preserving program. The expected run-time overhead of $\texttt{reviseProgram}(S)$ with respect to $Tree(S)$ is smaller than $size(S) \times size(delta\text{-}condition)$, i.e., $\mathcal{O}(size(S))$.*

4.3 An Example of the Effect Preservation Transformations

Finally, we demonstrate the transformation of a non effect preserving program into an effect preserving one. Consider the following artifical, but comprehensive, program $S(e_1, e_2, e_3)$, where P is and arbitrary condition:

$S(e_1, e_2, e_3)$ = `insert`$(table, e_1)$;
if P then `insert`$(table, e_2)$
`delete`$(table, e_3)$

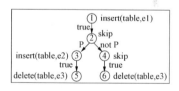

Clearly, `delete`$(table, e_3)$ might violate the effects of both insertions, depending on P and the value of e_3. The desired effects and delta-conditions of nodes are as follows:

node	$effects_D$	delta-condition
1	$e_1 \in table$	$true$
2	$e_1 \in table$	$true$
3	$e_1 \in table \wedge e_2 \in table$	$true$
4	$e_1 \in table$	$true$
5	$e_1 \in table \wedge e_2 \in table \wedge e_3 \notin table$	$e_1 \neq e_3 \wedge e_2 \neq e_3$
6	$e_1 \in table \wedge e_3 \notin table$	$e_1 \neq e_3$

The delta-conditions of the nodes 1, 2 and 4 reduce to *true*, since there is no previous action whose effects could be violated. The delta-condition of node 3 also reduces to *true* due to domain specific set considerations (an insertion does not interfere with set membership effects). The delta-conditions of nodes 5 and 6 reduce to comparisons of the inserted and deleted elements. Applying Algorithm reviseProgram to S returns the following program:

$S'(e_1, e_2, e_3)$ = insert$(table, e_1)$; ref:=childLeft(ref);
            if P then
               ref:=childLeft(ref);
               insert$(table, e_2)$; ref:=childLeft(ref);
            else
               ref:=childRight(ref);
               skip; ref:=childLeft(ref);
            if *delta-condition*(ref) then delete$(table, e_3)$ else *fail*;
               ref:=childLeft(ref)

5   Conclusion and Future Work

In this paper we defined the problem of effect preservation, and provided an efficient effect preservation algorithm with a linear run-time overhead. The algorithm relies on an exhaustive static analysis of a program, and on constraint reduction techniques. The static analysis includes path sensitive construction of effects, and reduction of interference conditions (delta-conditions). The resulting transformation is as expressive as the original program, but prevents effect violation.

The language considered in the paper is restricted to sequencing and conditional composite programs alone. In order to strengthen the approach, and enable partial transformations, it is necessary to extend the transformation to apply to a larger language of programs. In particular, it is important to add bounded loops to the language of programs.

Another extension is in the direction of more powerful dynamic effects, i.e., effects that allow simultaneous reference to initial and final values of state variables. Such effects are necessary for expressing evolution intentions such as "the value of a state variable can only grow".

Finally, we intend to apply our approach in multiple domains. For web based systems it is necessary to understand what are the characteristic effects of programs. For *Rule Triggering Systems* there is a need to study different modes of embedding an effect preservation algorithms within a system. For concurrent, reactive and mobile systems there is a need to study how effects of primitive actions should be defined. Our goal is to construct a generic open tool that can be extended in terms of language and effects, and can be applied to new domains.

References

1. E.W. Dijkstra and C.S. Scholten. Predicate calculus and program semantics. *Springer-Verlag, Texts and Monographs in Computer Science*, 1989.
2. K.D. Schewe and B. Thalheim. Limitations of Rule Triggering Systems for Integrity Maintenance in the context of Transition Specifications. *Acta Cybernetica*, 1998.
3. M. Balaban, S. Jurk. Improving Integrity Constraint Enforcement by Extended Rules and Dependency Graphs. In *Proc. 22th Conf. on DEXA*, 2001.
4. M. Balaban, S. Jurk. Intention of Updates - Characterization and Preservation. Technical report, Ben-Gurion University, Israel and BTU Cottbus, Germany, 2002.
5. F. Bry. Intensional updates: Abduction via deduction. In *Proc. 7th Conf. on Logi Programming*, 1990.
6. Greg Nelson. A generalization of dijkstras calculus. *ACM Transactions on Programming Languages and Systems*, 11:517–561, 1989.
7. P. Fraternali and S. Paraboschi and L. Tanca. Automatic Rule Generation for Constraints Enforcement in Active Databases. Springer WICS, 1993.
8. Joan Antoni Pastor. Extending the synthesis of update transaction programs to handle existential rules in deductive databases. In *Deductive Approach to Information Systems and Databases*, pages 189–218, 1994.
9. Joan Antoni Pastor-Collado and Antoni Olive. Supporting transaction design in conceptual modelling of information systems. In *Conference on Advanced Information Systems Engineering*, pages 40–53, 1995.
10. D. Plexousakis and J. Mylopoulos. Accommodating integrity constraints during database design. *Lecture Notes in Computer Science*, 1057, 1996.
11. K.D. Schewe and B. Thalheim. Towards a theory of consistency enforcement. *Acta Informatics*, 36:97–141, 1999.
12. S.Y. Lee, T.W. Ling. Further Improvement on Integrity Constraint Checking for Stratisfiable Deductive Databases. In *Proc. 22th Conf. on VLDB*, 1996.
13. J. Widom and S. Ceri. Deriving production rules for constraint maintenance. In *Proc. 16th Conf. on VLDB*, pages 566–577, 1990.
14. J. Widom and S. Ceri. *Active Database Systems*. Morgan-Kaufmann, 1996.

An Active Approach to Model Management for Evolving Information Systems

Henrik Gustavsson[1], Brian Lings[2], and Bjorn Lundell[1]

[1] University of Skovde, Department of Computer Science
P.O. Box 408, SE-541 28 Skovde, Sweden
{Henrik.Gustavsson, Bjorn.Lundell}@ida.his.se
http://www.his.se/ida/
[2] University of Exeter, School of Engineering and Computer Science
Prince of Wales Road, Exeter EX44PT, UK
B.J.Lings@dcs.exeter.ac.uk

Abstract. It is desirable to be able to interchange design information between CASE tools. Such interchange facilitates cooperative development, helps in avoiding legacy problems when adopting new tools, and permits the use of different tools for different life-cycle activities. Exchanging model transformation information is particularly demanding in the context of cooperative maintenance of evolving systems. In this paper we suggest an approach using active transformation rules. We show how transformation rules can be expressed using a modest extension of the Object Constraint Language of the UML standard, and actively interpreted. The approach allows existing UML-based tools or repository systems to be readily extended to actively manage models in evolving information systems.

1 Introduction

In CASE tools in general, and in repository systems in particular, it is desirable to be able to interchange information between different tools in a toolset [4], [9]. Such interchange can facilitate cooperative development, through the exchange of design documents. It can also help in preserving design information when a new tool is adopted. Under some circumstances it may also permit the use of different tools for different life-cycle activities.

Many CASE tools today use mappings or design transformations to automate different tasks within an IS lifecycle design process. Few tools, however, support user definable design transformations, and those that do use proprietary languages for their definition [13]. Interchanging a set of models for the purpose of cooperative development can therefore be problematic. In particular, if the interchange is between tools that do not support the same set of design transformations, inconsistencies will be introduced. We

A. Olivé (Eds.): ER 2003 Ws, LNCS 2784, pp. 112-123, 2003.

argue, therefore, that design transformations must themselves be interchanged, and in such a way as to facilitate their use in an importing tool.

What is required is an architecture which will allow efficient execution of design transformations in a tool, and the export of both transformations themselves and details of their usage in a design, for example in transforming a conceptual model into a logical one. The set of interrelated design models could then be successfully manipulated using an importing tool, without it previously having been configured to handle the transformations involved. Such extensibility in the IS modelling area is the goal of the research reported here.

1.1 Transformations

In the area of meta modelling and repository systems, adoption of the UML [26], MOF [27] and XMI [25] standards has made it possible to interchange information and to guarantee extensibility in meta modelling systems [9]. A number of implementations of repository systems that currently support UML also support XMI interchange of data, including the France Telecom model repository tool [1] and the SPOOL design repository [19]. These projects support extensible, standards based meta models. In addition to supporting an extensible meta model, the Microsoft Repository [3] also supports the expression of transformations. It uses a model called the OTM (open transformation model) to define and store transformations. The main purpose of this is to support transformations in data warehouses, so the model for transformations is affected by its roots within the data warehousing field. However, in most other cases, mappings and transformations (or *model management* features [2]) used in tools connected to repositories are neither interchangeable nor extensible.

The use of proprietary languages for transformations inhibits interchange between tools. The Microsoft Repository uses a proprietary combination of SQL and OLE software to execute transformations. The DB-MAIN project [13] mainly uses a procedural language with a constraint language to define pre and post conditions for transformations. A logic-based language has been proposed elsewhere [23].

Many different uses have been found for design transformations (see [12], [13], [15], [16], [23]). Most of these sources, however, do not discuss how the modelling decisions leading up to a design transformation are to be represented. Nor do they discuss how to represent the information required to perform a design transformation - not all relevant information is directly present in a model (for example, required parameters from the user). Other systems, such as the DAIDA project, use a knowledge-based approach to design transformations. This allows sophisticated deductions to be made from the knowledge base, for instance which transformations were used in mapping between models [17].

The DB-MAIN project, however explores the use of design histories as a means to represent design decisions [14]. The model before a transformation is not maintained in its entirety, but modelling decisions are indirectly captured through state transitions. Using this 'history', a model can be wound back to the time before a certain transformation was applied, so that the transformation can be reapplied with, for example, a different set of input parameters, resulting in a different destination model.

However, the use of design histories to achieve a higher degree of modelling transparency has a number of drawbacks. Firstly, a very sophisticated versioning system is required which supports multiple and branching histories. In addition, the system must be capable of inferring modelling decisions and properties from these histories. Secondly, it may in some cases be difficult to tell whether a certain change in a model is due to the application of a transformation or direct user intervention. This is because design histories serve a dual purpose, in that they support both historical information about previous versions of a model and an indirect representation of those modelling decisions. Knowledge based approaches, on the other hand, require sophisticated inference engines, and use proprietary languages and representation techniques which thus make them unsuitable for a scenario where interoperability between different tools is of prime importance.

In an earlier paper [10] we have suggested an approach by which design transformations can be freely interchanged between tools. Transformations are represented using a conservative extension of the OCL language. The approach is independent of proprietary languages and techniques. Further, since more and more tools are adding support for OCL [24], it will become increasingly straightforward to adopt this approach in existing tools. The approach in that paper, however, has a significant drawback: rule execution is independent of the event that triggers a transformation. This problem makes the approach less powerful and significantly less suitable for maintenance. In this paper we suggest how to remove this drawback, developing the OCL language to support reactive behaviour suitable for co-operative management of model evolution.

1.2   OCL as a Conceptual Language for Meta-modelling Constraints and Actions

Active databases have been proposed, over the years, for a wide variety of different tasks in many different application areas. In repository systems, active databases have been used to automate common tasks such as general model processing [18] and change management [8]. Such proposals, however, have relied in large part on platform dependent models or languages. This would impede successful application of the techniques to systems which do not share a common platform.

The Object Constraint Language [20] is part of the UML standard [26]. Amongst other things, it is used to introduce pre and post conditions to, and to place guards on, methods. The language is platform independent, declarative and efficient for querying and navigating object-oriented data. Even though the OCL language, as a conceptual language, is intended for object-oriented modelling, it can be used with other forms of modelling. It can, for instance, be used to specify constraints on SQL databases [7].

This versatility makes OCL a good language for platform independent specification of conditions in repository systems and meta models.

An extension to the OCL language to support actions [21] has been put forward, but the proposal stopped short of suggesting that such actions be executed using an OCL interpreter. However, to achieve a high degree of modelling transparency [5], the simultaneous update of interrelated parts of dependent models is needed. The most common way to achieve this is by transforming a model into one which reflects the required changes – that is, active behaviour.

1.3   A Novel Approach to Modelling Transparency

This project takes a novel approach to increasing modelling transparency in that transformation patterns representing modelling decisions made by a user are represented explicitly as part of the modelling information stored in a repository. The repository thus directly represents transformations, the parameters needed to perform each selected instance of a transformation, and the results of such transformations (in the form of updated models). In order to completely support the desired increase in modelling transparency, the objects that result from a transformation are also connected to the source objects using ordinary associations. This allows a connection to be navigated, for instance to allow a tool user to find the set of relational tables that result from the transformation of an entity type.

In a previous paper we have shown that transformation rules can be expressed using a conservative extension of OCL. In this paper we show how a tool can be made to react to state changes in its meta modelling repository through the addition of events to transformation rules. A further modest extension to the OCL language is proposed, to support context variables to receive parameters from event occurrences. We have tested the ideas through the implementation of an active repository system with an event detector and rule manager suitable for model management in a UML environment. The proof of principle system used to test the examples used in the paper is available on request (henke@ida.his.se).

2   Overview of Approach

Although the approach outlined is designed to be generally applicable for multi-model management, our chosen application context is CASE data interchange for cooperative design. We believe it is beneficial in such contexts to support the active interchange of design transformations.

In the general approach, each design transformation is represented by a set of rules which, given specific model and parameter information, can be used to bring about that transformation. This offers better support for the incremental update of models typical of cooperative design. The OCL language has been chosen to represent design transformations[1]. However, OCL traditionally supports neither updates nor active behaviour. Other authors have suggested extensions to OCL for introducing active behaviour [21]. In our work, we extend the OCL language and its interpreter to allow the expression of active behaviour with update. In general, the fundamental issues to be addressed in moving to active behaviour are [28]: event specification and detection, access to context information by rules, and access to state transition information.

The proposed extension uses an ECA (Event Condition Action) format for rules to provide support for active design transformations. The use of ECA rules gives a number of benefits over a condition action based approach [6]. Firstly, events and conditions play different roles in the system, allowing the repository to react directly to state changes in the context in which they occur. Making the event explicit thus allows finer grained control over when execution occurs. This increases flexibility in execution semantics. This latter is important, since this project strives to be as platform independent as possible so that the ideas in the approach can be adapted to fit existing tool environments. There is also a performance benefit in that by using an event to trigger a condition check, fewer conditions have to be evaluated for the same database state.

2.1   Meta-model Extensions for Active Behaviour

There are different ways in which reactive behaviour can be supported, each placing different requirements on the rule scheduler and event detection mechanism. One very important consideration for this project is the ease with which the techniques can be incorporated into existing CASE technology. The suggested methodologies should thus be simple enough to be easily implemented in existing tools or tool infrastructures.

It has only been found necessary to include primitive database events in the rule system; no transformations so far studied have required the introduction of temporal or composite events. Hence, the rule system proposed only recognises events that occur when objects are inserted into the model, when objects are updated in the model, and when objects are deleted from the model. However, it has been found useful to distinguish a separate set of event types for the modification of collections, i.e. the creation, deletion and update of associations between objects in models.

In order to support the specification of active OCL rules, it has been necessary to extend the OCL rule language beyond that suggested in our previous work [10] by the addition of a list of events that can trigger a transformation rule:

```
Contextclass: <Context class specification>
Event: <event specification>
Condition: <condition specification>
```

---

[1] An explanation of the rationale behind the choice of this language can be found in [8].

```
Declaration: <declaration specification>
Action: <action specification>
```

In order to be able to represent transformations directly within the models, some kind of meta modelling support is necessary. In order to achieve a high degree of interoperability this model has been kept as simple and as generic as possible, in contrast with, for example, the Microsoft Repository approach [3] that models transformations with proprietary and domain specific structures. A number of superclasses have been proposed previously [10] for this purpose in a non-active environment; these can be inherited by the other meta model classes. The only extension required is the addition of an event property to the rule class.

2.2   Event Types and Context Variables

The behaviour of an active set of models may be heavily dependent on the cascading of rules (if multiple levels of models are used). It has been found useful to differentiate between primary events and secondary events. Primary events occur as a direct result of user interaction, for example check-in of a model or direct modification of a modelling object. Secondary events occur when the model contents are modified by a transformation rule. By differentiating between the six primary event types and the six secondary event types, it is possible to perform different actions depending on whether an update came from inside or outside the repository. This gives increased control over rule cascades since a rule, through its triggering event, has knowledge of whether it is executing as the consequence of a cascaded event or as a direct result of an update by a tool user. For example, it allows increased control over cycles in rule cascades.

In active databases, context variables (event parameters [6]) contain information about the state of the data before and after updates, so that rule behaviour can be expressed in terms of state change. In order to support this type of behaviour for the active set of models it is necessary to extend OCL to allow the use of context variables in transformation rules. In earlier work [10], we introduced updates to the OCL language. In particular, the aliasing mechanism present in the OCL standard definition was used to allow new objects to be referenced, and thus be modified in different ways. In order to limit the scope of the necessary changes to an OCL interpreter, it would be beneficial to further use the aliasing mechanism in supplying context variables.

In the prototype implementation, user updates to the repository are taken to be atomic actions. Transformation rules are therefore executed only after the metadata updates corresponding to these atomic actions. We have introduced two new global aliases for use as context variables. They work in the same way as the "SELF" alias, which identifies the context object. The "OLD" alias identifies the object state before the triggering update, and the "NEW" alias the object state after the triggering update. These context variable aliases have slightly different meanings depending on the type of event triggering the rule using the aliases (see table 1).

Table 1. Event types and context variable descriptions

Event	Alias	Description
Insert	NEW	Provides access to the values of the newly inserted object. Since the object is new, there is no "OLD" variable.
Delete	OLD	Provides access to the object as it was before deletion.
Update	OLD NEW	Provide pointers to the information before and (respectively) after the update.
Collection Insert	NEW	Provides access to the object which has been added to the collection.
Collection Delete	OLD	Provides access to the object which is going to be removed from the collection.
Collection Update	OLD NEW	Only occurs for 0..1 or 1..1 cardinalities. In this case, the "OLD" alias provides access to the object in the collection before the update, and the "NEW" alias provides access to the object in the collection after the update.

Since the OCL language displays collections and properties in the same way, but since the actual handling of associations and properties must account for conceptual differences, this separation simplifies the management of these two types of event.

A specific update collection event type is also introduced for collections that contain at most one object. When this is changed so that it identifies some other object, an update collection event is fired, indicating an update of an existing collection. The main difference between collection events and property events is that in property events, the object in the new and old variables is of the context class type. In contrast, for collection events, the new and old variables refer to the object that was added/removed from a collection, which may not be of the same type as the context class.

3   Example of Approach

To allow easy comparison with existing approaches, an example rule set has been created which demonstrates some important types of transformation handled in the related work cited earlier (section 1.1). The set of example transformation rules and the example meta model (see figure 1) are not intended to be complete, but are designed to show the characteristics of an active approach. We have successfully captured the design transformations used in the real-world example cited in [22], where a company was unable to adopt CASE technology because none of the current generation of CASE-tools evaluated allowed import of the existing models.

The example in this paper uses a simplified version of a well known E-R notation [11]. It is not intended to suggest new or more advanced transformations than those used to demonstrate alternative approaches. However, through the use events the technique is also able to support incremental update of models without having to regenerate a complete schema, a feature important in maintenance scenarios.

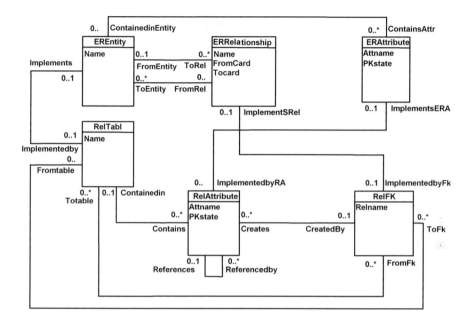

Fig. 1. A simple example meta model without transformation metadata included

The goal in the example is to transform an ER Entity to a relational model table, and transform ER attributes to table attributes while retaining the attribute names and the key attributes of the original entity. This simple transformation requires two separate rules, one that transforms the entities and one that transforms the attributes. An important feature of this rule set is that it can handle incremental updates of the attributes; when a new attribute is added to an existing entity, the corresponding attributes are generated automatically. Since supporting incremental updates of other modelling objects would require more rules, this example only supports incremental updates for the ER attributes. Rules expressed in logic for performing the inverse of this transformation were suggested in [23].

```
Contextclass: ERENtity
Event: INSERT
Declaration: RelTable T1
Condition: Implementedby->isempty
Action: T1.create;T1.name:=self.name;
T1.Implements:=self

Contextclass: ERAttribute
Event: INSERT
Declaration: Relattribute RA
Condition: IMPLEMENTEDBYRA->isempty
```

```
Action: RA.CREATE;SELF.implementedbyra:=RA; RA.attname
:=self.attname; RA.containedin :=
self.Containedinentity.implementedby;RA.Pkstate :=
self.PKstate
```

One well-known transformation suggested in another related paper [13] is the transformation of relationships into foreign keys. This transformation is performed by the rule listed below. Another rule would be required to deal with the case when the cardinalities are reversed. Further rules could also be added if options other than generating a foreign key are to be handled.

```
Contextclass: ERRelationship
Event: INSERT
Delcaration: RELFK FK
Condition: Fromcard="1" and Tocard="N" and implemented-
byfk->isempty
Action: FK.create; FK.relname:=self.name;
FK.implementsrel:=self; FK.fromtable :=
self.toentity.implementedby; FK.totable :=
self.fromentity.implementedby
```

```
Contextclass: RELATTRIBUTE
Event: IINSERT
Declaration: RELattribute RA
Condition: Referencedby->isempty and containe-
din.fromFK->notempty and PKstate="1"
Action: containedin.fromfk->iterate(
        FK| RA.create; RA.containedin:=fk.fromtable;
        RA.PKstate:="0"; RA.attname:=self.attname;
        RA.createdby:=FK; RA.references:=self)
```

The example rule set also contains rules to perform cascade update and cascade delete of ER attributes. These rules will allow the tool user to delete attributes or to rename ER attribute names without having to regenerate the whole relational model. Using events significantly reduces the number of conditions to be evaluated to support this type of behaviour.

```
Contextclass: ERATTRIBUTE
Event: DELETE
Condition: IMPLEMENTEDBYRA->notempty
Action: IMPLEMENTEDBYRA.REFERENCEDBY->iterate(RA |
RA.delete); IMPLEMENTEDBYRA.DELETE
Contextclass: ERATTRIBUTE
Event: UPDATE ATTNAME
Condition: IMPLEMENTEDBYRA->notempty
Action: IMPLEMENTEDBYRA.REFERENCEDBY->iterate(RA |
RA.attname:=self.attname); IMPLEMENTEDBYRA.attname :=
self.attname
```

4   Analysis and Discussion

We have proposed an approach to concisely representing design transformations through the use of reactive behaviour, implemented using active rules expressed in a conservative[2] extension of the OCL language. The approach allows a compliant tool to use an enhanced set of design transformations for a set of models without the tool itself having to be modified. Since the language used to represent transformations is based on standardized languages and representation techniques (UML/MOF), with standardised ways to interchange models (XMI), existing tools or repository systems can be extended for compliance with relative ease. The approach has advantages over proposals which use proprietary languages, such as [15] and [23]. Examples have been presented to illustrate efficient, incremental update of interchanged models is supported using the approach.

There are a number of implications for tool vendors wishing to benefit from the proposed approach; we perceive three different classes of tool that may utilize an imported model or export a tool-specific model.

Tools in the first class have no support for alternative design transformations, their representation or interchange. Design transformation information has no meaning to these tools, and will be ignored. Such a tool can only usefully export a model; any importing tool must be provided with the transformations used. Building the corresponding model connections would be a non-trivial task.

Tools in the second class allow a user to select from a set of alternative design transformations. For collaboration purposes, these selections should be interchangeable using standardised export formats. Translators must be written for this purpose. Any information that documents a transformation alien to the tool has no meaning to it. The importing translator for the tool has to distinguish the associations between ordinary modelling objects from those between modelling objects and transformation pattern objects, which behave differently. As with class 1, any tool importing from a class 2 tool must be provided with the transformations used.

Tools in the final (class 3) class support all of the different types of information. Such a tool has to distinguish between the various association types only by looking at the meta information. From our earlier analysis, this final class is likely to require support for global navigation between the different modelling objects, which together form a complete set of models for a given domain.

To turn a class 2 tool into a class 3 tool, it is only necessary to develop an extension of the internal transformation engine to interpret OCL actions. The prototype implementation has shown this to be a modest extension to existing OCL interpreters.

---

[2] In the sense that existing tools can be readily updated to support the extensions.

References

1. Belaunde, M.: A Pragmatic Approach for Building a Flexible UML Model Repository In: UML 1999, Lecture Notes in Computer Science, Vol. 1723. Springer-Verlag, Berlin Heidelberg New York (1999) 188-203.
2. Bernstein, P.A.: Generic Model Management: A Database Infrastructure for Schema Manipulation. In: 9th International Conference on Cooperative Information Systems, LNCS 2172, Springer (2001) 1-6
3. Bernstein, P.A., Bergstraesser, T.: Meta-Data Support for Data Transformations Using Microsoft Repository. IEEE Data Engineering Bulletin 22(1), IEEE (1999) 9-14
4. Blaha, M.R., LaPlant, D., Marvak, E., Requirements for Repository Software. In: WCRE'98 Honolulu, Hawaii, USA. IEEE Computer Society Press (1998) 164-173
5. Brinkkemper, S.: Integrating diagrams in CASE tools through modelling transparency. Information and Software Technology 35(2) (1993) 101-105
6. Dayal, U.: Ten Years of Activity in Active Database Systems: What Have We Accomplished? In: ARTDB 1995, Workshops in Computing, Springer-Verlag, Berlin Heidelberg New York (1995) 3-22
7. Demuth, B, Hußmann, H, Loecher, S.: OCL as a Specification Language for Business Rules in Database Applications. In: UML 2001, Springer-Verlag, Berlin Heidelberg New York (2001) 104-117
8. Gal, A., Etzion, O.: Handling Change Management using Temporal Active Repositories. In: OOER 1995, Lecture Notes in Computer Science, Vol. 1021 Springer-Verlag, Berlin Heidelberg New York (1995) 378-387
9. Gray, J.P., Liu, A., Scott, L.: Issues in software engineering tool construction. Information and Software Technology 42 (2000) 73-77
10. Gustavsson, H., Lings, B.: CASE-tool interchange of Design Transformations. In: 18th British National Conference on Databases: BNCOD 2001, Lecture Notes in Computer Science, Vol. 2097. Springer-Verlag Berlin (2001) 75-88
11. Elmasri, R., Navathe, S.B.: Fundamentals of Database Systems. 3rd edn. Addison-Wesley, Reading (2000)
12. Fahrner, C., Vossen, G.: A survey of database design transformations based on the Entity-Relationship model. Data & Knowledge Engineering 15(3) (1995) 213-250
13. Hainaut, J.-L.: Specification preservation in schema transformations – application to semantics and statistics. Data & Knowledge Engineering 19 (1996) 99-134
14. Hainaut, J.-L., Henrard, J., Hick, J.M., Roland, D., Englebert, V.: Database Design Recovery. In: CAiSE 1996 Lecture Notes in Computer Science, Vol. 1080. Springer-Verlag, Berlin Heidelberg New York, (1996) 272-300
15. Hainaut, J.-L., Englebert, V., Henrard, J., Hick, J.M., Roland D.: Database reverse engineering: From Requirements to CARE tools. Automated Software Engineering 3, 1996, Kluwer Academic Publishers (1996) 9-45
16. Halpin, T.A., Proper, H.A.: Database Schema Transformation & Optimization. In: OOER'95: 14th International Conference on Conceptual Modeling, Springer Lecture Notes in Computer Science, Vol. 1021, Springer-Verlag, Berlin (1995) 191-203
17. Jarke M., Rose T.: Managing Knowledge about Information System Evolution. In: Proceedings of the 1988 ACM SIGMOD International Conference on Management of Data, SIGMOD Record 17(3) (1988) 303-311
18. Jasper, H.: Active Databases for Active Repositories. In: ICDE 1994, IEEE Computer Society (1994) 375-384

19. Keller, R., Bédard, J.-F., Saint-Denis, G.: Design and Implementation of a UML-Based Design Repository. In: CAiSE 2001, Lecture Notes in Computer Science 2068, Springer-Verlag, Berlin Heidelberg New York (2001) 448-464
20. Kleppe, A., Warmer, J.: The Object Constraint Language: Precise Modeling with UML, Addison-Wesley (1999)
21. Kleppe, A., Warmer, J.: Extending OCL to include actions. In: 3rd International Conference on the Unified Modelling Language, UML, Springer-Verlag, Berlin Heidelberg New York (2000)
22. Lundell, B., Lings, B., Gustafsson, P.-O.: Method support for developing evaluation frameworks for CASE tool evaluation. In: 1999 Information Resources Management Association International Conference - Track: Computer-Aided Software Engineering Tools, IDEA Group Publishing, Hershey (1999) 350-358
23. McBrien, P., Poulovassilis, A.: A Uniform Approach to Inter-Model Transformations. In: Advanced Information Systems Engineering, 11th International Conference CAiSE'99, Lecture Notes in Computer Science, Vol. 1626, Springer-Verlag, Berlin Heidelberg New York (1999) 333-348
24. Medvidovic, N., Rosenblum, D.S., Redmiles D.F., Robbins, J.E.: Modeling software architectures in the Unified Modeling Language. ACM Transactions on Software Engineering and Methodology 11(1) (2002) 2-57
25. Object Management Group: XML Metadata Interchange (XMI) Document ad/98-10-06, http://www.omg.org/docs/ad98-10-05.pdf (1998)
26. Object Management Group: OMG Unified Modeling Language Specification, Version 1.3, June 1999 (1999)
27. Object Management Group: Formal MOF 1.3 Specification formal/00-04-04, http://cgi.omg.org/cgi-bin/doc?formal/00-04-03.pdf (2000)
28. Paton, N.W., Diaz, O.: Active database systems. ACM Computing Surveys 31(1) (1999) 63-103

Mobile Information Systems - Research Challenges on the Conceptual and Logical Level

John Krogstie[1], Kalle Lyytinen[2], Andreas Opdahl[3],
Barbara Pernici[4], Keng Siau[5], and Kari Smolander[6]

[1]Norwegian University of Science and Technology, Institute of Computer and Information
Sciences and SINTEF Telecom and Informatics, Norway
`John.Krogstie@sintef.no`
[2]Case Western Reserve University, USA
`kjl13@po.cwru.edu`
[3]University of Bergen, Norway
`andreas@ifi.uib.no`
[4]Politecnico di Milano, Italy
`Barbara.Pernici@Elet.PoliMi.IT`
[5]University of Nebraska-Lincoln, USA
`ksiau@unlnotes.unl.edu`
[6]Lappeenranta University of Technology, Finland
`kari.smolander@lut.fi`

Abstract. This paper discusses new challenges and possible approaches for developing and evolving *mobile information* systems, with focus on *model-based approaches* on the conceptual and logical level. We have experienced these new challenges through several research and industrial projects on mobile solutions, usability and model-based approaches over the last years. We summarize the main challenges on how model-based approaches can support the development of mobile information systems that are to be used together with other types of systems, primarily in a professional setting and indicate upcoming research issues in this very dynamic area. We argue that this research area is also timely, because the underlying technological infrastructure are just becoming sufficiently mature to make feasible research on conceptual and logical, and not only on technical issues.

1 Introduction

Today, the PC is only one of many ways to access information resources and services. On one hand, traditional computing technology is becoming more mobile and ubiquitous and, on the other hand, traditional mass-media are becoming richer as in interactive TV. Whereas information services related to interactive TV is projected to become prominent in a few years, mobility is perhaps the most important *current* market and technological trend within information and communication technology (ICT), although the development of UMTS infrastructure goes more slowly than originally envisaged. With the advent of new mobile infrastructures providing higher bandwidth and constant connection to the network from virtually everywhere, the way people use information resources is predicted to be radically transformed.

A. Olivé (Eds.): ER 2003 Ws, LNCS 2784, pp. 124-135, 2003.

According to Siau [29], the essence of mCommerce is to reach customers, suppliers and employees regardless of where they are located and to deliver the right information to the right person(s) at the right time. To achieve this, a new breed of mobile information systems [17] must be developed. This paper will highlight some of the research challenges in this field that can be related to the conceptual and logical levels of information systems development.

2   Novel Aspects of Mobile Information Systems

Mobile computing systems entail end-user terminals easily movable in space, operable independently of particular locations and typically with wireless access to information resources and services. We will in this section first described the different dimension of mobility, before highlighting the specific aspects of mobile information systems to support the different mobility dimensions.

2.1 Dimensions of Mobility

Mobility can be *spatial, temporal* or *contextual* [13]. The spatial and contextual dimensions are the ones most commonly considered and will be focussed on here. (Spatial) mobility is primarily about *people* moving in space, having wireless access to information and services. Secondarily, mobility relates to all sort of things in the environment (parcels, cars etc.) with the possibility to interact with other devices and people.

People in general are getting increasingly mobile, both in connection to their professional and private tasks. The user of mobile information systems is characterised by frequent changes in context, given by:

- The *spatio-temporal context* describes aspects related to time and space. It contains attributes like time, location, direction, speed, track, and place.
- The *environment context* captures the entities that surround the user, e.g. things, services, temperature, light, humidity, and noise
- The *personal context* describes the user state. It consists of the physiological context and the mental contexts. The physiological context may contain information like pulse, blood pressure, and weight. The mental context may describe things like mood, expertise, anger, and stress.
- The *task context*. This context describes what the user is doing. The task context may be described with explicit goals or the tasks and task breakdown structures.
- The *social context* describes the social aspects of the user context. It may, for instance, contain information about friends, neighbours, co-workers and relatives. The role that the user plays is an important aspect of the social context. A role may describe the user's status in this role and the tasks that the user may perform in this role. The term *social mobility* [22] refers to the ways in which individuals can move across different social contexts and social roles, and still be supported by technology and services.

- The *information context* – The part of the global and personal information space that is available at the time.

Luff and Heath [21] identify three types of mobility: Micro-mobility refers to how small artefacts can be mobilised and manipulated by hand. Local mobility involves real-time interaction between people and technology at the same location. Finally, remote mobility supports both synchronous and asynchronous collaboration among individuals who move around in distant physical locations. Several kinds of personal mobility have recently been identified in the literature. Kristiansen and Ljungberg [16] distinguish between *travelling, visiting* and *wandering*. *Travelling* is movement between different locations in a vehicle. *Visiting* is a prolonged period spent in one location before moving back to the original location or on to another one. *Wandering* is moving about — usually on foot — in the local area. To this, Esbjörnsson [6] adds *mobile work* proper, which is kinds of work where an essential aspect of the work process itself is mobility. Since mobile information systems is also relevant in non-working situations, we may extend this category to *mobility proper*, i.e., activities were mobility is an essential aspect of the activity itself, such as going on a hike or scenic tour or visiting an outdoor museum.

People also 'move' between different ways of organising their time. Hall [9] distinguishes between *monochronocity* and *polychronicity*. In the former, people seek to structure their time sequentially doing only one thing at a time, if possible according to a plan. In the latter, people accept — and maybe prefer — doing several things simultaneously, placing less importance on planned order. The new technologies seem to be increasing monochronicity in some situations and polychronicity in others. On the one hand, increased monochronicity appears in the interfaces of many contemporary enterprise systems, which often require business process steps to be carried out in strict sequence with little flexibility for individual variations of temporal order and few possibilities for carrying out several processes in parallel. Because mobile devices have small screen sizes and memories, monochronicity is strengthened, because it is less convenient to operate on several windows running different applications in parallel. On the other hand, the need for polychronicity is increased in many mobile settings. A larger proportion of work is today done by symbolic analyst [31], whose main work pattern is (often many parallel) knowledge intensive projects, both within and across organisational borders. Symbolic analysts such as consultants, reporters, and researchers will typically have many tasks going on concurrently, and will be interested in a lot of different information there and then, much of which can not be anticipated fully beforehand.

Thus mobile technologies inherently tend towards providing monochronic services, while at the same time they tend to place their users in contexts with polychronic demands.

2.2 Differences between Mobile and Traditional Information Systems

From an application point of view, mobile information systems differ from more traditional information systems [10,18,19,29]. We have grouped the differences within four areas:

User-Orientation and Personalization: Mobile information systems often address a wider user-group, which means that user-interfaces should feature prominently and early in the design process and that user-interfaces often need to be extremely simple. The resulting user-interfaces often cannot presume previous acquaintance with computers at all, and input and output facilities may be severely restricted (no keyboard, small screen-size etc.) or based on new modalities (speech-recognition and –synthesis etc.). This means that *individualisation* of mobile information systems becomes increasingly important, both at the individual level where user-interface details such as commands and screen layout is tailored to personal preferences and hardware, and the work level where functions are tailored to fit the user's preferred work processes. Individualisation means both information systems that automatically *adapt* themselves to the preferences of the user, and systems that can be explicitly *tailored* by users through a specific user-interface.

Technological Aspects Including Convergence and Multi-channel Support: Mobile devices have severely limited processing, memory and communication capacities compared to other kinds of computers. Performance considerations therefore become increasingly important during design. Analytically-based predictive methods are necessary in order to assess a large number of design alternatives during design of mobile information systems.

Because the new mobile devices integrate functions that were previously offered by physically separate tools (*convergence technology*), they probably signal the arrival of a plethora of new types of applications. Mobile and other new technologies provide many different ways to offer the same or similar services to customers. For example, broadcast news in the future will be available through plain-old television, enhanced television, Internet TV, 3G mobile phone and numerous other information appliances (the door of the glove compartment in your car, your living-room wall etc.). At the same time as new channels to information is provided, existing channels such as traditional PCs over a LAN will still be used in combination with the mobile information systems, thus one need to support a multi-channel approach, where the same functionality and information resources is available across a large range of processing devices.

Methodology for Development to Ensure Organizational Return: Mobile information systems are radical and therefore reward increased focus on idea generation early during design. This also means that there are not always existing services or situations in which to anchor problem analysis efforts. Another effect of the radically new approaches enabled by the technological solutions is that the introduction of mobile information systems often spawns several other initiatives for changed information systems.

The mobile clients still develop rapidly, which means that idea generation should not be limited by currently available technologies. It also means that systems must be designed for change. There is little accumulated experience on how to design software for the new technologies. As a consequence, lightweight design techniques and early prototyping is the natural choice for practical development projects at the moment. In addition, research is needed on accumulating experience from early development projects and packaging this knowledge into comprehensive, integrated and model-based development methodologies. There is also a need for user-interface guidelines and standards for mobile solutions.

Security and Other Quality Aspects: Mobile information systems pose new challenges to information systems security, for instance by rendering traditional firewall thinking unusable. Exacerbating a problem already introduced by the emergence of wireless LANs, mobile communications can in principle and easily be wiretapped by anyone. In addition, the mobile devices themselves are easily stolen, lost etc., sometimes without the loss being identified immediately.

Whereas these challenges to traditional software design are not new when seen in isolation, the emerging generation of new information and communication technologies increases their importance because (1) each challenge is *amplified by* the new technologies and (2) the new technologies *combine the challenges* in ways that are not yet understood.

3   Background on Our Structuring of the Research Area

We have for many years been engaged in the areas of information systems analysis and design methods, their application, evaluation and engineering in general, and has followed the development from mainframe to client-server, ERP, and web-applications. It is on this basis that we address research challenges within mobile information systems.

In our community, a distinction has traditionally been drawn between issues on the conceptual, logical, and physical level.

Conceptual Level: On the conceptual level the IS-problems are looked upon regardless of what part of the current or future IS in the broad sense that is (or is to be) supported or automated by information technology. Thus a conceptual data model for instance map the relationship between concepts as they are perceived to be by humans in the real world (normally within organisation). This level is by some also called the essential level.

Logical Level: On the logical level, it is taken into account that one is dealing with information technology, but without being overly constrained with detailed aspects of the concrete implementation technology. Data models for instance on this level would take into account e.g. the structuring and relationship of data in several relational tables.

Physical Level: Finally, at the physical level, all implementation details are regarded, including for a database e.g. things like physical indexes, tablespaces etc.

We have structured the main research issues and areas in connection to mobile information systems in the same way. For this paper, we focus specifically on aspects on the conceptual and logical level. Our focus is on the support of model-based approaches. The common approach is to not follow modeling-based approaches. Although most software engineers are aware of model-based methodologies and many companies claim to base their development processes on them, model-based methodologies are seldom followed in great detail in practise. In fact, in most real software engineering projects, if at all used, semi-formal modelling techniques mainly play a role during the initial development stages. Also most current multi-channel approaches do not focus on the use of rigorous model-based techniques. The Oxygen Project [4], developed at MIT, focuses on the concept of "pervasive computing" from a technical point of view introducing a novel network technology in which mobile devices can recognise each other, and dynamically configure their interconnection in order to form "collaborative regions". Odyssey [25] defines a platform to manage adaptive applications for different mobile devices using mobile agents. The Portolano Project [7] investigates the emerging field of invisible computation. It envisions a user interface that combines the data gathered from location sensors, identification tags, and on-line databases in order to determine user intents rather than relying on user commands. In contrast to these projects that focus on automating the support by partly guessing what the worker is interested in, the Ninja Project [8] aims at developing a software infrastructure for the next generation of Internet applications which is more open for adaptation in use, although not taking full benefit from a model based approach.

4   Research Challenges for Mobile Information Systems

We below highlight main research areas on mobile information systems at the conceptual and logical levels, structure according to the four areas described in section 2 as applicable.

4.1 Conceptual Level

User-Orientation and Personalization: Traditionally, support for workers in actually performing its processes has not been provided. Functions of the mobile information system should be tailored to fit the user's preferred work processes, which typically involve other persons as well. To support group and teamwork, awareness of the status of knowledge resources is increasingly important in a mobile setting. Given that knowledge resources both include individuals and technology that can be mobile, one should look into interactive systems to improve group performance. Peter Wegner's interaction framework [32] was triggered by the realization that machines involving users in their problem solving, can solve a larger class of problems than algorithmic systems computing in isolation. The main characteristic of an *interaction machine* is that it can pose questions to human actors (users) during its computation. The problem solving process is no longer just a user providing input to the machine which then processes the request and provides an answer (output), it is a multi-step conversation between the user and the machine, each being able to take the initiative. A major research question in this area is how to specify and utilize interaction machines on a multi-channel platform. To enable interaction machines, process support technology is a natural choice. Process support technology is typically based on process models, which need to be available in some form for people to change them to support their emerging goals. Thus interactive models should be supported [11,12]. The outset for this thinking is that models can be useful tools in a usage situation, even if the models are changing and are partly incomplete and inconsistent. The user is included as an interpreter and changer of the models, based on underlying interaction machines. Emergent workflow systems [11] represent a different approach to static and adaptive workflow systems with respect to their use of models. They target very different kinds of processes: Unique, knowledge-intensive processes where the structure emerges. It can be argued that this is not specific for mobile information systems utilizing GPRS and UMTS networks, but this area will be even more pronounced in such systems since future information appliances (and a multitude of services across the network) will be always available (and thus more likely to be used in an emergent or ad-hoc fashion). Awareness mechanisms are linked to our emergent workflow systems, and should be enriched with supporting giving notice of the additional changes in context.

Approaches such as ServiceFlow [34] points to the need for such flexible solutions, although not taking a model-based approach. In the ongoing EXTERNAL-project [20], we are involved in developing such a model-based approach that enables the change and adaptation of instance-models by the users themselves. The operating environment is currently available through a traditional web-interface using a PC, but we have started to experiment with PDAs as clients.

Methodology for Development to Ensure Organizational Return: Siau [29] highlights as an important application-oriented research area the development of mCommerce business models. Within eCommerce, many new business models have appeared. The mobile environment in which mCommerce applications reside will require further adaptations of these models. In order for mCommerce to succeed, it is vital to ensure that all the related applications and services can be accessed with ease and little cost. Thus, in addition to externalize the business models in an computing independent way, it is important to integrate these models with the internal enterprise models and enterprise architecture, to be able to pinpoint the links to e.g. internal systems for the efficient billing of services provided

Requirements Engineering for business solutions have so far primarily dealt with the elicitation, specification, validation, management and change to information systems to be accessed through PCs and workstations [17]. As multi-channel solutions including also mobile front-ends are applied in more and more situations, additional challenges will meet those that specify the requirements to these applications. The traditional view of requirements engineering [15], where a requirement specification is developed early in a project, and then undergoes only minor changes under development and further system evolution, only partly applies. Rather it will be important to deal with unstable, unclear, and inconsistent user requirements that evolve and emerge through actual use.

Security and Other Quality Aspects: To enhance social mobility, organisations and industries need to develop "social ontologies", which define the significance of social roles, associated behaviour and context [22]. These ontologies would need to be available as explicit models to be useful for the development and ensuring necessary security of the mobile information systems.

4.2 Logical Level

User-Orientation and Personalization: The new separation between content and medium found in mobile information systems serves as a major challenge. Design of new systems need to take a minimum set of assumptions about physical devices to provide a maximum level of personalisation. *Personalisation* of mobile information systems becomes increasingly important, where user-interface details such as commands and screen layout is tailored to personal preferences and hardware using information about the current context and context trace [27] of the user. Personalisation here means both information systems that automatically *adapt* themselves to the preferences of the user, and systems that can be explicitly *tailored* by users through a specific user-interface. Generally the context should be explicitly modeled to be able to keep an overview of, analyze, and simulate the multitude of possibilities open for adapting to the context, and the use of context traces. For the more general use of mobile applications, it is also important to be able to adapt these systems to the user at hand, thus making a case for simple user-models to guide the adaptation.

Recently, work within user interface modeling has focused increasingly on mobile user interfaces [5,23,26]. This is often done to facilitate some level of common models for the mobile user interfaces and more traditional ones. A central element in this is the development of model-based approached that are powerful enough to be used as a basis for the development of user-interfaces on the multitude of platforms needed, but still general enough to represent the commonalties in a single place. One approach is to define user-interface patterns with general usability principles as powerful building blocks. Several other researchers have examined how patterns can be used in usability-oriented work [1,30,33] and have described how patterns can fit into all the different phases of a usability-engineering life-cycle.

A main challenge for model-based approaches for developing multi-interfaces is to have a set of concepts that are, on the one hand, abstract and general enough to express specifications across a number of quite different platforms and, on the other hand, powerful and expressive enough to support mapping to different platforms. Thus, there is a need to combine generalization and specialization. A model-based technique that is abstract enough to be able to describe user interfaces with significant differences may run the risk of being banal. By this we mean that the model is not able to describe a sufficient number of aspects of the user interfaces in a way that renders it possible to transform the models to concrete user interfaces without adding so much additional information to the mapping process for each platform, that the interfaces might as well have been developed from scratch on each platform (Nilsson, 2002). A model based approach for such system might also prove efficient when needing to run the system on new mobile devices.

Technological Aspects Including Convergence and Multi-channel Support: There are currently (and will be for the foreseeable future) a multitude of competing technologies for providing the underlying infrastructure for distributed and mobile applications. A central element when addressing this is the development of model based specification techniques that are powerful enough to be used as a basis for the development of systems on a large number of technical platforms, but still general enough to represent the commonalties at one place only. The current major initiative within OMG, on Model-driven architectures (MDA), where both platform independent and platform specific modeling notations including refinement techniques are specified, highlights the current industry-focus on such an approach. In connection to this, it is interesting to note how meta-modeling techniques and domain-specific modeling (DSM) have found a special application for the design of mobile phone software [14]. Mobile information systems can be argued as a particular good area for using domain-specific modeling:

- The software (on the client side) is partly embedded, needing higher reliability than traditional software, which can be supported by restricting choices through adding modeling rules and code-generation.
- You need many, very similar variants of the same application.
- There are a number of standards to adhere to, and the technology and standards change rapidly. One wants to define e.g. GSM only once, and use this definition in a range of product. When necessary one would like to plug in e.g. UMTS or US analog system in its place

Several approaches to customize the presentation of the contents of distributed information systems wrt. the terminal device are reported. A literal translation from the web to wireless is inadequate. Merely squeezing data into small screens detracts from the user experience on mobile devices [2]. Most of the proposals concentrate on the generation of HTML pages for the web, and WML pages for WAP. Nowadays, the research interest is devoted to the automatic generation of multi-channel access systems. The most prominent approaches for the development of multi-channel interfaces can be summarized as follows:

- Terminal-independent form management such as XForms
- Vocal services such as using VoiceXML
- Transcoding: Several automatic transcoding tools have been developed to convert HTML documents into new languages, such as WML or HDML.
- Common languages such as XHTML Basic
- Comprehensive multi-channel language for a virtual universal device that includes all the characteristics of the devices through which the developed service should be accessed. CDI-ML and MaxML represent this approach.
- Finally WebML is a conceptual model for specifying data-intensive Web sites. WebML includes a structural model, to describe data, and a hypertext model, to describe how data are organized in pages and the navigation among pages. Generative techniques allow sites to be produced automatically even in a multi-channel context; also personalisation facilities are provided.

Methodology for Development to Ensure Organizational Return: Mobile information systems are often radical and therefore reward increased focus on idea generation early during development phases. This also means that there are not always existing services or situations in which to anchor problem analysis efforts, e.g., using As-is analysis as a starting point for To-be design [28]. Technology in the field still develops rapidly, which means that idea generation should not be limited by currently available technologies. It also means that systems must be designed for change. Applications of the new technology call for highly distributed systems that comprise new user-interface systems on the client side, new and existing back-end systems, as well as new bridging systems (which port information between other systems.) The new technologies therefore highlight the need for principled, long-term IS-architecture management and for integrating architecture management with software development methodologies. Often there is a need to interface to existing enterprise systems and architectures to enable the new workflow. Another aspect is how to integrate the user-interface models discussed above with other parts of the requirements and design model, for instance the entity model, process model and goal model. On both the process and the user-interface side, the challenges can be attacked by extending existing approaches to modeling, although research is needed to investigate both which techniques that should be extended and how they could be best adapted to the new problem areas. Looking at the architecture for general existing mobile information systems framework and solutions [3], we notice that the generic architecture is geared towards the modeling of data, business processes and tasks, events and behavior, rules, user interfaces and general context information.

Security and Other Quality Aspects: An important aspect is the dependability of the systems made. Laprie defines dependability as the "ability to deliver service that can justifiably be trusted" and identifies six dependability attributes: availability, reliability, safety, confidentiality, integrity and maintainability. Model-based development will in general be able to support dependability analyses, i.e., use of methods, techniques and tools for improving and estimating dependability, e.g., risk analyses, probabilistic safety assessment, testing, formal walkthrough, simulation, animation, exhaustive exploration and formal verification. Many of the dependability areas will be even more complex in mobile information systems than in traditional business systems. As an example, consider new issues arising in connection to security and privacy. The same device will often be used as a personal tool across the user's commitment to many different organizations and projects, and one must assure that data does not "leak" across different domains. Another area of concern is the users (lack of) control over the context traces they leave behind when they use location-based or other context-based general services.

5   Conclusion and Future Work

We have in this overview paper highlighted research areas for mobile information systems on the conceptual and logical level. We have primarily focused at the use of modelling-oriented tasks and approaches for business, process, requirements and design models. Although our focus is on user-oriented and traditionally 'early' phases of system development, the need for rapid and continuos development of new releases of a number of different variants brings forward a higher degree of reuse and integration of models of different nature. A major research question in connection to these areas is to what extent existing modelling-techniques based on e.g. UML can be applied, when these techniques should be extended, and when they need to be replaced all together due to the changes of the possibilities and limitations of the underlying infrastructure.

References

1. Borchers, J. *A pattern approach to interactive design.* New York: John Wiley & sons, Inc. 2001.
2. Billsus, D, Brunk, C. A., Evans, C. Gladish, B., and Pazzani, M. Adaptive interfaces for ubiquitous web access. In Communications of the ACM Volume 45, No. 5, May pp. 34-38, 2002.
3. Celesta Universal mBusiness Platform (http://www.celesta.com/pdf/products/mBusiness_Platform.pdf), June 6, 2001.
4. Dertouzos et al, The future of Computing, Sc. Am. 1999.
5. Eisenstein, J. , Vanderdonckt, J., and Puerta, A. *Applying Model-Based Techniques to the Development of UIs for Mobile Computers.* In "Proceedings of ACM Conference on Intelligent User Interfaces IUI'2001"
6. Esbjörnsson, M. "Work in Motion: Interpretation of Defects along the Roads", Proc. IRIS24, Bjørnestad, S., Moe, R., Mørch, A., Opdahl, A. (Eds.), Univ of Bergen, Norway, 2001.
7. Esler et al. Data-centric Networking for Invisible Computing: The Portolano Project, 5th ACM/IEEE Conf. on Mob. Comp. and Netw. 1999
8. Fox et al, Adapting to Network and Client Variation Using Active Proxies: Lessons and Perspectives, IEEE Pers. Comm., 1998
9. Hall, E.T. Beyond Culture. Anchor Books, Doubleday, 1976
10. Hirsch, R., Coratella, A., Felder, M., and Rodriguez, E. A Framework for Analyzing Mobile Transaction Models. Journal of Database Management: 12(3) July-September, 2001.
11. Jørgensen, H.D., and Carlsen, S. (1999) Emergent Workflow: Integrated Planning and Performance of Process Instances, Proceedings Workflow Management '99, Münster, Germany.
12. Jørgensen, H.D. (2001) "Interaction as a Framework for Flexible Workflow Modelling", Proceedings of GROUP 2001, Boulder, Colorado, October 2001.
13. Kakihara, M., and Sørensen, C., "Mobility Reconsidered: Topological Aspects of Interaction", Proc. IRIS24, Bjørnestad, S., Moe, R., Mørch, A., Opdahl, A. (Eds.), Univ of Bergen, Norway, 2001.
14. Kelly, S., and Tolvanen- J-P. Visual Domain-specific modelling: Benefits and Experiences of Using Metacase Tools, Metacase Consulting, 2001.
15. Kotonya, G.. and Sommerville, I. Requirements Engineering: Processes and Techniques, Wiley, 1998.
16. Kristiansen, S., and Ljungberg, F., "Mobility — From stationary to mobile work", chapter 6 in Planet Internet, Braa, K., Sørensen, C. & Dahlbom, B. (Eds.), Studentlitteratur, Lund, 2000.
17. Krogstie, J. Requirement Engineering for Mobile Information Systems. Proceedings of REFSQ'2001 Interlaken Switzerland, 2001.
18. Krogstie, J., Brandtzæg, P.B. , Heim, J.. and Opdahl, A.L. Usable mCommerce Systems: The Need for Modeling-Based Approaches. To be published in Lim, Ee-P.and Siau, K. Advances in Mobile Commerce Technologies, IDEA Group Publishing, 2002.
19. Kvalsøren, G.M.; Langeland, P.F.; Moe, R.E.; Opdahl, A L.; Solberg, J.O.; Thornquist, B., and Wikenes, M. Early Design of Enhanced ETV Services. I: Bjørnestad, Solveig; Moe, Richard Elling; Mørch, Anders I. og Opdahl, Andreas Lothe, red. Proceedings of IRIS24: The 24th Information Systems Research Seminar in Scandinavia,Bergen, Norway: Institutt for informasjonsvitenskap, UiB; s. 465-478 Ulvik, 11. - 14. aug, 2001.

20. Lillehagen, F. , Dehli, E. , Fjeld, L., Krogstie, J., and Jørgensen, H.D. Active Knowledge Models as a Basis for an Infrastructure for Virtual Enterprise PRO'VE 2002 - 3rd IFIP Working Conference on infrastructures for virtual enterprises. Sesimbra, Portugal, May 2002.
21. Luff, P., and Heath, C. Mobility in collaboration. In: *Proceedings of the CSCW'98*, Seattle, USA, 305-314, 1998.
22. Lyytinen and Yoo. The Next Wave of Nomadic Computing: A Research Agenda for Information Systems Research, Accepted for publication in Information systems research, 2002.
23. Muller, A., Forbig, P., and Cap, C. *Model Based User Interface Design Using Markup Concepts*. In "Proceedings of The Eighth Workshop on the Design, Specification and Verification of Interactive Systems, 2001.
24. Nilsson, E.G. Combining compound conceptual user interface components with modelling patterns – A promising direction for model-based cross-platform user interface development. In 9ᵗʰ International Workshop on the Design, Specification and Verification of Interactive Systems, Rostock, Germany, June 12-14, 2002.
25. Noble et al. Agile Application-Aware Adaptation for Mobility, 16th SOSP, 1997.
26. Pribeanu, C., Limbourg, Q., and Vanderdonckt, J. Task Modelling for Context-Sensitive User Interfaces. In "Proceedings of The Eighth Workshop on the Design, Specification and Verification of Interactive Systems, 2001.
27. Rahlff R., Rolfsen, R.K., and Herstad, J.*"Using Personal Traces in Context Space: Towards Context Trace Technology"*, Springer's Personal and Ubiquitous Computing, Special Issue on Situated Interaction and Context-Aware Computing, Vol. 5, No. 1, 2001.
28. Rolland, C.,and Prakash, C., "Bridging the Gap Between Organisational Needs and ERP Functionality", RE Journal 5(3):180–193, Springer, 2000.
29. Siau, K., Lim , E.-P., and Shen, Z. Mobile Commerce: Promises, Challenges, and Research Agenda Journal of Database Management: 12(3) July-September, 2001.
30. Sutcliffe, A., and Dimitrova, M. *Patterns, claims and multimedia.* Paper presented at the INTERACT'99 7th International Conference on Human-Computer Interaction, Edinburgh, UK, 1999.
31. Thompson and Warhurst. Workplaces of the Future, Macmillan Business, 1998.
32. Wegner, P. Why interaction is more powerful than algorithms, Communications of the ACM, vol. 40, no. 5, 1997.
33. Welie, M. v., and Trætteberg, H. *Interaction Patterns in User Interfaces.* 7th. Pattern Languages of Programs Conference, Allerton Park Monticello, Illinois, USA, 2000.
34. Wetzel, I., and Klischewski, R. Serviceflow beyond Workflow? Concepts and Architectures for Supporting Interorganizational Service Processes. In Pidduck, A. B., Mylopoulos, J. Woo, C. C., and Ozsu, M. T. (Eds.) Proceedings from CAiSE'14, Toronto, Canada, 2002.

A Cooperation Model for Personalised and Situation Dependent Services in Mobile Networks

Michael Amberg[1], Stefan Figge[2], and Jens Wehrmann[1]

[1]University of Erlangen-Nürnberg
{amberg,jens.wehrmann}@wiso.uni-erlangen.de
[2]CSC Ploenzke AG
sfigge@csc.com

Abstract. Situation dependent services are services that significantly depend on the user's context. Considering the individual needs, such services are regarded to be more beneficial to the customer than non-individual services. In this paper we present a conceptual framework and characterise a service platform for the cooperative development of situation dependent services. The framework pays attention to the current market situation and considers legal, economical and technical conditions that are relevant for providing situation dependent mobile services. The cooperative service platform which is hosted by the mobile network operator gives service providers access to the usage situation of their customers. Taking advantage of that platform, the provided services can be adopted effectively according to the customer's situation and needs.

1 Introduction

Due to the high investments in the technical infrastructure the mobile network operators are under pressure to ensure a certain amount of transaction volume with mobile (data) services. In spite of their former efforts to develop and provide mobile services by their own, they now incline to concentrate on their own core competencies while opening their data networks to specialised service providers. For that purpose, the mobile network operators have to develop and provide service platforms that supply service providers with the infrastructure for mobile data communication, billing of services as well as the handling of the collection procedure.

As the experiences with mobile services are showing, service concepts known from the stationary internet can not be transferred into the mobile environment. Instead, only those mobile services tend to be successful that take the specific features of the user's context into account and apply this information to generate an added value for the mobile customer. Services that automatically adapt to the context are termed *Situation Dependent Services* (SDS). Initial examples for SDS are mobile *Location Based Services* (LBS) or personalised internet services. By now, LBS are based on a low level of situation dependency and use mostly simple filtering techniques with database lookups.

A popular example of a service platform is i-mode that has been developed in Japan and was recently launched in Europe. In I-mode only simple situation dependent services are supported by now. The situation concept as introduced in this

A. Olivé (Eds.): ER 2003 Ws, LNCS 2784, pp. 136-146, 2003.

paper assists in structuring the mobile user's context and supports a cooperative development of situation dependent mobile services. It outlines a situation concept that can be technically handled and discusses the aspects that are relevant for conveying context information to the service providers.

1.1 Fundamental Conditions to Provide Mobile Services

For the development and commercialisation of situation dependent mobile services fundamental conditions such as legal, technical and economical conditions have to be considered.

Legal Conditions: As providing situation dependent mobile services is closely connected with the collection, storage and interpretation of personal information, it is obvious that this kind of data processing has to be supervised by some kind of data protection act. Even if penalties caused by violation against laws do not mean an immediate economical thread for a service provider, it might cause customers to decline a service or a service provider [1]. The Compass approach emphasises the customer's privacy and regards it as an influencing factor of success.

Technical Conditions: This category includes technical standards and specifications that are relevant for the exchange of data between the cooperation partners. While the internet provides a common communication infrastructure, the open questions are which interfaces to define between the involved participants and which format to use to convey the content.

Economical Conditions: As the providers of situation dependent mobile services are economically organised companies some kind of clearing has to take place for supplementary services. Especially, the value of the customer's situation data has to be clarified.

2 Compass – A Cooperation
Model for Personalised and Situation Dependent Services

The Compass approach that is outlined in this paper defines a methodological framework to provide situation dependent mobile services cooperatively.

The Compass approach integrates four major components (see Fig. 1). Considering these components in a balanced way, is understood to be a critical success factor within the development of mobile services.

- The **Compass Situation Concept** structures the mobile usage context and makes the situation information accessible for the cooperative service production.
- The **Compass Interaction Model** describes the flow of services and information between the cooperation partners.
- The **Compass Usage Cycle** presents the process to provide situation dependent mobile services and describes several service types.
- The **Compass System Architecture** details the technical adoption of the situation concept and suggests an underlying system infrastructure.
In the following, each of these four components is covered in more detail.

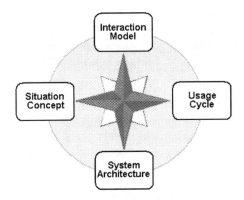

Fig. 1. The Compass Approach

3   The Compass Situation Concept

The Compass approach is based on the idea that the adoption of a mobile service according to the customer's situation provides a real benefit and an improved user experience. A mobile service that is able to access the context is much more able to solve a problem efficiently and to provide a certain added value compared to a service without this information.

Depending on the scope of interest, there are several definitions of the term "situation". For the development of SDS, it is sufficient to define a user's situation as all aspects that have a measurable influence on the individual, are measurable over mobile devices and are relevant for customising a service. Table 1 compares existing classifications focused on mobile as well as internet services with the classification proposed in this paper.

Hitz et al.[5] distinguish four dimensions and use these to adapt web applications. The dimensions are significantly abutted to the demands of the technical infrastructure for web applications. Scheer et al.[9] differentiate four types of context that are almost similar to the dimensions proposed here. They regard the person dimension in more detail and distinguish between *Personal* and *Action Based Context* of a person. Their classification is solely used to outline context sensitivity and not to develop and improve SDS. Gessler and Jesse [3] classify *Time*, *Location* and *Context*. Context is further subdivided into *User Context* (the user's characteristics), *Object Context* (other relevant objects nearby i.e. a restaurant) and *General Context* (other information for example weather). We believe that the *Object* and *General Context* do not directly belong to the user's situation but may help to identify the user's behaviour.

Table 1. Comparison of Different Classifications of a User's Situation

Proposed here	Hitz et al. [5]	Scheer et al. [9]	Gessler and Jesse [3]
- **Time**	- Time	- Time Context	- Time
- **Place**	- Location	- Local Context	- Location
- **Person**	- Terminal Equipment	- Personal Context	- User Context
	- Network Parameters	- Action Based Context	- Object Context
			- General Context

In this paper we propose to distinguish the measurable aspects of a user's situation according to three dimensions: *Time*, *Place* and *Person*. These dimensions correlate with the primary situation determinants that are presently transmittable in mobile networks. *Time* and *Place* are the common and most obvious dimensions that are easy to measure. The *Person* summarises all measurable aspects of a person. It includes the identity and demographic information as well as information about the specific behaviour.

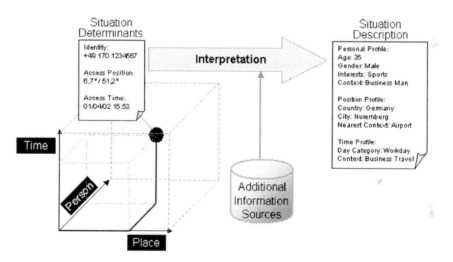

Fig. 2. The Compass Situation Concept

The **Compass Situation Concept** includes a three-step process to determine the user's situation for a mobile service:

a) **Determination:** In a first step, the elementary situation information (called situation determinants here) are measured. For the **identification** of a mobile customer in mobile GSM networks the *Mobile Subscriber International Subscriber Directory Number* (MSISDN) can be used. To calculate the **position** of the mobile terminal network or terminal based solutions exist. By merging these information with the world time the user's **local time** can be calculated.

b) **Interpretation:** On the basis of the situation determinants and by consulting additional data sources detailed information about the user's situation is derived.

c) **Description:** The derived knowledge about the user's situation is than coded in a suitable mark-up language.

The situation determinants are used in the interpretation process to derive a semantically richer description about the user's situation. A good example is the interpretation of the degree of longitude and latitude of the geo coordinate into information about the country, the city or street. To do such an interpretation, additional information sources are needed.

INPUT   OUTPUT

		General Attributes	Personal Attributes	Situation description
Situation determinants	Person	Demographic databases	Personal profile (hobbies, age, occupation, etc.)	Age: 28 Gender: Male Interests: Sports Context: Business Man
Identity: +49 170 1234567 Access Position: 6,7°/51,2° Access Time: 01.04.02 15:53	Place	Digital maps, Points of Interest	Location preferences (home, work, etc.), Routes (way to work, etc.)	Country: Germany City: Nuremberg Nearest Site: Airport
	Time	General calendar (events, public holiday, etc.)	Personal calendar (dates, travel, vacation, etc.)	Day Category: Workday Context: Business Travel

Fig. 3. Information Sources for the Interpretation of the Situation Determinants

An approach for structuring the required sources of information is given by the combination of dimensions and a degree of individualisation (Fig. 3). The degree of individualisation is differentiated in general and personal attributes. The first include attributes that are valid for all mobile customers while the personal attributes depend on the individual. After the interpretation process the result has to be coded adequately into a situation description that can be exported in a document.

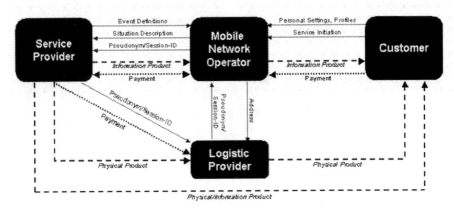

Fig. 4. The Compass Interaction Model

4   The Compass Interaction Model

The **Compass Interaction Model** describes the service and information relationships between the involved participants. From a conceptual perspective of providing situation dependent mobile services, three or four market participants can be differentiated (Fig. 4). Information products are offered by the service provider, procured by the mobile network operator and paid by the customer. For physical products a logistic provider is involved for the physical transportation between service provider and customer.

In the scope of the Compass Interaction Model, the mobile network operator takes an important role as an intermediate between service provider, customer and if necessary logistic provider. From the customer's view he is the contact for all customer specific concerns. He ensures the access to the mobile network, manages the personal settings and profiles (e.g. privacy protection), receives and processes the user requests, transmits the information products and is responsible for billing. From the service provider's view he provides a widespread service platform. This platform enables the service provider to offer any service. The resulting central role of the mobile network operator is obvious. Thus, aspects like protection of privacy or data security have to meet high demands. Considering the security aspects, the mobile network operator has to establish himself as a party of trust, commonly termed as *Trusted Third Party* (TTP). The authors consider emotional barriers to be very important. Concepts to ensure and guarantee trustability are an important field of research.

Typically, the used services are charged to the users mobile phone account bill. The mobile network operator may account the service fees to the service provider and a revenue sharing can be realised. The possible tariff models and different possibilities for accounting the services are not discussed in this paper.

The mobile network operator is the only involved party, who has the infrastructure to measure the situation determinants. This is an essential reason for being the only one who can handle the interpretation and description of situations efficiently. The strict borders of data protection and legal regulations [1] on the one hand and the sensibility of customers regarding their personal data on the other hand determine that the mobile network operator should only transfer anonymous situation descriptions. Most information products provided over the platform of the mobile network operator do not depend significantly on the user's identity. A practical concept for ensuring the privacy is using alias or session-IDs instead of a personal ID.

If a service includes the transportation of physical products, the observance of anonymity – if necessary - is more difficult to assure. For this case the Compass Interaction Model includes a specific interface to a logistic provider.

5   The Compass Usage Cycle

The **Compass Usage Cycle** describes the main process steps for providing situation dependent mobile services and differentiates the following three basic (not disjunctive) categories of services: **Individualised Services** are any kind of user initiated services. They are adapted to the individual customer's needs. **Proactive**

Services are automatically generated services which are triggered by special events. **Evolutionary Services** are services which are updated and enhanced successively by analysing and evaluating them in continuous time steps.

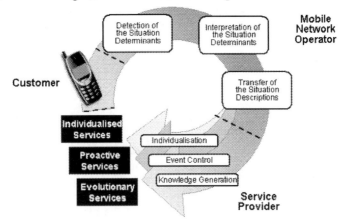

Fig. 5. The Compass Usage Cycle

Fig. 5 illustrates the Compass Usage Cycle. The main process steps are:

- **Detection of the Situation Determinants:** The mobile network operator detects the situation determinants. Objects of the detection are position, time and user identity.
- **Interpretation of the Situation Determinants:** The mobile network operator enriches the information by consulting additional information sources.
- **Transfer of the Situation Descriptions:** The mobile network operator encodes the situation description and transfers it to the service provider.
- **Individualisation of Mobile Services:** The service provider uses the situation description for the individualisation of user initiated services (pull services).
- **Event Control in Mobile Services:** The service provider can define situation based rules. The mobile network operator compares these rules with the situations. If a rule matches with a situation a proactive service is generated (push service).
- **Knowledge Generation in Mobile Services:** Knowledge generation for mobile services enables a long-term analysis, evaluation and extension of services.

The first two tasks have already been outlined. In the following, the remaining tasks of the Compass Usage Cycle will be discussed.

5.1   Transfer of the Situation Descriptions

After the situation description has been generated, an interface for the transfer to the service provider is needed. To ensure the protection of privacy, any information about the identity of the customer is removed and the situation description can be transferred in a pseudonymous or anonymous manner. The challenge is to reduce some of the elements without decreasing the significant information content. The following information elements have to be transferred: Pseudonym or session-ID, situation determinants as an atomic description of the situation and a set of interpreted information about the situation (e.g. town, customer age etc.).

Suitable interfaces must be defined for the transfer. For example the transfer of location data can use the *Mobile Location Protocol* (MLP) provided by the *Location Inter-operability Forum* (LIF). As the situation description includes valuable information, several accounting models between network and service provider are imaginable.

5.2   Individualisation of Mobile Services

The individualisation of mobile services is a tool for customer orientation and the manageability of services. The adaptation of services should lead to a rising user acceptance. As introduced in the Compass Situation Concept, three categories of individualisation can be differentiated:

Adaptation Referring to the Location: Services considering the location are well-known and Location Based Services (LBS) are discussed in literature sufficiently [2,6,8].

Adaptation Referring to the Time: There is a wide spectrum from week and daytime up to an adaptation to individual dates including the social context.

Adaptation Referring to the Person: Important components for an individualisation are preferences, profiles, knowledge and the interests of a customer.

5.3   Event Control in Mobile Services

A great potential of mobile services is the ubiquitous addressability of customers which is founded in the close interconnection of customer and personal mobile device. This allows services to get activated or initiated by a particular circumstance and enables active notification services. This makes mobile services to a tool for the marketing of the future [7]. Regarding the legal aspects and Godin's permission marketing concept [4], a complete new dimension of services for customers and service providers is imaginable. To control the matching of predefined rules, the mobile network operator has to investigate predefined rules and the situation of the customers continuously. The service provider as well as the customer must be able to control (set, modify, delete and limit) the rules and any kind of notification functionality.

5.4   Knowledge Generation in Mobile Services

A service provider may use the historical data about customer transactions and the respective user's situation as a valuable source for an evaluation of their mobile services. Thus, he can conclude to the demographic properties, the regional allocation or many other attributes that help to enhance or upgrade a service. Additional tools may further assist the service provider to understand the intentions, purposes and the special needs of users in special situations better. An evaluation of services by the customer may help to identify wrong adaptations. Depending on the success and the influencing factors, a service can be stopped or advanced in an evolutionary style.

6   The Compass System Architecture

The **Compass System Architecture** focuses on the implementation of the cooperation platform. The Compass components that have been conceptually outlined in the former chapters are discussed concerning the present realisation alternatives (Fig. 6).

The Compass Usage Cycle is initiated by the mobile customer at the time he or she is trying to access a mobile service. The determination of the user's situation is the basic challenge to provide situation based mobile services. With positioning and identification technologies that are available in mobile networks it is already possible to retrieve the selected situation determinants. The mobile network operator is able to use these information to consult databases that might have their origin in *Customer Relationship Management* (CRM) or portal activities. With these databases the situation determinants can be interpreted and semantically richer information derived. In the next step these information have to be conveyed to the service provider. Commonly, an *Extensible Markup Language* (XML) schema is used to define the structure and content of a data interface. All involved participants have to agree upon the necessary data interfaces before a concrete coding and transmission of a user's situation can be executed.

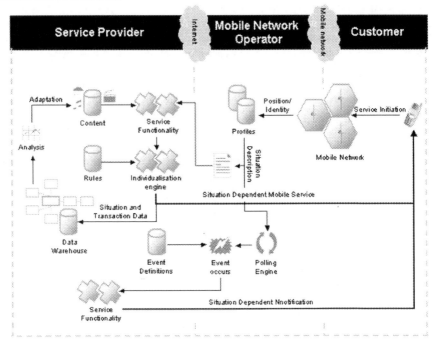

Fig. 6. The Compass System Architecture

The situation description that is conveyed from the mobile network operator to the service provider normally contains a reference to the identity of the user. The type of reference depends on the degree of intensity that characterises the relationship between the mobile customer and the service provider. The customer must have the choice to select the type of reference that he wants to transmit to the service provider:

- **Anonymity** (e.g. Session-ID): The service provider only gets a weak reference that points to the current data session of the customer. The customer-ID can not be resolved by the service provider.
- **Pseudonymity** (e.g. X-ID or Nickname): The service provider receives a pseudonym for the user that remains the same over all data sessions. Therefore, the service provider can recognise a mobile customer without knowing his identity.
- **Identity** (e.g. MSISDN): The service provider gets access to the technical address of the mobile terminal that enables him to resolve the customer's identity.

The anonymity as the weakest reference still provides all potential of the situation concept. Additionally, the other two types of reference allow the service provider to adapt the service even more comprehensively. To transmit the real identity might be desirable if the customer already has a trusted relationship with the service provider and if settings and preferences are already stored within the service provider's scope.

To implement the individualisation of a service, the service provider may define a set of rules and use the so called rule based matching concept to specify and control the service's behaviour. If the customer has decided to reveal his or her identity or the pseudonym to the service provider it will be possible for the service provider to store and process profiles and transaction data.

The second approach to use the situation concept is to leverage the situation description to generate knowledge at the service provider. To do this, transactions done by the customer are related to their current situation description. That information is then stored within a data warehouse. With the analysis of this information through *Online Analytical Processing* (OLAP) or *Data Mining* tools it is possible in the following to get a deeper understanding about the customers intentions and needs. On the basis of this information it is possible to redesign and enhance the service offering and make the service more successful.

7   Summary

Compass is a methodological approach that describes a conceptual framework and the fundamental requirements for a service platform to cooperatively develop and provide situation dependent services. In the authors opinions, cooperation platforms are one of the most important issues of research for mobile business. The added value generated by cooperation platforms may lead to an increasing usage intensity of mobile services and influence the revenue of service providers and mobile network operators positively.

This paper introduces Compass as a high-level framework. Future papers will discuss aspects of the methodological approach in detail. Although the Compass System Architecture discusses major implementation issues of a cooperation platform, the development of prototypes is already in progress to help verify the practicability of the outlined concepts.

References

1. Enzmann, M, Pagnia, H., Grimm, R. (2000): Das Teledienstedatenschutzgesetz und seine Umsetzung in der Praxis. In: *Wirtschaftsinformatik 42*. Wiesbaden, Germany: Vieweg Verlag, 5/2000, S. 402-412
2. Figge, S. (2001): Situation Dependent m-Commerce Applications. In: Dholakia, R., Kolbe, L., Venkatesh, A., Zoche, P. (Hrsg.): *Conference on Telecommunications and Information Markets Proceedings (COTIM 2001)*. Kingston, USA: University of Rhode Island
3. Gessler, S., Jesse, K. (2001): Advanced Location Modeling to enable sophisticated LBS Provisioning in 3G networks. In: Beigl, M., Gray, P., Salber, D. (Hrsg.): *Proceedings of the Workshop on Location Modeling for Ubiquitous Computing*. Atlanta, Georgia: http://www.teco.edu/locationws/9.pdf
4. Godin, S. (1999): *Permission Marketing*.: Finanzbuch Verlag, München, Germany
5. Hitz, M., Kappel, G., Retschitzegger, W., Schwinger, W. (2002): *Ein UML-basiertes Framework zur Modellierung ubiquitärer Web-Anwendungen*. In: Wirtschaftsinformatik 44. Wiesbaden, Germany: Vieweg Verlag, 3/2002, S. 225-235
6. May, P. (2001): *Mobile Commerce – Opportunities, Applications, and Technologies of Wireless Business*. Cambridge, UK: Cambridge University Press
7. Möhlenbruch, D., Schmieder, U. (2001): Gestaltungsmöglichkeiten und Entwicklungspotenziale des Mobile Marketings. In: Heilmann, H. (Hrsg.): *HMD - Praxis der Wirtschaftsinformatik*. Heidelberg: dpunkt Verlag, Heft 220, S. 15-26
8. Ovum (2000): *Mobile Location Services - Market Strategies*. London, UK: http: http://www.ovum.com/MOBILE
9. Scheer, A.W., Feld, T., Göbl, M., Hoffmann, M. (2002): Das Mobile Unternehmen. In: Silberer, G., Wohlfahrt, J., Wilhelm, T. (Hrsg.): *Mobile Commerce – Grundlagen, Geschäftsmodelle, Erfolgsfaktoren*. Wiesbaden, Germany

Sequence Diagrams for Mobility[1]

Piotr Kosiuczenko

kosiucze@informatik.uni-muenchen.de
Institute of Computer Science, Ludwig-Maximilian-University
Oettingenstr. 67, Munich, Germany

Abstract. There are several kinds of UML diagrams for convenient modelling of behaviour, but these diagrams can be hardly used for modelling mobility. The situation is not very different in the case of agent languages. There exist already some proposals for modelling mobility of interacting agents by graphical notations, but these notations are rather not very intuitive and hard to read if the specification becomes a bit complex. In this paper we propose a new graphical notation for modelling interaction of mobile objects. The notation is based on UML sequence diagrams. We model behaviour of mobile objects using a generalized version of lifelines. For different kinds of actions like creating, entering or leaving a mobile object we use stereotyped messages. We provide also a zoom-out, zoom-in facility allowing us to abstract from specification details. We explain our notation in a series of examples, study its applicability and limits.

1 Introduction

The emergence of World-Wide-Web and WAN provided a qualitatively new computational infrastructure which changed our view of computing. Its emergence fostered new concepts of location like virtual location for administrative domains, fire-walls, physical location for computing devices operating in different places and so on. The Web provides rather a dynamic collection of several independent administrative domains which are very different and where the communication latency matters (cf. [9]). The computing devices differ in their power, availability and the network links differ in capacity and reliability. The network topology, which was carefully hidden in LAN, starts to play a fundamental role; it is dynamic and very complex.

There are many different concepts of computing which exploit the Web infrastructure. One of the most important is the paradigm of mobile computing which gains more and more interest. Code mobility emerged in some scripting languages for controlling network applications like Tcl. There are agent languages like Telescript and place based languages like Linda. Agents mobility has been supported by Telescript, AgentTcl or Odyssey (cf. e.g. [9]). Mobile hosts like laptops, WAPs or PDAs can move between networks. Entire networks can be mobile too like for example the IBM's Personal Area Network, networks of sensors in airplanes or trains. Here the administrative barriers and multiple access pathways interact in very complex ways. Mobile computations can cross barriers and move be-

---

1. This research has been partially sponsored by the IST project Architectures for Mobility funded by the European Commission as a part of the Global Computing Initiative.

tween virtual and physical locations, they can turn remote calls to local calls avoiding the latency limits. There exist several formalisms and some notations for modeling mobility, but the most relevant for our approach are Ambient Calculus [5], Maude [12], Agent UML [2] (see below). There exists still a discrepancy between these formalisms and on the other hand the graphical modeling languages capable of specifying mobility. One of the major advantages of UML [13] is its expressiveness. UML provides a variety of different kinds of diagrams which allows one for specification of software systems from different points of view. UML proved to be very useful in describing various aspects of behavior, but at the moment offers limited support for modeling mobility. In particular its sequence diagrams can be hardly used to specify even simple cases (see section 3). Similarly, the graphical languages for agent systems capable of specifying mobility become very hard to understand when the complexity increases.

In this paper we present Sequence Diagrams for Mobility (SDM), an extension of UML sequence diagrams for modeling mobile objects. The idea is similar to the idea of ambients or Maude, in that a mobile object can migrate from one host to another and it can be a host for other mobile objects. It may interact with other objects. Like a place, a mobile object can host other mobile objects, it can locally communicate and receive messages from other places. Objects can be arbitrarily nested, generalizing the limited place-agent nesting of most agent and place languages. To model nested and dynamically changing structure, we generalize the concept of object lifeline of UML sequence diagrams. First, we blow up the lifeline to an action box which now plays the function of lifeline and of object boundary. Second we stretch the lifeline to contain also the paths of objects migrating from one host to another. Our idea generalizes the idea of Use Case Maps [4, 1] and it allows us to specify ambients with their nested structure and mobility, in particular moving objects are treated the same way as their hosts (i.e. the hosts can be mobile too, cf. [9]). We provide also the possibility to abstract from certain details of SDM if they are unnecessary for a view, i.e. we develop the concept of zoom-in and zoom-out view, where certain details may be shown or abstracted away if not necessary for the description. The qualitatively new ideas in our approach are:

- the blowing up of object's lifeline and message arrows to model not only the communication but also the changing topology and in particular mobility
- the zoom-in, zoom-out modelling facility

The paper is organized as follows. In section 2, we present related work. In section 3, we gradually introduce the basic concepts of our notation. In section 4, we present more advanced concepts; we discuss the problem of identifying mobile object across complex lifelines and present pattern matching algorithm for that. Finally in section 5, we consider a bit more complex example trying to push our graphical notation to its limits.

2   Related Work

There exist several formalisms and some notations for modeling and specification of mobility. We mention here those most relevant for our approach. A very interesting formal notation is provided by the Ambient Calculus [5]. In this formalism, on one hand the ambients are playing the role of physical or logical locations and on the other hand they are playing the role of processes. The ambients can move around entering or leaving other ambients and performing computations. The topology can be explicitly observed and constraints the communication and mobility. The ambients barriers model security constraints like those provided by fire-walls. This calculus is based on local synchronous communication and mobility. The advantage of this calculus is that it provides nice abstractions for modeling mobility across nested locations and allows one to specify security constraints.

One of the earliest formal notation capable of specifying mobile objects was Maude [12], although specification of mobility was not its primary goal. Maude is a very flexible formalism for specifying complex communication patterns where synchronous as well as asynchronous communication is supported and where hierarchical object structures are allowed, like in ambient calculus. Mobile Maude is an agent language extending Maude for specification of mobile computation [6].

UML [13] gained wide acceptance as a modeling language. There exist already several proposals for extending UML to model new artifacts. There is an extension, called Agent UML, for modeling agents and their interactions protocols [2, 3]. Class and interaction diagrams are extended for specification of complex agent interaction protocols. Sequence diagrams are extended by several constructs analogous to MSC inline expressions [8].

There exist two interesting extensions of UML which can be used for modeling mobility. The first one [10] is similar to an early idea of Use Case Maps, where for example the behavior of a traveler was modelled by a line going from one location to another [4, 1]. To model locations, stereotyped classes are used, object moves are modeled by stereotyped messages. This approach is well suited for the case when there are only mobile objects and static locations, but not for modeling objects like ambients which are both locations able to host other ambients and mobile devices. The second one [14] extends UML collaboration diagrams to model dynamic change of composition relationship. It was not meant to model mobility, but it can be used for this goal too. This approach is well suited for simple cases and provides very compact but hard to read specifications for larger ones, specially when the objects perform many jumps (cf. section 5). Let us mention an approach to three-dimensional animation of UML diagrams [7]. We have to mention also Message Sequence Charts (MSC) [8], a graphical language similar to sequence diagrams but with much more constructs included for specifications like inline expressions or High Level MSC. Unlike sequence diagrams, MSC are aimed at strictly asynchronous systems and can not model method calls.

3   The SDM Language

Mobility is the ability to cross barriers. Mobile objects may interact with other mobile objects, by sending messages and changing locations. In our approach, a mobile object is also a location where interaction may happen. Different locations are separated by action boxes. The action boxes describe what happens inside and what is outside and allows one to show in a transparent way message exchange and object's migration. Locations can be arbitrarily nested and form a tree structure, this is aimed at modeling firewalls, administrative domains networks and so on. For example, a personal area network may be located in a car located in a ferry which may enter a harbor and so on.

In ambient calculus communication across a single barrier is synchronous; communication across multiple barriers is performed via other ambients which navigate from one location to another. In UML but also in Maude, objects can communicate in synchronous or asynchronous way. We stick to this principle. Unlike ambients, in our notation it is possible to express actions at a distance (like RMI) even if many barriers are involved, so that multiple steps can be rendered atomic. In general, we do not want to restrict the language artificially; if something is easy to specify in our notation, then we allow it without bothering whether it is easy to implement or not. But of course if necessary one can define a dialect disallowing some expressions.

A mobile object can change its location in a jump action. For example an object may try to cross a firewall in a message; in this case the topology changes too (cf. [9]). To model this, the object lifelines in sequence diagrams are blown up to action boxes; it models actions performed by a mobile object and indicates the boundaries of the object. Consequently, in our two dimensional representation we have two lines which denote the same thread. This implies that different arrows must be attached to different levels of an action box. Unfortunately, we can not use here dashed lines for the action boxes as in sequence diagrams, since the pictures become very hard to grasp when the complexity increases. To avoid the visual clutter we use continuous lines.

A description of a mobile object's behavior starts with a box containing optionally the object name or class. A mobile object may jump into another object, or jump out of an object. If an object jumps into or out of another object, then the action box ends in the former location and the object is moved to another location. This move is indicated by a stereotyped message arrow which starts with a black circle; we call it jump arrow. We use UML state machines notation to indicate that after the jump the moving object starts its operation in a new location. A mobile object can not continue its operation outside of its new host, if it is already inside another host; consequently the arrow starts strictly at the end of the first action box to indicate that all action in the box must precede the jump. We assume, that the mobile objects can not be bi-located or merged, therefore an object box may have at most one jump arrow attached to the top and at most one arrow attached to the bottom. If a mobile object starts its operation (and was not active before anywhere else), then this is indicated by a special box like in the case of sequence diagrams. If a mobile object was already active somewhere else, then there must exist a jump arrow such that its sharp end is attached to the left or right upper corner of the corresponding action box (see figure 1). This requirement corresponds to the fact that mobile objects can not be merged, nor appear out of nowhere. We indicate the end of mobile object description by two horizontal lines, where the upper line is dashed. Let us point out that it does not mean that the object was terminated (see below).

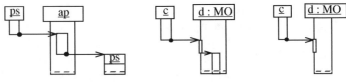

Fig. 1. Object mobility

Figure 1 shows what a mobile object looks like. As in the case of sequence diagrams, the object's names must be underlined. In the left hand side of figure 1, passanger ps enters airplane ap. Since there is no conflict concerning the identity of objects inside ap. The corresponding action box does not bear any name. Then ps deplanes ap and starts its operation outside ap, the name in the action box is not necessary either, since the identity of ps can be uniquely traced. No message arrow is attached to the corresponding action box except of the jump. In the middle of figure 1, a mobile object c enters object d of class MO by activating an operation of d (like a virus which sends itself in an e-mail). After the operation is finished the objects starts to operate inside d. In the right hand side, another scenario is shown, the object c does not manage to cross the barrier and disappears. We do not indicate it in any special way.

Figure 2 shows two communicating objects a1 and a2 inside the object a. The objects a1 and a2 reside inside a from the very beginning.

Fig. 2. Communication

Figure 3 shows an object b which creates a new object c. We use here a message arrow with stereotype <<create>>. Similarly for cloning an object, we use a message with stereotype <<copy>> [13], the copy is then assumed to behave as its original would do inside the new location (cf. [2]). Let us observe that the end line of the action box of the virus and the end line of the action box of the 131 PC are different. This does not have any meaning, but allows us for better grouping of object boxes (see sections 4 and 5).

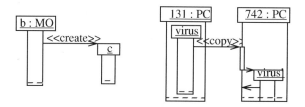

Fig. 3. Object createation and cloning

Another important operation is open, this operation opens an object making its hosted objects visible. If a mobile object is opened, then it ends its life, but its sub-objects continue to operate. This operation is similar to operation open in ambient calculus [5], but it may be synchronous as well as asynchronous, depending on the type of message used.

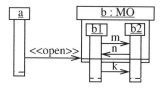

Fig. 4. Opening an object

In figure 4, we have shown an object b, which is opened by object a. The opening of an object is indicated by a horizontal line. Object a sends message open to b, then b is opened and the hosted objects b1 and b2 continue to operate. A mobile object can be terminated, in this case all its hosted objects are terminated too. The recursive termination is indicated by a continuous line. For the recursive termination caused by an other object we use a message with stereotype <<destroy>> (cf. [13]). The SDM diagrams can model immediate open (cf. figure 4) and destroy (see the left hand side of figure 5) as well as cases where the opened or destroyed objects continue to operate, in this case the sharp end of the message arrow is placed above the termination line (see the right hand side of figure 5) .

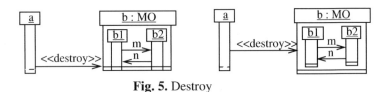

Fig. 5. Destroy

In figure 5, object a terminates object b. After terminating b, all its sub-objects are terminated too. The termination is indicated by a continuous line stretching across all objects. The left hand side of the figure shows immediate termination and the right hand side shows asynchronous termination.

4   Advanced Concepts

In this section we present some more advanced concepts and study the topology of nested objects more carefully. In the first subsection, we introduce the concept of zoom-in and zoom out view. In the second subsection, we define the notion of lifeline in general terms and give an example of a complex lifeline. In the third subsection, we present an algorithm which can be used to figure out an object's identity along complex lifelines.

4.1   The Zoom-in and Zoom-out View

In this subsection we show how to zoom into and zoom out of objects to see or to abstract from the internal details, respectively. The left hand side of figure 6 shows communicating mobile object c, in the zoom-in view, which displays the hosted object c1 with its topological details. The zoom-out view of c does not show its sub-objects but only its external communication. The right hand side of figure 6 shows the open operation performed by object a on object b. In this case the two sub-objects emerge, this is indicated by the fork operation which is analogous to the fork operation of state machines (cf. [13]).

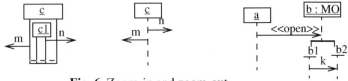

Fig. 6. Zoom-in and zoom-out

Let us observe that in the case of high parallelism zooming out may yield a more complex diagram, especially when the diagram contains a hierarchy of nested and in parallel operating objects. In such a case not only parallel forked lifelines for the emerging traces may be necessary, but also more powerful forms of combining lifelines such those provided by MSC inline expressions [8].

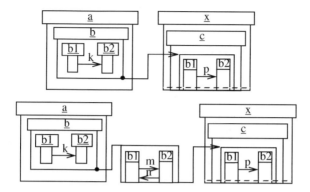

Fig. 7. Zooming into a message

It is possible also to zoom into an object's jump arrow to see the behavior of the participating objects. Figure 7 shows object b which, together with its hosted objects, jumps into object c contained in object x. In the top of the figure, the jump is shown in the zoom-out view. Below we show the zoom-in view of the jump. It displays the communication between b1 and b2. The zoom-in version of this arrow has only one black circle and one sharp end. We introduce this notation in order to make explicit that the communication happens between start of the jump and the end of the jump. Let us observe that it is not equivalent to the combination of jump out of a and jump into x, which would mean that the communication took place outside a and x (see section 5).

The possibility to mix the views is very convenient, since a specifier may chose the appropriate level of details displaying or abstracting from details. Figure 10 shows an example, where we abstract from the details of a flight which are not visible for an observer (see section 5).

4.2   Lifelines

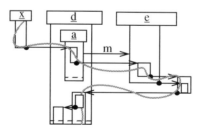

Fig. 8. Object's lifeline

The topology of nested objects changes during objects life. Therefore, we have to trace objects along performed jumps. An object's lifeline starts there where in the diagram the object appears for the first. The lifelines contains all jump arrows of the object and its hosts. We have to consider also the jumps of hosts, since the object may move with its hosts. The lifeline ends there where the object's description ends or there where the object terminates.

Figure 8 shows objects performing complex jumps. The object x jumps into the object a which is already in d. Then a communicates this fact to e and afterwords x leaves a (and d) and jumps into e. It jumps out of e, then e jumps into x. x jumps into d, and then e jumps out of x. The curve shows the lifeline of object x.

4.3   Matching Action Boxes

To figure out an object's lifeline, it is necessary to trace the object's identity. In order to do this, we have to match nested action boxes before and after a jump. If the zoom-in view of the arrow is concerned, we have to consider also the action boxes before the jump, in the beginning of the jump as well as at the end of the jump and after the jump. The matching must be consistent along all object's lifelines. It may prove hard since the hosted objects may be rearranged and moved without changing the semantics.

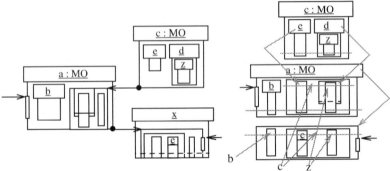

Fig. 9. Matching action boxes

Matching of object boxes can be formalized using a pattern matching algorithm. The tree structure of terms mirror well the tree structure of complex objects. We formalize the snapshots of the mobile objects by terms, so the object's states before and after a jump will be modeled by two terms. We use the function symbol

$$f : \text{Names} \times \text{Objects} \longrightarrow \text{Objects}$$

to model mobile objects. Each object is assumed to have a name and may contain other objects. To compose objects we use the commutative and associative operation (cf. [12])

$$* : \text{Objects} \times \text{Objects} \longrightarrow \text{Objects}$$

To model the fact that an object does not contain any other object we use the constant

$$\varepsilon : \longrightarrow \text{Objects}.$$

If an action box does not have name, then we use a variable for the unknown name.

For example, the state of object c before it performs a jump can be formalized by the term $f(c, f(e, \varepsilon) * f(d, f(z, \varepsilon)))$. The action box corresponding to object x after the first jump is formalized by the term $f(X_1, f(X_2, f(X_3, \varepsilon)) * f(X_4, \varepsilon))$.

A lifeline provides a set of pairs of terms corresponding to object's states before and after a jump (like those two terms above). These pairs of terms have to be unified using the same substitution. We require that for a sequence of term pairs $t_1, t_1{}', ..., t_n, t_n{}'$ there exists exactly one substitution σ such that $t_i{}^\sigma$ equals $t_i{}'^\sigma$ modulo commutativity and associativity, for $i = 1, ..., n$. The existence condition assures that a consistent naming exists and the uniqueness condition assures that naming is uniquely determined.

Let us consider the following rather sophisticated example (see figure 9): The object c contains object e and object d which in turn contains object z. c jumps into object a, which already contains object b. Then one of the nested objects within a is opened. Further, object a, with all its sub-objects, jumps into the object x.

It is not easy to identify the object names in host x. We use the matching algorithm to identify the object's identities through this complex history.

The snapshot of the object c before jump can be formalized by the term
$$t_1 = f(c, f(e, \varepsilon) * f(d, f(z, \varepsilon)))$$
The snapshot of object a after c jumps in can be formalized by the term
$$f(a, f(b, \varepsilon) * f(X_1, f(X_2, f(X_3, \varepsilon)) * f(X_4, \varepsilon)))$$
In particular the snapshot of x after the jump is
$$t_1' = f(X_1, f(X_2, f(X_3, \varepsilon)) * f(X_4, \varepsilon))$$
The snapshot of object a before its jump is given by the term
$$t_2 = f(a, f(b, \varepsilon) * f(X_1, f(X_3, \varepsilon) * f(X_4, \varepsilon)))$$
The snapshot of object x is formalized by the term
$$f(x, f(Y_1, f(Y_2, f(Y_3, \varepsilon) * f(e, \varepsilon)) * f(Y_4, \varepsilon)))$$
The snapshot of object a after its jump is formalized by the term
$$t_2' = f(Y_1, f(Y_2, f(Y_3, \varepsilon) * f(e, \varepsilon)) * f(Y_4, \varepsilon))$$
We have to unify the terms t_1 and t_1' and at the same time the terms t_2 and t_2'. The unification is performed modulo associativity and commutativity of *. It is not hard to check that the following function unifies these terms:
$$\{X_1 \to c, X_2 \to d, X_3 \to z, X_4 \to e, Y_1 \to a, Y_2 \to c, Y_3 \to z, Y_4 \to b\}$$
The right hand side of figure 9 shows the result of the matching algorithm.

5   A More Complex Example

In this section we consider an example of a flight (cf. [5]) seen from two different perspectives. The first version is very simple. Then we refine this version adding several details pushing our notation to its limits. Let us point out that specifying this system using a process algebra for mobility or collaboration diagrams would be much harder.

Figure 10 shows a simple story of a passenger x1 who boards an airplane in Warsaw airport, flies to Munich and publishes a picture in a WAN. This story is described from the perspective of an observer on the polish side. The person x1 together with other passengers enters the airport and then boards the airplane A7. The airplane flies to Munich (the flight number is 99), but the only thing the observer can see is that the airplane is airborne but not what happens inside the airplane nor further details of this flight. The next event which the observer is able to notice is the appearance of a picture in the WAN. To model several passengers (i.e. objects of class Pass), we use the multi-object notation [13], which allows us to present in a compact way several passengers playing the same role. Person x1 is distinguished using composition relationship. The observer does not care about the order in which the passengers board or leave the plane and what they do during the flight. We abstracted here from the architecture of WAN and the person's possession.

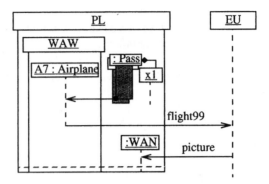

Fig. 10. Flight example

This simple view shows some of the barriers person x1 has to cross while flying from Warsaw to Munich. There are political boundaries which regulate the movement of people and devices, like airplanes, computers and so on. Within those boundaries, there are other boundaries like those protecting airports and single airplanes against intruders. Only people with appropriate passports and tickets may cross those boundaries. Therefore, in our model we make explicit such boundaries as well as moving acrossthem.

In the view presented in figure 10, we have abstracted from several details. The view of passenger x1 is much more detailed. He can see that the airplane A7 is a very active mobile computing environment, full of people who are talking, working with their laptops, calling their families, making pictures or connecting to Web via phones/modems provided in the airplane.

Figure 11 shows refined and extended version the previous example. We can see there, what happens inside the airplane during the flight; the jump arrow contains the action box of the airplane A7. Passenger x1 makes pictures with his digital camera, the pictures are send then to the WAN. As usual, a digital camera does not allows him to send pictures directly to WAN. It is also forbidden to use mobile phones during the flight. Therefore the passenger saves the pictures to his notebook nb, logs into the onboard network and then transmits the pictures to WAN via the onboard network. We abstract here from the structure of the WAN network (indicated by dashed line).

Let us point out that the sending of the picture by passenger x1 is not temporally related to crossing any border like those over PL, EU and so on. The only thing we can say is that it happens between the start of the airplane and its landing. Finally, all the passengers leave the airplane and the airport. The passenger can see that the airplane is boarded by new passengers. The dashed line in the head of the last box of passenger x1 means that the story of this passenger started earlier and that the head is a not beginning of his history.

Let us observe that the airplane is empty before the new passengers board. We assume that the action boxes determine the ordering of events, in this case the jump out arrows cross only one barrier of the airplane action box. Namely, if an arrow crosses both barriers of an action box then it means that the object is not involved in the corresponding event; inthis case the arrow ordering does not matter for figuring out the behavior of the object and the corresponding ordering of events. If an arrow starts or ends at a barrier, then it is

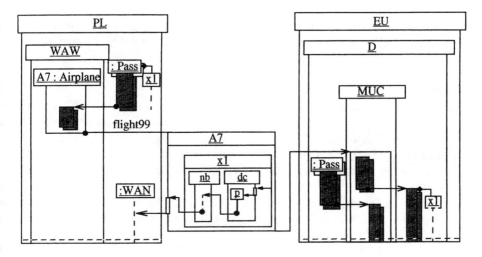

Fig. 11. Flight details

meant that the object produces or receives the event, respectively. If an arrow crosses only one barrier, then this means that another object within the barriers is involved in the event, and therefore the event can be perceived by an observer of the host object. In both cases the relative ordering of such events matters.

It is very useful to have not only asynchronous communication which uses objects to transfer messages between remote objects as in the case of ambient calculus [5], but also to have synchronous messages, which in this case mirror more exactly events like a phone call. The behavior presented here was a simply a sequence od events. To specify more complex behavior we would need constructs like the MSC's inline expressions. Let us observe that this example can hardly be specified in a notation like [10] since a mobile host like the airplane plays the role of host and the role of mobile object at the same time (cf. [10]). The regions, packages or agencies can hardly be used for that purpose.

Concluding Remarks

UML provides a variety of different kinds of diagrams which allows one for specification of software systems from different points of view. It is beneficial to have the possibility to specify a software system using different kinds of diagrams. UML sequence diagrams can be hardly used to specify mobility; therefore we proposed a new graphical notation for modeling object mobility. This notation proved to be very convenient and powerful; it extends sequence diagrams in a natural way.

In the future, we are going to define a UML profile for modelling mobile systems. This profile will extend/adjust different kinds of UML diagrams. We are going to study the duality between sequence diagrams and collaboration diagrams. We plan to perform a realistic case study which will test the appropriateness of our diagrams. Finally, we are going to provide a formal semantics for SDM which will allow one for precise analysis of systems, for proving or disproving their properties and which will facilitate tool support.

Acknowledgment

The author wants to express cordial thanks to Martin Wirsing for stimulating this research as well as to Hubert Baumeister, Alexander Knapp, Nora Koch and the anonymous referees for their helpful remarks.

References

1. Amyot, D., Mussbacher,G.: On the Extension of UML with Use Case Maps Concepts. In: Evans, A., Kent S. (eds.). The 3rd International Conference on the Unified Modeling Language, UML 2000, LNCS 1940, Springer, Berlin, 2000.
2. Bauer, B., Müller, J., Odell, J.: An Extension of UML by Protocols for Multiagent Interaction. Proc. 4th International Conference on Multi Agent Systems. IEEE Press, 2000.
3. Bauer, B., Müller, J.: Agent UML: A Formalism for Specifying Multiagent Software Systems. International Journal of Software Engineering and Knowledge Engineering, Vol. 11(3), 2001, 207-230.
4. Buhr, R. J. A. Casselman, R.S.: Use Case Maps for Object-Oriented Systems. Prentice-Hall, USA, 1995.
5. Cardelli, L.: Mobility and Security. Bauer, F., Steinbrüggen, R. (eds.): Foundations of Secure Computation. Proc. NATO Advanced Study Institute. IOS Press, 2000, 3-37.
6. Durán, F., Eker, S., Lincoln, P., Meseguer, J.: Principles of Mobile Maude. In: Kotz, D., Mattern, F. (eds.). Agent Systems, Mobile Agents, and Applications. 2000, LNCS 1882, Springer, Berlin, 2000, 73-85.
7. Gogolla, M., Radfelder, O., Richters, M.: Towards Three-Dimensional Animation of UML Diagrams. In: France, R., Rumpe, B. (eds.): UML'99 -The Unified Modeling Language. Beyond the Standard. LNCS, Vol. 1723, Springer, Berlin, 1999, 489-502.
8. ITU-TS, 2000, Recommendation Z.120. Message Sequence Charts (MSC). ITU-TS, Geneva.
9. Jing, J., Helal, A., Elmagarmid, A.: Client-Server Computing in Mobile Environments. ACM Computing Surveys. Vol. 31(2), 1999, 117-157.
10. Klein, C., Rausch, A., Sihling, M., Wen, Z.: Extension of the Unified Modeling Language for Mobile Agents. Idea Publishing Group, 2001.
11. Knapp, A.: A Formal Semantics for UML Interactions. In France, R. and Rumpe, B (eds.). Proc. 2'nd Int. Conf. UML, LNCS, Vol. 1723, Springer, Berlin, 1999, 116-130
12. Meseguer, J.: Parallel Programming in Maude. In Banatre, J. le Metayer, D. (eds.) Research Directions in High-Level Parallel Programming Languages, LNCS 574 Springer, Berlin, 1992, 253-293.
13. UML-OMG. Unified Modeling Language Specification. Version 1.4, September 2001.
14. Wienberg, A., Matthes, F., Boger, M.: Modeling Dynamic Software Components in UML. In France, R., Rumpe, B. (eds.): UML'99. Proceedings of the Second International Conference. LNCS 1723, Springer, Berlin, 1999, 204-219.

A Pattern-Based Approach to Mobile Information Systems Conceptual Architecture

Walter A. Risi and Gustavo Rossi

LIFIA, Universidad Nacional de La Plata, Argentina
{walter,gustavo}@@lifia.info.unlp.edu.ar

Abstract. As mobile access to information becomes a common trend in most commercial and corporate information systems, new software engineering challenges arise. While the most visible problems in mobile systems are the communication infrastructure and technical constraints of portable devices, there are also conceptual architecture issues that must be properly addressed.

This paper describes our work in progress towards categorizing and analyzing conceptual architectures for mobile information systems. We have defined the basics of a domain-specific architectural pattern catalog for this domain, and mined several patterns from existing, well-known systems. Our approach does not concentrate on the technical issues, but rather on identifying those architectures that better fit business goals regarding mobility.

Our goals are twofold. First, we aim to build a catalog of architectural solutions proven successful in industrial practice. On the other hand, we want to define a high-level, common-language to describe mobile architectural solutions.

1 Introduction

As mobile access to information becomes a common trend in most commercial and corporate information systems, new software engineering challenges arise. While the most visible problems in mobile systems are the communication infrastructure and technical constraints of portable devices (e.g. mobile phones and PDAs), there are also architectural issues that must be properly addressed at the conceptual level.

Current research in software artifacts regarding mobility concentrates primarily on fine-grained technological issues, such as wireless networking [14] and constrained hardware [13]. Unfortunately mobile information systems are seldom stable (because of technological improvements or changes in the underlying business model) and must be continuously upgraded or improved. Though it is widely known the importance of emphasizing design issues in applications that evolve fast, little attention has being paid to analyzing the conceptual issues that must be addressed when building a mobility-enabled information system

A. Olivé et al. (Eds.): ER 2002 Ws, LNCS 2784, pp. 159–172, 2003.

architecture. Only recently some design problems related with mobile software have been addressed in the literature [10].

Despite the hype around the technological issues, we claim that the architectural issues to address are even more critical. The design of a mobile information system architecture has challenges that simply go beyond the purely technological restrictions. For example, a mobile information system may require customizing its service for different types of users (mobile or not). On the other hand, a mobile information system may need to give mobile service to very different type of mobile users (e.g. wired and wireless).

This paper describes our work in progress towards categorizing and analyzing conceptual architectures for mobile information systems. We have defined the basics of a domain-specific architectural pattern catalog for this domain, and mined several patterns from existing, well-known systems. Our approach does not concentrate on the technical issues, but rather on identifying those architectures that better fit business goals regarding mobility.

We are building a catalog of architectural solutions proven successful in industrial practice. This catalog should be the basis of a high-level, common language to describe mobile architectural solutions. This language can be used during the process of conceptual modeling of this kind of applications, both to provide specificity to a general purpose modeling language (such as UML) and to face modeling and design problems at a higher abstraction level by reusing successful solutions.

This paper is organized as follows. In Sect. 2, we briefly review some of the concepts underlying this paper - such as software architecture and patterns. In Sect. 3, we present the general motivation for our approach. In Sect. 4, we present a preliminary classification of our patterns. In Sect. 5, we present some of the patterns we mined. Sect. 6 presents shows how our approach relates to the actual process of building and analyzing applications . Finally, in Sect. 7 we draw some conclusions and describe our lines for future work.

2   Software Architecture and Patterns

In recent years, there has been some discussion regarding the software architecture definition. In this paper, we use the term software architecture to refer to a structural plan that describes the elements of the system, how the interact together, and how these interactions fit the business goals. In other words, we adopt the *software blueprint* view of architecture [12,9]. We believe this is the most suitable view for today's industrial practice.

Though there are differences among the existing approaches to architecture, most of them agree in separating architectural concerns into several views [12]. This paper concentrates on what has been called the *conceptual view* [9]. This view describes the architecture in terms of the high-level computational elements that comprise the solution. In this view, the architect organizes the domain-specific computational elements (components) and the interactions between them (connectors), building a solution that meets the business requirements. For example, an architect designing a compiler may produce an architecture consisting of several components (e.g. parser, lexer), connected to each other by specific connectors (e.g. direct procedure calls).

The concept of *architectural patterns* emerged several years ago [15] and it is indeed similar to the widely spread notion of design patterns [7]. They share the intent of capturing, recording and conveying design experience. A pattern allows describing a recurrent design problem, together with its solution in an abstract way, such that the solution can be applied to different (though similar) problems. They provide a design vocabulary for the domain to which they are applied. However, while design patterns are used at the so-called micro-architectural level in which the design components are classes, objects and the interaction mechanisms are messages, architectural patterns deal with a higher-level view of the system in which primitives are components and connectors.

3   Why Mobile Architecture Patterns?

The definition of a mobile information system architecture is nowadays rather ad-hoc by current software engineering standards. The software architect relies on existing approaches to general software architecture, well-known solutions to fine-grained issues (e.g. underlying technology) and commercial solutions. However, the architect's toolbox lacks a catalog of vendor-independent architectural solutions. Indeed, most approaches consist in buying a predefined solution without a previous architectural analysis of the underlying problem.

While choosing commercial solutions is in general a cost-effective approach, performing an high-level architectural analysis of both the problem and the candidate solutions can help choose the best-fit solution for the problem. Instead of choosing an architecture based on vendor's claims about it, an architect could define a candidate architecture, analyze available architectures, and then decide on buying or building a solution.

Recognizing this need, we have defined a general strategy towards the classification and analysis of mobile architectures proven successful in industrial practice. Our strategy consists in the definition, maintenance and usage of a *pattern catalog*, providing a handbook for the architect facing this kind of engineering task. As mentioned before, these patterns help to improve the conceptual vocabulary of the designer, thus providing meaningful abstractions during conceptual modeling and architectural design.

4   Pattern Classification

Mobile devices are highly constrained in nature. Distinct devices have very different types of limitations, and where one device is strong another may be very weak. However, a mobile information system may have to consider the availability of the service to those very different devices. On the other hand, mobile users are not interested in exactly the same kind of information that standard users are. The classification we describe in the following was defined to reflect the different dimensions of these problems in the light of the already mined patterns – that is, following a bottom-up approach . We believe that this classification may evolve and even grow as new patterns are mined.

Physical Accessing. This category addresses the issues about how to physically access an information source from a mobile client, depending on the constraints imposed by requirements and device restrictions. Hardware limitations have a strong impact on the way mobile devices access to information.

For example, a mobile phone has better accessing facilities than a standalone PDA (i.e. without a modem) depending on a synchronization to a desktop machine to retrieve information. A PDA with a dial-up modem has better accessing facilities than a standalone PDA, but less autonomy than a wireless-enabled PDA. However, a dial-up connection is likely to be available in almost every city of the world, while today's wireless network areas are reduced.

While some alternatives may be preferable to others in certain contexts, the designer of the information system architecture may have to provide a solution that works both for a high-end autonomous clients and also for a client very limited in terms of information accessing. A common reason for this is that most adequate devices are also the most expensive ones, and the majority of users have devices that stand in the middle-ground, or even in the low-end of the spectrum.

Logical Addressing. This category addresses the issues that arise when a mobile client has to address a space of information sources. While a desktop client of an information system has a context suitable for freely navigating through the space of information sources, the choice of a mobile client is generally more reduced. A mobile client may be capable of processing only a subset of the whole universe of information – e.g. a subset of the web –, and even if capable, may only be interested in seeing a subset of it.

For example, most PDA devices have specialized browsers to access information from the web. However, most of these browsers do not work well with any page, but only with a subset that are encoded in such a way that they are suitable for mobile devices – e.g. smaller screens and a limited HTML syntax. A mobile user may not want to see the whole universe of information sources, but rather the subset that its suitable for its device and its needs – e.g. a set of mobile channels, suitable for PDA accessing.

Constrained devices are weaker and more specialized than mainstream devices. The choice of available information sources that the device can access is generally a subset of the whole universe of choices, not only because of hardware limitations but also because of the specialized interests of the mobile user . A mobile client in these conditions should not have to deal with the complexity of addressing the whole universe of information sources, but rather the subset in which it is interested.

Customization. This category provides architectural patterns that address the problems of customizing the information sources themselves. Again, the constrained nature of mobile devices poses physical and conceptual restrictions to the information that can be deployed in such a device. A mobile device may

Fig. 1. Using the UML to Describe Conceptual Architecture Concepts

not be capable of interpreting any information source encoding. Even if so, the mobile device user may not be interested in the same view of the information that a desktop client is.

For example, while most PDA devices have web-browsers, the screen limitations makes some web pages impossible to be viewed on such devices. Some browsers even do not support the complete HTML syntax, and therefore cannot access arbitrary pages on the web. Finally, a mobile user accessing a web site may be interested only in information relevant to its mobile context - e.g. a businessman accessing a financial company web site is more interested in finding market information rather than the history of the company.

A mobile user may be interested in the same information source that a non-user user is interested in, but not exactly in the same view of that source. Mobile devices may not be powerful enough to process the information source – e.g. for limitations in parsing the information format. Even if so, mobile users are interested in a view of the information source that is relevant to their mobile context.

5   Pattern Catalog

In this section we present some of the patterns we have mined in the categories mentioned in the previous section. We use a format similar to the one used in [7], though slightly customized to better fit the higher-level nature of architectural patterns. We have also included references to commercial implementations of each pattern, so that the practicing architect can use it to evaluate existing alternatives to the implementation of the pattern. Actually, the list is reduced in this paper for space reasons – and included in the *Known Uses* section – but shows the general intent of serving as a suggestion list. Again for space reasons, we have only included the *Related Patterns* section in those patterns for which we consider it more valuable.

Our pattern format includes an *UML* [8] diagram to explain the structure of the solution. While the UML is not particularly oriented to architecture description, there are several approaches to the usage of the UML for software architectures. We have deliberately chosen the one defined in [9] for being both simple and expressive. Note that we have actually simplified the mentioned notation for simplicity reasons, and instead we compliment our diagrams with textual explanations.

The diagram depicted in Fig. 1 shows an example of the notation we adopted. The diagram shows a component connected to a connector. A *component* is an

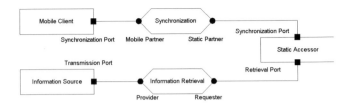

Fig. 2. Static Accessor

architectural entity that represents a conceptual unit of computation. The component exposes its functionality through one or more ports. The component can interact with other components through connectors, which represent a communication mechanism. A *connector* connects two or more components, through their ports. These elements are actually *stereotyped classes* - for more information about the usage of these stereotypes in this context, refer to [9].

5.1   Physical Accessing Pattern: Static Accessor

Intent. Provide a mobile client with the possibility of accessing an information source, when the client itself is not capable of accessing the information source on its own.

Problem. You have to deploy information into a constrained device that does not have enough capabilities to gather information on its own (e.g. a PDA without a modem, and without wireless capabilities). It may happen that the most common configuration of such a device does not provide such facilities (e.g. most Palm and PocketPC devices do not provide a modem in its basic configuration). It may also be the case that the targeted line of devices does not have such facilities at all.

Solution. Make the mobile client dependent of a more powerful, non mobile device. Provide a way so that the dependable client can be fed from the static device – the static accessor. The responsibility of interacting with the data source belongs to the static device, and the dependent client takes the information through the static accessor. See Fig. 2.

Participants. The *Mobile Client* is the mobile device interested in the information available from the information sources. The *Static Accessor* is a non-mobile device capable of retrieving information from the sources. The *Synchronization* connector is a mechanism that allows the mobile client to get the retrieved information from the static accessor. The *Information Retrieval* connector is a mechanism that allows the static accessor to get information from the information source. Finally, the *Information Source* is the information source in which the mobile client is interested.

Collaborations. Whenever the Mobile Client requires information from the Information Source, the Synchronization mechanism is activated. The latter can be activated from the Mobile Client side, or from the Static Accessor side (e.g.

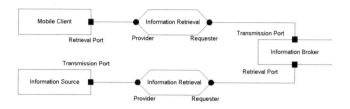

Fig. 3. Information Broker

when the static accessor discovers that there's new information available from the Information Source). The Static Accessor communicates with the Information Source through an Information Retrieval mechanism, getting the information in which the Mobile Client is interested.

Consequences. Any portable device gets the possibility of interacting with an information system as long as a suitable accessor is built. The autonomy of the client is reduced, since the information retrieval process requires the presence of the static accessor. The mobile client part is simplified, but having to provide a suitable accessor may involve additional work for the developers.

Known Uses. The mobile information system AvantGo [2] uses Palm OS's Hot-Sync [3] technology to transfer information from information sources (AvantGo channels) to the dependable clients (Palm OS handhelds) through a static accessor (a desktop machine). AcroClip [1] for Casio OS handhelds also uses this pattern.

5.2 Logical Addressing Pattern: Information Broker

Intent. Take control of a mobile client's addressing capabilities. Have the address space of available information sources preprocessed by an intermediary.

Problem. You have to allow the mobile user to retrieve information from an arbitrary or predefined set of information sources (e.g. web sites). You want to keep the mobile client simple (e.g. due to hardware restrictions), and therefore you need to reduce the information addressing capability of the mobile device. It may also be the case that you want to prevent mobile clients to access arbitrary information sources – e.g. for corporate security reasons. In that case, you need an intermediary capable of assuming the responsibility of addressing the whole universe of information sources – e.g. the whole web – and presenting a transformed universe to the mobile client – e.g. a set of corporate channels.

Solution. Provide a broker capable of interacting with the whole universe of information, presenting the mobile client with a transformed (possibly reduced) view of that universe, where that view is suitable for mobile access. See Fig. 3.

Participants. The *Mobile Client* is the mobile device interested in the information available from the information sources. The *Information Retrieval* connector is a communication mechanism that allows information transfer between components. The two appearances of the information retrieval connectors in the

Fig. 4. Custom Authoring

diagram does not imply that both appearances are identical. The *Information Broker* is software component that can address information sources and retrieve data that can be delivered to the clients. Finally, the *Information Source* is the information source in which the mobile client is interested.

Collaborations. The Mobile Client gets information from the Information Broker through an Information Retrieval mechanism. The Information Broker retrieves information from a set of available Information Sources using another Information Retrieval mechanism

Consequences. The mobile client addressing system may be simplified, but having to provide a suitable broker may involve additional work for the developers. The broker provider has control on the information that the mobile clients access.

Known Uses. AvantGo [2] centralizes the access to a growing set of channels, where AvantGo's M-Commerce server acts as a broker between the information sources and the actual mobile clients. The AcroClip [1] service also offers access through channels, controlled by a proprietary broker.

5.3   Customization Pattern: Custom Authoring

Intent. Provide the mobile client with information suitable for its direct manipulation, so that no expensive customization is required.

Problem. You have to deploy information from information sources (e.g. web sites) in a constrained device that does not support the format in which those sources encode their information (e.g. Palm's m100 handheld, for which a full-blown web browser is not available).

Solution. For each information source of interest, provide a customized version of that source, so that the format is exactly the one suitable for the client. See Fig. 4.

Participants. The *Mobile Client* is the mobile device interested in the information available from the information sources. The *Customized Source* is an information source that represents information in a format that can be handled directly by the mobile client. Finally, the *Information Retrieval* connector is a mechanism that allows the mobile client to get information from the information source.

Collaborations. The Mobile Client retrieves information directly from the Information Source, through the Information Retrieval mechanism. Since the Information Source is already customized for the Mobile Client, no additional processing is necessary.

Fig. 5. Transcoder

Consequences. The information is specially designed for the mobile clients in mind, so there is no possibility that it does not suit perfectly its clients. The content provider has additional work, since it has to provide a customized version of its information sources for each of the mobile clients in mind. Updating the information can be a heavy task, if there are several customized versions to be maintained.

Known Uses. AvantGo [2] provides an infrastructure so that clients provide their own customized versions of the information they provide.

5.4   Customization Pattern: Transcoder

Intent. Automate the process of adapting information from arbitrary sources for mobile clients' manipulation.

Problem. You have to deploy information from information sources (e.g. web sites) in a constrained device that does not support the format in which those sources encode their information (e.g. Palm's m100 handheld, for which a full-blown web browser is not available). The cost of making customized versions of the information sources is too high (e.g. because the number of information sources is too big, or because the number of different targeted devices is high).

Solution. Create a component able to convert data from arbitrary information sources to a format suitable for the potential clients. See Fig. 5.

Participants. The *Mobile Client* is the mobile device interested in the information available from the information sources. The *Information Retrieval* connector is a communication mechanism that allows information transfer between components. The two appearances of the information retrieval connectors in the diagram does not imply that both appearances are identical. The *Transcoder* is software component that can translate information represented in an particular format to a format that can be handled by the mobile client. Finally, the *Information Source* is the information source in which the mobile client is interested.

Collaborations. The Mobile Client receives information from the Trans-coder using an Information Retrieval mechanism. The Transcoder receives information in its original format from the Information Source using another Information Retrieval mechanism.

Consequences. The information provider has no additional work in the customization of the information for the mobile clients. The transcoder automat-

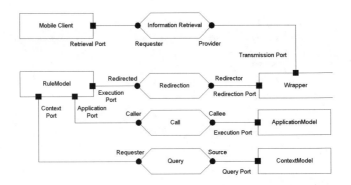

Fig. 6. Customized Behavior

ically handles this task. Building the transcoder can be a difficult task. There maybe several mobile clients in mind, with significant differences that the transcoder must support. The parsing of the original information source can be difficult in itself.

Known Uses. PumaTech [4] provides a service that allows accessing to standard web pages via Palm OS devices. PumaTech's solution relies on conversion heuristics that convert pages to version suitable for constrained hardware, in a way that semantics are preserved. IBM also provides a transcoder-based solution as part of its *Websphere* family of products [5]. AcroClip [1] has built-it transcoders for several web sites, and also allows users to define their own.

5.5   Customization Pattern: Customized Behavior

Intent. Provide different application response according to the mobile client.

Problem. In many situations you need to adapt an applications functionality to the kind of interface device (a web browser, a mobile appliance) in a dynamic way. Suppose that you are building an Internet application for selling products in the style of *amazon.com*. You may want to give special offers to users of some mobile devices: for example you have just signed an agreement with a cellular phone company and you want to induce customers to use that device. Unfortunately this business rule may change often; the discount rate may change, the condition on products that the customer must buy may vary, etc. If you tie the business rules either to the application model or to the components standing for the interface device you may have maintenance problems

Solution. Decouple the business rules from the application model and these from a context model that describes the current users state (device, network connection, etc). See Fig. 6.

Participants. The *Mobile Client* is the mobile device interested in the information available from the information sources. The *Application Model* contains the base application objects and behaviors. It should be built in such a way of being independent of different adaptation policies (for example to different mobile devices, types of network connections, etc) The *Rule Model* contains the logic of customization; by interacting with the context model it triggers corresponding application behaviors. The *Context Model* represents the actual user profile, including the information on the current mobile device The *Wrapper* redirects client requests to the application model, to the customization model

Collaborations. For each client request that must be customized (for example according to the mobile device) the wrapper mechanism redirects the request to the Rule Model. Rules interact with both the context model (they usually represent conditions) and the application model triggering the corresponding actions. The result of the rules execution is returned to the client.

Consequences. The application model remains stable when we add new business rules related with mobile devices or new devices. The rule model may get monolithic if you add many flat rules.

Known Uses. In the *UWA (Ubiquitous Web Applications)* project [10] rules are separated from the application and the context model is itself composed of user, device and network sub-models. In the *Munich Reference Architecture* for adaptive hypermedia applications [11] a similar approach is used. WebML [6] also uses a variant of this pattern.

Related Patterns. The Transcoder pattern is similar to the Customized Behavior in that it provides an automated way of presenting different views of the information to the mobile clients. However, while the Transcoder focuses mainly on the *looks* of the information, the Customized Behavior pattern focuses on the *guts* of the information generation process. Therefore the Transcoder acts like a facade over a system, being an information-unaware solution. In the Customized Behavior pattern, the rules and context which comprise the customization mechanism are aware of the kind of information the system provides.

6 From Patterns to Applications

In this section we show how the patterns we presented can help in both describing a commercial solution and defining a solution to fit a business goal. We present three examples on the usage of patterns, that go from representing commercial architectures to potential usages of these patterns in an enterprise context.

6.1 Representing AvantGo's Dynamic Mobility Model

The *Dynamic Mobility Model* (DMM) [2] is the solution suggested by AvantGo to provide mobile access to web-based information systems.

In Fig. 7 we show the conceptual architecture of the DMM. The *Static Accessor* pattern is used to allow non-wireless devices to access the system. An *Information Broker* provides the mobile clients with a reduced version of the internet, based on *channels*. Finally, the *Custom Authoring* pattern is used to provide information encoding in a format directly suitable for mobile clients.

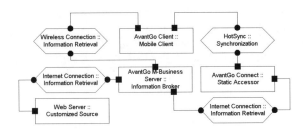

Fig. 7. AvantGo's Dynamic Mobility Model

Having a conceptual description of a technological infrastructure such as AvantGo enables architects to analyze the solution in a completely objective way. Given an actual problem, the architect can define the best-fit architecture and then compare it to AvantGo's to see if it really fits the business goals.

6.2   Customized Mobile Access to a Corporate Database

A software company wants to provide access to its corporate database to both their vendor force and also its customers. For its vendor force, it wants to provide updated information about their products, solutions and prices. Instead, for their customers, it wants to provide information about special offers and customized support. The first problem the architect faces is providing a customized view of its information database for the different users that may be interested in that information.

Since the vendor force needs updated information, the company decides to provide its vendors with wireless-enabled, high-end PDA devices. However, the customers have a variety of mobile devices, most of them not-wireless enabled. Thus, the second problem the architect faces is providing both wired and wireless access to the information. Also, the information encoding may be different for the high-end vendor devices, compared to the possibly-low-end customer devices.

Following the approach mentioned in section 3, the architect browses the architectural pattern catalog and selects those patterns that can help in solving the problem at hand. The resulting conceptual architecture is depicted in Fig. 8.

The proposed architecture is a high-level view of the solution. The *Static Accessor* pattern is used to provide wired access to the information source. The *Customized Behavior* pattern is used to provide different views on the same information source - the corporate database. Once the architecture is depicted, the architect can then discuss about building or buying a solution, depending on the available schedule and expense.

6.3   Mobile Access to a Commercial Website

A small company runs an entertainment web portal, which provides information about latest movies and movie theaters. The company believes that mobile infor-

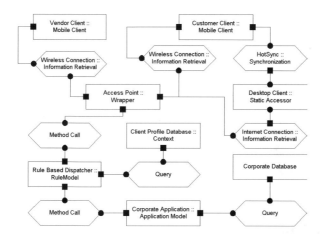

Fig. 8. Architecting Customized Mobile Access to a Corporate Database

mation access will provide it with an interesting advantage over its competitors. Moreover, since the company already has a website running, it wants to avoid having to author a parallel website for mobile access. Also, since the company has a small staff, management is heavily concerned about doubling the website maintenance effort.

The software architect browses the architectural pattern catalog and sees that a *Transcoder* based solution can solve both the development time effort and the staffing problems. The architect takes the suggested commercial component list from the pattern description and browses the web for commercial solutions, comparing prices and making a report about both the architecture and the prices the commercial tools involves. The architect also discards building a transcoder in-house for the development effort it involves. However, the architect also considers a *Custom Authoring* solution and calculates the approximate development and maintenance costs associated to it. The latter solution was also considered, since the commercial component providing access to customized sources has a significantly lower price than the transcoder-based solutions. The architect elaborates a report afterwards, and presents it to management for its cost/benefit evaluation.

7   Conclusions and Future Work

The current work on mobile information system architectures is mainly focused on the technological aspect of this kind of systems. While there is considerable research in approaches for implementing systems using a certain wireless technique or other, there are no studies about how the mobility aspect conceptually relates to an information system.

This paper presented an approach to describing, categorizing and analyzing conceptual architectures for mobile access to information systems. Our approach is based on the architectural pattern concept. We presented several patterns that represent common mobility configurations existing in current industrial practice.

Abstracting existing configuration as architectural patterns provides the designer with a catalog of architectures. The practitioner can then choose the architectural structures that best fit the business goals, without having to rely on vendor-specific solutions or terminology.

We are currently working on mining other architectural solutions that occur in existing mobile systems. Our intention is to grow a complete and solid architectural pattern language for providing mobile access to information systems. We are also working on defining an architectural methodology for the better usage of these patterns. Our main intention is to integrate these patterns into existing modeling tools and/or languages, in order to provide the architect with a toolbox of primitives so he can describe his mobile applications in a higher-level of abstraction.

References

1. AcroClip. http://www.pcsync.de.
2. AvantGo M-Commerce Server. http://www.avantgo.com.
3. HotSync Technology. http://www.palm.com.
4. PumaTech BrowseIt Server. http://www.pumatech.com.
5. Transcoding Publisher. http://www.websphere.ibm.com.
6. WebML. http://www.webml.org.
7. R.J. Erich Gamma, Richard Helm, and J. Vlissides. *Design Patterns, Elements of Reusable Object-Oriented Software.* Addison Wesley Professional Computing Series, 1994.
8. O.M. Group. *UML (version 1.3).* OMG, June 1999.
9. C. Hofmeister, R. Nord, and D. Soni. *Applied Software Architecture.* Addison Wesley, 2000.
10. G. Kappel, W. Retschitzegger, and W. Schwinger. Modeling Ubiquitous Web Applications: The WUML Approach. In *International Workshop on Data Semantics in Web Information Systems (DASWIS)-2001), co-located with 20th International Conference on Conceptual Modeling (ER2001), Proceedings*, November 2001.
11. N. Koch and M. Wirsing. The Munich Reference Model for Adaptive Hypermedia Applications. To be presented at the 2nd International Conference on Adaptive Hypermedia and Adaptive Web Based Systems, 2002.
12. P.B. Kruchten. The 4+1 View Model of Architecture. *IEEE Software*, 12(6):42–50, Nov. 1995.
13. J. Noble, C. Weir, and D. Bibby. *Small Memory Software: Patterns for Systems with Limited Memory.* Addison-Wesley, 2000.
14. S. Schaefer, S. Marney, T. Willis, and K. Parkkinen. OOPSLA Workshop on Architectural Patterns for Wireless Computing. 2001.
15. M. Shaw. Patterns for Software Architectures. In J. Coplien and D. Schmidt, editors, *Pattern Languages of Program Design*, chapter 24, pages 453–462. Addison-Wesley, 1995.

Support of Integrated Wireless Web Access through Media Types

Klaus-Dieter Schewe

Massey University, Department of Information Systems
Private Bag 11 222, Palmerston North, New Zealand
K.D.Schewe@massey.ac.nz

Abstract. Ideally, the demand for wireless access to web servers should not lead to a duplication of services. The major restriction imposed by mobile clients concerns the amount of information that is to be transferred from a server to the client and the presentation capability. We show that the theory of media types is suitable to cope with these restrictions having just one server specification that can automatically be tailored to the client needs. In particular, it is possible to generate presentations that are suitable for mobile clients.

1 Introduction

In order to support the increasing demand for wireless access to web-based services we have to be aware of the serious restrictions that are imposed by mobile clients. First, there is a strictly limited channel bandwidth, which implies that the amount of information that is transferred to a mobile client should not exceed a certain threshold. Of course, bandwidth may or will improve in the future, and information can be transferred in a compressed form, but it can hardly be expected in the short run that the same amount of information can be transferred in a wireless and a wire-based way.

Second, mobile devices usually provide only a mini-screen with restricted presentation facilities. This imposes again a restriction on the amount of information that is transferable, but also a restriction on the used presentation facilities.

The easy technical solutions for these problems are to use compression techniques in order to exploit the available bandwidth at its best, and to use WML instead of HTML. As most web-services are just HTML-based, this implies that services are either not available for mobile clients or that the server has to be duplicated. Obviously, the costs of duplicate services and the problems arising from keeping them consistent, lead to the desire to provide for an integration.

Ideally, there should only be one server-side specification of web services with the client presentation generated out of them. The need for well-structured web-sites is now agreed [5], but there are different opinions on what a well-founded site specification would be. The authors of [3,7,8,15] all agree on the separation of content from presentation and the linkage with databases, but only the theory

A. Olivé et al. (Eds.): ER 2002 Ws, LNCS 2784, pp. 173–181, 2003.

of media types [8,14,15] emphasizes the need for an integration of operations, the need to support different user profiles, different end-user devices, and different communication channels. Therefore, in order to support wireless web access, we continue the direction of the media type approach.

Media types are defined as extended views. The major extensions involve the association of operations in order to model a system's functionality, and a subtyping mechanism in order to allow information to be shared. The queries that are used to define the views must be able to create links between media objects similar to the references in object oriented databases [10]. General query algebras with this feature have been investigated in [11] and applied to web-based information systems in [12]. Creating identifiers and links is also a major point of discussion in [1] in the context of semi-structured data and XML, as it is felt that existing query languages such as XML-QL [6], LOREL [2], UnQL [4] and XQuery [18] lack the required functionality.

The idea underlying the application of the theory of media types to mobile clients is that the type of the mobile end-device and the used channel determine the maximum information capacity that could be treated as a transfer unit from the server to the client. At the server-side this information will be used to tailor a media type to fit with this restriction. The media type itself abstracts from all presentational issues. It just describes content and functionality, and provides the necessary tailoring mechanisms. The most significant issue is the ability to split the content automatically. In order to do so, the specification includes information, which parts of a media type content are preferably to be kept together, and which parts can be separated. We shall discuss two mechanisms for this, one based on subtyping, the other one on numeric proximity values.

Media types provide two ways to adapt themselves to the requirements of various users, channels and technical environments: cohesion pre-orders and proximity values. Both ways exploit the set of supertypes of the content type. This set also allows hierarchies to be defined. Together with added measurement units and ordering facilities, these additional extensions define the feature of *adaptivity* of media types, i.e., media types can be automatically tailored to different needs of a client.

Outline. Section 2 of the paper will give a brief summary of the fundamentals of media types without going into formal details. These can be found in [8,15]. Section 3 takes a deeper look into the issue of cohesion/adhesion, i.e., the controlled loss of information that would allow a media type to be split and tailored to the restrictions arising from channels and end-user devices. This also includes tailoring to different user profiles, but this aspect is not emphasized here. Section 4 contains a summary and conclusion.

2   Fundamentals of Media Types

The notion of *media type* was introduced in [8] extending the previously defined *information units* from [7] and combining them with the theory of *dialogue types* from [13]. They were introduced as a means to formalize descriptive means for web sites. The major intention was to abstract completely from presentational issues, but nevertheless to keep in mind the capability for presentation. Media types should combine descriptions of content and functionality.

As to the content media types provide abstract structural descriptions based on type systems including navigation structures. They also support database connections via views. The data provided by a media object may include hidden data, e.g., links, as well as context and escort information. In order to support different presentations to end-users and various end-devices media objects allow different granularity and density of content.

As to functionality this is achieved by adding functions. These can be internal functions such as database processes, internal search and navigation, or external connections such as general search, links to other sites, etc., or support functions such as marking, extraction in connection with metaphorical structures.

The core of a media type is defined by a *view* on an underlying database, i.e., we assume an underlying database schema $\mathcal{S}$, a view schema $\mathcal{S}_V$ and a defining query q_V, which transforms databases over $\mathcal{S}$ into databases over $\mathcal{S}_V$.

It is not important which datamodel is used for the underlying database. We could have a relational, entity-relationship [17] or object oriented database [10], or the data could have been described in XML [1,9]. However, in order to provide navigation links with the media types, the used query language must be able to create links as emphasized in [8]. In order to introduce links, we we must create anchors in the result of a query.

This can be done by transforming a set $\{v_1, \ldots, v_m\}$ or list $[v_1, \ldots, v_m]$ of values into a set $\{(u_1, v_1), \ldots, (u_m, v_m)\}$ or list $[(u_1, v_1), \ldots, (u_m, v_m)]$ of pairs with new created anchors u_i. Such query languages are called to have a *create-facility*.

It is also important to provide also escort information, which can be realized by a supertyping mechanism, i.e., a media type M basically consists of a content data type $cont(M)$, a finite set $sup(M)$ of super (media) types M_i, and a defining query q_M with create-facility such that $(\{t_M\}, q_M)$ defines a view. The introduction of supertypes in media types allows repeated parts to be shared. In particular, it is possible to associate general functionality or escort information with supertypes.

In order to model the required functionality we add operations to media types. This is completely analogous to the d-operations on dialogue types [13]. An *operation* on a media type M consists of an operation signature, i.e., name, input-parameters and output-parameters, a selection type which is a supertype of $cont(M)$, and a body which is defined via operations accessing the underlying database. The discussion in [7] listed several standard operations that are of particular interest in web information systems.

This is not yet the full definition of a media type. It combines content and functionality issues, but is not sufficient for modeling web information systems because of a lack of the information content to be tailored to specific user needs and presentation restrictions, e.g., those arising from mobile clients.

Therefore, media types are extended in four ways: providing measure units, order, cohesion/adhesion, and hierarchical structures.

For many of the values we have to provide not only the type, but also the *measure unit*, e.g. Joule or kcal, PS or kW, cm, mm or m, etc. There exist fixed means for the calculation between the different units. Formally, each base type b should come along with a set $unit(b)$ of possible measure units. Each occurrence of b in the database or the raw media types has to accompanied by one element from $unit(b)$. This lead to an implicit extension of the defining queries q_M.

Since the media types are used to model the content of the information service, order is important. Therefore, we claim that the set constructor should no longer appear in content expressions. Then we need an *ordering-operator* $ord_\leq$ which depends on a total order $\leq$ defined on a type t and is applicable to values v of set type $\{t\}$. The result $ord_\leq(v)$ has the list type $[t]$. We shall tacitly assume that ordering operators are used in the defining queries q_M.

Cohesion/adhesion introduces a controlled form of information loss. Roughly speaking we specify which information should preferably be kept together, and which information can be separated. Restrictions imposed by the client, e.g., a mobile client, may force us to split the media type in several small ones. The theory of media types provides two mechanisms to support cohesion/adhesion based on a total (pre-)order or proximity values. We shall discuss these two mechanisms in detail in the next section.

Hierarchies refer to a structuring of information as in OLAP systems. Flattening of dimensions results in information growth, its converse in information loss. Such a hierarchy is already implicitly defined by the component or link structures, respectively.

A formal introduction to the theory of media types is contained in [8,14].

3   Two Mechanisms to Adapt to Mobile Clients

We stated that cohesion should introduce a controlled form of information loss. In order to introduce this formally, we have to be more specific with respect to our data types. Let the type system be

$$t = b \mid (a_1 : t_1, \ldots, a_n : t_n) \mid \{t\} \mid [t]   .$$

Here b represents an arbitrary collection of *base types*, e.g., *BOOL* for boolean values **T** and **F**, *OK* for a single value *ok*, *TEXT* for text, *PIC* for images, *MPIC* for video data, *CARD* and *INT* for numbers, *DATE* for dates, *URL* for URL-addresses and anchors, *MAIL* for e-mail-addresses, etc. The constructors $(\cdot)$, $\{\cdot\}$ and $[\cdot]$ are used for records, finite sets and finite lists. We allow nesting of these constructors to an arbitrary depth.

For the content data type $cont(M)$ of a media type M we need a little extension. The place of a base type may be occupied by a pair $\ell : M'$ with a label ℓ and the name M' of another media type. This is necessary for modeling links. The type t_M used for the view definition arises from $cont(M)$ by substitution of *URL* for all pairs $\ell : M'$.

Next define a partial order $\leq$ on content data types, which extends subtyping:

- For any expression exp we have $exp \leq OK$.
- For link expressions we have $(\ell : M') \leq (\ell : M'')$ iff M'' is a direct or indirect (via transitive closure) supertype of M'.
- For record expressions we have $(a_1 : exp_1, \ldots, a_m : exp_m) \leq (a_{\sigma(1)} : exp'_{\sigma(1)},$ $\ldots, a_{\sigma(1)} : exp'_{\sigma(n)})$ with injective $\sigma : \{1, \ldots, n\} \rightarrow \{1, \ldots, m\}$ and $exp_{\sigma(i)} \leq exp'_{\sigma(i)}$.
- For list and set structures we have $\{exp\} \leq \{exp'\}$ (or $[exp] \leq [exp']$, respectively) iff $exp \leq exp'$ holds.

If $cont(M)$ is the content data type of a media type M and $sup(cont(M))$ is the set of all content expressions exp with $cont(M) \leq exp$, then a total (pre-)order $\preceq_M$ on $sup(cont(M))$ extending the order $\leq$ on content expressions is called a *cohesion (pre-)order*. Clearly, $cont(M)$ is minimal with respect to $\preceq_M$.

Defining a cohesion (pre-)order on a media type provides the first mechanism for tailoring information to reduced capacity. Small elements in $sup(cont(M))$ with respect to $\preceq_M$ define information to be kept together, if possible.

Applying a cohesion (pre-)order $\preceq_M$ in the case of a mobile client requires to determine first the maximum amount of data that should be transferred. The calculation has to take into account the capacity of the mini-screen at the client-side, the bandwidth of the channel, the compression rate, if compression is applied, and the percentage required for style information. Then we determine the least element t_1 with respect to $\preceq_M$ that requires not more than the available capacity. Note that if we only provide a preorder, not an order, than there may be more than one such t_1.

Taking just t_1 instead of $cont(M)$ means that some information is lost, but this only refers to the first data transfer. When transferring t_1, we must include a link to a possible successor containing detailed information. In order to determine such a successor we can continue looking at all content types $t' \in sup(cont(M))$ with $t_1 \npreceq_M t'$. These are just those containing the complimentary information that was lost. Again we can choose a least type t_2 among these t' with respect to $\preceq_M$ that requires not more than the available capacity. t_2 would be the desired successor.

Proceeding this way the whole communication is broken down into a sequence of suitable units $t_1, t_2, \ldots, t_n$ that together contain the information provided by the media type. Of course, the cohesion (pre-)order suggests that the relevance of the information decreases, while progressing with this sequence. The mobile user may decide at any time that the level of detail provided by the sequence $t_1, \ldots, t_i$ is already sufficient for his/her needs.

Example 1. Let us ignore the defining query as well as operations. Just take the following content type of a media type REGION:

(name: $STRING$, central : h: CITY, cities : { c : CITY }),

which contains a link to another media type CITY. So we could have the following instance:

$$(\&o_{11}, (\text{name} : \text{Taranaki}, \ \text{central} : \&o_{21}, \text{cities} : \{\&o_{21}, \&o_{22}\})) \ .$$

We used the convention to denote anchors and links with a starting $\&$. So, the anchor for this instance of a media type—in [8] this is called a *media object*—is $\&o_{11}$, and it links to other media objects $\&o_{21}$ (twice) and $\&o_{22}$, both of type CITY.

Postponing for the moment that the inner set type we could define a cohesion order (not just a preorder) by

$$(\text{name} : \ldots, \text{central} : \ldots, \text{cities} : \ldots)$$
$$\preceq (\text{name} : \ldots, \text{central} : \ldots)$$
$$\preceq (\text{name} : \ldots, \text{cities} : \ldots)$$
$$\preceq (\text{central} : \ldots, \text{cities} : \ldots)$$
$$\preceq (\text{name} : \ldots)$$
$$\preceq (\text{central} : \ldots)$$
$$\preceq (\text{cities} : \ldots)$$

Then assume that the capacity suffices to transfer $t_1 = (\text{name} : \ldots, \text{central} : \ldots)$. This would leave us with

$$(\text{name} : \ldots, \text{central} : \ldots, \text{cities} : \ldots)$$
$$\preceq (\text{name} : \ldots, \text{cities} : \ldots)$$
$$\preceq (\text{central} : \ldots, \text{cities} : \ldots)$$
$$\preceq (\text{cities} : \ldots)$$

Thus, the first part of the information that we transfer for the media object above would be

$$(\&o_{11}, (\text{name} : \text{Taranaki}, \ \text{central} : \&o_{21}, \ \text{more} : \&o_{11}^1)) \ .$$

Next, we could choose $t_2 = (\text{name} : \ldots, \text{cities} : \ldots)$. The second bit of transferred information of the media object above would be

$$(\&o_{11}^1, (\text{name} : \text{Taranaki}, \ \text{cities} : \{\&o_{21}, \&o_{22}\})) \ .$$

In fact, we could stop here, as further processing would not lead to more information. We would be left with just

$$(\text{name} : \ldots, \text{central} : \ldots, \text{cities} : \ldots) \quad \preceq \quad (\text{central} : \ldots, \text{cities} : \ldots)$$

Here, all maximal elements in $sup(cont(M))$ have disappeared, which indicates that no information has been left out. $\square$

Of course, we could now have a closer look into supertypes of (cities : ...),
which would lead to a larger set $sup(cont(M))$, but we omit further details.

An alternative to cohesion preorders is to use *proximity values*. For this, let
$exp_1, \ldots, exp_n$ be an antichain with respect to $\preceq$. A symmetric $(n \times n)$-matrix
$\{p_{ij}\}_{1 \leq i,j \leq n}$ with $0 \leq p_{ij} \leq 1$ is called a *set of proximity values*. The antichain in
the definition represents a possible split of the information content. The higher
the proximity value, the more do we wish to keep the components together.

Applying proximity values $\{p_{ij} \mid 1 \leq i,j \leq n\}$ requires also to determine
first the maximum amount of data that should be transferred. Then for each
$X \subseteq \{1, \ldots, n\}$ determine its *weight*, i.e.,

$$w(X) \quad = \quad \sum_{i,j \in X, i < j} p_{i,j}$$

and its *greatest common subtype* $gcs(X)$, i.e., the greatest element $t_1 \in$
$sup(cont(M))$ with $t_1 \leq exp_i$ for all $i \in X$. We choose the X with largest weight
such that the $gcs(X)$ does not require more than the available transport capacity. Proceeding this way we also construct a sequence of content types $t_1, \ldots, t_n$,
all appearing in the chosen anti-chain, such that together they provide the information of the media type. Same as for cohesion preorders the relevance of the
information decreases, while progressing with this sequence, and the mobile user
may decide to stop the transfer, after receiving $t_1, \ldots, t_i$.

Example 2. Let us take the same media type as in Example 1. We choose the
antichain $exp_1 = $ (name : ...), $exp_2 = $ (central : ...) and $exp_3 = $ (cities : ...)
and the proximity values $p_{1,2} = 0.8$, $p_{1,3} = 0.5$ and $p_{2,3} = 0.1$. Then we get the
following weights and greatest common subtypes:

X	$w(X)$	$gcs(X)$
{ 1 }	0	(name : ...)
{ 2 }	0	(central : ...)
{ 3 }	0	(cities : ...)
{ 1, 2 }	0.8	(name : ..., central : ...)
{ 1, 3 }	0.5	(name : ..., cities : ...)
{ 2, 3 }	0.1	(central : ..., cities : ...)
{ 1, 2, 3 }	1.4	(name : ..., central : ..., cities : ...)

Assuming that the whole information, i.e. $gcs(\{2,3\})$ exceeds the maximum
capacity, the result would be the same sequence of types as in the previous
example.   □

There is no general preference for cohesion preorders or proximity values. The
major difference is that the proximity values provide an information split that is
defined a priori, whereas the use of a cohesion (pre-)order would determine such
a split. This means that cohesion (pre-)orders are more flexible for the price of
being more costly with respect to the determination of the split.

4   Conclusion

In this article we briefly reviewed the theory of media types from [8,14] and emphasized its suitability for supporting integrated wireless web access. Media types combine content and functionality for web-sites, and provide mechanisms to tailor the information to the restrictions imposed by particular clients. So, there is just *one* specification on the server side serving various clients including mobile clients. The restrictions imposed by mobile clients refer to bandwidth and restricted presentation facilities. Both together imply a bound on the information that should be transmitted as a unit. However, the cohesion/adhesion facility of media types allows the information to be tailored to the restrictions of the mobile clients, as it allows information to be split if necessary.

The theory of media types has been applied in the development of large database-backed, web-based information services in the Lausitian region in Germany [16]. These services are available via the internet, but also via cable-TV-based videotext, a technology with significant restrictions on the presentation of information. This demonstrates that the theory can cope with end-user restrictions, and thus is suitable for mobile clients as well. Media types are a means to integrate wire-based and wireless services with a single server specification.

References

1. S. Abiteboul, P. Buneman, D. Suciu. *Data on the Web: From Relations to Semistructured Data and XML*. Morgan Kaufmann Publishers 2000.
2. S. Abiteboul, D. Quass, J. McHugh, J. Widom, J. Wiener. The LOREL Query Language for Semi-Structured Data. *Int. Journal on Digital Libraries*, vol. 1(1): 68-88. 1997.
3. P. Atzeni, A. Gupta, S. Sarawagi. Design and Maintenance of Data-Intensive Web-Sites. *Proc. EDBT'98*: 436-450. Springer LNCS 1377, 1998.
4. P. Buneman, S. Davidson, G. Hillebrand, D. Suciu. A Query Language and Optimization Techniques for Unstructured Data. *Proc. SIGMOD'96*: 505-516.
5. O. De Troyer. Designing Well-Structured Websites: Lessons Learned from Database Schema Methodology. In T.W. Ling, S. Ram, M.L. Lee (Eds.). *Conceptual Modeling – ER'98*: 51-64. Springer LNCS 1507, 1998.
6. A. Deutsch, M. Fernandez, D. Florescu, A. Levy, D. Suciu. A Query Language for XML. *International World Wide Web Conference* 1999.
7. T. Feyer, K.-D. Schewe, B. Thalheim. Conceptual Modelling and Development of Information Services. in T.W. Ling, S. Ram (Eds.). *Conceptual Modeling – ER'98*. Springer LNCS 1507, 7-20.
8. T. Feyer, O. Kao, K.-D. Schewe, B. Thalheim. Design of Data-Intensive Web-Based Information Services. In *Proc. 1st International Conference on Web Information Systems Engineering*. Hong Kong (China) 2000.
9. C.F. Goldfarb, P. Prescod. *The XML Handbook*. Prentice Hall. New Jersey 1998.
10. K.-D. Schewe, B. Thalheim. Fundamental Concepts of Object Oriented Databases. *Acta Cybernetica*, vol. 11 (4), 1993, 49-84.
11. K.-D. Schewe. On the Unification of Query Algebras and their Extension to Rational Tree Structures. In M. Orlowska, J. Roddick (Eds.). *Proc. Australasian Database Conference* (ADC 2001).

12. K.-D. Schewe. Querying Web Information Systems. In S. Jajodia, H. Kunii, A. Solvberg (Eds.). *Conceptual Modeling – ER 2001*. Springer LNCS 2224.
13. K.-D. Schewe, B. Schewe. Integrating Database and Dialogue Design. *Knowledge and Information Systems*. vol. 2: 1-32. 2000.
14. K.-D. Schewe, B. Thalheim. Modeling Interaction and Media Objects. In E. Métais (Ed.). *Proc. 5th Int. Conf. on Applications of Natural Language to Information Systems* (NLDB 2000). Versailles (France) 2000. Springer LNCS.
15. K.-D. Schewe, B. Thalheim. *Conceptual Modelling of Internet Sites*. Tutorial Notes. ER 2000.
16. B. Thalheim, Development of database-backed information services for Cottbus-Net. Report CS-20-97, BTU Cottbus 1997.
17. B. Thalheim. *Entity-Relationship Modeling – Foundations of Database Technology*. Springer 2000.
18. The World Wide Web Consortium (W3C). *XQuery*.
    http://www.w3c.org/TR/xquery

Domain-Specific Modelling
for Cross-Platform Product Families

Steven Kelly and Risto Pohjonen

MetaCase Consulting
{stevek,rise}@metacase.com

Abstract. Domain-specific modelling has proved its worth for improving development speed and dependability of applications. By raising the level of abstraction away from the code and towards the structure and behaviour of an application, it also offers good possibilities for generating the same application from the same models, but for a wide variety of client platforms. This paper examines one example of domain-specific modelling for an embedded application, and how that was extended to a mobile platform.

1 Introduction

This paper presents a modelling language for implementing software applications for cross-platform digital wristwatch applications. In general it is an example of how such a domain-specific modelling environment (later referred to as DSM environment) can be implemented in a metaCASE tool such as MetaEdit+. In particular, we are interested in how well a DSM approach can adapt to cope with new platforms.

In this section we discuss DSM and the watch modelling language from the point of view of a modeller using it. Section 2 describes the architecture behind the watch example from the point of view of a metamodeller creating the DSM environment. Section 3 looks at the extension of the watch example to the MIDP world. MIDP is the Mobile Information Device Profile, a Java platform for building applications to run on small devices such as mobile phones or PDAs. As the MIDP platform did not even exist when the watch example was originally made, it provides a good test of how well a DSM solution can cope with major unforeseen changes in the platform.

First, a proviso: the watch example is not strictly a real industrial example, since the authors are not in the business of making digital watches. It was included with the authors' MetaEdit+ metaCASE tool as a fully-worked example, and thus aims to be as realistic as possible. With the advent of mobile phones supporting MIDP, it is now a true application with real users. Given the dearth of experience reports on DSM, hopefully even with the proviso this report will still prove useful.

A. Olivé (Eds.): ER 2003 Ws, LNCS 2784, pp. 182-194, 2003.

1.1   Introduction to Domain-Specific Modelling

Why develop a DSM environment for modelling watches? Why not adopt some pre-existing general-purpose modelling language and a 'standard' CASE tool, then write code by hand? While it would be possible to apply such 'standard' technology here, there is much more to be gained by using a DSM. Let us consider the following reported benefits of the use of DSM in software development:

1. **Productivity increases by as much as a factor of 10.**
   Traditional software development has required several error-prone mappings from one set of concepts to another [5]. First the domain concepts must be mapped to the design concepts and then further mapped to the programming language concepts. This is equivalent to solving the same problem over and over again. With DSM, the problem is solved only once by working with pure domain concepts. After that, there is no need for mapping as the final products are automatically generated from these models. Studies have shown that this kind of approach is 5-10 times faster than the usual current practices [2,3,7].
2. **Better flexibility and response to change.**
   Focusing on design rather than code results in a faster response to requests for changes. It is easier to make the changes at the domain concept level and then let the tool generate code for multiple platforms and product variants from a single set of models.
3. **Domain expertise shared with the whole development team.**
   The usual problem within development teams is the lack of platform knowledge among the developers. It takes a long time for a new developer to learn enough to become productive. Even the more advanced developers make mistakes in coding. In the approach presented here, an expert defines the domain concepts, rules and mapping to code. Developers then make models with the concepts guided by the rules, and code is automatically generated.

These are vital issues if development involves more than one of the following: domain-specific knowledge, product families (variants of similar products), medium to large development teams, critical time-to-market factors, and a strong need for quality. Other papers have described DSM in more detail [1,6]; here we shall concentrate on an experience report about the watch example and its extension to the MIDP platform. First we will look from a modeller's point of view.

1.2   The Watch Modelling Language

The watch modelling language itself consists of two diagram types. First there is a WatchFamily diagram that describes the models in the watch family. It also describes the displays and logical watch applications that have been used to create the models. Fig. 1 shows such a diagram, with a family of related wristwatch models in the **Models** group at the top of the diagram, and the logical watch application and

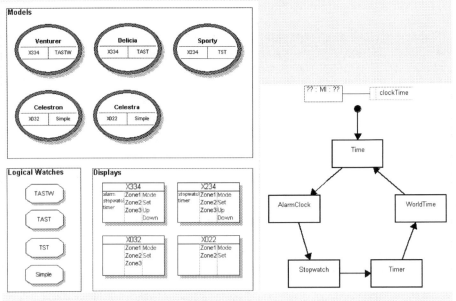

Fig. 1. The WatchFamily diagram   **Fig. 2.** The WatchApplication diagram

display components are presented in the two groups at the bottom of the diagram. Each Model consists of one LogicalWatch and one Display.

Displays are kept deliberately simple: all their information is displayed in this graph. Each Display specifies its available icons, zones for displaying time digit-pairs, and buttons. Logical Watches are more complex and are further defined in sub-graphs. For instance, the sub-graph defining the contents of the 'TASTW' Logical Watch is the 'TASTW' WatchApplication diagram as shown in Fig. 2.

This diagram shows the configuration of the logical watch application. It only contains the top-level logical configuration of sub-applications, basically showing which sub-applications have been included into this specific logical watch and in which order they are invoked. When the logical watch application is started (i.e. the watch is powered up), the basic Time sub-application will be invoked. If this sub-application is exited, an AlarmClock sub-application will be started. The cycle is completed when Time will be re-activated when exiting from the WorldTime sub-application. The name 'TASTW' comes from these sub-applications' initials in order.

Each sub-application is further defined in a sub-graph, which describes the implementation of that sub-graph. A simple example for the Time sub-application is shown

in Fig. 3. Whilst the type of this graph is actually the same as that of TASTW, it is clearer here that this is not an ordinary state transition diagram. The basic states and transitions can be seen, but there are customized semantics and many domain-specific additions, to enable the use of such domain-specific concepts as buttons and alarms.

The Mode button triggers transitions between the three states. While in one of the Edit states, the Hours or Minutes zone on the display will flash, and the Set button triggers Actions that increment the Hour or Minute components of the clockOffset variable. The DisplayFn at the top left defines that the time displayed by the watch will simply be the current clockTime.

1.3   The Watch Modelling Language as a Development Platform

Breaking the watch apart in this way results in a high level of reusability. Since sub-applications, logical applications and displays can be defined separately from each other, and they communicate via pre-defined interfaces, they make natural components. This enables the developer to build new watch variants quickly by combining sub-applications into new logical watch applications and then combining these with displays (new or existing).

When developing using the Watch Modelling Language, there is no need to write any code. The graphical models form the complete specification of a watch and its behaviour, and the code generated from them is complete.

2   The Watch Architecture,
Code Generators, and Framework Code

Having looked at the Watch Modelling Language from the point of view of a modeller, we now turn to look at how it actually works. These details are hidden from the modeller, who can thus concentrate on building new watches and applications without knowing them or considering them.

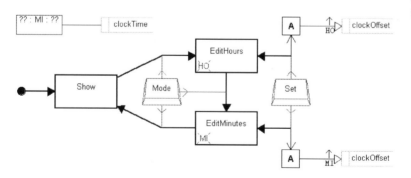

Fig. 3. The Time WatchApplication diagram

In real life the platform in this kind of case would be an electronic device controlled by a microchip. For an example to accompany MetaEdit+ this was of course not a viable option. As we wanted our test environment to run on any desktop, Java was chosen as the implementation language, and browsers as the runtime platform.

For the record, the whole project of designing and implementing the first working version of the Watch DSM language with one complete watch model took eight man-days for a team of two developers. Neither developer had prior experience of Java programming, or of building watch software, and there were of course no pre-existing in-house watch components. It took five days to develop the Java framework, two days for the modelling language, and one day for the code generator. These times include design, implementation, testing and basic documentation.

Since then, new watch models with new functionality have been implemented in fifteen minutes with this environment. As we estimated that it would have taken five to six days to develop the first watch model manually, and then one day for each additional watch model, it is fair to assume that the third watch model completed the development effort payback.

2.1   The Watch Architecture

The architecture for a DSM environment like our watch example generally consists of three parts: a modelling language, a code generator and a domain framework. To understand the role of each these within the architecture, we have to understand how the responsibilities are distributed among them. The basic principle of this distribution is illustrated in Fig. 4.

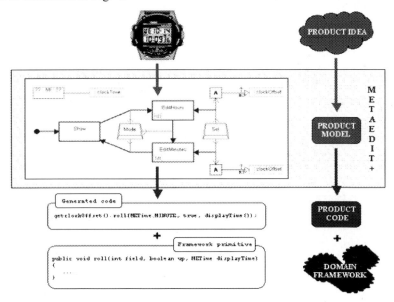

Fig. 4. The watch architecture

While designing and implementing the architecture for our watch example, we wanted to solve each problem in the right place and on the best possible level of abstraction. The modelling language was assigned to capture the behavioural logic and static aspects of watch models and applications, while the domain framework was created to provide a well-defined set of services for the code generator to interface to. Having already covered the modelling language, in the rest of this section we will examine the code generator and the domain framework classes the generated code interfaces with.

2.2   The Code Generator

The basic idea of the code generator within a DSM environment is simple: it runs through the models, extracts information from them and translates it into code for the target platform. With the models capturing all static and dynamic logical aspects and a framework providing the required low-level support, the code generator can produce completely functional and executable output code.

The MetaEdit+ report generator used to produce the code also provides a flexible tool to automate integration of the DSM environment with other tools. An example of this kind of integration within the watch example is the auto-build mechanism that enables us to automatically compile the generated code and execute it on a testing environment. This automation results in major savings of both the effort and time during the testing.

In the watch example, the auto-build proceeds with following steps:

1. **The scripts for compiling and executing the code are generated.** As the mechanism of automated compilation and execution varies between the platforms, the number and content of generated script files depend on the target platform.
2. **The code for framework components is output.** All framework code has been included into the watch models as attached Java files and is output from there as needed. This way we ensure that all required components are available at the time of compilation and have the control over the inclusion of platform specific components.
3. **The code for logical watches and watch applications is generated.** The state machines are implemented by creating a data structure that defines each state transition and display function. For each action the code generator creates a set of commands that are executed when the action is invoked.
4. **The generated code is compiled and executed as a test environment for the target platform.** Basically this step requires only the execution of the scripts created during the first step.

The structure of the code generation is show in Fig. 5 and 6. The code generators in MetaEdit+ are defined with a dedicated textual report definition language. Each report definition is associated with certain graph type and thus can operate on models made according to that specific graph type. These report definitions – that could be also referred to as sub-generators – can be arranged in a hierarchical fashion. The top level of the code generator architecture of the watch example (i.e. the sub-generators associated with WatchFamily graph type) is presented in Fig. 5 (a '*' in the name of a sub-generator denotes an individual version for each target platform).

The top-level generator is called 'Autobuild'. It handles the whole generation process by simply calling the sub-generators on the lower level. The sub-generators on the next level relate closely to those steps of the auto-build process presented earlier in this section. As '_JavaComponents' only outputs the pre-defined Java code for the framework components and '_compile and execute *' only executes scripts produced during the earlier steps of the generation process, we can concentrate on '_create make for *' and '_Models'.

The basic task of '_create make for *' sub-generators is to create the executable scripts that will take care of the compilation and execution of the generated code. As this procedure varies between platforms, there is an individual version of this sub-generator for each supported target platform. If there are any specific platform-related generation need like HTML for browser-based test environment in Fig. 5, they can be integrated with the '_create make for *' sub-generator.

The responsibility of the '_Models' and '_Model' sub-generators is to control the generation of code for the watch models, logical watches and watch applications. For each watch model, three pieces of code are generated: an applet as the physical implementation of the user interface, a display definition about the model specific user interface components, and the definition of the logical watch.

To understand how the code for a logical watch and a watch application is generated, we need to explore the code generator architecture further. The lower level of the architecture (i.e. the sub-generators associated with the WatchApplication graph type) is presented in Fig. 6.

The sub-generators '_JavaFile' (which is the same as in Fig. 5) and '_Java' take care of the most critical part of the generation process: the generation of the state machine implementations. To support the possibility to invoke a state machine from within another state machine in hierarchical fashion, a recursive structure was implemented in the '_JavaFile' sub-generator. During the generation, when a reference to a lower-level state machine is encountered, the '_JavaFile' sub-generator will dive to that level and call itself from there.

Reading the third level of generators (below '_Java'), we can see the main parts of the code generation for each Watch Application. First, any variables defined in the model are defined, along with getter and setter functions. The next three generators fill in data structures that record the states, their display functions, transitions, actions and decompositions. The generators under '_Actions' generate functions containing procedural code to execute the various actions specified in the models by the types with the same names. '_DisplayFns' works similarly to generate the code needed to calculate the time to be displayed.

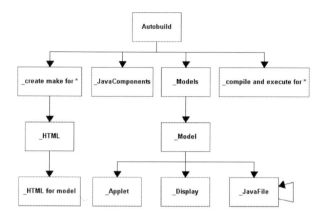

Fig. 5. The watch code generator architecture, part 1

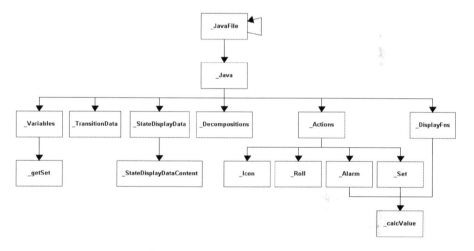

Fig. 6. The watch code generator architecture, part 2

2.3   The Domain Framework

From the point of view of the DSM environment, the domain framework consists of everything below the code generator: the hardware, operating system, programming languages and software tools, libraries and any additional components or code on top of these. However, in order to understand the requirements set for the framework to meet the needs of a complete DSM environment, we have to separate the domain-specific parts from the general platform related parts of the framework. The platform is considered to include the hardware, operating system, Java programming language with GUI classes, and an environment to test our generated code (either browser or MIDP emulator). The architecture of the watch domain framework is presented in

Fig. 7. Solid line arrows indicate the instantiation relationship while dotted line arrows indicate inclusion relationships between the elements.

The domain architecture of the watch example consists of three levels. On the lowest level we have Java classes that are needed to interface with the target platform. The middle level is the core of the framework, providing the basic building blocks for watch models in the form of abstract superclass 'templates'. The top level provides the interface of the framework with the models by defining the expected code generation output, which complies with the code and templates provided by lower levels.

There are two kinds of classes on the lowest level of our framework. METime and Alarm were implemented to raise the level of abstraction on the code level by hiding platform complexity. For example, the implementation of alarm services utilizes a fairly complex thread-based Java implementation. To hide this complexity, class Alarm implements a simple service interface for setting and stopping alarms, and all references from the code generator to alarms were defined using this interface. Similarly, METime makes up for the shortcomings of the date and time implementation of the Java version used. During the code generation, when we need to set an alarm or apply an arithmetic operation on a time unit, the code generator produces a simple dispatch call to the services provided by these two classes.

The other classes on the lowest level, AbstractWatchApplet and WatchCanvas, provide us with an important mechanism that insulates the watch architecture from platform-dependent user interface issues. For each supported target platform, there is an individual version of both of these classes and it is their responsibility to assure that there is only one kind of target template the code generator needs interface with.

On top of the platform interface and utilizing its services is the core of the framework. The core is responsible for implementing the counterparts for the logical structures presented by the models. The abstract definitions of watch applications, logical watches and displays can be found here (the classes AbstractWatchApplication and AbstractDisplay). When the code generator encounters one of these elements in the models, it creates a concrete subclass of the corresponding abstract class.

Unlike the platform interface or the core levels, the model interface level no longer includes any predefined classes. Instead, it is more like a set of rules or an API of what kind of generator output is expected when concrete versions of AbstractWatchApplet, AbstractWatchApplication or AbstractDisplay are created.

3   The Watch Example for MIDP

Mobile Information Device Profile [4] is a set of Java APIs which provides a standard application runtime environment targeted at mobile information devices, such as cellular phones. The phone contains a Java virtual machine, and the user can download mini-applications as .jar files and run them on the phone. Application size is often restricted to 30kB, in particular for downloading applications wirelessly.

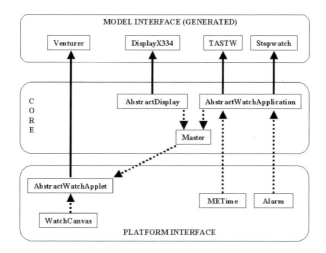

Fig. 7. The watch domain framework

Such an environment provides an interesting application for the previously ficti-
tious watch example. It also presents a challenge: is the solution we developed for
digital watches still viable if we extend the domain to include watch applications on
a MIDP phone? Changes could be necessary on four levels:

- The domain-specific modelling method and its metamodel
- The models
- The code generator
- The framework code

A moment's thought reveals that changes to the models (or certain changes to the
metamodel which do not update models automatically) are the worst kind: many developers would potentially need to update many models. If the initial domain analysis
has been good these can hopefully be avoided, or at least limited to backwards-
compatible additions to support new functionality in the new platform.

Changes to the code generator or framework code will require only the metamodeller's time, similarly for changes to the metamodel which automatically update relevant parts of the models. In particular, code generator changes can allow us to support a new platform with a fraction of the time normally needed — even though there
are changes needed throughout the whole body of code.

3.1   Changes to Support MIDP

Extending the Watch example to support MIDP required surprisingly few changes.
In fact, more changes were made because of minor problems noticed in the initial
code than because of MIDP.

Meta-models

No changes were required to the metamodels to support MIDP. To simultaneously support generation of both MIDP and the older Java, a new property was added to the top-level graph type. This allowed each framework classes to specify the target platforms for which it was intended.

Models

No changes were required to the models to support MIDP.

Generators

We had made three different implementations of a Java state machine whilst making the original watch, with ideas sketched out for another two. The implementation we went with required the reflection abilities of Java, which unfortunately are not present in MIDP. Hence we moved to a switch case based implementation, using initialised static final variables as labels.

This required an addition to the _Variables generator to generate the new static final variable for each Action and DisplayFn. Similarly, a minor change was made to the _TransitionData generator to generate the variable names rather than a string containing the same text.

The _Actions and _DisplayFn generators were similarly changed to place their body inside a case statement, rather than a similarly-named function.

A larger amount of work was required for the new '_create make for MIDP' generator. MIDP compiles its Java as for other platforms, but it also requires a preverify step, and a couple of configuration files naming and providing information about the MIDP suite (Watch family) and the MIDP applications (Watch models) it contains. Normally these configuration files would be written by hand, or filled in to a form, but in our case all the information needed can be obtained from the models.

Framework Code

The original code was much in need of refactoring, having been the authors' first Java application, and not really intended to be maintained. First we refactored out the mass of user-interface, control and state machine behaviour from the applet into their own classes. From this, it was easier to see what had to be done.

The majority of classes were platform independent, requiring only basic Java functionality. The user interface and control APIs are different for MIDP, so a separate WatchCanvas class had to be made for MIDP. Being a second attempt at the same functionality, with more Java experience than before, it was soon noticed that the same solutions could be applied to the WatchCanvas class for applets too. This resulted in smoother updating in the applet, as well as keeping the applet and MIDP versions more visually similar.

MIDP does not have the Applet class, so our Applet was replaced with a Midlet, the MIDP equivalent. As our generated applet classes subclass from Abstract-WatchApplet, our framework subclass of Applet, they work as subclasses of AbstractWatchApplet just fine, even when it is a subclass of Midlet. Thus, no changes were needed to the generation of the applet/midlet for each WatchApplication.

3.2   Results

With the above changes, the Watch modelling environment is now capable of making applications that run on a variety of MIDP and other Java platforms, adapting its display and user interface to the platform. For example, display size and fonts vary widely, as do buttons: some phones have up and down buttons physically available, other buttons are implemented as soft-keys or via menus. The modeller does not have to worry about these details: they are handled by the domain framework code.

4   Conclusion

Domain-specific modelling offers product family developers a high level of insulation from surrounding platform changes. The same Watch models have survived virtually untouched through changes from Java to Java2 to MIDP, with the main changes required being made by one person in only one place. Without DSM, the majority of developers would have to update most of their features for each platform change.

In particular, DSM offers excellent support for a family of products across a family of platforms. The current Watch models are capable of generating code for each of the three platforms, and on a variety of operating systems. Without DSM, there would quickly be no hope of maintaining one code base for all platforms.

These advantages are over and above those which come from making products by visual domain-specific modelling instead of writing textual code — a change which in itself normally increases productivity by 5 to 10 times. As always, however, DSM is only appropriate if there is a sufficient body of similar applications to be developed. Our experiences concur with those of Weiss et al. [7]: three watches would have been enough to offset the cost of building the DSM environment.

In supporting the MIDP platform, the majority of changes were in the new MIDP framework code and its build script. Minor changes were necessary to the code generation to work in the more restricted MIDP environment. Altogether, the changes took four man-days: 2 for the MIDP framework code, 0.5 for the MIDP build script, 1 for refactoring existing framework code, and 0.5 for adapting the code generation.

Fig. 8. Watch application in Nokia, Motorola and Sun emulators, and IE

References

1. Kelly, S., Tolvanen, J-P, Visual domain-specific modelling: Benefits and experiences of using metaCASE tools, In: International workshop on Model Engineering, ECOOP 2000, Ed. J. Bezivin, J. Ernst (2000)
2. Kieburtz, R. et al., A Software Engineering Experiment in Software Component Generation, In: Proceedings of 18th International Conference on Software Engineering, Berlin, IEEE Computer Society Press (March 1996)
3. MetaCase, Nokia case study, http://www.metacase.com/ (1999)
4. MIDP, JSR-000037 Mobile Information Device Profile (MIDP), Final Release, http://jcp.org/jsr/detail/37.jsp (2000)
5. Seppänen, V., Kähkönen, A.-M., Oivo, M., Perunka, H., Isomursu, P., Pulli, P., *Strategic Needs and Future Trends of Embedded Software*. Technology Development Centre, Technology review 48/96, Sipoo, Finland (1996)
6. Tolvanen, J-P, Kelly, S., Modelling Languages for Product Families: A Method Engineering Approach, In: Proc. of OOPSLA Workshop on Domain-Specific Visual Modeling Languages, Jyväskylä University Press, (2001) 135–140
7. Weiss, D., Lai, C. T. R., *Software Product-line Engineering*, Addison Wesley Longman (1999)

Dynamic Database Generation
for Mobile Applications

Ralf Mühlberger

School of Information Technology and Electrical Engineering
The University of Queensland, Brisbane Qld 4072 Australia

Abstract. Mobile devices can be seen as components of distributed information systems, with applications executed on these devices requiring a fragment of the global schema allocated to the device and implemented through materialised views. As mobile devices become more powerful we would like to minimise modifications to application code and thus reduce the cost of migration for large numbers of applications to mobile devices. Ideally an application should run mobile without any modification.

It is possible to implement dynamic database creation for application instances in an architecture with a light-weight database management system on the mobile device and an application manager.

This eliminates the need for the applications to be modified to manage their data requirements in mobile environments, with mobile dynamically created databases acting as the expected server database to the mobile applications. This is particularly useful in environments where tasks are scheduled by a workflow management system that is readily modified to act as an application manager.

1 Introduction

Writing applications for portability such that they can easily be executed on mobile devices requires taking into account their data requirements. When such data is an individual document, e.g. word processing or email, this is quite simple. However applications that rely on an underlying database are more difficult to make mobile, generally requiring modifications to the application code to use a check out/check in data management strategy.

As mobile devices become more powerful and more prevalent we would like to minimise modifications to application code and thus reduce the cost of migration for large numbers of applications to mobile devices. Ideally an application should run without any modification at all.

Our aim is to serve data to all existing fixed network applications on mobile devices without re-implementation of the application and without moving the overhead of modifying the applications to creating mobile databases for each application, or worse, each application instance. To this end, we require a materialised view on the mobile device that can be created and populated dynamically and that provides the data required for an application instance.

A. Olivé et al. (Eds.): ER 2002 Ws, LNCS 2784, pp. 195–204, 2003.

This paper outlines an architecture that uses light-weight databases created and populated dynamically by an application manager for application instances. The mobile database acts as the desktop/server database for an application, eliminating the need for modification of application code.

Essentially we are proposing an advanced data replication mechanism similar to the two-tier solution given in [1], and our focus on the implementation of the replication mechanism, rather than the transaction management, may be used in conjunction with that work.

[2], [3] and [4] describe a similar replication scheme that supports weak, partial and variant connectivity and manages the information consistency through methods to adjust the degrees of divergence. Our work has stricter assumptions on the re-connection of information but takes into account the issues as they apply to the information re-integration.

Configurable replication strategies are discussed in [5]. These do not include analysis of data semantics and application requirements to completely generate a mobile database, but are useful for adding to our work extra configurationability, such as impending dis/connection. [6] describes a semantic caching scheme used at a lower level of information management to more efficiently provide data to mobile applications. This is useful for faster access to the data, but also does not address the modification problem of mobile applications to access the data.

In [7] the global constraints on a distributed information environment that incorporates mobile devices are reformulated to achieve better localisation, and thus improve the applications' transactions. This complements our work, particularly the analysis of potential inter-application conflict.

2   Mobile Devices as Materialised Views

We are seeing a dramatic increase in the power of mobile devices, such as the Clie Palm implementations by Sony, Linux Personal Digital Assistants (PDAs) and Microsoft Windows Embedded machines. This is shifting the use of these devices from their initial role as PDAs only to a role that includes more advanced business applications. An ideal case would not only allow us to manage to-do lists, calendar and scheduling functions, and receive, compose and send email using a mobile device, but also transfer other tasks to be worked on. In the past this has required specific applications to be ported to the mobile device, and the data for the application to be transferred manually or extracted by the application.

Driven in part by the cross platform needs of the world wide web, applications are now developed that either run on virtual machines such as the Java Virtual Machine (JVM), or through complex and functionally rich interpreted languages such as PHP. As the power of mobile devices also increases, virtual machines and interpreters are available on these devices, with applications able to be executed as for larger desktop computers.

However, unless the data used by an application can also be made available on the mobile device, and in the same manner as for its desktop execution, application mobility still requires code modification. Continuous wireless connection of the mobile device is expensive and only available at a sufficiently high bandwidth in selected areas. This is therefore not a viable solution, particularly when the connection between the device and the server may be dropped. A standard, fixed network application has a continuous connection to the database through the DBMS using connectivity technology such as ODBC, JDBC and CORBA and an access language such as SQL.

When the application is on a mobile device, and thus potentially disconnected from the database, application relevant data is required on the mobile device. The most common implementation is for the application to extract all required data, manage it locally, and then return the data at reconnection. This requires modification to the application code however, both to extract the information rather than just access it, and also to manage the dataset that has been checked out – potentially including constraint and data type management.

To provide the required data to the mobile application so that it does *not* have to extract and manage the data itself, we use a light-weight mobile database management system that is also located on the mobile device. This mobile database is created and populated by an application manager with which an application registers its data requirements and that interacts with the fixed network database that the application would normally use. Light weight database management systems for mobile devices are already being developed, including an Oracle client for the Palm PDA device.

This architecture is illustrated in figure 1, where an application may interact with a database management system if on the desktop, or in the same manner with a database on a mobile database management system that is created by an application manager. For this environment we require a database management system that can handle application granularity data locking (or field/tuple level managed by application manager), an application manager and a mobile database management system. These components are described in more detail below.

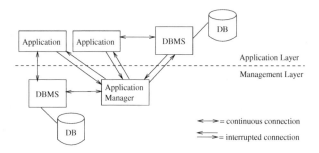

Fig. 1. Database/Application Environment with Application Manager

2.1   Components

The first component of our mobile computing architecture is an application schema manager on the fixed network that is aware of the applications and their data requirements. This awareness is implemented by a semantically richer schema, the Global Application Schema (GAS) expressed in our Application Data Demand Modelling (ADDM) language. ADDM, application schemata and the GAS are described further in section 3. The GAS DBMS requires a number of maintenance methods for adding, deleting and modifying an application schema, including the mapping from an application schema to the database implementation. These are described in [8]. With the GAS in place, we then also require the following Application Scheduling/Support Methods:

- Query the GAS wrt overlap of a number of applications, ie to see if the execution of an application may be allowed given the currently running applications. This requires a check of what operations an application may wish to perform (stored in the AS) and whether the data that the application instance would operate on overlaps the data currently being operated on by an active application.
- Query the GAS to get the database structure needed by the application.
- Query the GAS to get the data to populate the database needed by the application.
- Manage the gap of the data that will be operated on by an application, ie that has been 'checked out' by the mobile database, possibly including a locking mechanisms.
- On checking data back in, unlock and update the relevant records in the central database and log the transactions from the mobile device on the central database log. This may even be done continuously through the execution of the application as it periodically re-connects.

The *mobile database* sits on a light weight database management system on the mobile device. It serves the mobile client application instance the required data extracted from the fixed server database, and thus needs to support the access technology used by the applications. The mobile database is created and populated as required by the application manager.

The final component, other than the applications, is the application manager. This is used to invoke applications, check out data from the GAS DBMS, create and populate the mobile database and manage the check in of data when the application reconnects. These interactions occur during the check-out and the check-in methods of the application manager, which we describe in more detail in section 4.

2.2   Approaches to Implementation

Architecturally we have several choices for how such a mobile environment could be constructed, depending on the location of the application manager:

1. Internal DBMS extension
2. External system
3. Internal Mobile DBMS extension

In the first approach the application manager becomes another component of both the fixed network and mobile DBMS. This is probably the wisest in the long run, as local applications can also be managed with relation to mobile applications, which is of particular use where the application manager checks for conflict situations.

An external system implements the application manager as a separate component to the fixed network DBMS and interacting with a separate mobile DBMS. The second approach is the easiest to implement without access to database management system internals. We have successfully built extensions to workflow management systems as external solutions, see [9,10].

In an internal mobile DBMS extension the application manager is external to the main DBMS, but internal to the mobile DBMS. In essence this is like having an external application manager that includes the data management function on the mobile device. This approach may lend itself better to optimisation for mobile devices, taking into account other requirements specific to the device and its connectivity options.

3 Application Modelling

Having described the architecture in which the applications we consider are deployed, we now go on to describe the applications themselves. This is fundamental to how we can manage and support the applications' data requirements.

3.1 Applications

An application in the terms of this paper is some code that manipulates data maintained in a database through a data manipulation language. An application instance is a specific invocation of an application that accesses only a subset of the data in the database.

When an application instance is invoked we first specify some identifying information, such as an Insurance Claim Number or a Customer ID. This sets the context of the application instance and is a standard requirement of applications executed by workflow managements systems, where applications are invoked for a specific business task. The context setting may be performed from within the application, or by passing parameters during invocation.

Once the context is set the application executes a number of operations before finishing. For a normal application this is a process of opening a connection to the database, executing different transactions on the database and then closing the connection. For mobile applications this approach holds problems in that disconnection during the execution of an application may result in the currently active transaction being managed by the database management system, but subsequent transactions not being possible until re-connection.

For an application to check out a data set sufficient for its' execution has a number of problems. As the application operates on internally stored data, constraints on the data declared in the database must either be enforcable by the application or left until check in time. The later can obviously cause difficulties for applications with many constraints and much effort. The former is often difficult to implement, adding major complexity to the application code, as well as redundancy of the replicated constraint definitions to be maintained.

Checking out data dependant on the operations to be performed, i.e. with different degrees of 'check out', can alleviate the problem of extended resource locking also associated with disconnected applications. Some operations an application performs may not require the checked out data to be made unavailable to other applications, e.g. reads. Other operations may require some temporary information to be inserted into the database before the execution proper of the application, e.g. creation of a new Customer ID to be used by the application and reserving that ID during the disconnected execution of the application.

Requiring applications to manage the potential for disconnection is similar to requiring applications to manage the data itself. Not only does it rely on the application programmers understanding of the issues, it replicates functionality that can be abstracted out. There is also the potential for the interaction of different applications to be more complex than can be anticipated from a single application's point of view.

Specifically related to this work, [11] describe the use of *hoard keys* based on an analysis of access patterns by applications to address the problem of data allocation to mobile clients. They do not however take into account the different types of operations that may be performed by an application, nor the *specific* data requirements of an application as captured by our application schema.

3.2   Application Schema

An application's demand of the database is captured in three aspects:

1. the subschema of the database that contains the data to be used
2. an indication of what subset of data within the subschema may be used by a particular application instance, e.g. all information relevant to an insurance claim identified by an insurance claim number
3. the operations the application may perform on that data during the execution of the application

We refer to these respectively as the *data schema*, the *context* and the *operation range* of the application, and capture all three in an Application Schema (AS).

We use a conceptual schema language to model the Application Schema for the usual reasons of physical implementation independence and the clearer understanding that a conceptual schema diagram gives to a human reader. The two main conceptual schema modelling languages used for designing relational databases are the Entity Relationship (ER) model and Object Role Modelling (ORM). We extend the ORM, as it has a more powerful constraint specification language and does not suffer from the entity/attribute confusion. We refer to our dialect of ORM as Application Data Demand Modelling (ADDM). For an introduction to ORM database design see [12].

For the *data schema* we use the standard ORM constructs. The model essentially consists of entity types and the relationships or fact types that combine entity types. The ORM languages also allow us to specify the roles that an entity type plays in a relationship. Extensions to include interdatabase dependencies in the ADDM let us model applications that execute over distributed databases, however this class of applications is outside the scope of this paper.

The *context* over which the application is to perform its operations is indicated by the context entity types. Specifying the entity instances for these entity types allows us to select the subset of the data that populates the data schema in the underlying database for an application instance. Context entity types are marked up as such by a subscript of the Entity Type name.

For the application schema we also add the *operation range* that an application may cover. Operations are performed on the entities in relationships, and the operation range is added to the fact types in ADDM. An operation on a fact type is made up of the operations that may be performed on each role of the fact type. The role level operations are Read, Delete, Insert (new and existing), Modify and Replace (with new and existing). These give us combinations for fact type level operations such as (D,D), (R,R), (I_N,I_N), (I_N,I_E) etc for a binary fact type. The operation range is the set of fact type operations that may be performed by an application instance.

The operation range for any particular fact type may be extended by a schema expansion method that checks for operations performed on other fact types that may need to be cascaded based on the constraints on the schema. This cascading may also increase the schema when mapped onto an existing database, i.e. through constraints not taken into account or known during the initial application design.

More information on the Application Data Demand Model and the construction of an Application Schema using the Application Schema Design Methodology is described in [8].

3.3   Global Application Schema

Having defined an application schema, the next step is to map this to the database schema on which the application is to be run. Ideally there are application schemata for every application that has been built on a database, and all of these are mapped onto the database schema, providing a complete cover for the schema. The union of these application schemata is called the Global Application Schema (GAS) and can be used to see what parts of the schema affect what applications.

The GAS includes a mapping down to the relational schema that directly represents the implementation of the database, allowing us to use the GAS for the creation of the mobile database with the correct naming required by the application.

More significantly however, the GAS also allows us to investigate the effect that an application instance has on another application instance of either the same, or a different, application type. We see whether two application instances would perform operations on the same data, and if those operations could cause conflicts due to the required locks. The algorithm for finding potential conflict is as follows:

1. Add every fact type in the GAS that has an operation range for both applications to the potential conflict list.
2. Remove every fact type from the potential conflict list where the facts populating that fact type for the two applications are disjoint.
   - If the context entity types (CETs) are the same but the context entity instances for the two applications are different, e.g. two insurance claims with different claim numbers, then all fact types where the CET is part of the key will have disjoint fact populations.
   - This also holds for any fact types where the key includes an entity type that has a one to one relationship to the CET, e.g. Customer Number or a complex object consisting of the Customer Name, Address and Date of Birth.
3. Remove any fact types from the list where the operations to be performed by the applications are *only* reads. There are other combinations that may not cause conflicts, depending on what can be preset. For example inserting new orders may use generated order numbers that are created at application invocation time and can thus be assured to be disjoint.

This algorithm highlights any applications that may perform conflicting operations on the same data. How we deal with potential conflict, e.g. restricting an application from execution if another application that may conflict is already active, and further checks at run time to determine if the potential conflict has actualised is dealt with by the application manager described in section 4.

For a more detailed discussion of the Global Application Schema, including its construction and maintenance and how the GAS is used for multidatabase schema integration, see [8]. In [13] database transactions from mobile devices over distributed databases are discussed. Although our work assumes that data is reconciled at a fixed network site, this is not always the case. A transaction mechanism for mobile transactions may be a good extension to the application manager's mechanism of updating the fixed network database, rather than our current use of classical transactions.

4   Application Manager

The application manager is called as part of the invocation of all applications. Although it does not need to create a mobile database for applications running on the fixed network, awareness of what application instances are active, including their context, helps with the advanced scheduling functions.

One example of application management technology is a workflow management system (WfMS). Applications are associated with tasks in the workflow processes and the WfMS schedules and invokes the applications as needed. Workflow management systems also manage some data flow between tasks within process instances, including, at least, the data required to set the context of invoked applications.

The functionality of the application manager is focused around two application methods:

Check Out of the data required by an application from a database, providing it to the application through a mobile database.

Check In to the fixed network database the data and transaction log returned by the application and clean up the mobile database.

These basic functions can be extended by using the knowledge of other applications, either scheduled on worklists or already invoked, to improve on the allocation of applications to minimise data locking and potential conflicts.

5 Conclusion

We address the problem of data management for mobile applications initially at the conceptual schema level, modelling an application schema and mapping this to the schema of the database used by the application. By enhancing the database schema in the DBMS with the union of application schemata, the Global Application Schema (GAS), we show how a database management system can be made application aware.

The addition of an application manager that is used for application invocation can assist in the data management for mobile applications, anticipating and preparing for both disconnected work and potential associated isolation issues. Adding a lightweight database management system to the mobile device, applications can be run with minimal modification to account for the different data source, and with no modifications to manage the disconnected data. In this way applications can be invoked, the data requirements for an application secured and execution of applications carried out regardless of the connectivity.

The check in of data sets may face problems of conflict resolution if local updates have been made. Rather than relying purely on optimistic check in methods, proactive and reactive conflict resolution strategies can be specified for application conflicts at design time. These can trigger a number of different approaches at run time, for example users checking out data may be warned of possible conflicts when invoking an application.

This work applies to data management in environments where we have some awareness of a number of applications that are intended to be executed, including mobile applications. Such an environment exists in workflow management systems, and the application granularity data modelling used can be applied to other database issues including control of database design scope and rapid integration of multidatabases to consistently support global applications.

References

1. Gray, J., Helland, P., O'Neil, P., Shasha, D.: The dangers of replication and a solution. (1996) 173–182
2. Pitoura, E.: A replication schema to support weak connectivity in mobile information systems. In: 7th International Conference on Database and Expert Systems Applications (DEXA). (1996)
3. Pitoura, E., Samaras, G.: Data Management for Mobile Computing. Volume 10. Kluwer Academic Publishers (1998)
4. Pitoura, E., Bhargava, B.K.: Data consistency in intermittently connected distributed systems. Knowledge and Data Engineering **11** (1999) 896–915
5. Heuer, A., Lubinski, A.: Configured replication for mobile applications (2000)
6. Ren, Q., Dunham, M.H.: Using semantic caching to manage location dependent data in mobile computing. In: Mobile Computing and Networking. (2000) 210–221
7. Mazumdar, S., Chrysanthis, P.K.: Achieving consistency in mobile databases through localization in PRO-MOTION. In: DEXA Workshop. (1999) 82–89
8. Muhlberger, R.M.: Data Management for Interoperable Systems. Phd thesis, The University of Queensland, Qld, Australia (2001)
9. Kiepuszewski, B., Mühlberger, R., Orlowska, M.E.: Flowback: Providing backward recovery for workflow systems. In: Proceedings of the 1998 ACM SIGMOD International Conference on Management of Data. (1998)
10. Muhlberger, R., Orlowska, M.E., Kiepuszewski, B.: Backward step: The right direction for production workflow systems. In: Proceedings of the 1999 Australian Database Conference. (1999)
11. Badrinath, B.R., Phatak, S.: Database server organization for handling mobile clients. DCS Technical Report DCS-342, Rutgers University, New Brunswick, NJ, USA (1997)
12. Halpin, T.A.: Information Modeling and Relational Databases. Morgan Kaufmann Publishers (2001)
13. Elmagarmid, A., Jing, J., Bukhres, O.: An efficient and reliable reservation algorithm for mobile transactions. In: Proceedings of the 4th International Conference on Information and Knowledge Management (CIKM'95). (1995)

m-WOnDA: The *"Write Once 'n' Deliver Anywhere"* Model for Mobile Users

Dionysios G. Synodinos[1] and Paris Avgeriou[2]

[1]National Technical University of Athens, Network Management Center
Heroon Polytechniou 9, Zografou 157 80, Greece
dsin@noc.ntua.gr

[2]National Technical University of Athens, Software Engineering Laboratory
Heroon Polytechniou 9, Zografou 157 80, Greece
Tel: +3010-7722487, Fax: +3010-7722519
pavger@softlab.ntua.gr

Abstract. The design and development of hypermedia applications that are deployed on the Wireless World Wide Web is a daunting task because of the various available platforms and the restrictions and capabilities imposed by the lack of established standards and the exponentially increasing number of emerging platforms. There are now justifiable research and development efforts that attempt to formalize the engineering process of such applications in order to achieve certain quality attributes like modifiability, maintainability and portability. This paper presents such an attempt for designing a conceptual model for hypermedia applications that allows for easy update and alteration of its content as well as its presentation and also allows for deployment in various mobile platforms. In specific this model explicitly separates the hypermedia content from its presentation to the user, by employing XML content storage and XSL transformations. Our work is based upon the empirical results of designing, developing and deploying hypermedia applications for mobile platforms, and on the practices of well-established hypermedia engineering techniques.

1 Introduction

During the last years there has been a lot of hype about the wireless World Wide Web (W4), where hypermedia applications can be accessed by wireless clients and especially mobile users. Emerging technologies and the penetration of mobile computing in our daily lives, have led to the need for mobile access of common web sites. The technology behind the mobile access to the Web usually draws upon a subset of HTML, like the cHTML (compact HTML) of NTT DoCoMo's i-mode with its millions of users in Japan, or is XML-derived like WML (Wireless Markup Language), the markup language of WAP, heavily deployed in Europe and abroad.

The anticipation of faster and cheaper W4 (Wireless World Wide Web) that the 3rd generation (3G) wireless networks and more sophisticated mobile devices will bring, results in a growing number of organizations that plan to deploy parts of their traditional web sites for mobile users. This task though can be overwhelmingly difficult since several problems have derived in building and maintaining hypermedia applications for mobile users.

A. Olivé (Eds.): ER 2003 Ws, LNCS 2784, pp. 205–216, 2003.

To begin with, there is a vast demand for the adaptation of content into a growing number of presentational templates, each one of them suitable for a different device. Only in the case of WAP-enabled phones, the developer must provide numerous templates that comply with the potential user's device capabilities and restrictions. These can be device characteristics like the screen size, e.g. a site should be deployed in a different way for a Nokia 7110 with its 96x46 pixels screen and for an Ericsson RS with its generous 360x120 pixels display. Also resolution and available bandwidth is an issue. For instance the site author should make provisions for slow GSM access, faster GPRS networks or even lightning fast 3G and beyond. Furthermore, the input peripherals bring in another degree of freedom, ranging from the standard numerical pad to Nokia 's 9210 PC-like keyboard. To make matters worse, mobile clients might need different versions of web pages as a side effect of the different level of support for WMLScript, the WAP client-side scripting language. In situations like these, updating content and performing version control can become tremendously resource-consuming if not impossible.

On top of everything else, web pages have evolved to a point of becoming too complex with all the inline client scripts and styles rules in order to facilitate the ever-growing and often conflicting demands for enhanced usability and impressive 'look and feel'. Therefore the daily task of updating content can no longer be performed by a novice in markup languages, but instead designated professionals with a solid background on web authoring and a clear understanding of the architecture of the certain site must be utilized.

The World Wide Web Consortium had an early provision to such problems with the launch of XML and the related family of technologies, in order to separate the content from the rest of the information such as presentation rules, metadata, active components etc. The question now is, given the XML technology, how can a site be engineered in order for it to achieve modifiability, maintainability and portability. In specific, the problem that hypermedia application authors have at hand, is comprised of the following secondary problems:

- How can one maintain the site content by updating it, at will, without requiring him or her to master the underlying technology of presentation style sheets, client-side scripts etc. for the target mobile platforms?
- How can one modify the layout, presentation and active components of the site without affecting the content associated with them?
- How can one port the hypermedia application to alternative versions for existing mobile platforms and still make provisions for future delivery platform versions?

In this paper we attempt to solve the above problems by proposing an XML-based multi-tier model, which is established upon the separation of the actual content, active widgets, presentation rules and the page generation process. This model is a refinement of the **WOnDA (Write Once, Deliver Anywhere)** model [1] for mobile clients. The presentation rules are themselves separated into a set of rules for transforming the actual content, the various widgets and the layout of the pages for every one of the presentational domains. The proposed model is based on an XML repository that holds the actual (textual) content and utilizes the power of eXtensible Style Sheet (XSL) transformations in a hierarchical manner that is well suited for providing a rich set of formats for every page to be deployed in. It also facilitates easy administration, the ability to easily add new formats and fast/clear refactoring of old ones. Also, since there is a complete separation between data and presentation, the development of content can become a streamlined process that doesn't deal with the complexity of the underlying structure of the chosen presentational domains.

The structure of the rest of this paper is as follows: Section 2 introduces a short literature review, comprised of the most significant approaches in designing hypermedia applications for several presentational domains and mobile clients. Section 3 analyses the proposed model and its philosophy. Section 4 presents a case study of a demo site that is created with the aid of the model and deployed in four mobile clients. Finally section 5 wraps up with ideas for future work.

2   Literature Review

There is already work in progress by the World Wide Web Consortium, under the title of **Composite Capabilities/Preference Profiles (CC/PP)** [2] towards the direction of serving the same content to different clients according to their profile. In particular, the CC/PP framework aims to provide a common way for clients to express their capabilities and preferences to a server that originates content. The server then uses this information to adapt the content in a way appropriate for the client device. This approach is particularly valuable for the case of mobile devices where the variety of clients is overwhelming. The WOnDA model can be integrated with the CC/PP model in the manner that different presentation formats can be created in an asynchronous way to satisfy the device profiles collected from a central or various distributed profile registries. On the other hand WOnDA proposes that creation of hypermedia context is done prior to user request (static content), and has no provision for dynamic adaptation of content according to the capabilities of the device by reading the device's profile in real time. Such a scenario though will be examined in future additions of WOnDA in order to serve the needs of a database-driven website where dynamic page generation from queries to a database is a requirement.

Another important approach of serving the same content to different clients is **Several Interfaces, Single Logic (Sisl)** [3]. This is an architecture and domain-specific language for designing and implementing services with multiple user interfaces. It aims to the decoupling of interface from service logic, by employing an event-based model of services that allows service providers to support interchangeable user interfaces to a single source of service logic or data. The need to provide content in a hypermedia format to a mobile client can be satisfied using the Sisl approach, in the sense that a web site can be modeled and developed using standard Sisl architecture, so that it can later facilitate interchangeable user interfaces. In fact, Sisl targets a wider variety of services and deals in greater depth with issues like how to manage the fundamental differences in the nature of interaction across the spectrum of user interfaces. As a result it doesn't elaborate on the actual process of creating the hypermedia documents. Also the broader spectrum of applications that Sisl aims to, causes it to grow in complexity, making its use in smaller projects, an overkill.

The IBM's T.J. Watson Research Centre has established a vision, named **Platform-Independent Model for Applications (PIMA)** [4], http://www.research.ibm.com/PIMA/) about next generation pervasive computing that can be described by the following three dimensions: use of mobile computing devices, creation/deployment of applications to such clients, and the environment and how it is enhanced by the emergence and ubiquity of new information and functionality. WOnDA is actually oriented towards the second dimension and especially on the deployment of hypermedia applications and it elaborates on the "*design-time*" part of the proposed application model of IBM. Both approaches suggest that applications are not written with a specific device in mind. So the developer should not make any assumptions about the client's device restrictions and capabilities in a manner that restricts the applications functionality, thus resulting to the fact that the task logic should not be secondary to the user interaction. Since the model proposed by IBM requires that application description captures the purpose of the user interaction at a high level, the user interface definition should include a decomposition of the interaction that is driven by the definition and structure of the user tasks. Because the above model should also be context-aware, the developer should not make assumptions about the services available and so these services should not be explicitly named, but rather specified in an abstract manner. This is in contrast with the WOnDA model for hypermedia applications where the application is deployed asynchronously into a format desired by the target clients, where the set available services, restrictions and capabilities are well defined and available to the designer at design-time. Also in the WOnDA universe there is no need for a specific client-side adaptation of content, which means that clients with smaller footprints can be utilized

It is also important to mention the **User Interface Markup Language (UIML)** [5] that provides a high device-independent method to describe a User Interface (UI). UIML looks at any UI from six orthogonal dimensions: the parts comprising the UI, the presentation of these parts, the content, the behaviour, the mapping of UI controls in some domain (e.g. HTML) and the business logic connected to this UI. It is implemented as a declarative XML-compliant meta-language that allows for the implementation of many UIs without learning the language or API specific for that device. The same philosophy is adopted by WOnDA, which supports content creation without mastering the underlying technology of any of the supported platforms. UIML's latest version supports multi-modal UI that can be used simultaneously and kept synchronized. For example a UI might offer a voice and a screen based front-end and the user can at any time switch between the two interaction modes. It supports a variety of supported domains (not only Markup Languages) and provides a canonical representation of any UI that is suitable for mapping to existing languages. Due to its view of a UI as a tree whose parts can change dynamically, it is well suited for applications that need to be multilingual.

A final interesting approach for mobile access to hypermedia applications is presented at [6], where the authors advocate the need for an automated approach to the adaptation of the User Interface that uses artificial intelligence and statistical techniques. The adaptation model proposed is incremental and iterative and focuses on the user's interests as depicted by his actions and not by explicit content rating. In this way the system learns from the user's preferences and adapts the UI in a way that provides an easy access to a vast amount of information. This approach is still at a very theoretical level and remains to be tested in real-world applications.

3   The Model

Before describing the WOnDA model in detail, it is useful to examine the way this
model is used for writing content once and delivering it to multiples clients. An
overview of the model 's modus operandi is illustrated in Fig.1. The content is
authored in a text editor that provides XML authoring facilities in a transparent way to
the author. This could be implemented as a MS Word plug-in [YAWC Pro,
http://www.yawcpro.com/], an ActiveX component [XMLSpy document editor
browser plug-In, http://www.xmlspy.com/download_plugin.html], or a different
editor [XMLSpy IDE, http://www.xmlspy.com/products_ide.htm l]. This means that
content can be created and updated by people with no web-authoring background, by
letting them write in simple text and have it automatically converted to XML. In
sequence, XSL transformations are utilized to impose style rules and presentation
layout, add active objects, and generate the page in its final form, e.g. WML page, a
handheld-compatible page etc. The final page is then published to a Web Server and
served to the appropriate clients through the Internet.

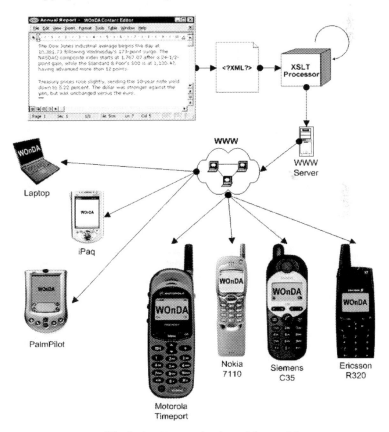

Fig.1. A macroscopic view of the model

What is the mechanism that deals with the XML files and XSL Transformations that
translate raw content into a specific delivery platform? What are these XML files, how

do the XSL transformations take place and what does the final result look like? These questions will be answered in the remainder of this section in the form of a guide for the construction of maintainable, modifiable, and portable hypermedia applications for mobile clients.

In order to describe this mechanism we propose a conceptual model by utilizing the Unified Modeling Language [7] (http://www.rational.com/uml), a widely adopted modeling language in the software industry and an Object Management Group standard [http://www.omg.org/]. Furthermore in order to define the syntax and semantics of the conceptual model we have designed a UML meta-model, i.e. a model that defines the language for expressing the conceptual model [8].

The conceptual model described here considers only static hypermedia pages and every page is comprised of the following elements:

1. The actual content of the page that consists of text, hyperlinks, images, videos, animation etc.
2. A set of navigational or promotional active objects or widgets like navigation bars, search boxes, menus, logos, ads, banners etc.
3. The general layout of the page meaning the positioning of all the above in the browser window and the rest of the markup envelope that is needed in order for the page to be syntactically valid.
4. Hyperlinks to other hypermedia pages

It is noted that this is a simplified and superficial model of a hypermedia page because the aim of WOnDA is not to model hypermedia applications in general but merely to separate content from the rest of the information and generate multiple versions of hypermedia applications. In other words the proposed model is considered to be in a lower abstraction layer than usual hypermedia design models such as HDM [9], RMM [10], WebML [11] etc.

We now move on to specify the meta-model that will define the language for expressing the conceptual model. The principles of the meta-model are the following:

1. The actual content (text, links, references to media files) of each hypermedia page is kept in one XML file. These files will be referred to as **Page Contents** (PCs). PCs represent published pages as abstract data entities without taking into account any presentation aspects derived by the desired formats.
2. The task of providing content rendering information is left up to a set of XSL files, which will be referred to as **Content Transformers** (CTs). The idea behind CTs is that if we define a set of N versions for the site under construction, every version is exactly identical to all the others in terms of textual information since this information is provided by the PCs, but the versions differ in the layout, functionality, style and the markup that they're written in. For every one of the versions we define a CT which describes the rules necessary to transform the content provided by the respective PCs.
3. In the fashion of PCs and CTs for the textual content we define **Page Widgets** (PWs) and **Widget Transformers** (WTs), which hold the necessary data and presentation rules respectively for the widgets used.
4. Metadata that are specific to the content page, as in the WML, cHTML, HTML <META> element, used throughout a version or even throughout the entire site are kept in an XML file, which will be referred to as **Content-Specific Metadata** (**CSM**).

5. Metadata that are specific to a certain version, e.g. character encoding information, are kept in another XML file, called **Version-Specific Metadata (VSM).**

6. Both content page-specific and version-specific metadata are rendered by another transformer XSL file called **Metadata Transformer (MT).**

7. For every one of the different versions we define an XSL file, which describes the rules necessary to generate the page layout that is restricted in the context of the version. These XSL files, which will be referred to as **Version Builders (VBs)**, do not contain any information about the rules we need to render the textual content drawn from the PCs nor the widgets used. They rather define the general layout of the page meaning the positioning of all the above in the browser window and the rest of the markup envelope that is needed in order for the page to be syntactically valid for the corresponding presentational domain. The information about client-side scripts or additional client-side style rules (e.g. CSS), are referenced by the VB or included in it depending on the capabilities of the syntax of the relevant domain. For example for the HTML domain this can be accomplished by the <LINK> element.

Fig. 2 depicts the relationship between the above model elements. Page Contents, Page Widgets and Content-Specific Metadata are XML files and are all specializations of the class "Generic Hypermedia Page Element". They are also connected with an aggregation relationship with the "Hypermedia Page" class, which means that they are all part of a hypermedia page. Content Transformer and Widget Transformer are XSL files that render the corresponding Page Contents and Page Widgets. Furthermore it is obvious that Content-Specific Metadata are related to Page Contents, in the sense that metadata describe the content. Moreover, Content-Specific Metadata and Version-Specific Metadata are rendered by the Metadata Transformer. Finally Version Builder uses all the other transformers to render the layout of the hypermedia page and insert the appropriately transformed content, widgets and metadata into the final version-specific hypermedia page. Content Transformers, Widget Transformers and the Version Builder are specializations of the "Version-Specific Transformer" class. Finally it is noted that the names of the classes "Generic Hypermedia Page Element", "Hypermedia Page", "Version-Specific Transformer" are written in italics, since they are abstract classes in this meta-model.

8. For every page there is a registry specific for it, called **Page Registry (PR),** which link together all the page elements and their transformers for the various versions.

9. For every site there is a main registry, the **Site Index Page (SIP)**, which holds all the file system (or network) paths to the Page Registries.

10. All the above are parsed by a processing shell, which will be referred to as *Site Builder* and provides the web site administrator with a web interface to generate or update certain pages, entire versions of the site etc.

Fig.3 depicts the page creation process that takes place with the aid of the last three elements. The Page Registry gathers all the necessary data from the Page Content, the Content Transformer, the Content-Specific Metadata and the Version Builder. The Site Builder parses the Site Index Pages to look for all the Page Registries, performs the transformations and generates the hypermedia page of the appropriate format.

The last thing to be clarified about WOnDA is the way that the model is applied. A simple process model for harnessing WOnDA is depicted in Fig.4 is a UML activity diagram, showing the discrete activities as well as the artifacts that activities produce or take as input

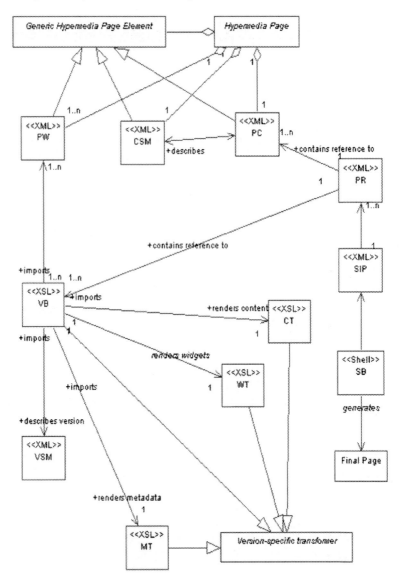

Fig. 2. The hypermedia page elements and the transformers

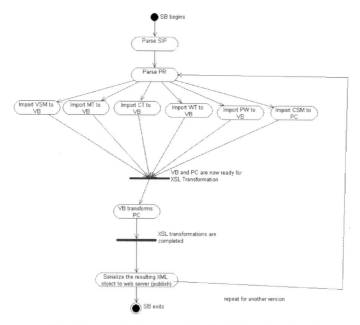

Fig. 3. An activity diagram of the Site Builder functionality

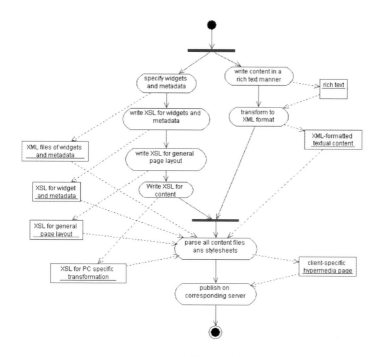

Fig. 4. A process model for applying WOnDA

4   Mobile City Guide of Athens: A Case Study

In order to examine the feasibility and effectiveness of WOnDA in a real world scenario, a demo website has been developed. The purpose of this site is to provide tourists that visit Athens for the 2004 Olympic Games and have mobile Internet access, with information about the city, the Games and the various events. The aim of our effort was to provide custom access to both textual information and images e.g. maps, for a certain number of predefined mobile devices. The scenario described by the following pictures is one where 4 users with 4 different mobile clients, access the home page of the site and choose to browse a map of the city.

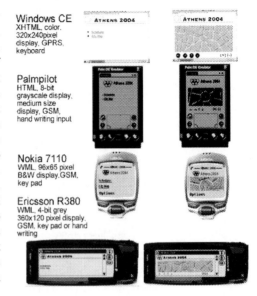

Fig. 5 Screenshots of mobile clients

It is important to mention that since there are multiple versions of the site, one for every version available, there is a need for a mechanism that redirects any device that visits the top-level URL (e.g. www.mobile2004.gr), to the part of the site that corresponds to the device used (e.g. www.mobile2004.gr/nokia7110/index.wml). This can be easily implemented by parsing the HTTP headers of the client's original request and identifying his/her browser by the "User-Agent" header [12]. Even in the case that the information exposed by this header doesn't match a client known to the system then the user can be redirected to a generic version of the site, which proves functional for his device, although not customized.

Fig. 6 depicts the implementation of the meta-model described earlier in the case of the aforementioned demo site, focusing on the page with the city map. This page consists of a picture with the map, a header with the Athens 2004 logo and a footer with navigational widgets. This is an instance of the meta-model, i.e. a model per se that is described using all the necessary meta-model elements. The diagram shows only the elements for Nokia7110 and PalmPilot in order not to overload the diagram, even though the other two clients are represented in a similar way. Also with the intention of keeping the diagram simple, the relationships between the elements that were defined in the meta-model are note repeated here. Every model element in this diagram is distinguished by having a stereotype defined for it. Stereotypes are a UML mechanism for extending the core of the language and are denoted by brackets in this diagram.

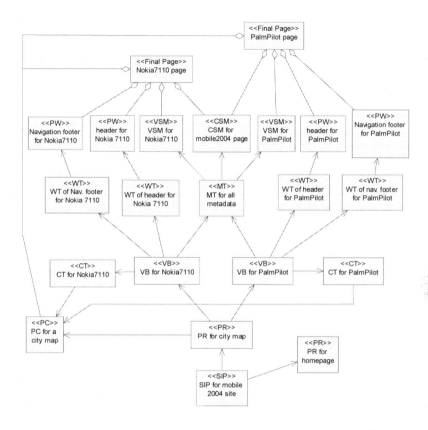

Fig. 6. The model for the mobile 2004 site

5 Future Work

Although the principles described above provide a solid foundation, they do not deal with the entirety of the diverse scenarios that are popular in contemporary hypermedia applications for mobile clients. Therefore we plan to extend this model in various ways in order to accommodate certain features that are currently missing. First of all dynamic content must be provided to the user in situations where the user needs to systematically draw information from a database or merely execute HTML-embedded server side scripts. Furthermore the model needs to take provisions about multiple languages used for the same content, a strongly emerging need especially for sites like the one illustrated in the case study section.

Another issue that concerns the model per se is the use of the Object Constraint Language (OCL) [13] to define the model more formally with the use of well-specified constraints. OCL is the UML's recommended language for specifying constraints and can help in formalizing the various model elements and the relationships between them.

A formal evaluation of the model's effectiveness is another step thaw we plan to take in order to measure the quality of this work. This is already under way with the use of the model in new hypermedia applications for mobile users.

Finally, an interesting issue that is under research is the way that WOnDA can benefit from all the work recently done in the database area in order to deal with XML documents. This is caused by the variety of proposed models for storing and accessing XML information both natively and on object-relational databases.

References

1. D. Synodinos and P. Avgeriou, "WOnDA: An Extensible Multi-platform Hypermedia Design Model", in proceedings of Efficient Web-based Information Systems (EWIS), September 2nd, 2002, Montpellier, France, Lecture Notes in Computer Science series, Springer-Verlag.
2. World Wide Web Consortium (W3C), "Composite Capabilities/Preference Profiles: Requirements and Architecture", W3C Working Draft, 28 February, 2000.
3. T. Ballz, C. Colby, P. Danielseny, L. Jategaonkar Jagadeesany, R. Jagadeesan, K. L'aufer, P. Matagay, K. Rehory, "Sisl: Several Interfaces, Single Logic", Journal of Speech Technology, Kluwer Academic Publishers, 2000.
4. Guruduth Banavar, James Becky, Eugene Gluzbergy, Jonathan Munson_, Jeremy Sussman, and Deborra Zukowski, "Challenges: An Application Model for Pervasive Computing," Sixth Annual ACM/IEEE International Conference on Mobile Computing and Networking (Mobicom 2000), 2000. http://www.research.ibm.com/PIMA/
5. MarcAbrams and Constantinos Phanouriou, "UIML: An XML Language for Building Device-Independent User Interfaces", in proceedings of XML '99, Dec. 1999, Philadelphia.
6. Daniel Billsus, Clifford A. Brunk, Craig Evans, Brian Gladish, and Michael Pazzani, "Adaptive Interfaces for Ubiquitous Web Access", Communications of the ACM, May 2002, Volume 45, Number 5.
7. G. Booch, J. Rumbaugh, and I. Jacobson, The UML User Guide, Addison-Wesley, 1999.
8. The Rational Unified Process, 2000, v. 2001.03.00.23, Rational Software Corporation, part of the Rational Solutions for Windows suite.
9. F. Garzotto, D. Schwabe, P. Paolini, "HDM- A Model Based Approach to Hypermedia Application Design", ACM Transactions on Information Systems, Vol. 11, #1, Jan. 1993, pp. 1-26.
10. T. Isakowitz; E. Stohr; P. Balasubramaniam, "RMM, A methodology for structured hypermedia design", Communications of the ACM, August 1995, pp 34-48
11. S. Ceri. P. Fraternali, A. Bongio, "Web Modeling Language: A modeling language for designing Web sites", proceedings of WWW9 Conference, Amsterdam, May 2000.
12. IETF RFC 1945, Hypertext Transfer Protocol - HTTP/1.0
13. OMG, Object Constraint Language Specification, version 1.3. Framingham, MA, 1999.

Basic User Requirements for Mobile Work Support Systems - Three Easy Steps

Asbjørn Følstad and Odd-Wiking Rahlff

SINTEF, Forskningsvn. 1, Pb 0124 Blindern, N-0314 Oslo, Norway
{asf,owr}@sintef.no
http://www.sintef.no

Abstract. Due to shortage of time and resources in the early phases of mobile work support development processes, it is necessary to develop a 'quick and clean' method for user requirements modelling. The method consists of three easy steps that anyone with an interest in human factors should be able to complete: (1) The explication of a common vision, (2) observations in the field, and (3) problem oriented focus group processes. The method is designed to generate results that may serve as a foundation for more comprehensive later stage system modelling. As an illustration of the method, a case of use is presented: The development of an electronic delivery guide (EDG) for the newspaper deliverers of a major Norwegian newspaper distribution.

1 Introduction

Mobile work support systems are aids and devices that enable mobile workers to do their job in an effective and efficient manner. What may be expected from a mobile work support system is that the worker, wherever he or she may be, is enabled to:

- retrieve necessary information.
- save notes and input.
- communicate with the right people.

Organisations with a mobile workforce embrace mobile ICT as a welcome solution to the challenge of increasing the efficiency and effectiveness of the individual workers, and the corporate flow of information alike. Pen and paper are replaced with stylus and PDA, paper-based order forms and instructions are traded for intangible bit-streams, and the social call of the nearest leader is substituted with brief phone calls. However, the new tools introduced in the old ways of the workers must fit the needs and characteristics of those that will be using them. The development process leading to new mobile work support systems must include proper user requirements modelling, and user evaluation of early implementations.

1.1 The Problem of Time and Resources

In spite of the importance of adequate user requirements modelling, this part of the system development process is easily overlooked [1]. There may be two causes for this. One: Not enough time; the ICT business sector is characterised by an increasing demand for shorter product development time. Two: Not enough resources; development activities that are directly oriented towards implementing code are often prioritised at the cost of user involvement. Consequently it is necessary to rethink the way the basic user-oriented work in the development process is conducted. There is a need to refine user centred methods and techniques in a way that makes them simple

A. Olivé (Eds.): ER 2003 Ws, LNCS 2784, pp. 217-228, 2003.

and time-saving. To use the words of Wichansky [2], what is needed is a 'quick and clean' (as opposed to 'quick and dirty') framework for user involvement.

The early phases of a new work support system based on mobile ICT will most likely be a replacement of an old work support system that may or may not include electronic devices. Of course, new work support systems may be introduced in synchrony with a revolution of the existing organisational structures, but just as likely the new system will initially imply only a modest evolution of the old ways. The reason for this may be as follows: Someone higher up in the company has agreed that new mobile ICT represents interesting opportunities for the enterprise. At the same time there is no guarantee that this new technology will prove to be beneficial. The competitors probably have not started using the technology yet, and who wants to be the first to introduce a potential disaster. As a consequence one decides to go for a short-term, low-cost pilot project where mobile ICT is introduced to a small part of the organisation. No major organisational changes are involved, the dedicated development team is small, and most important in regard to the present paper: There is no organisational incitement to initiate resource-consuming modelling efforts. What is needed, from the short term perspective of the development team is to get this first system version to work - fast. Even so, the results of this first introductions may have important bearings for the future development of mobile work support in the company and the importance of user requirements modelling is paramount; even though the company CEO may see it differently.

1.2 Basic Assumptions

The user requirements of a new work support system will be dependent on the actual implementation of the old system, and the benchmark 'acceptable low' of the user requirements will be that the new system does not make the users workday more difficult. If the mobile workers are to consider the new mobile work support system a success, it must at least be as efficient, effective and reliable in use as the old system. This implies:

- The new system must provide as efficient and effective access to all necessary information as the old system.
- The input mechanisms of the new system must be as efficient and effective as those of the old.
- The new system must provide the same opportunity for necessary communication as the old.
- The new system must be as reliable as the old.

Making any system comply with the four principles above demands user requirements identification. When time and resources are short, it is necessary to make this as simple as possible. One favourable aspect of the situation may be a small sized development team, which loosens the demands on the formality of the requirements, and the success of the requirements work is more dependent on a good dialogue with a few persons.

1.3 The Purpose of this Paper

The purpose of this paper is to present a quick and clean refinement of traditional methods for user requirements identification, particularly suited for mobile work support systems when time and resources are too scarce for in-depth modelling. The method consists of three easy steps that anyone with an interest in human factors should be able to complete, and should produce a set of prioritised user requirements necessary for the actual implementation of the system, compatible with the necessary business and technical requirements documentation.

The three steps of the method consist of methods belonging to most tool-boxes of user requirements identification [3,4]. However, the tailoring of these methods to comprise one single low-cost approach is an effort that we hope will enable more developers to include adequate user requirements engineering in the development process. The three steps are:

- Collecting a common vision through stakeholder interviews.
- Observing the old system in the field.
- Requirements identification in focus groups.

1.4 The Case: User Requirements for an Electronic Newspaper Delivery Guide

The methodological approach was developed in association with the collection of user requirements for an electronic newspaper delivery guide (EDG) developed by a Norwegian company for newspaper distribution. The EDG was to be implemented as a replacement of the paper based delivery guide used by the newspaper deliverers on their paper route. The old delivery guide included information regarding subscriber names, addresses and products to be delivered, as well as the order of delivery and a route map. Furthermore, the guide was subject to daily updates by way of paper forms attached to the packets of newspaper delivered at the regular drop point.

The old newspaper delivery guide system had several weaknesses: Its updating was cumbersome, costly, and depended on the conscientiousness of the workers. Also any input provided by the workers (written input and the particular sequence of the route) would be lost with the paper copy of the guide. At the same time the paper based delivery guide had several advantages: It was sturdy and could take a beating, involving being dropped in the floor, exposed to rain, used in cold weather etc.

The suggested new system implied an evolution of the old. Whatever information the paper deliverers got from the paper based delivery guide, they would in the future get from a PDA-like terminal, preferably with online connection to a central database. The early phases of development should not involve any major changes of the business processes of the organisation. Rather the paper-based work support system was replaced with an electronic one. The technology chosen for the first running version was a Compaq iPaq running PocketPC 2002, using Internet Pocket Explorer and GPRS data transfer via Bluetooth from a central database. The project period for the development and implementation of this first version was 6 months, at the end of which 25 newspaper deliverers should have permanently replaced their old paper-based delivery guides.

Fig. 1. Old paper-based and new electronic delivery guides

The plans for the first phase of the project included proper system modelling activities, but these were discarded for the time being due to pressure on time and resources. It was however realised that this new way of updating the delivery guides will enable a more flexible distribution system, that can enable the organisation to provide distribution of weekly or monthly magazines of nearly every kind in addition to the daily newspaper.

2   Step One: Explicate a Common Vision

Any system to be designed already exists as a figment of the customer's imagination. The commission given to the development team is founded on an idea of what kind of application the users of the system are to be provided and the effect it will have on the organisation. This basic idea of the customer may be contaminated with two problems:

1. The user aspects of the system have not been thoroughly analysed. The system in question may imply consequences that are unwanted or antagonistic relative to the users' work situation.
2. The idea is developed by the members of a group or organisational unit, and the different actors of the group have different conceptions of the system in question.

To conquer the first problem there is need for an explication of the customer's vision of the system. The quick and clean way to do this is through interviews with each actor in the 'customer group', in addition to reviews of relevant documentation. In the interviews the following is mapped:

*   Users - including administrators, maintainers and end users.
*   Context and organisational structure.
*   Tasks to be assisted.
*   Possible gains and risks for the different users when introducing the new system.
*   System success criteria.

Through an explication of the customer's vision, possible mismatches between user needs and system concepts may be identified. And, just as important, this exercise ensures that user requirements are made an explicit part of the customer's vision of the system, which in turn will have bearings on the incorporation of user requirements in the overall requirements specification. The duration of each interview will typically be one hour.

The second problem to be solved through the explication of a common vision is that of possible mismatches between the visions existing in the heads of the different members of the customer group: The vision of the CEO does not match that of the CTO etc. To side-step this, the interviews are conducted with each representative of the customer separately. Individual differences in opinion may thus be uncovered, and may be made the focus of attention at an early developmental stage.

Based on the information from the interviews, a memo containing lists of items from each of the five categories above is generated. The items of the lists are described in prose text, and wherever there are mismatches in the information given by the different members of the customer group this is accentuated. The lists of this memo may be called the intermediate customer vision.

Following the interviews the members of the customer group are invited to a plenary presentation of the intermediate common vision. Differences in opinion are addressed, and a revised common vision is agreed on. In the case of unresolved disagreements, appropriate actions are defined. An explicit agreement on the common vision is important to ensure the customer's and development team's commitment to user requirements. The lists that are finally agreed on are to be reckoned as the explicated customer vision, and constitute the foundation for later user requirements.

The Case: Explicating the Vision of an Electronic Newspaper Delivery Guide

The development and implementation of an EDG was based on an old idea. A group of people at the newspaper distribution company had been thinking about the possible gains of making an electronic version of the paper-based delivery guide for several years, but obstacles like immature technology and the lack of basic funding had earlier been to great to surmount. Finally resources were allocated to a project that was to develop a first running version of the EDG. Technical and business requirements were taken care of by personnel within the project; the generation of user requirements were handed to an external organisation. The timeframe and resources allowed to identify user requirements implied that this was to be done "quick and clean". The explicating of the vision included the following steps:
- Review relevant documentation.
- Interview of half a dozen key persons in the EDG project and the distribution company.
- One plenary meeting where the explicated vision was presented and agreed on.

The interviews resulted in a general list of involved user groups and organisational units, tasks and intended gains. In the final plenary meeting a list of system success-criteria was agreed on. The list later served as evaluation criteria for the first running version.

3   Step Two: Observe in the Field

If the minimum user requirements to a new system is implicitly decided by the design of the existing system, a successful introduction of a new routine for mobile workers demands that it is perceived as at least as effective, efficient and reliable as the old. Thus sorting out the user requirements of the new system involves understanding the old way of doing things.

In general there are two primary sources to the ways things are done; using concepts from the domain of organisational theory, these may be labelled tacit and explicit knowledge [5]. Explicit knowledge includes formal work descriptions, procedures etc. Tacit knowledge refers to the knowledge in the heads of the workers and their non-formalised daily routines. Major amounts of research on how to access the knowledge associated with the behaviour of workers in an organisation have been done, and the prescribed methods may involve complex methodological efforts way out of the range of the resources allowed within the paradigm of 'quick and clean'. What is needed is a simple and effective method for describing the mobile work that is to be supported. This work description may follow the pattern of traditional task analyses.

A traditional task analysis requires that one major task (getting the work done) is broken down in several sub-tasks that are described and again broken down in lower-level tasks [6,7]. This exercise is usually conducted without differentiating between those tasks that depend on work support and those that don't. The reason for this approach is that traditional task analysis is designed to analyse the total work situation of a user, e.g. when all the work is done through a stationary PC. However, in the case of mobile work support the situation is different; the users are not using their work support all the time. On the contrary, a lot of the sub-tasks the users are engaged in probably will be conducted without the need for any work support at all. This allows for cutting some corners in regard to the traditional task analysis, by an early identification of those tasks that demand work support and a focusing of attention on these. Consequently a task analysis for mobile work support systems should include no more than the following:

- Superficial description of sub-tasks and their sequence.
- Identification of those lower level tasks that require work support for information retrieval, information input, or communication.
- Minute description of the information, input or communication required in the lower level tasks identified in step 2.

The 'quick and clean' way to conduct a task analysis for mobile work support systems is that of observation by participation, validated through focus groups. One way of arranging an observation by participation may be that the user requirements engineer goes through on-the-job training, where she is given the basic training routine of the work in question. Information to be gathered:

- The sequence of tasks conducted by the user.
- The information that is used in carrying out particular tasks.
- The access and structure of the necessary information.
- The different kinds of notes and inputs made by the user during particular tasks.
- The users communicational needs.

The observer should also take photos or video-clips for later presentation in the focus group of step 3. The information gathered is to be collected in a systematic work description. The what, where and how of the tasks are to be described briefly; the tasks explicitly associated with necessary information retrieval, note-taking, or communication are elaborated.

The resulting task analysis is to be validated in a focus group, where a representative selection of the workers in question are participating. The validation is conducted as a walk-through of the sequence of tasks. When the validation is finished and there exists one agreed-on task analysis, the same focus group is used in step 3 of the method.

The Case: Analysing the Task of Paper Delivery

The future users of the EDG are currently equipped with a work support system consisting of a paper based delivery guide, a mobile phone and a paper form on the pack of papers indicating the subscriber changes and delivery complaints of the day. To conduct a 'quick and clean' task analysis two observers followed two newspaper deliverers on their daily route. The observers were given the introduction routine for new paper deliverers, and assisted in delivering the papers. Data were collected in the form of notes and photographs.

The observation resulted in the following list of sub-tasks:
- Picking up the papers at the drop-point.
- Delivering the papers:
    - In areas of detached houses.
    - In areas of non-detached houses.
    - In areas of 'high-rise buildings'.
- Communicating with the 'district leader'.
- Updating the delivery guide.

The list of tasks was elaborated in regard to the sub-tasks that depend on work support. One example of a task broken down in sub-tasks is given below.

Picking up the papers at the drop-point
Find packs of paper belonging to the route; the reference number of the route is given at the front page of the delivery guide
Count papers; the number of papers is given on the paper forms on the packs
Check changes in the delivery guide; new or stopped subscriptions are given on the paper forms on the packs
Check for messages or complaints; given on the paper forms of the packs

---

The task analysis was validated in the first part of two subsequent focus groups, one with a representative selection of newspaper deliverers and one with a representative selection of district leaders.

4   Step Three: User Requirements through a Focused Group Process

The final step of the 'quick and clean' path to user requirements of mobile work support systems is to elicit the requirements on the basis of the explicated vision of the new system and the task analysis of the old. The bulk of user requirements is already given through the task analysis of step 2, in particular if the new work support system represents a mere evolving of the old ways. However a new system also represents an opportunity for more efficient, effective and reliable work support, also as seen from the users' point of view.

Knowledge related to the possible improvements in regard to existing work support may be stored in different places, but is certainly exists in the heads of the users. Their knowledge represents a prime source to the different small or large frustrations and difficulties of an ordinary workday. Some of these frustrations may be linked to the lack of work support in the old system. Given that we are right in locating the key to possible improvements of work support in the everyday knowledge of its users, the challenge is to elicit this knowledge. So, how does one reveal possible improvements from users? One could always ask 'how can we improve your current mobile work support?', but chances are that this will not turn out to solve the problem. Our suggestion is to elicit user knowledge not through focusing on (technological) solutions, but through focusing on their problems. If you want to get inside the problems and difficulties of a particular work situation, put the workers employed in it together in a group and get them to talk. The final methodological step of the 'quick and clean' process to user requirements is problem-oriented focus groups.

Traditionally, focus groups are not reckoned as a particularly valid instrument for identification of user requirements [7,8]. The users are taken out of their workplace and may therefore not be reliable sources to their actual ways of work. Also the discussions of the focus groups are easily biased. However, the use of focus groups as the third step in a quick and clean methodology for user requirements identification for mobile work support systems is quite adequate. Due to the earlier steps there already exists a task analysis, based on observing the users in the field. This ensures that the moderator of the focus group knows the workplace of the users first hand. Furthermore, the users are reminded of their work through a task analysis validation with both verbal descriptions and pictures from the workplace. It may also be added that the discussions are focused through the structure of the sub-tasks, which should minimise bias. However, in order to minimise the risk of seriously biased results, it is recommended to conduct two separate focus groups with different persons.

The participants of the focus group should be a representative selection of the general user population, a moderator, a referent, and (preferably) representatives from the customer and development group. The users are encouraged to present whatever problems they may experience in their daily work, without worrying weather or not the problems they present are relevant in regard to the new work support system. However, the discussions should follow a certain structure:

- Reach a common understanding of the tasks involved.
- Identify present problems.
- Discuss requirements and possible solutions.
- Prioritise the problems.

Reach a Common Understanding

A common understanding of the tasks involved is reached through the validation of the task analysis presented in step 2. The moderator of the focus group conducts a walk-through of the work, structured according to the sub-tasks identified in the task analysis and presented through verbal descriptions and photos taken during the observation. The participants of the focus group are encouraged to criticise the task analysis, and a final task analysis is agreed on.

Identify Problems

Each of the different sub-tasks identified in the final task analysis is assigned one poster-size sheet of paper on the wall. The moderator goes through the sub-tasks one by one. The participants are first encouraged to elaborate in detail on what the different tasks involve and are then asked what problems they may experience when conducting the task. Identified problems are jotted down on post-it notes, and posted on the sheet of paper assigned to the particular sub-task.

Discuss Requirements and Possible Solutions

When all sub-tasks have been treated, there is a summary discussion of the problems that has been identified and what user requirements these imply. The participants of the focus group are invited to think loud around the shaping of the requirements, but the final revision of the requirements must be done after the focus group. The moderator also initiates a short discussion on possible solutions to the different problems.

Prioritise the Problems

Finally the participants of the focus group are asked to assign all identified problems a priority value from 1 (not important) to 3 (very important). The priorities are written by each participant directly on the post-it note on each sheet of paper. The sum average of the priority values is interpreted as the measure of priority, and the final list of requirements is sorted on the basis of the priority assigned to the identified problem associated with the requirement.

The process results in a validated list of tasks and associated present work support. In addition a prioritised list of present user problems, new system requirements and suggested design solutions are generated.

Fig. 3. Focus group participants posting sub-task-related problems

**The Case: Eliciting User Requirements
from a Room Full of Newspaper Deliverers**

In the case of the EDG, two problem-oriented focus groups was conducted. One with four newspaper deliverers, another with four of their nearest leaders ('district leaders'). The participants were assigned to a group on the basis of employment status; as we wanted input from both groups, and it was reckoned that the paper deliverers would speak more freely when their immediate leaders were not present. The focus groups progressed fairly similarly, thus only the group of the paper deliverers will be referred in detail.

The focus group started with an initial presentation of all people present, followed by a presentation of the purpose of the meeting. Then a walk-through of the task analysis of newspaper delivery was conducted. The work of a paper deliverer was in the task analysis divided into three sub-tasks, each with three to four lower level tasks requiring mobile work support. Each sub-task with lower level tasks was presented by way of PowerPoint, including textual bullet points and pictures from observations in the field. The participants were invited to ask questions and freely criticise the way their work was presented; be it that sub-tasks were missing or distorted. Afterwards each of the three sub-tasks was assigned a poster on the wall and discussed. The newspaper deliverers explained in detail what they did during the different sub-tasks, and for each sub-task the moderator guided their discussion over to concrete problems associated with particular tasks. The participants in the group of paper deliverers were not particularly eager to write down their experienced problems themselves; this was done continuously by the referent who also posted the notes on the appropriate sheet of paper on the wall.

Working out the full set of problems related to each sub-task was met with great enthusiasm from the participants, and was also the most time consuming activity of the workshop. After summarising the problems related to each task, possible user requirements following from these problems were discussed. Finally possible solutions were briefly debated. The latter activities were more difficult for the participants of the group than working out the set of problems. A few ideas and suggestions for possible requirements and solutions to problems were generated, but the user requirements team had to work out most of the user requirements afterwards.

Taking the Requirements Further

Based on the 'quick and clean' activities of the three-step identification of user requirements, a written report is produced and handed over as a final delivery to the customer. The report is an important document as a starting point for in-depth modelling activities, and valuable for the customer as documentation. Even so, the immediate value of the user requirements work depends on the communication of user requirements to the key persons of the development team. Allowing for the fact that the development team is of limited size, this may be done as presentations, workshops, or informal dialogue between the human factors experts and the system developers. This communication shall ensure that the user requirements are taken into consideration when developing the mobile work support system, and it may also work as a lever for selling in more extensive modelling work at the next stages of development.

The user requirements are also to be used as criteria of evaluation when testing the first version of the system on users in the organisation. The description of 'quick and clean' evaluation of mobile work support systems will follow in a later paper.

The Case: Further Work with the EDG

In the EDG project, user requirements were communicated to the development team through presentations and discussions. This dialogue was regarded as useful by the developers, and the identified user requirements had important bearings on the design of the PDA application as the system front-end.

When the first running version of the EDG was introduced, several user evaluations were conducted, including focus groups, observations and questionnaires. The limited size and scope of the present paper prevents a detailed presentation of the evaluation results, but the overall impression was that the users were truly happy with their new mobile work support system. In an adapted version of the IBM satisfaction measurement questionnaire PSSUQ [9], the EDG was rated as easy to use, easy to learn and pleasant to use (as opposed to difficult to use, difficult to learn and unpleasant to use). It was rated as neither increasing nor decreasing work efficiency, but it was generally held that it would increase work effectiveness by helping the newspaper deliverers to avoid customer complaints.

5   Discussion

As a response to limited time and resources available in mobile work support system development processes, a 'quick and clean' three step method for basic user requirements modelling has been presented. In addition it has been presented a case where the method has been successfully used. It has been argued that the method is to be regarded as a substitute for more time-consuming and thorough modelling efforts, and that it should generate a result that may be deployed in modelling work later on in the development process. The method may also be a useful first step in promoting the importance of modelling work to the development team and company administration. One important aspect that should be discussed is that of validity. How to be confident in a method that produces user requirements based only on a few interviews, observations and focus groups? The main argument in defence of the method is its multi-method approach. All three basic methods utilised have major flaws when it comes to validity, both internal validity and generalisation. However, when they are used together they will serve as each other's sources of triangulation, and the scewed results that may be produced with one method should be corrected with one of the others. Also the focus of attention when using the methods is on the work support system of today 'as is', and not the new system. The user requirements of the new system are generated as the sum of requirements and problems belonging to the old and familiar system. Only when the requirements and problems of the old system are established, the users are asked about requirements, wishes, and wants for the new.

Taking this method further will involve its integration in a complete framework for system modelling and evaluation. The next steps will be to focus on the evaluation method for the first running version of the system and the integration of comprehensive system modelling techniques in the later developmental stages.

References

1. Vredenburg, K., Mao, J., Smith, P.W., and Carey, T.: A survey of User Centred Design Practice. CHI letters, Vol. 4-1. (2002) 471-478
2. Wichansky, A.M.: Usability testing in 2000 and beyond. Ergonomics, Vol. 43-7 (2000) 998-1006
3. Maguire, M.C.: User-Centred Requirements Handbook (Report D5.3): HUSAT Research Institute, UK (1998)
4. Inuse. A practical handbook on user-centred design for assistive technology. HUSAT Research Institute, UK (1996)
5. Nonaka, I., and Takeuchi, H.: The knowledge-creating company. New York: Oxford University Press (1995)
6. Wickens, C.D., Gordon, S E., and Liu, Y.: Human Factors Engineering. NY: Longman (1997)
7. Usabilitynet [Online 20.06.2002] Available at: http://www.usabilitynet.org
8. Nielsen, J.: The use and misuse of focus groups. [Online: 20.06.2002] Available at: http://www.useit.com/ (1997)
9. Lewis, J.R. (1995). IBM Computer Usability Satisfaction Questionnaires: Psychometric Evaluation and Instructions for Use. Journal of Human-Computer Interaction,. 7(1), pp. 57-75

Accounting and Billing of Wireless Internet Services in the Third Generation Networks

Päivi Kallio[1], Giovanni Cortese[2], Roberto Tiella[2], and Alessandro Zorer[2]

[1]VTT Electronics, Kaitoväylä 1, 90571 Oulu, Finland
Tel. :+358 400 963 214, Fax: +358 8 551 2320
paivi.kallio@vtt.fi

[2]Sodalia S.p.A, Via Valentina Zambra n.1, 38100 Trento, Italy
Tel.;+39 0461 316111, Fax: +39 0461 316663
{cortese,tiella,zorer}@sodalia.it

Abstract. The development of the wireless Internet market and its structure is driven by differing industry fundamentals and the revenue derived from content and content-related services is expected to increase significantly for all actors within the wireless industry. Providing flexible and scalable accounting and billing systems will be essential for success when offering wireless services to end customers. The wireless service providers have difficulties in billing their customers due to their inability to associate customer transactions with network usage, correlate data from multiple sources and flexibly support the emerging billing models. In this paper an accounting and billing model for the two wireless services is presented. The evaluation of the services proved that the number of roles and partners in the wireless services is huge and that solutions like accounting agents and billing mediation servers are needed for tracking customer transactions and directing the accounting and billing between the partners.

1 Introduction

Differing industry fundamentals have been driving the development of the wireless Internet market and its structure in Europe, USA and Japan. In Europe the air interface standards are uniform, the network quality is good and messaging is highly used and fixed-line Internet relatively highly used.

The revenue derived from content and content-related services is expected to increase significantly for all actors within both the wireless and Internet Protocol (IP) industries, and, therefore, a well-formulated business model will give a competitive advantage over the other wireless companies [1]. The increased number of actors in the wireless value chain is faced with the following challenges:

- A growing complexity of interoperability among providers' service elements.
- Settling revenue throughout the value chain should be manageable and software driven.
- The absence of industry standards for interfacing all the involved service elements.
- The unique character of General Packet Radio Service (GPRS) infrastructure requires a new accounting and billing model.

A. Olivé (Eds.): ER 2003 Ws, LNCS 2784, pp. 229–240, 2003.
© Springer-Verlag Berlin Heidelberg 2003

230 Päivi Kallio et al.

Accounting is according to the definition:

" ... *the process of keeping track of a user's activity while accessing the network resources, including the amount of time spent in the network, the services accessed while there and the amount of data transferred during the session. Accounting data is used for trend analysis, capacity planning, billing, auditing and cost allocation.*"[3]

The providers of wireless services cannot currently effectively bill their customers for the wireless services due to their inability to:

- Associate customer transactions and network usage in real-time;
- Correlate data from multiple sources, such as network usage events, transactions and content purchases;
- Flexibly support emerging billing models

The aim of this research is to develop an accounting and billing model for the wireless services by researching the literature and evaluating two wireless services that are under development for the Third Generation (3G) networks. The first service is a trading service for banks and brokers, and the other is a multi-player game. In this paper the roles of the companies in the wireless business are handled first, then the requirements of accounting and billing in wireless services and, finally, an accounting and billing model for the two case-example services is presented.

2 The Roles of the Companies in a Wireless Business and their Billing Roles

In a wireless business all companies can play several roles and communicate directly with each other in spite of their role. Several categorizations of the company's roles in the wireless business exist, and as many speculations about its future roles. The possible roles of the wireless companies ([5],[2]) are presented in Table 1 :

Table 1. Roles of the companies in a wireless business

Role	Description
Content Provider (CP)	Develops original content for various distribution channels or aggregate content that others have created.
Network Operator (NO)	Sells network capacity to consumers via service providers enabling the use of services
Technology Provider	Produces mobile-enabled devices, application platforms and components and storage technologies and basic operating environments.
Application Service Provider (ASP)	Provides remote hosting, services, maintenance and upgrades of applications and thus enable businesses to contact their customers via a mobile channel.
Service Provider	Sells mobile telecommunications services to the subscribers and takes care of the billing, customer relationships and marketing.
Customer	Uses services defined by the service architecture

In the case-example services, multiple providers are involved in the value chain, supplying part of the end-to-end service delivered to the final customer. Each of the partners in the value chain should be paid for the part of service provided.

Fig.1describes the transaction flows for billing to the final customer and for revenue settlement between the service providers.

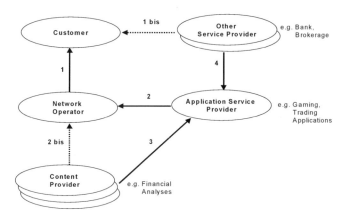

Fig. 1. Billing roles of the companies in the case-example services

In relationship 1 (Figure 1), the NO is likely to 'interface' with the customer for invoicing since they already have a contract. The bill provided to the final customer includes fees for network access and usage, and fees for service usage. The revenue provided to the CP (2 bis) refers to the content provided directly or through the application service provider's applications. So far, the NOs have determined the functionality of the services, and the operators, who want to gain a customer base without deploying the infrastructure, have acquired many service operators.

The billing of the customer could be based on:
- Monthly fees to access the service.
- Initial download of the service and download of additional services.
- Links to service-based fashion/retail websites.

In relationship 2, interconnection and settlement agreements between the ASP and the NO should be considered for revenue sharing. The revenue provided to the ASP may refer to the entire charge for the value-added service or only the ASP service.

The content providers sell their content to portals and service providers. The critical success factors for the CPs are whether or not they are producing high-quality content and their knowledge of the control of mobile user interfaces. Aggregating and repackaging content will probably be one of the main sources of revenue for content providers. The content providers charge for their services based on the content.

Additional sources of revenue for the actors in the 3G- field are:
- Advertising.
- % of revenues of service providers.
- % of data download/airtime revenue.
- Standard or premium usage rates paid by the end user.
- Flat rate or as part of bigger service.

- License revenues for software developers.
- Service revenues for operators, integrators and software developers to enable the wireless corporate Local Area Network (LAN).

The density and duration of the service usage sessions will be completely dependent on the service and will vary from 60 seconds (location-based entertainment) to 40 minutes [8](games).

3   Requirements of Accounting and Billing in Wireless Services

The billing includes invoicing, rating and discounting, and network data management [4]. In this research billing is handled mainly from the aspect of invoicing. The aim of billing is to provide a correct bill and, if there is a billing problem, resolve it quickly. [6] The requirements of the accounting and billing in wireless services include:

1. The ability to collect, exchange and reconcile *billing data from multiple sources*. The end-user service involves services provided by many providers and at least one of the providers will be responsible for end-user billing. This may be the network provider in some business models, but not always.
2. *Support for a variety of billing schemes*, like content or volume. For the billing, the following are foreseen possibilities:
   - Flat rate where the user subscribes a contract, which gives the customer unlimited access to the service. Flat rate is often combined with some form of usage-based tariff scheme.
   - Usage-Based, that can be based on time, volume, transaction or content and on a combination of different rating attributes, such as Quality of Service (QoS), time (e.g. prime-time vs. off-peak) and location.
3. *Batch and Real-Time Support.*
   The following major phases are foreseen in the processing chain:
   - Data collection that generates raw accounting data from network element/ application server
   - Aggregation and correlation of multiple sources of data. This involves generating call and service data records for all the 'service components' within a service usage instance.
   - Rating by using contract data.
   - Billing that includes applying discount policies for a service, generating an invoice to the customer and generating revenue sharing data to the third-party providers involved.
   The above steps can be performed in batch, involving transfer and processing of large blocks of data. Alternatively, they can be performed on an event basis (real-time). Real-time processing for some or all of the steps can only be for improving the timeliness of the billing process, or, in some cases, to achieve a specific functionality. This requires feedback from the billing processing chain to the application or infrastructure services
4. *Open Interfaces*
   A set of selected resources that contribute to the end-user service has to be equipped with an accounting 'agent' that is able to exchange data through public, open interfaces that are related to the service. When the service is web- or WAP-

based, it is likely that the agent is a generic agent based on interpretation of the web/WAP server logging.

5. *Dynamic configuration*
    The accounting agent must support all the above behaviours and be remotely configurable from a properly authorized software entity, and should be able to select the appropriate behaviour at run-time.

4   Accounting and Billing in the Case-Example Services

The fundamental question for the wireless services is "What to bill and how to account?". As the volumes of data being filtered by mediation devices increases, the key to an effective billing system is scalability. The players in the wireless service area must think carefully about the complexities of the service delivery channel and balance the requirements for accounting and billing simplicity and clarity for the customer [7]. In the case-example services, the network operator is assumed to be the interface and thus to have the billing relationship with the customer.

4.1   Objectives of the Accounting and Billing in the Case-Example Services

The main goal of accounting and billing in the case-example services is to define the functionalities and Application Programming Interfaces (APIs) needed to develop an end-to-end mobile service charging solution for value-added and content services, and to propose an architectural framework where this solution can be implemented. Other goals of accounting and billing in the case-example services are:

1. Demonstrate the dynamic configuration of the behaviour of accounting agents attached to the service elements.
2. Demonstrate the ability to collect and correlate usage data from multiple sources driven by the end-to-end view of the service. The sources of income are very different in terms of the role played within the service, and with respect to the level of support provided to the accounting and billing process.
3. Support multiple rating schemes. The different events coming from the user can be paid for differently and this type of logic can be flexibly defined in the business model.
4. Support real-time billing, from event collection to transaction/volume rating, in order to support the prepaid charging model or service usage checks.
5. Provide data for supporting different business models. Whenever feasible in the service, the advertising model could also be supported. In practice this means that the customer could be provided with advertisements for discounts or free service, while the advertiser pays the fees.

   The solution encompasses data collection from all the relevant service elements of the multiple service providers via accounting agents, data mediation and analysis, end-to-end service rating and revenue sharing. API exported to billing [4] is standard compliant in order to use any billing product for constructing the invoice.

4.2   Main Components of the Billing Chain

This section describes the major components of the billing chain used in the case-example services. It is assumed that all the parties involved in the supply chain allow access to their service elements in order to collect the raw usage data needed to perform the rating and billing functions.

Typically, not all the service elements need to be interfaced in order to collect usage data related to data and value-added services. For example, in the network part of GPRS/UMTS access services it is necessary to receive data from the Gateway GPRS Support Node (GGSN) and extract information about the connectivity between the mobile terminal and the IP network, and, from the authentication server, to correlate information about the mobile terminal equipment and IP Address assigned to the session.

The level of support provided to the accounting process by the different service elements varies considerably. Some kinds, such as network nodes, are able to provide raw usage records in a standard format, while some others - such as Wireless Application Protocol (WAP) and web servers - don't care about accounting and thus do not provide any standard or vendor-specific usage records. For the latter, some kind of application function, here named Accounting Agent, should be provided in order to extract usage data from sources such as log files and database tables. Accounting and billing components receive data from the relevant service elements that co-operate in providing the end-to-end service to the final customer.

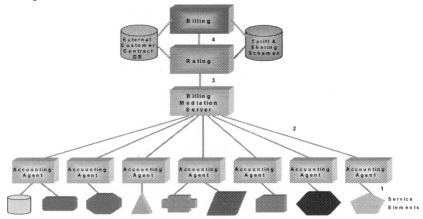

Fig. 2. Logical Architecture of the Billing Chain

Fig.2 illustrates a logical view of the architecture of the billing chain, providing the main components and their relationships (the interfaces are numbered).

It is important to be noted that Interface 1 (between Service Element and Accounting Agent) and/or Interface 2 (between Accounting Agent and Billing Mediation Server) introduces some critical security issues when they are located between the boundaries of different Providers. Mature technologies, such as PKI infrastructure provides the basic instruments in order to face of the problem, providing the needed security to all the involved parties.

4.2.1   Accounting Agents

Accounting agents are attached to all the relevant service elements in order to collect raw usage data (interface 1 in Fig.2). To achieve better performance and reduce management traffic overhead, it is better to run accounting agents close to service elements.

The management function performed by accounting agents depends on the type of application/ network node interfaced. It provides the following functions:

- Acts as an interface for the service elements supporting multiple protocols.
- Converts raw usage data from multiple source data formats to a set of standard detail records [4].
- Filters, validates and aggregates raw usage data extracted from the source service elements.
- Translates usage detail records to a common eXtensible Markup Language (XML) syntax, possibly an encoded format [9].
- Acts as an interface for the billing mediation server on an event basis or in batch mode to provide usage detail records.
- Provides feedback to service elements in a prepaid or service usage check .

The accounting agent need to interface a variety of usage data sources and to provide collected data encoded into different output formats. Furthermore, it is it should be extensible in order to support new data source types and output formats in the future. To achieve such goals without introducing heavy-weighted platform, for the case-example services an architectural framework has been adopted, that allowed the Accounting Agent to be designed as a set of pluggable modules that could be assembled at runtime and remotely managed and configured.

4.2.2   Billing Mediation Server

The billing mediation server receives all the usage detail records from accounting agents distributed over the network (interface 2 in Fig.2).

It should be able to receive usage data on an event basis or in batch mode. Communication between the mediation server and the agent could be asynchronous for receiving single events, for example using Java Messaging Service (JMS), or scheduled for collecting massive usage data The ability to receive asynchronous messages is needed in order to support the prepaid charging model or service usage checks.

An application protocol should be used to guarantee the correct and complete transfer of the usage data. The billing mediation server also provides some elaboration of usage data, such as aggregation of records coming from different sources, filtering of duplicated records and synchronization.

4.2.3   Rating

The rating engine receives all the usage detail records from the billing mediation server (interface 3 in Fig.2) in standard formats and correlates them on an end-to-end service generating records related to the entire service to be billed. The customer services are rated according to tariff schemes, and support multiple options such as volume, content, time, service and combinations thereof.

The service usage records are correlated to the contract data in order to rate customer services according to the subscribed contracts. Deny of Service notifications are sent back to Billing Mediation Server that dispatch them to the proper Service Element by means of the related Account Agent.

All the elaboration functions, like record correlation, aggregation, rating, and verification, should be configurable. The flexibility in defining and modifying these steps is fundamental to meet the requirements in terms of complexity and time-to-market of today's Wireless Internet Services. One of the most promising and established technology for this purpose, adopted in the case-example services, is rule languages and engines. In the billing domain rule technology allows to easily define through configuration and maintain all the business logic that performs correlation and rating functions.

The rated service usage record is exported to billing on an event basis or in batch mode. Two types of service usage records can be exported: records related to the final customer usage of the service and records aggregated to the partner service provider. In the latter, only the portion of the service (e.g. content) owned by the partner is taken into account.

4.2.4   Billing

Billing applies pricing and discounting polices to the received service usage records (interface 4 in Fig.2) by generating an invoice to the final customer. It also generates revenue sharing data to third-party providers, only including details of the their portion of service. The billing function takes into account the pricing and discounting schemes configured in the billing system.

4.3   Service 1 - A Multi-player Game

Service 1 is a multi-player game that is known as the "Labyrinth Game". It is an arcade game where multiple players move in a big labyrinth or dungeon and complete a mission. The client side is implemented using MIDP (Java MIDlets) and a GPRS/UMTS (Universal Mobile Telecommunications System) connection is used on terminal side clients, while on the server side J2EE (Java 2, Enterprise Edition) is used. The user can download the game "on the air" through a serial cable or infrared connection.

4.3.1   Billing Roles in Service 1

Fig.3 shows the billing roles of Service 1. The user of Service 1 pays for access to the service and for playing it for a certain time. The NO delivers the invoice to the customer and receives the fees, part of which is afterwards paid to the other partners for revenue sharing.

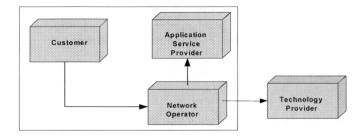

Fig. 3. Billing roles in Service 1

The billing of Service 1 takes place according to the number of bits transferred, but it could also be based on different kinds of packages.

4.3.2   Accounting and Billing-Scenario for Service 1

As depicted in Fig.4, in Service 1 the accounting agents can be attached to:

- A GPRS backbone network for collecting usage data in order to evaluate the network service usage in terms of data volume/time;
- An authentication server for collecting accounting records in order to correlate the IP address information to the subscriber;
- A gaming server for collecting value-added service usage data in order to charge for the service per-transaction.

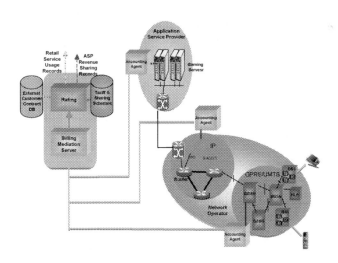

Fig. 4. The Billing Context of Service 1

The service components Rating and Billing Mediation Server collect the usage data and correlate the usage records as explained in section 4.2.

After all the collection, filtering/validation, correlation and rating phases, the service accounting records are aggregated for the different roles:

- To bill the final customer.
- To define incoming revenue of the network operator, and
- To define the revenue sharing fees for the application service provider.

4.4   Service 2 – A Trading Solution

Service 2 is a trading solution that provides

- Easy and precise online stock exchange information.
- A complete set of advanced analysis tools, and
- Real-time, direct, electronic trading.

for professional traders and serious Internet investors. It is a service for Direct Access Trading (DAT) on the major European and North American exchanges from one professional, effective and reliable platform that is fully functional for operations throughout the entire world.

4.4.1   Billing Relationships in Service 2

As in Service 1, the NO delivers the invoice to the customer and receives the fees, part of which is afterwards paid to the other partners for revenue sharing. The customer of Service 2 has to be a customer of a bank and subscribed to the service as a bank customer. The service connection is transparently carried out with the service provider. In the Service 2, performance and reliability are the most important quality requirements. The NOs share revenue by paying the application service, service and content providers. Fig.5 illustrates the billing relationships of Service 2.

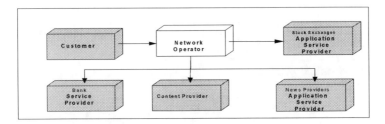

Fig. 5. Billing roles in Service 2

The price of Service 2 is based on:

1. The subscriptions for software functionalities.
2. Exchanges fees - from how many exchanges do they want to receive the quotes.
3. Trading fees.
4. Content fees, such as financial news or financial analysis.

The main revenue streams for Service 2 are licensed per year, with a changeable cost based on the number of functions enabled by the license and trading fee.

4.4.2   Accounting and Billing Scenario for Service 2

As depicted in Fig.6, in Service 2 the accounting agents could be attached to:

- A GPRS backbone network for collecting usage data in order to evaluate the network service usage in terms of data volume/time;
- A server for collecting accounting records in order to correlate the IP Address information to the subscriber;
- Servers of ASP and other service providers for collecting value-added service usage data in order to charge for the service per transaction and per content .

After collection, filtering, correlation and rating, the service accounting records are aggregated:

- To bill the final customer (retail model);
- To define the incoming revenue of the network operator and other SP, and
- To define the revenue sharing fees for the ASP, CP and other SP.

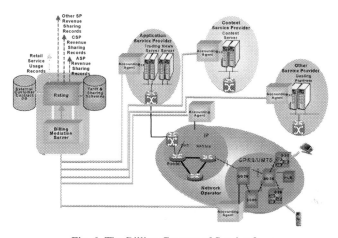

Fig. 6. The Billing Context of Service 2

4.5   Implementation of the Components in the Future

In the implementation of the illustrated case-example services it is assumed that the network operator works as the provider of the billing services to the final customer and accounts for the sharing of revenues with the Internet service providers and/or content providers.

The components can be used to implement advanced billing models in a complex value-chain that provides wireless data and value-added services. For these services, it could be demonstrated how an entity, acting as a provider of billing services, is able to collect, correlate and rate the end-to-end service for the final customer and the different parties involved. The provider of these billing services could be the wireless network service provider, some other party involved in the supply-chain - such as a bank - or a party not involved in delivering the service.

5   Conclusions

Providing flexible and scalable accounting and billing systems will be essential for success in the wireless services of the 3G-networks. The increased number of partners in the wireless value chain causes difficulties when defining the division of income between the partners, and the wireless service providers typically also have difficulties in billing their customers due to their inability to:

- Associate customer transactions and network usage in real-time;
- Correlate data from multiple sources and
- Flexibly support emerging billing models

The wireless services require defined needs models for accounting and billing, and methods of putting them into practice. In this paper an accounting and billing model for the two wireless services was presented. The evaluation of the services proved that the number of roles and partners in the wireless services is huge and some kind of solution needs to be defined for tracking the customer transactions and directing the accounting and billing information between several partners. In the billing chain of the case-example services, four main components were used: rating, billing, billing mediation server and accounting agent. We regard these as the most important parts of the wireless billing chain of the future. The presented billing and accounting model will be technically implemented in the future as a real-case service, as it was presented in this paper.

Acknowledgements

This work was done in the Wise (Wireless Internet Service Engineering) project funded by the European Union and the participating five European companies and three research institutes.

References

1. Afuah, A.; Tucci, C.L., 2001. Internet Business Models and Strategies. McGraw et Hill, New York, USA. ISBN 0-07-239724-1. 358 p.
2. Durlacher, 2000. UMTS Report, an Investment Perspective. 146 p.
3. Internet.com, 2002.Webopedia. On-line at:
    http://www.webopedia.com/TERM/A/AAA.html
4. Ipdr.org, 2002. Network Data Management -Usage (NDM-U) For IP-Based Services; Version 3.1. On-line at: http://www.ipdr.org/documents/NDM-U_3.1.pdf . 100 p.
5. Lymysalo, M. ,2000. Evolution of Mobile Electronic Commerce- Opportunities for One-to-one Marketing. VTT Information Technology. Research Report TTE1-2000-31. 88 p.
6. TMForum, 2000. Process Invoicing and Collections (Telecom Operations Map- version 2.1). On-line at: http://www.tmforum.org/clickmap/tomv2.1/pr5.htm
7. UMTS Forum, 2000a. Enabling UMTS/ Third Generation Services and Applications. p.72
8. UMTS Forum, 2000b. Shaping the Mobile Multimedia Future- An Extended Vision from the UMTS Forum. On-line at: http://www.umts-forum.org/reports/report10.pdf . 113 p.
9. IETF, 1995. RFC 1832, XDR: External Data Representation Standard, August 1995.

Quality in Conceptual Modeling –
New Research Directions

Geert Poels[1], Jim Nelson[2], Marcela Genero[3], and Mario Piattini[3]

[1] Department of Management Information, Operations Management
and Technology Policy, Ghent University
Hoveniersberg 24, 9000 Gent, Belgium
Geert.Poels@rug.ac.be

[2] Department of Accounting and MIS, Fisher College of Business
The Ohio State University
2100 Neil Avenue, Columbus, Ohio, USA
nelson_j@cob.osu.edu

[3] Department of Computer Science, University of Castilla-La Mancha
Paseo de la Universidad, 4, 13071, Ciudad Real, Spain
{mgenero,mpiattini}@inf-cr.uclm.es

Abstract. Quality is currently one of the main research topics in conceptual modeling. In this paper nine new research contributions are organized using a classification framework that is based on the well-known framework for conceptual modeling quality of Lindland, Sindre, and Sølvberg. The aim of this work is to identify new directions in conceptual modeling quality research.

1 Introduction

Quality has been identified as one of the main topics in current conceptual modeling research [6]. In this paper we classify nine new research contributions, accepted for the first International Workshop on Conceptual Modeling Quality[1], using the framework of conceptual modeling quality that was proposed by Lindland, Sindre, and Sølvberg [4] in the mid-nineties. Although since its proposal, the Lindland et al. framework has been repeatedly extended and several alternative frameworks have been developed, its role as inaugural work in this field of research is undisputed. The comprehensive nature of the framework allows us to link, compare and differentiate the workshop contributions in order to identify related work and current areas of interest and to sketch a (necessarily incomplete) state-of-the-art in conceptual modeling quality.

We hope that this paper will help to better evaluate the different contributions in order to assess their scope and value. We also hope that this exercise will help to

---

[1] The first International Workshop on Conceptual Modeling Quality (IWCMQ'02) was held in conjunction with the 21st International Conference on Conceptual Modeling (ER'02) in Tampere, Finland, on October 11, 2002.

A. Olivé (Eds.): ER 2003 Ws, LNCS 2784, pp. 243–250, 2003.

discern uncovered areas, remaining research questions, and future opportunities for research in conceptual modeling quality.

The rest of this paper is structured as follows. In section 2 the basic ideas underlying the Lindland et al. framework and some of its extensions are presented. We further discuss how the framework can be used to classify and structure the nine workshop papers. The actual classification and comparison of the workshop contributions is presented in section 3. Finally, in section 4 we summarize our work by distilling the new research directions in conceptual modeling quality as observed in the workshop contributions.

2   A Classification Framework

High quality conceptual models are critical to the success of system development efforts. Despite this importance, quantitative methods for evaluating conceptual model quality are virtually nonexistent. Even definitions of quality (when they are given) are vague and complicated, and there is no underlying structure that helps the user to understand how the properties relate to one another. Lindland, Sindre, and Sølvberg [4] addressed this problem with a systematic examination of the nature of quality in conceptual models.

The original framework consisted of three types of model quality: syntactic, semantic, and pragmatic quality. Syntactic quality describes how well the model follows the rules of the modeling language. Semantic quality describes how well the model captures the domain of interest within the context of the user. Pragmatic quality captures how well a conceptual model is understood by its audience. Within each of these types of quality are two main quality concepts: completeness and validity. A model is complete if it contains all of the elements of the domain. It is valid if it does not contain any elements that are not in the domain.

This framework was extended by Nelson, Monarchi, and Nelson [5] to include two types of quality that cover the earliest stages of modeling and one type that gives an overall assessment of model quality. Perceptual quality measures how well the actors within the domain of interest understand that domain. Descriptive quality measures the ability of the modeler to elicit a description of that domain. Finally, inferential quality measures how well the conceptual model as understood by the audience matches the original domain.

These six types of quality form the first dimension for classifying conceptual model quality research. Another useful dimension is the object of the study. Quality research can focus on any (or all) of three modeling objects. The first object is the conceptual model itself, the product of the modeling activity. The second object is the process of creating the model. In general, the quality of the modeling process is directly proportional to the quality of the model produced by the process. If the modeling process is of high quality, then the conceptual model that is produced should also be of high quality. The third object is the modeling facility. The modeling facility includes all of the tools, techniques, and controls that are used to direct the modeling process.

The final conceptual model quality research classification dimension is the research goal. There are five research goals in the classification framework: understanding, measuring, evaluating, assuring, and improving conceptual model quality. Research into understanding quality seeks to define the various dimensions, or measures, of quality. It develops the scales that can be used to determine quality. Measuring quality examines how to apply those dimensions against conceptual models. Research that evaluates quality explores the correlation between the quality measurements and real-world experiences with the model. For example, how various measurements correlate with model understanding, model maintenance, and so on. Quality assurance research examines how to ensure that the process that produces the conceptual model actually does produce a quality model. Finally, the research into improving quality examines how to make conceptual model quality better.

The three classification dimensions that form the framework are summarized in the table below. In the next section, we will use the classification framework to organize the research contributions in the workshop.

Table 1. Quality research classification dimensions

Type of Quality	Object of Study	Research Goal
perceptual quality	product	understanding quality
descriptive quality	modeling process	measuring/assessing quality
syntactic quality	modeling facility	evaluating quality
semantic quality		assuring quality
pragmatic quality		improving quality
inferential quality		

3   Classification of New Research Contributions

In this section we classify the nine papers along the dimensions proposed in the previous section. The section is structured according to an initial grouping that is roughly based on the type of conceptual model considered. The same structure has been used for the workshop agenda. We end this section by summarizing our classification efforts.

3.1   Requirements and Entity Relationship Models

Two of the papers propose techniques to improve the quality of conceptual data models developed using Entity Relationship (ER) modeling. In his paper, Bowers presents and demonstrates an algorithm to detect redundant relationships in ER models. The presence of such relationships may cause automatically generated relational schemas to be un-normalized. In terms of the Lindland et al. framework, this work contributes towards developing a modeling activity (i.e. using an algorithm, implemented in a CASE tool, to detect and subsequently remove redundant relationships) to ascertain the presence of a quality-carrying property (i.e. the absence of redundant relationships) with the goal of improving quality. The type of quality considered is pragmatic quality, in the sense of making the conceptual model easier to use by the techniques that generate relational schemas from ER diagrams. It should be noted that in the Lindland et al. framework, users of conceptual models include technical actors, like for instance CASE tools, which need to 'understand' the model.

In another paper related to ER modeling, Danoch, Shoval, and Balaban present a method, called HERD, to create hierarchical ER diagrams starting from a 'flat' diagram. In their paper, Danoch et al. describe the design and results of an experiment to compare the user comprehension of hierarchical and flat ER diagrams. Like Bowers, the authors propose a means (i.e. the HERD method) to assure a quality-carrying model property (i.e. being hierarchically structured) to improve pragmatic quality. The experiment aims at evaluating the effectiveness of this method.

The paper of Matulevicius and Strasunskas is different from the other workshop contributions in the sense that it does not focus on the quality of a conceptual model as a product, but on the quality of modeling facilities. Their proposal concerns a new quality framework to evaluate the validation and verification capabilities of requirements engineering (RE) tools. The authors show that their evaluation framework covers all quality dimensions in the semiotic framework for conceptual modeling quality by Krogstie, Lindland, and Sindre [3][2]. They further test the framework on a set of commercial RE tools and compare the results of their evaluation with an independent survey of RE tools.

3.2 Class Models and Architectures

The quality of UML class diagrams is the topic of two workshop papers. But apart from the object of study these papers take different positions in our classification framework.

Letelier and Sanchez present a graphical animation environment that is used to animate the behaviour of an object system that is specified in a UML class diagram. They propose animation as a means to help assuring the 'right' product functionality. Through animation differences between stakeholder requirements and the conceptual model can be detected. The type of quality concerned is therefore semantic quality. As a proof of concept the authors apply their animation tool on a simple banking example.

Instead of quality assurance, the goal of the work of Genero, Olivas, Piattini, and Romero is quality prediction. They propose a set of metrics to measure the structural complexity (i.e. a quality-carrying property) of UML class diagrams and conduct a controlled experiment to show a relationship with the maintainability (i.e. a pragmatic quality issue) of the diagrams. By means of a machine learning technique called Fuzzy Prototypical Knowledge Discovery, the authors were able to build a

---

[2] This framework is another extension of the Lindland et al. framework. It adds two lower-level, technical quality aspects (i.e. physical quality and empirical quality) and one higher-level, social quality aspect (i.e. social quality) to the syntactic, semantic, and pragmatic quality types.

maintainability prediction model based on structural complexity metrics. This work addresses the need for 'quantization' of conceptual modeling quality, as suggested by Lindland et al. [4]. The metrics-based prediction model can be considered as an indirect measurement instrument for UML class diagram maintainability.

The paper of Avgeriou, Retalis, and Skordalakis is different from the other contributions as the object of study is a high-level systems design artifact, rather than a conceptual model. This paper describes the use of a new architectural quality evaluation framework, similar to the quality frameworks for conceptual modeling, to evaluate a proposed software architecture for learning management systems. By applying their framework the authors show that pragmatic quality attributes are built into the architecture.

3.3 Web and Interactive Models

Two of the workshop papers propose instruments to measure and evaluate the quality of conceptual representations of web artifacts. Comai, Matera, and Maurino present a new quality model for conceptual schemas that are specified using the WebML modeling language. This quality model is related to the Lindland et al. framework in the sense that it incorporates different types of quality, including syntactic quality (e.g. syntactic correctness), semantic quality (e.g. semantic correctness) and pragmatic quality (e.g. usability attributes). As a quality model (instead of a purely conceptual framework) the proposal of Comai et al. also addresses the need to decompose quality goals into measurable attributes, as suggested by Lindland et al. in [4]. The authors further present and demonstrate an XSL-based framework, called WebML Quality Analyzer, as a tool to automatically measure and evaluate the quality attributes of WebML conceptual schemas.

Abrahao, Olsina, and Pastor describe the WebFP_QEM methodology for evaluating the quality of operative web sites and applications. This methodology considers both quality aspects related to nonfunctional requirements (i.e. pragmatic quality) and functional requirements (i.e. semantic quality). In their paper, the authors specifically discuss the interplay between conceptual modeling (using the OOWS modeling approach) and measurement (using new structural complexity metrics for object models, agents, navigational maps and navigational context). They demonstrate their ideas using a simple example of adaptive maintenance of an e-commerce web application. The empirical validation of the metrics, as in the previously mentioned paper of Genero et al., is listed as a topic for further work.

In the final paper we discuss here, Krogstie and Jorgensen propose a further extension of the conceptual modeling quality framework of Krogstie et al. [3]. Their new framework is specifically intended to better understand the quality of interactive models, which are a special type of active models.

3.4 Summary

Table 2 summarizes our classification efforts. Each paper is identified by its first author.

Table 2. Classification of new contributions to conceptual modeling quality research

Paper	Type of Quality	Object of Study	Research Goal
Bowers	pragmatic	product	improving
Danoch	pragmatic	product	improving
Matulevicius	syntactic semantic pragmatic other	modeling facility	evaluating
Letelier	semantic	product	assuring
Genero	pragmatic	product	measuring
Avgeriou	pragmatic	product	evaluating
Comai	syntactic semantic pragmatic	product	measuring, evaluating
Abrahao	semantic pragmatic	product	measuring, evaluating
Krogstie	syntactic semantic pragmatic other	product	understanding

4   Conclusions

The diverse nature of the conceptual representations that are the object of study in the papers accepted for IWCMQ'02 demonstrates the bridge function fulfilled by conceptual modeling. As an early stage activity, conceptual modeling plays a crucial role in software, database, and web development. Therefore the success of systems development strongly depends upon the quality of the conceptual models that are produced. The massive response to the workshop's call for papers[3] is another evidence of the huge importance of quality in conceptual modeling products, processes, and facilities. It also shows that quality issues are nowadays high on the agenda of conceptual modeling researchers.

Although the workshop papers cover diverse application domains and focus on many different types of conceptual models, our classification shows that the main emphasis of current research efforts is product quality. In spite of the need for quality-related process guidelines and quality assurance of modeling processes in general (already recognized in the frameworks of Krogstie et al. [3] and Nelson et al. [5]), it seems that current research has largely disregarded quality aspects of conceptual modeling processes and facilities. Given that quality processes result in quality products, we identify this topic as a major opportunity for future research in conceptual modeling quality.

---

[3] The nine accepted papers represent less than half of the submitted papers.

Regarding the types of quality considered in the papers, the main focus is on pragmatic quality and, to a lesser extent semantic quality. The concern for pragmatic quality issues is not unrelated to the current interest in the quality of software development artifacts. Syntactic quality issues seem to be well understood and supported by automated tools. The other quality types, added by the Nelson et al. framework, are not addressed, perhaps because they do not lend themselves easily to objective measurement [5].

In section 2, the goals of conceptual modeling quality research were organized into a hierarchical structure. According to our classification, workshop papers are found at each level. Some papers focus on understanding quality by elaborating a conceptual framework or multi-level quality model for specific types of model (or modeling facilities). A subset of these papers go further by using the framework or model as a practical quality assessment and evaluation instrument. Other papers aim at developing objective and automatically computable measurement instruments (i.e. metrics) for quality attributes of conceptual models. In domains were quality seems to be reasonably well understood (e.g. static conceptual models like Entity Relationship diagrams and class diagrams), research aims at techniques to assure and improve model quality. In other domains, like web development, the quality of the conceptual models is a relatively new research topic that needs to be further elaborated.

As another idea for future research we like to stress that, to our knowledge, little work has been done towards measuring, evaluating and assuring the quality of conceptual representations of behavior, activities, processes, etc.. The need for more research on the quality of functional and dynamic models has also been pointed at in the recent software engineering literature (see e.g. [1]).

We end this paper by drawing the attention upon the research method employed in the papers that we discussed. Although some papers include a well-designed experiment or a representative case study, in most papers new research ideas are only illustrated by means of some proof of concept. We believe that to grow into a mature research discipline more scientific validation is needed. Again we refer to recent developments in software engineering research, where there is a remarkable increase in empirical validation efforts of existing or new theories, methods, techniques, and tools. We believe that research in conceptual modeling quality can benefit from the experiences and guidelines of empirical software engineering research (see e.g. [2], [7]). Clearly more quality models and metrics are needed, but also a thorough validation of these models and metrics in a real (or realistic) environment.

References

1. Brito e Abreu, F., Henderson-Sellers, B., Piattini, M., Poels, G., Sahraoui, H.: "Quantitative Approaches in Object-Oriented Software Engineering", In: *Lecture Notes in Computer Science*, 2323, Object-Oriented Technology, ECOOP'01 Workshop Reader, 2002, Springer, Berlin, pp. 174-183.
2. Juristo, N., Moreno, A.: *Basics of Software Engineering Experimentation*. Kluwer Academic Publishers, 2001.

250   Geert Poels et al.

3. Krogstie, J., Lindland, O.I., Sindre, G.: "Towards a Deeper Understanding of Quality in Requirements Engineering", In: *Lecture Notes in Computer Science*, 932, Proceedings of the 7th International Conference on Advanced Information Systems Engineering (CAiSE'95), Jyvaskyla, Finland, June 12-16, 1995, Springer, Berlin, pp. 82-95.
4. Lindland, O.I., Sindre, G., Sølvberg, A.: "Understanding Quality in Conceptual Modeling", *IEEE Software*, 11(2), 1994, pp. 42-49.
5. Nelson, H.J., Monarchi, D.E., Nelson, K.M.: "Ensuring the "Goodness" of a Conceptual Representation", In: *Proceedings of the 4th European Conference on Software Measurement and ICT Control (FESMA 2001)*, Heidelberg, Germany, May 8-11, 2001.
6. Olivé, A.: "Specific Relationship Types in Conceptual Modeling: The Cases of Generic and with Common Participants", unpublished keynote lecture, 4th International Conference on Enterprise Information Systems (ICEIS'02), Ciudad Real, Spain, April 3-6, 2002.
7. Wohlin, C., Runeson, P., Höst, M., Ohlson, M., Regnell, B., Wesslen, A.: *Experimentation in Software Engineering: An Introduction.* Kluwer Academic Publishers, 2000.

Evaluation Framework
of Requirements Engineering Tools for
Verification and Validation

Raimundas Matulevičius and Darijus Strašunskas

Dept. of Computer and Information Science, Norwegian Univ. of Science and Technology
Sem Sælands vei 7-9, NO-7491 Trondheim, Norway
{raimunda,dstrasun}@idi.ntnu.no

Abstract. This paper presents an evaluation framework for requirements engineering tools (RETs). We provide a list of qualitative requirements to guide the customer in evaluating the appropriateness and features functionality of RET. Verification and validation (V&V) activities should be an on-going process throughout life cycle of system development. The paper discusses the framework for evaluating the requirements engineering tools capability for V&V. We tested our proposed evaluation framework on eight different commercial requirements engineering tools. Proposed framework guides the participants (developers and end-users) in evaluating the RET features for assessing the accuracy of RE process.

1 Introduction

Requirements engineering (RE) is the branch of software engineering concerned with the real world goals for, functions of, and constraints on software systems. It is also concerned with the relationships of these factors to precise specifications of software behavior and to their evolution over time and across software families [28]. RE includes different activities – like elicitation, specification, negotiation, analysis and other.

Verification and validation (V&V) are the generic name given for checking processes, which ensure that system conforms to its specification and meets the needs of customer. Verification deals with the building the model right, validation – building the right model. As no model is absolutely accurate, the purpose for V&V is to ensure that conceptual model is sufficiently accurate. To ensure validity of the conceptual model, V&V should be performed in a RE stage as well as in all system engineering phases.

We are interesting in how requirements engineering tools (RETs) ensure the process and product quality and how they support V&V of information between project stakeholders during RE activities. V&V is difficult to make automatically, but semi-automatic V&V is desirable feature of RET, as an automatic validation of the further phases.

There are several attempts to evaluate and classify the RET [10, 13, 26]. Some of them are evaluations of few tools at a certain time [13, 26]; some [10] are being up-

A. Olivé (Eds.): ER 2003 Ws, LNCS 2784, pp. 251-263, 2003.

dated periodically. The latter is a good up-to-date guidance to the RET market, but it may be not precise enough, because it relies too much on vendors' response. Tools surveys at a certain moment have little long-term value, as new tools are being created and features of existing ones are being continuously improved. Moreover, no review is done about RETs support of V&V.

Tool evaluation and testing could be performed in different ways. RETs can be evaluated from theoretical point of view - using information provided by vendor. They could be tried out on some realistic examples. It is also possible to gather development experience from industry. The evaluation would be more structured, complete, effective, accurate and objective if evaluation framework for RET is applied.

The evaluation framework, proposed in this work, analyses qualitative requirements to guide the customer in evaluating the appropriateness and features functionality of RET. It benefits to companies looking for an RET, reduces the evaluation process cost and helps to evaluate RETs. The paper contributes in development of RET by evaluating currently available commercial RETs using proposed evaluation framework and clarifying current shortcomings in V&V functionality of RETs.

The rest of the paper is structured as follows: first we discuss the existing quality frameworks for conceptual models. Next we provide the framework for evaluation of RETs. Then we survey some commercial RETs and apply our evaluation framework. Finally conclusions and future works of work are presented.

2   Related Works

Creation of a good conceptual model means insurance that model is understandable and understood by all stakeholders, that it provides essential elements of the problem domain and relationships among these elements. The choice of an appropriate representation of a model is one of the most crucial tasks in software development. Although modeling represents only a proportion of the total system development effort, its impact on the quality of the final system is probably greater than any other phase [18].

According to [8], the distinction is frequently made between product quality and process quality. Modeling of product and modeling of process are absolutely separate activities [9]. Product quality is concerned with evaluating and improving the quality of the model (product) while process quality is concerned with improving process of analysis [18].

The literature [1, 12, 15, 23] provides different frameworks for process and product quality. A semiotic framework for quality of conceptual models [12, 15] distinguishes between goals and means to achieve these goals. Quality has been defined referring to the main quality types:

• Physical quality. There are two basic quality means on the physical level: externalization, that the explicit knowledge of some person has been externalized in the model by the use of a modeling language, and internalizeability, that the externalized model is persistent and available, enabling the other persons involved to make sense of it.

- Empirical quality deals with error frequencies when a model is read or written by different users, coding and ergonomic of computer-human interaction for modeling tools.

- Syntactic quality is the correspondence between the model and the language extension of the language in which the model is written.

- Semantic quality is the correspondence between the model and the domain. The framework contains two semantic goals: validity and completeness.

- Perceived semantic quality is the similar correspondence between the participants, interpretation of a model and his or her current explicit knowledge.

- Pragmatic quality is the correspondence between the model and audience's interpretation of it.

- Social quality. The goal defined for social quality is agreement among participant interpretations.

Agreement about the requirements among all stakeholders is one of the major activities in classical approaches of RE [16, 11]. Pohl suggests a three dimensional framework of RE [20]. In this framework the requirements specification process, which often includes conceptual modeling, is stretched out along three orthogonal dimensions:

- the *specification* dimension, which deals with the degree of requirements understanding.

- the *representation* dimension, which deals with the degree of formality.

- the *agreement* dimension, which deals with the degree of agreement between stakeholders.

At the beginning of the RE process the knowledge about the system is vague. Therefore the specification is very *opaque*, based on *personal views,* and mainly *informal representations* are used. The desired output of the requirements specification process is a *complete specification*, which is expressed using *formal language, commonly agreed* by all stakeholders.

RETs influence both – process quality, since they support a large part of software engineering part; and product quality, since the output of RE is requirements specification, which itself should be of high quality for further software engineering stages.

A formal software specification is the end product of a large number of decisions, negotiations and assumptions made throughout the RE process. It is therefore important to be able to recreate the rationale behind some specification items in order to question its appropriateness and validity in the light of changing circumstances [16, 19].

3 Evaluation Framework

3.1 Framework for Evaluating RETs

Evaluation framework describes steps of evaluation. It could provide an effective way of comparison of different tools and features. Evaluation framework could serve as the classification of RETs. Evaluation framework could also be used to answer question about the investment to RET, or it could be used for the analysis if company's investment strategy failed. Evaluation of RET using an evaluation framework provides more accurate and objective assessment than doing it without the framework.

Different evaluation criteria sets could be taken into account. They depend on the features, which are evaluated. We are aware of the importance of evaluation issues such as purchase and training costs, support, vendor reliability, usability, robustness and etc in a concrete evaluation task. Here we are focusing on evaluation of functional characteristics and looking what V&V activities are supported by RETs.

Our evaluation framework (Figure 1) is based on dimensions of Pohl's framework [20] and Land/Duggan requirements [14]. Pohl's framework provides three orthogonal dimensions of RE. Lang/ Duggan requirements for requirements management focus on collaborative work between different stakeholders. But they are not structured to any framework, and could mislead, during the process of RET evaluation. We refine Lang/ Duggan requirements and fit them in three-space RE process dimensions.

Requirements, shown in fig.1, are requirements categories, which should be analyzed during the RET evaluation. An organization, which would apply our framework for RET acquisition, would have to deal with a lot of detailed requirements in order to determine, which tool fits organization's need best. We extend these requirements with *the basic activities* (table 1), which should be tested during RET evaluation process.

How framework covers a RET is evaluated by setting evaluation by *High* (very good coverage), *Medium* (average coverage), *Low* (poor coverage). In the framework we do not consider the relative importance of the criteria, although it is necessary that some features must be covered better in the evaluation process than others. In such cases the weighting mechanism should be used to stress the importance of the features. In some cases we have to extend our evaluation scale with additional options (for example *not exists*). The final evaluation for the feature is the total of activity evaluations.

3.2 Discussion

The use of informal, semi-formal as well as formal representation languages must be possible. Four traceability mechanisms [5] could be defined – backward/ forward from traceability, and backward/ forward to traceability. Traceable relationships are especially important during requirements representation, which should start with informal (natural language) description, follow by semi-formal and formal descriptions. Traceability between these descriptions ensures that all they uniquely identify requirement.

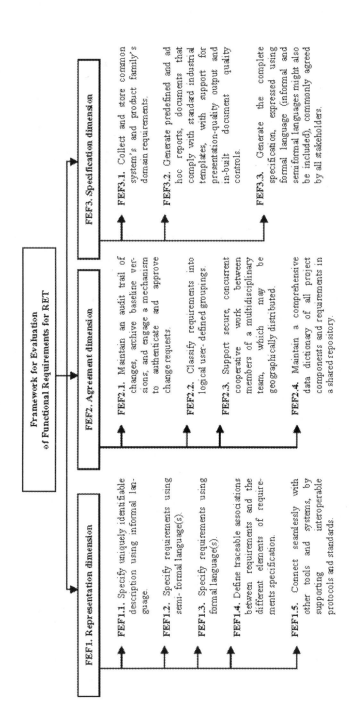

Framework for Evaluation of Functional Requirements for RET

FEF1. Representation dimension

FEF1.1. Specify uniquely identifiable description using informal language.

FEF1.2. Specify requirements using semi-formal language(s).

FEF1.3. Specify requirements using formal language(s).

FEF1.4. Define traceable associations between requirements and the different elements of requirements specification.

FEF1.5. Connect seamlessly with other tools and systems, by supporting interoperable protocols and standards.

FEF2. Agreement dimension

FEF2.1. Maintain an audit trail of changes, archive baseline versions, and engage a mechanism to authenticate and approve change requests.

FEF2.2. Classify requirements into logical user-defined groupings.

FEF2.3. Support secure, concurrent cooperative work between members of a multidisciplinary team, which may be geographically distributed.

FEF2.4. Maintain a comprehensive data dictionary of all project components and requirements in a shared repository.

FEF3. Specification dimension

FEF3.1. Collect and store common system's and product family's domain requirements.

FEF3.2. Generate predefined and ad hoc reports, documents that comply with standard industrial templates, with support for presentation-quality output and in-built document quality controls.

FEF3.3. Generate the complete specification, expressed using formal language (informal and semi-formal languages might also be included), commonly agreed by all stakeholders.

Fig. 1. Framework for Evaluation of Functionality for RET

Table 1. Activities for Framework for Evaluation of RET

	Features	Activities for evaluating the features. How does the RET …
Representation dimension	FEF1.1.	a) provide natural language description at the early requirements engineering stage (RET must provide the natural language description, since this is essential criteria for non-technical stakeholders)? b) allow specifying unique identification (ID) for each separate requirement? c) allow importing of requirements and their description from textual document? d) provide other techniques (drawing tools, model-based, etc) for informal description?
	FEF1.2.	a) provide tools for semiformal language description (ER-diagrams, UML diagrams, DFD, OMT, etc)? b) provide forward/ backward traceability between informal, semiformal, formal descriptions?
	FEF1.3.	a) provide tools for formal language description (Z-schemas, algebraic specifications, action semantics, B-notations, etc)? b) provide forward/ backward traceability between informal, semiformal, formal descriptions?
	FEF1.4.	a) provide V&V functions for testing traceability between informal, semiformal and formal requirement description? b) create parent-child traceable relations between requirements? c) create peer-to-peer traceable relations between requirements? d) create traceable relation between different related information? e) maintain forward/ backward traceability between source of requirements, requirements and design?
	FEF1.5.	a) allow importing/exporting requirements description from/to textual documents? b) allow importing/exporting requirements description from/to graphical documents?
Agreement dimension	FEF2.1.	a) maintain user authentication to the system (provide user name, password)? b) allow grouping users into different groups? c) allow creating different functionality views (according to documents, requirements, attributes) for different groups of stakeholders? d) register agreement/ rationale/ discussion/ negotiation/ changes/ history of requirements and by how it was achieved? e) call the earlier requirement description/ versions and register them into history context?
	FEF2.2.	a) allow specifying attributes/ properties of the requirement? b) provide sorting according to different attributes/ properties? c) provide filtering according to different attributes/ properties?
	FEF2.3.	a) deal with usability (standalone application, Intranet, Internet based program)? b) provide www-based interface for geographically distributed users? c) allow making copy for modification of already approved version of requirements description in different abstract levels (document, requirement, attribute)? d) provide change approval cycle for multiple change negotiation and approval before posting into common repository?
	FEF2.4.	a) provide the single repository or data dictionary? b) provide separate data dictionaries for non-technical users and technical users? c) provide the help system to the users?
…tion dimension	FEF3.1.	a) enable selection and extraction of common domain requirements? b) incorporate common requirements to concrete project? c) adapt/ spread changes in domain requirements to concrete projects within domain? d) provide comparison of domain requirements feasibility?

Features	Activities for evaluating the features. How does the RET ...
FEF3.2.	a) provide wizards for report generation? b) provide possibility to print report according views and sorting? c) provide possibility to print results of rationale, brainstorm and etc? d) provide techniques for error checking?
FEF3.3.	a) correspond to standards of software documentation? b) support formal languages for complete, commonly agreed requirements specification?

Table 2. V&V support by Framework for Evaluation of RET

	Features	V&V support
Representation dimension	FEF1.1.	Transformation process between informal, semi-formal and formal representations must be supported. Automatic or semi-automatic transition between formality levels facilitates V&V of specification and agreement between different stakeholders. V&V ensures that each requirement is unique.
	FEF1.2.	
	FEF1.3.	
	FEF1.4.	The impact of changes in one fragment have to be traced to related elements. This benefits in more efficient validation, re-validation could be avoided.
	FEF1.5.	Connection with other tools benefits in easier verification and ensures interchange of produced and validated fragments between different tools used in different system development steps.
Agreement dimension	FEF2.1.	Version control and configuration management helps to track changes after V&V was performed and benefits in facilitated re-validation process and understanding the rationale behind the change.
	FEF2.2.	Cooperative work increases the confidence of product by facilitating the understanding and discussing the model produced. It also facilitates the development of consensus between stakeholders and ensure sufficient accuracy of the model. Possibilities of cooperative work for geographically distributed team reduce expenses for V&V.
	FEF2.3.	
	FEF2.4.	
Specification dimension	FEF3.1.	This feature rise only necessity to validate domain appropriateness and to reuse already validated and verified set of common requirements. It benefits in reduction of delivery time.
	FEF3.2.	The specification could benefit in increased confidence of product. V&V techniques have to be applied. V&V errors and gaps within the specification can be detected. Reuse of requirements specification of already existing systems leads to better insight of the systems behavior and avoids misspecifications.
	FEF3.3.	

Since formal requirements are built out of informal ones, the V&V process must allow less restriction. Stakeholders should verify different descriptions not only when they trace from informal thought semiformal to formal descriptions, but also when requirements are imported from/ exported to another tools.

The different views and specifications must be maintained during RE process. They help to collect information about conflicts and to determine who causes conflicts. Views help to aquire knowledge for V&V. An agreement could only be gained through communication among the involved participants. The maintainance of communication, conversation, coordination and collaboration processes between participants as well as decision support leads to better and faster agreements and V&V of the RE process. RET must support concurrent cooperative work between members of the multidisciplinary team, which may be geographically distributed. In this case participants could save time and money while performing V&V. This way of validation helps to increase the confidence of model/specification and develop a consensus of opinions.

The specification of the system could be improved by applying techniques for requirements V&V. The final RE product – requirements specification - must be complete, expressed in formal language, commonly agreed among all participants and correspond to predefined standards. V&V support by our framework is provided in table 2.

Our framework covers the semiotic framework for quality [12, 15] of conceptual models (table 3), distinguishes the variety of elements, looks for error frequency, diagram layout in documents, previews, reports, graphs and diagrams (semi-formal, formal requirements specification). RETs have to prevent and detect errors. In such a way empirical quality is covered. Goal of syntactic quality is syntactic correctness, so requirements descriptions should be according to the syntax and vocabulary of the language. Semantic quality deals with consistency and validity checking, statements insertion and deletion, traceability between statement setting. Percieved semantic quality covers correspondence between the actor interpretation of a model and current knowledge of domain. The comprehensive common repository would allow better understanding on the domain. Social quality deals with knowlegde of participants, social and technical audience interpretation.

4   Testing the Framework for Evaluation of RETs

We adopt the requirements management (RM) definition provided in [11]: "Requirements management is the process of managing changes to system's requirements." RM is understood as part of requirements engineering process: elicitation, analysis, negotiation and validation. To avoid ambiguity, further we are using term 'requirements engineering tools (RET)' instead of 'requirements management tools' as usually vendors call these tools. Functionality of those tools covers more requirements engineering (RE) activities, such as elicitation, analysis, negotiation and validation, not only management of changes.

4.1   Survey of RETs

The list of RETs - candidates for testing our evaluation framework- was formed from other evaluation reports and papers [10, 13, 14, 26], also performing search on the Internet with a keyword "requirements management/ engineering tool". This was done trying to distinguish set of representative tools (leaders in the market) as evaluation of all tools is time consuming and does not make sense due to frequent appearance of new tools in the market.

We applied for the tools to the different companies and got eight evaluations, trial or demonstration versions of RETs. They are[1]: *Core 3.1 Trial* [3], *DOORS 5.2.* [6], *Caliber-RM Web v.4.0.* [2], *RequisitePro* [22], *Vital Link* [25], *XTie-RT 3.1.* [27], *RDT Version 3.0* [21], *Cradle-4* [4].

Table 3. Coverage of Semantic quality framework by RET evaluation framework

Semantic quality framework / RET evaluation framework	Physical		Empirical	Syntatic	Semantic		Perceived semantic		Pragmatic	Social
	Ext.	Int.	Min. err. freq.	Correct.	Valid.	Comp.	Perc. valid.	Perc. compl.	Compr.	Agr.
Representation Dimension FEF1.1				✔						✔
FEF1.2			✔	✔					✔	
FEF1.3			✔	✔	✔				✔	
FEF1.4					✔		✔		✔	
FEF1.5	✔				✔	✔				
Agreement Dimension FEF2.1							✔	✔		✔
FEF2.2									✔	✔
FEF2.3									✔	✔
FEF2.4							✔	✔		
Specification dimension FEF3.1		✔			✔	✔				
FEF3.2			✔				✔	✔		✔
FEF3.3						✔			✔	✔

4.2 Evaluation Methods

In order to get the evaluation results we were working individually with separate tools. Afterwards, we compared our evaluations and had a discussion in order to decide about the final evaluation of the tool feature. We evaluated tools from theoretical point of view since we could easily obtain manuals and documentation of RET in Internet. We performed tools exploration, trying them out on small examples, looking at what features each tool has. We were using trial, demonstration and evaluation versions of RETs, the functionality of these versions were limited. We used our evaluation framework to coordinate the activities of evaluation.

One of the best evaluation methods, of course, is on-hands product evaluation. Unfortunately that is almost impossible, or at least it is very expensive process (in a sense of time consumption) due to a variety of existing commercial tools. It is important to reduce the quantity of tools before on-hands evaluation.

---

[1] Detailed descriptions of the tools could be found in vendors Internet pages.

4.3   Evaluation and Results

To support V&V processes RET could play a vital role. RETs provide assistance for the requirements specification process. Automated assistance of the tool helps to manage development process. Usually RETs help to perform all range of requirement management tasks: manage versions and track changes, link requirements to other system elements, control access, negotiate changes, communicate with stakeholders, etc. The evaluation of RETs is summarized in table 4.

During the tool evaluation using the proposed evaluation framework, we noticed that most RETs provide strong traceability possibilities. But only some of the RETs provide a more complete set of description languages (informal, semiformal, formal). This makes difficult to automate V&V and agree about accuracy of requirements captured.

Most of RETs have very good possibilities for filtering and sorting requirements according to different attributes. They provide views, according to user needs, they help to increase the confidence of specification and to achieve sufficient accuracy in validation of product. Some RETs focus only on the standalone work of individual users and do not provide any possibilities for collaboration work. The problem is lack of collaboration tools. This decreases the possibility to achieve common understanding of product, as requirements specification is mainly natural language documents, which is difficult to validate automatically. None of RETs are ideally suited for use by a multidisciplinary, distributed team where the stakeholders have diverse skills and needs. Possibilities for geographically distributed team work could save time and financial resources. In many cases import, export of files, association with other tools expand functionality of the RET. RETs lack reuse possibilities and functionality.

RETs are specially designed for use by skilled specialists who are proficient both in the software engineering methods and functionality of the tool itself. Because of complex functionality, RETs are not comfortable for non-technical stakeholders [7, 14, 24]. Additional features increase the functionality of the tools, but often users do not use all functionality because it is too complex to get familiar with all features including the appropriate V&V ones.

The purpose of the evaluation was not to choose the "best" product for any concrete customer, but rather to evaluate applicability of the framework as such. However the highest score was assigned to RequisitePro (6 high and 6 medium), the lowest scores to XTie-RT (1 high, 7 medium, 4 low). Comparing to other similar evaluations, for instance [10], the results show high confidence, as the RequisitePro looks[2] one of the best and XTie-RT - one "from the bottom". Our framework performed quite well, covering the important aspects of each tool. But we also should have in mind the limitations of demonstration, evaluation and trial versions of RETs.

---

[2] [10] does not provide final score for the evaluation. Both our and [10] evaluations are quite subjective since they mainly rely on usability of the tools, but the compared RET features corresponds each other in many cases in both evaluations.

Table 4. Evaluation of representation, agreement, and specification features

Features	Core 3.1 Trial	DOORS 5.2	Caliber-RMWeb v.4.0	Requisite Pro	Vital-Link	Xtie-RT 3.1	RDT Version 3.0	Cradle-4
FEF1.1	High	Medium	Medium	Medium	High	Medium	High	Medium
FEF1.2	High	Medium	Medium	High	Low	Low	Low	Medium
FEF1.3	Medium	Low	Low	High	Low	Low	Low	High
FEF1.4	High	Medium	Low	Medium	Medium	Medium	High	High
FEF1.5	Medium	Medium	Medium	High	Low	Medium	Medium	High
FEF2.1	Medium	Medium	High	High	Medium	Medium	Medium	Medium
FEF2.2	Medium	High	Medium	High	High	High	High	Medium
FEF2.3	Low	Medium	Medium	Medium	Low	Low	Low	Low
FEF2.4	Low	High	Medium	Medium	Medium	Low	Medium	Low
FEF3.1	Low	Medium	Medium	Medium	Low	Medium	Medium	High
FEF3.2	Medium	High	Medium	High	High	Medium	Medium	Medium
FEF3.3	Medium	Low	Low	Medium	Low	Medium	Medium	High

Our framework, as it is, could not be used directly to select the tool for acquisition. It must be customized for the particular need of the user, by: a) selecting and weighing various features according to importance depending on the development methods used by the company, or the learning goals of the university course; b) adding non-functional evaluation criteria like purchase cost, upgrade costs, support, perceived usefulness and perceived ease of use (the latter two would require on-hands experience to evaluate).

5   Conclusions and Future Works

We have provided a list of general features to guide requirements engineers and RE tool constructors in evaluating the suitability of available options, in order to minimize the costs and risks involved in selecting or developing RET. We presented the concrete evaluation framework that covers the major steps and activities of the RE process, it fits to Pohl's framework [20], and satisfies framework for quality of conceptual model [12, 15]. As features of proposed framework is based on the list of Lang/Duggan requirements for RET described in [14], we contribute in a better coverage of requirements engineering process and in a more complete list of vital features for up-to-date RETs.

We tried out the evaluation framework on the set of commercial RETs by evaluating how those tools support validation and verification. We looked at validity, reliability and usability of the proposed framework. We can state that validity of our framework is pretty *high*, as results correspond to requirements management tools survey provided in [10]. At the moment reliability of the framework is not clear, because we were not able to test our framework with statistically reliable corpus of users. The same problem is with usability of the framework, but from our own experience the framework is easy to use in a way it shows the concrete steps and activities, while testing and evaluating RET.

From the perspective of the PORE method [17] our proposed evaluation framework is supposed to be used during the early stages of requirements acquisition and tool selection, when one has to rely on the vendor data in white papers, technical documents, and Web site information.

As future work we would explore the distinction of features of RET and assign the weights to features. After weighting the features we will perform reliability test on the framework, involving experts from industry and/ or students' work in university. It is also considered to extend framework for PORE method templates, product demonstration and on-hands product evaluation, respectively.

References

[1]   Bielkowicz P., Tun T.T.: A Comparison and Evolution of Data Requirement Specification Techniques in SSADM and Unified Process. In: K.R. Dittrich, A. Geppert, M.C. Norrie (Eds.): CaiSE 2001, LNCS, Springer=Verlag, Berlin Heidelberg (2001) 46-59

[2]   Caliber-RM: URL: http://www.starbase.com/

[3]   CORE: A Guided Tour. Release 3.0. 12.2000,
      URL: http://www.vtcorp.com/productline.html

[4]   Cradle: Cradle User Guide & Tutorial, URL: http://www.threesl.com/

[5]   Davis, A.M.: Software requirements, Prentice Hall (1993)

[6]   DOORS: Using DOORS, 12.06.2001, URL: http://www.telelogic.com/

[7]   Duitoit A.H., Paech B.: Developing Guidance and Tool Support for Rationale-based Use Case Specification, In: Proceedings REFSQ'2001. Interlaken, Switzerland (2001)

[8]   Evans, J.R. and Lindsay, W.M.: The Management and Control of Quality. 5th edn. South-Western (Thomson Learning), Cincinnati, Ohio (2002)

[9]   Gordjin, J., Akkermans, H., van Vliet, H.: Business Modelling is not Process Modelling. In: Proceedings ECOMO 2000, Salt Lake City, USA (2000)

[10] INCOSE: Tools Survey: Requirements Management (RM) Tools by International Council on Systems Engineering (INCOSE) URL: http://www.incose.org/tools/tooltax.html (checked: 06.09.2002)

[11] Kotonya G., Sommerville I.: Requirements Engineering: Processes and Techniques, Wiley, (1998)

[12] Krogstie J.: Integrating the understanding of Quality in requirements Specification and Conceptual Modeling. Software Engineering Notes 23 (1), (1998) 89-91

[13] LaBudde Ed. V.: Finding the Right Off-the-Shelf Requirements Management Tool, (MDDI, Oct 1997, p. 48). URL: http://www.devicelink.com/mddi/archive/97/10/013.html (checked: 06.09.2002)

[14] Lang M., Duggan J.: A tool to support collaborative software requirements management, Requirement Engineering 6 (2001) 161-172

[15] Lindland O.I., Sindre G., Sølvberg A.: Understanding Quality in Conceptual Modelling, IEEE Software 11, 2 (1994) 42-49.

[16] Loucopoulos P., Karakostas V.: System Requirements Engineering, McGraw-Hill, (1995)

[17] Maiden N. A., Ncube C.: Acquiring COTS Software Selection Requirements. IEEE Software (1998) 46-56

[18] Moody, D.L., Shanks G.G.: Improving the Quality of Data Models: Empirical Validation of a Quality Management Framework. International Journal of Information Systems (in press)

[19] Nguyen L., Swatman P. A.: Managing the Requirements Engineering Process, In: Proceedings REFSQ'2001. Interlaken, Switzerland (2001)

[20] Pohl K.: The three dimensions of requirements engineering: a framework and its applications, Information systems Vol. 19, No 3 (1994) 243-258.

[21] RDT: Product Overview, URL: http://www.igatech.com/rdt/

[22] RequisitePro: Rational RequisitePro v2002. Evaluators Guide with a Requirements Management Overview. URL: http://www.rational.com/

[23] Hommes B.J., van Reijswoud V.: Assessing the Quality of Business Process Modelling Techniques. In Proceedings of the 33rd Hawaii International Conference on System Sciences (2000)

[24] Urquhart C., Analysts and client in organizational contexts: a conversational perspective, Journal of Strategic Information Systems 10 (2001) 243-262

[25] VitalLink: Vital Link Tutorial & Help, URL: http://www.complianceautomation.com/

[26] Wiegers K. E.: Automating Requirements Management.
URL: http://www.processimpact.com/articles/rm_tools.html (checked: 06.09.2002)

[27] XTie-RT: Cross Tie, Version 3.1.03 Tutorial, URL: http://www.tbe.com/

[28] Zave, P., Jackson M., "Four dark corns of requirements engineering", ACM Transaction on Software Engineering and Methodology, 6 (1), (1997) 1-30.

Hierarchical ER Diagrams (HERD) -
The Method and Experimental Evaluation

Peretz Shoval*, Revital Danoch, and Mira Balaban

Department of Information Systems Engineering
Ben-Gurion University of the Negev P.O.Box 683, Beer-Sheva 84105, Israel
{shoval,danochav}@bgumail.bgu.ac.il, mira@cs.bgu.ac.il

Abstract. HERD (Hierarchical Entity-Relationship Diagram) is a semi-algorithmic, bottom-up method for creating hierarchical ER diagrams (ERD) from a given "flat" diagram. The method is based on three packaging operations, which group entity and relationship types according to certain criteria. The packaging operations are applied in several steps on a given (presumably large) ERD. The result is a hierarchy of simple and interrelated diagrams - ER structures - with external relationships to other structures. We conduct an experimental comparison of HERD and flat ERD from the point of view of user comprehension; time to complete comprehension tasks, and user preference of models. Results of the comparison reveal that there is no significant difference in comprehension of the two diagram types and in the time it takes to complete the comprehension tasks, but we found that users prefer HERD diagrams.

1 Introduction

Conceptual modeling is an important phase in designing a successful database application [6]. The concepts in a data model are usually represented in a diagrammatic form. A conceptual schema diagram must be powerful in its semantic expressiveness and easily comprehensible, as it serves as a communication medium between professional designers and users (including managers) who interact during the stage of requirement analysis and modeling, and validate the design [13]. Once approved by users (as a proper representation of reality), the conceptual schema is converted into a specific database schema, depending on the data model and DBMS that is used for implementation [14]. The major problem, however, is to create a good conceptual schema that is semantically correct, complete, easy to use, and comprehensible.

Entity-Relationship (ER) model is one of the most widely used conceptual data models. An ER diagram (ERD) models the data structure of a reality in terms of entities, relationships and attributes. However, in case of a large-scale application, the ERD may become very big, and it may be very difficult to understand and to manage it, especially for end users or managers [15]. As database application requirements increase in size and complexity, comprehensibility and maintainability of the specification degrades rapidly [10]. A mechanism is needed to improve ERD comprehensibility

---

*Corresponding author (Tel. +972-8-6472221; Fax. +972-8-6477527).

A. Olivé (Eds.): ER 2003 Ws, LNCS 2784, pp. 264-274, 2003.
© Springer-Verlag Berlin Heidelberg 2003

and to simplify its maintainability, in particular if we want to effectively apply the ER model on large-scale applications. Indeed, the common ER model includes some abstraction mechanisms that support comprehensibility, mainly generalization (sub typing of entity types) and aggregation (whole-part relationships). However, these abstraction mechanisms alone do not solve the problem of too much detail in too small space [10]. Layering of diagrams has been a key tool of abstraction, thus removing complexity of large schemas generated by enterprise modeling [7]. For example, layered diagrams are common in system analysis, where functional decomposition is carried out with data flow diagrams [4]. Hierarchical structuring is common in software engineering; UML class diagrams include the *package* construct, but only as an organizational tool (like a folder in file management) - not as a first class construct.

In [5] we proposed a method for creating hierarchical ERDs - HERD - in a bottom-up fashion, namely, from a given low-level "flat" ERD. The method is semi-algorithmic, and it consists of three packaging operations, which are applied in several steps on the flat ER diagram, to create from it a hierarchy of simple and interrelated diagrams. To enable this, we enrich the common ER diagrams by introducing new constructs: **structure** and **composite-relationship**. A *structure* is a (partial) ERD that consists of entities and relationships; it may also contain other structures (hence, it is similar to a package in UML), and is related to other structures by external relationships. An external relationship is a relationship of an entity within a structure with other entities that belong to another structure. A *composite-relationship* is a relationship between structures or between entities and structures. In other word, it is an aggregation of one or more specific relationships among entities not belonging to the same structure.

The method for creating HERD diagrams consists of three packaging (grouping) operations, which are applied in several steps. In the first step, the grouping operations are applied on the flat (bottom-level) ERD, creating leaf-level structures and external-relationships. In subsequent steps, the grouping operations are applied recursively on the bottom-level ERD as well as on the already created structures, thus creating higher-level structures (with external relationships to other entities) and composite-relationships (within subordinate structures and entities). In the final step, a top-level diagram, termed HERD-Tree, is created, showing the tree structure of the model.

As a new data model, it must be evaluated on various dimensions, e.g. quality of its product, comprehensibility, learn ability, ease of use, maintainability, preference by users and professionals, etc. In this paper we present an evaluation of HERD from the points of view of users, namely: comprehensibility of the diagrams by users; time to complete tasks of comprehension; and user preference of model. The evaluation is based on an experimental comparison of HERD with flat ERD. Results of the comparison revealed that there is no significant difference between the two diagram types with respect to comprehension and time, but that users prefer the HERD diagrams.

Section 2 presents related studies on evaluation of data models and methods, mainly from the point of view of user comprehension. Section 3 describes briefly the HERD models and the method for creating HERD diagrams. Section 4 presents the experimental comparison of HERD with flat ERDs; and Section 5 summarizes and suggests further research issues.

2 Related Studies

Numerous studies evaluate and compare various data models and methods in experimental settings. Many of the studies compare ERDs with normalization of relations, or with object-class diagrams. In almost all those studies the subjects of the experiments were students with varying degrees of training in information systems and databases. Some studies compared the models/methods from a user perspective, attempting to find out which of the compared models/methods is easier to comprehend or apply. Other studies compared the models/methods from a designer perspective, attempting to determine which model/method yields more accurate and precise products, or requires less time to complete the analysis or design task, or which is preferable by designers. Here are a few relevant examples.

Shoval and Frumermann [13] compared EER and OO Schemas (class diagrams) from the perspective of user comprehension. Two groups of users were given equivalent EER and OO diagrams. Comprehension of schemas was based on a questionnaire consisting of statements concerning various constructs of the two data models. Subjects of the experiment were students of behavioral science and management, who were trained to "read" each of those diagrams. The authors found a significant difference in comprehension of ternary relationships in favor of the EER model, and no significant difference in comprehension of other constructs (e.g. binary relationships).

In a following study, Shoval and Shiran [14] compared the same EER and the OO models from the point of view of quality, namely correctness of schemas specified by designers. They also measured the time to complete the design tasks and the designers' preferences of the models. The subjects of this experiment were graduates of Information Systems. Subjects in two groups were given similar design tasks, each group using a different model. Performance was measured according to the number of correct/incorrect constructs created with each model. The authors found that EER model is better than the OO model in specifying unary and ternary relationships, with no significant differences in other constructs; that it takes less time to create EER schemas; and that the designers prefer modeling with EER more than with OO.

Chechen and Prashant [13] investigated similarities and differences in the quality of data representations produced by end-users using the relational model (RM), extended entity relationship model (EERM), and object oriented model (OOM). By performing laboratory experiments using MIS students, quality was evaluated on five constructs of data models (entity/objects, descriptor, identifier, relationships and generalization hierarchy) and six facets of relationship (unary 1:1, unary 1:n, binary 1:1, binary 1:n, binary n:n and ternary n:n:n). The research focused on two major issues: data model design and data model conversion. The fist issue investigated the difference in user performance between RM, EERM and OOM. The second investigated the differences in user performance between RM and the relational conversions of EERM and OOM models. For the first issue, EERM and OOM scored much higher than the RM in correctness of binary 1:n and binary n:n relationships. RM and OOM scored much higher than EERM on unary 1:1 relationships. OOM required significantly less time than EERM to complete the task. For the second issue, RM and the relational conversion of OOM scored significantly higher than the relational conversion of EERM on unary 1:1 relationships.

3 The HERD Model and Method

3.1 The HERD Model

HERD model and method are described in detail in [5]); here we provide only a brief description. The creation of HERD starts from a given flat (large-scale) ERD, with the application of packaging operations that gather entities and relationships into higher-level ERDs called ***structures***. The process is iterative, where packaging operations are applied on the bottom-level (flat) diagram, as well as on the already created structures. A leaf-level structure includes entities, relationships and their attributes – namely a partial ERD. A higher-level structure includes also lower-level structures and composite-relationships, where a composite-relationship is an aggregation of relationships that exist among structures and entities. To ease comprehension, every structure shows also external-relationships, i.e. relationships of entities within the structure with entities belonging to other structures. On top of all diagrams a top-level diagram, called HERD-Tree, is created, showing the whole tree of structures in the hierarchy.

For clarity of the explanation of the HERD model, we first show an example of a "flat" ERD. Fig. 1 shows an example from a hospital domain. The diagrammatic notation that we use is similar to that in [1] and [6]. We can distinguish entity types (rectangles), attributes (ovals) and relationships types (diamonds). Weak entity types (dashed rectangles) are related to their strong entities with dashed diamonds and links. Identifying attributes are underlined, and bold circles signify multi-valued attributes. Arrows linking sub-entities to their super-entities, signify supertype-subtype hierarchies. The example, though not trivial, is still relatively small, as it fits into a single page. Yet, it's already not to understand "what's going on". (Note, for example, that in order to avoid crossing lines, we had to duplicate the rectangle of entity *Physician* – this is marked at the upper left corner.) In reality, ERDs may be much more complex, and therefore they must be split in several pages or screens, like road maps.

HERD extends ERD with two new constructs: *structure* and *complex-relationship*.

A. Structure
Structure is a higher-level entity type; it is an aggregation of entity and relationship types. A structure is represented as a large bold rectangle with a small rectangle (a "tab") attached on its upper left corner, like a folder. A leaf-level structure contains only (elementary) entities and the relationship between them, along with their attributes (see examples in Figures 2 and 3). A higher-level structure contains also one or more subordinate structures (see examples in Figures 4-6). When a structure is contained within a super-structure, its details are not shown; only its name and its number are written within the bold rectangle.

A structure has external-relationships, namely, relationships of entities within a structure with entities not belonging to the structure - they appear outside the frame of the structure (Note also that non-leaf structures contain composite-relationships - they will be explained later on). Structures may be created in several steps/levels. The top-level structure shows the most general view of the whole data model, and it contains mainly lower-level structures, but it may also contain elementary entities and relationships. Fig. 6 shows the top-level structure of the example.

It is important to note that every entity belongs to one structure only (at any level). Hence, the structure hierarchy is a strict tree. This ensures that structures are non-overlapping (disjoint), and therefore minimize redundancy between them [11]. Note, however, that an entity may appear more than once as part of an external relationship of some structures. Attributes of an entity are shown only once, in the structure where the entity belongs. (But attributes of a relationship may appear more than once, if that relationship is an external - as will be described later).

A structure is given a name, which is supposed to describe its contents. (The name may be identical to the name of a major entity contained in it). Every structure is given a unique decimal number to indicate its level. For example, a leaf-level structure is numbered 1.x (where x is a serial number); a subsequent-level structure -- 2.x, etc. A higher-level structure may contain structures from different levels. For example, Structure 3.1 (Fig. 6) contains structures 1.1, 1.2, 2.1 and 2.2. (Note that due to space, only structure 1.2 and 2.1 are shown in separate figures.) Structure numbers help recognizing and navigating between structures, and finding entities and relationship belonging to each structure.

An entity within a structure may have relationships with other entities that are not part of that structure (besides entity relationships within the structure). Such external relationships appear outside the frame of the structure, along with the related entities and the relationship attributes. For ease of comprehension, next to every external entity name, we write (in parentheses) the structure number to which it belongs.

Similar to external relationships, a structure may also have external abstractions, namely external generalizations (subtype-relationships) as in Fig. 3, and external aggregations (whole-part relationships).

B. Composite Relationship

A non-leaf structure contains subordinate structures that may be related to other subordinate structures or entities. Since a subordinate structure "hides" its component entities, each of which may have relationships to entities that are external to that structure, we must aggregate these individual relationships and represent them in one symbol. We term it *composite-relationship*. A composite-relationship is represented as a bold diamond. It is given a name that is assumed to represent the relationships that it aggregates. For example, in Fig. 6 there are five composite-relationships. One of them, *Hospitality,* relates two structures: *Patient-Hospitalization-1.1* and *Staff and Reassert –2.1*. It is an aggregation of several specific relationships that relate different entities contained in those structures: one such specific relationship is *Surgeon*, which relates *Physician* and *Actual-Surgeon;* another specific relationship is *Physician-Diagnosis*, which relates *Physician* and *Diagnosis*. (Both can be seen in Fig. 3.)

While every specific relationship has its specific cardinalities, a composite-relationship does not show any cardinality because the member (specific) relationships it aggregates may have different cardinalities. Similarly, a composite-relationship does not have attributes, because each of its member relationships may have other attributes.

Similar to composite-relationships, are also possible composite generalizations. A composite-generalization aggregates one or more specific generalizations existing among super- and sub-entities or structures not belonging to the same structure. A composite-generalization is represented as a bold line with an arrowhead pointing to the super entity or structure - see examples in Figures 5-6.

3.2   The Method for Creating HERD Diagrams

The method for creating HERD diagrams consists of three packaging operations that are applied is several steps. Packaging operations gather entities and relationships to form structures. We distinguish between three types of packaging operations:

(a) **Dominance grouping** groups weak entities together with their strong entities (See example in Fig. 3). In case that a weak entity dependents on more than one entity, it is arbitrarily grouped with one of them. (Hence, the method is not deterministic). In case that a weak entity dependents on another weak entity, the "chain" of weak entities are grouped together with the top-level strong entity.

(b) **Accumulation**: An entity that is related to only one other entity (namely, has only one relationship type) is grouped together with that entity. Examples are entities *Supplier* and *Medical Equipment, which* are related only to *Organizational Unit* (Fig. 2). The accumulation operation can be applied also on a structure that is related to another structure (see Figures 4-5), or to a structure that is related to an entity – depending on the packaging step.

(c) **Abstraction grouping**: *Multi*-level data objects that are related as generalization/ specialization (super/sub-types) or aggregation (whole-parts) may be grouped into an entity cluster. Subtypes are grouped together with their supertype, as shown in Fig. 2, and participating entities are grouped together with the aggregating entity.

The above packaging operations are applied in four steps.

- **Step 1: Create leaf-level structures.** The first step in the process is forming leaf-level structures, by applying the grouping operations **(a)**, **(b)** and **(c)** on the flat ER diagram. Every structure thus created is given a number (1.x). Within a frame of each structure are included entities and relationships that are grouped by following one or more of the above operations. Outside the frame are shown the external relationships. We add to every external entity the number of the structure to which it belongs. In our example we obtain 6 leaf-level structures as result of the application of Step 1. (Two of them are shown in Figures 2 and 3.)
- **Step 2: Create higher-level structures.** Higher-level structures are constructed by applying packaging operations **(b)** and **(c)** recursively, on the leaf-level structures produced in Step 1, and on entities that have not been grouped yet. (Operation **(a)** is no longer relevant at this stage.). For example, Fig. 4 shows Structure 2.1, which contains subordinate Structures 1.4 and 1.3. Another example for the creation of a higher-level structure is Structure 2.2 (Fig. 5), which groups subordinate structures 1.5 and 1.6. Structure 2.2 is created because structure 1.5 is related only to Structure 1.6, so they are grouped together due to Operation **(b)**.

  Step 2 is applied recursively, until the grouping operations **(b)** and **(c)** cannot be applied any more on the remaining elements (i.e. entities and structures). In the last iteration of Step 2 we obtain the top-level structure (in our example, Structure 3.1 in Fig. 6). Note that this structure consists mainly of structures and composite-relationships, but not only -- have we had also the entity *Medicine*, which could not be grouped into a structure earlier in the process, because of its various relationships with other entities.

To summarize Step 2, in its first iteration we created Structures 2.1 (Fig. 4) and 2.2 (Fig. 5); and in the second/last iteration - Structure 3.1 (Fig. 6).

- **Step 3: Change and improve structures.** While steps 1 and 2 apply the packaging operations algorithmically, in Step 3 we may apply heuristic rules to improve the resulting structures. One such rule is to combine related structures that contain a few elements only, thus reducing the number of structures in the model. For example, Structure 2.2 (Fig. 5) is relatively small; since Structures 1.5 and 1.6 (which are not shown) are included within Structure 2.2, the former can be eliminated and its components be incorporated within the latter. The result of this combination is presented in Fig. 7.

  Contrary to combining small structures, we may opt to split a too large structure into two smaller structures. If we split a structure, we also have to update the external relationships. Another possible change involves weak entities: if a weak entity has several strong entities, each placed in a different structure; we may opt to combine those structures (if they are not too big already).

- **Step 4: Create the HERD-Tree**. After all changes of structures, in Step 4 we create the HERD-Tree, which shows the tree of structures. Fig. 8 shows the HERD-Tree created from the original structures (before any changes made in Step 3). Note that in addition to the structures hierarchy, at the bottom of each structure in the HERD-Tree are listed the entity names it includes. This facilitates orientation: to find a certain entity and its attributes or relationships, one has to review the HERD-Tree diagram, locate the structure to which that entity belongs, and see the details in that structure. The HERD-Tree is built bottom-up: at the bottom are the leaf-level structures (numbered 1.x); then the secondary-level structures (numbered 2.x), and so on – till the top-level structure.

4   Experimental Comparison of HERD and Flat ERDs

4.1   Hypotheses and Experimental Design

In an experimental setting, we compared flat-ER and HERD diagrams from a user perspective, in order to find out which of the two diagram types is more comprehensible. Comprehensibility was examined mainly in terms of correctness of answers to questions (statements) posed to users, dealing with the facts represented in the diagrams. Additional criteria included time to complete tasks of comprehension, and the users' preferences of models.

Although in many areas it has been proven that hierarchy has many advantages [2], [4], [9], [12] we have no a-priori reason to assume that one model is more comprehensible than the other is. Therefore we hypothesize that there is no difference in comprehension of the two types of diagrams. We defined null hypotheses with respect to comprehension of nine different constructs of the two models, plus the time aspect, as follows:

(1) There is no difference in comprehension when dealing with attributes of an entity.
(2) There is no difference in comprehension when dealing with a binary relationship.
(3) There is no difference in comprehension when dealing with a ternary relationship.

(4) There is no difference in comprehension when dealing with an abstraction (generalization).
(5) There is no difference in comprehension when dealing with two binary relationships.
(6) There is no difference in comprehension when dealing with more than two relationships.
(7) There is no difference in comprehension when dealing with both an abstraction (generalization) and a relationship.
(8) There is no difference in comprehension when dealing with a week entity.
(9) There is no difference in the **overall comprehension** of the two diagram types.
(10) There is no difference in time to complete the comprehension tasks.

The dependent variables were, according to the above hypotheses: (a) correctness of answers to statements, and (b) time to complete the task. The independent variables were the ER and HERD diagrams. For the experiment, we prepared an example – an extended version of the hospital example presented here. First, we created a flat ER diagram. Since it could not fit into a single page, we had to split it into a number of pages. Then we applied the packaging steps, creating HERD diagrams and the HERD-Tree, explained in Section 3.

To measure comprehension, we prepared a questionnaire consisting of 41 "true"/"false" statements, which we classified in 8 categories, according to the above hypotheses; namely, statements dealing with attributes of an entity; a binary relationship; a ternary relationship; an abstraction (generalization); two binary relationships; more than two relationships; an abstraction and a relationship; and a weak entity. The reason for this classification is that we wanted to be able to distinguish differences in comprehensibility of the various constructs of each model. We prepared four sets of questionnaires, each with a different ordering of the (same) statements – in order to avoid bias due to order of statements. Table 1 shows examples of a few statements.

Table 1. Example of True and False Statements

Category	Statements
Binary relationship	A physician cannot participate in different researches. *(False)*
Ternary relationship	A supplier can supply a certain organizational unit with many types of medical equipment, and a supplier can supply a certain type of medical equipment to many organizational units. *(True)*
Abstraction	A nurse has an ID number, name, address, role and degree. *(True)*
Two relationships	A research can be conducted by different physicians and be financed by different funds. *(False)*
Weak entity	An actual surgery is identified by the patient ID and surgery code. *(False)*

The subjects of the experiment were 42 students of Software Engineering who took the same courses, including Databases, where they studied the two models. (They first studied and exercised with the "traditional" ER model, and then with the HERD model, on which they spent less time and did less exercises. This fact might have influenced the experiment results, as will be discussed later on.)

In the experiment, the subjects were randomly divided into two groups. Each subject in one group received a set of flat ER diagrams, while each subject in the other group received a set of HERD diagrams. Along with the diagrams the subjects received a questionnaire. (Recall that we prepared four sets of questionnaires, with different ordering of the statements; they were distributed to the subjects randomly). Subjects were asked to mark the correct answers, by marking "true" or "false" next to each statement.

To enable measuring the time it takes to complete the comprehension tasks, we recorded, for every subject, the start and end time of completing the questionnaire. At the end, the subjects were asked to express to what degree they liked the model which they used – using a 1-7 point scale.

Table 2. Results

No	Category	Model	Mean Grade	# of Observ.	t-Statistic	P(T<=t) two-tail	Significant Difference?
1	Attributes of an entity	HERD	0.900	20	0.843	0.404	No
		Flat ER	0.867	21			
2	Binary relationship	HERD	0.850	20	1.759	0.087	Weak-HERD
		Flat ER	0.816	21			
3	Ternary relationship	HERD	0.700	20	-2.433	0.020	Yes-flat ER
		Flat ER	0.857	21			
4	Abstraction	HERD	0.975	20	1.000	0.324	No
		Flat ER	0.929	21			
5	Two relationships	HERD	0.839	20	0.141	0.889	No
		Flat ER	0.830	21			
6	More than two relationships	HERD	0.726	20	1.601	0.118	No
		Flat ER	0.646	21			
7	Relationship and abstraction	HERD	0.917	20	1.019	0.315	No
		Flat ER	0.873	21			
8	Weak entity	HERD	0.640	20	-0.361	0.720	No
		Flat ER	0.667	21			
9	Overall comprehension	HERD	0.8124	20	0.580	0.565	No
		Flat ER	0.7943	21			
10	Time (minutes)	HERD	42.950	21	-1.919	0.063	Weak-flat ER
		Flat ER	37.524	20			

4.2 Experiment Results

For each subject, we counted the number of correct answers ("true" or "false") within each of the eight categories of statements. Based on that, we computed each subject's grade per category (using a percentage scale). This enabled us to compute the mean grade of all subjects, per category and the overall grade - within each model. We applied t-statistic to test the significance of differences between the mean grades, per category and overall grade. Similarly, we computed the time it took each participant to complete the task, and based on that we computed the mean times per model, and tested the significance of mean differences using t-test. Finally, we computed the average preference of each model, as expressed by the users, and tested the significance of difference using t-test.

The results of 'Comprehension' and 'Time' are presented in Table 2. The *Significant Difference?"* column indicates weather or not the results are significant (at α=0.05). As can be seen, we found no significant difference in comprehension in almost all categories and in overall comprehension. Only in the Ternary Relationships category there was a significant advantage to flat-ER diagrams, while in the Binary Relationships category there was a slight (insignificant) advantage to HERD diagrams. With respect to Time, we found that it takes slightly (not significantly) less time to complete the comprehension task with flat ER diagrams.

The results of User Preference of Model are presented in Table 3. As can be seen, subjects preferred the HERD model.

Table 3. Model Preference

Model	Mean	Observations	t-stat.	Significance
HERD	5.683	41	3.826	0.000
Flat ER	4.805	41		

5   Summary and Further Research

The results of the experiment seem to be surprising. On one hand, we found that users prefer the hierarchical model; on the other hand - from the point of view of comprehension – we did not find that there is an advantage to using hierarchical diagrams. Although psychological researches (e.g. [9], [2], [4] and 12] showed superiority to hierarchy in many areas, like items organization and libraries organization, we did not find a clear advantage to hierarchy in comprehension of a data model.

The question is how valid are the results of this experiment. Should we abandon the hierarchical model because of these results? Not necessarily, it is possible that the "surprising" results are due to flaws in the experiment. One possible explanation to the results is the order of learning effect: the subjects learned flat ER diagrams first, and then HERD. Moreover, they spent more time on learning and exercising with flat ER diagrams – two 3-hour lectures, including several examples, plus 3 homework problems - compared to only one 2-hour lecture on HERD, including a single example only, and with no homework assignment.

We plan to conduct more experiments in which we'll control the order of learning and the time of learning effects. We also plan to use examples of various sizes (namely with varying numbers of entities and relationships), in order to see the interactions between model and example size. We hypothesize that the advantage of hierarchy will show as the example size gets bigger and more complex.

Another further research issue is to extend the method to create hierarchical ER diagrams from top down. Namely, starting from user requirements, we plan to propose a method to create a top-level ER structure first, and then to decompose it, following certain steps and rules of decomposition, until bottom-level ER diagrams are obtained.

References

[1] Batini, C., Ceri, S., and Navathe, S. *Conceptual Database Design: An Entity Relationship Approach*, Benjamin Cummings, Redwood City, California, 1992.
[2] Bower, G. "Organization factors in memory", *Cognitive Psychology*, Vol. 1, 1970, pp. 18-46.
[3] Chechen, L., and Prashant, C.P. "The impact of data models and task complexity on end users performance: an experimental investigation", *Int. J. Human-Computer Studies*, Vol. 52, 2000, pp. 831-845.
[4] De Marco, T. *Structured Analysis and System Specification*, Yourdon Press, 1978.
[5] Danoch, R., Shoval, P., and Balaban, M. "Hierarchical evolution of Entity-Relationship diagrams – a bottom-up approach", *Proc. of the Sixth CaiSE/IFIP8.1 Int'l Workshop on Evaluation of Modeling Methods in Systems Analysis and Design (EMMSAD'01)*, Interlaken, Switzerland, June 2001.
[6] Elmasri, R., and Navathe, S.B. *Fundamental of Databases Systems*, Benjamin Cummings, Redwood City, California, 2000.
[7] Gandhi, M., Robertson, E., and Gucht, D. "Leveled Entity Relationship model", *Proceedings of the 13th International Conference on the Entity-Relationship Approach*, Manchester, Untied Kingdom, December 1994, pp. 420-433.
[8] Kerlinger, F. *Foundation of Behavioral Research*, 3rd Ed. Orlando, FL: Holt, Rinehart, and Winston, Inc. 1986.
[9] Mandler, G. "Organization and Memory". In: *The Psychology of Learning and Motivation: Advances in Research and Theory*, K.W. Spence, and J.T., Spence (ED), Vol. 1, New York: Academic Press, 1967.
[10] Moody, D. "Graphical Entity Relationship models: toward more user understanding representation of data", *Proceedings of the 15th International Conference on Conceptual Modeling*, Cottbus, Germany, October 1996, pp. 227-244.
[11] Moody, D. "A methodology for clustering Entity Relationship models - a human information processing approach", *Proceedings of the 18th International Conference on Entity-Relationship Approach*, 1999, pp. 114-130.
[12] Najarian, S.E. "Organizational factors in human memory: implications for library organization and access systems", *Library Quarterly*, Vol. 51(3), 1981, pp. 269-291.
[13] Shoval, P., and Frumermann I. "OO and EER conceptual schemas: a comparison of user comprehension", *Journal of Database Management*, Vol. 5(4), 1994, pp. 28-38.
[14] Shoval, P., and Shiran, S. "Entity-relationship and object–oriented data modeling – an experimental comparison of design quality", *Data & Knowledge Engineering* Vol. 21, 1997, pp. 297-315.
[15] Teory, T., Wei, G., Bolton D., and Koenig, J. "ER model clustering as an aid for user communication and documentation in database design", *Communication of the ACM*, Vol. 32(8), 1989, pp. 975-987.

Figures: Due to space limit, the figures are not included in this paper. They can be found at: ***http://www.ise.bgu.ac.il/faculty/shoval/HERD-ER-IWCMQ-02.pdf***

Detection of Redundant Arcs
in Entity Relationship Conceptual Models

David S. Bowers

Computing Department, The Open University
Walton Hall, Milton Keynes, MK7 6AA, UK
d.s.bowers@open.ac.uk

Abstract. One measure of the quality of a conceptual model is the quality of
design that can be derived from it. Redundant relationships in an Entity
Relationship model cause a generated relational schema to be un-normalised.
Since a relationship is redundant only if some other path in the model implies
both its set theoretic signature and its semantics, determination of redundancy is
not mechanical, and always requires interaction with the client or user. A path
composition and search algorithm is presented to detect potentially redundant
relationships, and strategies are discussed for the incorporation of this type of
algorithm in a CASE environment.

1. Introduction

The principal justification for quality in conceptual models is that such models form
the basis for designs and implementation. Well-understood, deterministic rules to
transform a conceptual model into a design can be automated, in which case, a
conceptual model of poor quality would result in an inadequate implementation.

Within the scope of a short paper, a tractable example is the generation of a
relational schema from an Entity Relationship (ER) Model. Various authors,
including Teorey [1] and Bowers [2], have proposed algorithmic approaches for the
synthesis of a relational schema from an Entity Relational Model, and such techniques
are now widely adopted. Despite the essential rigour of such techniques, however,
normalization is invariably applied to the generated schemas, since they reproduce
faithfully any redundancy present in the original conceptual models.

This paper addresses the detection of redundant relationships within ER models. A
relationship is redundant when both its mapping and its semantics are implied by
some alternative path. Relational schemas synthesized from conceptual models that
include redundant relationships may not be in Third Normal Form, and will not be in
Fifth Normal Form. Conversely, posted-key synthesis techniques, such as that
described by Bowers [2], should generate schemas always in fourth normal form, and
often in fifth normal form, from ER models that are both free of redundant
relationships and contain neither multi-valued attributes nor merged entity types.

Detection of redundant relationships within an ER model supports interaction with
the client at the conceptual level to resolve redundancy. The traditional alternative of
deferring the resolution to the normalization of the generated schema seems both to be

A. Olivé (Eds.): ER 2003 Ws, LNCS 2784, pp. 275-287, 2003.

too late and, moreover, inappropriate: too late because much of the semantic content of the model has been discarded prior to normalization, and inappropriate because normalization based solely on functional dependency analysis can itself introduce ambiguity into the schema.

The algorithms presented in this paper can be incorporated into CASE tools to support the systematic detection of redundancy, and its resolution through a dialogue with the tool user. Such support allows modellers to err on the side of including rather than excluding relationships, but still to address the issue of redundancy.

The context for this discussion is presented in Section 2, and the interaction between redundancy in ER models and normalization criteria are reviewed in Section 3. The basic algorithm for determining potential path equivalence is introduced in Section 4, and strategies for its application are discussed in Section 5. Finally, issues still to be resolved are outlined in Section 6.

2. Context

The issue of redundancy within Entity Relationship models results from what is both the greatest strength and the greatest weakness of the approach: its perceived simplicity. This has led to the almost universal adoption of ER techniques, or one of its derivatives, for modelling data structures, with widespread belief that such models are readily comprehensible by both analyst and client. Unfortunately, there is ample evidence that the comprehension of ER models is difficult, and that their construction can be error-prone [7,8,9,10]. The quality of an ER model, and of any database schema derived from it, remain fundamental issues. Whilst the former has attracted some attention [11,12,13], the latter seems still to be subsumed into a pervasive assumption that any "initial" relational schema, whatever the "quality" of the ER model from which it has been derived, will always need to be "improved" by normalization[14] – an unprovable act of faith that, in many cases, is not justified by the resulting normalised model. Indeed, normalization is normally a technical activity effected entirely on the basis of perceived dependencies between fields of a schema; the semantic information expressed in an ER model is invariably discarded during its transformation to a relational schema. Furthermore, normalization is often regarded as a purely implementation issue, and therefore performed without reference to the client, quite possibly without full understanding of the client's domain.

It is irrelevant to argue that expert analysts would not make mistakes in ER diagrams. The principal purpose of such diagrams is to act as a communication medium between an analyst and a client , who is almost certainly a novice, at least as far as ER diagrams are concerned. During consultation with the analyst, it is quite possible that the client might suggest - or insist on - a relationship being drawn between two entities, even if it is already implied by another path. Thus, redundant relationships could be introduced merely through interaction with a client..

Systematic approaches to redundancy in ER Models seem to have attracted relatively little attention in the literature. Simple redundancy between a single relationship and paths of two relationships are explored exhaustively by means of occurrence diagrams in [3]. The authors suggest a set of heuristics that an analyst could use to determine redundancy in an ER model.

Our work seeks resolution of redundancy at a semantic level, rather than by mechanical consideration of rules against possible, or actual, data occurrences. Further, our work considers paths of arbitrary length, although the equivalences we deduce for paths of length one and two are the same as in [3].

The focus of the superficially similar approach in [4] seems to be on the rearrangement of the generated relational schema to reduce redundancy. There is, however, an interesting analysis of implicit relationships, represented within an ER diagram by "posted" keys not derived from any explicit relationship. Whilst such "errors" might be contrary to the ethos of ER modelling, it would be interesting to explore how the techniques of [4] could be integrated with those presented here.

An apparently related issue is explored in [5]. Given multiple paths between entities, cardinality constraints, both explicit and implicit, might prevent instantiation of the model. However, a redundant relationship and its alternate path imply precisely the same mapping; hence, they cannot affect the satisfiability of any model.

Similarly, the exploration in [6] of extensional "Int-cardinality" constraints is concerned primarily with satisfiability rather than redundancy, and is therefore also not relevant to the approach presented here.

The problem of identifying redundant relationships in an ER model is similar to that of identifying redundant connections within logic circuits [15,16]. Similar problems arise also with redundancy in production rules [17]. The path composition algorithms are only slightly simpler than those presented in Section 4.

Finally, path composition relates closely to transitive closure algorithms, as developed extensively for knowledge-based systems and deductive databases; which are known to be expensive [18, 19]. Such algorithms have been used for the analysis of functional dependencies [20, 21], but not yet, it seems, related directly to conceptual-level models, such as ER. Also, although efficiency of the transitive closure algorithms is crucial in the examples cited, it is perhaps less so for design activities, where the problems do have to be solved, but, in principle, only once.

3. Redundancy, Synthesis, and Normalization Criteria

Normalization, at least to Third Normal Form (3NF), has long been accepted as a quality criterion for relational schemata. This section summarizes the "errors" in an ER model that, if synthesized into a relational schema using a "posted key" algorithm would cause violations of each of the common Normal Forms.

The absence of redundant relationships in a conceptual model is one of three correctness criteria for an ER model enumerated in [12], although, curiously, it is distinguished from "third normal form violations". This separation may be somewhat misleading, since synthesised redundant relationships would, specifically, violate the criteria for third normal form, by introducing transitive dependencies.

Repeating groups in a schema, which would violate first normal form (1NF), could arise either from multi-valued attributes or from the incorrect "posting" of a relationship. In relational synthesis, a relationship is represented by "posting" the identifier of the entity at the "one" end of a relationship into the relation representing the entity at the "many" end; thus, a posted key can only be single valued. Hence, a

278   David S. Bowers

schema synthesised from an ER model will always satisfy 1NF, provided that no entity type has multi-valued attributes.

This is sufficient also to ensure that there are no multi-valued dependencies in the schema. Thus, if the synthesised schema is in 3NF, it will also be in 4NF.

Synthesis algorithms never merge relations for separate entities: at most, keys are posted to represent relationships. Hence, attributes in a synthesised relation are always fully dependent on the identifier of the corresponding entity, provided that no entity in the model has attributes drawn from more than one "real-world" entity.

underlying entity, or they are posted keys of entities in a many-to-one (or one-to-one) relationship Third Normal Form (3NF) requires that there must be no transitive dependencies. Attributes functionally dependent on the primary key are either attributes of the with that entity. Since the non-key attribute on which a transitively-dependent attribute depends must itself be a (primary) key of some entity, it follows that the determining non-key attribute must be a posted (foreign) key.

Hence, the issue is how a relationship between two entities - represented by the determination of the transitively-dependent attribute by a foreign key - might be included in the relation for a third entity. In the simplest case, it will be because there is a redundant relationship in the ER model.

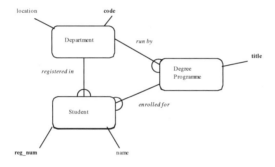

Fig. 1. A simple example of potential redundancy

This is best illustrated by an example, as in Figure 1. Synthesis of this model results in the following schema, in which in the relation *Student* contains an apparent transitive dependency of *department_code* on *reg_num* via *degree_programme_title.*:

Department (code, location)
Degree_programme (title, department_code)
Student (reg_num, name, degree_programme_title, department_code)

The problem lies in the ER model of Figure1, since the relationship *registered in* might be implied completely by the pair of relationships *enrolled for* and *run by*. The potential implication depends on whether or not the fact that a *student* is *enrolled for* a *degree programme run by* a particular *department* means that the *student* is also *registered in* that *department*. If the relationship is redundant, then the resulting schema violates Third Normal Form.

In the more general case, in which the relationships involved are not constrained to have degree one-to-many, the synthesised schema will contain a join dependency, rather than a transitive dependency. However, the elimination of redundant relationships alone is not sufficient to ensure that synthesised schemas will satisfy 5NF, since, rather than being "redundant", the relationship may be part of a representation of a higher-order relationship between three or more entity types, such as the cyclic many:many-many:many-many:many structure.

4. Path Composition and Equivalence

An algorithm to detect (potentially) redundant relationships within an ER diagram needs three components: a means of composing transitive relationships, a strategy for comparing each relationship with every alternative (composed) path between the entities it connects, and a way of comparing the semantics of alternative paths that have the same signature. A path composition algorithm is presented in this section, the available strategies are discussed in section 5.

Each relationship in an ER diagram has a set theoretic signature which is a {partial or total} {function or multifunction} from one entity (say, A) to a second (C), and an inverse signature, drawn from the same set, from C to A. Two paths between A and C are equivalent if they have both the same signatures **and** the same semantics; at this stage, we ignore any explicit numerical cardinality constraints, but take account of optionality in the relationships. Thus, in Figure 2, the relationship C-A, which is optional for entity A, represents a partial multifunction from A to C, and a total function from C to A. These are the same as the composed signatures of relationships B-A and C-B; however, although the two paths from A to C have the same signatures, they are equivalent **only** if they also have the same meaning.

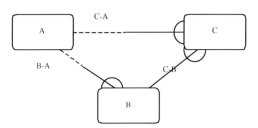

Fig. 2. A generic Entity Relationship loop

More generally, consider an arbitrary path between two entities, E_1 and E_n. Denoting a path from entity i to entity j as $R_{i,j}$, a composite path from E_1 to E_n will comprise:

$$R_{1,n} = [E_1], R_{1,2}, [E_2], R_{2,3},.....R_{n-1,n}, [E_n] \tag{1}$$

An informal proof of the composition $R_{1,n} = R_{1,2}.R_{2,3}....R_{n-1,n}$ follows.
Consider first the signature of the path $R_{1,n}$, from E_1 to E_n.

Degree: If any $R_{i,j}$ ($j > i$) of the relationships $R_{1,2}.R_{2,3}....R_{n-1,n}$ is a multifunction, then the whole path is a multifunction.

Proof: If R_{ij} is a multifunction, then some $e_i \in E_i$ maps to several $e_j \in E_j$. Even if the degree of all the remaining $R_{j,j+1}..R_{n-1,n}$ is one, e_i therefore maps to several $e_n \in E_n$. Further, even if the degree of all $R_{1,2} .. R_{i-1,i}$ is one, so that some $e_1 \in E_1$ maps only to e_i, it follows that e_1 will map to several e_n.

Optionality: If any $R_{i,j}$, from E_i to E_j, of the relationships $R_{1,2}.R_{2,3}....R_{n-1,n}$ is partial ($j>i$), then the whole path from E_1 to E_n is partial.

Proof: If $R_{i,j}$ is partial, then there can be some $e_i \in E_i$ that does not map to any $e_j \in E_j$. Since the path from E_i to E_n is via E_j, then e_i may therefore not map to any $e_n \in E_n$. Further, any $e_{i-1} \in E_{i-1}$ that maps only to e_i may also not map to any e_n, and so, recursively, any $e_1 \in E_1$ which maps only to e_i can not map to any e_n. Hence, there may be an e_1 which does not map to an e_n, and $R_{1,n}$ is partial.

The converses of each of these proofs – that path $R_{1,n}$ is a function if all $R_{i,j}$ are functions, and that path $R_{1,n}$ is total if no $R_{i,j}$ is partial – follow trivially.

Hence, the overall degree of $R_{1,n}$ is one IFF the degree of ALL $R_{i,j}$ in $R_{1,n}$ is one, and the path is mandatory IFF all $R_{i,j}$ are mandatory. Analogous arguments apply to $R_{n,1}$ for the inverse signature.

Thus, if the optionality, $O_{i,j}$, of relationship $R_{i,j}$ (i.e., the required participation of E_i in the relationship $R_{i,j}$) is represented by boolean values '1' if it is mandatory and '0' otherwise, then the optionality of the composition $R_{1,n}$, using the same convention, is

$$O_{1,n} = O_{1,2} \wedge O_{2,3} \wedge ... \wedge O_{n-1,n} \tag{2}$$

Similarly, representing the degree, $D_{i,j}$, of $R_{i,j}$ by '1' if the degree is one and '0' otherwise, the degree of the composition $R_{1,n}$ is

$$D_{1,n} = D_{1,2} \wedge D_{2,3} \wedge ... \wedge D_{n-1,n} \tag{3}$$

The four components of the complete signature, $S_{i,j}$, of a binary relationship, $R_{i,j}$, may be coded as four binary values; the order corresponds to the graphical representation of the relationship:

$$S_{i,j} = (D_{j,i}, O_{i,j}, O_{j,i}, D_{i,j}) \tag{4}$$

For example, the relationship $R_{a,c}$ ("C-A") in Figure 2 has signature $S_{a,c} = (1010)$. The overall signature of a composite path, $R_{1,n}$, is found as:

$$S_{1,n} = S_{1,2} \wedge S_{2,3} \wedge ... \wedge S_{n-1,n.} \tag{5}$$

For the alternate path in Figure 2, $S_{a,b} = (1010)$ and $S_{b,c} = (1110)$. Hence, the signature of the alternate path, $S'_{a,c} = (1010) \wedge (1110) = (1010)$.

This coding provides a general method for composing the relationships in a path within an Entity Relationship model, and for comparing alternate paths. For paths of length 2, the results are the same as those obtained by exhaustive search in [3].

5. Detection Strategies

Given an algorithm to compose the signature of a path of arbitrary length, it is necessary then to have a strategy to apply that algorithm.

There are three obvious strategies, all of which imply an exhaustive search of the ER model. The first is to consider each relationship in turn, and all alternative paths, if any, between the entities connected by that relationship. The second is to focus on each entity in turn, and the set of relationships starting from that entity, and to compose all possible paths from that entity, until all possible alternative routes have been considered for each relationship. The third strategy is to consider the ER model as a whole, building, first, all paths of length 2, comparing those paths with the initial relationships, and, after eliminating any redundant relationships implied by paths of length 2, continuing the search with paths of length 3, and so on.

The first two strategies are fundamentally similar, differing only slightly in their termination criteria. Termination depends, in both cases, on inconsistency between the signatures of a path and a relationship. If the signature of the relationship R is S_R, and that of the path P is S_P, then, applying Equation (5), P is inconsistent with R if:

$$S_R \wedge S_P \neq S_R \qquad (6)$$

In both cases, particular sub-paths may be composed several times, and both also suffer from the lack of clear termination conditions, discussed in Section 6, in the presence of loops, cycles and multiple relationships between pairs of entities.

Nevertheless, the first strategy has been used as the basis for a prototype CASE environment constructed using Peerlogic's Toolbuilder meta-CASE tool [22]. That prototype has demonstrated that it is feasible to generate an appropriate dialogue to guide the interaction with the analyst to resolve the issue of semantic equivalence, and, furthermore, to modify the ER diagram as a result of that interaction.

The third strategy seems attractive, since it reduces a graph search problem to a one analogous to matrix multiplication. The ER model is represented by an adjacency matrix, in which each cell contains the signature S of the relationship from its "row" entity to its "column" entity. The signatures for paths of length 2 are then found by pre-multiplying the adjacency matrix by itself, to give a matrix of order 2. In this matrix, each cell contains a list of signatures, derived using equation (5), each associated with an intermediate entity, so that the path can be reconstructed as ("from", "intermediate", "to"). Paths of greater length are found by pre-multiplying the higher-order matrix, repeatedly, by the original matrix, appending new "intermediate" entities to the cell entries to represent the appropriate partial paths.

At each stage, the path signatures are compared with those of the relationships in the initial matrix. If any path signature is equal to that of the corresponding simple relationship, then the relationship is potentially redundant, and clarification can be sought from the client. Relationships found to be redundant are removed from the base matrix, and paths containing them from the higher order matrices.

We introduce here an assumption that renders the algorithm tractable, sound but incomplete; the extent of the incompleteness is discussed in Section 6. We assume that no path may visit any entity more than once - that is, loops (and cycles) are not considered. This implies both that there can be no diagonal elements in the adjacency matrix, and that any paths which include an entity more than once can be discarded.

The algorithm is illustrated by an example. Figure 3 represents a scenario for a small software house that uses contract employees to work on projects sponsored by clients. The contract employees' time is billed directly to the client who sponsors their project, and the projects are managed by managers within the software house. The managers may also act as the contact for specific clients, and may supervise a number of contract employees.

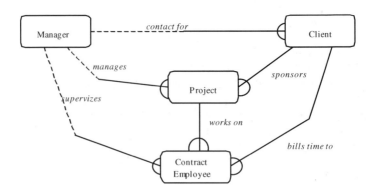

Fig. 3. An ER diagram with potential redundancy

Table 1 is the initial adjacency matrix for this simple scenario, although the signatures are represented by relationship lines rather than by the corresponding 4-tuple of (4). It is clear that the matrix is anti-symmetric, as are all matrices of higher order. In higher-order matrices, not only are the directions of the relationships reversed in diagonally symmetric cells, but so also is the order of entities in any partial path. These entities are represented in the partial paths by the letters M (*Manager*), C (*Client*), P (*Project*) and CE (*Contract Employee*).

Table 1. The Initial Adjacency Matrix

From \ To	Manager	Client	Project	Contract Emp
Manager		- - - —∈	- - - —∈	- - - —∈
Client	∋— - - -		———∈	———∈
Project	∋— - - -	∋———		———∈
Contract Emp	∋— - - -	∋———	∋———	

In Table 2, there are four paths (each appearing twice) that have the same signature as the corresponding simple relationship. These paths are highlighted in the table, and suggest that the corresponding relationships may be redundant. So, for example, it may be that a *Manager* manages a *Project* because (s)he is the contact for the *Client* who sponsors that *Project*; thus, the path *Project - Client - Manager* may imply the relationship "manages". Similarly, the path *Contract Employee - Project - Client* may imply the relationship "bills time to", but it may be that, in this particular company, neither of the paths *Contract Employee - Project - Manager* or *Contract Employee - Client - Manager* imply the relationship "supervizes".

Table 2. Adjacemcy Matrix of Order 2

From \ To	Manager	Client	Project	Contract Emp
Manager		P ∋- - - ──∈ CE ∋- - - -∈	C - - - ──∈ CE ∋- - - ──∈	C - - - ──∈ P - - - ──∈
Client	P ∋──- - -∈ CE ∋── - - -∈		M ∋- - - - - -∈ CE ∋────∈	M ∋- - - - - -∈ P ────────∈
Project	C ∋──── - - - CE ∋── - - -∈	M ∋- - - - - -∈ CE ∋────∈		M ∋- - - - - - -∈ C ∋────∈
Contract Emp	C ∋──── - - - P ∋──── - - -	M ∋- - - - - -∈ P ∋────	M ∋- - - - - -∈ C ∋────∈	

Removing the two redundant relationships (*manages* and *bills time to*) from the initial matrix, the 2nd order matrix reduces to Table 3. This is then premultiplied by the (reduced) initial matrix, to give the 3rd order matrix in Table 4. The matrix is, again, anti-symmetric, but, for clarity, the lower triangle includes the four paths formed during the multiplication that are discarded because they are loops.

There is just one path in the 3rd order matrix with the same signature as the corresponding simple relationship: *Manager - Client - Project - Contract Employee*. As before, let us assume that this path does not imply the relationship "supervizes".

Table 3. Adjacancy Matrix, Order 2, after removal of redundant relationships

From \ To	Manager	Client	Project	Contract Emp
Manager			C - - - ──∈ CE ∋- - - ──∈	
Client				M ∋- - - - - -∈ P ────────∈
Project	C ∋──── - - - CE ∋──- - -∈			
Contract Emp		M ∋- - - - - -∈ P ∋────		

If loops are not permitted, the longest path possible in a model with four entities will involve three relationships. Hence, the order 3 matrix is the last that needs to be calculated, and the final model is that shown in Figure 4. In general, the algorithm terminates sound at the matrix of order N-1, when the ER model contains N entities.

Clearly, however, the contents of the matrix grow rapidly as paths of increasing length are derived. Fortunately, this can be mitigated by several heuristics. First, the removal of redundant relationships at the earliest opportunity can reduce significantly the number of paths in higher order matrices.

Second, the complexity of paths retained in the matrix can be limited. For example, if all the relationships in the ER diagram had degree no more than one to many, a criterion could be set to exclude all paths "less constrained" than one to many. Defining the signature S_0 to be that for a fully optional one to many signature, $(1,0,0,0)$, and S_0^T as its inverse, $(0,0,0,1)$, the criterion for inclusion of a path P, with signature S_P, in a higher-order matrix is then:

$$(S_0 \wedge S_P = S_0) \vee (S_0^T \wedge S_P = S_0^T) \qquad (7)$$

Finally, the initial adjacency matrix will normally be sparse, unlike the relatively dense example discussed here. Furthermore, the large number of paths that populate the higher order matrices are precisely the same as those that would be derived in either of the first two strategies, but that, using the matrix approach, the partial paths are derived only once rather than for each entity or relationship.

Table 4. Adjacancy matrix of Order 3

From \ To	Manager	Client	Project	Contract Emp
Manager		CE.P ∋- - - —∈		C.P - - - —∈
Client	P.C ∋— - - -∈ P.CE ∋— - - -∈		M.CE ∋-- - - -∈	
Project		CE.M ∋ - - - -∈ CE.P ∋——∈		C.M ∋- - - - -∈
Contract Emp	P.C ∋—- - - P.CE ∋— - - -∈		M.C ∋- - - - -∈ M.CE ∋-- - - -∈	

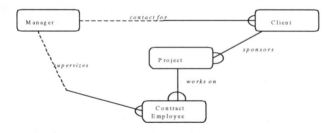

Fig. 4. ER Diagram after removal of redundant relationships

6. Outstanding Issues

The algorithm presented herein is an exhaustive search for closed paths within an ER model, and a search for possible redundancies within each closed path. As such, it does not scale well: the complexity of the matrix algorithm can be shown to be potentially $O(N^{N+1})$, where the model contains N entities. Restricting the search to cycles, in which no entity is visited more than once, reduces the complexity to $O(N^3.(N-2)!)$, which still seems somewhat impractical.

Fortunately, the initial adjacency matrix is likely to be sparse. If the average number of relationships in which an entity participates is 2ϕ, then the likely complexity of the search could fall to $O(N^3.\phi^N)$. Experience suggests that ϕ is likely to be of the order of 2 or less, indicating that the sheer computational complexity of the approach may be high but, conceivably, attainable.

This analysis ignores the interaction with the client. Whilst such interaction may result in the removal of one or more redundant relationships, the more significant issue is that the number of interactions with the client could, itself, be huge. Even a model containing no redundant relationships may contain several which *could* be, if the semantics were ignored. Each potential redundancy requires an interaction with the client for the distinct semantics to be confirmed. Empirical studies of the scale of this problem will be explored as the next phase of this research.

A related issue is the order in which potential redundancies might be tested. The algorithm detects cycles in order of increasing length, and removal of any redundancies thus exposed can eliminate longer cycles before they are even detected.

Further, adoption of a filter such as (7) could restrict the search to potentially redundant 1:many relationships. Not only would this reduce the effective complexity of the search, but clarification would no longer be sought for a large number of "implied" unconstrained (many to many) relationships. The matrix algorithm is particularly suited to successive relaxation of such a filter, and, again, empirical studies will be undertaken with the implemented algorithm.

Empirical studies will be required also to establish the effectiveness of asking the client - albeit working with an analyst - to decide whether or not a path carries the same semantics as a single relationship. The comprehension difficulties that trigger the inclusion of a redundant relationship, rather than relying on its implication by a path, may make it difficult to decide on the equivalence of the two sets of semantics.

Although there is a tacit assumption in Section 5 that there will be only a single relationship in the ER model between any pair of entities, it is clear that a simple extension of the matrix representation could accommodate reflexive or multiple relationships. Unfortunately, this would also complicate the termination condition for the algorithm. Specifically, it may not be possible to justify restricting the search to simple cycles; indeed, it is possible to envisage examples, such as that in Figure 8, in which the reflexive "supervizes" relationship might be implied by the fact that one employee manages a project on which other employees work.

Hence, the algorithm presented in this paper, whilst sound, is not complete, in that it is possible to conceive ER models containing specific types of redundancy, involving loops and parallel relationships, that might not be detected. These issues are being explored currently, and extensions to the algorithm are being considered.

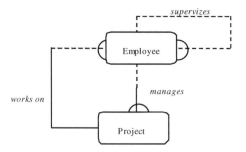

Fig. 5. An ER model in which a relationship may be implied by a cycle

A further issue is the identification of structures that misrepresent higher-order relationships. The best known of these is the cyclic many:many:many structure. Typically, such structures are "resolved" either by the introduction of an entity to represent a ternary relationship between the three entities, or by recognising the join dependencies between relations representing the explicit relationships. In the latter case, the schema violates 5th normal form. The algorithm presented here could draw attention to the cyclic structure, but can suggest no appropriate resolution until the detection of such cliches has been incorporated.

This investigation has been pursued in the context of Entity Relationship models, since the underlying semantics of the notation are well understood. Once the problems identified in this section have been resolved, it should be trivial to extend the approach to other graphical notations - such as Class Diagrams in UML.

7. Conclusions

The issue of redundant relationships within Entity Relationship models has been identified as one that is significant for model quality. A technique has been presented for locating relationships whose set theoretic signature is implied by some alternative path within the model. This alone is insufficient for the relationships in question to be redundant; it is necessary for the semantics also to be equivalent, and determining this always requires interaction with the client for whom the model has been constructed.

Although the algorithm is sound, it is both computationally expensive and incomplete for certain special cases. This suggests a number of issues, including the most important question of usability, which are currently receiving attention.

Nevertheless, the technique as presented in this paper seems already to be a useful tool for improving the quality of Entity Relationship models, and which should reduce the requirement for normalization of generated relational schemas. Furthermore, the approach should generalise to more complex notations.

References

1. Teorey, T.J., Yang, D., Fry, J.P.: A logical design methodology for relational databases using the extended entity-relationship model. ACM Computing Surveys **18**(2) (1986) 197 - 222

2. Bowers, D.S.: From Data to Database. Van Nostrand Reinhold, London (1987), 164 - 179

3. Dullea, J., Song, I-Y.: An Analysis of Cardinality Constraints in Redundant Relationships, Proc. CIKM 97 (1997) 270-277

4. Rosenthal, A., Reiner, D.:Tools and Transformations - Rigorous and Otherwise - for Practical Database Design, ACM Transactions on Database Systems **19** (2) (1994) 167 - 211

5. Lenzerini, M., Nobili, P.: On the Satisfiability of Dependency Constraints in Entity-Relationship Schemata, Proc. 13th International Conference on Very Large Databases, Brighton (1987), Morgan Kaufmann, 147-154

6. Hartmann, S.: On the Consistency of Int-cardinality Constraints, Proc. ER-98, 17th International Conference on Conceptual Modelling, Singapore (1998), 150-163

7. Shanks, G., Darke, P.: Understanding corporate data models, Information & Management **35**, (1999) 19-30

8. Batra, D., Antony, S. R.: Novice errors in conceptual database design, European Journal of Information Systems, **3**(1) (1994) 57-69

9. Atkins, C., Patrick, J.: NaLER: A natural language method for interpreting E-R models, Proc. International Conference Software Engineering: Education and Practice, (1998) 2-9

10. Hay, D.C.: Making data models readable, Information Systems Management, **15**(1), (1998) 21-33

11. Kesh, S.: Evaluating the quality of entity relationship models, Information & Software Technology, **37**(12) (1995) 681-689

12. Moody, D.L..: Metrics for evaluating the quality of entity relationship models, Proc. ER-98, 17th International Conference on Conceptual Modelling, Singapore (1998), 211-225

13. Moody, D.L., Shanks, G.G., and Darke, P, Improving the quality of entity-relationship models – experience in research and practice, Proc. ER-98, 17th International Conference on Conceptual Modelling, Singapore (1998), 255-276

14. Morris, A., The Key, the Whole Key, and Nothing But..., Application Development Adviser, **2**(4) (1999) 64-67

15. Agrawal, W.D., Bushnell, M.L, Lim, P.: Redundancy Identification Using Transitive Closure, Proc. ATS-96, 5th Asia Test Symposium (1996) 4-9

16. Chang, S.-C., Cheng, D.I., Yeh, C.-W.: Removing multiple redundancies in combinational circuits, IEE Proc. Comput. Digit. Tech. **149**(1) (2002) 1-8

17. Schmolze, J.G., Snyder, W.: Detecting redundancy among production rules using term rewrite semantics, Knowledge Based Systems **12** (1999) 3-11

18. Dar, S., Ramakrishnan, R.: A Performance Study of Transitive Closure Algorithms, Proc. ACM - SIGMOD - 94, (1994) 454-465

19. Agrawal, R., Borgida, A., Jogadish, H.V.: Efficient Management of Transitive Relationships in Large Data and Knowledge Bases, ACM - SIGMOD - 89 (1989) 253 - 262

20. Sridhar, R., Iyengar, S.S.: Efficient parallel Algorithms for Functional Dependency Manipulations, Proc. 2nd International Symposium on Databases in Parallel and Distributed Systems, Dulbin (1990) 126 - 137

21. Ausiello, G., D'Atri, A, Sacca, D.: Graph Algorithms for Functional Dependency Manipulation, Journal of the ACM **30** (4) (1983), 752 - 766

22. Bowers, D, Database Schema Improvement Techniques for CASE Tools, proc. UKAIS 2000 (2000) 266-275

Assessing Object-Oriented Conceptual Models Maintainability

Marcela Genero, José Olivas, Mario Piattini, and Francisco Romero

Department of Computer Science, University of Castilla-La Mancha
Paseo de la Universidad, 4, 13071, Ciudad Real (Spain)
{marcela.genero,joseangel.olivas,mario.piattini}@uclm.es

Abstract. Conceptual modeling has become a key task in the early phases of object oriented (OO) software life cycle. In the development of OO software class diagrams represent the conceptual schema that reflects not only the objects of the application domain but also the behaviour of them. Indeed, class diagrams constitute the backbone of OO software so, their quality has a great impact on the quality of the product which is finally implemented. To assess class diagram quality, it is useful to have quantitative and objective measurement instruments. After having thoroughly reviewed existing OO measures applicable to class diagrams at a high-level design stage, we defined a set of metrics for UML class diagram structural complexity (and internal quality attribute), with the idea that it is related to maintainability of such diagrams. In order to gather empirical evidence that the proposed metrics could be early indicators of class diagrams maintainability, we carried out a controlled experiment. The main goal of this paper is to show each of the steps of the experimental process, and how we have built a prediction model for class diagram maintainability based upon the data collected in the experiment using a novel process, the Fuzzy Prototypical Knowledge Discovery process.

1 Introduction

Conceptual modeling has become a key task in the early phases of OO software life cycle. The proof of this is that modern approaches towards OO system development, like Catalysis [12] and Rational Unified Process [30], includes conceptual modelling as a relevant task. In the development of OO software, class diagrams represent the conceptual schema that reflects not only the objects of the application domain but also the behaviour of them. Indeed, the class diagram is a key early artifact that lays the foundation of all later design and implementation work. Hence, class diagram quality is a crucial issue that must be evaluated (and improved if necessary) in order to obtain quality OO software, which is the main concern of present day software development organisations.

It is in this arena where software measurement plays an important role, because the early availability of metrics contributes to class diagram quality evaluation in an objective way avoiding bias in the quality evaluation process. Moreover, metrics

A. Olivé (Eds.): ER 2003 Ws, LNCS 2784, pp. 288-299, 2003.

provide a valuable and objective insight into specific ways of enhancing each of the software quality characteristics.

Given that maintenance was (and will continue to be) the major resource consumer of the whole software life cycle, maintainability has become one of the software product quality characteristics [20] that software development organisations are more concerned about. However, we are aware that maintainability is an external quality attribute that can only be measured late in the OO software life cycle. Therefore, it is necessary to have early indicators of such qualities based, for example, on the structural properties of class diagrams [4].

After a thorough review of some of the existing OO measures, applicable to class diagrams at conceptual level [6, 10, 22, 23] we have proposed [16, 18] a set of UML class diagram structural complexity measures brought on by the use of UML relationships, such as associations, generalizations, aggregations and dependencies (see table 1).

Table 1. Metrics for UML class diagram structural complexity

Metric name	Metric definition
Number of Classes (NC)	The total number of classes.
Number of Attributes (NA)	The total number of attributes.
Number of Methods (NM)	The total number of methods .
Number of Associations (NAssoc)	The total number of associations.
Number of Aggregation (NAgg)	The total number of aggregation relationships within a class diagram (each whole-part pair in an aggregation relationship).
Number of Dependencies (NDep)	The total number of dependency relationships.
Number of Generalisations (NGen)	The total number of generalisation relationships within a class diagram (each parent-child pair in a generalisation relationship).
Number of Aggregations hierarchies (NAggH)	The total number of aggregation hierarchies (whole-part structures) within a class diagram.
Number of Generalisations hierarchies (NGenH)	The total number of generalisation hierarchies within a class diagram.
Maximum DIT	It is the maximum of the DIT (Depth of Inheritance Tree) values obtained for each class of the class diagram. The DIT value for a class within a generalisation hierarchy is the longest path from the class to the root of the hierarchy.
Maximum Hagg	It is the maximum of the HAgg values obtained for each class of the class diagram. The HAgg value for a class within an aggregation hierarchy is the longest path from the class to the leaves.

However, the proposal of metrics is of no value if their practical use is not demonstrated empirically, either by means of case studies taken from real projects or by controlled experiments. Empirical validation is crucial for the success of any software measurement project [2, 15, 21, 31]. Therefore, our main motivation is to investigate, through experimentation, if the metrics we proposed for UML class diagram structural complexity (internal quality attribute) are related to class diagram maintainability (external quality attribute). If such a relationship exists and is confirmed by empirical studies, we will have really obtained early indicators of class diagram maintainability. These indicators will allow OO software designers to take better decisions early in the OO software development life cycle, thus contributing to the development of better quality OO software.

We performed a previous controlled experiment [17], pursuing a similar objective. In it, as in this one, the independent variable is the UML class diagram structural complexity. In the previous experiment the dependent variables were three maintainability sub-characteristics (understandability, analysability and modifiability) measured by means of user ratings on a scale composed of seven linguistic labels. Even though the results obtained in the previous experiment reflect that the metrics we proposed were highly related to class diagram maintainability, we are aware that the way we choose to measure the dependent variable was subjective and relies solely on judgment of the users, which may have biased the results. Therefore, we decided to carry out another experiment measuring the dependent variable in a more objective way. In the experiment we present in this paper, the dependent variable is the maintainability of the class diagrams measured by the time spent in modification tasks, called maintenance time. Maintenance time is the time taken to comprehend the class diagram, analyse the required changes and to implement them.

The data collected in the present experiment was analysed using an extension of the original Knowledge Discovery in Databases (KDD) [14]: the Fuzzy Prototypical Knowledge Discovery (FPKD) [25, 26] that consists in the search for fuzzy prototypes [34] that characterise the maintainability of a class diagram. These prototypes lay the foundation of the prediction model that will lead us to predict class diagram maintainability.

This paper is organised as follows: In section 2 we describe the controlled experiment we have carried out in order to evaluate if there is empirical evidence that UML class diagram structural complexity metrics are correlated with maintenance time. In section 3 we use the data collected in the experiment to build prototypes, that characterises UML class diagram maintainability and to show how we use these prototypes to predict UML class diagram maintainability early in the OO software development life cycle. Finally in section 4, we present some concluding remarks and future trends in metrics for OO models.

2   Empirical Validation of the Proposed Metrics through a Controlled Experiment

In this section we describe an experiment we have carried out to empirically validate the proposed measures as early maintainability indicators. We have followed some suggestions provided in [4, 28] and [32] on how to perform controlled experiments and have used (with only minor changes) the format proposed in [32] to describe it.

Using the GQM template [1], for goal definition, the experiment goal is defined as follows:

Analyse	*UML class diagram structural complexity metrics*
For the purpose of	*Evaluating*
With respect to	*their capability of being used as class diagram maintainability indicators*
From the point of view of	*OO software designers*
In the context of	*Undergraduate Computer Science students and professors of the area of Software Engineering at the Department of Computer Science in the University of Castilla-La Mancha*

The subjects were ten professres and twenty students enrolled in the final-year of Computer Science at the Department of Computer Science in the University of Castilla-La Mancha in Spain. The subjects were chosen for convenience, i.e., they have experience in the design of OO Software using UML.

The independent variable is the UML class diagram structural complexity. The dependent variable is UML class diagram maintainability.

The objects were UML class diagrams (all the expeimental material is published on our web site http:\\alarcos.inf-cr.uclm.es). The independent variable was measured by the metrics (NC, NA, NM, NAssoc, NAgg, NDep, NGen, NAggH, NGenH, MaxHAgg, MaxDIT). The dependent variable was measured by the time the subjects spent carrying out the tasks required in the experiment. We called this time "maintenance time". Maintenance time comprise the time to comprehend the class diagram, to analyse the required changes and to implement them. Our assumption here is that, for the same modification task, the faster a class diagram can be modified, the easier it is to maintain.

We wish to test the following hypotheses:

- Null hypothesis, H_0: There is no significant correlation between structural complexity metrics (NC, NA, NM, NAssoc, NAgg, NDep, NGen, NAggH, NGenH, MaxHAgg, MaxDIT) and maintenance time.
- Alternative hypothesis, H_1 : There is significant correlation between structural complexity metrics (NC, NA, NM, NAssoc, NAgg, NDep, NGen, NAggH, NGenH, MaxHAgg, MaxDIT) and maintenance time.

We selected a within-subject design experiment, i.e., all the tests (experimental tasks) had to be solved by each of the subjects. The subjects were given the tests in different order.

At the time the experiments were carried out, the subjects had taken two courses of Software Engineering. In these courses they learnt how to design OO software using UML. The subjects were given an intensive training session before the experiment took place. The material we gave to the subjects, consisted of a guide explaining UML notation and nine UML class diagrams of different application domains, that were easy enough to be understood by each of the subjects. The diagrams have different structural complexity, covering a broad range of metric values.

Each diagram had an enclosed test that included a brief description of what the diagram represented and two new requirements for the class diagram. Each subject had to modify the class diagrams according to the new requirements and to specify the start and end time. The difference between the two is what we call maintenance time (expressed in minutes and seconds). The modifications to each class diagram were similar, including adding, updating and deleting attributes, methods, classes, associations, etc.

The subjects were given all the materials described in the previous paragraph. We explained how to do the tests. We allowed one week to carry out the experiment, i.e., each subject had to do the test alone, and could use unlimited time to solve it.

We collected all the data including the modified class diagrams with the maintenance time obtained from the responses of the tests and the metrics values automatically calculated by means of a metric tool we designed.

Once the data was collected, we controlled if the tests were complete and if the modifications had been done correctly. We discarded the tests of seven subjects, which included a required modification that was done incorrectly. Therefore, we took into account the responses of 23 subjects.

2.1   Analysis and Interpretation

We had the metric values calculated for each class diagram (see table 5), and we calculated the mean of the maintenance time. So this is the data we want to analyse to test the hypotheses stated above. We applied the Kolmogrov-Smirnov test to ascertain if the distribution of the data collected was normal. As the data were non-normal we decided to use a non-parametric test like Spearman's correlation coefficient, with a level of significance $\alpha = 0.05$, correlating each of the metrics separately with maintenance time (see table 2).

Table 2. Spearman´s correlation coefficients between metrics and maintenance time

Metrics	Spearman´correlation coefficients
NC	0.941 p=0
NA	0.803 p=0.009
NM	0.795 p=0.01
NAssoc	0.671 p=0.006
NAgg	0.667 p=0.049
NDep	0.411 p=0.272
NGen	0.728 p=0.04
NAggH	0.759 p=0.018
NGenH	0.719 p=0.029
MaxHAgg	0.840 p=0.005
MaxDIT	0.669 p=0.04

For a sample size of 9 (mean values for each diagram) and $\alpha = 0.05$, the Spearman cutoff for accepting H_0 is 0.66 [5, 11]. Because the computed Spearman's correlation coefficients (see table 6) for all the metrics, except for NDep, are above the cutoff, and the p-value $< 0,05$, the null hypothesis H_0, is rejected . Hence, we can conclude that there is a significant correlation between all the metrics (except NDep) and the maintenance time. So, NDep is the only one that has a no correlation, but this could be explained by the fact that in most of the selected diagrams NDep took the value 0. So in future experiments we have to select diagrams with more representative NDep metric values.

2.2   Validity Evaluation

We will discuss the various issues that threaten the validity of the empirical study and how we attempted to alleviate them:

- **Threats to conclusion validity.** The conclusion validity defines the extent to which conclusions are statistically valid. The only issue that could affect the statistical validity of this study is the size of the sample data (243 values, 9 diagrams and 23 subjects). We are aware of this, so we will consider the results of the experiment as preliminary findings.
- **Threats to construct validity.** The construct validity is the degree to which the independent and the dependent variables are accurately measured by the measurement instruments used in the study. The dependent variable we used is maintenance time, i.e., the time each subject spent performing the tasks related to the modifications arising from the new requirements, so we consider this variable constructively valid. The construct validity of the measures used for the independent variables is guaranteed by Poels and Dedene´s framework [28] used for their theoretical validation [16].
- **Threats to internal validity.** The internal validity defines the degree of confidence in a cause-effect relationship between factors of interest and the observed results. Seeing the results of the experiment we can conclude that empirical evidence of the existing relationship between the independent and the dependent variables exists. We have tackled different aspects that could threaten the internal validity of the study, such as: differences among subjects, knowledge of the universe of discourse among class diagrams, precision in the time values, learning effects, fatigue effects, persistence effects and subject motivation.
- **Threats to External Validity.** External validity is the degree to which the research results can be generalised to the population under study (UML diagrams used as design artifacts for developing OO software) and to other research settings. The greater the external validity, the more the results of an empirical study can be generalised to actual software engineering practice. Two threats to validity have been identified which limit the ability to apply any such generalisation, and we tried to alleviate them: materials and tasks and subject selection.

3   Building a Prediction Model
for UML Class Diagram Maintainability

In the previous section, we have found, by analysing the empirical data, that the metrics we proposed for measuring the structural complexity of UML class diagram seems to be correlated with the class diagram maintainability (expressed as the maintenance time). This fact leaded us to think about building a prediction model for class diagram maintainability based on metric values. Seeing the encouraging results obtained of the application of the FPKD process for building prediction models applied to different domains [25, 26] we decided to use it for our purpose.

First the FPKD process is followed to find fuzzy prototypes that characterise class diagram maintainability. These prototypes form the foundation of the prediction model that allows us to predict class diagram maintainability. The use of fuzzy schemas allows us to achieve better and more understandable results, concerning patterns and prediction results. Next, we will explain each of the steps we have followed in the FPKD process, an we will also show how to predict class diagram maintainability.

We have taken, as a starting set, a relational database that contains 207 records (with 12 fields, 11 represent metrics values, 1 represents the maintenance time).

We built a unique table with 9 records (one record for each class diagram) and 12 fields (11 metrics and 1 field for the maintenance time). The metric values were calculated measuring each diagram, and the values for the maintenance time were obtained aggregating maintenance time using the mean of time.

In order to detect the relationships between the class diagrams, to obtain those, which consume low, medium or high maintenance time, we have carried out a hierarchical clustering process by Repertory Grids [3]. The set of elements is constituted by the 9 class diagrams and the clustering data are the mean of the maintenance time to accomplish an analysis of clusters on elements, we have built a proximity matrix that represents the different similarities of the elements, a matrix of 9 x 9 elements (the diagrams) that above the diagonal represents the distances between the different diagrams. Converting these values to percentages, a new table is created and the application of Repertory Grids Analysis Algorithm returns a graphic as a final result (see figure 1).

The selected algorithm for data mining process was summarise functions (calculating factors such as medium, minimum and maximum maintenance time). Table 3 shows the parametric definition of the prototypes. These parameters will be modified taking into account the degree of affinity of a new class diagram with the prototypes. With the new modified prototype we will be able to predict the maintainability of a new class diagram.

The prototypes have been represented as fuzzy numbers, which are going to allow us to obtain a degree of membership in the concept. For the sake of simplicity in the model, they have been represented by triangular fuzzy numbers. Therefore, in order to construct the prototypes (triangular fuzzy numbers) we only need to know their centrepoints (centre of the prototype), which are obtained by normalising and aggregating the metric values corresponding to the class diagrams of each of the prototypes.

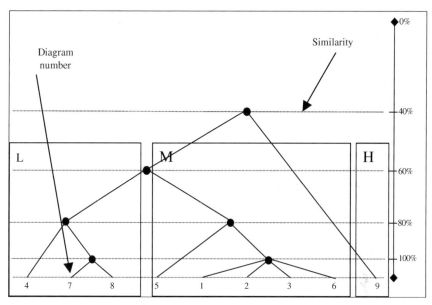

Fig. 1. Clustering results (L: Low time-consuming to maintain, M: Medium time- consuming to maintain, H: High time-consuming to maintain)

Table 3. Definition of the prototypes

	Maintenance Time
High time-consuming to maintain	
Average	7 minutes 10 seconds
Maximum	18 minutes
Minimum	2 minutes
Medium time-consuming to maintain	
Average	4 minutes 40 seconds
Maximum	9 minutes 40 seconds
Minimum	2 minutes
Low time-consuming to maintain	
Average	3 minutes
Maximum	7 minutes
Minimum	1 minute

Hereafter, we will show how we have applied our prediction model. Given a new class diagram, if you want to predict its maintainability there are two possibilities:

1. Evaluate which prototype has more affinity with, the new class diagram and, give as a result the maintenance time of a new class diagram the values taken from table 2. This is very trivial, and there is lose of information.
2. Using Fuzzy Deformable Prototypes [26] we can deform the most similar prototype to a new class diagram, and define the factors for a new situation, using a linear combination with the degrees of membership as coefficients. This solution is better than the previous because it adapts the prototype instead of basing it on fixed values. It also takes into account the degree of membership with other prototypes, without loosing valuable information.

We will show an example of how to deform the fuzzy prototypes found above. Given the metric values corresponding to a new class diagram shown in table 4 and normalising their values, the final average is 0.79.

Table 4. Metric values for a new class diagram

NC	NA	NM	NAssoc	NAgg	NDep	NGen	NAggH	NGenH	MaxDIT
21	30	70	10	6	3	16	2	3	2

The most similar prototype for this new class diagram is "High time-consuming to maintain", with a degree of membership of 0.81. The predicted values for the maintenance time related to the new class diagram is shown in table.

Table 5. Predicted maintanence time for a new class diagram

Average time	Minimum time	Maximum time
6 minutes 15 seconds	2 minutes	15 minutes 10 seconds

4   Conclusions and Future Work

Due to the growing demand of quality OO software, continuous attention to and assessment of class diagrams is necessary to produce quality OO software. As in the OO software development field it is generally accepted that the quality of software is highly dependent on decisions made early in the development, it is necessary to have measurement support for class diagrams early in the development life cycle in order to contribute to the quality of the OO software which is finally delivered.

In this paper we have presented a set of metrics for assessing the structural complexity of UML class diagrams, obtained at early phases of the OO software life cycle.

We have also carried out a controlled experiment, corroborating by means of it that there seems to be high correlation between the proposed metrics and the maintenance time. We have also shown how to predict UML class diagram maintainability based on the metrics values and the time spent on maintenance tasks, by a prediction model built using the FPKD process. Even though the FPKD has been used in other domains such forest fire prediction, medical diagnosis, etc. [25][26], we are aware that it is pending for future work the validation of the model presented in this paper.

Nevertheless, despite the encouraging results obtained more metric validation is needed in order to assess if the presented metrics could be really used as early quality indicators. Also, data of "real projects" on UML class diagram maintainability efforts would be useful, as well as time spent on maintenance tasks in order to predict data that can be highly fruitful to software designers and developers. However the scarcity of such data continues to be a great problem we must fin other ways to tackle validating metrics. Brito e Abreu et al. [7, 8, 9] suggested the necessity of a public repository of measurement experiences, which we think would be a good step towards the success of all the work done on software measurement.

In future work, we will focus our research on measuring other quality factors like those proposed in the ISO 9126 [20], which not only tackles static diagrams, such as class diagrams, but also evaluates dynamic UML diagrams, such as, statechart diagrams, activity diagrams, etc. To our knowledge, little work has been done towards measuring dynamic UML diagrams [13, 29, 33].

Acknowledgements

This research is part of the DOLMEN project supported by CICYT (TIC 2000-1673-C06-06) and the CIPRESES project supported by CICYT (TIC 2000-1362-C02-02).

We want to thanks Geert Poels for his valuable and encouraging comments while we are writing this work.

References

1. Basili, V., Rombach, H.: The TAME project: towards improvement-oriented software environments, IEEE Transactions on Software Engineering, Vol. 14 N° 6 , (1988) 728-738
2. Basili, V., Shull, F., Lanubile, F.: Building Knowledge through Families of Experiments. IEEE Transactions on Software Engineering, Vol. 25 N° 4, (1999) 435-437
3. Bell, R.: Analytic Issues in the Use of Repertory Grid Technique. Advances in Personal Construct Psychology 1, (1990) 25-48
4. Briand, L., Arisholm, S., Counsell, F., Houdek, F., Thévenod-Fosse, P.: Empirical Studies of Object-Oriented Artifacts, Methods, and Processes: State of the Art and Future Directions. Empirical Software Engineering, Vol. 4 N° 4, (1999) 387-404
5. Briand, L., El Emam, K., Morasca, S.: Theoretical and empirical validation of software product measures. Technical Report ISERN-95-03, International Software Engineering Research Network, (1995)
6. Brito e Abreu, F., Carapuça, R.: Object-Oriented Software Engineering: Measuring and controlling the development process. 4th International Conference on Software Quality, Mc Lean, Va, USA, (1994)

298   Marcela Genero et al.

7. Brito e Abreu, F., Henderson-Sellers, B., Piattini, M., Poels, G., Sahraoui, H.: Quantitative Approaches in Object-Oriented Software Engineering. Object-Oriented technology: ECOOP 2001 Workshop Reader, Lecture Notes in Computer Science, Vol. 2323, Springer-Verlag, (2002) 174-183
8. Brito e Abreu, F., Poels, G., Sahraoui, H., Zuse, H.: Quantitative Approaches in Object-Oriented Software Engineering. Object-Oriented technology: ECOOP 2000 Workshop Reader, Lecture Notes in Computer Science, Vol. 1964, Springer-Verlag, (2000) 326-337
9. Brito e Abreu, F., Zuse, H., Sahraoui, H., Melo, W.: Quantitative Approaches in Object-Oriented Software Engineering. Object-Oriented technology: ECOOP'99 Workshop Reader, Lecture Notes in Computer Science, Vol. 1743, Springer-Verlag, (1999) 326-337.
10. Chidamber, S., Kemerer, C.: A Metrics Suite for Object Oriented Design. IEEE Transactions on Software Engineering, Vol. 20 N° 6, (1994) 476-493
11. CUHK- Chinese University of Hong Kong - Department of Obstetrics and Gynaecology – Available: http://department.obg.cuhk.edu.hk/ResearchSupport/Minimum_correlation.asp (Last visited on July 22nd, 2002)
12. D'Souza, D., Wills, A.: Objects, Components and Frameworks with UML: the Catalysis Approach. Addison-Wesley, (1999)
13. Derr, K.: Applying OMT. SIGS Books. Prentice Hall. New York, (1995
14. Fayyad, U., Piatetsky-Shapiro, G., Smyth, P.: The KDD Process for Extracting Useful Knowledge from Volumes of Data. Communications of the ACM, Vol. 39 N° 11, (1996) 27 – 34
15. Fenton, N., Pfleeger, S.: Software Metrics: A Rigorous Approach. 2nd. edition. London, Chapman & Hall, (1997)
16. Genero, M.: Defining and Validating Metrics for Conceptual Models, Ph.D. thesis, University of Castilla-La Mancha, (2002)
17. Genero, M., Olivas, J., Piattini, M., Romero, F.: Using metrics to predict OO information systems maintainability. CAISE 2001, Interlaken, Switzerlarnd, Lecture Notes in Computer Science, Vol. 2068, (2001) 388-401
18. Genero, M., Piattini, M., Calero, C.: Early Measures For UML class diagrams. L'Objet. Vol. 6 N° 4, Hermes Science Publications, (2000) 489-515
19. Henderson-Sellers, B.: Object-Oriented Metrics - Measures of complexity. Prentice-Hall, Upper Saddle River, New Jersey, (1996)
20. ISO/IEC 9126-1.2. Information technology- Software product quality – Part 1: Quality model, (2001)
21. Kitchenham, B., Pflegger, S., Fenton, N.: Towards a Framework for Software Measurement Validation. IEEE Transactions of Software Engineering, Vol. 21 N° 12, (1995) 929-943
22. Lorenz, M., Kidd, J.: Object-Oriented Software Metrics: A Practical Guide. Prentice Hall, Englewood Cliffs, New Jersey, (1994)
23. Marchesi, M.: OOA Metrics for the Unified Modeling Language. Proceedings of the 2nd Euromicro Conference on Software Maintenance and Reengineering, (1998) 67-73
24. Melton, A. (ed.): Software Measurement. International Thomson Computer Press, London, (1996)
25. Olivas, J., Romero, F.: FPKD. Fuzzy Prototypical Knowledge Discovery. Application to Forest Fire Prediction. Proceedings of the SEKE 2000, Knowledge Systems Institute, Chicago, Ill. USA, (2000) 47-54
26. Olivas, J.: Contribution to the Experimental Study of the Prediction based on Fuzzy Deformable Categories, PhD Thesis, University of Castilla-La Mancha, Spain, (2000)
27. Perry, D., Porter, A., Votta, L.: Empirical Studies os Software Engineering: A Roadmap. Future of Software Engineering. Ed:Anthony Finkelstein, ACM, (2000) 345-355

28. Poels, G., Dedene, G.: Distance-based software measurement: necessary and sufficient properties for software measures, Information and Software Technology, Vol. 42 Nº 1, (2000) 35-46
29. Poels, G., Dedene, G.: Measures for Assessing Dynamic Complexity Aspects of Object-Oriented Conceptual Schemes. 19th International Conference on Conceptual Modeling (ER 2000), Salt Lake City, Lecture Notes in Computer Science, 1920, Springer-Verlag, (2000) 499-512
30. Rational Software: Object Oriented Analysis and Design, Student Manual. http://www.rational.com/, (1998)
31. Schneidewind, N.: Methodology For Validating Software Metrics. IEEE Transactions of Software Engineering, Vol. 18 Nº 5, (1992) 410-422
32. Wohlin, C., Runeson, P., Höst, M., Ohlson, M., Regnell, B., Wesslén, A.: Experimentation in Software Engineering: An Introduction, Kluwer Academic Publishers. (2000)
33. Yacoub, S., Ammar, H., Robinson, T. (1998).: Dynamic Metrics for Object Oriented Designs. Proceedings of the Sixth IEEE International Symposium on Software Metrics
34. Zadeh, L.: A note on prototype set theory and fuzzy sets. Cognition 12, (1982) 291- 297

Validation of UML Classes through Animation[*]

Patricio Letelier[1] and Pedro Sánchez[2]

[1]Department of Information Systems and Computation
Technical University of Valencia, Valencia, Spain
letelier@dsic.upv.es

[2] Department of Information Technologies and Communications
Technical University of Cartagena, Cartagena, Spain
pedro.sanchez@upct.es

Abstract. Animation is the validation of formal software specifications by means of automatically generated prototypes. Animation is an effective way of validating a specification against the stakeholder requirements. *OASIS* is a formal language for conceptual modeling. We have carried out experiments animating *OASIS* specifications. In this work we take advantage of our experience animating *OASIS* specifications to provide animation support for UML classes. We illustrate that it is possible to use *OASIS* as a formal semantic framework for UML specifications. Obviously, *OASIS* does not cover as many model aspects as UML. We will concentrate on some UML diagrams, particularly in classes modeled in class diagrams to validate them through animation. To explain our approach, we give an example of a bank account and we show its UML model and its corresponding *OASIS* specification. Our aim is to build a module for animation and validation of specifications integrated in a CASE tool. We present a prototype of this module.

1 Introduction

Conceptual models, representing the functional requirements of information systems, are a key factor when linking the problem and solution domains. Building a conceptual model is a discovery process, not only for the analyst but also for the stakeholders. The most suitable strategy in this situation is to build the conceptual model in an iterative and incremental way, through analyst and stakeholder interaction. Conceptual modeling involves four activities: elicitation of requirements, modeling or specification, verification of quality and consistency, and eventually, validation. Formal methods for conceptual modeling provide improvements in soundness and precision for specifications, simplifying their verification. However, when considering elicitation and requirements validation, prototyping techniques are more often used. The purpose is to obtain a prototype exposing the main aspects of the system functionality, those included in the conceptual model. Hence, it is interesting to obtain a combination of

---

[*] This work is supported by CICYT (Project DOLMEN-SIGLO) TIC2000-1673-C06-01.

A. Olivé (Eds.): ER 2003 Ws, LNCS 2784, pp. 300-311, 2003.

both approaches (formal methods and prototyping) to validate the conceptual model, this combination is named animation [8, 12]. Although other aspects such as efficiency, security and user interface design are important to the final quality of the software product we will concentrate on the product functionality.

Regarding the way how the animation should be oriented, scenarios techniques [9] are a suitable way to capture requirements from stakeholders, and to compare the expected behavior of the system with the animation of the conceptual model [10]. Scenarios are concentrated on the most critical aspects of the system establishing the main restrictions of the system. The key point using scenarios is that they are easy to build and to be verified by the stakeholders. From a process perspective at each stage in the conceptual model construction, it would be possible to validate the behavior of the prototype against the expected behavior, established by the set of scenarios. The analysis of these results could lead to modify the conceptual model or the set of scenarios. This cycle continues until stakeholder and analyst reach an agreement regarding the behavior of the conceptual model and the desired set of scenarios.

We are interested in prototypes automatically generated, and we have taken advantage of using a formal framework for specifying the conceptual model. *OASIS* (**O**pen and **A**ctive **S**pecification of **I**nformation **S**ystems) [4] is the formal framework we are using, it is an object-oriented language for conceptual modeling. We have carried out experiments using Object Petri Nets and Concurrent Logic Programming as execution domains for *OASIS* specifications [5, 10, 11].

We recognize that formal methods and languages are not easy to use and they require some previous training. This is the reason why semi-formal techniques for modeling software systems are more accepted. Nowadays UML is without discussion the most popular notation for object-oriented modeling. UML is neither perfect nor a radical innovation, but it represents a useful consensus regarding the previous approaches (and the corresponding gurus). UML includes notation support to model many aspects of a software system. However, as far as the conceptual model is concerned, we are interested in the class diagrams, the state diagrams and the activity diagrams. In addition, considering the interest in specifying scenarios, UML interaction diagrams (sequence diagram and collaboration diagram) are very suitable.

The aim of this work is to illustrate how UML classes can be validated by animation. We show a preliminary version of an animation environment. This work is based on our previous experience animating *OASIS* specifications. We establish the basic correspondences between UML classes and *OASIS* classes, in this way we use UML for modeling and *OASIS* as a semantic animation framework.

This work is organized in seven sections. After this introduction, next section presents the example of a bank, which we will use throughout the paper. Section three gives a brief introduction to *OASIS* and illustrates the basic correspondences between UML and *OASIS* classes using the bank example. In section four we summarize the execution model of *OASIS*. Section five presents a graphical environment to validate UML classes through animation. In section six we comment some related works and tools supporting animation or simulation of software models. Eventually we present the conclusions of this work.

2 An UML Example

Fig. 1 and 2 show a bank example using a UML class diagram and an activity diagram, respectively. We have used UML comments linked to the class account to include visually the preconditions and semantic of the account operations. The activity diagram is used to model the trigger action occurring each time the condition "times=5 and good_balance=false and rank=0" is satisfied. The attribute times represents the number of operations performed with the account. Thus, when the condition is satisfied the account pays a commission and times is reset. This example will be used throughout the paper.

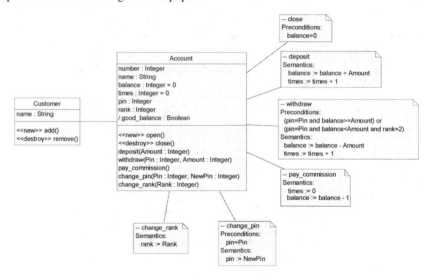

Fig. 1. UML class diagram of our example

3 *OASIS* Semantic for UML Classes

An *OASIS* specification is a presentation of a theory in the used formal system and is expressed as a structured set of class definitions. Classes can be simple or complex. A complex class is defined in terms of other classes (simple or complex). Complex classes are defined by establishing relationships among classes. These relationships can be aggregation or inheritance. A class has a name, one or more identification mechanisms for its instances (objects) and a type or template that is shared by every instance belonging to the class. We present next the basic concepts of *OASIS*.

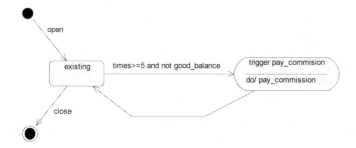

Fig. 2. Activity diagram modeling a trigger based on a condition

Definition 1. Template or type. *A class template is represented by a tuple* ⟨ *Attributes, Events, Formulae, Processes* ⟩ .

Attributes is the alphabet of attributes. For all *att* ∈ *Attributes* exists the function *att*: *sort of names* → *sort of values*. *Events* is the alphabet of events. For all *e* ∈ *Events* it is possible to get $\underline{e} = \theta e$ being θ a basic substitution of the parameters of the event. *Formulae* is a set of formulae that are organized in sections and their underlying formalism depends on the section where they are used. *Processes* is the set of process specifications, classified in protocols and operations.

Definition 2. Service. *A service is either an event or an operation. The former is an instantaneous and atomic service. An operation is a non-atomic service and, in general, has duration.*

Definition 3. Action. *An action is a tuple* ⟨ *Client, Server, Service* ⟩. *It represents the action in the client object, associated to requiring the service, as well as the action in the server object, associated to providing the service.*

For each class we assume the implicit existence of *A*, a set of actions obtained from the services that objects in the class can request (clients) or provide (servers). For all *a* ∈ *A* it is possible to obtain $\underline{a} = \theta a$, being θ a basic substitution of client, server and service.

Definition 4. Object state. *The object state is a set of evaluated attributes. It is expressed by well-formed formulae in First Order Logic.*

Definition 5. Step. *A step is a set of actions occurring simultaneously in the life of an object.*

Definition 6. Object life or trace. *The life or trace of life of an object is a finite prefix of object steps.*

To express the object behavior *OASIS* uses a variant of Dynamic Logic that includes Deontic Logic operators [7]. The basic deontic operators are represented in the following formulae:

$\psi \rightarrow [a]\, \phi$ "in states where ψ is satisfied, immediately after the a occurrence, ϕ must be satisfied"

$\psi \rightarrow [a]\, false$ "the occurrence of a is forbidden in states where ψ is satisfied"

$\psi \rightarrow [\overline{a}]\, false$ "the occurrence of a is obligatory in states where ψ is satisfied"

where ψ is a well-formed formula that characterizes the state of an object when the action a occurs and $\overline{a}$ represents the non-occurrence of the action a (i.e. only other actions different from a could occur). Furthermore, there is no state satisfying the atom *false*. This represents a state of system violation. Thus, one action is forbidden if its occurrence leads the system towards a violation state, and one action is obligatory if its non-occurrence leads the system towards a violation state. The *OASIS Formulae* and *Processes* are mapped to the formulae previously presented.

Next we present the corresponding *OASIS* representation for our example.

```
conceptual schema banking_system
  class account
  identification
    number:(number);
  constant attributes
    number:nat;
    name:string;
  variable attributes
    balance:nat(0);
    times:nat(0);
    pin:nat(0);
    rank:nat(0);
  derived attributes
    good_balance:bool;
  derivations
    good_balance:={balance=100};
  events
    open new;
    close destroy;
    deposit(Amount:nat);
    withdraw(Pin:nat,Amount:nat);
    pay_commission;
    change_pin(Pin:nat,NewPin:nat);
    change_rank(Rank:nat);
  valuations
    [deposit(Amount)] balance:=balance+Amount,times:=times+1;
    [withdraw(Pin,Amount)] balance:=balance-Amount,
                           times:=times+1;
    [self:pay_commission] balance:=balance-1,  times:=0;
    [change_pin(Pin,NewPin)] pin:=NewPin;
    [change_rank(Rank)] rank:=Rank;
  preconditions
    withdraw(Pin,Amount) if (pin=Pin and balance=Amount) or
```

```
                    (pin=Pin and balanceAmount and rank=2);
      change_pin(Pin,NewPin) if (pin=Pin);
      close if (balance=0);
    triggers
      pay_commission when
         (times=5 and good_balance=false and rank=0);
    end class

    class customer
    identification
      name:(name);
    constant attributes
      name:string;
    events
      add new;
      remove destroy;
    end class

    interface customer(someone) with account(someone)
      services(deposit,withdraw,change_pin);
    end interface
end conceptual schema
```

customer objects have an interface with account objects enabling to require actions associated with the visible events.

4 The *OASIS* Execution Model

Our execution model is an abstract animator for formulae of obligation, permission and change of state associated to an object. Next we describe briefly the concepts included in the *OASIS* execution model.

The sequence of steps in the life of an object is sorted by time. We assume there is a "clock object" sending special actions - called ticks - to every object in the system. The received ticks by an object are correlative with natural numbers, t_1, t_2, etc. Hence, being i and j natural numbers then $i < j \Leftrightarrow t_i < t_j$.

Definition 7. Mailbox. *A mailbox is the set of actions that can be included in a step executed by one object at one tick. The mailbox at instant t_i is denoted by $Mbox_i$.*

Definition 8. State of an object at tick. *The state of an object at tick is denoted by $State_i$ and represents the object's state in the interval $[t_i, t_{i+1})$. That is, between t_i (included) and t_{i+1} the state is considered constant.*

The processing of the actions inside the mailbox implies their classification. Next we present all possible actions that might be present in a mailbox. They are characterized as subsets of $Mbox_i$ (that is at instant t_i).

— **Obligated actions**: these are actions associated to obligated service requests (which have as a client the object itself) and **have to** occur. The set of obligated actions is denoted by $O\,Exec_i$. These actions are determined by obligation formulae, that is, their form is: $\psi \rightarrow [\overline{a}]\,false$.

— **Non-obligated actions**: these are actions corresponding to services requested by other objects (or itself) which could be provided or not depending on prohibitions established over those actions and verified in $State_i$. The set of non-obligated actions is denoted by $\overline{O}\,Exec_i$.

— **Rejected actions**: these are non-obligated actions whose occurrence is prohibited in $State_i$. The set of rejected actions is denoted by $Reject_i$. These actions are determined by prohibition formulae, that is, their form is: $\psi \rightarrow [a]\,false$.

— **Candidate actions**: these are non-obligated actions whose occurrence is permitted in $State_i$. The set of candidate actions is denoted by $Cand_i$.

— **Executed actions**: these are actions forming the step executed at t_i. The set of executed actions is denoted by $Exec_i$. A step is composed by $O\,Exec_i$ joined with a subset of $Cand_i$.

— **Actions in conflict**: These are a subset of $Cand_i$ formed by actions in conflict[1] with some obligated or candidate action just selected. The set of actions in conflict is denoted by $Conf_i$.

A simple criterion is used in order to choose actions from $Cand_i$: when two actions are in conflict, the action which first arrived to the mailbox will be chosen. The actions in conflict $Conf_i$ are copied to the next mailbox ($Mbox_{i+1}$). The object behavior is characterized by an algorithm that manipulates each mailbox (at each tick) obtaining the subsets previously defined and producing the change of the object state.

5 A Graphical Animation Environment

In the *OASIS* context, the system behavior is determined by the behavior of its objects. An object behavior can be observed by analyzing the actions occurred and the states reached by the object. In this sense, the animation of an *OASIS* specification allows examining actions and states of the objects. Next we present the animation module that would be integrated in a CASE tool environment. Thus it is supposed that using the CASE facilities the conceptual model would be built. Our module takes as an input the representation of the conceptual model or a part of it. We are now achieving this by reading from a file simulating this input. The first step is to generate a prototype according to the specification. This task is carried out by a translator from the input representation to KL1[2] (a concurrent logic programming language). Then the prototype is started and the user interface begins to interact with the prototype, showing graphically the objects, its states and occurred actions. In the prototypes generated by our implementation each object has its own thread.

---

[1] Two actions are in conflict if they could change the value of a non-disjoint set of attributes.
[2] http://www.klic.org/ .

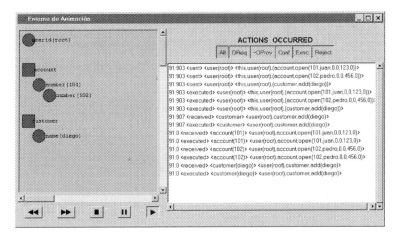

Fig. 3. Animation session after creating three object instances

Fig. 3 shows an animation session. The object society is drawn in the upper left corner, on the right the traces of actions of an object (or object group) are listed. At the beginning one metaobject appears for each class of the model. Furthermore, there is always by default a `root` object that will allow activating the events that still do not have an explicit client in the specification. Other objects only have access to the services established by the interfaces in which they participate as clients. This represents the association between classes in the UML class diagram.

In the object society area objects can be selected, one can select one object, an object group or all the objects (clicking in the background of this area. According to the selected objects, on the right, the trace (list of actions) can be filtered according the kind of actions defined ($O\,Exec_i$, $\overline{O}\,Exec_i$, $Conf_i$, $Exec_i$ and $Rejected_i$) and occurred until the last meaningful clock tick (when the last change of state occurred). Buttons *play*, *pause*, *stop*, *forward* and *review* are provided in order to control the session of animation. When the animation is paused it is possible to explore the traces of actions and states at previous instants.

When only one object is selected the windows in Fig. 4 appear. One of them shows the current state of the object. The other allows the analyst to introduce actions on behalf of the selected object. This window shows all the classes, objects and services that are accessible for the selected object. In this way the analyst can activate some object operation that still are without a specified client object. In this window the analyst can prepare several actions and trigger them at the same time.

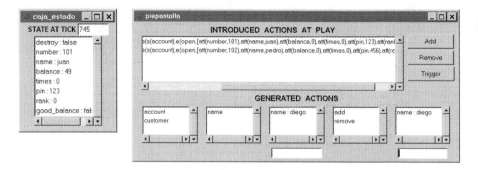

Fig. 4. Current state of `account(101)` and window to introduce actions

In the window on the right in Fig. 4 the creation of two instances of `account` class (numbers `101` and `102`) and one instance of `customer` class ("diego") are being created. After triggering these actions and clicking in the background of the object society area the we would obtain the window of Fig. 3.

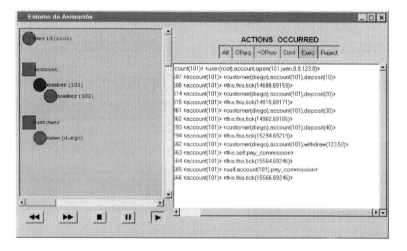

Fig. 5. Executed actions by `account(101)` object

Next, we are going to establish a scenario in which a customer object performs four deposits and one withdraw in an account. The requested operations are: `deposit(10)`, `deposit(20)`, `deposit(30)`, `deposit(40)` and `withdraw(50)`. Selecting the object `customer(diego)` we would reach a window similar to the one on the right in Fig. 4. In this window we introduce the actions corresponding to request the operations we want to trigger on behalf of the object `customer(diego)`. These five actions will be sent to the object `account(101)`. If after this we select the object `account(101)` and press the button *Exec*, we will obtain a window like the one in Fig. 5 showing the list of actions executed in this object. Furthermore, because only one object is selected, the window showing the state of the object will also appear (see window on the right in Fig. 4).

6 Related Works

We have studied the documentation available of 34 CASE tools[3] looking for validation through animation. Few of them said explicitly that they support specific facilities for animation. Some common characteristics of these CASE tools are:

- They are oriented to the construction of embedded or real-time systems, where validation is frequently a critical aspect.
- Even they use UML as visual modeling language, they have a more formal language to support precise verification and animation. For instance, some CASE tool use SDL (Specification Description Language), a language to specify systems principally in telecommunication applications.

Although it does not intent to give a complete list, the following CASE tools mention that they have animation facilities: Telelogic Tau SDL, System Architect, SILDEX v.5, SoftModeler 3.0, RationalRose RealTime, Raphsody, Artisan and iUML.

Most research and technology about code generation in CASE tools are concerned with obtaining the final product from models. But, even if they have an acceptable program from this automated generation, the execution of the final product is not the best way of exploring exhaustively the behavior of the system. In addition, in this case the executable code is normally obtained later in the development process, when the specification is complete enough, not at the same time as we are building and validating the conceptual model. This is explained by the fact that most of these works are not based on a formal approach and in this situation animation is difficult.

Gibson in [2] exposes reasons why a validation phase is necessary in the requirements engineering. He points out the importance of using formal methods in this activity. Furthermore, a basic incremental and iterative process is described. In this line of work, Mokhtari et al [8] show how temporal logic is a suitable formalism for automated animation of specifications. It is also pointed out the interest in using different notations, integrating graphical notations (with or without formal basis) with formal notations, taking advantage of both.

Regarding the utilization of scenario techniques in order to validate requirements specifications, some works in this research line are: Haumer et al in [3], Maiden in [6] and Filippidou et al in [1].

---

[3] They were selected from
http://www.objectsbydesign.com/tools/umltools_byPrice.html.

7 Conclusions

Validation of conceptual models is a difficult task. We are dealing with informal requirements used as input to build a software specification. This is a discovery process and the communication between stakeholders and requirements engineers is crucial. In order to help this activity we have presented in this work an approach for validating conceptual model based on animation. In our approach the stakeholders express their requirements as scenarios, the analyst builds the conceptual model and by means of an animation environment a prototype is generated automatically. Thus regarding the stakeholders scenarios and using the animation environment, such a scenarios can be executed in order to detect and study the possible differences.

The current state of our module for animation only deals with the computed behavior obtained as a result of the execution of the prototype. Another important part of the environment should be considered in order to allow introducing the expected behavior of the system. Using a scenario notation, which would correspond to interaction diagrams of UML, the expected behavior could be specified, maybe taking advantage of those diagrams provided by the CASE tool in which the animation would be integrated. Then, having the expected and computed behavior these could be compared automatically, helping in the validation activity. The prototype environment for animation we have showed in this paper has been developed using the Tcl/Tk script language[4] for user interfaces and KL1 a concurrent logic programing language for the conceptual model prototype. In order to make more portable our approach and to integrate it in a CASE tool we are migrating our environment to Java language and including it as a module in the Together CASE tool[5].

There is an initiative to obtain the execution of UML models, and it has been included as a part of the standard UML specification with the name of Action Semantics[6]. We are studying the relationship between our *OASIS* execution model and the Action Semantics proposal in order to establish the possible correspondences. Initially our execution model is more abstract, we are not interested in generating the final product code in some programming languages what is the intended purpose of UML Action Semantics, but we want only animate the conceptual model, according to the needs of our animation environment.

---

[4] http://www.tcl.tk.
[5] htttp://www.togethersoft.com.
[6] http://www.umlactionsemantics.org.

References

1. Filippidou D., and Loucopoulos P. *Using Scenarios to Validate Requirements in a Plausibility-centered Approach.* In Proceedings of the 9th International Conference on Advanced Information Systems Engineering, CAISE'97, pp 47-60, Barcelona, 1997.
2. Gibson P. *Formal object oriented requirements: Simulation, validation and verification.* In Proceedings: European Simulation Multi-conference, ESM'99 , Warsaw, Poland, June 1999. Also published in: Modelling and Simulation: A tool for the next millennium , vol II. SCS, pp. 103-111.
3. Haumer P., Heymans P., and Pohl K. *An Integration of Scenario-Based Requirements Elicitation and Validation Techniques.* Technical Report CREWS 98-28, Cooperative Requirements Engineering with Scenarios, 1998.
4. Letelier P., Ramos I., Sánchez P., and Pastor O. *OASIS 3.0: Object oriented Conceptual Modeling using a Formal Approach.* Servicio de Publicaciones Universidad Politécnica de Valencia, SPUPV-98.4011, 1998. (in Spanish)
5. Letelier P., Sánchez P., and Ramos I. *Prototyping a requirements specification through an automatically generated concurrent logic program.* First International Workshop on Practical Aspects of Declarative Languages (PADL'99), New Mexico, USA, LNCS 1551, pp. 31-45, 1999.
6. Maiden N.A.M. *Scenarios for Acquiring and Validating Requirements.* Cooperative Requirements Engineering with Scenarios, Technical Report CREWS 98-03, 1998. http://sunsite.informatik.rwth-aachen.de/CREWS/reports98.html
7. Meyer J.-J.Ch. *A different approach to deontic logic: Deontic logic viewed as a variant of dynamic logic.* In Notre Dame Journal of Formal Logic, vol.29, pp. 109-136, 1988.
8. Mokhtari, Y., and Merz, S. *Animating TLA specifications.* In Ganzinger, H.; McAllester, D., and Voronkov, A., eds., 6th International Conference on Logic for Programming and Automated, volume 1705 of LNAI, pp. 92-110. Springer-Verlag, 1999.
9. Rolland C., Ben Achour C., Cauvet C., Ralyté J., Sutcliffe A., Maiden N.A.M., Jarke M., Haumer P., Pohl K., Dubois E., and Heymans P. *A Proposal for a Scenario Classification Framework.* Requirements Engineering Journal, Vol. 3, No. 1, pp.23-47, Springer Verlag, 1998.
10. Sánchez P., Letelier P., and Ramos I. *Validation of Conceptual Models by Animation in a Scenario-based Approach.* Proceedings of OOPSLA 2000 Workshop: Scenario-based round-trip engineering, Tarja Systä (Ed.), Report 20, pp. 32-37, Tampere University of Technology, Software Systems Laboratory.Minneapolis, Minnesota USA. 2000. http://www.cs.uta.fi/~cstasy/oopsla2000/schedu-le.html.
11. Sánchez P, Letelier P., and Ramos I. *Animating Formal Specifications with Inheritance in a DL-based Framework.* Journal of Requirements Engineering, vol. 4(4), pp. 198-209, Springer-Verlag London Limited, 1999.
12. Siddiqi J., Morrey N.A.M., Roast C.R., and Ozcan M.B.*Towards quality requirements via animated formal specifications.* Annals of Software Engineering, n.3, 1997.

Building Quality into Learning Management Systems - An Architecture-Centric Approach

Paris Avgeriou[1], Simos Retalis[2], and Manolis Skordalakis[1]

[1] National Technical University of Athens
Department of Electrical and Computer Engineering
Software Engineering Laboratory, Zografou, Athens, 15780, Greece
{pavger,skordala}@softlab.ntua.gr
[2] Department of Computer Science, University of Cyprus
75 Kallipoleos St., P.O. Box, 20537, CY-1678 Nicosia, Cyprus
retal@softlab.ntua.gr

Abstract. The design and development of contemporary Learning Management Systems (LMS), is largely focused on satisfying functional requirements, rather than quality requirements, thus resulting in inefficient systems of poor software and business quality. In order to remedy this problem there is a research trend into specifying and evaluating software architectures for LMS, since quality attributes in a system depend profoundly on its architecture. This paper presents a case study of appraising the software architecture of a Learning Management through experience-based assessment and the use of an architectural prototype. The framework of the evaluation conducted, concerns run-time, development and business qualities. The paper concludes with the lessons learned from the evaluation, emphasizing on the compromise between them.

Keywords: Software architecture, architectural evaluation, quality attributes, quality requirements, nonfunctional requirements, Learning Management System, Unified Modeling Language, Unified Process.

1 Introduction

Governments, authorities and organizations comprehend the potential of the Internet to transform the educational experience and envisage a knowledge-based future where acquiring and acting on knowledge is the primary operation of all life-long learners. In order to realize this vision, the use of **Learning Management Systems** is being exponentially augmented and broadened to cover all fields of the new economy demands. LMS are software systems that synthesize the functionality of computer-mediated communications software (e-mail, bulletin boards, newsgroups etc.) and on-line methods of delivering courseware (e.g. the WWW) [1].

LMS that are in use today are either commercial products (e.g. WebCT, Blackboard, Intralearn), or customized software systems that serve the instructional purposes of particular organizations. The design and development of LMS though, is largely focused on satisfying certain *functional* requirements, such as the creation and distribution of on-line learning material, the communication and collaboration be-

A. Olivé (Eds.): ER 2003 Ws, LNCS 2784, pp. 312-324, 2003.
© Springer-Verlag Berlin Heidelberg 2003

tween the various actors and so on. On the contrary, the *quality* requirements of LMS are usually overlooked and underestimated. This is due to the fact that even though quality is always of prime interest to the software vendors, they usually give priority to functionality because it is more tangible and a better argument for marketing purposes. In other words, LMS vendors are competing in a race of implementing as much functionality as possible. This is rather obvious in LMS comparative evaluations, where only functionality is evaluated, and quality requirements are completely ignored [2]. This naturally results in inefficient systems of poor software and business quality. Problems that typically occur in these cases are: bad performance which is usually frustrating for the users; poor usability, that adds a cognitive overload to the user; increased cost for purchasing and maintaining the systems; poor customizability and modifiability; limited portability and reusability of learning resources and components; restricted interoperability between LMS.

The question that arises is how can these deficiencies be remedied, i.e. how can the quality attributes be incorporated into the LMS being engineered? Quality attributes in a software system depend profoundly on its architecture and are an immediate outcome of it [3, 4, 5, 6]. Therefore the support for qualities such as performance, security, availability, and usability should be designed *into the architecture* of the system [5, 6, 7]. These principles have only recently been widely accepted and adopted and have lead to a research trend into defining software architectures that support quality attributes in the field of LMS [8, 9, 10].

Similarly, the key idea behind our endeavor is to design for quality. In specific, this paper presents a case study of applying an evaluation framework to the software architecture of a Learning Management System so that quality can be built inherently into the system. The latter is achieved by appraising the quality of the architecture, in each development iteration, and using the feedback to re-design the architecture in order to enhance the quality of the system. For that purpose, certain criteria, as well as heuristics derived from experience, are adopted for assessing the quality attributes of the system under development and indicating, "where the system is at", in terms of quality. A most significant assistant in this evaluation is an architectural prototype of a Learning Management System that has been engineered to implement the architecturally important design decisions. The conclusions inferred from the evaluation process, concern an estimation of each criterion, complemented with appropriate justification. Furthermore, the evaluation interestingly reveals the compromise between the quality requirements, as they are very tightly inter-connected and are either in conflict or in accordance with each other.

The structure of the paper is as follows: Section 2 very briefly demonstrates the proposed architecture and the architectural prototype. Section 3 introduces an evaluation framework with certain methods and quality attributes and moves on to present the results of the quality evaluation. Finally Section 4 contains conclusions, as well as future plans.

2   A Learning Management System Architecture

The proposed architecture is a result of a prototype *architecting process* that is characterized of five key aspects: it is founded on the higher-level architecture of IEEE LTSC Learning Technology Systems Architecture [8]; it uses a prototype

LTSC Learning Technology Systems Architecture [8]; it uses a prototype architecture of a Web-based Instructional System [11] to build a complete business model and refine and constrain the requirements for the Learning Management System; it adopts and customizes a big part of the well-established, software engineering process, the Rational Unified Process (RUP) [7, 12]; it uses the widely-adopted Unified Modeling Language [13, 14] to describe the architecture; and it is fundamentally and inherently component-based. The latter is justified by the fact that great emphasis has been put, not only in providing a pure component-based process, that generates solely components and connectors, but also in identifying the appropriate binding technologies for implementing and integrating the various components. Further study of the architecting process can be found at [15].

2.1   The Architectural Description

The first and most sizeable part of the architectural description is the views of the 5 models dictated by the RUP. Due to lack of space, it is not practical to illustrate even a small representative sample of the numerous diagrams produced in the 5 models. A rather extensive description of the architectural description can be found at [16]. Instead we will only provide the first-level decomposition of the system, by specifying the coarse-grained discrete subsystems in the design model. The decomposition is combined with the enforcement of the "Layered Systems" architecture pattern [17, 18, 19], which helps organize the subsystems hierarchically into layers, in the sense that subsystems in one layer can only reference subsystems on the same level or below. The RUP utilizes the aforementioned architectural pattern by defining four layers in order to organize the subsystems in the design model.

The proposed layered architecture is depicted in Figure 1, which, besides identifying all first-level subsystems and organizing them into layers, also defines dependencies between them, which are realized through well-specified interfaces. The plethora of dependencies between the different sub-systems is indicative of the complexity of LMS. The architectural description continues to decompose each one of these subsystems into smaller subsystem until it reaches the 'tree leaves', i.e. individual classes. Of course, in every subsystem identified, we also design its required and provided interfaces, as well as interaction diagrams that depict the run-time behavior of that subsystem.

Additional issues of the architecture description, such as the legacy systems, the commercial software, the architectural patterns to be used etc. are also quite important for the evaluation to follow and are outlined as following. In the proposed architecture there are a few legacy systems, such as some communication components and some courseware delivery components, but fortunately they were all written in the Java programming language, and thus were relatively easy to integrate into the new system. As far as the commercial systems, we have adopted several of them such as the mySQL RDBMS [   ] and the Resin Web Server and Servlets engine [   ] etc. The architectural patterns that have been used, as seen in the catalogues composed in [17, 18, 19] include: the *layered* style as aforementioned; the *Client-Server* style has been used extensively, especially in the communication management components; the *Model-View-Controller* style in the GUI design, which is inherent in all Java Swing UI components; the *blackboard* style in the mechanisms that access the database in various ways; the *Virtual Machine* and the *object-oriented* style which are both a result of the implementation in Java; the *event systems* style for the notification of GUI components about the change of state of persistent objects.

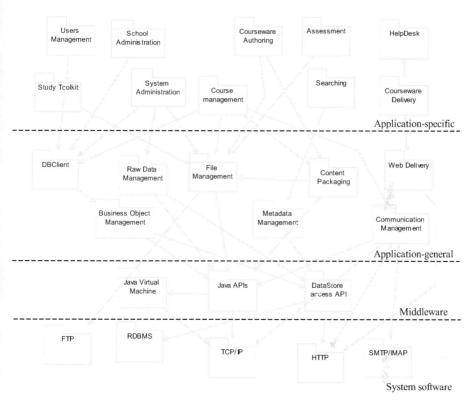

Fig. 1. The layered, component-based architecture of a Learning Management System

2.2   The Architectural Prototype

An architecture is a visual, holistic view of the system, but it is only an abstraction. In order to evaluate the architecture in terms of the quality attributes it promotes, we must build a significant part of it. Therefore, the software architecture must be accompanied with an **architectural prototype** that implements the most important design decisions sufficiently to validate them - that is to test and measure them [3, 6, 12]. The architectural prototype is the most important artifact associated with the architecture itself, which illustrates the architectural decisions and help us evolve and stabilize the architecture.

Therefore, in order to assess and validate the proposed architecture, a prototype was engineered, named "Athena" that implements the main architectural elements. Our choice between Java and Microsoft platforms was the former because it is an open technology, rather than proprietary, and based on a Virtual Machine, thus promoting portability. The specific technologies used are applets, servlets, Java Beans, Enterprise Java Beans, Java Server Pages, as well as the JFC/Swing, RMI, JDBC, 2D Graphics, JMF and JAF Java APIs. The eXtensible Markup Language (XML) was used as the default language for the representation of data that were not stored in the database. About 75% of the total number of components have been implemented or acquired and put into operation, even though some of them do not offer the complete functionality prescribed in the system design.

Finally there was an attempt on adopting international standards within the various components in order to promote interoperability of LMS. For that purpose we have developed the metadata management component conforming to the IEEE LTSC Learning Object Metadata working standard [20] and the assessment component in order to adopt the IMS Question and Testing Interoperability Standard [21].

3   Evaluating the Architecture for Quality

3.1   Theoretical Underpinnings

Software Architectures cannot be classified as either inherently good or bad; instead they are either more or less appropriate to achieve some declared objectives. Therefore architectures can be evaluated according to specific criteria and are designed to fulfill certain quality attributes [3, 6, 19]. It is noted that no quality can be maximized in a system without sacrificing some other quality or qualities, instead there is always a trade-off while choosing on supporting the different quality attributes [3, 6, 19].

The question is how to evaluate the quality attributes of architectures since they are not tangible products but abstract designs that came from the minds of architects. One solution would be to measure the qualities after the system is built but there is an obvious disadvantage in that: it usually takes such an amount of resources to re-engineer the system in order to better support certain qualities, that it is unrealistic to perform [3]. Therefore, since it is too expensive to fix up a system when it is completed, we need to find a way to evaluate the qualities of the system before it is constructed.

The answer to this problem is the *assessment techniques* that have been especially created for the purpose of evaluating the quality attributes of architectures *before* they are implemented into real systems. Therefore these techniques do not estimate the qualities of the actual system, but rather measure the potential of the architecture to fulfill the required quality attributes. For that purpose, in [19] they propose the method of architecture reviews, as well as the Software Architecture Analysis Method (SAAM), which is better demonstrated in [22]. In [23] the Architectural Tradeoff Analysis Method (ATAM) studies the tradeoff between the different quality requirements in architectural evaluation. In [6] the authors perform a thorough and comparative presentation of architecture evaluation through the SAAM, ATAM and ARID methods. In [3], the author identifies the following methods for assessment of software architectures with respect to quality attributes:
- **Scenario-based evaluation** – to evaluate a specific quality attribute, a set of scenarios is created that captures the meaning of that particular attribute.

- **Simulation** – where the main parts of the application are developed, while the rest are only simulated, providing an overall executable system. Therefore the system under evaluation is an implementation of the complete software system at a high level of abstraction.
- Another approach, similar to the simulation method is to use an **architectural prototype**, where only parts of the application are implemented and executed. The simulation and the architectural prototype methods are best for evaluating operational quality attributes, that is qualities that can be measured at the system's run time.
- **Mathematical modeling** – where special-use mathematical models are devised and formalized in order to evaluate quality attributes, especially the ones that concern the operation of the system.
- **Experience-based assessment** - which is rather an intuitive approach based on former experiences of the architects and reasonable argumentation. Even though this is not a formal technique, it is very often used, since the experience of the architects, especially in a certain domain, is priceless, particularly when it is supported by the appropriate line of reasoning.

Regarding the quality attributes themselves, there is also a plethora of qualities proposed by various researchers as well as international standards [24, 25]. Fortunately, these sets of qualities that have been proposed, revolve around the same concepts, even when they are named differently. Probably the most comprehensive catalogue of qualities is given in [19], where four different categories of these qualities are identified:

1 **System quality attributes discernable at runtime:**
   a. **Performance** – the responsiveness of the system, the time required to respond to stimuli (events) or the number of events processed in some interval of time. This quality depends highly on the communication and interaction, taking place between components.
   b. *Security* – the system's ability to resist unauthorized attempts at usage and denial of service while still providing its services to legitimate users. It can be strengthened by incorporating specialized components into the system such as authentication servers.
   c. *Availability* – the proportion of time the system is up and running. It is measured by the length of time between failures as well as by how quickly the system is able to resume operation in the event of failure. It can be enhanced by duplicating critical components and connectors that take over when the primary ones fail, and by closely monitoring the system to detect failure. It also depends on the separation of concerns between the components, as well as their modifiability. A closely related quality is *reliability*, the ability of the system to keep operating over time.
   d. *Usability* – this quality is comprised of other partial qualities: how quick and easy is it for a user to learn to use the system's interface (**learnability**)? Does the system respond with appropriate speed to a user's request (**efficiency**)? Can the user remember how to do system operations between uses of the system (**memorability**)? Does the system anticipate and prevent common user errors (**error avoidance**)? Does the system help the user recover from errors (**error handling**)? Does the system make the user's job

easy (**satisfaction**)? Since usability is concerned with human-computer interaction (HCI) issues, the flow of information to the user through the various components is of great significance to this quality attribute. Also the modifiability quality generally assists in achieving usability. Finally efficiency is directly linked to the system's performance.

2 **System quality attributes not discernable at runtime (development qualities):**
   a. *Modifiability* – the ability to make changes quickly and cost-effectively. It is also widely known as **maintainability**. It relies heavily on locality of change, which in turn depends on the encapsulation of functionality and the coupling between components through dependencies.
   b. *Portability* – the ability to run under different computing environments. It depends on the existence of a layer that is interposed between the application and the environment.
   c. *Integrability* – the ability to make the separately developed components of the system work correctly together. It is governed by specification of the components interfaces and their interactions, as well as the separation of concerns between them. A special case of integrability is *interoperability:* the ability of a system to work with another system.
   d. *Reusability* – the ability to reuse the system's structure or some of its components again in future applications. It is related to how coupled each component is with the rest; the loosely-coupled components are more reusable. Also the modifiability of the system entails reusability.
   e. *Testability* – the ease with which software can be made to demonstrate its faults through (typically execution-based) testing. It is determined by the level of architectural documentation, the separation of concerns and information hiding.

3 **Business qualities:**
   a. *Time to market* - It is reduced when pre-built components such as Commercial Off The Shelf (COTS) products are purchased or reused from existing development projects. Of course the issue of inserting pre-built components is a matter of integrability.
   b. *Cost.* It can be reduced by reusing pre-existing assets such as components.
   c. **Projected lifetime of the system** - This quality attribute can be supported if the system scores well on the modifiability and portability attributes. If the system is modifiable and portable it has an extended lifetime but there is also an increase in the time-to-market quality.
   d. *Targeted market* - This is also a quality that depends on other quality attributes, such as portability, usability, performance and of course the functional requirements that are out of the scope of this paper.

3.2   Evaluation of Quality Attributes

The evaluation framework that we shall use to assess the architecture is based on the methods and attributes described in the previous subsection. More specifically the methods used are the 3rd and the 5th, i.e. the evaluation results of the architectural prototype, as well as architectural experience combined with the appropriate line of reasoning.

3.2.1 System Quality Attributes Discernable at Runtime

1. *Performance* - This attribute is compromised by the use of the 'layered systems' architectural pattern, which, even though causes the system to be flexible and modifiable, brings a lot of overhead due to inter-component communication. So performance is naturally limited because of the layered nature of the system. The use of Java has an effect on performance as well, since it is an interpreted language. However, by putting a lot of functionality on the client, i.e. implementing a thick client, the system 's performance is greatly enhanced since there is limited client-server communication overhead. In addition, Java performs comparatively better than other similar technologies, like for instance, CGI scripts, where every operation leads to at least an HTTP request. Java applets perform much better since the performance bottlenecks are limited to downloading the bundled classes. So this attribute could be evaluated as fair enough.
2. *Security* - the sole precaution taken in order to improve security of the system, is choosing communications ports to be non-standard HTTP ports, and place the system behind a firewall so as to block unauthorized requests. On the other hand there is no provision in the architecture about denial of service or IP source address spoofing attacks. Therefore the system is rather vulnerable to attacks.
3. *Availability* – according to the implementation model of the architecture, there are 7 different server components (application server, WWW server and servlets engine, FTP server, E-mail server, RDBMS, Chat server, Whiteboard server) and they are all independent of each other. Therefore the failure of one server component does not affect the others. Good practice would also be to disperse the server components in different workstations, so that the crashing of one workstation will not affect the others and further improve availability, though that would cause extra communication overhead. However there are no redundant components foreseen in the architecture to take over when the primary ones fail, or an error reporting mechanism. In conclusion the system has a mediocre availability.
4. *Usability* – This quality attribute is probably the most difficult to assess in terms of the system's architecture, because it concerns the user interface and is mostly subjectively appraised. In general we could claim that the flow of information to the user is straightforward, correct and complete. Efficiency is not rated highly due to the corresponding performance insufficiency. More evaluation results in this quality should be made available when the prototype is tested within its context of use, i.e. with students participating in Open and Distance Learning courses.

3.2.2 System Quality Attributes not Discernable at Runtime

1. *Modifiability* – Modifiability is met by the proposed architecture since the component-based nature of the system causes it to be inherently modular, making **dependencies explicit** and helping to reduce and control these dependencies [4]. This means that a component can be changed to improve or adapt its functionality if necessary, or it could even be replaced by another new and better component without affecting the overall system. In other words, since the component in-

terfaces are clearly defined, components can be treated as black boxes and a change in a component will not propagate changes to the other components it interacts with. That is after all what locality of change is all about. Even if changes need to occur to a society of components instead of a single one, this society can still be isolated so that changes to it are made transparently to the rest of the system. Another argument for the good modifiability of the LMS architecture is that the architectural design and the implementation of the system are both performed in object-oriented languages, so if changes occur in either the design or the code it is trivial to transfer them to the other. Furthermore, except from the component nature of the architecture, the layered structuring also leads to separation of concerns and therefore to locality of change. To sum up, the architecture scores pretty high in this quality.

2. *Portability* – The architectural prototype is to some extent portable since both the client-side and the server-side code are written in Java, which is an interpreted platform-independent language. In other words the Java Virtual Machine plays the role of a portability layer between the Learning Management System and the environment. Of course, in reality, Java does not run on all platforms and therefore 100% portability can't be achieved. In addition, a lot of the GUI is also written in standard HTML, which is apparently platform-independent. As far as the third-party components, such as the MySQL RDBMS or the Resin Web Server and servlets engine, they have also been chosen to be portable or available in multiple platforms. Therefore the architecture can be claimed to be acceptably portable.

3. *Integrability* – This is also a quality that is satisfied because of the component-based nature of the system, the explicit definition of components and connectors, the predefined protocols of component interaction and the clearly defined interfaces of the different components. In cases where the interfaces of the components under integration are incompatible and cannot be changed for various reasons, e.g. they are COTS products, methods such as gap analysis [26] have been used to leverage the incompatibility. The layered structure of the system also assists in partitioning the functionality into separate components and thus promoting integrability. Finally, since the legacy systems were all written in Java, they did not have to be re-written or wrapped inside Java wrappers, but it did take some adaptation to make them interoperable with the new components.

4. *Reusability* – According to the same arguments as in the modifiability and integrability quality, the components developed within the proposed architecture, having clearly defined functionality and interfaces, and thus being loosely-coupled, can be reused in different applications, may they be other LMS or not. This was an anticipated result, since reusability and modifiability tend to support each other and the system was evaluated as highly modifiable.

5. *Interoperability* - This quality attribute is satisfied by the fact that, not only internal component interfaces are identified, i.e. interfaces that allow the system's components to interoperate, but also external ones. For example the Metadata Management System has an external interface, defined as a Java API, that can be used to import or export sets of metadata that conform to an international standard, in our case IEEE LTSC Learning Object Metadata [20].

6. *Testability* – The proposed architecture promotes testability in a considerable degree for the following reasons: the design is made using object-oriented UML constructs that have a one-to-one mapping to the code, making the architectural documentation clearly articulated and illustrating the exact system built; therefore the testers can understand exactly where the error is caused and why. Furthermore, the concepts of information hiding and separation of concern that have been achieved in the component design, lead to tracing of faults to unique components. Again, sources of errors are easy to distinguish inside a society of inter-operating components. On the other hand, the kinds of errors that have to do with the overall system operation, such as system-wide failures, deadlocks in process synchronization etc. cannot be tested explicitly with the proposed architecture, but rather implicitly by creating test cases from the corresponding use cases. These are, of course, huge classes of errors, but unfortunately don't depend on software architecture.

3.2.3 Business Qualities
1. *Time to market*. Instead of developing all the components from scratch, some of them were located as COTS products, as seen in the architectural prototype description, and that has affected in a great reduction in time to market. Of course the time of integrating COTS in the system is still not minimal, since it takes time to search for them and customize the rest of the system so that they can be properly integrated. Fortunately they were relatively easy to integrate, thanks to the component, layered nature and pre-defined interfaces, as explained above.
2. *Cost*. The use of COTS has also reduced the cost of the system under development. It is noted though that for the sake of our architectural prototype, the COTS were not purchased, since their license allows their use for non-commercial or instructional purposes. If they were indeed bought, then there would probably be a considerably added cost. It is speculated though that still the cost of COTS is less than the cost of developing them from scratch.
3. *Projected lifetime of the system*. Since the system was evaluated to be quite modifiable, it will manage change easily and thus extend its lifetime. Additionally the portability of the system allows for it to claim a bigger share in the market and establish itself in many platforms, thus having better possibilities to last longer.
4. *Targeted market*. Since the system was evaluated highly in the quality attribute of portability, and fairly enough in usability and performance, it is estimated that the system has increased potential for a good market share.

4   Conclusions and Future Work

There is little doubt anymore that a well-specified architecture is able to build quality inherently into a system [4, 6, 7, 12]. Software architecture allows for the evaluation of the system before it is built, thus saving a lot of resources that would have otherwise been unnecessarily spent. It assists the architect into making the right design decisions to correct the development process and finally to achieve the target qualities.

The general conclusion derived from the evaluation presented in this paper, is that the proposed architecture scores pretty high as far as the development qualities are concerned, but it fails to adequately meet most of the run-time qualities. The business qualities are somewhere in the middle: the architecture achieves an acceptable score in the business section. This result makes sense from an architectural point of view, since the development qualities are often in direct conflict with the run-time qualities while, on the other hand, development qualities usually promote business qualities. The controversy between the development and the run-time qualities are further documented in these remarks:

1. The layered nature of the system supports modifiability and integrability but has a considerable cost on performance since there is a lot of communication overhead between independent components.
2. The use of the Java programming language has a negative effect on performance since it is an interpreted language. On the other hand being an interpreted language and relying on a virtual machine, Java is platform-independent, thus allowing portability to an extent. Moreover, Java allows for a direct mapping, from the object-oriented architectural design into the implementation language, thus leading to increased modifiability of the system.

Conversely, the mutual support between the development and the business qualities is illustrated in the following observations:

1. The use of COTS and other third-party components is feasible due to the high integrability and modifiability of the system. This in turn promotes the business qualities, such as reduced time to market as well as reduced cost.
2. The system's modifiability guarantees the effective management of change, therefore it promotes an increased lifetime. Portability also promotes the system's lifetime as well as its targeted market.

It is rather evident that the various qualities of the system are quite mingled and interdependent and might support or diminish one another. It is the job of the architect to try and maximize the more desirable ones, and at the same time, minimize the consequent effect for the less desirable qualities. This is quite a challenging problem with many daunting tradeoff issues, but it could be performed more easily and systematically with the adoption and use of a formal evaluation method that provides more hard data and quantifiable results.

Another conclusion is that the evaluation method based on the architectural prototype is best for evaluating quality attributes discernable at runtime. On the other hand experience-based assessment, fits better with development qualities such as modifiability, portability etc.

The work presented in this paper is part of research conducted on the software engineering of a Learning Management System, with emphasis on software architecture. Future work in this area initially includes the adoption of a custom, formal evaluation method to assess the quality attributes and produce more accurate, solid results as well as tradeoff analysis. Furthermore, the feedback from the evaluation presented in this paper is being used to re-engineer the system in order to improve some of the low-score quality attributes. It is of paramount importance to inspect the methods, as well as the effort required to re-engineer the system under development. Finally the adoption and use of architectural patterns [17] will also be investigated with respect to the effect such patterns have on the quality attributes.

Acknowledgement

The work described in this paper was performed as part of the MENU project (Model for a European Networked University), which is partly funded under contract NO001ELEARN011of the European Community.

References

1. Oleg, S., Liber, B.: A framework of pedagogical evaluation of Virtual Learning Environments. Available online at [   ], (1999).
2. Avgeriou, P., Papasalouros A. and Retalis, S.: Web-based learning Environments: issues, trends, challenges. Proceedings of the 1st IOSTE symposium in Southern Europe, Science and Technology Education, Paralimni, Cyprus, (2001).
3. Bosch, J.: Design and Use of Software Architectures. Addison-Wesley, (2000).
4. Szyperski, C.: Component Software: Beyond Object-Oriented Programming. Addison-Wesley, (1999).
5. Eriksson, H. and Penker, M.: Business Modeling with UML - Business Patterns at work. John Wiley & Sons, (2000).
6. Clements, P., Kazman, R., Clein, M.: Evaluating Software Architecture. Addison-Wesley, (2002).
7. Jacobson, I., Booch, G., Rumbaugh, J.: The Unified Software Development Process. Addison-Wesley, (1999).
8. IEEE Learning Technology Standards Committee: Draft Standard for Learning Technology Systems Architecture (LTSA). Draft 9, (2001).
9. Thorne, S., Shubert, C., Merriman, J.: OKI architecture overview. OKI project document, (2002).
10. Cisco Systems: Blueprint for Enterprise E-learning. white paper, (2002),
11. Retalis S., Avgeriou P.: Modeling Web-based Instructional Systems. Journal of Information Technology Education, Volume 1, No. 1, pp. 25-41, (2002).
12. Kruchten, P.: The Rational Unified Process, An introduction. Addison-Wesley, (1999).
13. Booch, G., Rumbaugh, J., Jacobson, I.: The UML User Guide. Addison-Wesley, (1999)
14. Rumbaugh, J., Jacobson, I., Booch, G.: The UML Reference Manual. Addison-Wesley, (1996).
15. Avgeriou, P., Retalis, S., Papasalouros, A., Skordalakis, M.: Developing an architecture for the Software Subsystem of a Learning Technology System – An Engineering approach. Proceedings of International Conference of Advanced Learning Technologies, Madison, Wisconsin, IEEE Computer Society Press, (2001), pp. 17-20.
16. Avgeriou, P., Retalis, S., Skordalakis, M.: A Software Architecture for a Learning Management System. Post-proceedings of the 8th Panhellenic Conference in Informatics, to be published in the Lecture Notes in Computer Science series, Springer-Verlag, (2002).
17. Buschmann, F., Meunier, R., Rohnert, H., Sommertland, P., Stal, M.: Pattern-Oriented Software Architecture, Volume 1: A System of Patterns. John Wiley & Sons, (1996).
18. Shaw, M., Garlan, D.: Software Architecture: Perspectives on an Emerging Discipline. Prentice Hall, (1996).
19. Bass, L., Clements, P., Kazman, R.: Software Architecture in Practice. Addison-Wesley, (1998).
20. IEEE Learning Technology Standardization Committee (LTSC): Draft Standard for Learning Object Metadata, P1484.12/D6.1.   , (2001).
21. IMS Global Learning Consortium: IMS Question & Test Interoperability Specification-Best Practice and Implementation Guide, version 1.2.1.   /, (2001)

22. Kazman, R., Abowd, G., Bass, L., Clements, P.: Scenario-Based Analysis of Software Architecture. IEEE Software 13, 6, (1996), pp. 47-55.
23. Kazman, R., Klein, M., Clements, P.: ATAM: Method for Architecture Evaluation. TECHNICAL REPORT CMU/SEI-2000-TR-004 ESC-TR-2000-004, (2000).
24. IEEE: Recommended Practice for Software Requirements Specifications, IEEE Std. 830-1993. (1993)
25. ISO/IEC 9126: Information technology-Software product evaluation-Quality characteristics and the guidelines for their use. (1993).
26. Cheesman, J., Daniels, J.: UML Components: A Simple Process for Specifying Component-Based Software. Addison-Wesley, (2000).

Towards the Quality Evaluation of Functional Aspects of Operative Web Applications[*]

Silvia Abrahão[1], Luis Olsina[2], and Oscar Pastor[1]

[1] Department of Information Systems and Computation
Valencia University of Technology
Camino de Vera s/n, P.O. Box: 22012, E-46022, Valencia, Spain
{sabrahao,opastor}@dsic.upv.es
[2] Software Engineering R&D Group (GIDIS)
Department of Informatics, Engineering School, UNLPam
Calle 110 esq. 9, 6360 General Pico, La Pampa, Argentina
olsinal@ing.unlpam.edu.ar

Abstract. The development and maintenance approaches for web applications (WebApps) have often been ad hoc, lacking systematic strategies not only for development but also for quality assurance. One of our current concerns is assessing the quality of operative WebApps considering both functional and non-functional (F&NF) requirements. We claim that an operative web application should be assessed not only from the quality perspective of the nonfunctional requirements, but also from a functional viewpoint like informational and navigational architecture. In this paper, we specifically discuss how to deal with the functional side, i.e., the re-engineering and evaluation of conceptual models of a WebApp in the maintenance phase using the Web Function Points and Quality Evaluation Methodology (WebFP_QEM).

1 Introduction

With the rapid evolution of the web, WebApps have become increasingly more complex. Nowadays it is widely accepted that a Web site is not merely a matter of content and aesthetic, but the functionality is also required, combining navigation with complex services and transactions. Because of the increasing size, complexity, quality needs and market demands for WebApps, several problems have frequently been reported [5] such as exceeding budgets, unknown or bad product quality, in addition to a lack of requirements and architectural documentation.

From the quality evaluation point of view, some methods and techniques currently exist for evaluating different quality characteristics and metrics. However, in practice, they provide only partial solutions because they separately focus on either nonfunctional or on functional requirements. Indeed, integral solutions are needed.

---

[*] This work is partially supported by the CYTED Program, in the VII.18 research project, WEST; the CICYT project: TIC 2001-3530-C02-01 (Spain), and by the UNLPam-09/F022 research project (Arg.).

A. Olivé (Eds.): ER 2003 Ws, LNCS 2784, pp. 325–338, 2003.

An interesting (though partial) solution to the restructuring and maintenance problem of WebApps is given in [13], where authors define a set of analyses that automatically extracts a description of a site's main architectural features as well as its evolution. This solution is partial because it must add abstraction techniques to support a high-level view (conceptual models and primitives). WebFP_QEM is a systematic and flexible approach aimed for analyzing the informational and navigational architecture and for evaluating the quality of complex WebApps in the operative phase [1]. It permits capturing goals for different audiences, specifying conceptual models (the functional requirements -FR), specifying quality models and assessment criteria (the nonfunctional requirements -NFR), analyzing outcomes in order to give recommendations for improvements, as well as drawing up cost prediction reports. Thus, we claim that an operative site should be assessed not only from the quality perspective of the NFR, but also from the FR viewpoint like informational and navigational architecture.

In order to represent FR, the proposed methodology uses conceptual modeling techniques to capture the informational and navigational structure of operative WebApps [11]. To modeling NFR, a quality model is considered. In this model, quality characteristics have to be specified in an operational way. That is, for each quality characteristic and sub-characteristic, not only a sound specification should be given, but associated attributes, metrics and criteria should also be designed [10]. Ultimately, by using the underlying process of WebFP_QEM, evaluators can give recommendations by assessing both functional and nonfunctional requirements of a WebApp in the operative phase. If a change is suggested, the estimation of the maintenance cost can be done using a Web-centred Function Points measure [1].

The rest of this paper is structured as follows. Section 2 provides an overview of the WebFP_QEM methodology with descriptions of the main steps. Section 3 explains the conceptual modeling phase and the analyses of the outcomes. We discuss a comprehensible example in the e-commerce field in order to illustrate the strategy (mainly on the functional side). In addition, we propose a set of metrics to perform the analysis of conceptual models. Finally, concluding discussions and further works are presented.

2   Overview of the Strategy

The WebFP_QEM methodology covers the major process steps underlying the modeling and analysis of the information and navigation architecture and the quality assessment of complex WebApps in the operative phase. The final goal is to obtain a document with strategic recommendations for decision-makers. These recommendations are based on the strengths and weaknesses of a WebApp obtained from conceptual modeling, quality measurements, and analysis activities. Thus, maintenance changes in F&NF requirements can be identified. Figure 1 shows the evaluation process model underlying the WebFP_QEM methodology, which includes the main steps, the models and tools used and the inputs and outputs. These steps are grouped in the following six major technical processes: *Goal-Oriented Restructuring Analysis, Conceptual Model-*

ing, Quality Requirements Modeling, Quality Assessment, Results Analysis and *Functional Size Measurement*. A thorough discussion of these steps can be seen in [1].

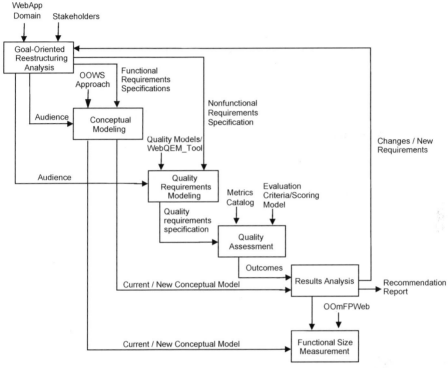

Fig. 1. The evaluation process underlying the WebFP_QEM methodology

3   Conceptual Modeling and Analyses of Outcomes

3.1   Detecting a New WebApp Goal: The Wish List Example

Let us suppose that, in the Goal-Oriented Restructuring Analysis process, a new functionality for an e-commerce application was detected with stakeholders, namely: the incorporation of a Wish List. Many WebApps provide a wish list as an area where the users can add items for later potential purchases. This goal can imply an adaptive maintenance. Figure 2 shows the details of this restructuring goal. For instance, specific information about goal definition, scope and audiences as well as FR and NFR can be recorded. For example, a description of this goal can be *"to incorporate a wish list functionality to the current web application"*. This goal concerns the application scope because it directly affects the components of the WebApp. For this goal, the selected audience is a *Registered User*. Also, the *objective, preconditions, category, main steps*, *alternative steps* and *priority* are specified for each functional requirement.

The objective of a FR can be *"to place an item on the wish list to possibly be purchased at a later time"*. Preconditions express constraints under which the FR will work properly. For the above example, the precondition is that the user should be viewing an item. The category indicates the level of the web application (i.e., information, navigation or interface, etc.) involved in the FR specification. For example, the *category* in Fig. 2 indicates that interface objects are responsible for mediating user interaction with navigation objects.

Goal: To incorporate a "wish list" functionality to the current web application.	Scope: Application

Audiences: Registered User	
FR 1:	**Objective:** To place an item into the wish list to possibly be purchased at a later time.
	Preconditions: The user is currently viewing an item
	Category: navigation and interface
	Main Steps: Registered user selects an item to add to the wish list. System displays the current contents, if any, of the list with the addition of the new item Registered user selects to modify the Quantity of an item in the list. System updates the quantity and displays the contents of the list.
	Alternative Steps: System detects that the wish list is at its maximum capacity.
	Priority: high
FR 2:	...
NFR 1:	**Objective:** To provide feedback (e.g. by means of a linked control) to return to the previous context.
	Category / Attributes: usability / availability of feedback to the previous context
	Priority: high
NFR 2:	...

Fig. 2. Template to specify goals, audiences, F&NF requirements

3.2   Conceptual Modeling of the Wish List

We argue that the conceptual modeling process is necessary in order to develop correct WebApps as well as to support the documentation of complex ones. Moreover, we consider navigation to be a critical feature in the conceptual modeling of WebApps. The following questions must be stated when introducing a conceptual modeling approach: a) What are the specific conceptual constructs that should be used when dealing with a WebApp? b) Where the new features such as navigation and presentation definitely relevant?, and 3) What notation is provided to properly capture those conceptual modeling constructs?

In order to accomplish this objective, we introduce the conceptual patterns proposed by the Object-Oriented Web-Solutions (OOWS) modeling approach [11], justifying their use from the point of view of what is required by a web conceptual schema in terms of information and navigation structure. This approach uses well-known UML-compliant diagrams to represent the required conceptual information.

When dealing with the conceptual modeling step, the abstractions derived from the problem domain are specified in terms of classes, their structure, behavior and functionality. The information structure results in the acquisition of content and functionality within the WebApp, while the navigation establishes the structure of the WebApp and the flow of user interactions. We represent this information in the following conceptual models: the *Object Model* and the *Navigation Model*.

According to the OOWS approach, two complementary conceptual models are specified: the Dynamic Model and the Functional Model. In the former, valid object life cycles and inter-object communications can be represented. In the latter, the semantics associated to any change of an object state is captured as a consequence of a service occurrence. However, for reasons of brevity, we consider the Object and Navigation models sufficient to get a generic view of the underlying semantics of an operative WebApp.

The *Object Model* is a graphical model where system classes including attributes, services and class relationships (i.e., aggregation and inheritance) are defined. In an aggregation hierarchy, it is necessary to define whether there is an association or a composition. In an inheritance hierarchy, it is necessary to specify whether a specialization is permanent or temporal. Additionally, agent relationships are specified to state the services that objects of a class are allowed to activate.

Figure 3 shows a simple schema for the wish list functionality. Two kinds of users are represented: anonymous and registered. Anonymous users can register themselves by performing the *signIn* service, thereby passing to the registered user category. The registered user is a temporal specialization of the anonymous user, inheriting its properties and behavior. Each registered user has a wish list to add, modify and delete items (references to products) to possibly be purchased at a later time.

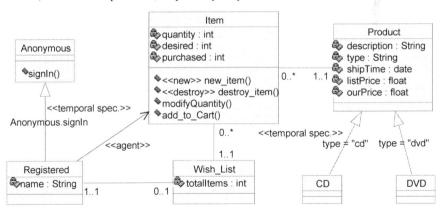

Fig. 3. The Object Model schema for the wish list functionality

A *Navigation Model* is obtained by adding a navigational view over the Object Model. The navigational semantics of a web application is captured based on the point of view of each *agent* (audience) identified in the Object Model. This model is essentially composed of a *navigational map* that represents the global view of the application for a specific audience. It is represented by a directed graph where nodes are navigational contexts and arcs are navigational links. A *navigational context* represents the perspective a user has on a subset of the Object Model, while a *navigational link* allows navigating from one context to another. Navigational contexts can be classified into two types: *exploration contexts* (E) and *sequence contexts* (S). The former can be reached at any moment independently of the current context (e.g. landmarks), whereas the latter can only be reached following a predefined sequence of navigation paths.

Figure 4 shows a part of the navigational map for the registered user of the Amazon WebApp. There are four exploration contexts for organizing the navigation space. These contexts are related to the landmarks that appear in the Amazon main navigational menu.

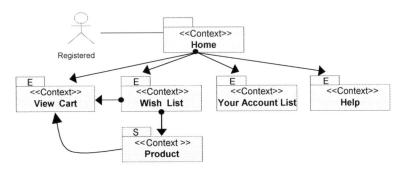

Fig. 4. A Navigational Map schema of the registered agent

A navigational context is composed by a set of classes which is stereotyped with «view», and connected by navigational relationships. These classes are called *navigational classes* and they represent views over specific classes in the Object Model. These views make a restriction to a given subset of attributes and services of the involved classes. For each navigational context there is a main class that is called *manager class* from where navigation starts. The others classes are called *complementary classes* and they contribute to giving additional information to instances of the manager class. These classes are connected using navigational relationships, providing related information between them. Service links can be defined and associated to class services. A *service link* connects with a target navigational context when the execution of the associated service is completed.

A navigational relationship is a unidirectional binary relationship between two navigational classes that must be defined over an existing aggregation or inheritance class relationship in the Object Model. There exist two types of navigational relationships: context relationships and contextual dependency relationships. A *context relationship* is a navigational relationship that also defines a directed navigation from this navigational context towards the target one, where the target class of the context relationship acts as the manager class. Graphically, it is represented using solid arrows.

Four kinds of attributes can be specified for this type of relationship: a) *context attributes*, which specify the target navigational context of a navigational link, b) *link attributes*, which specify which attribute of the target class is involved in the connection, c) *role attributes*, which indicate the referenced relationship-role when two classes have more than one relationship, and d) *filter attributes*, which introduce selection criteria on the population of the target class, based on the value of the attribute involved.

In a *contextual dependency relationship*, the navigational semantic towards the target class is not defined: this kind of relationship is used to provide the required additional information in the current context without denoting any further navigation. Graphically it is represented using dashed arrows.

Finally, the following information can be specified during the design phase: population filters and order. A *population filter* establishes a selection of objects over the manager class. It is represented by a logical expression evaluated on the state of these classes. The *ordering* primitive indicates a traversal order of the context elements. A brief example which includes the above comments is shown in Figure 5. This example shows how a Wish List of an e-commerce application can be specified using the OOWS approach. The Wish_List context describes all the products selected by a Registered user.

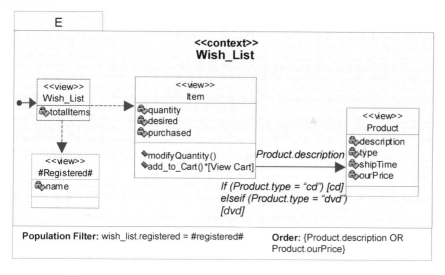

Fig. 5. A Navigational Context schema for the wish list example

The navigation starts in the Wish_List class which acts as the manager class. The totalItems attribute from the Wish_List class and the name of the connected user will be shown. The *Registered, Item,* and *Product* classes are complementary classes and provide additional information related to the manager class. In order to provide this information, the Wish_list class has a contextual dependency relationship with them.

For instance, the relationship between Wish_List class and Item class presents the *quantity, desired* and *purchased* attributes of a wish list. Also, the user can modify the quantity of an item or add it to a shopping cart, beginning the sale process. The service link associated to the add_to_Cart service indicates the target navigation context after the service execution. Additionally, a context relationship appears: from an Item, users can obtain more details of a Product (Product_Details context) by selecting its description. In addition, a population filter over the wish_list class is performed in order to restrict the retrieved information about the interactive registered user. The items can be arranged by their description or price.

We claim that by using these basic conceptual constructs it is possible to specify the semantics attached to the information architecture and navigation requirements for WebApps. At the end of this process, a Current Conceptual Model which represents the functional structure of a WebApp is produced.

3.3   Towards the Analysis of Conceptual Models

Once the conceptual model of a current WebApp and the quality requirements process are performed, decision-makers are ready to analyze the results and draw up recommendations (see the Analyzing the Results process in Fig. 1). With regard to the conceptual model the key issues are what primitives and structures in the conceptual modeling affect the quality of a WebApp. The main concern related to the information architecture focuses on analyzing whether the conceptual model (Object and Navigation Models) of the current WebApp represents all the information and functionality required for the business and application goals.

In practice, the quality of conceptual models is often evaluated in an ad hoc way, based on common sense and experience. Few guidelines exist to evaluate the quality of the conceptual models and there is little agreement among experts about what makes a "good" conceptual model [8]. In addition, there are an abundance of design recommendations and guidelines for building usable Web sites [9]. These guidelines address a broad range of website features, from the amount of content on a page to the breadth and depth of pages in the site. However, there is little consistency and often overlap among them making it difficult to know which guidelines to adhere to. Furthermore, there is a wide gap between a heuristic and its operationalization in metrics.

To bridge this gap, we have proposed a set of metrics for the different primitives of the OOWS conceptual models. The explanation of the importance of assessing quality measures at the high design level is discussed in [4]. Specifically, we have elaborated a set of metrics for Object Models, Agents, Navigational Maps, and Navigational Contexts. These metrics provide quantitative measures of *completeness* and *complexity* of the information content and navigation structure of a WebApp. For instance, completeness refers to whether the conceptual model contains all the information required to meet actual user requirements, while complexity refers to structural issues such as compactness, shortest navigation path, breadth and depth of hierarchies, among others.

In fact, the analysis of conceptual models involves the following tasks: 1) assessing the quality of a current conceptual model; 2) contrasting the results with identified restructuring goals; 3) identifying different possibilities of maintenance (i.e., corrective, adaptive, perfective or preventive); 4) conceptual modeling of changes or new functional requirements, and 5) measuring the new conceptual model with respect to the current conceptual model.

As stated above, some of the proposed metrics can be interpreted as the degree of completeness of the Current Conceptual Model with respect to the New Conceptual Model taking into account the restructuring goals. Others, for instance, can be useful for analysing the structural complexity of Navigational Maps and Contexts. Table 1 shows a set of metrics for the Object Model.

Table 1. Some Metrics for the Object Model

Metric Name	Metric Definition
Ratio of Added Classes (RAC)	Ratio of new classes with respect to a *com**.
Ratio of Deleted Classes (RDC)	Ratio of deleted classes with respect to a *com*.
Ratio of Modified Classes (RMC)	Ratio of modified classes with respect to a *com*.
Ratio of Added Attributes (RAA)	Ratio of new attributes with respect to a *com*.
Ratio of Deleted Attributes (RDA)	Ratio of deleted attributes with respect to a *com*.
Ratio of Modified Attributes (RMA)	Ratio of modified attributes with respect to a *com*.
Ratio of Added Services (RAS)	Ratio of new services with respect to a *com*.
Ratio of Deleted Services (RDS)	Ratio of deleted services with respect to a *com*.
Ratio of Modified Services (RMS)	Ratio of modified services with respect to a *com*.

*com means current object model

For instance, the ratio of added classes (RAC) in the new conceptual model with respect to the current object model can be expressed in the following formula:

$$RAC = \frac{\#NewClasses}{\#CurrentClasses + \#NewClasses} \tag{1}$$

The ratio of deleted classes (RDC) with respect to the current object model can be expressed in the following formula:

$$RDC = 1 - \left(\frac{\#CurrentClasses - \#DeletedClasses}{\#CurrentClasses} \right) \tag{2}$$

Finally, the ratio of modified classes (RMC) with respect to the current object model can be expressed in the following formula:

$$RMC = \frac{\#ModifiedClasses}{\#CurrentClasses} \tag{3}$$

The same idea can be applied in order to measure the ratio of added, deleted and modified attributes and services with respect to the current Object Model.

While modeling the navigational structure of a WebApp, several aspects should be taken into account such as: what the underlying structure of navigation is (i.e., how the navigation space is organized); which objects will be navigated, as well as what the effects of a navigation action are. According to the OOWS approach, the navigation space is organized by defining a unique navigational map for each agent. It is important to remark that we could add (or delete) a Navigational Map without adding a new audience, as was the case with the Wish List. Or, we can add a new Agent for a new Navigational Map, among other possibilities. Table 2 shows some metrics for Agents that can be useful for observing the impact of changes regarding added or deleted audiences in a maintenance process.

Table 2. Some Metrics for Agents

Metric Name	Metric Definition
Ratio of Added Agents (RAAg)	Ratio of new agents with respect to a current Navigational Model.
Ratio of Deleted Agents (RDAg)	Ratio of deleted agents with respect to a current Navigational Model
Number of Final Agents (NFAg)	Total number of agents in a new Navigational Model.

Table 3 shows some metrics for Navigational Maps. Features such as depth level of a (current) navigational map and breadth of a navigational map for a given Agent are considered. It is worthwhile noting that we could follow a heuristic-based approach in order to guide the analysis process [9].

Table 3. Some Metrics for Navigational Maps

Metric Name	Metric Definition
Depth of a Current Navigational Map (DCNM)	We can measure the maximum, minimum and average depth of a current navigational map for each agent.
Breadth of a Current Navigational Map (BCNM)	We can measure the breadth of a navigational map for each audience (e.g. for exploration contexts).
Minimum Path Between Navigational Contexts (MPBNC)	This metric determines the minimum quantity of navigational links that are necessary to transverse from a source to a target navigational context.
Number of Path Between Navigational Contexts (NPBNC)	This metric indicates the number of alternative paths to reach two contexts within a navigational map.
Number of Navigational Contexts (NNC)	The total number of navigational context in a navigational map.
Number of Navigational Links (NNL)	The total number of links in a navigation map.
Compactness (Cp)	The degree of interconnectivity of a navigation map.

The *Depth of a Navigation Map* (DNM) is just the distance of a root navigational context to a leaf context. It indicates the ease with which the target navigation context can be reached and likely the importance of its content. The interpretation is: the bigger the distance of a leaf navigation context from the root, the harder is for the agent to reach this context, and potentially the less important this context will be in the map. We can measure the maximum, minimum and average depth of a navigation map for each agent. The *Breadth of a Navigation Map* (BNM) is the number of exploration navigational contexts (i.e. at the first level of contexts). The interpretation is: the bigger the number of exploration navigation contexts, the harder is for the agent to understand the web application (too many options at once).

The *Compactness* metric (Cp) refers to the degree of interconnection between nodes pertaining to a hypermedia graph. It is a value between 0 and 1, where 0 implies that there are no connections between nodes and 1 implies total connection. The experience and the analysis on different domains recommend (according to [3]) a rank between 0.3 and 0.8 as appropriate. The degree of interconnectivity of navigation contexts is obtained by applying this metric on the navigation maps. For example, when there are few links in a navigational map, nodes (navigational contexts) could be difficult to reach by following links. In addition, users may become disoriented because they need to go through many steps to get a piece of information. Also, some parts of a navigational map may not even be connected by links at all (known as orphan or dead-end nodes). The formula for computing compactness is:

$$Cp = \frac{Max - \sum_i \sum_k D_{i,k}}{Max - Min} \tag{4}$$

Where, $Max = (n^2 - n) * k$; $Min = (n^2 - n)$; $n =$ quantity of navigational contexts in the map; $k =$ constant superior to the amount of contexts; $\sum_i \sum_k D_{i,k} =$ the sum of distances taken from the matrix of converted distances (with factor k); and $D_{ik} =$ the distance between the contexts i and k (refer to [3] for more details).

During the analysis, high compactness means that each navigational context can easily reach any other node in the map (this may indicate a highly connected map that can lead to disorientation). Low compactness may indicate an insufficient number of links, which may indicate that parts of a map are disconnected. Lastly, the ratios of added, deleted or modified navigational maps are similar to those shown for object models.

Table 4 shows some metrics for Navigational Contexts. One commonly used metric is the fan-in / fan-out metric, which is based on the ideas of coupling. The interpretation is: the larger the number of couples, the greater the degree of interdependence and difficulty of maintenance, and the lower the potential for reuse. The cohesion level of a navigational context is the extent to which the individual classes are needed to perform the core task. The main idea of the cohesion level of a navigational context is the same as in the traditional O-O concept of cohesion, but instead adds the aspect of cohesiveness of classes in a navigational context. The higher the degree of "similarity" of classes in a context, the greater the cohesiveness and the higher the degree of encapsulation of the context.

The metrics presented represent a quantitative measure of the informational and navigational aspects of a WebApp. These metrics can allow a structural analysis as well reveal potential navigational problems such as unnecessary circular (link) paths and dead-end nodes.

Table 4. Some Metrics for Navigational Context

Metric Name	Metric Definition
Fan-In of a Navigational Context (FINC)	It counts the number of invocations a navigational context calls.
Fan-Out of a Navigational Context (FONC)	It counts the number of navigational links that call a navigational context.
Number of Navigational Classes (NNC)	The total number of classes (manager and complementary) within a navigational context

3.4 The Estimation of the Size of Change

The current estimation models must be adapted to be able to address the estimation challenges for controlling projects involved in WebApps production. To achieve this goal, we extended a measure for O-O systems from conceptual models [12] to the web environment. The functional size measurement of a web application is accomplished by mapping Function Point concepts defined by the IFPUG [7] to the OOWS conceptual model primitives.

This mapping is conducted in four steps: 1) the conceptual models are analyzed to determine the application boundary, and the measuring scope; 2) the conceptual models are analyzed to identify the data and transactional candidate function types; 3) the complexity of each identified function is determined. The logical functions are mapped for low, average and high complexity levels in accordance with IFPUG tables [7]; 4) the complexity levels are mapped into values. The total value results in unadjusted OOmFP-Web. Based on these considerations, we have identified the functions and a set of counting rules.

In line with this strategy, we propose an approach to predict the size of change of evolving WebApps based on the current / new conceptual models (see Fig. 1). With the current conceptual model measurement, the functional size of an operative WebApp can be determined in its current state (before the quality evaluation). By measuring the new conceptual model, the functional size of a WebApp can be estimated after recommended changes. This is made counting the number of functions that have been added (ADD), changed (CHG), and deleted (DEL) during the maintenance of a WebApp. Thus, the final size change can be estimated by the following equation:

$$OOmFP_{Web} = \sum_{i=1}^{n} ADD_i + \sum_{j=1}^{m} CHG_j + \sum_{k=1}^{l} DEL_k \qquad (5)$$

4   Discussions and Further Work

In this paper, we claim that an operative WebApp should be assessed not only from the quality perspective of nonfunctional requirements, but also from the functional viewpoint such as conceptual modeling. WebFP_QEM can be a useful approach for analyzing, and potentially restructuring a WebApp in the operative phase. Thus far, we have used our approach in a real case study. Specifically, the CYTED web site was assessed in order to determine the current functional size and quality. The informational and navigational architecture for a specific audience was obtained (see [2] for more details). A recommendation report was delivered, however, the restructuring of the site is still an ongoing project.

Even if we have only focused the discussion on conceptual modeling and on a set of metrics useful for analyzing conceptual models, WebFP_QEM is an integral approach, which allows for capturing goals for different audiences, specifying informational and navigational models, defining quality models and assessment criteria, analyzing outcomes in order to give recommendations as well as drawing up cost prediction reports. In the restructuring process, the type of maintenance, the audiences involved, the scope of the modification (the size and cost of changes), and the consequences of the modification such as the impact in the navigational structure, usability, maintainability, etc., should be considered.

It is worth noting that effective and efficient assessment and restructuring processes require both methodological and technological support. There are some issues we need to address in the near future: a) A design of experiments in order to empirically validate the presented metrics, following for instance the approach proposed in [6]; b) A smooth integration of the Recommendation Report [1]. This should include not only specific sections for the quality report (as currently used in the WebQEM_Tool [10]), but also the sections for conceptual modeling analyses.

References

1. Abrahão S., Olsina L., and Pastor O. "A Methodology for Evaluating Quality and Functional Size of Operative WebApps", *In Proc. of 2ⁿᵈ International Workshop on Web Oriented Software Technology*, ECOOP'02 Workshops, Málaga, Spain, 2002, pp. 1-20.

2. Abrahão, S. M., Pastor, O., Olsina L., and Fons, J.J. 2001. Un Método para Medir el Tamaño Funcional y Evaluar la Calidad de Sitios Web. In *Proc. of VI Jornadas de Ingeniería de Software y Base de Datos*, Almagro, Spain, 2001, 478-491. (In Spanish).

3. Botafogo, R, Rivlin, E., and Shneiderman, B.,1992, "Structural Analysis of Hypertexts: Identifying Hierarchies and Useful Metrics". *ACM Transactions on Office Information Systems*, 10(2), pp. 142-180.

4. Briand, L., Morasca, S., and Basili, V. "Defining and Validating Measures for Object-based High-level Design", IEEE Transactions on Software Engineering, 25(5), 1999, pp. 722-743.

5. Cutter Consortium, "Poor Project Management – Problem of E-Projects", October 2000, http://www.cutter.com/consortium/press/001019.html

6. Genero, M. "Defining and Validating Metrics for Conceptual Models". PhD. Thesis, Department of Informatics, University of Castilla-La Mancha, Spain, 2001.

338   Silvia Abrahão et al.

7. IFPUG: Function Point Counting Practices Manual, Release 4.1, International Function Points Users Group – IFPUG, Mequon, Wisconsin, USA, April 1999.
8. Lindland, O. I., Sindre, G., and Sølvberg, A. Understanding Quality in Conceptual Modeling, IEEE Software, Vol. 11, N° 2, pp. 42-49, 1994.
9. Nielsen, J. Designing Web Usability: The Practice of Simplicity, New Riders Pub., 2000.
10. Olsina, L., Rossi, G, A Quantitative Method for Quality Evaluation of Web Sites and Applications, *IEEE Multimedia*, Vol. 9, N° 4, 2002.
11. Pastor, O.; Abrahão, and S.M.; Fons, J. J. *"Object-Oriented Approach to Automate Web Applications Development"*, 2nd Int. Conference on Electronic Commerce and Web Technologies (EC-Web'01), Munich, Germany, Springer Verlag, 2001, 16-28.
12. Pastor, O., Abrahão, S. M., Molina, J. C., and Torres, I. "A FPA-like Measure for Object-Oriented Systems from Conceptual Models", 11th International Workshop on Software Measurement (IWSM'01), Montreal, Canada, Shaker Verlag, 2001, 51-69.
13. Ricca, F., and Tonella, P. "Understanding and Restructuring Web Sites with ReWeb", *IEEE Multimedia*, Vol 8, N° 2, pp. 40-51, 2001.

A Model and an XSL Framework for Analysing the Quality of WebML Conceptual Schemas

Sara Comai, Maristella Matera, and Andrea Maurino

Dipartimento di Elettronica e Informazione - Politecnico di Milano
Via Ponzio, 34/5, 20133 – Milano, Italy
{comai,matera,maurino}@elet.polimi.it

Abstract. Web conceptual models certainly represent a successful approach to the design of complex Web applications. Wrong uses of conceptual models may however introduce problems, which void the numerous advantages deriving from their exploitation in Web applications design. In this paper, we present a quality model for WebML, an XML-based Web conceptual model having a graphical notation. We also introduce an XSL-based framework able to automatically verify a set of quality attributes identified for WebML conceptual schemas. Our quality framework was born as a WebML-specific framework, but it is flexible enough to be applied to other Web conceptual models based on an XML specification.

1   Introduction

It is widely accepted that conceptual models are a prerequisite for successfully planning and designing complex software systems. Current Web applications are more and more complex software systems; Web conceptual models [1–4] have therefore recently emerged as a solution to face such a complexity.

The great advantage offered by Web conceptual models is that they allow reasoning at a high level of abstraction about the overall organization of a Web application, avoiding to early committing to detailed architectural and implementation issues. By providing common domain level concepts, they also support reuse of high-level artefacts [5], [11]. However, despite these advantages, conceptual modelling often results into a number of problems, which decrease the quality of the obtained artefacts, and in turn reduce the effectiveness of the development process.

Based on these promises, the need arises for methods to analyse the quality of conceptual schemas. However, schema quality strictly depends on the adopted modeling language - consider for example the numerous issues related to the semantic and syntactic correctness of a model-based specification. Therefore, this paper discusses an approach for analysing the quality of conceptual schemas based on WebML, a modelling language for visually specifying the content organization and the hypertext structure of a Web application that is also formally defined through an XML-based specification [4]. In particular, the paper presents the quality model on which our analysis is founded, and describes the features of *WebML Quality Analyser*, an XSL-

A. Olivé (Eds.): ER 2003 Ws, LNCS 2784, pp. 339–350, 2003.

based software framework, that is able to automatically verify and measure some quality attributes on WebML conceptual schemas. Although our discussion concentrates on issues related to WebML modeling, we however believe that the overall approach can be easily adopted in the context of other conceptual modeling methods.

The paper is organized as follows: Section 2 shortly describes the WebML model for the design of Web applications. Section 3 discusses about our notion of quality for WebML conceptual schemas, and introduces some measurable attributes that drive the quality analysis. Section 4 illustrates our analysis technique, and Section 5 presents the WebML Quality Analyser software architecture. Finally, Section 6 draws our conclusions.

2   WebML in a Nutshell

WebML (Web Modelling language) is a visual language for specifying the content structure of a Web application and the organization and presentation of such content in a hypertext [4]. Besides having a visual representation, WebML is also provided with an XML-based textual representation that is used to specify additional detailed properties, not conveniently expressible in the graphic notation. XML representation enables the automatic processing of WebML conceptual schemas by means of WebRatio (http://www.webratio.com), a CASE tool that is able to translate WebML visual specifications into concrete page templates.

WebML mainly consists of the *Data Model* and the *Hypertext Model*.

The WebML Data Model adopts the Entity-Relationship primitives for representing the organization of the application data. Its fundamental elements are therefore *entities*, defined as containers of data elements, and *relationships*, defined as semantic connections between entities. Entities have named properties, called *attributes*, with an associated type. Entities can be organized in *generalization hierarchies* and relationships can be restricted by means of *cardinality constraints*.

The WebML Hypertext Model enables describing how data specified in the data schema are assembled into information units and pages, and how these elements are interconnected to constitute a hypertext. The WebML hypertext model includes a *composition model*, concerning the definition of pages and their internal organization in terms of elementary interconnected units, and the *navigation model*, describing links between pages and content units to be provided to facilitate information location and browsing. The model also includes a *content management model*, offering a set of operations for the specifying management and update of content. These three models are detailed in the following sections. A broader description of the language and its formal definition can be found in [4] and at http://webml.org.

2.1   Composition Model

Composition modelling establishes the overall structure of the hypertexts, and mainly focuses on the definition of pages, which are the actual containers of information delivered to the user. Pages are made of *content units*, which are the elementary pieces of information extracted from the data sources and published within pages. Units (see Table 1 for their visual notation) denote one or more instances of the elements of the data schema, typically selected by means of queries over entities, attributes, or relationships. In particular, they allow displaying a set of attributes for a single entity instance (*data* unit), all the instances (or a subset of them) for a given entity (*multidata* unit), list of properties, also called descriptive keys, of a given set of entity instances (*index* unit), and also scrolling the elements of a set with commands like next/previous (*scroller* unit). An additional unit represents a form for collecting input values into fields (*data entry* unit).

Table 1. The five content units in the WebML composition model

Data Unit	Multi-data unit	Index unit	Scroller unit	Data Entry unit
Data unit	Multidata unit	Index unit	Scroller unit ◁ ▷	Entry unit

2.2   Navigation Model

The navigation model is based on the definition of links that connect units and pages, thus forming the hypertext. Links can connect units in a variety of legal configurations, yielding to composite navigation mechanisms. Links between units are used to carry some information (called *context*) from the source unit to the destination unit.

As an example, Fig. 1 depicts a simple hypertext, consisting of two pages. Papers Page includes an index unit showing the list of all the instances of the entity Paper, from which one single paper can be selected and its details shown through the data unit. The link between the index unit and the data unit carries the information (i.e., the context) about the paper selected from the index. The data unit uses this context for displaying the instance details. A further link allows instead navigating from Papers Page to Authors Page, where a multidata unit shows data about all the instances of the entity Author. Links between pages do not carry any context: in the example the content of Authors Page is independent from the content of Papers Page.

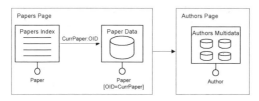

Fig. 1. Example of contextual and non-contextual navigation

A link can be tagged as *automatic* to specify that the link is "navigated" without needing user intervention. Going back to the example of Fig. 1, we can note that the user must explicitly select an item from the index to populate the data unit. If we alternatively define the link between the index unit and the data unit as automatic, the achieved effect is that, even without the user intervention, the data unit is filled with some default content coming from the index unit: for example, the first item of the index is displayed. Automatic links are visually denoted through a label "A" placed over the link arrow.

2.3   Content Management Model

WebML supports also the specification of Web applications requiring write access to information content. WebML primitives for expressing content management operations, whose notation is reported in Table 2, allow creating, deleting or modifying an instance of an entity (respectively represented through the *create*, *delete* and *modify* units), or adding or dropping a relationship between two instances (respectively represented through the *connect* and *disconnect* units).

From the user point of view the execution of an operation is usually a side effect of navigating a link: for example, users fill in a form and when they clicks on a submit button a create operation is performed to insert the new data into the application data source.

Table 2. WebML operation units

Create unit	Delete unit	Modify unit	Connect unit	Disconnect unit

3   A Quality Model for WebML Conceptual Schemas

Web conceptual models provide a valuable support for reasoning at a high level of abstraction and systematically defining the overall organization of an application. On the other hand, their use may arise several problems, which decrease the effectiveness and the efficiency of the development process, especially when conceptual schemas are to be automatically translated into a running application. Appropriate techniques can therefore be adopted for conceptual schemas analysis, so that problems can be discovered early at design time, when error recovery requires less effort.

This section presents a quality model for WebML, i.e., the set of the quality attributes that are relevant for the analysis of WebML schemas, and the measurement methods that can be used to assess such attributes [7]. In particular, the presented model focuses on two quality factors, *correctness* and *usability*, that in order to be measured have been decomposed into a number of finer-grained attributes.

It is worth noting that other factors or attributes could contribute to make our quality model more complete. However, aim of this paper is not being exhaustive on all the possible quality analysis dimensions. Rather, we want to provide a flexible framework, which could be further extended for the analysis of the WebML schema quality, and possibly adopted for the analysis of others Web conceptual models.

3.1   Correctness Attributes

The correctness of a conceptual schema representing a Web application can be approached from two different perspectives:

- A conceptual schema is *syntactically* correct if all the constructs used in the model are correct and consistent with respect to a given syntax: for example, looking at Fig. 1, all the units are correctly defined over an entity of the data model, links connect two units or two pages, and it does not occur that a unit is erroneously connected with a page.

- A conceptual schema is *semantically* correct if the corresponding Web application runs correctly, according to the semantics associated with each single unit and navigation link. For example, the two pages of Fig. 1 have the following semantics: when Papers Page is entered, the content of the index unit is first computed; every time the user clicks on one anchor of the index, the content of the data unit is calculated using the context passed through the link; finally, when the user clicks on the link exiting the page, Authors Page is displayed. In this example, the behaviour of the described hypertext is unambiguous and correct.

Syntactic correctness verification is quite straightforward, consisting of a check over syntactic properties of WebML primitives. We will therefore concentrate on semantic correctness only, which can be studied by adopting formal methods. In [6] the WebML model semantics has been formally specified in terms of Statecharts [9], with the aim of analysing and predicting semantic problems. From this analysis, a list of possible semantic correctness criteria have emerged:

- **Absence of conflicts:** A conflict arises when, starting from a particular state in the Web application (i.e., a particular composition of units and links), two alternative states (i.e., different compositions of units and links) can be reached, and one of them must be chosen. Two classes of conflicts have been identified by [9] for generic systems; they may apply to Web conceptual models conflicts as well, according to the following definitions:
  - *Deterministic conflicts* arise when two different states can be reached, but one of them has an implicit higher priority and is therefore followed.
  - *Non-deterministic* conflicts arise when two different states can be reached, and no priorities can be implicitly assigned to them.
- **Absence of racing conditions**: A racing condition arises when different (but legal) execution orders in computing a set of units provide different results. An example of racing condition will be shown in Section 4.1.
- **Absence of deadlocks:** in WebML a deadlock occurs when two (or more) units cannot be computed, because they depend from each other, and each of them is waiting for the other to be computed.

The list we present here is not complete and may be enriched with several other criteria, referring for example to the reachability of all the pages, the reachability of all the units inside a page, and so on.

3.2   Usability Attributes

Besides correctness issues, some other properties can be analysed in WebML conceptual schemas, which refer to consistency and completeness issues having impact over the usability of the final application. Usability is traditionally evaluated by means of inspections or user-based testing conducted over running releases of the application, being them intermediate prototypes or the final application. When the development process is based on the adoption of a conceptual model, some structural properties influencing usability can be however analysed at design time.

Several attributes may be associated to the notion of usability, many of them being related to aesthetic aspect of pages [10]. Our analysis is however focused on a set of structural hypertext properties, which refer to navigation definition, page content composition, and invocation within pages of content management operations and external services, and therefore concentrates on the following attributes:

- **Consistency:** It refers to the use throughout the application hypertext of coherent patterns for page composition, navigation, and operation invocation, whenever the same situations occur. Consistency must be privileged, because it helps users identify reliable expectations about the overall application structure, and easily recognize the way information can be accessed and operations activated.
- **Ease of Navigation:** It refers to the availability of links for supporting users while exploring the Web application. The minimum set of links expected in a Web application is the one directly induced by the relationships defined among entities in the data schema. However, having only these links may be too limiting for users, and a richer set of links is recommended for efficiency purposes. For example, navigation can be improved at least by providing each page in the hypertext with persistent links to the Home Page. Also, if a hypertext consists of different areas, then entry points to such areas must be provided in each page.
- **Low Page Density:** It refers to the number of content units and operation invocations within single hypertext pages. According to a well-established usability principle [10], a high page density may affect the users understandability of the provided contents and operations. It also greatly affects the complexity of page computation, because unit population translates into a high number of queries over data sources.

4   The Analysis Method

Our analysis method is centered on the identification, within the WebML conceptual schemas, of *patterns* representing potential sources of problems. A pattern consists of a chain of units and links within one or more pages. For each quality attribute it is possible to identify one or more patterns that represent hypertext configurations to be retrieved within the schema and analysed in order to identify potential attribute violations. Each attribute is therefore associated with a set of *pattern descriptions*, specifying the WebML compositions that need to be retrieved, and with an *analysis method*, specifying the procedure to be executed for analysing the retrieved patterns. In particular, the analysis method may consist of a *metric computation*, generating aggregated numerical values that quantify the level in which the analysed attribute is satisfied, or of a *condition checking*, generating warnings that highlight potential problems. The following sections describe some examples of patterns and analysis methods.

4.1 Semantic Correctness Analysis

By analysing the formal specification of WebML, it is possible to find out possible patterns of units and links giving rise to non-determinism, racing conditions and so on. Semantic correctness can then be expressed as a condition over the pattern description.

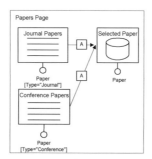

Fig. 2. Example of racing condition

As an example of pattern description, consider the *racing condition pattern* depicted in Fig. 2: two indexes allow the reader to select either a conference paper or a journal paper; the selected paper is then detailed through a data unit. If the two links between the index units and the data unit are defined as automatic, a default paper for both indexes is determined, and their contexts are automatically propagated through the two links. This results into an unpredictable navigation context to be passed to the data unit, and represents a racing condition.

This particular case of unit composition generating a racing condition can be extended to the general pattern where a unit receives its context from two different paths, both contemporarily "navigable" and having automatic links. For each correctness criteria, patterns like the previous one can be described and verified in the application specification.

4.2   Usability Analysis

In case of usability analysis, pattern description and analysis method can vary depending on the attribute to be measured.

In some cases, pattern description can refer to single WebML primitives, or to very simple compositions. For example, page density can be measured by insulating pages in the hypertext specification, and calculating the number of included content units and operations departing from them. Therefore, the pattern description for Low Page Density analysis simply specifies a page, and the analysis method then consists in computing the number of content units and operation per page.

In other cases, pattern description and analysis method require a more complex specification, as it happens for consistency analysis. Consistency analysis is aimed at verifying if one or more patterns, providing solutions to well-defined problems, are applied consistently. In WebML, a pattern typically consists of a *core specification*, representing the invariant WebML unit composition that characterizes the pattern, and a number of *pattern variants*, which extend the core specification with all the valid modalities in which the pattern can start (*starting* variants) or terminate (*termination* variants). Starting variants describe which units can be used for passing the context to the core pattern composition. Termination variants describe instead how the context generated by the core pattern composition is passed to successive compositions in the hypertext.

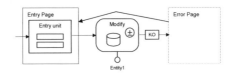

Fig. 3. Core specification of the modify pattern

Sometimes it happens that, even when the same pattern is adopted along the whole application, some consistency problems are caused by the use of different pattern variants. Consistency analysis may therefore correspond to verifying if a same pattern is applied with the same starting and termination variants, whenever the same problem occurs [8]. For this analysis, the pattern description consists of the core pattern specification, plus all the starting and termination variants - these compositions must indeed be extracted from the schema and analysed. The analysis method corresponds to quantifying the distribution of pattern variants throughout the application conceptual schema, highlighting the most adopted variant and the number of times in which different variants have been used. Further analysis of such data can then highlight pages where possible inconsistencies occur.

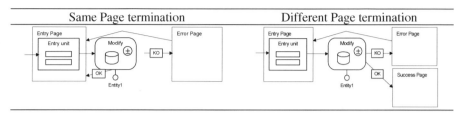

Fig. 4. Two termination variants for the Modify pattern

As an example of pattern description for consistency analysis, let us consider the *Modify pattern*: it consists of a hypertext configuration centered upon the WebML Modify unit (see Table 2), used for specifying the invocation of an operation for modifying an entity instance. This pattern is used whenever users must insert some data for updating old ones, as for example it happens when users want to change the quantity of ordered items in a shopping cart. As reported in Fig. 3, the core pattern specification consists of an entry unit, providing a form for inputting new data, and a modify operation unit. The link defined between the entry unit and the operation transports the new attributes values inserted by users, and the OID of the entity instance to be modified, passed to the entry unit by some other units external to the core pattern specification. If the operation fails, an error page is displayed with a message inviting users to repeat the operation, and a link to the initial page.

The modify pattern can have at least three starting variants, *Start-with-data-unit*, *Start-with-index-unit*, *Start-with-multidata-unit*, depending on the unit that precedes the entry unit and supplies the OID of the entity instance to be modified. As illustrated in Fig. 4, it can also have two termination variants, *Same Page* and *Different Page*, that after the operation completion respectively lead back users to the same page in which the operation has started or in a different page. In the first case, users are allowed to further modify the same entity instance or, depending on the adopted starting variant, they can also choose to modify a different entity instance. In the second case, a further modification of the same entity instance or of a different one requires one or more additional navigation steps for going back to the initial page.

5   An XSL Framework for the Automatic Analysis of WebML Schemas

The analysis technique previously illustrated is suitable to be automatically performed by means of a software tool. In this section we describe the architecture of the *WebML Quality Analyser* (from now on simply WQA), an XSL-based framework that can be applied over the XML specification of WebML conceptual schemas, for analysing their quality [8].

WQA employs XSL rules to measure the quality attributes described in Section 3. As shown in Fig. 5, the framework is based on two repositories: the *Pattern Descriptions* repository contains the XSL description of the pattern to be used in the quality analysis; the *Quality Criteria* repository includes the XSL specifications of the quality criteria, in terms of the corresponding analysis procedures to be performed over patterns.

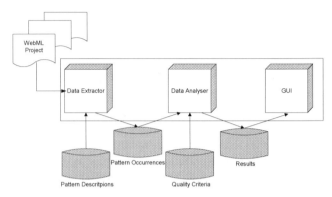

Fig. 5. WQA software architecture

Given an XML specification of a conceptual WebML schema, first the *Data Extractor* module applies the XSL rules stored in the *Pattern Descriptions* repository, to detect all the occurrences of the described patterns in the WebML specification. The identified patterns are returned in XML format and stored in the *Pattern Occurrences* repository. The *Data Analyser* module then executes the analysis procedures coded as XSL rules in the *Quality Criteria* repository, for verifying if the extracted patterns satisfy the quality criteria. The result of this analysis is a further XML document, stored in the *Results* repository, containing the aggregate values of measured attributes or a set of warnings, depending on the adopted analysis procedure. Finally, a GUI module displays the analysis results by showing the aggregate values in form of charts and warnings as textual sentences.

This framework is very flexible and extensible: new measures can be easily specified by means of XSL rules and added to the WQA repositories. In this way, each design team can define its own quality criteria, and code their measures within WQA by simply writing XSL code, an extensively used W3C standard.

Fig. 6 shows a simplified version of an XSL rule from the Pattern Description repository, which is used to identify occurrences of the Same Page termination variant for the Modify pattern. The Data Extractor module invokes the fragment of Fig. 6, which finds a data entry unit tag in the XML specification of the WebML conceptual schema (line 1). Three variables are then defined (lines 2-4) to identify the modify unit, the target of the link exiting the modify unit, and the page containing the entry unit from which the operation starts. If this page coincides with the target of the link exiting the modify unit (line 5), then a Same Page termination pattern variant is found: the XSL rule creates a new tag in the resulting document, called ELEMENT (line 6), having only one attribute named page (lines 7-9), whose value is taken from the variable corresponding to the starting page. Notice that, by changing the condition in the IF clause also the Different Page termination pattern can be described.

```
1 <xsl:template match="ENTRYUNIT">
2    <xsl:variable name="modify" select="(id(LINK/@to)[self::MODIFYUNIT])"/>
3    <xsl:variable name="target" select="$modify/LINK/@to"/>
4    <xsl:variable name="page" select="../@id"/>
5    <xsl:if test="(id($target)[self::PAGE[(@id = $page)]]) >
6      <xsl:element name="ELEMENT">
7        <xsl:attribute name="page">
8          <xsl:value-of select="$page"/>
9        </xsl:attribute>
10     </xsl:element>
11   </xsl:if>
....
```

Fig. 6. A simplified version of an XSL rule

6   Conclusions and Future Works

This paper has presented some preliminary results about the WebML approach to the quality analysis of Web conceptual schemas. The approach is based on the definition of a quality model for WebML, and on the use of the WQA software tool, which is able to automatically analyse the XML specification of WebML conceptual schemas according to the defined quality model.

The overall approach is under evolution. First of all, we are trying to validate the reliability of the defined attribute measurements. Also, we are trying to extend the quality model, by discovering new quality factors and attributes that can be relevant for quality in WebML modeling, as well as their corresponding measures. Part of our work is also devoted to improving the tool user interface on two different directions, one related to the visualization of analysis results, the other related to the extension of the tool with a new module for the visual definition of new quality attribute measurements to be computed by WQA.

Although the tool is still available in a prototype version, it has been already used for the quality analysis of very large applications, thus providing proof of its effectiveness (see [8] for more details).

References

1. Atzeni, P., Mecca, G., Merialdo, P.: Data-Intensive Web Sites: Design and Maintenance. *World Wide Web*, vol. 4 (2001) 21-47

2. Baresi, L., Garzotto, F., Paolini, P.: Extending UML for Modeling Web Applications. In: Proc. of the 34th Hawaii Int. Conf. on System Sciences, Hawaii, USA, IEEE Press (2001)

3. Bieber, M., Isakowitz, B.T. (eds.): Special issue on "Designing Hypermedia Applications". *CACM*, Vol. 38, no. 8 (1995)

350   Sara Comai et al.

4. Ceri, S., Fraternali, P., Bongio, A., Brambilla, M., Comai, S., Matera, M.: *Designing Data-Intensive Web Applications*. Morgan Kaufmann, December 2002.

5. Ceri, S., Fraternali, P., Matera, M.: Conceptual Modeling of Data-Intensive Web Applications. *IEEE Internet Computing*, Vol. 6, no. 4 (2002) 20-30

6. Comai, S., Fraternali, P.: A semantic model for specifying hypermedia applications using WebML. In: Proc. of Int. Semantic Web Workshop, Infrastructure and Applications for the Semantic Web, Stanford University, California, USA (2001)

7. Fenton, N.E., Pfleeger, S.L.: *Software Metrics* (2nd ed.). Thompson Publishing (1997)

8. Fraternali, P., Matera, M., Maurino, A.: WQA: An XSL Framework for Analyzing the Quality of Web Applications. In: Proc. of IWWOST 2002 - 2nd Int. Workshop on Web-Oriented Software Technologies, Malaga, Spain (2002) 46-61

9. Harel, D., Naamad, A.: The STATEMATE Semantics of Statecharts. *ACM TOSEM*, Vol. 5, no. 4 (1996) 293-333

10. Nielsen, J.: *Designing Web Usability: The Practice of Simplicity*. New Riders Publishing, Indianapolis (2000)

11. Schwabe, D., Esmeraldo, L., Rossi, G., Lyardet, F.: Engineering Web Applications for Reuse. *IEEE Multimedia*, Vol. 8(1) (2001) 20-31

Quality of Interactive Models

John Krogstie and Håvard D. Jørgensen

Norwegian University of Science and Technology
Institute of Computer and Information Sciences
and SINTEF Telecom and Informatics, Norway
{hdj,jok}@sintef.no

Abstract. Interactive models have been proposed as a general technique for increasing the flexibility of computerised information systems. Interactive models are first made during development, but are also available for manipulation by the users at run-time, and the model contents influence the behaviour of the system. Such models are more immersed in day-to-day work activities than the models conventionally developed during software development. Consequently, they face stronger requirements, particularly regarding comprehensibility, simplicity and flexibility. A comprehensive overview and classification of these requirements is currently lacking in the literature on interactive models. We have earlier developed a framework for understanding and assessing the quality of models in general, with emphasis on conceptual models. The framework has earlier been specialised in several directions, but primarily for passive models such as enterprise and requirements models. In this paper we extend our quality framework towards assessing interactive models. These extensions are based on our experiences from implementing interactive modelling languages and support systems. Whereas parts of the framework can be used as originally defined, other areas give quite different results due to the much tighter interplay between model changes and domain changes than what is found when using traditional modelling and system development approaches. This results in a useful deepening of our framework, and improvement of its practical applicability for understanding the quality of interactive models.

1   Introduction

Today's organisations are characterised by dynamic, only partially understood and error-prone environments. The constantly changing nature of the competitive environment in the global network economy creates emergent organisational forms, where "every feature of social organisations are continually emergent" [39]. Traditional enterprise systems tend to be quite inflexible, hardly adaptable at runtime, and primarily support the organisationally agreed processes. Extensions of these systems have typically been focused on dealing with exceptions and have thus offered some support for adaptive processes. These types of systems, however, have typically overlooked emergent processes, which seem to encompass an increasing part of organised activity. An emergent process is not totally predefined, but partly emerges as one is working on the tasks of the process. An alternative approach is to support

A. Olivé (Eds.): ER 2003 Ws, LNCS 2784, pp. 351-363, 2003.

interactive models as a general technique for increasing the flexibility of computerised information systems. With interactive models, the IS makes the models available to the users at runtime, and the behaviour of the system is partly controlled by the models. By altering the models the users can thus modify the behaviour of the system to fit their needs.

Over the last years, a lot of effort has been made to improve the understanding on quality of models and modelling languages used in IS development e.g. on business process models [20], data models [33], requirement specification models [26], design models e.g. in UML [25], and conceptual models in general [24,26,27]. What characterises most of this work, is that these traditional IS models are passive relative to the end-users use of the information system. Little has been done do look specifically at quality for interactive models. We will in this paper extend and deepen our quality framework [26] to also be a help in connection to the assessment and evaluation of quality of interactive models.

The following section describes in more detail the needs for and characteristics of interactive models. Section 3 describes briefly the original quality framework, whereas section 4 describes the specialisation of this frameworks for interactive models. In the conclusion we highlight the contribution of the paper, both relative to the quality framework, and specifically relative to our increased possibility for developing support environments that enable interactive models of high quality.

2   Interactive and Conceptual Models

Research into conceptual modelling has concentrated on systems *development* activities. Models of work environments have long been used to analyse the problem domain, to capture and structure user requirements. Most of these approaches focus on the relationship between model elements and the real world objects that they represent. Individual, social and situational aspects of model *usage* have had less influence upon mainstream information systems engineering. The modellers are mostly systems developers and experts, not end-users. A fresh look at the role of models to manage and change system *operation* can complement this, enabling information systems to better meet local user needs and changing environments. Supporting learning and knowledge management is another main motivation [22]. Chen et al [11] has pointed to active modelling as a major future direction for research in conceptual modelling, including model execution, end user participation, and interaction. Greenwood et al [18] argue that active models can enable IS to meet many business needs that current technologies fail to support.

Models are generally defined as explicit representations of some portions of reality as perceived by some actor [42]. A model is *active* if it directly influences the reality it reflects, i.e. if changes to the model also change the way some actors perceive reality. Actors in this context include users as well as software components and services. *Model activation* is the process by which a model affects reality. Model activation involves actors interpreting the model and to some extent adjusting their behaviour accordingly. This process can be

- *Automated*, where a software component interprets the model alone,
- *Manual*, where the model guides the actions of human actors, or
- *Interactive*, where prescribed aspects of the model are automatically interpreted and ambiguous parts are left to the human actor to resolve.

Fully automated activation implies that the model must be formal and complete, while manual and interactive activation also can handle incomplete and partly informal models. Completing this conceptual framework, we define a model to be *interactive* if it is interactively activated. That a model is interactive entails a co-evolution of the model and its domain. A model that does not change will not be able to reflect aspects of reality that changes, nor can it reflect evolution of a human actor's understanding. Consequently, an interactive model that does not evolve will deteriorate. It contributes to change but does not reflect this change. The process of updating an interactive model is traditionally called *articulation*. The interplay of articulation and activation reflects the mutual constitution of interactive models and the social reality they reflect. The software components that support intertwined articulation and activation are termed *model activators*.

The most developed theoretical approach to this field is Peter Wegner's interaction framework [41, 42]. Its development was triggered by the realisation that machines involving users in their problem solving, could solve a larger class of problems than algorithmic systems computing in isolation [23,41]. The primary characteristic of an *interaction machine* is that it can pose questions to users during its computation. The process can be a multi-step conversation between the user and the machine, each being able to take the initiative.

2.1   Information Systems with Interactive Models

Workflow [6], document classification and retrieval [4], product data management [17], co-operation support, knowledge based systems and reflective systems are areas where active and interactive models have been applied. Our primary practical experience with interactive models is through the ongoing EXTERNAL project [14,31,32], where our aim is to facilitate inter-organisational co-operation also in knowledge intensive tasks. Three different case studies are currently underway; one in business consulting, the second a network of co-operating small and medium-sized enterprises (SMEs), and the third an international research project.

The EXTERNAL infrastructure integrates four model activators:

- METIS [30], a general purpose enterprise modelling and visualisation tool,
- CHIPS [19], a co-operative hypermedia tool integrated with process and communication support,
- SimVision [29], a project simulator that can be used to analyse resource allocation, highlighting bottlenecks and actor backlogs.
- WORKWARE [21], an emergent workflow management system available over a standard web-browser with to-do-lists, document sharing, process enactment, awareness mechanisms and email integration.

Although focussing on instance level models, we can also model on a generic level, and bridge generic (type-level) models and instance models. A first version of a model on the type level can often be developed in the traditional way, or be reused based on an existing reference process, with no immediate interaction by a user. In addition to task breakdown and decision points of the overall workflow, the language we use (based on [8,21]) includes description of roles linked to the task which can be filled by concrete resources (i.e. persons, organisations, tools, or information objects) when instantiated.

The resulting instance model can later be reused, either as a starting point for another instance, or by looking at discrepancies between how work has actually been done, and how it is described in the generic model, and use this as a basis for updating the generic model.

3   Framework for Model Quality

The model quality framework [24,26,27] we use as a starting point has several distinguishing properties:

- It is closely linked to linguistic and semiotic concepts because we recognise that modelling is essentially making statements in some language. In particular, the core of the framework including the discussion on syntax, semantics, and pragmatics is parallel to the use of these terms in the semiotic theory of Morris [36], and the full framework is based on work in organisational semiotics [16].
- It is based on a constructivist world-view [2], recognising that models are usually created as part of a dialogue between the participants involved in modelling, whose knowledge of the modelling domain changes as modelling takes place, and where the domain is also developed (socially (re) constructed) as a side-effect of the modelling activity.
- It distinguishes between goals and means that supports the achievement of the goals. Even if it can be argued from both activity theory [13] and decision theory [37] that the interrelationships between goals and means are being determined through the preference function of the modeller applied at the modelling task at hand, we have found that most modelling techniques in practice can be said to contribute directly primarily to a specific model quality goal, and only indirectly to other quality goals.

The main concepts of the framework and their relationships are shown in the Figure 1. We have taken a set-theoretic approach to the discussion of model quality at different semiotic levels, which has been defined as the correspondence between statements belonging to the following sets:

- *G,* the (normally organisationally defined) goals of the modelling task. In connection to e.g. a requirements specification model, this includes goals related to what the system to be made is to achieve in organisational terms, when it should be available for users etc. Such goals are often in conflict with each other and a trade-off is often done based on the priorities of the organisation.

- **L**, the language extension, i.e., the set of all statements that are possible to make according to the graphemes, vocabulary, and syntax of the modelling languages used.
- **D**, the domain, i.e., the set of all statements which can be stated about the situation at hand. Note that the domains we are normally dealing with in information systems development has been socially constructed, and are more or less inter-subjectively agreed. That the world is socially constructed does not make it any less important to model that world [12], to be able to understand and potentially reconstruct it.
- **M**, the externalised model, i.e. the set of all statements in someone's model of part of the perceived reality written in a language.
- **K_s**, the relevant explicit knowledge of the set of stakeholders being involved in modelling (the audience **A**). A subset of the audience is those actively involved in modelling, and their knowledge is indicated by **K_M**.
- **I**, the social actor interpretation, i.e. the set of all statements which the audience think that an externalised model consists of.
- **T**, the technical actor interpretation, i.e. the statements in the model as 'interpreted' by the different model activators.

The main quality types are indicated by solid lines between the sets, and are described briefly below, basically following the levels of a semiotic ladder as described in [16].

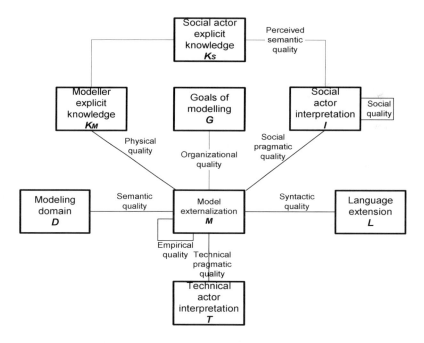

Fig. 1. Main parts of the quality framework

- Physical quality: The basic quality goals on the physical level is externalisation, that the knowledge K of the domain D of some social actor has been articulated with the help of a modelling language, and internaliseability, that the externalised model M is persistent and available enabling the audience to make sense of it.
- Empirical quality: deals with predicable error frequencies when a model is read or written by different users, coding (e.g. shapes of boxes) and ergonomics of computer-human interaction for documentation and models.
- Syntactic quality is the correspondence between the model M and the language extension L of the language in which the model is written. This includes aspects of lexicon correctness, syntax correctness and structural quality [15].
- Semantic quality is the correspondence between the model M and the domain D. The framework contains two semantic goals; Validity which means that all statements made in the model are correct relative to the domain and completeness which means that the model contains all the statements which is found in the domain.
- Perceived semantic quality is the similar correspondence between the participants interpretation I of a model M and his or hers current knowledge K of the domain D. Whereas the primary goal for semantic quality is a correspondence between the externalised model and the domain as indicated above, this correspondence can neither be established nor checked directly. To build a model, one has to go through the participant's knowledge regarding the domain, and to check the model, one has to compare with the participant's interpretation of the externalised model. Hence, what we observe at quality control is not the semantic quality of the model, but a perceived semantic quality based on comparisons of the two interpretations.
- Pragmatic quality is the correspondence between the model M and the audience's interpretation of it (I).
- The goal for social quality is agreement among participants' interpretations I.
- The organisational quality of the model relates to that all statements in the model directly or indirectly contributes to fulfilling the prioritised goals of modelling (organisational validity) , and that all the prioritised goals of modelling is addressed through the model (organisational completeness).

Goals and means to achieve these goals being model and language properties and modelling activities have been identified, and we will return to these in more detail throughout the paper. One of these means is the use of appropriate modelling languages. We have elsewhere discussed a process model for the dynamic use of the quality framework [38]. A large-scale empirical trial of applying the core of framework is reported in [5].

4   Interactive Models in the Light of the Quality Framework

Compared to traditional models used during the early phases of systems development, interactive models are faced with a different set of requirements, which we have elicited through the EXTERNAL case-studies. We summarise these using the sets in the quality framework, before outlining how these requirements influence the discussion of quality at the different levels within the quality framework.

- G, the goals of modelling is more related to have an up to date, tailored model to support the individual users in their actual tasks, and is less directly linked to overall goals of an organisation. Note that this is here a balance, since one should only be able to change parts of the model that it is not defined as very important for the organisation to keep stable and traceable. Secondarily the model should support organisational learning.
- L, the language extension: Local modifications to match the needs of a particular enterprise are supported by instance modelling. This limit the scope of a change to the local situation, removing much of the complexity that has prevented modelling by end users at the more generic level. It is also a prerequisite for establishing an immediate connection between the domain and the interactive model, enabling learning and knowledge management anchored in practice, as discussed above. For externalisation and user participation, it is important to keep the core modelling languages simple, and represented in such a way that a large number of people with a diversity of backgrounds are able to use them.
- D, the domain. More closely related to the task at hand, and not to a generic support of an abstract domain. It is also more obvious to see how the modelling quite instantly are able to have organisational effect and change the domain through articulation of new knowledge.
- M, the externalised model: Whereas traditional models in most cases are on the type level, most of the work with interactive models are on an instance level.
- K_m and K_s. A wider range of people are actively involved in modelling, amplifying the social, psychological and organisational aspects. More people (potentially all users) act as modellers, thus the difference between the set of modellers and general social actor is smaller.
- I, the social actor interpretation: need to be able to quickly update the interpretation of model changes done by one person, that also influences other people
- T, the technical actor interpretation, the model as interpreted by information systems. The models are available at run-time, but might only be partly defined, i.e. the model activators used must be made with interaction possibilities in mind.

A main difference between interactive and traditional IS-models is how rapid changes in the different sets influence each other. The main quality types are specialised in the following way.

Physical Quality. The physical quality goal of externalisation is closely linked to aspects of language *quality* as means. For interactive models, the modellers include not only software professionals, but also normal end users. Hence, stronger requirements to support physical quality are likely, both because end users lack experience with conceptual modelling, and one will want to update the models more frequently due to learning, and this needs to be supported. The possibility to rapidly update the model (and thus the underlying support system) is one of the main advantages with this approach. In systems engineering, new approaches like incremental development and extreme programming attempt to shorten these learning cycles, but they are still hampered with a relatively long time-span from learning of the end-user to model and system-change compared to the what can be achieved with interactive models. Also, users are likely to have more in-depth knowledge K of their domain D than software developers who have seldom taken part in the practice of the domain. Consequently, the potential for high semantic quality is greater. Hence, simplicity, adaptability and user-orientedness of the modelling language are even more crucial for interactive models than for their traditional counterparts. Meta-modelling involves changing the modelling language and is typically carried out in order to improve its suitability with respect to the domain

Internaliseability has two primary means, persistence and availability: Many of the general activities in connection to this part of physical quality are based on traditional database-functionality using a repository-solution for the long-term internal representation of the model.

Empirical quality deals with error frequencies when a model is read or written by different users, coding, and ergonomics of computer-human interaction. For computer-output based on the process models specifically, many of the principles and tools used for improved human-computer interface are relevant at this level. The general guidelines for diagrammatic and textual models at this level can to a large extent be reused when discussing the quality of interactive models.

Syntactic quality has the goal of *syntactic correctness*, i.e. that all statements in the model are according to the syntax and vocabulary of the modelling language. As a result of providing user oriented models, interactive model approaches will have to enhance formal syntax means by providing more functionality in the area of error detection, prevention and recovery; especially regarding allowing the continued enactment of completed, error-free parts. For the parts of the model that is only manually activated on the other hand, syntactic quality is of lesser importance.

Semantic quality has the quality goals of *feasible validity* and *feasible completeness*. Validity here means all statements in the model are correct and relevant to the problem, while completeness means the model contains all statements that *would be* correct. Since we normally cannot proceed with modelling endlessly, we have introduced the notion of *feasibility* in these quality goals relative to the goal of modelling. Consistency checking here is regarded as means to achieve semantic quality goals of feasible validity and feasible comprehension. Other general semantic quality means are formal semantics and model reuse.

Actions often involves changing the domain D, and should thus be reflected in the model M. If an action is supported by an information system with interactive models, it can be automatically captured, increasing the semantic quality of the interactive model without extra work for the users.

Perceived semantic quality covers the correspondence between actors' interpretation of the model and their current knowledge of the domain and has the goals of *perceived validity* and *perceived completeness*. Important means to achieve high perceived semantic quality are the same as those for achieving semantic quality, with the addition of participant training and *requisite variety*, i.e. to maintain several, possibly conflicting, model views since the domain may not be intersubjectively agreed upon. Since we are able to support different variants on the instance level, the potential variety of models of the 'same' generic process can be beneficial for organisational learning and development.

Pragmatic Quality. General means to increase pragmatic quality include executability, animation and simulation, but also advanced techniques like model transformations, model filtering, model translation, and explanation generation explaining both the model, the meta-model and model execution through the generation of natural language explanation. The core of active models is how models are *activated*. Activation implies *interpretation* of the model and corresponding *action* by either the social or the technical actors [7]. Technical pragmatic quality demands complete models with an operational semantics, while the social pragmatic quality of the models and the cognitive economy of externalisation (K→M) often demands more flexible, informal approaches. Interactive model interpretation enables models with user-controlled levels of formality, detail and preciseness, bridging the gap between theory and practice

This immediate nature of interactive models, stemming from the interaction of the real world domain and model, can also enhance the social pragmatic quality of the models. When both the real world and the model that reflects it are available and adaptable for the users, the connections between them are easier to understand. Simulation and training methods can be developed that utilises this connection.

Social quality has the goal of *feasible agreement*, where agreement covers agreement in knowledge, agreement in interpretation and both relative and absolute agreement. Feasible agreement does not have to imply consensus, it only implies resolving inconsistencies by choosing alternatives where benefits of choosing exceed the costs of working out an agreement. Means to achieve high social quality include inconsistency modelling, model integration and conflict resolution; but also the so far seemingly untapped potential of linking modelling tools with argumentation support tools. In systems development, agreement among participants about the requirements is crucial since they form the basis for a lot of detailed technical work that cannot easily be redone. Interactive models have a more immediate connection to the system and the environment it represents, so users have access also to the domain when negotiating a shared understanding. Social quality is thus perhaps not as important when assumptions readily can be tested immediately in the real world.

If an interactive model is to be reused in another setting, agreement is more important. Social quality of interactive models influences the processes of negotiating meaning and domesticating reusable model fragments into the local situation and work practice [40]. In these processes, the ability to represent conflicting interpretations and the argumentation underlying this, and make local modifications, is just as important as the ability to represent agreement (the end result) in an unambiguous way. Also, since people learn through their work and use of the models, agreement is likely to be partial and temporary.

Organisational Quality. When using interactive models, the models are more a work tool for the individual and group, utilising instance models. Thus the primary goal for the model to fulfil is those of the user and group in their situated action. When reusing models that of some reason are not to be changed (e.g. because they decode a procedure that need to be done in a certain way to be legally correct), these organisational rules have to be enforced by the support-system, thus it must be possible to differentiate which parts of the model that can be changed and those that can not. Support for this can be integrated with generic access control mechanisms of the systems. Tracking of model elements back to organisational goals or earlier base-lined models is traditional means for supporting the organisational quality.

Interactive models should be coupled to organisational learning. At the organisational level; process models are particular knowledge representations resembling organisational images [1]. An organisation's theory of action is embedded in a behavioural world which shapes and constrains its theory-in-use; To achieve double-loop learning – i.e. "doing the right things" instead of "doing the things right" – models must include links to intentional aspects [9]. The gap between real and modelled processes has been highlighted as a major inhibiting factor of process support systems and organisational learning [1] alike. Thus interactive models has a great potential for supporting knowledge management and process improvement. Nonaka and Takeuchi's theory on knowledge creation [34,35] also has implications for modelling and activation. Knowledge creation is a *collective* endeavour, hence modelling also should be viewed as a dynamic and collective endeavour [10]. Interactive models as an articulation of work also play the role of boundary objects for supporting perspective making and perspective taking [3]. By giving users control over the models, we empower them to externalise and share knowledge.

5   Conclusions and Further Work

As earlier stated, Chen et al [11] has pointed to active modelling as a major future direction for research in conceptual modelling. This paper has focussed on interactive models, which is a kind of active models created and used during the operation of information systems, as a general technique for increasing the flexibility of computerised systems. Differences in the development and use of these kinds of models and the models conventionally used for systems development have been discussed. We have earlier developed a framework for understanding and assessing the quality of models in general, with emphasis on conceptual models. In this paper we have extended our quality framework towards supporting the assessment of interactive models. These extensions are based on our experiences from implementation and usage of interactive models and support systems, mainly in the EXTERNAL project. Whereas parts of the framework can be used as is, specifically most of the discussion around physical, empirical, and syntactic quality, other areas (the more high-level, social aspects) give quite different results due to the much tighter interplay between model changes and domain changes than what is found in traditional modelling approaches. This results in a useful specialisation of our framework, and improves its practical applicability for discussing the quality of interactive models. More important is how the framework gives us further input on improving the possibility for developing support environments that enable interactive models of high quality.

Further work on the approach needs to be done to more clearly differentiate the requirements of interactive models on traditional externalisation of models, activation, articulation and reuse. Another focus area is a process model (methodology) indicating how the different quality levels should be supported in concert. Early work on this indicates that quite different mechanisms are at play here than what has been found appropriate for supporting the development of e.g. requirements specification models [38].

References

1. Argyris, C., and Schön, D. *Organizational Learning: A Theory of Action Perspective.* Reading, MA, USA: Addison Wesley, 1978.
2. Berger, P., and Luckmann, T. *The Social Construction of Reality: A Treatise in the Sociology of Knowledge.* Penguin,1966
3. Boland, R.J., and Tenkasi, R.V. (1995). Perspective Making and Perspective Taking in Communities of Knowing. *Organization Science, 6*(4), 350-372, 1995.
4. Brasethvik, T., and Gulla, J.A. Semantically accessing documents using conceptual model descriptions, *Workshop on Web and Conceptual Modelling*, ER'99, Paris, France, 1999.
5. Brasethvik, T., Moody, D., Sindre, G., and Sølvberg, A. *Evaluating the quality of process models: empirical analysis of a quality framework*, In Proc. 21st International Conference on Conceptual Modeling (ER'2002), Tampere, Finland, 7-11 Oct 2002.
6. Carlsen, S. *Conceptual Modeling and Composition of Flexible Workflow Models*, PhD-thesis, NTNU - Norwegian University of Science and Technology, Trondheim, Norway, 1997.
7. Carlsen, S., Johnsen, S.G., Jørgensen, H.D., Coll, G.J., Mæhle, Å., Carlsen, A., and Hatling, M. *Knowledge re-activation mediated through knowledge carriers*, MICT'99, Copenhagen, Denmark, 1999.
8. Carlsen, S. *Action Port Model: A Mixed Paradigm Conceptual Workflow Modeling Language*, 3rd IFCIS Conference on Cooperative Information Systems, New York, 1998.
9. Carlsen, S., and Gjersvik, R. *Organizational Metaphors as Lenses for Analyzing Workflow Technology.* GROUP '97, Phoenix, Arizona USA, 1997.
10. Carlsen, S., Jørgensen, H.D., Krogstie, J., and Sølvberg, A. *Process Models as a Knowledge Creation Arena.* EURAM 2002, Stockholm, Sweden, 9-11 May 2002.
11. Chen, P.P. Thalheim, B., and Wong, L. Y. *Future directions of Conceptual Modelling* in LNCS vol 1565, Springer, 1999
12. Dahlbom, B. The idea that reality is socially constructed in Floyd, C., Zullighoven, H., Budde, R., and Keil-Slawik, R. *Software Development and Reality Construction* Springer 101-126, 1991.
13. Engeström, Y., et al. (eds.), *Perspectives on Activity Theory.* Cambridge University Press, 1999.
14. EXTERNAL *EXTERNAL - Extended Enterprise Resources, Networks And Learning*, EU Project, IST-1999-10091, *New Methods of Work and Electronic Commerce, Dynamic Networked Organisations.* Partners: DNV, GMD-IPSI, Zeus E.E.I.G., Computas, SINTEF Telecom and Informatics, 2000-2002.
15. Fabbrini, F., Fusani, M., Gervasi, V., Gnesi, S., and Ruggieri, S. Achieving Quality in Natural Language Requirements, in *Proceedings of the 11th International Software Quality Week (QW'98)* San Francisco, California, USA 26-29 May, 1998
16. Falkenberg, E.D. et al. (eds.) A framework of information systems concepts. The FRISCO Report, December, 1996.

17. Farshchian, B.A. *Gossip: An Awareness Engine for Increasing Product Awareness in Distributed Development Projects*, in *Advanced Information Systems Engineering - Proceedings of CAiSE 2000*, vol. LNCS 1789, B. Wangler and L. Bergman, Eds. Stockholm, Sweden: Springer, 2000.

18. Greenwood, R.M., Robertson, I, Snowdon, R.A., and Warboys, B.C. *Active Models in Business*, 5th Conference on Business Information Technology, CBIT '95 1995

19. Haake, J.M., and Wang, W. *Flexible Support for Business Processes: Extending Cooperative Hypermedia with Process Support*, GROUP '97, Phoenix, Arizona USA, 1997.

20. Hommes, B.-J., and Reijswoud, V van. The Quality of Business Process Modeling Methods. in Falkenberg, E. D., Lyytinen, K. and Verrijn-Stuart, A. A. (eds.) Proceedings of the IFIP8.1 working conference on Information Systems Concepts (ISCO4); An Integrated Discipline Emerging. Leiden, Netherlands, 20-22 September, 1999.

21. Jørgensen, H.D., and Carlsen, S. *Emergent Workflow: Integrated Planning and Performance of Process Instances*, Workflow Management '99, Münster, Germany, 1999.

22. Jørgensen, H.D. *Software Process Model Reuse and Learning*, Process Support for Distributed Team-based Software Development (PDTSD'00), IIIS and IEEE, Orlando, Florida, 2000.

23. Jørgensen, H.D. *Interaction as a Framework for Flexible Workflow Modelling*. GROUP'2001, Boulder Colorado, 2001

24. Krogstie, J. *Conceptual Modeling for Computerized Information Systems Support in Organizations*, PhD-thesis, University of Trondheim, The Norwegian Institute of Technology, Trondheim, Norway, 1995.

25. Krogstie, J. *Using a Semiotic Framework for the Development of Models of High Quality*, in *Unified Modelling Language: Systems Analysis, design, and Development Issues*, K. Siau and T. Halpin, Eds.: IDEA group, 2000.

26. Krogstie, J., Lindland, O.I., and Sindre, G. *Defining Quality Aspects for Conceptual Models*, Proceedings of the IFIP8.1 working conference on Information Systems Concepts (ISCO3): Towards a Consolidation of Views, Marburg, Germany, 1995.

27. Krogstie, J., and Sølvberg, A. *, Information Systems Engineering - Conceptual Modeling in a Quality Perspective*, Tapir academic publisher, Trondheim, Norway, 2003.

28. Krogstie, J.A. Semiotic Approach to Quality in Requirements Specifications: IFIP 8.1 Conference on Organizational Semiotics, Montreal, July 2001.

29. Kuntz, J.C., Christiansen, T.R., Cohen, G.P., Jin, Y., and Levitt, R E. *The Virtual Design Team: A Computational Simulation Model of Project Organizations*, Communications of the ACM, vol. 41, no. 11, 1998.

30. Lillehagen, F. *Visual Extended Enterprise Engineering Embedding Knowledge Management, Systems Engineering and Work Execution*, IEMC'99, IFIP International Enterprise Modelling Conference, Verdal, Norway, 1999.

31. Lillehagen, F., Dehli, E., Fjeld, L., Krogstie, J., and Jørgensen, H. D. *Active Knowledge Models as a Basis for an Infrastructure for Virtual Enterprise* PRO'VE 2002 - 3rd IFIP Working Conference on infrastructures for virtual enterprises. Sesimbra, Portugal, May 1-3, 2002

32. Lillehagen, F., Krogstie, J. Jørgensen, H.D., and Hildrum, J. *Active Knowledge Models for supporting eWork and eBusiness*. Accepted at ICE'2002 June, Rome, Italy, 2002.

33. Moody, D.L., and Shanks, G.G. *Improving the quality of data models: Empirical validation of a quality management framework*, to be published *in Information Systems* 2002

34. Nonaka, I. *A Dynamic Theory of Organisational Knowledge Creation*, Organisation Science, vol. 5, no. 1, pp. 14-37, 1994.

35. Nonaka, I., and Takeuchi, H. *The Knowledge Creating Company: How Japanese Companies Create the Dynamics of Innovation*. New York: Oxford University Press, 1995.

36. Nöth, W. *Handbook of Semiotics* Indiana University Press, 1990.

37. Schuette, R. *Architectures for Evaluating the Quality of Information Models – A Meta and an Object Level Comparison*, in Conceptual Modeling-ER'99 18th International Conference on Conceptual Modeling, 490-505 Paris, November, 1999.

38. Sindre, G., and Krogstie, J. *Process Heuristics to Achieve Requirements Specification of Feasible Quality*, in Editors Pohl, K., and Peters. P (eds.) Second International Workshop on Requirements Engineering: Foundations for Software Quality (REFSQ'95), Jyvälskylä, Finland, 92-103, 1995.

39. Truex, D.P., Baskerville, R., and Klein, H. *Growing Systems in Emergent Organisations* Communications of the ACM vol 42 no 8, 1999.

40. Voss, A., Procter, R., and Williams, R. *Innovation in Use: Interleaving day-to-day operation and systems development*, Participatory Design Conference, New York, NY, USA, 2000.

41. Wegner, P. *Why interaction is more powerful than algorithms*, Communications of the ACM, vol. 40, no. 5, 1997.

42. Wegner, P., and Goldin, D. Interaction as a Framework for Modeling, in *Conceptual Modeling. Current Issues and Future Directions, Lecture Notes in Computer Science 1565*, P. P. Chen, J. Akoka, H. Kangassalo, and B. Thalheim, Eds. Berlin, Germany, Springer, 1999.

Process Models and Business Models –
A Unified Framework

Maria Bergholtz, Prasad Jayaweera, Paul Johannesson, and Petia Wohed

Department of Computer and Systems Sciences
Stockholm University and Royal Institute of Technology
Forum 100, SE-164 40 Kista, Sweden
{maria,prasad,pajo,petia}@dsv.su.se

Abstract. In e-Commerce, there are two fundamental types of models, business models and process models. A business model is concerned with value exchanges among business partners, while a process model focuses on operational and procedural aspects of business communication. Thus, a business model defines the *what* in an e-Commerce system, while a process model defines the *how*. The purpose of this paper is to analyse the contents of business models and process models and to show how they can be integrated. We are using ebXML as a conceptual and notational framework for our approach. The theoretical foundations of our approach are based on the Language/Action approach and REA. We illustrate how our approach can be used to facilitate integration, process specification and process pattern interpretation.

1   Introduction

With the growing interest and activities in e-Commerce, there is an increasing need for methods and techniques that can help in the design and management of e-Commerce systems. In e-Commerce, systems design is based on two fundamental types of models, business models and process models. A business model is concerned with value exchanges among business partners, while a process model focuses on operational and procedural aspects of business communication. Thus, a business model defines the *what* in an e-Commerce system, while a process model defines the *how*. This means that the process of designing e-Commerce systems consists of two main phases. First, a business requirement capture phase focusing on value exchanges, and secondly, a phase focused on operational and procedural realisation.

In the business requirement capture phase, coarse-grained views of business activities as well as their relationships and arrangements in business collaborations are represented by means of business model constructs at an abstract level. In contrast, the specification of a process model deals with more fine-grained views of business transactions, their relationships and choreography in business collaborations. Although the two phases in e-Commerce design, and their related models, have different focuses, there is clearly a need for integrating them. A unified framework covering coarse-grained business modelling views to fine-grained process specification views provides several benefits. It can be used for supporting different user views of the system being designed, and it can form the basis of a precise understanding of

A. Olivé (Eds.): ER 2003 Ws, LNCS 2784, pp. 364–377, 2003.

modelling views and their inter-relationships. Another advantage of a unified framework is that it can be used for process integration, i.e. to provide measures for the establishment of correspondences between different structures in process models.

The purpose of this paper is to analyse the contents of business models and process models and to show how they can be integrated. We use ebXML [3] as a conceptual and notational framework for our approach, more specifically BPSS (Business Process Specification Schema) for process models and UN/CEFACT UMM [17] for business models. The theoretical foundations of our approach are based on the Language/Action approach and REA.

The rest of the paper is organised as follows. Section 2 gives an overview of related research. Section 3 introduces the UMM Business Requirement View. Section 4 describes process models according to BPSS. Section 5 contains the main contribution of the paper and shows how to integrate business and process models based on a Language/Action approach. Section 6 illustrates two applications of the introduced framework. Section 7 presents conclusions and suggests future research directions.

2   Related Research

The approach proposed in this paper is based on elements from the Language/Action approach and the REA ontology [5]. The Language/Action approach to information systems design (based on speech act theory [1]) focuses on communication aspects when analysing and developing a system. A speech act is defined as an action changing the universe of discourse when a speaker utters it and a recipient grasps it. It may be oral as well as written, or even expressed via some other communication form such as sign language. Searle has developed speech act theory [14] by introducing a taxonomy of five different kinds of speech acts: assertive, directive, commissive, expressive, and declarative, also called illocutionary points.

An *assertive* is a speech act the purpose of which is to convey information about some state of affairs of the world from one agent, the speaker, to another, the hearer. For example, the utterance "The father of speech act theory was Austin". A *commissive* is a speech act, the purpose of which is to commit the speaker to carry out some action or to bring about some state of affairs. An example is the utterance "I will complete and submit the paper to eCOMO02". A *directive* is a speech act, where the speaker requests the hearer to carry out some action or to bring about some state of affairs, e.g.. "You shall complete and submit the paper to eCOMO02". A *declarative* is a speech act, where the speaker brings about some state of affairs by the mere performance of a speech act. An example is the establishment of accepted papers, e.g. "Paper no 23 is accepted". Finally, an *expressive* is a speech act, the purpose of which is to express the speaker's attitude to some state of affairs, e.g. "I like the ideas presented in this paper".

In addition to its illocutionary point, a speech act also has a propositional content. For instance, the speech acts " I hereby pronounce you husband and wife" and "You are hereby divorced", which are both declaratives, have different propositional contents. Furthermore, speech acts with different illocutionary points may have one and the same propositional content, which is the case with the examples for directive and commissive given above. A speech act is often viewed as consisting of two parts, its propositional content and its illocutionary force. The illocutionary force is the illocutionary point together with the manner (for example ordering, asking, begging) in which the speech act is performed and the context in which it occurs.

Some well-known and recent Language/Action approaches are Action Workflow [11], Business Action Theory (BAT) [6], and Dynamic Essential Modelling of Organisations (DEMO) [2]. The second building stone of our approach, the Resource-Event-Agent (REA) framework, [15], has been designed for representing and reasoning about economic phenomena, more specifically about economic exchanges.

The REA framework is based on three main components: Economic Agents, Economic Resources, and Economic Events, see **Fig. 1**. An Economic Agent is a person or organisation that is capable of controlling Economic Resources and interacting with other Economic Agents. An Economic Resource is something, e.g. goods or money that is viewed as being valuable by Economic Agents. An Economic Event is the transfer of control of an Economic Resource from one Economic Agent to another one.

Fig. 1. Resources, Events, and Agents (REA) [5]

A central component in REA is the *Duality* existing between two Economic Events, i.e. one agent transfers some resource to another agent and receives in return another resource from that agent. This *Duality* of resource transfer is essential in commerce.

3   UMM Business Requirements Views

The REA framework has recently been applied in the UN/CEFACT Modelling Methodology (UMM) [17], where it is used as a theoretical foundation of the Business Requirements View. UMM is based on the Unified Modelling Language (UML) [13], and it provides a procedure for modelling business processes in a technology-neutral, implementation-independent manner. In UMM, a number of different view metamodels are defined to support an incremental model development and to provide different levels of specification granularity. Among these is the Business Requirement View (BRV), see **Fig. 2**, capturing the business transactions with their interrelationships, which makes it the most relevant meta-model for our work.

Like REA, BRV models Economic Events, the Economic Resources transferred through the Economic Events, and the Economic Agents, here called Partner Types between whom the Economic Events are performed. Furthermore, an Economic Event fulfils an Economic Commitment. An Economic Commitment can be seen as the result of a commissive speech act and is intended to model an obligation for the performance of an Economic Event. The *duality* between Economic Events is inherited into the Economic Commitments, represented by the relationship *reciprocal*.

In order to represent collections of related commitments, the concept of Economic Contracts is used. An Economic Contract is an aggregation of two or more reciprocal commitments. An example of an Economic Contract is a purchase order with several order lines, which are the Economic Commitments involved in the purchase order contract. The products specified in each line are the Economic Resource Types that are the subject for the Economic Commitments.

Moving one level up, the Economic Contracts are often made within the boundaries of different Agreements. An Agreement is an arrangement between two Partner Types that specifies the conditions under which they will trade. Furthermore, a Business Collaboration choreographs the Business Collaboration Task performed in a contract formation when the contract formation requires a number of requesting and responding business interactions.

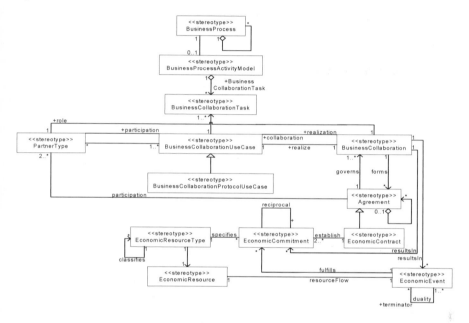

Fig. 2. UMM Business Requirements View (BRV) [17]

4   Business Process Specification Schema

There are well-established modelling techniques for e-Commerce development. However, there is still a considerable gap to be covered between e-Commerce process modelling and specification of software components. One major framework intended to bridge this gap is the ebXML Business Process Specification Schema (BPSS), [3]. In BPSS, a collaboration consists of a set of Business Transactions choreographed to obtain a control flow of the transactions. Each transaction consists of a pair of request and response activities carried out by two Business Partners in different roles as well as document flows between the activities, see **Fig. 3**. A collaboration may be between two parties, a Binary Collaboration, or between several parties, a Multi Party Collaboration. A UML class diagram of BPSS is shown in **Fig.4**.

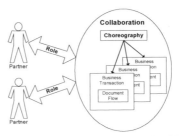

Fig. 3. Collaborations in ebXML (reprinted from the ebXML BPSS [3])

A Business Transaction is an atomic unit of work; it consists of one Requesting Business Activity, one Responding Business Activity, and one or two document flows between them. There is always a Request document flow, while there does not have to be a corresponding Response document flow. A pair of Request and Response document flows is needed in cases where some kind of agreement is to be established. Some transactions, however, have the function of notifications, and in such cases only a Request document flow is needed. There is a common super class, Business Action, for Requesting Business Activity and Responding Business Activity, which holds common attributes specifying conditions on intelligibility checks, authorisation, time to acknowledge, and non-repudiation. An example of a Requesting Business Activity is "Request Purchase Order", an example of a Responding Business Activity is "Accept Purchase Order" – together these two Business Actions constitute a Business Transaction.

Business Transactions are the basic building blocks of Binary Collaborations. A Binary Collaboration is always between two roles, and it consists of one or more Business Activities. These Business Activities are always conducted between the two roles of the Binary Collaboration. One of these roles is assigned to be the *initiatingRole* (from) and the other to be the *respondingRole* (to). An example of a Business Collaboration is "Manage Purchase" which could involve several Business Activities for querying about products or establishing the individual purchase order lines.

There are two kinds of Business Activities: Business Transaction Activities and Collaboration Activities. A Business Transaction Activity is the performance of a Business Transaction within the context of a Binary Collaboration. Thus, the same Business Transaction can be performed by multiple Business Transaction Activities within different Binary Collaborations or even within the same Binary Collaboration.

A Collaboration Activity is the performance of a Binary Collaboration. Analogous to Business Transaction Activities, a Binary Collaboration can be performed by multiple Collaboration Activities within different Binary Collaborations or even within the same Binary Collaboration.

A Binary Collaboration is not just an unordered set of Business Transaction Activities and Collaboration Activities. The Business Activities need to be ordered, which is done by means of a choreography. A choreography is specified in terms of Business States and Transitions between these states. The most important kind of a Business State is a Business Activity. Furthermore, there are a number of auxiliary Business States corresponding to diagramming artefacts on a UML activity chart: Start, Completion State, Fork, and Join.

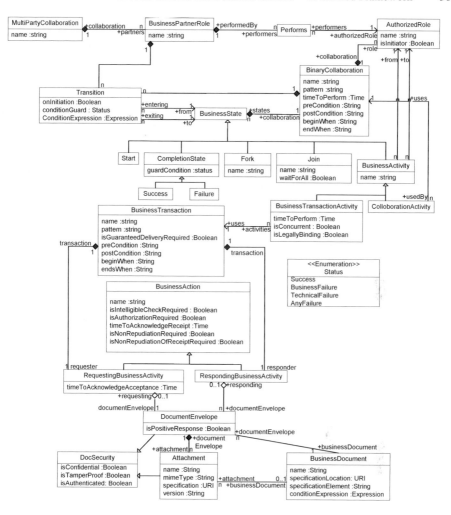

Fig. 4. ebXML Business Process Specification Schema [3]

5   Pragmatics of Business Actions

In the UMM Business Requirements View, there is only a very general relationship between economic concepts (i.e. Economic Event, Economic Contract, Economic Commitment, Economic Resource, Economic Resource Type, Agreement, and Partner Type) and process concepts. Essentially, the relationship states that a commitment or agreement is created by means of a collaboration, but there is no indication of how the constituents of the collaboration are related to the economic concepts. In order to get a more fine-grained view of the relationships between collaborations and economic concepts, we need to specify how the individual **Business Actions** involved in a collaboration are related to the economic concepts.

5.1   Pragmatic Actions

The basic notion introduced for relating **Business Actions** to economic concepts is that of a pragmatic action, see Fig. 5. A **Pragmatic Action** is a speech act, as defined in Section 2, and consists of two parts: a content and an illocutionary force. In e-Commerce applications, the content is always an economic concept. The illocutionary force of a pragmatic action indicates in what way the action is related to its content. An agent can perform a pragmatic action and thereby influence an economic concept in a specific way.

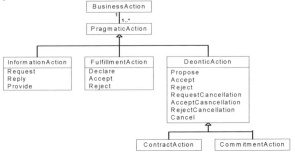

Fig. 5. Business Actions and Pragmatic Actions

Depending on which economic concept a pragmatic action addresses, different illocutionary forces are applicable. The pragmatic actions are, therefore, divided into several subclasses as indicated in **Fig.5.** The three main subclasses are information actions, deontic actions, and fulfilment actions. The underling intuition for identifying these three sub classes of pragmatic actions is that in an e-Commerce scenario, trading partners exchange business information, then establish different obligations, and finally exchange **Economic Resources**, thereby fulfilling the obligations.

An **Information Action** can have any economic concept as its content and requests or provides information about the concept. There are three possible illocutionary forces for information actions: **Request** asks for information, **Reply** answers a preceding request, and **Provide** provides information without a preceding request. E.g. "query for price and availability".

A **Fulfilment Action** has an **Economic Event** as its content. The action may declare that an **Economic Event** has been performed, or it may express that such a declaration is accepted or rejected. There are three possible illocutionary forces for information actions: **Declare** states that an **Economic Event** has been performed, **Accept** states that a preceding declaration of performing an **economic event** is accepted, **Reject** states that such a declaration is rejected. E.g. "declare shipment completed".

A **Deontic Action** can have a commitment or contract as its content. Thus, a deontic action concerns obligations to carry out events in the future. There are seven possible illocutionary forces for deontic actions: **Propose** means that an agent proposes the establishment of a commitment or contract. **Accept** is the acceptance of such a proposal while **Reject** is the rejection of a preceding proposal, **RequestCancellation** is a request to cancel an established commitment or contract, AcceptCancellation is the acceptance of such a request, while RejectCancellation is the rejection of a preceding request to cancel, Cancel is a unilateral cancellation. E.g. "request purchase order".

5.2   Abstraction Levels of Business and Process Views

In the analysis of the relationships between the UMM/BRV and the BPSS process model (**Fig. 2** and **Fig.4**) parts of the corresponding concepts in the respective models are modelled on different levels of abstraction. Two common abstraction levels defined in [**4**] and [**5**], are the operational level and the knowledge level. The *operational level* models concrete, tangible individuals in a domain. The *knowledge level* models information structures that characterise categories of individuals at the operational level. Martin and Odell, [**10**], employ the concept of *power types* to refer to the correspondence between the objects of the knowledge and operational levels. A power type is a class whose instances are subtypes of another class. The Economic Resource Type of **Fig. 6** is a power type of Economic Resource. Instances of the Economic Resource Type are the different categories of Economic Resources, for instance "real estate". An instance of the Economic Resource class is a particular piece of land, e.g. "Hyde Park Mansions".

In BPSS, classes like Business Activity and Business Transaction are defined at the knowledge level only. Business Activities do not possess properties related to actually transferred recourses, nor are they associated with the agents or roles between whom the transfer occurs. This is, however, not the case with the economic concepts of UMM/BRV. An Economic Event of UMM/BRV is explicitly related to an actual Economic Resource on the operational level.

An Economic Resource refers to an actual and tangible resource, whereas an Economic Resource Type is the corresponding power type defined on the knowledge level, serving as a template for concrete Economic Resources. Pursuing this line of analysis it is possible to identify templates on several levels, each of which is the power type of the other.

To facilitate the integration with BPSS, several economic concepts need to be added to UMM/BRV to include classes defined on the knowledge level. In the case of an Economic Contract, an Economic Contract Type is introduced to distinguish between the description of a contract and the actual contract between parties or abstract roles to be played by parties. The Economic Contract Type class models properties such as the types of conditions that may initiate or terminate a future contract, whereas an Economic Contract is associated to the authorised roles or partner types between whom a contract is established.

The introduction of new knowledge level classes into the economic concepts of UMM/BRV can be seen as schema conforming [**16**], i.e. transforming the schemas to be integrated in order to increase their similarity. The individual constituents of the BPSS model become possible to relate to the economic concepts of UMM/BRV as the two views now contain corresponding concepts defined on the same level of abstraction. The global, integrated view of UMM/BRV and BPSS is shown graphically in **Fig. 6**. The glue in this integrated view are the pragmatic actions defined in Section 5.1. Each individual Business Action of BPSS carries one or more Pragmatic Actions, which serve as categorisations of the Business Action. The categorisations are, in turn, defined in terms of the economic concepts of UMM/BRV. In **Fig. 6**, the original BPSS-parts are grouped with a dotted line boundary, UMM/BRV-parts are grouped with a dashed line boundary and the pragmatic actions that relate the two are depicted without any line boundary.

6   Applications

In this section, two applications of the proposed framework are introduced. First, different process views for incremental development are suggested. Finally, we outline a number of rules for governing the choreography of Business Collaborations.

6.1   Process Views

A process model may easily become complex and difficult to understand. One way to manage this complexity is to introduce a series of views of (partial) processes that move from the most basic actions to the finest details. A series of such views is given below, based on the notions introduced in the previous section. Each view is an extension of the previous one and adds new components to the model. The background behind the order of the views is that the purpose of an e-Commerce process is to exchange Economic Resources. The first view, therefore, specifies the actual Economic Events taking place. The second and third views specify the contracts and commitments needed to manage the Economic Events. The following two views provide optional actions on information exchanges and cancellations.

As a working example, we will introduce a business model of an on-line e-Catering business, shown in **Fig. 7**. Here a customer places a meal order within a contract with an e-Caterer. Upon the receipt of a customer order, the e-Caterer purchases beverage from the beverage supplier and food from the food supplier, and packages it all into a customer meal delivery. The e-Caterer requests the customer to complete a down payment for her meal delivery and then completes a down payment for the beverage prior to the beverage delivery. Finally, the e-Caterer settles final payment for the beverage and payment for the food after receiving final payment from the customer for her meal delivery.

Due to space limitations we have chosen to collapse every pair of Requesting and Responding Business Activity into one Business Transaction and **Fig. 8** shows integrated view of the Activity Diagrams of transaction groups identified below. Thus the activity symbols of **Fig. 8** refer to Business Transactions and every symbol can be placed on the swim lane between the Partner Roles (Customer, E-caterer etc.) to whom the Requesting and Responding Business Activities refers.

View 1. Fulfilment Transactions
This view contains only Business Transactions of Business Actions related to Fulfilment Actions. These transactions represent the Economic Events taking place in the collaboration in which the transactions appear. In the e-Catering case, a number of fulfilment transactions are depicted in V1s of the final choreography in **Fig. 8**.

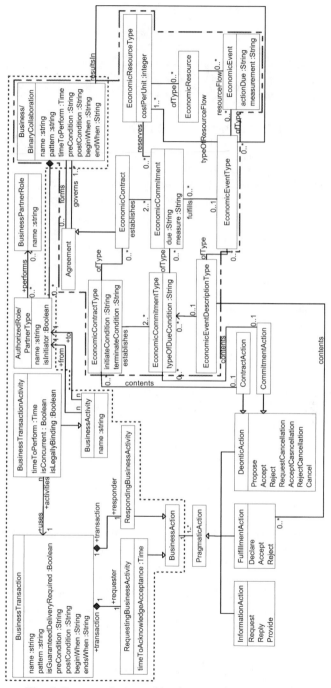

Fig. 6. Integrated view of business and process model

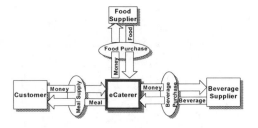

Fig. 7. The Business Model for an e-Caterer System

View 2. Contract Transactions
This view adds Business Transactions of Business Actions that are related to Contract Actions. These transactions represent the contracts needed for regulating the Economic Events of the collaboration. A number of contract transactions from the e-Catering case are depicted in V2s.

View 3. Commitment Transactions
This view adds Business Transactions of Business Actions that are related to Commitment Actions. These transactions represent the detailed content of the contracts. In the e-Catering case, a number of commitment transactions are shown in V3s.

View 4. Information Transactions
This view adds Business Transactions of Business Actions that are related to Information Actions. These transactions can, e.g., be about checking status of contracts and commitments. In the e-Catering case, a number of information are depicted in V4s.

View 5. Cancellation Transactions
This view adds Business Transactions of Business Actions that are related to deontic actions concerning cancellations. In the e-Catering case, a number of cancellation transactions are depicted in V5s.

View 6. Choreography
The final process diagram consists of the completed choreography of the Business Collaboration, see **Fig. 8**.

6.2   Choreography Rules

In this section, we introduce three rules governing the choreography of business collaborations. Recall from Section 4 that a *choreography* of a Business Collaboration is specified in terms of Business States. The relationships between these Business States are given by a directed graph, where an edge refers to a transition from one Business State to another. Furthermore, every Business State refers to exactly one Business Transaction, which means that we can restrict our attention to the choreography of Business Transactions without loss of generality.

When a designer constructs a choreography for a collaboration, it is helpful to consider the dependencies that exist among the transactions of the collaboration. There exist two kinds of dependencies that occur across many domains: trust dependencies [8] and flow dependencies [9].

A *trust dependency* is an ordered pair of transactions <A, B>, which expresses that A has to be performed before B as a consequence of limited trust between the initiator and responder. As an example, it is possible to require that a product be paid before it can be delivered.

A *flow dependency* is an ordered pair of transactions <A, B>, which expresses that A has to be performed before B because the **Economic Resources** obtained in A are needed for carrying out B. As an example, the different components of a meal to be delivered must be transferred to the e-Caterer before she can deliver the complete meal to the customer.

We define two partial orders, **Flow** and **Trust**, whose members are flow and trust dependencies, respectively.

Trust is a partial order over *(Ful ∪ Com ∪ Ctr)* X *(Ful ∪ Com ∪ Ctr)*.
Flow is a partial order over *Ful* X *Ful*.
Ful, Com, Ctr and *Can* refer to the sets of Fulfillment, Commitment, Contract, and Cancellation transactions, defined in views 1 – 5 above, respectively.

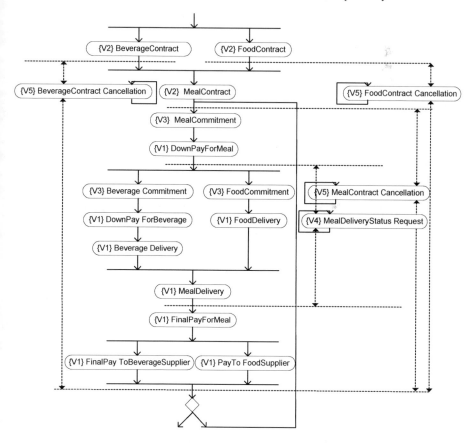

Fig. 8. View 6 – Choreography

The following rule can now be stated based on flow and trust dependencies:

Rule 1: If A and B are nodes in a choreography **C**, and <A,B> ∈ {Flow ∪ Trust} then there must exist a path from A to B in **C**.

Furthermore, we observe that the establishment of a commitment or contract must precede the cancellation of the same, which gives rise to the following rule:

Rule 2: If A and B are nodes in a choreography **C** and A ∈ {*Com* ∪ *Ctr*} and B ∈ *Can* where B is cancelling the contract or commitment established by A then there must exist a path from A to B in **C**.

Returning to the relationships between Economic Commitment, Economic Contract and Economic Event, we observe that Economic Contracts are subtypes of Agreements carrying Economic Commitments that some actual economic exchange will be fulfilled in the future. Thus we identify the following rule:

Rule 3: If A and B are nodes in a choreography **C** and A ∈ {Com ∪ Ctr} and B ∈ Ful, where B is establishing the Economic Event that fulfils the commitment established by A, then there must exist a path from A to B in **C**.

7   Concluding Remarks

The main contribution of this paper is a unified framework to facilitate the analysis and integration of business models and process models in e-Commerce. The approach suggested bridges the gap between the declarative aspects of a business model and the procedural aspects of a process model. The work has been carried out and expressed in the context of the ebXML standard, but the results can easily be adapted to other frameworks.

Recent approaches to e-Commerce systems design, [7], [3], stress the distinction between business models and process models. They also suggest that business models should be developed independently of process models. This is a valid design approach as it separates concerns, i.e. separates reasoning on declarative economic aspects from procedural control flow aspects. However, these aspects have to come together in the final design. The framework proposed in this paper can help in merging business and process aspects in a systematic way.

References

1. Austin, J.L., *"How to do things with Words"*, Cambridge, MA: Harvard Uni. Press, 1962.
2. Dietz, J.L.G., and Mallens P.J.M., "Business Process Modeling as a Starting Point for Information Systems Design", *Data2Knowledge Newslette,(may 2001)*.
3. ebXML Deliverables, http://www.ebxml.org/specs/index.htm .
4. Fowler, M., *"Analysis Patterns: Reusable Object Models"*, Addison-Wesley, 1997
5. Geerts, G., and McCarthy W. E., "The Ontological Foundaton of REA Enterprise Systems", *working paper, Michigan State University*.
6. Goldkuhl, G., "Generic business frameworks and action modelling", *Conference Language/Action Perspective*, Springer Verlag, 1996.

Process Models and Business Models – A Unified Framework 377

7. Gordijn, J., Akkermans, J.M., and Vliet, J.C., "Business Modeling, is not Process Modeling", *eCOM 2000 workshop, ER* 2000.
8. Jayaweera, P., Johannesson, P., and Wohed, P., "Process Patterns to Generate eCommerce Systems", *eCOMO 2001, ER 2001*, Springer LNCS.
9. Malone et al.: "Towards a handbook of organizational processes", *MIT eBusiness Process Handbook*, http://ccs.mit.edu/21c/mgtsci/index.htm .
10. Martin, J., and Odell, J.: *Object-Oriented Methods. A Foundation,* Prentice Hall 1994
11. Medina-Mora, R., et al.: "The Action Workflow Approach to Workflow Management Technology", *4th Conference on Computer Supported Cooperative Work*, 1992.
12. Object Constraint Language Specification, Version 1.1, 01 September 19997, http://www.omg.org/docs/ad/97-08-08.pdf .
13. OMG Unified Modeling Language Specification, Version 1.4, September 2001, ftp://ftp.omg.org/pub/docs/formal/01-09-67.pdf .
14. Searle, J.R., "A taxonomy of illocutionary acts", K. Gunderson (Ed.), *Language, Mind and Knowledge*, Minneapolis: University of Minnesota, 1975.
15. Significant *REA Model* papers: http://www.msu.edu/user/mccarth4/paplist1.html .
16. Spaccapietra, S., Parent, C., and Dupont, Y., "Model Independent Assertions for Integration of Heterogeneous Schemas", *The VLDB Journal*, vol. 1, no.2, pp. 81-126, 1992.
17. TMWG N090R10: UN/CEFACT Modeling Methodology (UMM). N090, http://www.ebxml.org/project_teams/jdt/resources/.
18. Weigand, H., and de Moor, A., "A Framework for the Normative Analysis of Workflow Loops", *ACM SIGGROUP Bulletin*, August 2001/Vol 22, No.2.

Behavior-Consistent Composition of Business Processes from Internal and External Services

Günter Preuner[1] and Michael Schrefl[2]

[1] Institut für Wirtschaftsinformatik, Data & Knowledge Engineering
Universität Linz, Austria
preuner@dke.uni-linz.ac.at
[2] School of Computer and Information Science
University of South Australia, Mawson Lakes, Australia

Abstract. E-business processes are typically developed by composing internal processes and external processes offered by service providers. Whereas e-service integration has received considerable interest recently, the relationship between the behavior of the composite process and the behavior of the constituting service processes has not yet been thoroughly investigated.

It is natural to expect that the behaviors of the composite process and the service processes are related as follows: (1) The composite process synchronizes the execution of activities from different service processes. (2) The composite process provides a complete overview of the service processes in that business transactions can be tracked ("observed") over their entire life time across all services. (3) If an activity can be invoked according to the composite process, it can be successfully invoked in the respective service process. (4) The description of the composite process, focusing on coordination, abstracts from local details as far as possible. Based on these requirements, the paper introduces formal correctness criteria for business-process composition and sketches an accompanying algorithm that determines a "behavior-consistent" composition.

1 Introduction

Organizations, in handling their business transactions, typically interact with services of other organizations. For example, a university's library may select the service of a wholesale trader to buy books and the service of a bank to transfer the amount due.

Different to business transactions occurring only rarely, the processing of business transactions that occur regularly should be pre-defined through business processes. *Service providers* specify offered service processes in terms of activities and an execution order of these activities. *Service requesters* use service processes of service providers *(external service processes)* and integrate them with services performed by the requester's organization *(internal service processes)*.

Requesters observe the current processing state of business transactions and execute activities of service processes, e.g., via a web interface. For example, the

A. Olivé et al. (Eds.): ER 2002 Ws, LNCS 2784, pp. 378–389, 2003.

library places orders via the book trader's web interface and later observes that the order is prepared for shipment.

If a business transaction is processed by several un-integrated service processes, it is difficult for the requester to track the processing state of the business transactions and the activities that have to be invoked by him/her in the service processes.

This gives rise to the need to define a *composite process,* which (1) represents temporal dependencies ("synchronization") between activities of different service processes (e.g., the money transfer is initiated after the order has been placed), (2) enables the requester to track the processing states of business transactions during their complete life time across all service processes, (3) ensures that if an activity can be invoked on a business transaction in the composite process, a corresponding activity in a service process can be invoked, as well, and (4) comprises all activities needed for synchronizing activities of the involved service processes, but abstracts from other details.

This paper presents — after dealing with modeling and composition of processes in Sect. 2 — formal consistency criteria for these informal behavioral requirements in Sect. 3 and presents an accompanying algorithm for service composition in Sect. 4. The definition of a composite process from the requester's perspective with clear correctness criteria complements previous approaches on the design of inter-organizational business processes and the integration of e-services as explained in Sect. 5. Section 6 concludes this work.

2 Modeling and Composing Service Processes

We present the concept of behavior-consistent composition of business processes using *Object/Behavior Diagrams (OBDs)* [6] as "research vehicle". This choice is motivated as follows: OBDs define the overall behavior of objects with a notation based on Petri nets and have been successfully employed for modeling business processes (cf., e.g., [1]). Formal consistency criteria together with necessary and sufficient checking rules have been identified for the specialization of OBDs in [15,17]; behavior-consistent composition can be defined upon that. Different to UML [14], OBDs clearly separate between extension and refinement, whereas in UML, intended extensions may need to be mimicked by a refinement [16,19]. This difference is particularly important for composition, where the composite process basically combines existing service processes by "extension" in that one service process is "extended" by the other ones. Nevertheless, the concepts of composition presented in this paper may be applied to UML state charts if their restricted refinement concept is relaxed. Behavior Diagrams are presented in Sect. 2.1 as far as necessary for composition; composition of service processes is introduced in Sect. 2.2.

2.1 Modeling Service Processes with Behavior Diagrams

In OBDs, business transactions are represented by instances of business-object classes; they are referred to as *business objects* in the following. A Behavior Di-

agram describes the behavior of business objects by *activities,* which are atomic
units of work that can be performed on a business object, by *states,* in which a
business object may reside, and by *arcs,* which connect activities with states.

Behavior Diagrams can be extended with labels [15] in order to distinguish
different aspects of a business object. Labels may be compared to copies of a
form in traditional paper work and are assigned to arcs, indicating the "flow" of
"copies" between activities and states.

Definition 1. *A* Labeled Behavior Diagram (LBD) $B = (S, T, F, L, l)$ *consists
of three kinds of elements, states $S \neq \emptyset$, activities $T \neq \emptyset$, and labels $L \neq \emptyset$, as
well as of arcs $F \subseteq ((S \times T) \cup (T \times S))$ and an assignment of labels to arcs
$l : F \to 2^L \setminus \{\emptyset\}$. The labels of an element $e \in (S \cup T)$ follow from the element's
incident arcs, i.e., $l(e) = \{x \in L | \exists (e', e'') \in F : x \in l(e', e'') \wedge (e' = e \vee e'' = e)\}$.*

The analogy between copies of a form and labels holds as far as the net
structure of Behavior Diagrams is concerned, but different to traditional paper
work, only "object identities" but no "copies" reside in states (cf. [15]). The paper
analogy gives rise to the following *labeling properties:* (1) For each activity, the
union of the labels of its incoming arcs is equal to the union of the labels of its
outgoing arcs (*label preservation*), (2) all incoming arcs as well as all outgoing
arcs of an activity have disjoint sets of labels (*unique label distribution*), (3) for
each state, all its incident arcs carry the same labels (*common label distribution*),
and (4) for each label, there is exactly one *initial state* α that carries this label
and has no incoming arcs (*unique and complete initial label distribution*). For
brevity, the sets of pre-states and post-states of t are denoted as $^\bullet t$ and $t^\bullet$,
respectively, in the remainder.

Example 1. Figure 1 shows business process BTraderA *(abstract book trader).* Its
labels d and p represent aspects *delivery* and *payment,* respectively. The sole
initial state α is depicted by dashed lines and will be omitted in the remainder.

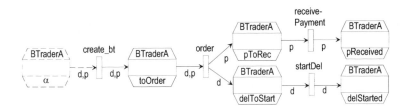

Fig. 1. LBD of business process BTraderA

The *life-cycle state* $\sigma \subseteq 2^{(S \cup T) \times L}$ of a business object indicates which of
its labels reside in which states or are currently processed by which activities.
As with Petri Nets, an activity can be invoked on a business object if this

business object resides in all pre-states of the activity. When an activity is completed, the business object resides in all post-states of the activity. During the activity execution, the business object resides in an implicit activity state. A sequence of life-cycle states of a business object is called a *life-cycle occurrence* $\gamma = [\sigma_1, \ldots, \sigma_n]$, where $\sigma_1 = \{(s, x) | \not\exists t \in T : (t, s) \in F \wedge x \in l(s)\}$ is the initial life-cycle state, and each subsequent life-cycle state σ_{i+1} results from invoking or completing an activity on σ_i. Two life-cycle occurrences are *equal* (=) if their sequences of life-cycle states are the same once subsequent duplicate life-cycle states have been removed.

Example 2. Each business object of process BTraderA resides initially in life-cycle state $\{(\alpha, d), (\alpha, p)\}$. Invoking activity create_bt leads to life-cycle state $\{(create\_bt, d), (create\_bt, p)\}$.

One particular kind of specialization, *refinement,* is relevant to composition. Refinement means that an activity in LBD B can be refined to a set of alternative activities in LBD B', a state into a sub-net comprising several activities and states in B', and a label into a set of labels.[1]

The correspondence between elements in B' and elements in B is defined by a total refinement function $h : S' \cup T' \cup L' \rightarrow S \cup T \cup L$. The abstraction of a life-cycle state σ' in B' to B is defined as $h(\sigma') = \{(h(e'), h(e''))|(e', e'') \in \sigma'\}$. The abstraction of a life-cycle occurrence γ, denoted $h(\gamma')$, results from abstracting all its life-cycle states.

LBD B' is an *observation-consistent refinement* of LBD B if for any life-cycle occurrence γ' in B' holds that $h(\gamma')$ is a valid life-cycle occurrence in B [17].

Example 3. The LBD of BTrader in Fig. 2 is an observation-consistent refinement of the LBD of BTraderA. It refines the aspect delivery (label d) into two aspects, *carrier* (dc) and *shipment* (ds), and state delToStart into several activities and states. One possible life-cycle state is $\{(carToSel, dc), (smPrepd, ds), (pToRec, p)\}$, its abstraction according to BTraderA is $\{(delToStart, d), (pToRec, p)\}$. Ignore state ordered for the moment.

2.2   Composition of Service Processes

Service processes involved in processing a particular kind of business objects are composed to a composite process together with synchronization requirements, describing temporal dependencies between activities of different service processes. The synchronization requirements are described by an LBD, the *synchronization service,* and a *synchronization function* mapping each activity of the synchronization service to at most one activity of a service process. Hence, the composite process consists of elements that "wrap" elements or sub-nets of service processes and elements that are introduced in the synchronization service.

---

[1] According to [15], an activity may be refined into several states and activities; for compatibility with UML state charts, refinement of activities is restricted to alternatives, cf. [19].

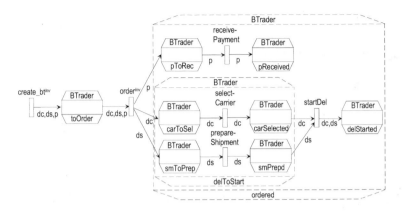

Fig. 2. LBD of service process BTrader

Service processes may contain "invocable" activities that are to be invoked by the requester, whereas the provider waives the right to invoke them, and "observable" activities that are executed by the service provider and observed by the requester. To distinguish between these two, we extend LBDs by a boolean function i on T, where $i(t)$ holds iff t is to be invoked by the requester.

In the remainder, we need the notion of the restriction of an LBD to a set of labels:

Definition 2. *The restriction of LBD $B = (S, T, F, L, l, i)$ to a set of labels $\tilde{L} \subseteq L$, denoted as $B_{/\tilde{L}} = (S_{/\tilde{L}}, T_{/\tilde{L}}, F_{/\tilde{L}}, L_{/\tilde{L}}, l_{/\tilde{L}}, i_{/\tilde{L}})$, is defined by $S_{/\tilde{L}} = \{s \in S | l(s) \cap \tilde{L} \neq \emptyset\}, T_{/\tilde{L}} = \{t \in T | l(t) \cap \tilde{L} \neq \emptyset\}, F_{/\tilde{L}} = F \cap ((S_{/\tilde{L}} \times T_{/\tilde{L}}) \cup (T_{/\tilde{L}} \times S_{/\tilde{L}})), L_{/\tilde{L}} = \tilde{L}, \forall f \in F_{/\tilde{L}} : l_{/\tilde{L}}(f) = l(f) \cap \tilde{L}$, and $\forall t \in T_{/\tilde{L}} : i_{/\tilde{L}}(t) = i(t)$.*

The correspondence between elements in a service process $B_i = (S_i, T_i, F_i, L_i, l_i, i_i)$, for $i \in [1, \ldots, n]$, and elements in the composite process $\hat{B} = (\hat{S}, \hat{T}, \hat{F}, \hat{L}, \hat{l}, \hat{i})$ is represented by a total function h_i, which maps labels in B_i to labels in $\hat{B}$, maps transitions in B_i to transitions and states in $\hat{B}$, and maps states is B_i to states in $\hat{B}$. The composite process embeds the synchronization service B_s; activities from service processes that are referenced by an activity of B_s by synchronization function f_s must map to this activity in $\hat{B}$.

We define composition based on the following assumptions, reflected by conditions (3) to (6) in the subsequent Definition 3 of a composite process.

1. Different service processes focus on different aspects, e.g., "money transfer" and "delivery"; hence they have no elements in common.
2. Since invocable activities can be invoked only be the requester, all of them are included in the composite process as invocable activities.
3. For simplicity, each invocable activity in the composite process maps to at most one activity in a service, i.e., does not wrap more than one activity from service processes.

4. All activities from B_s are invocable since all synchronization requirements between service processes are to be handled by the composite process.

Definition 3. *A composite process $\hat{B} = (\hat{S}, \hat{T}, \hat{F}, \hat{L}, \hat{l}, \hat{i})$ integrating service processes $B_1, \ldots, B_n$ according to synchronization service B_s and synchronization function $f_s : T_s \to \bigcup_i T_i$, is defined by a set of total composition functions $h_i : S_i \cup T_i \cup L_i \to \hat{S} \cup \hat{T} \cup \hat{L}$ for $i \in [1, \ldots, n]$, where (1) $\forall e \in S_i \cup T_i \cup L_i : h_i(e) \in \hat{L} \Leftrightarrow e \in L_i$ and $\forall e \in S_i \cup T_i \cup L_i : h_i(e) \in \hat{T} \Rightarrow e \in T_i$, (2) $\hat{B}_{/(\hat{L} \setminus \bigcup_i (\{h_i(x) | x \in L_i\}))} = B_s$, where $\forall t \in T_s : f_s(t)$ is defined $\Rightarrow \exists i \in [1, \ldots, n] : h_i(f_s(t)) = t$, (3) $\forall i, j \in [1, \ldots, n], i \neq j, e_1 \in S_i \cup T_i \cup L_i, e_2 \in S_j \cup T_j \cup L_j : h_i(e_1) \neq h_j(e_2)$, (4) $\forall i \in [1, \ldots, n], t \in T_i : i_i(t) \Rightarrow (h_i(t) \in \hat{T} \wedge \hat{i}_i(h_i(t)))$, (5) $\forall \hat{t} \in \hat{T}, \hat{i}(\hat{t}), i \in [1, \ldots, n], t_1 \in T_i, t_2 \in T_i : h_i(t_1) = h_i(t_2) = \hat{t} \Rightarrow (t_1 = t_2 \wedge i_i(t_1))$, and (6) $\forall t \in T_s : \hat{i}(t)$.*

Example 4. A library maintains a local service process for invoking book orders and receiving incoming books (cf. Fig. 3). Books are ordered via an online book trader, whose service process is depicted in Fig. 2. The library uses the service process of its bank for transferring money from the library's bank account to the book trader (cf. Fig. 4). Invocable activities are marked with superscript *Inv*.

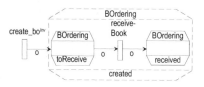

Fig. 3. Internal service process BOrdering

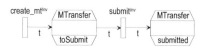

Fig. 4. External service process MTransfer

The composite process BO-Comp, depicted in Fig. 5, integrates the service processes according to the synchronization service depicted in Fig. 6. Elements appearing in BO-Comp at the same level of detail as in a service process keep their names (e.g., activity create_bt). If a sub-net of a service process is abstracted to a single element, the abstraction is illustrated in the respective service process. For example, several activities and states of BTrader have been abstracted to one state ordered (cf. Fig. 2). Labels dc, ds, and p of BTrader have been abstracted to b, all other labels appear as such in some service process or in the synchronization service. Different shadings of activities and states as well as label subscripts indicate their "origins" as described in the figure's legend.

3 Behavior Consistency

We informally identified four requirements for the composite process in the introduction, where the first one on *synchronization* is naturally captured by the definition of a composite process given in the previous section. The second and

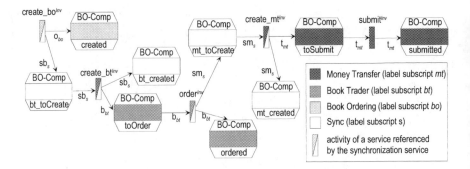

Fig. 5. Composite process BO-Comp

Fig. 6. Synchronization service Sync

third requirement concern *behavior-consistent composition*, which is formally defined in Sect. 3.1. The fourth requirement states to select the most abstract process from the candidate processes and is formally defined in Sect. 3.2.

3.1 Behavior-Consistent Composition

A requester should be able to observe the processing of business objects in the service processes as a correct processing according to the composite process *(observability consistency)*. More precisely, for each service process B_i, the processing of a business object in B_i must be observable as a correct processing according to the composite process $\hat{B}$ if only labels that correspond to labels in B_i are considered. For a selected aspect, this requirement corresponds to observation-consistent refinement (cf. Sect. 2.1). Further, it must be ensured that at any time when $\hat{t}$ can be invoked in the composite process, it can be invoked in the respective service process, as well *(invocability consistency)*.

Definition 4. *Composite process* $\hat{B}$ *is a* behavior-consistent composition *of* $B_1, \ldots, B_n$ *with composition functions* $h_1, \ldots, h_n$ *iff two conditions hold:*

1. Observability consistency: $\forall i \in [1, \ldots, n], \hat{\gamma} = [\hat{\sigma}_1, \ldots \hat{\sigma}_m]$ *of* $\hat{B}, \gamma = [\sigma_1, \ldots, \sigma_n]$ *of* $B_i, \hat{\gamma}_{/B_i} = h_i(\gamma), t \in T_i : (t$ *can be started or completed on* σ_n, *gaining new life-cycle state* $\sigma_{n+1}) \Rightarrow$
   (a) $h_i(\sigma_n) = h_i(\sigma_{n+1})$ *or*
   (b) $h_i(t)$ *can be started or completed, resp., on* $\hat{\sigma}_m$, *yielding* $\hat{\sigma}_{m+1}$,
       with $(\hat{\sigma}_{m+1})_{/B_i} = h_i(\sigma_{n+1})$,

where $\hat{\sigma}_{/B_i} := \{(s,x) \in \hat{\sigma} | x \in \bigcup_{x' \in L_i}(h_i(x'))\}$ *and* $\hat{\gamma}_{/B_i} := [(\hat{\sigma}_1)_{/B_i}, \dots,$
$(\hat{\sigma}_m)_{/B_i}]$.

2. Invocability consistency: $\forall i \in [1, \dots, n], \hat{\gamma} = [\hat{\sigma}_1, \dots, \hat{\sigma}_m]$ *of* $\hat{B}, \gamma = [\sigma_1, \dots,$
   $\sigma_n]$ *of* $B_i, \hat{\gamma}_{/B_i} = h_i(\gamma), \hat{t} \in \hat{T} : (\hat{t}$ *can be started or completed on* $\hat{\sigma}_m$ *gaining*
   $\hat{\sigma}_{m+1}) \Rightarrow$
   (a) $(\nexists t \in T_i : h_i(t) = \hat{t}) \wedge (\hat{\sigma}_{m+1})_{/B_i} = h_i(\sigma_n)$ *or*
   (b) $\exists t \in T_i : h_i(t) = \hat{t} \wedge i_i(t) \wedge t$ *can be started or completed, resp., on* σ_n,
   yielding σ_{n+1}, *with* $h_i(\sigma_{n+1}) = (\hat{\sigma}_{m+1})_{/B_i}$.

Theorem 1. *A sufficient condition to check whether observability consistency is fulfilled by* B_i *(*$i \in [1, \dots, n]$*) with respect to* $\hat{B}$ *is that (1)* B_i *is an observation-consistent refinement of* $\hat{B}_{/\{h_i(x')|x' \in L_i\}}$ *and (2) for each* $t \in T_i$ *one of the following conditions holds: (a)* $h_i(t) \in \hat{S}$ *or (b)* $h_i(t) \in \hat{T} \wedge \forall \hat{s} \in {}^{\bullet}(h_i(t)) \exists s \in {}^{\bullet}t :$ $\hat{s} = h_i(s)$.

Theorem 2. *If observability consistency is fulfilled, a sufficient condition to check whether invocability consistency is fulfilled, as well, is that for each invocable activity* $\hat{t} \in \hat{B}$*, (a) there is no activity* t' *in* B_i *with* $h_i(t') = \hat{t}$*, or (b) there is exactly one invocable activity* t' *of* B_i *where* $h_i(t') = \hat{t}$*, and each pre-state of* $\hat{t}$ *is the image of one or several pre-states of* t'*, i.e.,* $\forall e' \in (S_i \cup T_i) : h_i(e') \in {}^{\bullet}\hat{t} \Rightarrow$ $e' \in {}^{\bullet}t'$.

Proofs: see [13].

Example 5. Business process BO-Comp is a behavior-consistent composition of BOrdering, BTrader, and MTransfer. It fulfills *observability consistency:* For example, process BTrader is an observation-consistent refinement of BO-Comp, if BO-Comp is restricted to label b and all elements labeled with b. It fulfills *invocability consistency:* For example, invocable activity order in BO-Comp corresponds to the invocable activity order in BTrader; pre-state toOrder in BTrader is defined as pre-state of order in BO-Comp, as well.

3.2   Most-Abstract Behavior-Consistent Composition

If several composite processes fulfill behavior-consistent composition, the most abstract one is selected. Hence, there must not be another composite process $\bar{B}$ (a) that fulfills behavior-consistent composition, (b) that is not isomorphic to $\hat{B}$ and (c, d) that is more abstract than $\bar{B}$, where the abstraction function $\hat{h}$ and the composition functions h_i of $\hat{B}$ and $\bar{h}_i$ of $\bar{B}$ are coherent in the sense that the image of each element in a service process under $\bar{h}_i$ is the same as the image under the function composition of h_i and $\hat{h}$.

Definition 5. *Composite process* $\hat{B}$ *is the* most-abstract behavior-consistent composition *of service processes* $B_1, \dots, B_n$ *according to synchronization service*

B_s and synchronization function f_s iff (1) $\hat{B}$ is a behavior-consistent composition of $B_1, \ldots, B_n$ according to B_s and f_s and (2) there is no business process $\bar{B}$ that fulfills the following criteria: (a) $\bar{B}$ is a behavior-consistent composition of $B_1, \ldots, B_n$ according to B_s and f_s with composition function $\bar{h}_i :$ $S_i \cup T_i \cup L_i \rightarrow \bar{S} \cup \bar{T} \cup \bar{L}$ for $i \in [1, \ldots, n]$; (b) $\bar{B}$ is not isomorphic to $\hat{B}$; (c) $\bar{B}$ is an observation-consistent abstraction of $\hat{B}$ with an abstraction function $\hat{h} : \hat{S} \cup \hat{T} \cup \hat{L} \rightarrow \bar{S} \cup \bar{T} \cup \bar{L}$; (d) abstraction function $\hat{h}$ is defined such that $\forall i \in [1, \ldots, n], e \in (S_i \cup T_i \cup L_i) : \bar{h}_i(e) = \hat{h}(h_i(e))$.

Example 6. Consider the behavior-consistent compositions BO-Comp (cf. Fig. 5) and BO-Comp', which is equal to BO-Comp except that it includes elements toReceive, receive, and received from BOrdering instead of abstract state created. Process BO-Comp is the most abstract one of them.

4   Algorithm for Service Composition

The algorithm for constructing a composite process takes a set of service processes $B_1, \ldots, B_n$, synchronization service B_s, and synchronization function f_s as input. It produces the most-abstract behavior-consistent composition $\hat{B}$ together with mapping functions $h_i : S_i \cup T_i \cup L_i \rightarrow \hat{S} \cup \hat{T} \cup \hat{L}$ as output. The algorithm is illustrated by an example; its formal definition is found in [13].

1. *Initial construction of $\hat{B}$:* Initially, $\hat{B}$ is constructed by embedding all elements of B_s and creating one element for each element in B_i; activities t' in B_i that are referenced by an activity t_s in B_s are mapped to t_s. Function h_i is continuously updated throughout the algorithm to map elements in B_i to the corresponding elements in $\hat{B}$.
2. *Abstraction of states and activities to a state:* An abstract state may comprise a sub-net consisting of several states, activities, and connecting arcs. The algorithm identifies a set of activities and states that can be abstracted consistently according to the rules of observation-consistent refinement [15], [17]; this set must not include invocable activities or pre states of invocable activities in order to fulfill invocability consistency.
3. *Abstraction of states:* A set of states is abstracted to one state if the set of activities producing into these states and the set of activities consuming from these states are the same.
4. *Abstraction of activities:* A set of alternative observable activities (i.e., activities with the same set of pre- and post states) can be abstracted to one single activity. Invocable activities are not abstracted according to the assumption that each invocable activity in a B_i is invocable in $\hat{B}$ without abstraction.
5. *Abstraction of labels:* A set of labels is abstracted to one label if these labels are assigned to the same set of arcs.

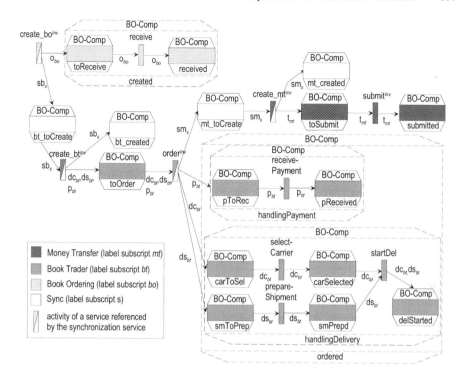

Fig. 7. Composite process BO-Comp: Initial construction and abstraction

Example 7. The initial construction of process BO-Comp is recognized in Fig. 7 in that each element's origin is indicated by shadings and label subscripts.

Sub-nets of activities and states are abstracted to a single state as indicated in Fig. 7 by state symbols with dashed lines: Starting with activities receive, receivePayment, and startDel, the abstraction process leads to abstract states created, handlingPayment, and handlingDelivery. Notice that activities are selected iteratively as starting points for determining sets of elements for abstraction. A different selection (e.g., starting with selectCarrier) would lead to the same result, yet possibly with more "intermediate" abstract states. Afterwards, states handlingPayment and handlingDelivery, which are post-states of the same activity order are abstracted to ordered. Labels dc, ds, and p, which are assigned to the same set of arcs, are abstracted to one single label b (cf. Fig. 5).

5   Related Work

Related work falls into two main areas: the design of inter-organizational business processes and software architectures for service composition.

Different from our approach, *top-down* design of inter-organizational business processes is discussed in [3,9], where a conceptual business process is split into different parts, each one being assigned to an involved organization. In [21], proclets are introduced as autonomous processes that interact with each other via communication channels (e.g., e-mail), thereby constituting an inter-organizational process. Our approach is different in that services can be incorporated into the requester's process, e.g., via a web interface, thereby shifting control over service execution to requesters. In [5], workflow views, describing the public interface to services, communicate with each other. View mechanisms are supported in our approach, as well (yet are not the focus of this paper). Service flows are introduced informally in [7] as sequences of service points that represent communication relationships between organizations. In [2], service providers may offer external services via a public interface, yet integration of processes in the realm of our paper is not discussed there.

Replacing a service by an alternative one that fulfills a similar task is discussed in [11]. This problem is different from the problem discussed in this paper, yet our approach could support different alternative services, as well. Integration of conceptual processes as discussed in [12] in the realm of view integration is different from service composition: In view integration, different users define by views how they perceive processing of business transactions, based on their experiences from everyday work. Hence view integration does not integrate *existing* processes, but process descriptions that exist only at the level of design.

Several papers focus on the software and protocol aspects of integration [8,10,18]. Processes are represented in [18] by a conceptual notation, yet without considering composition.

6   Conclusion

In this paper, we investigated the behavioral relationship between a composite process and its constituting service processes. The composite process should fulfill the following goals: On the one hand, it should give a full, comprehensive overview of all services without ignoring any aspect of a service. On the other hand, it should abstract as many details as possible from its constituting service processes and focus on their synchronization.

Based on earlier work on behavior specialization in object-oriented systems, we defined *behavior-consistent composition* requiring observability consistency and invocability consistency and *most-abstract behavior-consistent composition* that requires to abstract process elements taken from a service process as far as possible without violating behavior consistency. Finally, an algorithm was introduced to generate the most-abstract behavior-consistent composition from a set of service processes and synchronization requirements.

The results of this paper found the formal basis for the integration of services. Yet web services are usually not defined by a formal notation like OBDs, but by service description languages based on XML, like WSFL [4], XLANG [20], and XRL [22]. These languages support the definition of activities and control flows between activities, like sequences and choices. Therefore, we consider them appropriate for implementing our concepts, which will be part of our future work in this field.

References

1. P. Bichler, G. Preuner, and M. Schrefl. Workflow Transparency. In *Proc. Int. Conf. on Advanced Information Systems Engineering*. Springer LNCS 1250, 1997.
2. A. Eyal and T. Milo. Integrating and customizing heterogeneous e-commerce applications. *VLDB Journal*, 10(1):16–38, 2001.
3. V. Guth, K. Lenz, and A. Oberweis. Distributed Workflow Execution based on Fragmentation of Petri Nets. In *Proc. IFIP World Computer Congress*, 1998.
4. IBM. Web Services Flow Language (WSFL 1.0), May 2001.
5. E. Kafeza, D.K.W. Chiu, and I. Kafeza. View-based Contracts in an E-service Cross-Organizational Workflow Environment. In *Proc. 2nd Int. Workshop on Technologies for E-Services (TES)*. Springer LNCS 2193, 2001.
6. G. Kappel and M. Schrefl. Object/Behavior Diagrams. In *Proc. Int. Conf. on Data Engineering*, 1991.
7. R. Klischewski and I. Wetzel. Modeling Serviceflow. In *Proc. Information Systems Technology and its Applications*. German Informatics Society, 2001.
8. R. Krithivasan and A. Helal. BizBuilder — An E-services Framework Targeted for Internet Workflow. In *Proc. 2nd Int. Workshop on Technologies for E-Services (TES)*. Springer LNCS 2193, 2001.
9. K. Lenz and A. Oberweis. Modeling Intergorganizational Workflows with XML Nets. In *Proc. 34th Hawaii Int. Conf. on System Sciences*, 2001.
10. M. Mecella and B. Pernici. Designing wrapper components for e-services in integrating heterogeneous systems. *VLDB Journal*, 10(1):2–15, 2001.
11. M. Mecella, B. Pernici, and P. Craca. Compatibility of e-Services in a Cooperative Multi-Platform Environment. In *Proc. 2nd Int. Workshop on Technologies for E-Services (TES)*. Springer LNCS 2193, 2001.
12. G. Preuner, S. Conrad, and M. Schrefl. View Integration of behavior in object-oriented databases. *Data & Knowledge Engineering*, 36(2):153–183, 2001.
13. G. Preuner and M. Schrefl. Behavior-consistent Composition of Business Processes from Internal and External Services. Technical Report 02.02, Universität Linz, Institut für Wirtschaftsinformatik, Sept. 2002.
14. J. Rumbaugh, I. Jacobson, and G. Booch. *The Unified Modeling Language Reference Manual*. Addison Wesley, 1999.
15. M. Schrefl and M. Stumptner. Behavior Consistent Refinement of Object Life Cycles. In *Proc. Int. Conf. on Conceptual Modeling*. Springer LNCS 1331, 1997.
16. M. Schrefl and M. Stumptner. On the Design of Behavior Consistent Specialization of Object Life Cycles in OBD and UML. In M. Papazoglou, S. Spaccapietra, and Z. Tari, editors, *Advances in Object-Oriented Data Modeling*. MIT Press, 2000.
17. M. Schrefl and M. Stumptner. Behavior Consistent Specialization of Object Life Cycles. *ACM Trans. Software Engineering and Methodology*, 11(1):92–148, 2002.
18. G. Shegalov, M. Gillmann, and G. Weikum. XML-enabled workflow management for e-services across heterogeneous platforms. *VLDB Journal*, 10(1):91–103, 2001.
19. M. Stumptner and M. Schrefl. Behavior Consistent Inheritance in UML. In *Proc. 19th Int. Conf. on Conceptual Modeling*. Springer LNCS 1920, 2000.
20. S. Thatte. XLANG: Web Services for Business Process Design. Microsoft, 2001.
21. W. van der Aalst, P. Barthelmess, C. Ellis, and J. Wainer. Proclets: A Framework for Lightweight Interacting Workflow Processes. *Int. Journal of Cooperative Information Systems*, 10(4):443–482, 2001.
22. W. van der Aalst, H. Verbeek, and A. Kumar. XRL/Woflan: Verification and Extensibility of an XML/Petri-net based language for interorganizational workflows. In *Proc. 6th Conf. on Information Systems and Technology*, 2001.

Process-Oriented, Flexible Composition of Web Services with UML

Sebastian Thöne[1,2], Ralph Depke[2], and Gregor Engels[2]

[1] International Graduate School of Dynamic Intelligent Systems
[2] Department of Computer Science
University of Paderborn, 33098 Paderborn, Germany
{seb,depke,engels}@upb.de

Abstract. The composition of elementary web services to larger-scale services has become an important means to enhance e-business collaborations. If such composite web services can also integrate legacy components that are not yet provided as web services, the number of possible compositions is increased. Following a process-oriented approach, the compositions can be described as control- and data-flow between available web services and components. This paper discusses the *Business Process Execution Language for Web Services* (BPEL4WS), an existing service composition language, and proposes *UML-WSC* as an alternative, visual language. For the advanced description of service interfaces, UML-WSC extends the type system of the established *Web Service Definition Language* (WSDL).

1 Introduction

Web services enable seamless application integration over the network regardless of programming language or operating environment. In their elementary form, they encapsulate existing applications under web accessible interfaces and enable remote calls to these proprietary applications [1, 5]. Certainly, there are also many software components which support internal business processes only and which are not published as web services. If enterprises want to automate their business processes with the help of these own software components and (third-party) web services, they have to compose them according to their individual processes. The resulting automated processes can then be exposed as advanced web services to customers and trading partners. For the realization of this scenario a *web service composition language* is required to describe the business processes as compositions of legacy components and third-party web services.

Since the *Extensible Markup Language* (XML [12]) is the standard data format for web service input and output, business collaborations can then be realized by the exchange of XML messages between these advanced services. Nowadays, also most of the legacy components provide XML interfaces similar to web services, e.g., XML connectors for databases. If this is not the case for certain components, they can be accessed through XML-compliant adaptors. Thus, we can specify both legacy components and web services with XML interfaces.

A. Olivé et al. (Eds.): ER 2002 Ws, LNCS 2784, pp. 390–401, 2003.

In order to make a web service addressable via internet, the service provider must describe its interface and publish this information to clients. The most commonly used language for this formal interface specification is the XML-based *Web Service Description Language* (WSDL [12]). A WSDL document describes the interface of a web service as one or more *port types*. Each port type contains a set of *operations* with input and output messages. If only the output message is given, the operation is called a *notification*; if only the input message is given, a *one-way* operation. But in most cases web services support both messages and realize *request-response* operations, which correspond particularly nice to the HTTP request-response model. The input and output messages are composed out of one or more *message parts*; each part represents a complete XML document. WSDL specifies the allowed document type by the document's root element whose structure and subelements are defined by an associated *XMLSchema* [12].

In order to raise the flexibility in designing the service compositions, one should apply small service units for dedicated tasks. Many of these services can then be flexibly composed to advanced services. Since those specialized services might work on certain parts of the incoming messages only, they are independent from the actual root element and solely require certain subelements. In this case, the type specification of the service interface should abstract from the root element and give only the required sub elements. This way, it minimizes the input requirements and maximizes the reusability of the service. Services with such *partial input requirements* mostly modify only the corresponding sub parts of the document and return the resulting document with the unchanged root element as output. The simple WSDL type system cannot be applied in this case: it neither allows the specification of mandatory subelements nor the description of the dependency between the output type and the input type. For this reason, we suggest extensions like *inout message parameters* towards a *more fine-grained, flexible type system* which considers also partial requirements.

It is advantageous to assemble the interface specifications in a *static* part and the processes in a *dynamic* part. Then the interface operations specified in the static part can be used in various process definitions of the dynamic part. The dynamic part describes the *control-* and *data-flow* between the process activities, which are performed by the available software operations. To enable more complex execution sequences, the description language should provide all of the usual *control-flow elements* including iterations, conditional branching and concurrency [11]. One further requirement for better maintainability and reusability is the *decomposition* of large process definitions into subprocesses.

Since the service operations expect XML documents as input and output, the data-flow can be considered as a *flow of XML documents*. A document-flow between the output and input of two successive operations is only consistent if the message type of the source matches the type of the target. This constraint restricts the variety of possible service connections. The composition language should integrate rules forbidding inconsistent connections, which can be checked, e.g., by a type checker.

Sometimes the types of two documents are different although their content is similar, e.g., due to different naming conventions. In order to enable a matching of those incompatible types anyhow, the description language should allow to integrate *transformation rules* into the document flow. For example, the *Extensible Stylesheet Language Transformations* (XSLT [12]) standard enables the specification of structural transformations on XML documents which can be used to overcome these type mismatches. Thereby, the flexibility in connecting the services and components is improved.

Since the descriptions of the compositions shall serve the automation of business processes, it is very important that they are *machine executable*, i.e., they should be complete and contain all details which are necessary for a process engine to take the description and process incoming request messages. If the description is executable, a subsequent time and cost consuming implementation is not necessary. This objective also requires the specification of suitable *service providers* and the location of service implementations, e.g., a concrete legacy class or a certain URL.

On the other hand, the description should be *well understandable* and easy to read for human engineers. This is important for good maintainability, and it enables the discussion with non-technical experts, e.g., from business departments. Since the requirement of understandability is usually satisfied by an abstraction from technical details, it contradicts the requirement of executability and completeness. As a compromise, one should at least abstract from too technical representations and use *visual models* instead. The understandability of such a model can be further increased by applying an already *well-known modeling language* like the *Unified Modeling Language* (UML [8]).

The following section exemplifies problems of existing approaches by confronting the *Business Process Execution Language for Web Services* (BPEL4WS) with the above outlined requirements (summarized in Table 1). As an alternative, Section 3 proposes the *UML-WSC profile* as a new visual composition language, which solves the identified problems. Section 4 shows how software tools can support the design and execution of composite services, and Section 5 concludes the paper.

2   Business Process Execution Language for Web Services

This section provides an overview of the *Business Process Execution Language for Web Services* (BPEL4WS [3]). This XML language was released by BEA, IBM, and Microsoft in July 2002, and it replaces the existing web service composition languages *XLANG* [2] by Microsoft and *Web Service Flow Language* [6] by IBM.

BPEL4WS is used to describe executable business processes which rely on the import and export of web services exclusively. The processes are specified on an abstract level disregarding any binding information of the service types to concrete service implementations. The static part of the process description including the participants of the business process interactions, i.e., the other third-party web services, relies on extended WSDL documents. Besides for describing the interfaces of the third-party web services, WSDL documents are used to define so-called *service link types*. These link types are basically a pairing of two WSDL port types to one link type, where each port type gets a certain *role name*. The WSDL documents are not extended concerning the WSDL message type system. Hence, it is neither possible to integrate services with partial input requirements or inout parameters nor to integrate (legacy) components which do not provide a WSDL-compliant interface.

The specification of a business process within a BPEL4WS document mainly consists of three sections: the *partners* for the participants in the process interactions, the *activities* with the corresponding control-flow, and the *containers* for the required messages and their data-flow.

- **The interaction partners.** This part of a BPEL4WS document declares web services imported or exported by the business process. It refers to service link types defined in some WSDL documents. One role of each link type is assigned to the partner, the other one to the business process. Hence, a suitable partner service has to provide the corresponding port type of that role. At execution-time, the business process calls the operations provided by the port types of the partners. This way, a collaboration between the business process and its partners is established. The details of these collaborations are defined in the activities section of the BPEL4WS document.
- **The process activities.** This part of the BPEL4WS document describes the activities of a business process and their allowed sequences using control-flow elements like sequences, decisions, concurrent sections, and synchronization points. A process usually starts with a *receive* activity for receiving an XML message, and it ends with a *reply* activity for sending an XML message. This is, because the business process itself realizes a new advanced web service with its own port type and corresponding input and output messages. The other activities of the process can be used for interactions with the web services provided by the partners.
- **The message containers.** This section of a BPEL4WS document specifies containers for XML messages which are shared among different activities of the business process. Therefore, these containers play an essential role for the data-flow of the business process. To each container a certain WSDL message type is assigned. If the output message returned by a partner service is of the corresponding type, it can be stored in the container. Later in the process, the content of the container can be used as input message for another service. Finally, one of the stored messages could be returned as result of the entire business process.

Table 1 summarizes the discussion of BPEL4WS by checking if the language supports the requirements given in the first section. Since BPEL4WS makes use of WSDL specifications of web services, it is possible to integrate WSDL-compliant web services, but not legacy components without WSDL interfaces. Also, the restrictions of the WSDL type system are transferred to BPEL4WS concerning the lack of interfaces with partial input requirements or inout parameters. If we consider the WSDL specification of the web service interfaces as the static part of the composition language, then this static part is clearly separated from the dynamic part, which is the process description. Although there are all relevant control-flow elements available for the process description, there are no means for subdividing complex processes into smaller subprocesses. The only way to do this, could be to define the subprocesses as new web services which are then in turn called by the more complex processes.

Since the containers for the used documents are typed with WSDL message types, the consistency of the data-flow can be checked against these types. On the other hand, it is not possible to apply sophisticated transformations to the current content of a container. Instead, it is possible to copy a part of the content into a part of another container. But this mechanism supports only minor changes which are not sufficient to restructure documents so that they match to a new message type.

As BPEL4WS is an XML language, it can be interpreted by a suitable tool [9] and is hence machine-executable. But this reduces its understandability, because a verbose, non-visual XML language like BPEL4WS is rather difficult to read and to understand for human engineers. This point is especially important, if business process-related aspects have to be discussed with non-technical staff.

Table 1. Evaluation of BPEL4WS

Requirements	BPEL4WS
integration of legacy components	−
integration of WSDL-based web service interfaces	+
interfaces with partial requirements	−
interfaces with inout parameters	−
separation of static and dynamic parts	+
all control-flow constructs available	+
decomposition possible	−
consistent XML data-flow	+
message transformations possible	−
machine-executable	+
visual language, well understandable	−

A previous approach towards visual modeling of service compositions is introduced in [1]. There, the authors use a subset of *UML statecharts* to express the control-flow of their compositions. Since they assign the execution of a service to each state of the statechart and use transitions without triggers only, their statecharts look similar to *UML activity diagrams*. Besides, activity diagrams enable the modeling of more sophisticated data-flows as shown in the next section. For these reasons, our proposal mainly relies on activity diagrams. We aim to satisfy the requirements of Section 1 both for visual modeling of service compositions and for an advanced type system.

3   Web Service Composition with UML

As already mentioned, the description language for web service compositions should visualize the processes in order to facilitate their understandability. For this reason, the following subsections present the *UML Profile for Web Service Composition (UML-WSC)* as a visual modeling language which is based on UML [8]. As a very well known modeling standard, UML offers different diagram types to model static and dynamic aspects of a system. In this case, *UML class diagrams* with extended interfaces are used for the static part and *UML activity diagrams* for the dynamic part of the compositions. As revealed in [4], activity diagrams are also well suited for workflow specifications, which are similar to the service composition processes concerning control- and data-flow.

3.1   Activity Diagrams and the Dynamic Model

UML-WSC uses an extended variant of activity diagrams for the description of process-oriented service compositions. Fig. 1 shows an example from the area of electronic business. The depicted process describes the activities for answering a customer's request for an individual product offer. After the customer has sent information about himself, the product he wants, and the required amount, the supplier has to query his inventory management system if that amount is available from stock. If not, he must ask another supplier for an offer by addressing the supplier's web service. Concurrently, the customer's credit rating has to be checked via the web service of a credit investigation agency because it influences the price calculation at the end of the process. Eventually, the offer including the price is returned to the customer. If the supplier realizes this business process as a web service, he can also address customers who, e.g., want to use an autonomous software agent that automatically gets and compares different offers.

The standard UML elements can be extended by so-called stereotypes: the rectangular *service states* with rounded corners and the hexagonal *transform states* are both stereotyped forms of the UML *call state* (see Fig. 1). The service states call operations from components and web services, while the transform states perform structural transformations on messages. The completion of one operation triggers the outgoing transition to the next activity. Although this concept of operation invocation only conforms to the *request-response* and *one-way* operations of the WSDL specification [12], it is still suited because most web services are used with the HTTP request-response model.

The control-flow is modeled by transitions and pseudo states for decisions, forks, joins, and synchronization. E.g., in Fig. 1 there is synchronization between the two concurrent control threads on the left and in the middle. Decisions are made through boolean XPATH expressions [12], which can directly access the current message contents. The last state of the example process illustrates the ability to integrate subprocesses as building blocks into a process definition. This is not possible in BPEL4WS processes.

The data-flow is indicated by the dashed transitions. According to UML, they also imply a control-flow. The rectangular *object flow states* represent the flowing

XML messages. Every flow state stands for a message of the indicated XML type, which is provided as output of one service operation and is then sent as input to the next. On this way the message might pass a transform state, where its format is adapted to the subsequent input requirements if necessary. In contrast to existing languages like BPEL4WS the integration of such transformations enables a very flexible data-flow between the operations, even if the interfaces do not match at first sight.

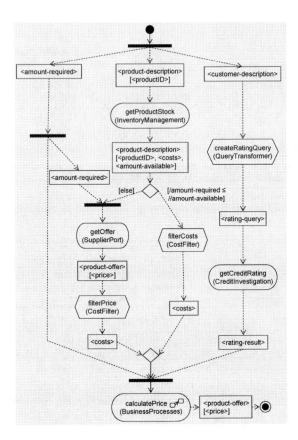

Fig. 1. Dynamic model as UML activity diagram

The detailed input and output interfaces of the operations are specified in the static model. Note that processes get input and output parameters, too. These correspond to the input and output messages of the web service operation realized by the process definition.

To summarize, the extensions of activity diagrams consist of the smooth integration of XML technology: Instead of objects, XML documents form the data-flow, and the object flow states represent certain XML document types. The introduction of the transform states allows an easy distinction of XML transformations from ordinary service calls. Finally, the application of XPath in guard conditions enables the selection from various branches depending on the actual document content.

3.2   The Static Model and Flexible Process Compositions

The static model of UML-WSC describes the available web services and components with their operations and parameters. This is done by stereotyped interfaces in a simple UML class diagram like Fig. 2. Similar to the dynamic model, we distinguish between *service* and *transformer* components: e.g., the service InventoryManagement provides the getProductStock operation, and the transformer CostFilter provides two transformations for extracting ¡costs¿ elements.

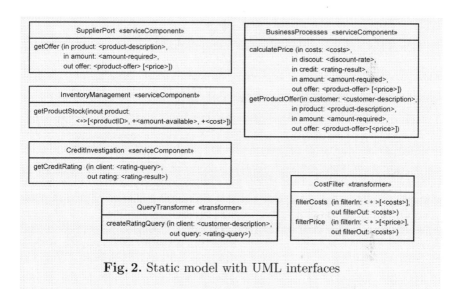

Fig. 2. Static model with UML interfaces

Each operation can have several in and out parameters that require or provide XML documents. For the integration of WSDL-compliant web services the operations of the WSDL port types become operations of the UML interfaces. Then, WSDL input message parts of an operation are mapped to *in* parameters, while the output message parts are mapped to *out* parameters. The *type* of each parameter is given by the XML root element of the respective WSDL message part. In Fig. 2 the namespaces of the elements are omitted for better readability, but normally they are required to uniquely identify XML elements.

This WSDL type system is not very flexible and can be improved by the addition of *wildcards* and *mandatory subelements*. The wildcard ¡∗¿ states that a message can have an arbitrary XML root element. An appended list of XML subelements in squared brackets states that the message must contain these elements somewhere in the document. These concepts are required to specify the interface of components which process only the mandatory subelements and do not rely on the rest of the document: e.g., the operations of CostFilter, which

just extract the ⟨costs⟩ subelement. As shown in Fig. 1, they can follow the
getProductStock as well as the getOffer operation, although both provide different root elements as input to the CostFilter. Thus, by leaving the root element
open, one gets weaker input requirements and the number of possible component
connections is increased.

Another important extension of the WSDL type system is the introduction of
inout parameters. They are required for operations which accept arbitrary root
elements as input and return them as output after some subelement modifications. As an example consider the operation getProductStock. It scans arbitrary
input documents for a product ID and adds information about the available
amount and the costs as subelements to the document. According to this functionality, its *in* parameter would read ⟨*⟩[⟨productID⟩] and its *out* parameter
⟨*⟩[⟨productID⟩, ⟨amount-available⟩, ⟨costs⟩]. Having such a partially specified *out*
parameter type, it is difficult to define a consistent data-flow to a subsequent
operation because the target *in* parameter would have to accept arbitrary root
elements (⟨*⟩[...]), too. But since most services are not that flexible, this restricts the number of possible service connections; e.g., the data-flow relation to
getOffer would not have been allowed in Fig. 1.

As we know that getOffer requires an input document of type ⟨product-
description⟩, we can only allow that data-flow if it is guaranteed that getProductStock always returns such documents. This condition is satisfied because in
the example the input to getProductStock is always of that type. Conditions of
this kind can only be checked for a concrete process model which is designed
successively from the start state. Then, one knows the actual input type to a
partially specified *in* parameter by the incoming data-flows, and the wildcard
⟨*⟩ can be replaced by the concrete incoming document type [10]. In order to
propagate this *binding* to the partial *out* parameter, one has to specify which
partial *out* parameter of an operation corresponds to which partial *in* parameter
of the same operation, because their might be several of them.

For this purpose, *inout* parameters tie the in and out parameters together
(see getProductStock). According to their semantics the operation's output message retains the original input type. Thus, only modifications of the subelements
are allowed. They are specified by *modifier symbols*: a + preceding a subelement says, the operation will add this element to the message, a − says, it will
remove this element. A subelement without any modifier will not be affected
by the operation. With the help of an inout parameter the binding of ⟨product-
description⟩ to the input wildcard also holds for the operation's output, which
becomes ⟨product-description⟩[⟨productID⟩, ⟨costs⟩, ⟨amount-available⟩]. As a result, the set of suitable subsequent operations is extended, and getOffer is now
possible, too. This advanced type system offers more flexibility than the basic
WSDL type concept.

Technical low-level details like the XSLT stylesheets, specifying the necessary
transformations, can be assigned to the interfaces as tagged values which are not
represented visually.

3.3   Language Definition by a UML Profile

The proposed description language is formalized by the *extension mechanisms* [8] of the UML metamodel. They enable the extension of syntax and semantics to domain specific needs by so-called *stereotypes*. A syntax extension is for example the introduction of hexagons for transform states, which are not included in the original UML. All stereotypes are collected in a *UML-WSC profile. Constraints* and *tagged values* can be added in order to define certain conditions or new meta attributes. Since there is not enough space to present the complete UML-WSC profile here, Figure 3 shows an extract containing the static part only. There, each stereotype is derived from a certain UML meta class. E.g., serviceComponent and transformer, which are known from Fig. 2, are stereotypes of the meta class Classifier. By these extension mechanisms UML-WSC conforms to UML and remains manageable by UML tools as described in the next section.

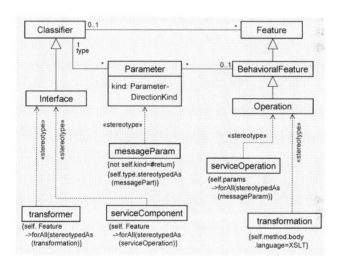

Fig. 3. Extract from the UML-WSC profile for the static model

4   Model Editing and Execution

Since the UML-WSC profile is a well-defined UML extension, the class and activity diagrams can be drawn and managed with every UML modeling tool that supports the definition of stereotypes. But in order to integrate advanced consistency checks, a dedicated tool was introduced in [7]. This tool can check the well-formedness of the control-flows and additional constraints as depicted in Fig. 3. Similarly, it prevents the process designer from creating inconsistent data-flows by checking the right interface matching of the data-flow sources and targets. In order to support the extended, more flexible type system, the type checker also considers the specified subelements and replaces the wildcards by concrete document types as described in Sect. 3.2.

One sophisticated design task is the development of the transformation rules (XSLT stylesheets) for bridging incompatible interfaces. For this task an XML expert is needed because it requires detailed knowledge of both the complex XSLT language and the internal structure of the source and target formats as given by their XML Schemas. Nowadays, an increasing number of tools is available which offer visual support for XSLT.

To enable an automated execution, the model editor saves the complete visual model in a machine readable format. Since existing formats like BPEL4WS do not support the advanced type system and the integration of transformations, a proprietary format for the entire language was developed.

The automated model execution including the specified control- and data-flow is performed by a *process engine*. If the process implements a new web service, then the process engine has to be called whenever the web service is invoked by a client. The engine acts like a mediator between all involved services and legacy components and directs the corresponding message-flow. For this purpose, the engine must be able to find suitable implementations of the specified operations using the given location information. Then it must invoke the respective operation and pass the required input messages. The engine can access involved web services over the internet, while legacy components must either offer a direct XML interface or a suitable adaptor in order to provide their functionality to the process engine. If there are any XSLT transformations associated with transform states, the engine can apply an *XSLT stylesheet processor* that performs the required format transformations.

For the correct processing of the resulting business transactions including the case of any fault, an exception handling mechanism is required. We distinguish between *local* and *global* exceptions. A local exception is thrown during the execution of a certain service or component and can be communicated to the process engine through a certain XML exception message instead of the usual XML output. During design time the engineer decides by conditional branches within the process diagram where the process execution should go to in this case. If the local exception is not caught or any other fatal error occurs, a global exception is thrown that stops the entire process. In order to re-establish a consistent state again, the designer can create *compensation processes* which undo the activities of the interrupted process. The details of these approaches are to be worked out in the future.

5   Conclusion

Our objective was to describe process-oriented compositions of web services and legacy components to larger-scale web service applications. The presented UML-WSC profile is an alternative to existing languages like BPEL4WS. In addition to their achievements like model executability, the used diagrams

- are well understandable as they allow a visual modeling of the processes,
- allow the integration of web services as well as of legacy components,
- use a more fine-grained type system than provided by WSDL, which allows the specification of additional operation interfaces by wildcards, mandatory subelements, and inout parameters,
- enable a more flexible connection of services by integrating transformations on incompatible message formats.

Future work will have to cope with an advanced exception handling and a concept to support the WSDL *solicit-response* and *notification* operations. Perhaps, the UML event mechanisms could be useful here. On the other hand, it would be interesting to model the public business protocol visually, too. A solution for this problem could apply UML sequence diagrams, which model the sequences and rules of service invocation and message exchange, which the trading partners want to follow when interacting over the internet.

References

[1] B. Benatallah, M. Dumas, M.C. Fauvet, and F. Rabhi. Towards Patterns of Web Services Composition. Technical Report UNSW-CSE-0111, The University of New South Wales, Sydney, Australia, November 2001.
[2] S. Thatte (Microsoft Corporation). XLANG, Web Services for Business Process Design, 2001. http://www.gotdotnet.com/team/xml_wsspecs/xlang-c/.
[3] F. Curbera, Y. Goland, J. Klein, F. Leymann, D. Roller, S. Thatte, and S. Weerawarana. Business Process Execution Language for Web Services, Version 1.0, July 2002.
http://www-106.ibm.com/developerworks/webservices/library/ws-bpel/.
[4] Marlon Dumas and A. H. M. ter Hofstede. UML activity diagrams as a workflow specification language. In *Proc. UML 2001, 4th Int. Conference,* volume 2185 of *Lecture Notes in Computer Science,* pages 76–90. Springer, 2001.
[5] B. Benatallah et.al. Declarative Composition and Peer-to-Peer Provisioning of Dynamic Web Services. In *Proc. 18th International Conference on Data Engineering (ICDE'02),* San Jose, California, 2002. IEEE Computer Society Press.
[6] F. Leymann (IBM Software Group). Web Service Flow Language 1.0, 2001. http://www-4.ibm.com/software/solutions/webservices/pdf/WSFL.pdf.
[7] B. Lütkemeier and S. Thöne. Process-Oriented Integration of Software Components by XML-Based Workflow Models. Diploma thesis, Univ.of Paderborn,2001.
[8] Object Management Group (OMG). Unified Modeling Language Spec. (Version 1.4), September 2001. ftp://ftp.omg.org/pub/docs/formal/01-09-67.pdf.
[9] IBM AlphaWorks Download Page. BPEL4J: BPEL4WS Java Run-Time, 2003. http://www.alphaworks.ibm.com/tech/bpws4j.
[10] R.Depke, G.Engels, S.Thöne, M.Langham, and B.Lütkemeier. Process-Oriented, Consistent Integration of Software Components. In *Proc. 26th International Computer Software and Applications Conference (COMPSAC'02).* IEEE, 2002.
[11] The Workflow Management Coalition. The Workflow Reference Model, 2002. http://www.wfmc.org/standards/model-desc.htm.
[12] W3C World Wide Web Consortium. Specifications of SOAP, WSDL, XML, XSLT, XMLSchema, XPath. http://www.w3.org.

Extracting Data behind Web Forms

Stephen W. Liddle*, David W. Embley*, Del T. Scott, and Sai Ho Yau

Brigham Young University, Provo, UT 84602, USA
{liddle,scottd}@byu.edu, {embley,yaus}@cs.byu.edu

Abstract. A significant and ever-increasing amount of data is accessible only by filling out HTML forms to query an underlying Web data source. While this is most welcome from a user perspective (queries are relatively easy and precise) and from a data management perspective (static pages need not be maintained and databases can be accessed directly), automated agents must face the challenge of obtaining the data behind forms. In principle an agent can obtain all the data behind a form by multiple submissions of the form filled out in all possible ways, but efficiency concerns lead us to consider alternatives. We investigate these alternatives and show that we can estimate the amount of remaining data (if any) after a small number of submissions and that we can heuristically select a reasonably minimal number of submissions to maximize the coverage of the data. Experimental results show that these statistical predictions are appropriate and useful.

1 Introduction

To help consumers and providers manage the huge quantities of information on the World Wide Web, it is becoming increasingly common to use databases to generate Web pages dynamically. Unlike ordinary Web pages mapped to standard URLs, information in this "deep Web" [1] or "hidden Web" [6,15] is not accessible through regular HTTP GET requests by merely specifying a URL and receiving a referenced page in response. Most commonly, data in the hidden Web is stored in a database and is accessible by issuing queries guided by HTML forms.

Automated extraction of data behind form interfaces is desirable when we wish to have automated agents search for desired information, when we wish to wrap a site for higher level queries, and when we wish to extract and integrate information from different sites. How can we automatically access this information? We began to answer this question in an earlier paper where we outlined our approach to automated form filling [10]. As our contribution in this paper we statistically streamline the process to make the information gathering process efficient, and improve our analysis of returned results. In the broader context of our project [7,5], information gathered during form processing will later be handed to a downstream data extraction process.

---

* Supported in part by the National Science Foundation under grant IIS-0083127.

A. Olivé et al. (Eds.): ER 2002 Ws, LNCS 2784, pp. 402–413, 2003.

1.1   Related Work

Others have also studied the problem of automatically filling out Web forms. Most common are tools designed to make it easier for an end user to fill out a form. Commercial services exist, for example, to provide information from a limited portfolio of user-specified information such as name, address, contact information, and credit card information [3,4,12]. These services, such as the Microsoft Passport and Wallet system, encrypt a user's personal information and then automatically fill in Web forms when fields can be recognized. Since many forms share common attributes (especially in the domain of e-commerce transactions), these tools can reliably assist users in entering personal information into Web forms.

One of the earliest efforts at automated form filling was the ShopBot project [2], which uses domain-specific heuristics to fill out forms for the purpose of comparison shopping. The ShopBot project, however, did not propose a general-purpose mechanism for filling in forms for non-shopping domains.

The most closely related work to our own is the Hidden Web Exposer (HiWE) project at Stanford [14,15]. HiWE provides a way to extend crawlers beyond the publicly indexable Web by giving them the capability to fill out Web forms automatically. Because of the formidable challenges to a fully automatic process, HiWE assumes that crawls will be domain specific and human assisted (we also rely on human assistance at key points, but we do not use domain specific information in retrieving data from a particular site). Although HiWE must start with a user-provided description of the search task, HiWE learns from successfully extracted information and updates the task description database as it crawls. Besides an operational model of a hidden Web crawler, a significant contribution of this work is the label matching approach used to identify elements in a form based on layout position, rather than proximity within the underlying HTML code. These researchers also present the details of several ranking heuristics together with metrics and experimental results that help evaluate the quality of the proposed process. The independently-developed details of our approach are complementary to HiWE. For example, we consider the task of duplicate record elimination and we use a statistics-based sampling approach to efficiently decide when a particular source has been sufficiently extracted.

1.2   Overview

In the remainder of the paper we describe the details of our contribution. We have created a prototype tool that automatically retrieves the data behind a particular HTML form. We refer the reader to [10] and [9] for details on our tool and approach. After briefly summarizing our approach, we discuss our form-submission plan in Section 2. In particular, we discuss the use of statistical procedures as a means to intelligently cover the search space and to determine how much of the available data has likely been retrieved and how close we are to completion. Section 3 presents the results of experiments we conducted to verify our approach to automatically extracting data behind Web forms. We summarize, report on our implementation status, and give plans for future work in Section 4

1.3   Summary of Our Approach

As described in [10], our approach to automated form filling starts with parsing the HTML page containing the target form. Next we construct an HTTP request that is equivalent to "filling in the form manually." This request is issued to the host Web server, and our tool analyzes the result page. If the result page contains links to other pages of results (e.g. the result displays, say, records 1–10 of 53), the tool follows the required links to retrieve all the result records. Often, it is the case that the default query (which consists of using the form's default values for all fields) returns all the records in the underlying database. But in most cases, we have to submit a variety of different queries in order to retrieve all the records. The same underlying records might be returned in response to different queries. So each time we add the results of a query to the accumulated extracted data, we first eliminate any duplicate records. The tool also deals intelligently with error pages and unexpected results.

2   Form Submission Plan

Our goal is to retrieve all the data within the scope of a particular Web form. One way to do this is to fill in the form in all possible ways. Ignoring the issue of fields with unbounded domains (i.e., text boxes), there are still two problems with this strategy. First, the process may be time consuming. Second, we may have retrieved all (or at least a significant percentage) of the data before submitting all the queries. Many forms have a default query that obtains all data available from the site. If the default query does not yield all data, it is still likely that we can extract a sufficient percentage of the data without exhaustively trying all possible queries.

Our strategy involves several phases: (1) issue the default query, (2) sample the site to determine whether the default query response is likely to be comprehensive, and (3) exhaustively query until we reach a limiting threshold. In the exhaustive phase, we can often save considerable effort by using limiting thresholds. For example, we can estimate the size of the database behind a form, and then continue issuing queries until we have reached a certain percentage of completeness. The user can specify several thresholds:

- *Percentage of data retrieved*: What percentage of the estimated data has actually been retrieved so far? Typical values for this threshold might be 80%, 90%, 95%, or 99%. This threshold controls the quality of the crawl.
- *Number of queries issued*: How many total queries have been issued to this site? It may be prudent to limit the burden placed on individual sites by terminating a crawl after a particular number of queries. This threshold controls the burden placed on crawled sites.

- *Number of bytes retrieved*: How many bytes of unique data have been retrieved so far?
- *Amount of time spent*: How much total time has been spent crawling this site? This threshold and the previous one control the resources required on the crawler side to support the crawl.
- *Number of consecutive empty queries*: How many consecutive queries have returned no new data? The probability of encountering new data goes down significantly as the number of consecutive empty queries goes up.

Each of these thresholds constitutes a *sequential stopping rule* that can terminate the crawl before trying all possible queries (by "all" we mean all combinations of choices for fields with bounded domains — we exclude fields with unbounded domains in this study).

2.1 Sampling Phase

Earlier we described the method for determining and issuing the default query. We now discuss the sampling procedure used to determine whether the default query is likely to have returned all the data behind a particular form.

There are several parameters of interest to us. First, we characterize each form field as a "factor" in our search space. Let $f_1, f_2, ...f_n$ be the n factors corresponding to fields with bounded domains, and let $|f_i|$ represent the number of choices for the ith factor. Then the total number of possible combinations N for this form is:

$$N = \prod_{i=1}^{n} |f_i|.$$

We are also interested in the cardinality c of the largest factor: $c = \max(|f_1|, |f_2|, ..., |f_n|)$.

Next, we define C to be the size of a sampling batch. We want each sampling batch to be large enough to cover the margins of our sample space — that is, we want to have fair coverage over all the factors. So we let $C = \max(c, \lceil \log_2 N \rceil)$. This accounts for the case where there are many factors of small cardinality. For example, if there were 16 factors each of cardinality 2, then $N = 2^{16} = 65536$, but $c = 2$. We want c to be representative of the size of our search space, so we require that it be at least $\log_2 N$, which is a statistically reasonable number to use when sampling populations of known size (consider, for example, the 2^k factorial experiments method [16,11]).

Our decision rule for determining whether the default query returned all the data available from a particular site is based on a sample of C queries. If all C queries return no additional data (i.e. after duplicates have been eliminated), then we assume the default query did indeed retrieve all available data.

However, we need to be careful about how we choose the C queries. Suppose the form of interest contains two bounded fields with choices of 7 and 4 possibilities respectively. Then we have $N = 7 \times 4$ and $C = \max(\max(4, 7), \lceil \log_2 28 \rceil) = \max(7, 5) = 7$. If we simply choose C random queries, we might end up with a sample set like the one shown in Table 1. This table shows a two-way layout [16,8,11,13] that helps us use a two-factor method [16,11,13] to choose a query sample. Notice that a_6, a_7, and b_3 were not considered in any of the sample queries, while b_1 is oversampled.

One solution is to keep track of how many times we have sampled each factor, and spread the samples evenly, as Table 2 shows. This approach for constructing a sampling search pattern yields "maximal coverage."

In Table 2 we use a regular pattern to cover both factors as broadly as possible. The sample consists of the sequence (a_1, b_1), (a_2, b_2), (a_3, b_3), (a_4, b_4), (a_5, b_1), (a_6, b_2), (a_7, b_3). If we were to continue, the next query we would choose would be (a_1, b_4). The algorithm chooses a next sample that is as far away from all previous samples as possible. Since we have categorical, not quantitative, data each of the a_i choices for factor A is equally distant from all others. Thus, our distance function simply measures the number of coordinates that are different. For example, the distance between (a_1, b_1) and (a_2, b_2) is 2, while the distance between (a_1, b_1) and (a_7, b_1) is 1.

To ensure that a regular pattern does not bias our results, we introduced a stochastic element by randomly choosing next samples from the list of all those that are equally furthest from the set selected so far. This yields a layout like the one in Table 3. Note that our technique is general for n dimensions, $n \geq 2$.

Table 1. Two-Way Layout with Random Sampling

		Factor A						
		a_1	a_2	a_3	a_4	a_5	a_6	a_7
	b_1	x	x		x			
Factor B	b_2		x		x			
	b_3							
	b_4			x		x		

Table 2. Regular Sampling with Maximal Coverage

		Factor A						
		a_1	a_2	a_3	a_4	a_5	a_6	a_7
	b_1	x				x		
Factor B	b_2		x				x	
	b_3			x				x
	b_4				x			

Table 3. Random Sampling with Maximal Coverage

		Factor A						
		a_1	a_2	a_3	a_4	a_5	a_6	a_7
	b_1				x			x
Factor B	b_2	x					x	
	b_3					x		
	b_4		x	x				

After issuing C queries stochastically in a maximally covering fashion, if we have received no new data we judge the default query to be sufficient and halt, claiming that we have successfully retrieved all data. In practice, this rule has been highly successful (as judged by human operators manually verifying the decision). Although this rule never reported that all data had been retrieved when it had not, we did encounter sites where our rule was too strict. (The copy detection system reported new bytes in subsequent queries, but there were not really any new records; this can be the result of personalized advertising information or other dynamic variations in Web pages).

Our decision rule for determining whether a query yields "new" data is based on a size heuristic. First we strip a returned page of its HTML tags, leaving on the special sentence boundary tags (<s.>) described in [10]. Then we use the copy detection system to remove duplicate sentences, and count the number of bytes U remaining. If U is at least 1000, we assume we have received new data. If U is less than 1000, we use order analysis to prune small results. We first find the minimum size M returned by the previous C queries. If U is greater than M then we assume we have received new data. We have also tested a percentage threshold, comparing U to the total number of bytes returned in the page (excluding HTML tags). Both heuristics perform reasonably well. Since we are using a statistical approach, some noise in the system is acceptable, and indeed some even cancels itself out.

Another way to test for uniqueness of data would be to call on our downstream record extraction process to actually extract and structure the records from this page. Then we could perform database-level record comparisons to determine when we have found unique records. However, this makes the Web-form retrieval less general by tying it to a specific domain ontology. In the future we will investigate more fully the ramifications of this alternate approach.

2.2 Exhaustive Phase

If the C sample queries yield new data, we proceed by sampling additional batches of C queries at a time, until we reach one of the user-specified thresholds or we exhaust all the possible combinations. Sampling proceeds according to the maximal covering algorithm discussed earlier — each new query is guaranteed to be as far away from previous queries as possible, thus maximizing our coverage of the factors.

However, before proceeding, we first estimate and report the maximum possible space needed for storing the results and the maximum remaining time needed to finish the process. We also give the user the choice of specifying the various thresholds for completeness of retrieved data, maximum number of queries to be issued, maximum storage space to use, and maximum time to take. Additionally, the user can decide to stop and use only the information already obtained. (All this information can also be specified ahead of time so the process can run unattended.)

We estimate the maximum space requirement S by multiplying the total number of queries N by the average of the space needed for data retrieved from

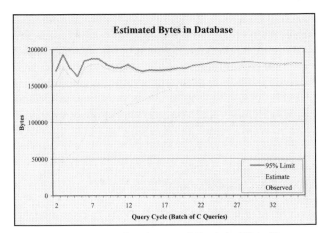

Fig. 1. Completeness Measures for Automobile Ads Web Site (www.slc-classifieds.com, Form 1)

m sample queries:

$$S = \left(\frac{N}{m}\right) \sum_{i=1}^{m} b_i$$

where b_i is the size in bytes of the ith sample query, and typically $m = C$. We estimate the remaining time required T similarly:

$$T = \left(\frac{N}{m}\right) \sum_{i=1}^{m} t_i - \sum_{i=1}^{m} t_i = \left(\frac{N-m}{m}\right) \sum_{i=1}^{m} t_i$$

where t_i is the total duration of the ith sample query. Note that we subtract the time already spent in the initial sampling phase. Also observe that since we follow "next" links, what we are calling a "query" could actually involve a fair number of HTTP GET requests. For larger sites, this can take a significant amount of time.

After establishing the user's preferences, we proceed to process additional batches of C query samples. At the end of each sample batch, we test the thresholds to see if it would be productive to continue processing. Note that each batch provides maximal coverage of the various factors, using unique combinations that have not yet been tried.

Figure 1 illustrates how we measure our progress with respect to the percentage of information retrieved so far. The "Observed" line indicates how many actual unique bytes we have seen after each query cycle. The "Estimate" line shows our estimate of the number of unique bytes we would encounter if we were to exhaustively crawl this Web site (trying all possible combinations of queries). The "95% Limit" line uses the standard deviation of our prediction estimate for the probability of finding additional data to determine the level at which we can claim 95% confidence about our estimate. That is, based on what we have seen so far, we are 95% confident that the real number is less than the "95% Limit"

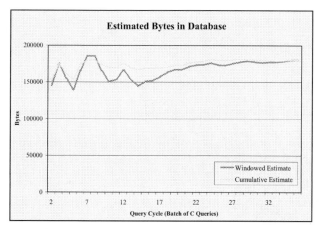

Fig. 2. Windowed vs. Cumulative Estimates

number. In this example, we cross the 80% completeness threshold in cycle 14 (out of 36 total). After 22 cycles we estimate that we are 90% complete. We reach 95% in cycle 25, and 99% in cycle 31. Only after all 36 cycles have been exhaustively attempted would we determine that we are 100% complete. In this example, $N = 2124$ and $C = 59$. Thus, if 80% completeness is sufficient for the user, we prune 1297 out of 2124 queries (61%) from the list.

The formula for estimating the database size D_i after i queries is shown in Equation 1:

$$D_i = O_i \left(1 + \frac{N - i}{i} p_i \right) \qquad (1)$$

where O_i is the number of unique bytes observed after i queries, and p_i is the estimate of the probability of finding new data in query $i + 1$. The only random variable in Equation 1 is p_i, which is defined as the number of queries that returned new data divided by i. Thus, p_i is a cumulative probability estimate reflecting the ratio of successful queries to total queries. We compute D_i by predicting that in the remaining $N - i$ queries the proportion that return new data will be approximately p_i. Further, we estimate that on average successful queries will return approximately $\frac{O_i}{i}$ new bytes. We can compute $\hat{D}_i$, that is, D_i with 95% confidence by including in p_i a measure of the standard deviation of p_i over the previous two query cycles, σ_i, as shown in Equation 2:

$$\hat{D}_i = O_i \left(1 + \frac{N - i}{i} (p_i + 1.645 \sigma_i) \right) \qquad (2)$$

Rather than using a cumulative estimate of database size, we could instead use a window to ignore older data points. For example, Figure 2 compares a cumulative estimate of D_i with a windowed estimate, where the probability p_i is only computed using the last two query cycles. One might think that a windowed probability estimate should be more accurate because it reflects more recent experience. But in practice the more stable cumulative estimate appears

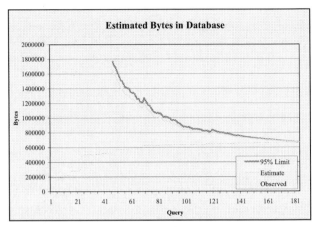

Fig. 3. A Contrasting Automobile Search (`www.slc-classifieds.com`, Form 2)

to give better performance among the sites we have examined. Both converge relatively quickly and show nicely declining variance over time.

3   Experimental Results

A considerable amount of our work was done by simulation, crawling a site once and then playing with different sampling scenarios to understand the ramifications of various approaches. However, we also tried our tool on 15 different Web sites from several different application domains to evaluate its performance empirically. In all cases, we manually verified the decision reported by the system regarding whether the default query retrieved all data. In six of the cases, the default query did indeed return all the data.

In our testing, processing a single HTTP request took anywhere from 2 to 25 seconds on average, depending on the Web site. A single query, which includes following "next" links, averaged between 5 seconds and 14 minutes. Some pages had no "next" links, but others had as many as 140 such links! Thus, the sampling phase could take anywhere from a few dozen seconds to several hours. Storage requirements were modest by modern standards, requiring anywhere from several megabytes to hundreds of megabytes per tested site.

We encountered two typical data patterns. First is the relatively sparse behavior exhibited by the site crawled in Figure 1. The second is fairly dense, as typified by Figure 3. Both of these data sets come from the same Web site, but through different forms to different sub-portions of the site. In this second example, there are only 8 query cycles of 23 queries each (8 choices for one bounded field, 23 for another), for a total of $N = 184$. However, it is not until the end of cycle 6 (query 138) that we estimate we have retrieved 80% of the available data. And even then, there is still an estimated 42% probability of obtaining additional data with another query. Thus, we can only save a small portion of the 184 queries (25% or fewer). Even in such cases, however, the 15-25% savings can be significant.

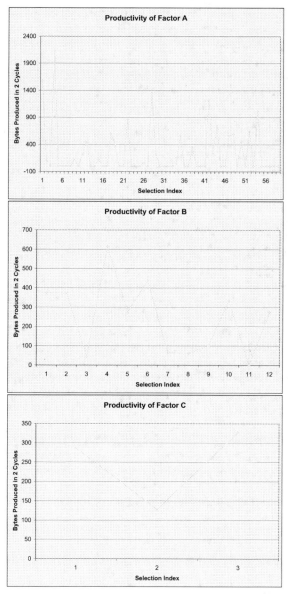

Fig. 4. Relative Productivity of Various Factors

412   Stephen W. Liddle et al.

4   Conclusion

In this paper we have described our domain-independent approach for automatically retrieving the data behind a given Web form. We have prototyped a synergistic tool that brings the user into the process when an automatic decision is hard to make. We use a two-phase approach to gathering data: first we sample the responses from the Web site of interest, and then, if necessary, we methodically try all possible queries until either we believe we have arrived at a fixpoint of retrieved data, or we have reached some other stopping threshold, or we have exhausted all possible queries.

We have created a prototype (mostly in Java, but also using JavaScript, PHP, and Perl) to test our ideas, and the initial results are encouraging. We have been successful with a number of Web sites, and we are continuing to study ways to improve our tool.

One improvement that seems particularly promising is to perform an analysis of the productivity of various factors in order to emphasize those that yield more data earlier in the search process. For example, Figure 4 shows that choices 1, 4, and 28 of Factor A have been significantly more productive than average in the first two query cycles. Similarly, choices 4 and 6 of Factor B, and choices 1 and 3 of Factor C are highly productive. A straightforward two-way interaction analysis indicates which pairs of choices for various factors are most productive. There are challenging issues with determining how best to partition the search space, but we are studying how a directed search algorithm might perform.

Our research group is generally working in the broader context of ontology-based data extraction and information integration. If we combine the hidden Web retrieval problem with the tool of domain-specific ontologies, we could automatically fill in text boxes with values from the ontologies. While this makes the retrieval process task-specific, it also increases the likelihood of being able to extract just the relevant subset of data at a particular Web site. (Our assumption in this paper has been that the user wants to retrieve all or most of the data at a given site.) Also, it is likely that we could avoid a fair amount of the manual intervention in our current process if we use ontologies.

Users need and want better access to the hidden Web. We believe this will be an increasingly important and fertile area to explore. This paper represents a step in that direction, but a great deal remains to be done. We look forward to continuing this promising line of research.

References

1. M.K. Bergman. *The Deep Web: Surfacing Hidden Value*. BrightPlanet.com, July 2000. Downloadable from http://www.brightplanet.com/deep_content/deepwebwhitepaper.pdf, checked August 10, 2001.
2. R.B. Doorenbos, O. Etzioni, and D.S. Weld. A scalable comparison-shopping agent for the World-Wide Web. In *Proceedings of the First International Confence on Autonomous Agents*, pages 39–48, Marina del Rey, California, February 1997.

3. Patil systems home page. `http://www.patils.com`. Describes LiveFORM and ebCARD services. Checked August 10, 2001.

4. eCode.com home page. `http://www.eCode.com`. Checked August 10, 2001.

5. D.W. Embley, D.M. Campbell, Y.S. Jiang, S.W. Liddle, D.W. Lonsdale, Y.-K. Ng, and R.D. Smith. Conceptual-model-based data extraction from multiple-record Web pages. *Data and Knowledge Engineering*, 31:227–251, 1999.

6. D. Florescu, A.Y. Levy, and A.O. Mendelzon. Database techniques for the World-Wide Web: A survey. *SIGMOD Record*, 27(3):59–74, 1998.

7. Home Page for BYU Data Extraction Group, 2000. URL: `http://www.deg.byu.edu`.

8. T. Leonard. *A Course In Categorical Data Analysis*. Chapman & Hall/CRC, New York, 2000.

9. S.W. Liddle, D.W. Embley, D.T. Scott, and S.H. Yau. Extracting data behind Web forms. Technical report, Brigham Young University, June 2002. Available at `http://www.deg.byu.edu/papers/`.

10. S.W. Liddle, S.H. Yao, and D.W. Embley. On the automatic extraction of data from the hidden web. In *Proceedings of the International Workshop on Data Semantics in Web Information Systems (DASWIS-2001)*, pages 106–119, Yokohama, Japan, November 2001.

11. R.A. McLean and V.L. Anderson. *Applied Factorial and Fractional Designs*. Marcel Dekker, Inc., New York, 1984.

12. Microsoft Passport and Wallet services. `http://memberservices.passport.com`. Checked August 10, 2001.

13. R.L. Plackett. *The Analysis of Categorical Data, 2nd Edition*. Charles Griffin & Company Ltd., London, 1981.

14. S. Raghavan and H. Garcia-Molina. Crawling the hidden Web. Technical Report 2000-36, Computer Science Department, Stanford University, December 2000. Available at `http://dbpubs.stanford.edu/pub/2000-36`.

15. S. Raghavan and H. Garcia-Molina. Crawling the hidden Web. In *Proceedings of the 27th International Conference on Very Large Data Bases (VLDB 2001)*, Rome, Italy, September 2001.

16. A.C. Tamhane and D.D. Dunlop. *Statistics and Data Analysis: From Elementary to Intermediate*. Prentice-Hall, New Jersey, 2000.

Managing Unstructured E-commerce Information[*]

Rui Gureghian Scarinci[1], Leandro Krug Wives[1], Stanley Loh [2, 3],
Christian Zabenedetti[1], and José Palazzo Moreira de Oliveira[1]

[1] Instituto de Informática, PPGC/UFRGS
Avenida Bento Gonçalves, 9500 - Campus do Vale - Bloco IV
Bairro Agronomia – Porto Alegre – RS, Brasil, CEP 91501-970 – Caixa Postal: 15064
{rgs,wives,palazzo}@inf.ufrgs.br, czambene@ucs.tche.br
[2] Universidade Luterana do Brasil (ULBRA)
Rua Miguel Tostes, 101 – Bairro São Luis, CEP 92.420-280, Canoas – RS, Brasil
[3] Universidade Católica de Pelotas (UCPEL)
Rua Félix da Cunha, 412 – Bairro Centro, Pelotas – RS, Brasil
loh@zaz.com.br

Abstract. This paper describes an e-commerce application build on the Electronic Trading Opportunities System. This system enables 'Trade Points' and trade related bodies to exchange information by e-mail. This environment offers an enormous trade potential and opportunities to small and medium enterprises, but its efficiency is limited since the amount of circulating messages surpasses the human limit to analyze them. The application described here aids this process of analysis, allowing the extraction of the most relevant characteristics from the messages. The application is structured in three phases. The first is responsible for analyzing and for providing structural information about texts. The second identifies relevant information on texts through clustering and categorization processes. The third applies Information Extraction techniques, which are aided by the use of a domain specific knowledge base, to transform the unstructured information into a structured one. By the end, the user gets more quality in the analysis and can more easily find interesting ideas, trends and details, creating new trade opportunities to small and medium enterprises.

1   Introduction

The increasing needs to transmit and manage accurate information for international trade are of high importance for business efficiency in today's competitive economies. Due to the high cost of advanced IT-systems and telecommunications, such services are not feasible for small companies, specially the ones from emerging countries. To provide a compensatory mechanism to the globalization processes, the Electronic Trading Opportunities (ETO) System was developed by the United Nations Trade Point Development Center (UNTPDC) to provide assistance to Small and Medium

---

[*] This research is partially sponsored by grants from CNPq and CAPES.

A. Olivé (Eds.): ER 2003 Ws, LNCS 2784, pp. 414–426, 2003.
© Springer-Verlag Berlin Heidelberg 2003

Enterprises (SME), offering the same benefits that were previously only enjoyed by large organizations. The ETO system enables Trade Points and trade related bodies to exchange information in standardized m on a global basis, using semi-structured text sent by e-mail. Trade Points are a source of trade-related information, which provides data to actual and potentials traders, offering data about business and market opportunities, potential clients and suppliers, trade regulations and requirements.

The ETO System connects 135 Trade Points and 10,000 trade related bodies in 75 developed countries, 60 developing countries and 20 Less Developed Countries (LDC). This System generates more than 130,000 records monthly, resulting in nearly 13 GB of messages about trade every month. Presently, the ETO switch transfers over 2 million e-mails a day with trade leads to 10,000 organizations in 148 countries [1]. The described environment offers an enormous trade potential and opportunities to enterprises in developing and LDC.

To support the information demand from Small or Medium Enterprise (SME), an automated system is needed as those enterprises have a little budget to invest in the human processing of the ETO. In this paper, we discuss the environment and the techniques employed to allow a SME to reach a competitive position. The present approach executes analyses of high-level textual characteristics over the ETO messages.

2   ETO Treatment and Management Process

The ETO System may be interpreted as a kind of semi-structured documents database. This system, in combination with Document Retrieval (DR) and Information Extraction (IE) techniques, allows identifying new trade opportunities to SME. We propose an automated environment to categorize, index and analyze the ETO, using an approach that we call Information Extraction in Multiple Layers (IE-ML).

The IE-ML is developed to manipulate e-commerce information through multiple conceptual layers, taking care of different information necessities from different users using the same initial database. Some users may want to know only the subject of the unstructured files (domain), while others may desire to select specific information from these files, storing them in a structured database. With the use of multiple conceptual layers, information may be discovered and retrieved on different abstraction levels [2].

The IE-ML framework is based on a set of individual and independent processes. Most IE systems are based on a set of processes, with well-defined functions, executed linearly [3]. The IE-ML approach uses intermediate databases to connect these processes (Figure 1). The flexibility offered by the multiple conceptual layers is a consequence of this modularization and the use of intermediate databases generated by a progressive information treatment. The user may obtain information of intermediate stages of data processing, analyzing and managing resultant information. The application of the intermediate database's approach to IE improves and modifies the traditional architecture of this kind of system. Han, Zaiane and Fu utilize a similar approach, known as Multiple Layer Databases, for Knowledge Discovery in Text - KDT [2] [4] thru information generalization while our approach specialize this information, focusing on specific interest domains for the user (the highest layers have more specialized information).

The IE-ML framework defines four conceptual levels for the treatment and management of e-commerce information. The progressive specialization and transformation of this information, level-by-level, performs the information processing, initiating from the original database (level 0 or primitive) until the relevant information is extracted and structured. The database technologies may be applied to manipulate and retrieve data in the higher levels [4]. A Data Mining system, for example, may be used to explore the data in the final level.

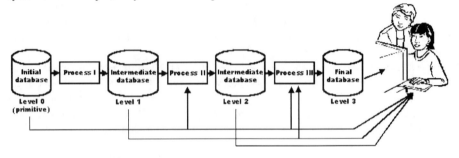

Fig. 1. Conceptual levels of the IE-ML framework

The IE-ML extracts the information progressively, through a sequence of extraction processes (Fig 1) that act on different input file characteristics, and make use of information from all lower data levels. In this framework, level 0 contains the original data files. Level 1 contains structural information about the storage format of the data files, defining each file's structural content. Level 2 contains the concepts that describe the domains and subjects present on each file. Finally, level 3 stores information, based in the user interests about each domain.

In contrast to many other extraction systems, this approach is not sequential. For instance, any process may be executed without the complete execution of the previous processes, using the partial information generated by the previous process and information stored in lower-level databases.

The use of intermediate databases presents many benefits, allowing the partition of the information extraction process in independent phases by the modules. The division of the overall extraction process in precisely defined phases makes possible the combination of different techniques of DR and IE in the extraction system. Such techniques will be used at different moments, partially searching the required data.

There are three major steps (sub-processes) in the overall process: Structural Classification (P1), to discover structural characteristics; Domain Classification (P2), to determine the documents domain (concepts); and Extraction (P3), to extract text segments and structure the relevant information for the user.

2.1   Structural Classification

IE is associated with a semantic procedure that is dependent of the input file type. A previous analysis of these files is executed, exploring the file extension or internal file structures to determine its class and the appropriated extraction process to be applied. The structural classification process allows the generation of groups of files based on different data storage structures. The use of specific extraction rules for each storage format improves the process efficiency considering the structural characteristics of the files to extract the relevant information from them. This technique has been used in the Essence system [5], which uses summarizers and special procedures to process each different type of file, generating the search index. The Structural Classification process is executed on the primitive data level, performing the following operations:

1. *Identification*: consists of the identification of the file's group, size and date of creation or last modification. These data are used for the extraction phases, maintaining the relationships between the primitive input files and the intermediate databases by the addition of a pointer to the corresponding file in L0. A knowledge base supplies information about the location of the primitive input files.
2. *Selection:* this operation selects the files to be processed in the next phase by the analysis of the external characteristics of these files. The user may build rules to select only the most recent files, or to discard larger files, reducing the amount of data to be processed in other phases.
3. *Splitting:* this activity splits physically grouped files such as zipped files or e-mails grouped structures, as those of Microsoft Outlook's ".pst" files. External procedures are used to split the files. Grouped files may contain other grouped archives. Consequently, the division of such files requires a recursive processing. The intermediate database L1 contains the URL pointing to the original grouped file and to the resultant files.
4. *Conversion*: this operation converts the files into standard ASCII format. The user should define Rules in the knowledge base to specify which file-types must be converted to the ASCII format.
5. *Classification:* this operation classifies (indexes) the files by its internal storage structure already identified in the previous phases.

2.2   Domain Classification

Once the documents are classified according to its structure, it is necessary to discover its semantics. All ETO are analyzed and classified in categories that extract their domain and relevant concepts.

This categorization process is very similar to an indexing process, since, on its termination, all ETO will have one or more concepts associated. In the present case, keywords are not used; the more powerful concept construct is employed instead [6]. We define a concept as being a set of words that represent some idea, object or domain. This set of words is used to infer/deduct the concept (see the details bellow, in the "Categorization" step).

With this kind of information, the ETO may be selected according to any specific need or context (the user can select the domain subset of the messages to be processed). In this case, only a subset of the entire ETO System messages will be used in the IE process, providing faster analysis and results that are more accurate.

The Domain classification process involves three sub-processes: Preprocessing, Concepts Definition and Categorization:

1. *Preprocessing*: this process combines "stop word" removal and stemming techniques that are used to "clean" the documents. Stop word is the name given to a word that should not be considered in the process (excluded of the analysis). Prepositions, pronouns, conjunctions, adverbs and other frequently used English words, plus ETO domain specific and structural words, are examples of stop words. The set of all selected stop words is known as "stop list", and it is used for the stop word removal process. For the stemming process it is employed the Porter's algorithm [7], which uses some heuristic rules to convert words into their root form.

2. *Concepts Definition:* consists of the application of clustering techniques on a representative sub-set of documents in order to aid the identification and the definition of the concepts. A simple disjoint clustering technique can be used to identify clusters of related documents and then these clusters can be analyzed in order to identify the words that are more common and representative. These words can then be used as suggestions to represent concepts. After the automated procedure, a person should make the final decision of which the suggested words must be used to represent a concept, and inform the importance of each word in the concept description.

   For the clustering process, we use an algorithm that compares each document surrogate (a list of words preprocessed in the previous step plus the information of its frequency) against the other document's surrogate. The pattern matching is performed by a variation of the Rocchio's algorithm [8]. The choice for this algorithm is due to its simplicity, easy implementation and relative efficiency [9]. Besides that, Ragas and Koster [10] carried out experiments using four different algorithms and found that Rocchio's and Bayes algorithms achieved better results.

3. *Categorization:* The goal of this task is to identify concepts present in texts. However, documents do not have concepts explicitly declared, but more exactly the concepts are embedded in the words composing the document [11]. Instead of using complex Natural Language Processing algorithms to analyze the syntax and the semantics of a document to identify embedded concepts, we use a simpler technique based in the hypothesis that concepts may be identified by the appearance of "hint" terms. It is possible to calculate the likelihood of a concept being present in a text using a fuzzy reasoning over the hints found in this text.

The algorithm we use to do the categorization of the texts uses a prototype-like vector (a centroid) of concepts to represent each class/category. The membership of an element (text) in a class is evaluated by a similarity function that calculates the distance between the element and each centroid (this is also a variation of the Rocchio's algorithm). The algorithm starts comparing all texts against each concept, assuming that concepts were defined early and the texts previously represented in an internal format. The comparison is done through a fuzzy reasoning process. Weights of common terms (those present in both text and concept) are multiplied. The overall sum of these products (limited to 1) is the degree of relation between the text and the concept (the relative probability of the concept to be present in the text with a specific degree of importance). Each word of a concept contributes with certain strength to the presence of that concept. Strong indicators receive higher weights in the concept definition.

That means that if words that describe a concept appear in a text, then there is a high probability of the presence of the concept in that text. The decision concerning whether a concept is present or not depends on a threshold used to cut off undesirable degrees. Our approach uses that threshold to decide whether a concept is present or not. As the user may set this threshold, it is possible that only one term indicates the concept presence. The decision is achieved by the context analysis. This threshold may be chosen in a training session before the classification task. Therefore, if a concept is considered to be present a text, the text can be considered to be in the category described by this concept. Moreover, we call the identification of concepts within texts a "categorization" process.

2.3   Extraction Process

At this point, the ETO files are classified and indexed; the concepts and implicit knowledge that could be used directly by the user to find any opportunity are identified. However, in this case the user would still have to read each trade opportunity in order to identify important information. To avoid this, the extraction process (P3) transforms an ETO collection in information that is more easily analyzed and read. This collection is defined according to the user's interest, based on the concepts associated with a sub-collection of ETO, using the index classes.

The extraction module is focused on the reduction of the process time and to obtain better information quality. This task isolates relevant text fragments, extracts relevant information from the fragments and then put the information together in a coherent framework (level 3). IE systems do not try to interpret the text. Instead, they analyze the portions that may contain relevant information [12]. The relevancy is determined by a set of predefined patterns that should specify, as accurately as possible, what kind of information the system is expected to find.

An IE system converts unstructured texts into entries in a structured database [13]. The entries in the output database can be generated from a fixed group of values or strings extracted from the original text. It allows the processing of information by other applications [14]. Moreover, it allows the user to understand the meaning of the information in a text without the need to read it completely analyzing only the extracted data. For each kind of text (defined by structural and by domain classification), a database table must be created, specifying the data fields that will be filled with the extracted data, and which extracted information will be stored in each of those fields (subject, product/service, etc) [12].

The search of knowledge in unstructured textual databases demands the understanding of the stored data. A reader acquires knowledge from text, easily and naturally, identifying the relevant information and memorizing it. The automation of this activity is as complex as building a system to understand natural language [15].

To avoid the complexity of the analysis, our approach for IE uses a simplified process without the manipulation of deep characteristics of the text's semantics. The information extraction process does not need to accomplish the understanding of natural language.

The goal is to emphasize the superficial cognitive aspects involved in text reading, understanding how human beings retrieve information and coding the reader knowledge as rules to guide the extraction process. Retrieval and information systems often demand adaptation of inference models of knowledge-based systems to the task of document analysis. The extraction process module analyzes the input text files according to the content of the knowledge bases defined by user, interpreting the rules. As result, an output file is generated. The knowledge representation, using production rules, is generic and can be applied to different domain description.

However, the use of this approach is only possible due to the classification processes (P1 and P2), which previously define the structure and the domain of the input files on which the extraction rules of the P3 process will be executed. The importance of this classification is evidenced through other works of IE that partially use superficial natural language analysis methods. Using the previous intermediate databases, in which the input files are classified, user associates to each classification the knowledge base defined for this extraction process. In fact, the extraction domain becomes more restricted, facilitating the configuration of the knowledge bases and magnifying the quality of the extracted data.

It is possible to create many knowledge bases defining multiple extraction domains, which are utilized according to the user necessities and different structural and conceptual classes. The rules represent empiric knowledge, generated from the user knowledge about textual characteristics that are explored to select the entry information. This module discovers the semantic knowledge in a text from superficial characteristics like individual words (lexicon), contextual characteristics and through patterns of sentences in the text. Cowie [16] confirms that the use of shallow techniques (i.e. superficial text characteristics) is simpler to extract and process and provides an effective mechanism to develop systems.

Each extracted word is processed as a "token" by the rules stored in the knowledge base. A term may be composed by one or more words: "Call for Papers" has a real meaning only if associated in this order. The expression "chemical product", for example, is a meaningful term in the ETO analysis. Some other expressions or single words may be identified only with an analysis process, as the string "10/01/2001", where the structure identifies the string as a date. The extraction process stores in dictionaries all the terms identifiable by the lexical analyzer. Each one of these dictionaries should describe a group of related terms (i.e. "country names" like Argentina, Brazil, Finland and so on).

On texts written in English or Portuguese, for example, the words starting with capital letters can help the identification of persons or company names. Moreover, many delimiters, as titles (Mr. and Dr.) and designations for companies (Co. and Inc.) allow that unknown words will be considered part of name patterns. The performance of the patterns identification process is between 40% and 90%, depending of the domain and the technique used [16].

The context and superficial patterns complete the lexically extracted information, increasing the process' precision. The goal is to find the structural properties of one individual term inserted in a document. The utilization of context and superficial patterns is also based in a simple relation between sentences and phrases. During the extraction process, a term is defined as the "search head", starting from which the other terms will be extracted. Usually this "head" term is the result of a previous lexical analysis, amplifying the meaning attributed to the "head" term through associated structural/superficial information extraction. The user must define the scope of terms relations in the extraction rules. According to the previous date example, it is possible to associate the string "10/10/95" with a previous word like "dead-line", adjoining a greater semantic meaning to that string.

3   Experiment

In this section, the application of the IE-ML methodology in the ETO System is described. The objective of this experiment is to give evidence of the multi-layer process of information extraction in a real-life application. Four steps are applied in the experiment: Gathering of ETO messages, Structural Classification and Filtering, Domain Classification and Extraction of Relevant Information. These steps are detailed bellow.

Step 1 - Gathering of ETO messages: We have collected 250 messages. Each message was saved in a separated file and those were mixed with other files, creating the N0 database. The intention was to test the system's ability to filter the relevant messages among other documents.

Step 2 - Structural Classification and Filtering: The second step is to analyze each document file and select those that match the filtering criteria: (a) files smaller than 20 KB; (b) files with the DOC, TXT, PS and PDF. This step also includes the decompression of ZIP files in order to find relevant documents and the conversion of DOC, PS and PDF files into TXT files. The resulting set of relevant documents consists of 250 text files (TXT) that form the L1 database.

Step 3 - Domain Classification: This step consists on tree sub-steps: Concepts Analysis, Concepts Definition and Indexing.

- **Concepts Analysis**: This phase consists on the application of an algorithm to perform the document collection and to identify clusters of closely related documents. The used algorithm is a variation of the "Stars" algorithm defined by Salton (1983). The purpose of this step is to find documents of closely related subjects (concepts). Once the clusters are found a processing is performed to find those words that are more statistically relevant and analyze its result in order to get some hints on the subjects stated on the documents.
- **Concepts Definition**: Based on the list of the most frequent words for each cluster, an expert on the field can identify the subjects and the more relevant concepts for the documents collection. Once those concepts are identified they are used to index

the documents. The concept's model described in the previous section expresses
the subjects. In the case the following concepts were:
- Mobile telephony: "mobile", "Nokia", "cellular", "batt" (and its variations, like
  battery) and "accessories".
- Computing: "motherboard", "motherboards", "byte", "bits", "computer",
  "computers", "software", "hardware", "notebook", "notebooks", "laptop" and
  "laptops".
- **Classification**: In this phase, the documents are analyzed to see which concepts
  can be found inside them. The identification of the concepts is done by the process
  stated in the previous section, and can be compared to a categorization task, in
  which the documents are categorized in all categories they are more likely to be
  present. Each category represents one of the concepts defined in the previous sub-
  step. After this phase, all documents are indexed and represented by the concepts
  found and not by the independent words they contain. In our experiment only one
  concept, the most relevant, was used. This is very similar to the classification
  process of documents, where a document is assigned to one category. The result is
  the L2 database.

The application of the first process (P1) resulted in 250 documents and they were
manually analyzed to identify its categories. These categories were used to test the
accuracy of our classification process. Table 1 shows the results of this test.

Table 1. Evaluation of the classification process

	Expected number of documents in each category (A)	Correctly classified (B)	Incorrectly classified (C)	Recall R=B/A	Precision P=B/(B+C)
Mobile telephony	33	32	3	96.97	91.43
Computing	140	54	0	38.57	100.00
Uncategorized	77	64	97	83.12	39.75
Average				72.89	77.06

The "Mobile Telephony" category presented better results than the "Computing"
one. This occurred because the concepts of the former had been refined based on the
results initially presented in L2. The "Computing" concept, however, was not refined,
generating low quality results. This comparison shows one advantage of the multiple
level databases, which allows the partial evaluation of a process before activating the
next extraction's phase.

Step 4 – Extraction of Relevant Information: After the structural and domain
classification are applied, the information extraction process may be started using
superficial techniques. The use of superficial techniques instead of deep linguistic
analysis is possible since it is feasible to define simple extraction rules that are
specific to the category of interest. A set of rules was established for each domain
(concept). The data desired was: subject, type, country, product, address, phone,
website, date-of-send, contact and validity of the proposal. The website and validity

information were extracted from the 'Computing' category only, to differentiate the rules applied to each domain. The 89 archives left in L2 were processed in P3.

In this process, three dictionaries of words were employed: *products, addresses,* and *countries*. The words in these dictionaries have been chosen after the human analysis of a sample set of documents, verifying the most frequent as indicative of a possible address, product or country.

For the product information extraction, six different rules were created to recover distinct characteristics. Moreover, the use of diverse rules improves the results quality. In the L3 database, six different fields were created; each is the result of a rule. The use of different rules for the extraction of the same information allowed to select the most efficient rule, or to combine them in the search of better results.

The same extraction technique was applied to the extraction of addresses. Two extraction rules were applied resulting in fields in L3: *base_address* and *simple_address*. The rules search for a term that indicates address information such as Street, Avenue and Block. Once it is found, there are two data structure possibilities considered by the rules. The first extraction rule, which stores the information in the *base_address* field, extracts all the text segments from the head (indicative) term until finding, in the next four lines, a term that indicates a country. This characteristic frequently occurs in the address information, allowing a better quality in the extraction (with little irrelevant information). The second rule, which stores information in the *simple_address* field, simply extracts all the text segments from the head term up to three lines, but it facilitates the extraction, in some cases, of irrelevant content. If the first rule extracts the address information, the second rule is not executed, as defined in the knowledge base (see the following example of an "address extraction rule").

```
IF Search_Base(address, CxFree, 8, 100)
AND Verify_Base(countries, CxFree, 1, 4, LINE, AFTER)
THEN BEGIN
    Move(1,Line,PREVIOUS);
    Copy_Until(base, countries, 1, CxFree, 4, LINE,
    AFTERINC, NMODIFIED, base_address);
    Move(1,Line,DEP);
END
ELSE BEGIN
    Copy(3, LINE, TOT, NMODIFIED, simple_address);
    Move(1, LINE, AFTER)
END;
```

The 89 documents in L2 were manually analyzed in order to define all the information that must be extracted. This analysis was employed to build a reference for the quality of the automated analyses. The results of the manual extraction were compared to the ones of the automated process.

The information of contact, date-of-sending, subject, type (offer or demand) and country, as being all in the ETO header (which is very similar to an e-mail header) had an index of recall and precision of 100%, as it should be expected for semi-structured data. From the 89 files processed, 48 were of the type "offer" and 41 of the type "demand".

The address information's extraction result was generated from the combination of the information stored in the *base_address* and *simple_address* fields of the L3 database. These results indicate that the information stored in the *base_address* field has greater precision than the information stored in the *simple_address* field (9.33% against 55.85%). On the other hand, the indices of recall lowered, since addresses without the presence of the country can exist, and these cases are not extracted for the first rule (20% against 6.49%). The remaining data (telephone, website, validity and so on) can be found in the text body and, even being unstructured, they had gotten excellent indices of recall and precision because the text usually has head-terms that indicate the occurrence of that information.

The result obtained for the product information was good, with high indices of ample precision (94.57%). The indices of ample recall (83.85%) could be improved, using a more complete dictionary of terms about products. It is important to emphasize that the values of the incorrectly extracted information is low (4.55%).

The average of recall and precision in the process P3 shows good results: 92.38% (RA), 97.71% (PA), 77.44% (RE) and 81.99% (PE). It shows the importance of the IE-ML for the treatment of this type of information.

4   Concluding Remarks

This paper presented the treatment and management of unstructured e-commerce information over Electronic Trading Opportunities (ETO) System. This is based on a mix of DR and IE technologies. These technologies were applied to a higher-level context that uses concepts instead of words as attributes, minimizing the vocabulary problem. A small experiment was developed with 250 ETO occurrences to give a first indication of the proposal validity. The small number of occurrences was necessary due the full human analysis to validate the extraction process. At present, an experiment on 14.000 ETO occurrences is under development to perform real scale experimentation. In this huge data volume case, the identification of concepts in the textual collection is performed by humans with support of software tools allowing the management of a great number of occurrences in a limited time.

The extraction process is aided by the use of a domain specific knowledge base (concept and rules base). This procedure adds more quality to the discovery process, allowing users to find interesting ideas, trends and information details present in texts. Moreover, this application is very useful in marketing analysis, competitive intelligence and so on.

The use of a multiple levels database allowed the evaluation of the results of each extraction process and its efficient configuration. It can be observed during the experiment that the "noise", or error introduction (irrelevant information) during the data processing, can be easily identified in each extraction phase, and each process can be adjusted to extend the precision of the extraction. On the other hand, the loss of relevant information also was reduced through refinements in the knowledge base associated with each intermediate process, generalizing it and recovering the missed information. Thus, the IE-ML methodology makes possible high extraction quality through the partial evaluation of the extraction process and refinements of the knowledge base in agreement of these partial results.

The IE-ML extract the information gradually, through a sequence of independent and integrated extraction processes, which act on different characteristics of the files, combining different RD and IE techniques. The process' cost is distributed among the extraction stages and allowed to discard irrelevant information and extract and structuralize relevant information.

The use of an extraction methodology based on the superficial analysis of documents (P3 process) revealed efficiency. However, the use of this approach is only possible because of the classification processes (P1 and P2), which previously defines the structure and the domain of the input files on which the extraction rules of the P3 process will be executed.

The system is domain portable. It is independent of the documents storage structure or application domain. It is possible to create many knowledge bases defining multiple extraction domains, which are used according to the user necessities. This allows reduced effort to obtain good extraction results, defining and identifying concepts in texts and obtaining structured information.

References

1. UNTPDC. Electronic Trading Opportunities (ETO) System, United Nations Trade Point Development Center, UNTPDC. http://www.wtpfed.org . Last Access Date: Sep, 2002

2. HAN, J., AND FU, Y. Discovery of Multiple-Level Association Rules from Large Databases, in Proc. of 1995 Int'l Conf. on Very Large Data Bases (VLDB'95), Zürich, Switzerland, September 1995. pp. 420-431.

3. HOBBS, J.R. Generic Information Extraction System. Artificial Intelligence Center SRI International, 2002. http://www.itl.nist.gov/iaui/894.02/related_projects/tipster/gen_ie.htm . 2002. Last Access Date: Sept, 2002.

4. ZAÏANE, O.R. From Resource Discovery to Knowledge Discovery on the Internet, Technical Report TR 1998-13, Simon Fraser University, August, 1998.

5. HARDY, D.R., and SCHWARTZ, M.F. ESSENCE: A Resource Discovery System Based on Semantic File Indexing. in USENIX WINTER CONVERENCE. 1993. San Diego, California: Boulder: University of Colorado. pp. 361-374

6. LOH, S., WIVES, L.K., and OLIVEIRA, J.P.M. Concept-based knowledge discovery in texts extracted from the WEB. ACM SIGKDD Explorations, 2000. 2(1):29-39.

7. PORTER, M.F. An algorithm for suffix stripping, *Program*, 14(3):130-137. 1980. Reprinted in Sparck Jones, Karen, and Peter Willet, 1997, *Readings in Information Retrieval*, San Francisco: Morgan Kaufmann, ISBN 1-55860-454-4.

8. ROCCHIO, J.J. Document Retrieval Systems: Optimization and Evaluation, 1966, Ph.D. thesis, National Science Foundation, Harvard Computation Laboratory.

9. COHEN, W.W., and SINGER, Y. Context-Sensitive Learning Methods for Text Categorization. ACM TOIS. 17(2):141-173. New York: ACM Press, 1999.

10. RAGAS, H., and KOSTER, C. Four Text Classification Algorithms Compared on a Dutch Corpus. in ACM-SIGIR'98. 1998. Melborne, AU: New York: ACM Press. pp. 369-370.

11. APTÉ, C., DAMERAU, F., and WEISS, S.M. Automated learning of decision rules for text categorization. ACM Transactions on Information Systems, 1994. 12(3):233-251.

12. LEHNERT, W. CRYSTAL: Learning Domain-specific Text Analysis Rules, 1996. CIIR Technical Report Computer. http://www-nlp.cs.umass.edu/ciir-pubs/te-43.pdf . Last Access Date: sep, 2002.

13. GRISHMAN, R. Information Extraction: Techniques and Challenges - Information Extraction - A Multidisciplinary Approach to an Emerging Information Technology. Lecture Notes in Artificial Intelligence, ed. M.T. PAZIENZA. 1997, Springer-Verlag: Berlin, Heldelberg. pp. 10-27.

14. CONSTANTINO, M., MORGAN, R.G., and COLLINGHAM, R.J. Financial Information Extraction Using Pre-defined and User-definable Templates in the LOLITA. CIT - Journal of Computing and Information Technology, 4(4):241-255, December 1996.

15. MOULIN, B., and ROUSSEAU, D. Automated knowledge acquisition from regulatory texts. IEEE Expert, 1992. 7(5):27-35.

16. COWIE, J., and LEHNERT, W. Information Extraction. Communications of the ACM. 39(1):80-91. 1996.

Modelling Web-Based Banking Systems: Story Boarding and User Profiling*

Klaus-Dieter Schewe[1,4], Roland Kaschek[1,4],
Claire Matthews[2,5], and Catherine Wallace[3]

[1] Massey University, College of Business
Department of Information Systems
[2] Department of Finance, Banking and Property
[3] Department of Communication and Journalism
[4] Information Science Research Centre
[5] Centre of Banking Studies
Private Bag 11 222, Palmerston North, New Zealand
{K.D.Schewe,R.H.Kaschek,C.D.Matthews,C.M.Wallace}@massey.ac.nz

Abstract. Electronic Business applications are often implemented using web-based Information Systems, in which human-to-human interaction is replaced by human-computer interaction. To design systems that meet both the users' needs and the business intentions of the service provider requires anticipating the users' behaviour. *User profiles* can be used to classify user needs as well as the various kinds of system support for them. For this end also analysis and description of *story boards*, i.e., navigation paths of users through the system can used. In this article the problems of story boarding and user profiling are approached in the context of loan application systems as a typical banking application.

Keywords. Banking, e-business, user profile, story boarding.

1 Introduction

Often Electronic Business technology is linked with web-based Information Systems. In particular, this holds for typical banking services such as loan applications. In web-based e-business systems human-to-human interaction is replaced by human-computer interaction. Thus satisfying customers' needs and meeting the expectations of the service providers, i.e., the bank, requires anticipating the users' behaviour. Only if the system is accepted by a large range of various users, can expectations regarding cost reduction or attracting new customers be met. Acceptance and use by customers is also important in that some customers dissatisfied by the offered web-based system might be lost to the business as they are expected to be able to find an alternative system that suits them better.

Anticipating users' behaviour requires forecasting the actual process of system use that is going to be made. Thus a reasonable design approach will be to

---

* The research reported in this article is supported by the Massey University Academy of Business Research Fund (Project "Story boarding for web-based services", 2002/03).

A. Olivé et al. (Eds.): ER 2002 Ws, LNCS 2784, pp. 427–439, 2003.

identify user types and their most likely occurring behaviour patterns. User types can be characterized by users' goals, intentions, application domain knowledge, i.e. knowledge concerning banking and loans, understanding of their financial abilities and necessities, their information technology abilities and the like. We refer to user type identification by the term *user profiling*. User behaviour pattern analysis we refer to using the term *story boarding*. This is the way users will navigate through a system, which (optional) web-pages they will look at, e.g., samples of filled-in forms, which level of detail they like to see on these pages, etc. While we denote a navigation path as a *story* and each page visited on the path as a *scene*, we denote the integrated stories as a *story board*.

Story boarding and user profiling provide two problems for conceptual modelling of web-based Information Systems, and thus for conceptual modelling of E-Business Systems. Our goal in this article is to present some techniques for solving these problems. We have chosen the field of banking services, specifically loan applications as an area to investigate these problems, and to see how the abstract methodology can be used for these applications.

Developing web-based Information Systems is a large area with many complicated problems besides user profiling and story boarding. The work in [1] emphasizes the design of *content* leading to databases, *navigation* leading to hypertext, and *presentation* leading to the pages layout. Other authors [2,7,11] follow the same lines of thought or concentrate on the "add-on" to database design, the hypertext design dealing with navigation structures [8,14]. The work in [5] presents the forerunner of the theory of *media types* [12], as it has been used in the Cottbus*net* project. Media types provide a theoretically sound way to integrate databases, external views, navigation structures, operations, and even support adaptivity to different users, environments and channels. The *adaptivity* feature distinguishes them from the *dialogue types* that are used to integrate database systems with their user interfaces.

The work in [12] already emphasizes that conceptual abstraction from content, functionality, and presentation of an intended site is not sufficient for the adequate conceptual modelling of web-based systems, even if complex media types are taken into consideration. The approaches in [1,2,7,8,11,14] miss out on the important aspect of story boarding, which is needed to capture the business content of the system. In [12] it is suggested that story boarding be supported through directed graphs called *scenarios*, in which the nodes represent the scenes and the edges correspond either to navigation or to actions issued by the user. This extends the work in [5], where simply partially ordered sets have been used. In addition, user profiling is approached by using *user dimensions* capturing various aspects of how to characterize users. The work in [3] presents a formalized language `SiteLang` to support the specification of story boards.

Our first goal is to extend the work on story boarding and user profiling. We emphasize the data communication between scenes, or between scenes and the user. We also show how to link story boards with media types. The second goal is to provide guidelines on how to develop story boards. The work in [15] suggests investigating metaphorical structures in the application domain to develop the story board. While metaphors are useful to increase user acceptance of a system, only a small part of the activities entering into the story board can be described by them. We therefore suggest analyzing the traditional loan application processing. This involves analysing forms, where this is appropriate. It further includes analyzing the communication between staff and customer. We expect this to give some insight in user profiles, and how problems are addressed by staff. We highlight some communication barriers since the general literature on business communication, e.g., [4,6,9,10], seems to focus on the issue only in terms of intra-organizational communication, not in terms of customer-staff communication.

In Section 2 we briefly describe the methodology underlying our approach to developing web-based Information Systems. We emphasize the parts of the methodology dealing with story boarding and user profiles. Sections 3 and 4 then look into more details in our banking application emphasizing stories associated with the different parts of a loan application, possible profiles of users, i.e., customers, and the communication between customers and banking staff in loan applications and communication barriers.

2   Developing E-business Systems

The general co-design approach to the development of web-based Information Systems [5,12] is based on several layers. On the top-most layer the goal is to capture the intentions concerning the system to be developed. This is called the *intention layer*.

The next layer is the *business layer*, in which the system is to be described in terms of the application domain. This is the layer where business processes, story boarding and user profiling come into play.

The third layer is the *conceptual layer*, in which media types and the underlying conceptual database schema will be developed. The general procedure assumes that the media types will be associated with the scenes appearing in the scenarios defining the story board. The media types provide the basis for the implementation of the system.

The implementation itself is captured in the *presentation layer*, in which style declarations are added to the media types, and in the final *implementation layer*, in which XML suites and transformation tools into HTML are used to derive the final system.

Our interest here is only devoted to the business layer. We define user types in order to address the user profiling problem, and we define scenarios in order to address story boarding.

To describe user profiles, we introduce a finite set Δ of *user dimensions*, e.g. $\Delta = \{$education, banking_knowledge, risk_awareness$\}$. The set of dimensions serves as a guideline for user type introduction, i.e. user classification.

For each dimension $\delta \in \Delta$ we assume to be given a scale $Sc(\delta)$. Formally, a *scale* is a totally ordered set. For example, the scale for risk_awareness may be $Sc($risk_awareness$) = \{$low, average, high$\}$ with low $<$ average $<$ high.

If $\Delta = \{\delta_1, \ldots, \delta_n\}$ is a set of user dimensions, then the *set of user profiles* (or the *user-grid*) over Δ is $gr(\Delta) = Sc(\delta_1) \times \cdots \times Sc(\delta_n)$. A *user type* over Δ is a convex region $U \subseteq gr(\Delta)$.

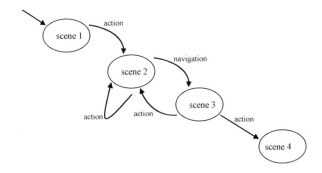

Fig. 2.1. Scenario with Actions

In addition to user profiles and user types we can model *roles* of users. These are normally associated with different access rights to the system. For instance, in an electronic management system for publications there may be roles for those who have the right to add entries, to delete entries, to maintain the whole system including the definition of users and access rights, and "normal" users who can just enter queries and search for publication entries.

As to story boarding we adapt the approach of `SiteLang` with some smaller additions. The story board will be described by scenarios.

A *scenario* is a finite, directed graph $\mathcal{G} = (V, E)$, where the nodes, i.e., the elements of V, are called scenes. With each scene $sc \in V$ we associate a view V_{sc} describing the information consumed by sc and an (optional) user type U_{sc}. Each edge $e \in E$ from sc_1 to sc_2 corresponds to a possible transition from the source scene sc_1 to the target scene sc_2. Such a transition should be triggered by an action initiated by the user. This action can simply be a navigation. Therefore, each edge is associated with the name of an action that can be issued in that scene. In addition, it is also associated with a data type expressing the information communicated from scene sc_1 to scene sc_2.

Figure 2.1 indicates a scenario with four scenes together with the actions associated with the navigation through these scenes. User types, information consumption and production, and communication data types have been omitted. It is quite obvious that in early stages of story boarding these data are not available. It is also possible that one does not yet have a formal specification for them, but only an informal descriptive name.

Instead of emphasizing the transitions between scenes and the triggering actions as done in Figure 2.1, we may want to emphasize the data communication between scenes. In this case it is advantageous to bundle all the information associated with a transition, i.e., we assume that for any two scenes $sc_1, sc_2 \in V$

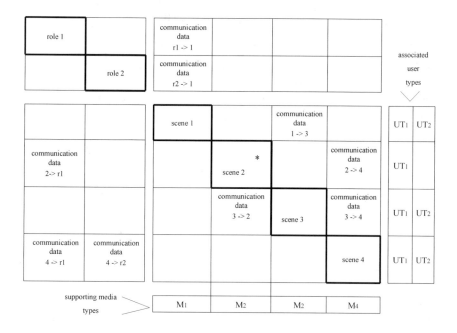

Fig. 2.2. Adjacency Matrix of a Scenario showing Communication Data

in the graph $\mathcal{G} = (V, E)$ representing the scenario there is at most one edge from sc_1 to sc_2. Thus, for $V = \{sc_1, \ldots, sc_n\}$ the graph $\mathcal{G}$ can be represented by its adjacency matrix $\mathcal{A} = \{a_{i,j}\}_{1 \leq i,j \leq n}$, where $a_{i,j} = 1$, if there is an edge from sc_i to sc_j, and 0, otherwise. We use this representation means to get rid of crossing labelled edges in diagrams. We however use it in a modified form. First we use a table T with n columns and rows to represent the matrix. We further fill the table's cells $T(i,i)$, for all $i \in \{1, \ldots, n\}$ with the name of scene sc_i and fill the table cell $T(i,j)$ with whatever labels were attached to edge (sc_i, sc_j), in case there is an edge from sc_i to sc_j. Otherwise we leave the cell blank. A loop in a scenario, i.e. an edge from, e.g. scene sc_i to itself is indicated in the table by means of an asterisk placed in cell $T(i,i)$ of T.

In case we wish to include roles in the scenario then we formally treat them like scenes and include them in the adjacency matrix of the scenario. This allows us to specify the communication the roles are involved in in the obvious way. We often wish to point out which user types we expect to make use of scene sc_i, so we list the respective types at the right side of the table in the form of additional columns. In analogous manner we indicate the media type that is going to be used in a specific scene but denote them as an additional row below the table. See Figure 2.2 as an example for all of this. The figure illustrates the same scenario as Figure 2.1.

3   Story Boarding in Loan Applications

Let us look at story boarding in loan application systems, which provide a nice banking application. The goal of such a system is to provide the loan best suiting the customer's purpose and to offer a loan in a way that the budget—payments in comparison to income, liabilities, etc.—can be justified. Of course, loan applications can be rejected, if no satisfactory budget can be set up or if the securities are insufficient. Note however that the respective decisions nowadays are highly rule based and don't leave much latitude to bank staff.

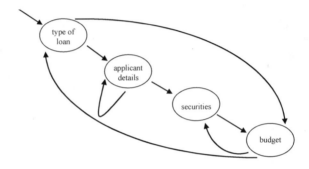

Fig. 3.1. Scenario for Loan Application

The analysis of application forms from various banks shows a lot of similarities. In general, we can detect four major parts in them (not necessarily in the order used below):

- The first part deals with the identification of *the loan type*. This type can be a mortgage for a house, a simple loan to purchase some goods, e.g., a car or furniture, an overdraft loan, etc. The customer is requested to select the type of loan, the amount of the loan including any extra costs, and to describe the purpose of using the loan.
- The second part deals with the *applicant details* and possible joint applicant(s), i.e., name, address, previous addresses if necessary, occupation, employer, contact details, etc. The requested information is normally the same for all applicants.
- The third part deals with *securities* offered to cover the loan, e.g., a dwelling, piece of land, life insurance, etc. If the security is owned by a third party, then an indication must be given that this party will guarantee the requested amount, i.e. that it acts as guarantor in the required manner.
- The fourth and largest part concerns setting up a *budget* for the customer. This contains all details about current income (salaries, rents, interest, etc.), commitments (existing loan payments, rates, living expenses, etc.), proposed payment for the requested loan, liabilities and assets.

Therefore, we can define a scenario with four scenes for each of these system parts as in Figure 3.1. Figure 3.2 contains more details for this scenario emphasizing the data communication and the user types. As this scenario is a very general one, there is no distinction between the user types.

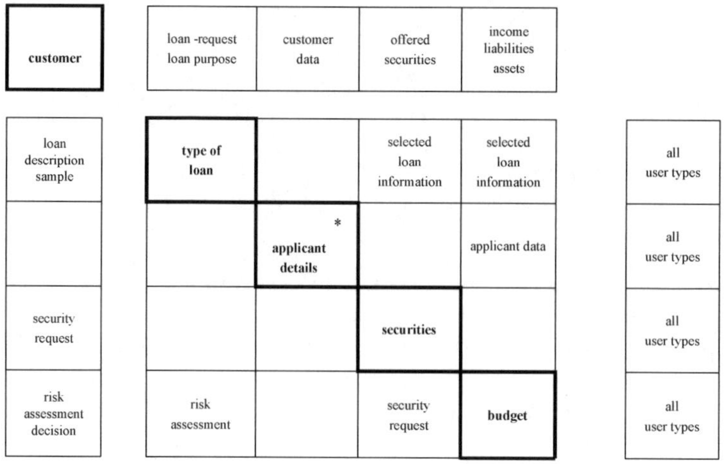

Fig. 3.2. Communication Scenario for Loan Application

For each of the scenes more detail, i.e., a refining or sub-scenario, can be given and a scene could be replaced by a complete sub-scenario. In the latter case the edges, which have the original scene as source or target, have to be replaced as well. Figure 3.3 illustrates a sub-scenario for the scene handling the selection of loans. In this sub-scenario the outgoing edge with source 'offered loans' defines edges from 'offered loans' to 'applicant details' and 'budget', as these scenes appeared in the original scenario.

It is likely that some users are not experts in the loan business. Furthermore, one can expect that some users do not know much about the spectrum of loan types offered by the bank. This will be reflected in the definition of user profiles in Section 4. Customers lacking deep knowledge concerning loans may require in-depth explanations for each of the loan types including possible samples and loan conditions. Since the loan business is a complicated one, it is likely that some customers will acquire knowledge of it while processing the application form. Thus one has to expect that they may change their initial goals. Some may even proceed to or stay in a state in which they have no idea which loan to apply for. It could further be the case that customers are not clear about the purpose of the loan. In these cases traditionally bank staff assist. This help may take several forms, i.e., suggestions concerning the loan's purpose and the loan type most suitable to the customer's living conditions may be made. Sometimes

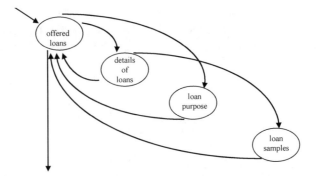

Fig. 3.3. Sub-Scenario for 'Loan Type Determination'

staff will even advise not to apply for a loan at all. In any case the scenario and the data communication requires further detail as described in Figure 3.4.

Enrichment also is required with respect to the other scenes in Figure 3.1. For instance, setting up the budget may again require samples to be shown to customers who are unsure about what data are required by the system. It would also be desirable to provide transparent assessment criteria and terms and conditions for the loans, so that the customer is able to anticipate, whether the loan application processing will be straightforward or not and whether the application is likely to be approved. In a traditional system this information would be provided by the bank staff in a face-to-face discussion.

There are metaphors we propose for use in setting up further refinements of the scenario. They correspond to message flaws to be dealt with below. These flaws are consequences of specific perceptions of the applicant itself, the bank and its staff. Since we are dealing with a quite formalized business we think these perceptions should be based on a conceptualization of this business. We identify three main roles (besides the decision-making) played by bank staff. The first role is that of an information provider, which leads to the metaphor of *dictionary*. The second role is that of a helpful assistant who answers questions on how to fill in the form. This gives an *operations manual* metaphor. The third role is that of an adviser who advises about the most suitable loan type or the acceptability of the customer for a particular loan. This gives an *adviser* metaphor. Whether the introduced metaphors really help can only be decided based on empirical studies. Obviously not only customer specifics but also design and implementation issues are going to impact the respective findings.

4   Communication in Loan Applications

Finally we look at the communication and user types in loan application systems. To describe the desired functionality of loan application systems—leaving aside additional aspects such as system security—we assume that we only need to be interested in the customers. Thus, there will be only one role.

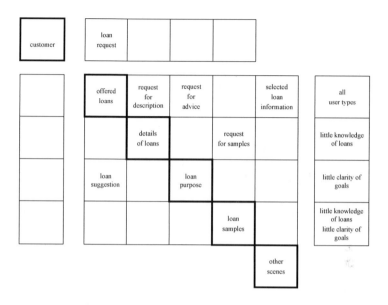

Fig. 3.4. Adjacency Matrix of Sub-Scenario 'Loan Type Determination'

Communication is an exchange of messages. Since we are interested in communication barriers we focus on successful communication, i.e. on both partners meeting their goals underlying the communication case. According to [13, pp. 23-35] with respect to a spoken message we distinguish four main dimensions:

- *Content*, i.e., what the message is about;
- *Presentation*, i.e., what the speaker tells about the message and the sender;
- *Relationship*, i.e., what the speaker thinks about the receiver and their relationship;
- *Appeal*, i.e., what the speaker wants the receiver to do.

These dimensions also apply to non-verbal communication. We use these message dimensions as a simple message meta model and suppose that communication is not successful if at least one message with respect to its instances of the dimensions is flawed. We therefore distinguish the following message flaws:

- *Content flaw*, i.e., the speaker does not say what s/he wanted to say;
- *Presentation flaw*, i.e., what the speaker tells about him/herself is inaccurate;
- *Relationship flaw*, i.e., what the speaker thinks about her relationship to the listener is incorrect;
- *Appeal flaw*, i.e., what the speaker wants the listener to do is not persuasive.

Clearly the above mentioned dimensions of message understanding are not really independent in a formal sense and neither are the flaws. But as can be seen below, they help to formulate and classify communication barriers that appear to be realistic. The project we are running shall show to what extent our view of communication barriers in loan applications is realistic and whether the proposed means to circumvent them can be expected to work in practice.

Since we believe banks and their staff to be sufficiently experienced in loan application processing we restrict our attention to the mentioned message flaws to those that may occur from the applicants' perspective. We then propose means to deal with these flaws so that the applicants will benefit immediately and the bank in the long term.

Clearly the system should be set up in a way that it can be used by all bank customers. These however are not a homogeneous group. The respective distinguishing characteristics are apparent in face to face communication and to some degree can be dealt with by experienced bank staff. The design problem raised by replacing human-to-human interaction by human-computer interaction thus is the simulation of human communication skills by the system. According to our approach we restrict our study to the above mentioned message flaws and propose means to deal with them in the above sense.

- *Message flaws*
    - Customers have a variety of levels of knowledge concerning loan types offered, their application areas, the terms and conditions, the assessment criteria, etc.
    - Customers may or may not have a clear picture about what the loan is needed or going to be used for. Some may have only a vague idea of the purpose.
    - Customers may—depending on their level of education—easily understand the differences between loan types and their respective suitability or not.
- *Presentation flaws*
    - Customers may have a clear mind about their financial capability, and thus be able to set up a reasonable budget. Others may over- or underestimate their capability to afford the payments that will be required in case of application approval.
    - Customers may have sufficient computer literacy to handle an electronic system without difficulties or need a lot of help in doing so.
    - Customers might—due to their insufficient language fluency—need specific support while filling the application form.
- *Relationship flaws*
    - Customers might—due to their personal background—tend to uncritically follow bank staff's advice.
    - Customers might—due to their cultural background, or family related reasons—not dare to apply for a loan.

– *Appeal flaws*
  • Customers might—due to their insufficient understanding of banking business or their difficult state of affairs— just appeal for help and overlook the fact that the bank only in rare cases can afford not to make profit from accepting a loan application.

From the message flaws we derive customer characteristics and turn them into customer dimensions: education, banking knowledge, loan knowledge, clarity about the application itself, clarity about their own financial situation, computer literacy, their cultural and family background including employment status, and language fluency. It appears not to be difficult to invent scales for these dimensions.

The communication between a customer applying for a loan and a bank employee dealing with loan applications is mainly determined by the metaphors described above, and some communication barriers. Recall that the identified metaphors mainly relate to the role of bank staff as seen by the customer. To some degree this is a consequence of the fact that the loan application processing is highly rule based and only leaves a little latitude to bank staff.

A customer might ask bank staff for information about the available loan types, their application area, etc. including illustrating examples, seek advice for which loan is best to apply for, or simply need help in filling forms. This should be reflected in the scenarios. The sub-scenario in Figures 3.3 and 3.4 already pays attention to the information and advice aspects, as it provides the in-depth information for customers with little banking knowledge or little clarity about the purpose of their application. The aspect of help in using computer systems must be incorporated.

Let us finally briefly consider communication barriers impacting the traditional loan application process. The level of education may be a barrier to successful communication between a customer and bank staff. This is reflected in the user dimensions and should lead to further explanatory system components. Another severe communication barrier is the customer's fear, or bluff as its counterpart. A customer might fear the loan application not being accepted, especially, if the loan is essential and the financial situation is tough. Communication barriers may also arise due to gender, age, ethnicity, cultural or family background.

Dealing with bluff and fear requires the system to be as transparent as possible and to emphasize the identified advice component. Inabilities with respect to language can be dealt with based on a multi language feasible design. Cultural background and ethnicity up to some degree can be reflected by the system supplying the applicable general legal regulations. Age and gender may be addressable by design and layout issues as well as focussing on the most required loan application areas and amounts.

5 Conclusion

In this paper we addressed an electronic business application in banking dealing with loan application systems. We addressed the problems of *user profiling* and *story boarding*.

We have shown that the analysis of the communication between customers and bank staff is a good starting point to recognize different types of users of the e-business system. These types of users can be described by various dimensions such as level of education, knowledge of loans and how they are assessed, clarity of goals, etc.

We have shown that story boarding with graphs is adequate to capture information consumption and production and user activities in terms of the banking application. At the same time the story board enables the definition and association of media types, which provides opportunities for developing maintainable, database-backed web-based systems.

We have shown that the story boarding and user profiling approach was able to highlight possible user expectations and communication behaviour of customers, possible communication barriers, the roles of banking staff as seen by the customers, and certain metaphors that may be helpful in designing system components. The resulting system will most likely differ significantly from one that is designed just by projecting existing paper-based forms on a web site.

Though loan application systems provide only a fairly small example of electronic business applications, the shown differences to ad-hoc systems development and the resulting benefits justify the conclusion that user profiling and story boarding are indispensable in the development of e-business systems and more generally web-based Information Systems. Furthermore, the techniques based on user-dimensions and graph-based scenarios are appropriate for these tasks.

References

1. P. Atzeni, A. Gupta, S. Sarawagi. Design and Maintenance of Data-Intensive Web-Sites. *Proc. EDBT'98*: 436-450. Springer LNCS 1377, Berlin 1998.
2. A. Bonifati, S. Ceri, P. Fraternali, A. Maurino. Building multi-device, content-centric applications using WebML, and the W3I3 tool suite. *ER Workshops 2000*: 64-75. Springer LNCS 1921, Berlin 2000.
3. A. Düsterhöft, B. Thalheim. *SiteLang: Conceptual Modeling of Internet Sites*. In H.S. Kunii et al. (Eds.). *Conceptual Modeling – ER 2001*: 179-192. Springer LNCS vol. 2224, Berlin 2001.
4. J. Dwyer. *The Business Communication Handbook*. Prentice-Hall, Australia 1993.
5. T. Feyer, K.-D. Schewe, B. Thalheim. Conceptual Modelling and Development of Information Services. in T.W. Ling, S. Ram (Eds.). *Conceptual Modeling – ER'98*: 7-20. Springer LNCS 1507, Berlin 1998.
6. D. Francis. *Unblocking Organisational Communication*. Cambridge University Press, Cambridge (England) 1987.
7. M. Gädke, K. Turowski. Generic web-based federation of business application systems for e-commerce applications. *EFIS 1999*: 25-42.

8. F. Garzotto, P. Paolini, D. Schwabe. HDM - A model-based approach to hypertext application design. *ACM ToIS* vol. 11(1): 1-26, 1993.
9. M.E. Guffey. *Business Communication: Process and Product.* South Western College Publishing, USA 1997.
10. M. McLaren, K.O. Locker. Business and Administrative Communication. Irwin, Australia 1995.
11. G. Rossi, D. Schwabe, F. Lyardet. Web Application Models are more than Conceptual Models. In P.P. Chen et al. (Eds.). *Advances in Conceptual Modeling*: 239-252. Springer LNCS 1727, Berlin 1999.
12. K.-D. Schewe, B. Thalheim. Modeling Interaction and Media Objects. In E. Métais (Ed.). *Proc. 5th Int. Conf. on Applications of Natural Language to Information Systems*: 313-324. Springer LNCS 1959, Berlin 2001.
13. F. Schultz von Thun. *Miteinander Reden 1: Störungen und Klärungen.* Rowohlt Taschenbuch Verlag. Reinbek bei Hamburg, Germany, 2000.
14. D. Schwabe, G. Rossi. An Object Oriented Approach to Web-Based Application Design. *TAPOS* vol. 4(4): 207-225. 1998.
15. B. Thalheim, A. Düsterhöft. The Use of Metaphorical Structures for Internet Sites. *Data & Knowledge Engineering* vol. 35 (2000): 161-180.

Communication: Key to Success on the Web*

Catherine Wallace[1] and Claire Matthews[2,3]

[1] Massey University, College of Business
Department of Communication and Journalism
[2] Department of Finance, Banking and Property
[3] Centre of Banking Studies
Private Bag 11 222, Palmerston North, New Zealand
{C.M.Wallace,C.D.Matthews}@massey.ac.nz

Abstract. Much has been written about what constitutes good principles of web design. Significantly less attention has been paid to the related communication issues. Critical success factors taken from a pilot study of nine organisations are listed in this paper. We show that they imply that communication aspects of design and implementation of web presence of organisations are key. We point out and classify typical communication barriers. We argue that using localisation abstraction and metaphors can help to overcome communication barriers, implying that their use may enhance the user's understanding and successful navigation through a web site. Our overall implication is that methods for the development of web applications need to shift their focus from technical aspects of applications to communication aspects in particular and on human factors in general.

Keywords. communication, e-business, success factors.

1 Introduction

We consider web applications as defining a space in which users are located somewhere and within which, at various locations, functionality is offered. To invoke functionality users need to identify and locate it, position themselves on the identified location and then trigger it. Functionality allows users to retrieve and process data and to present the data in the most convenient way.

Web applications differ from traditional information systems in that the space they create is essentially open, i.e. by means of following links, so-called navigation, users can reach locations of functionality that cannot be controlled by the application designer. Organisations and thus responsible designers wish to have open applications however at the same time there is the risk that designers will have insufficient experience or skills to fully comprehend the users' requirements. Consideration of security and safety issues requires that organisations have a log-in mechanism to protect key parts of applications. Successfully using

---

* The research reported in this article is supported by the Massey University Academy of Business Research Fund (Project "Story boarding for web-based services", 2002/03).

web applications is much more difficult than using traditional information systems. Consequently the users of web applications need much more sophisticated support than is required for traditional information systems.

The respective possibilities seem to exist because the web is a communication media able to integrate various sorts of digital media such as sound, video, picture and text. However most web sites still require users to approach the medium in a linear, text-based fashion. Doing so is likely to result in failure to select the communication style most appropriate for a given user aiming at solving a given task. Few business web sites have embraced the opportunity that exists for more communication with users who are aware of the characteristics of the web. To use a bank scenario, transaction elements such as querying an account's status, requesting further information or asking for account information to be represented in a more graphical form (such as account balances) can be enhanced with greater use of design features.

Web applications are often intended to restructure the workload of staff. A reduction of routine helpdesk enquiries is the aim as well as an increase of counselling in more advanced matters. The paper [Schewe et al., 2002] deals with more details regarding the modelling of online loan applications. This intent may lead to a reduction of staff time allocated to certain customer use cases. The human communication abilities that staff applied in traditional way of operating must now be partially realised by software. We propose that the communication aspects are more important than the technical ones.

Web applications often are too complex for users to have a sufficiently complete and detailed overview of them, thus users require aid in identifying their locations as well as the functionality in their neighbourhood. We believe that localisation abstraction is a key aid for the user in this matter. This abstraction represents the whole space such that the user's location and neighbourhood is emphasised. Distant locations are suppressed, only sketched or also emphasised in case it is expected that they are of major importance for the user. A very common example of an application of it is highway destination signs. We further believe that localisation abstraction should be combined with using metaphors to help users make appropriate decisions while using services. According to the discussion in [Thalheim and Düsterhöft, 2000] metaphors are language expressions used in an unconventional language context. They can make reasonable what was previously complex and provide a structure for the experience of phenomena. Metaphors also may highlight key attributes and obscure others. Unmasking the dominant metaphor reveals the way it implicitly structures information and knowledge, thereby allowing the user to more fully understand the strengths and weaknesses of any particular concept or conception [Clampitt, 2001].

Various techniques are used in the communication literature to audit and review communication strategies. These include questionnaires, incident reports, interviews, observations and network analysis. A common way of discussing communication strategies with participants and researchers is by referring to a range of metaphors such as client-server, the queuing model, the checkout trolley, transaction analysis etc. These models can be either implicitly or explicitly developed and discussed with participants.

Users construct their perception of the business, its services and the quality of these services through a blend of the expectations and successful use of identifiers on a site. These identifiers include logos, slogans, branding, using tone, icons, font and typeface choices, colour and animations. They open further chances to identify and use suitable metaphors.

The paper structure is as follows: In Section 2 we discuss critical success factors of web applications. In Section 3 we discuss communication aspects of web sites and in Section 4 identify and classify communication barriers. Section 5 contains our conclusions followed by the references.

2   Critical Success Factors of Web Applications

The first author, see [Wallace, 2002], conducted research to understand the ways organisations were using the Internet, i.e. web pages, intranets and email, for their various business functions. Assessment was made of best practice from these case studies.

The research objectives were to identify the nature and extent of Internet based business activity by organisations in New Zealand, to examine the motives and impacts of these initiatives and to determine factors that contributed to the success of these endeavours.

A longitudinal case study methodology was selected to provide a rich source of material relevant to the desired research outcome. The methodology included observations and interviews over time with key participants. Relevant business records were examined and changes to the process of planning, implementing and gaining an online presence were documented. Case study research aims to study social action as it takes place in interaction or communication as interpreted by respondents [Sarantakos, 1993].

Interviews were conducted with a range of personnel concerned with the organisation including management, communication and human resource people, employees and customers. Their comments were coded according to a predetermined five-point scale, all comments pertinent to that critical success factor were totalled and then the means were calculated. The data was analysed using principal component analysis (PCA). This is a data compression technique that summarises quantitative data into fewer key or principal dimensions. Qualitative interpretations of these key dimensions can then be made.

The analysis showed that those critical success factors that have the greatest impact on an organisation's successful Internet use are more strongly related to the human factors rather than the technical aspects. A closer examination revealed that they were in fact more specifically concerned with communication and customer service. The strongest factors in descending order of importance were:

- plan for dealing with site related communication,
- meeting customer demand,
- web site part of overall communication strategy,
- consideration of site's marketing aspects, and
- updating and refocusing of web site.

Various attributes were then examined to see whether they were affected by the critical success factors. The attributes of organisation type, organisation size, the amount of time the organisation had been online and the ways they were using the Internet as an organisation weren't associated with the critical success factors.

Other factors found to have limited relevance to an organisation's successful Internet use were:

- Plan for the organisation's web site
- Development of an integrated Internet package
- Formal Internet policy
- Internet training given and updated
- Support from top management
- Positive relationship with Internet Service Provider
- Intranet in place
- Secure server
- Importance of a project champion
- Being aware of the competition
- Organisational culture responsive to change
- Engaging in electronic commerce
- Use of outside expertise
- Consideration of web site on business effectiveness

3   Communication Aspects of Web Sites

The growth of web sites for businesses, institutions and individuals has led to a huge amount of advice about how to develop and maintain a successful site. More often than not, this advice is theoretical, prescriptive, based on conventions rather than evidence, or focused primarily on technical and commercial aspects of a site rather than its ability to engage with the site's visitors according to [Durham, 2000].

Some of the major communication faults of web sites are caused by not paying enough attention to the aims of the site and the audience's needs, leaving major choices concerning human-computer interaction and thus communication between the organisation and the customer to technical experts, an overly strong focus on the visual communication elements and lack of analysis about the communication effectiveness of the site. The poor quality of web sites is often due to missing "mission statements" according to [Troyer, 1998]. They suggest important questions such as "Who will use the service?", "Which user intentions and behaviour shall be supported?", "Which technical devices will be used by the users?" etc have not been sufficiently taken into account.

Research documented in [Durham, 2000, p. 3] resulted in four general findings that can add to the body of knowledge about web sites, their communicative nature and effectiveness:

1. "The number of studies about web sites is growing. The interest however is still predominantly on other aspects of the Internet, including more ephemeral or informal writing such as email messages and chat room dialogue.
2. The literature on effective web sites suffers from the same problem that until recently characterised writing in the technical writing field, that is, the popularity of unsubstantiated and idiosyncratic guidelines and the dearth of research-based information.
3. Empirical studies about web sites, especially considering the web sites as texts, are still small in number but the results help to identify communication issues.
4. The current empirical studies often lack theoretical frameworks to help make sense of web sites and the communication choices that they embody."

Some guidelines about web sites appear to rely on web writing and design "folklore" with little substantiated evidence. One commonly mentioned example is that readers should be no more than three clicks away from desired information but no rationale for this rule seems to have been given. A comment along similar lines is that while a site may contain 200 pages, the site is considered to work for users if they can find exactly what they are after by looking at two or three pages [Blyth, 1999]. Other guidelines provide principles or prescriptions that are difficult to quantify. One source is cited by [Durham, 2000] that identifies "bad" web pages as those that are "unattractive" or "lack a logical organisation" and another that tells the web site creator to "write clearly".

Web writing styles were researched by [Morkes and Nielsen, 1997] who manipulated a web site's text to create five different writing styles and then used readers to test for comprehension and reaction. They concluded that written material for the web needs to be concise, scannable (able to be read easily) and objective. Usability analysis of a document's language and visual design choices can suggest its impact on readers' ability to orient themselves in the document, find information and process it effectively [Truchard and Katz-Haas, 1998]. Until recently, usability research has been focussed on technical elements such as browser capability and design elements such as colour and font choice. More recently, attention has turned to elements directly affecting the communicative nature of sites as they engage users [Durham, 2000].

Organisations are considering the level of interactivity available on their site and moving from email links, a search function and downloadable files to subscription services, voter surveys, order facilities and in some cases bulletin boards and chat rooms. A study by one of the authors [Matthews, 1998] of New Zealand bank web sites in early 1998 found the TSB Bank included little more than an email address and a thank you message for visiting the site. A visit in mid 2002 to the same site allowed forms to be completed and sent online and loan calculators to be used. Another bank with limited functionality in 1998 was WestpacTrust. At that time it consisted of a one-page site showing logos and a question related to the merger of Westpac and Trust Bank. A comparative visit in July 2002 showed the site offered online banking, the latest rates and services prices and a currency calculator. The authors consider more research needs to be done about audience involvement on organisational web sites and the cost-benefit analysis of interactivity from a business perspective.

A number of studies in the human-computer interface (HCI) field analyse how well web sites communicate with their users. These studies primarily focus on the presentation aspects. Research done on the development of metaphors by [Carroll et al., 1988] paid attention to what may be intuitive for users to comprehend and use when working online. Other HCI studies consider the breadth or depth of structure in a Web site [Larson and Czerwinski, 1998] in terms of helping users to find and comprehend information. A study by [Anderson et al., 1998] of editing levels suggested what the authors called the 'big-picture issues' such as audience definitions, information categories and hierarchies and screen layouts. Our own work focuses on intentions of web sites, storyboarding and conceptual abstraction [Schewe et al., 2002].

4 Communication Barriers

Properly applied, metaphors can simplify the task of communicating complex ideas, create interesting relationships, and result in enthusiastic users as reported in [Thalheim and Düsterhöft, 2000]. In our previous paper [Schewe et al., 2002] we examined the role of story boarding and user profiling in the banking industry and established that anticipating the users' behaviours is needed to design systems that meet both the users' needs and the business intentions of the service. One aspect in this design is to identify the communication barriers that exist and seek to eliminate, or at least alleviate, both their occurrence and their consequences.

The transition from human-to-human interaction to human-computer interactions can be thwarted by a number of barriers. Transactions that were traditionally performed over the counter in a branch of the bank were aided by face-to-face communication using voice intonation, questions and answers in real time, feedback loops, eye contact, observance of nonverbal communication such as reference to computer screens or printed material for records. Online transactions are significantly lacking in verbal indicators and query possibilities. A common expectation of users is that human-computer interactions will be more efficient than traditional ones due to faster response times and fewer delays, less time spent on turn-taking or politeness strategies, a higher level of accuracy achieved and multiple queries or tasks performed within the one service encounter. However, this is not necessarily the case.

446 Catherine Wallace and Claire Matthews

4.1 Types of Communication Barriers

We introduce four types of communication barriers: content, navigation, presentation and technical. This paper explores each of them to illustrate the fundamental design concepts that are often problematic. A number of authors such as [Thalheim and Düsterhöft, 2000] attribute these failings to saying sites are often designer-centred, lack attention to detail and use inappropriate tone.

Content type barriers may consist of actual or potential users being overwhelmed by information overload. Information underload, another content type barrier, consists of insufficient data provision and results in users being unable to solve their problems. Both of these can be stressful and lead to service delivery being perceived as unsuccessful. Other content barriers include overuse or inappropriate use of jargon and terminology such as formal legal disclaimers being repeatedly displayed before the user reaches useful pages. Use of unnecessary concepts and terminology to explain to users his or her options or the actual state of affairs also belongs to this type as well as usage of appropriate but not or insufficiently explained concepts and terminology.

Navigation type barriers can be attributed to three main causes. Users may not know where they are located in the web application space, how to reach a desired location, or what functionality is required and where is it located. Examples include broken or badly labelled links, too many layers to "drill down" for information, "dead ends" when moving to the next step in a process, lack of ability to search the site with keyword, lack of an intuitive "look and feel" to the site, and insufficient overview information pointing out to the user what is available where. An example of a site that has poor navigation might have the facility to "Change Password" buried deep within a site.

Presentation type barriers may include poor choice of colour scheme, cluttered layout such as too much information on a page, lack of white space, font size too small, inappropriate typeface and no order to the links offered. An example of a site that is difficult to read would be red or dark green text on a black background as identified in the Bank Direct web site by [Matthews, 1998]. It is further worth mentioning for this type the popping up of advertisements and the blinking and flickering due to graphical objects changing colour, intensity, shape or position on the screen.

Technical type barriers include barriers that interfere with service delivery including non-recognition of user names and passwords, systems being "down" or out of service and lack of integration with the ledger and other accounting systems. Users may also be excluded from communication due to them using the wrong vendor's browser or a version of a recognised vendor, which is considered to be too old. Slow down of communication speed especially in remote or rural situations may result in users becoming impatient or the connection dropping out. Often it is not so much the actual computing speed as the perceived speed of the service due to either overloaded networks, servers or modems of insufficient quality that contribute to this barrier occurring. More than half of all attempted Internet transactions are abandoned out of frustration [Collier, 2002]. Finally the attempted installation of software on the user's computer can cause barriers due to lack of permission to do so or due to the software getting installed but not uninstalled and thus being a security risk or just consuming resources and possibly slowing down the respective machine.

4.2   Improving Communication via Localisation Abstraction

The communication we here have to deal with is a mediated human-to-human interaction. Various kinds of knowledge and ability have been represented inside the web application as data or program. The application then chooses the data or program best fitting to the user's inquiry. This requires having a model of the user represented inside the web application such that a sufficiently sharp distinction between users can be made based on the respective model. The web application further obtains an answer to the inquiry that can be just the identified data or the result of applying the program to the data. Finally the application actually delivers the answer to the user. Since the functionality required by the user is distributed over the application space, the user might not be able to access it immediately but first to position on the location best suited thus communication gets intermixed with navigation in application space. Simplifying navigation significantly can therefore result in reducing communication barriers. The simplification of choice is realised by supporting tools.

At least the following navigation functions appear worth being supported by tools:

- Position signalling, a function pointing out to the user his or her actual position in application space.
- Heading determination, a function determining the direction and also maybe the means best suited to approach a certain position[1].
- Short distance environment exploration, a function used to explore the immediate neighbourhood of a given location.
- Long distance environment exploration, a function used to explore the regions of the application space that are far away from a given location.

In web applications these functions can be supported by the use of what we call localisation abstraction. An application space model depending on the user and his or her location in the application space may be displayed to the user. The model may be presented in form of a graph. The vertices of it could represent locations and the edges the connections between vertices. The vertices could be labelled by the functionality, i.e. knowledge or ability that is available at the very location. After each navigational step obviously the model must be updated. Sufficiently performing algorithms are needed for obtaining and updating the models. It should be possible to obtain the needed results on the fly if the intended model is not too sophisticated.

---

[1] Positioning on far away locations does not necessary imply the user clicks through all the links to the target. Instead of this a shortest path from user location to user target could be determined and the final link could be offered as kind of soft or dynamic link.

Using the localisation abstraction properly can thus target navigation type barriers since it reduces the perceived complexity of the application space and thus increases the users' ability to aim for his or her purpose. Reasonably chosen metaphors additionally may help the users to apply their knowledge and abilities in a situation (i.e. while operating in application space) they are unfamiliar with. Using metaphors may cause users to be much more efficient in identifying the functionality required for their purpose, position to there, invoke the functionality and thus meet their goals more efficiently.

4.3   Improving Communication via Metaphors

We already pointed out that to generate the answer most suitable to the user depends on having a model of the user, i.e. on being able to group users into reasonably constructed types. Often it appears difficult to answer ill posed questions. To result in good answers the web application must be designed such that it is likely that good and relatively easy to answer questions, i.e. inquiries are issued by users. This can be aimed at using metaphors. They can help users understand their actual location in application space and what they can, shall, or shall not attempt there. This is due to the definition of metaphors given in [Thalheim and Düsterhöft, 2000] as being language expressions used in an uncommon language context. This allows the user, up to a certain degree, to master his or her actual state of affairs in the application space in terms of some area of knowledge or skill he or she already has mastered.

Human communication essentially is metaphorical. It is likely that the traditional human-computer interaction due to its lack of use of metaphors is responsible for some of the problems of this interaction. Approaching human-computer interaction to human communication by augmented use of metaphors appears thus as having the potential to reduce the number of communication barriers as well as their implications.

It may be the case that no engineering procedure can be constructed leading to usable metaphors in a sufficient high degree of cases. Therefore it is important to design applications that shall exploit the use of metaphors such that these easily can be built in after deployment and are maintainable. Supposing such design is found and implemented then by means of prototyping and perfective maintenance more suitable metaphors or metaphors at all may be found and incorporated into the web application. Such design needs to take into account that computer applications at least have three language levels: The tool language[2], i.e. the language in which the user interface signals the user the semantics of its functionality, the universe of discourse (UoD) language, i.e. the language used in the UoD to identify problems, their solutions and quality criteria of all of them. Finally there is the metaphor language, which helps the user understand the state of affairs in the UoD and what interface functions can be used to achieve

---

[2] We borrow this term from the PROMATIS INCOME Suite 4 of PROMATIS AG, which, e.g. allows to have German as Tool language, and English as UoD language, but has no independent metaphor language.

his or her goals. In our paper [Schewe et al., 2002], e.g. we proposed to use the metaphor 'dictionary' to support users in online loan applications in finding explanations concerning the technical terms of this UoD.

Generation of metaphors could be attempted by logically decomposing the application space into a small number of domains that appear somehow homogeneous with respect to the offered functionality. Then one can relate the domains to user types and expected user actions. Generation of metaphor appears then as being connected to finding characterizing names for the three valued relationships mentioned. It might be useful for this to omit user related information from the user type that for the expected behaviour appears not to be relevant. Further, methods from requirements engineering such as role-playing or brainstorming can be applied to generate first ideas on the metaphors to use. Clearly one must avoid for a given user type having confusingly many, conflicting or contradicting metaphors built into the web application.

5 Conclusion

Communication and collaboration are the critical success factors when building a successful knowledge enterprise [Raisch, 2001]. Building an open communication climate between employees, customers and partners is critical. One way of achieving this is via an organisation's web site that serves as a communication channel. Reducing barriers whether content, navigation, presentation or technical is essential.

The main implication from the case study research is that those involved with the design of web sites should start with the human factors rather than the technical issues.

Acknowledgement

The authors gratefully acknowledge the significant assistance received in the writing of this paper from Roland Kaschek and Klaus-Dieter Schewe.

References

Anderson et al., 1998. Anderson, S., Campbell, C., Hindle, Price, J., and Scasny, R. (1998). Editing a web site: Extending the levels of edit. *IEEE Transactions on Professional Communication*, 41(1):47–57.
Blyth, 1999. Blyth, D. (1999). Point and click content. In *New Zealand PC World's Web Guide*.
Carroll et al., 1988. Carroll, J., Mack, R., and Kellogg, W. (1988). Interface metaphors and user interface design. In Helander, M., editor, *Handbook of human-computer interaction*, pages 67–85. North-Holland: Elsevier Science.
Clampitt, 2001. Clampitt, P.G. (2001). *Communicating for managerial effectiveness*. Sage: London.
Collier, 2002. Collier, Y. (2002). Telemarketing: The present and the future. *B & FS*, 116(3):50.

Durham, 2000. Durham, M. (2000). Organisational web sites: How and how well do they communicate? *Australian Journal of Communication*, 27(3):1–14.

Larson and Czerwinski, 1998. Larson, K., and Czerwinski, M. (1998). Web page design: Implications of memory, structure and scent for information retrieval. In *Proceeding CHI'98*. Los Angeles, CA.

Matthews, 1998. Matthews, C. (March 1998). Internet banking in new zealand - A critique. *New Zealand Banker*, pages 26–28.

Morkes and Nielsen, 1997. Morkes, J., and Nielsen, J. (1997). Concise, scannable and objective: How to write for the web. http://www.useit.com/alertbox/9710.html. Jakob Nielsen's Alertbox.

Raisch, 2001. Raisch, W. (2001). *The eMarketplace: Strategies for success in B2B eCommerce*. McGraw Hill, USA.

Sarantakos, 1993. Sarantakos, S. (1993). *Social research*. South Melbourne: Macmillan.

Schewe et al., 2002. Schewe, K.-D., Kaschek, R., Matthews, C., and Wallace, C. (2002). Modelling web-based banking systems: Story boarding and user profiling. In H. Mayr and W.-J. Van den Heuvel, editors, *Proceedings of the Workshop on Conceptual Modelling Approaches to E-Commerce*. Springer-Verlag.

Thalheim and Düsterhöft, 2000. Thalheim, B., and Düsterhöft, A. (2000). The use of metaphorical structures for internet sites. *Data & Knowledge Engineering*, 35:161–180.

Troyer, 1998. Troyer, O.D. (1998). Designing well-structured websites: Lessons learned from database schema methodology. In T.W. Ling, S. Ram, and M.L. Lee, editors, *Conceptual Modeling- ER'98*, volume 1507 of *LNCS*, pages 51–64. Springer-Verlag.

Truchard and Katz-Haas, 1998. Truchard, A. and Katz-Haas, R. (1998). Ten guidelines for user-centred web design. *Usability Interface*, 5(1):12–13.

Wallace, 2002. Wallace, C. (2002). *The impact of the Internet on business*. PhD thesis, Massey University, Palmerston North.

Author Index